THE PERSIANS

Homa Katouzian is Iranian by birth, with an academic background in economics and the social sciences. He currently teaches Iranian history and literature at St Antony's College and the Oriental Institute, University of Oxford. He is the editor of the journal *Iranian Studies* and the author of numerous academic monographs and articles about Iran and its literature.

HOMA KATOUZIAN

THE
PERSIANS
*Ancient, Mediaeval
and Modern Iran*

YALE UNIVERSITY PRESS
NEW HAVEN AND LONDON

For information about this and other Yale University Press publications, please contact:

U.S. Office: sales.press@yale.edu yalebooks.com
Europe Office: sales@yaleup.co.uk www.yalebooks.co.uk

Set in Minion Pro by IDSUK (DataConnection) Ltd.
Printed in Great Britain by Clays Ltd, Eclograf S.p.A.

Library of Congress Cataloging-in-Publication Data

Katouzian, Homa.
  The Persians : ancient, medieval, and modern Iran / Homa Katouzian.
    p. cm.
  Includes bibliographical references and index.
  ISBN 978-0-300-16932-4 (alk. Paper) 1. Iran—History. I. Title.
  DS272.K375 2009
  955—dc22

                                                                2009005669

A catalogue record for this book is available from the British Library.

ISBN 978-0-300-16932-4 (pbk)

10 9 8 7 6
2021 2013 2012 2011 2010

Contents

Acknowledgements

The great Persian epic poet Abolqasem Ferdowsi once wrote in his immortal *Shahnameh*: 'in this book, among the renowned/Share Ali Deilam and Budolaf of this town'.[1] Many more share in this lesser book, though for its views and errors I alone am to blame.

In 2001 the Institute for Advanced Studies, Princeton, gave me a visiting post to launch a research project for a history of modern Iran from 1800 to 2000. I am therefore most grateful to them for their moral and material support. But it was the highly persuasive powers of Heather McCullum of Yale University Press that later convinced me to extend the project to an interpretive and comprehensive history of Iran. She also arranged for three reviewers of my initial proposal, to whom I am indebted for their very generous and encouraging comments; Stephanie Cronin was the one among them who chose not to remain anonymous. The libraries of the Middle East Centre, St Antony's College and the Oriental Institute, as well as the Ferdowsi Library of Wadham College and the Bodleian Library, all of the University of Oxford, were indispensable in providing many, and sometimes rare and inaccessible, sources, English as well as Persian, for a study which spans more than two and a half millennia of Iranian history. I am especially grateful to Mastan Ebtehaj, librarian of the Middle East Centre, for her unfaltering support.

Throughout the years in which this book came into being, my son Amir, who for a long time has been my sole companion in domestic life, helped to provide a home environment conducive to peaceful and uninterrupted work.

In 2007 I was a guest of Mohamad Tavakoli-Targhi in Toronto for six weeks, working mainly on this project, though also on a joint project which we hope to publish some time in the future. Mohamad's company was in itself a source of joy and energy, and his role as a perfect host was conducive to long hours of deliberation. I also benefited from the use of his extensive library, which is distinguished for its Persian books and journals, so rarely accessible elsewhere.

John Gurney briefly commented on early drafts of some chapters, which was helpful in developing the strategy of the study as it later evolved. Touraj Daryaee's comments on chapters 1 and 2 were useful in polishing my account of ancient Iranian history. But most of all, I benefited from the support of two matchless referees throughout the work, without whose cogent comments and suggestions the manuscript would not have reached its present stage. Hossein Shahidi of the Lebanese American University, and my co-editor of another book, read each chapter line by line and returned it to me with comments on both form and substance. Having responded to his comments, I then sent the chapter to my editor, Phoebe Clapham, who likewise read and commented on it. Hossein viewed the material from the point of view of a seasoned specialist, Phoebe as a highly intelligent, literate and acute non-specialist – incidentally demonstrating that she is a rising star in her profession.

Nasrollah Kasraian and Jassem Ghazbanpour, two leading professional photographers, kindly let us use copies of their works for the illustrations. I am most grateful to them as well as to Syma Sayyah (Afshar), Paul Sanford and Hossein Shahidi for facilitating their generous contribution. I am also grateful to Oxford University for their generous contribution towards the cost of the other illustrations.

Many more whose help has been less direct would have been acknowledged had I had more space. In wishing to express my deepest gratitude to them all, named and unnamed, I am reminded of the Arabic verse which simply says 'Say thank you and it will suffice'.

HK
St Antony's College and the Oriental Institute
University of Oxford
August 2008

List of Illustrations

Maps

Preface

⟶ ⚙ ⟵

Getting its history wrong is part of being a nation.   Ernest Renan

THIS BOOK IS A history of Iran – or Persia, as it was known in the West until the
1930s – from the foundation of the Persian empire until the present. The
introduction outlines the main features of Iranian history and society, setting the
framework for more detailed discussion in the chapters that follow, which also
include an account of Iranian myths and legends as well as Iranian cults and
religions, both pre-Islamic and post-Islamic.

There are differences of opinion, not least among historians themselves, as to
how history should be written or what constitutes 'real' history. Some put much
value on descriptive accounts of events, and usually regard detailed or micro-
historical studies as the right approach to historiography. To them, the discovery
of a hitherto unknown fact, however minute, may be more important than a new
analytical insight into broad historical trends. Others put much less emphasis on
the facts, and tend to use broad brushstrokes to map out the canvas of history,
searching for how and why things happened: in some extreme cases they go as far
as completely emptying history of its empirical content.

While I believe that history must have real empirical content, I also believe
that it must include analytical insights, which make sense of the facts and distinguish history from intelligent and disciplined storytelling. This book is about the
'what', the 'how' as well as the 'why' of Iranian history. In trying to fulfil all these
tasks at once, I have also made comparative observations on Iranian and
European history, in an attempt to show why Iranian society and history in their
richness have nevertheless been different from those of the West in some important respects: why, for example, the principal agenda of the Constitutional
Revolution was the establishment of law or why in the revolution of February
1979 society as a whole – rich and poor, young and old, traditional and modern
– was united against the state.

Chapters 1 to 6, covering the periods from ancient times to the mid-
nineteenth century, do not contain detailed notes and references but are
based on many sources, a selection of which are cited in the short bibliography
at the end of each of the chapters. On the other hand, Chapters 7 to 14, on the

mid-nineteenth century to the present period, are closely documented with direct references to primary and secondary sources. The reason is that the earlier period has been discussed more briefly and is less controversial; whereas the latter period has been dealt with in greater detail and opinions differ more widely regarding its various aspects.

This book is addressed to the general reader as well as the specialist. While it is not just a general review of Iranian history, I have done my utmost to present it in such a way that makes it intelligible, perhaps even enjoyable, for the lay reader as well. It is the story of a major human civilization told in one volume, laying bare and explaining the reasons for its unique aspects.

What remains may be summarized by the apposite Persian verse:

The story of our good and our evil will be writ
For history has a book, a pad, a page.

Modern Iran

INTRODUCTION

Iran and Iranians

How Great, Old and Mysterious is Iran! Sadeq Hedayat

THE GREAT PERSIAN POET Sa'di says in a verse, quoting Bozorgmehr, the legendary minister of Anushiravan, the great Sasanian emperor: 'To cast an opinion not by the ruler allowed / Would be to spill one's own blood.' Writing an interpretive general history of Iran could, metaphorically, result in similar punishment. Real blood is less likely to be spilled, but there is a risk of emotional, intellectual, even political blood being splashed on the floor of argument, discussion and criticism. Iran is such a controversial member of the world community at the time of writing that almost every power, race and community has its own view of Iran, which is sometimes considerably different from those of the others. Moreover, Iranians themselves are so divided, whether in Iran or as part of the Iranian diaspora, that, if not each one of them, then every group, class and creed has a conception of the country and its history more or less at odds with the rest. Not only are there Islamist, non-Islamist, pre-Islamist, nationalist, democratic, patriotic, leftist and ethnic separatist forces and sentiments current among Iranians at home and abroad, but there is even a greater variety of conceptions of Iran's past, present and future – which, however, is often based on little serious reflection or sober studies of the reality. And, moreover, each one is held as both absolute and sacred truth, so that any alternative view to each or all of them is regarded as no less than blasphemy and perhaps a product of a vicious conspiracy against the entire Iranian race.

To give one example, a few years ago a highly educated Iranian and ethnic Persian-speaker wrote an emotionally charged article in a leading Tehran cultural journal arguing that the British had invented the term 'Persia' for Iran because they intended to sow division in and break up the Iranian lands. On the other hand, there are ethnic separatists who regard the concept of Iran as a unified cultural entity in spite of its ethnic diversity as no less than a conspiracy to suppress the ethnic communities. Iran has many things but it is also a great treasure house of intense and conflicting sentiments and emotions. Therefore, the more competent, careful, detached and disinterested the author of an interpretative general history of Iran, the more likely he will be to run the risk of offending and alienating virtually everyone, precisely because he will not present the gospel according to any one of them.

Iran is a country with thousands of years of history, the great variety of every aspect of which is at least partly responsible for the diversity of opinions and emotions noted above. It is an ancient land of the utmost variety in nature, history, art and architecture, languages, literature and culture.

Persian literature is the most glittering jewel in the crown of Iranian history and culture, the greatest single contribution of Iran to human civilization and the collective product of countless poets and writers, both native and non-native Persian-speakers. Persian poetry in particular, famous the world over through the works of Rumi, Hafiz, Khayyam, Ferdowsi and Sa'di, is one of the most elevated poetical legacies of humankind, including literary giants who are unsurpassed by any other literary tradition. Iranian architecture, ancient as well as mediaeval, represented by such historic monuments as Persepolis and the Congregational Mosque of Isfahan, is one of the world's major cultural legacies. Spanning more than a thousand years of the visual arts, Persian miniature and modern painting and mosaic designs are related to other artistic traditions but unique in their distinct Iranian identity. Persian carpets in their great variety are the most advanced and most exquisite artworks of their kind. This does not exhaust the list of Iranian achievements but is sufficient to demonstrate the variety, originality and antiquity of Iran as a major civilization.

IRAN AND PERSIA

Despite the Iranian conspiratorial theories cited above, it was not a conspiracy for the British to call Iran 'Persia', the French 'Perse' the Germans 'Persien', and so on. When the Greeks (from whom European civilizations descend) first came across the Iranians, Persian Iranians were ruling that country as the Persian empire. It was therefore no more of a conspiracy for them to call it 'Persis' than for the Persians who first came into contact with Ionian Greeks to call the entire Greek lands 'Ionia'. To this day Iranians refer to Greece as Ionia (i.e., *Yunan*) and the Greeks as Ionians (i.e., *Yunaniyan*). Indeed, some scholars, such as Gnoli, have doubted if the Achaemenid Persians described their empire as Iran (or a variation of that term), but this is a generally unresolved question which need not detain us here.

The cultural and intellectual menace of the word *Farsi* needs a brief mention. In recent western usage the word *Farsi* has been used alternatively for the Persian language. *Farsi* is the Persian word for 'Persian' just as *Deutsch* is the German word for 'German' and *Français* for 'French'. But no one would use *Deutsch* for German or *Français* for French when speaking English, even though those words are more familiar than *Farsi* to the English-speaking peoples. Unlike Persian, *Farsi* has no cultural or historical connotations, and hardly any English-speaker would have heard of '*Farsi* literature', or would be able to locate it if he or she did. To many Europeans, Persian is known as a language of culture and literature, but very few of them would know the meaning of *Farsi* even as a language.

THE COUNTRY AND ITS BASIC FEATURES

Persia was only part of Iran insofar as the Persians made up one of the Iranian people. Yet at times it had an even wider meaning than Iran because what was historically known as Persia or the Persian empire included not only a much wider territory than present-day Iran but also encompassed non-Iranian countries and peoples such as Egypt (see Chapter 2). 'Persia' remained the European term for Iran until 1935 when the Iranian government insisted that all countries should officially call the country by the latter name (see Chapter 12). But 'Persia' survived in unofficial usage until the revolution of 1979 established 'Iran' in universal application. Still, for many western people, 'Persia' has a much wider historical and cultural connotation than is conveyed by 'Iran', which they sometimes used to confuse with Iraq. Many no longer know that Iran and Persia are the same, thinking that Iran is also an Arab country.

As noted, present-day Iran is part of the much larger Iranian plateau, the whole of which at times formed part of the Persian empire. The country is vast, bigger than Britain, France, Spain and Germany combined. It is rugged and arid and, except for two lowland regions, is made up of mountains and deserts. There are two great mountain ranges, the Alborz (Elburz) in the north, stretching from the Caucasus in the north-west to Khorasan in the east, and the Zagros, which extend from the west to the south-east. The two great deserts, Dasht-e Kavir and Dasht-e Lut, both in the east, are virtually uninhabitable. The two lowland areas are the Caspian littoral, which is below sea level, has a subtropical climate and is thick with rainforests, and the plain of Khuzistan in the south-west, which is a continuation of the fertile lands of Mesopotamia and is watered by Iran's only great river, the Karun.

Thus land is plentiful but water scarce, unlike a country such as Holland where land is scarce and water plentiful. The scarcity of water has played a major role not just in influencing the nature and system of Iranian agriculture but also a number of key sociological factors including the causes and nature of Iranian states and the relationship between state and society (see below). The extent of mountain and desert has naturally divided the Iranian population into relatively isolated groups. But aridity played an even greater role in this, and at the level of the smallest social units. In most of the country arable cultivation and the keeping of livestock was possible only where natural rainwater, a small stream, a subterranean water channel, known as *qanat*, or a combination of these provided the minimum necessary supply of water. *Qanat* or *kariz* is an ingenious technological development of ancient times, dating back to well before the foundation of the Persian empire. From an existing underground water table in the upland, a tunnel is dug under the ground, sloping downwards to the lowland (near the surrounding farms) where it comes to the surface. The water which flows from the source by the pull of gravity is then distributed via narrow canals to where it is needed for irrigation and other purposes.

The typical Iranian village, small, isolated and almost self-sufficient, was a product of the aridity of the land, the general scarcity of water typically putting a long distance between one village and next. The village thus became an isolated and self-sufficient social and productive unit, but too small to provide a feudal base: there was no or insufficient surplus of production to support a feudal lord, his court and his retinue. On the other hand, the villages were far too distant from each other to provide such a base taken together. The aridity of the land and isolation of the social units to which it was related thus combined to prevent the rise of a feudal society and state such as prevailed throughout much of European history. For this reason I have described Iran as 'the arid-isolatic society', which supplements my equally realistic designation of the country as 'the arbitrary society' and 'the short-term society', each of which terms describes a fundamental feature of the society, and each of which is closely interconnected with the other two. Independent long-standing social classes – feudal or other – did not exist as they did in Europe. Instead, the state exercised arbitrary power over all.

In a feudal society landlords formed the ruling classes, which were first and foremost represented by the state. The state was thus dependent on and representative of the ruling classes. In Iran, the landlords and other social classes depended on the state. In feudal Europe, as in other European and European-type class societies, the social classes formed a pyramid at the top of which was the state as their representative, and the higher the social class the greater was the state's obligation towards it. In Iran, the state stood over and above the social pyramid and looked upon the whole of the society, both high and low, as its servants or flocks. It had the power both to assign land to a person, thus turning him into a landlord, and to withdraw the title from an existing landlord and give it to someone else. It even had the power to take a part or the whole of a merchant's fortune. In general, Iranian states had the power of life and property over their subjects regardless of their social class, a power that not even the absolutist states of Europe – which flourished only for four centuries over the continent taken as a whole – ever possessed (see Appendix for a longer discussion of this issue.

The shah, normally addressed as shahanshah (meaning 'king of kings' or 'emperor') wielded the kind of power which no European ruler ever did, though some Russian rulers such as Peter the Great came close to it. All power and fortune emanated from him and all life and possessions were at his will. In principle he had the power of life and death over every member of the society, from princes of the blood and the chief minister downwards. And he could expropriate any prince, vizier, landlord or merchant so long as he had the physical power to do so at the time: no independent law or custom existed that could stop him from so doing. If he was not expressly worshipped as a divine being, he certainly was God's vicegerent on earth and several cuts above all other human beings, including his sons and other princes. Even if he was the first son of the previous shah, which he often was not, his fundamental legitimacy was not due to that fact or even to his belonging to the ruling dynasty: it came directly from God, His Grace or Divine Effulgence, called *farrah* in Middle Persian and *farr* in New Persian. It is important to emphasize this point, that the Persian shahs did not draw their legitimacy from an aristocratic and /or priestly class but *directly* from God by possessing the *farr* or divine grace. This concept of kingship survived into Islamic times, when both the term *farr* and such titles as *zellollah*, or Shadow of Almighty, and *qebleh-ye alam*, or Pivot of the Universe, were used to describe the shah's glory (see Appendix).

STATE–SOCIETY CONFLICT

Iranians typically opposed their rulers precisely because their lives and property were in the rulers' power. But they nearly always welcomed a ruler who emerged in the midst of chaos and brought order, although once this was done society went back to its habit of adopting a negative view of the state, even if through gossip, rumour-mongering and myth-making, or making jokes at its expense. And they became increasingly rebellious whenever the state was in trouble. With few exceptions, there was a fundamental antagonism between state and society throughout Iranian history. The state tended towards absolute and arbitrary rule (*estebdad*); society tended towards rebellion and chaos (*harjomarj, ashub, fetneh*, etc.). *Estebdad* literally means arbitrary behaviour or arbitrary rule. It is not the same as the absolutism or despotism that prevailed in Europe between 1500 and 1900 approximately, either in its literal meaning or in its social function. One of four situations normally prevailed in Iranian history: absolute and arbitrary rule; weak arbitrary rule; revolution; chaos – which was normally followed by absolute and arbitrary rule.

According to the theory of Divine Grace, a ruler will be abandoned by God if he stops being just to the people, and will therefore fall. This would normally happen as a result of a successful rebellion (or a foreign invasion), the first example of which in ancient mythology was the rise of Kaveh the Blacksmith and Fereydun against Zahhak. In his turn, Zahhak toppled and killed Jamshid, who had lost Grace by claiming divinity (see Chapter 1). Therefore, by definition, anyone who succeeded to the throne was presumed to have Grace and his rule to be in that sense legitimate; and anyone who was brought down was assumed to have been unjust and to have lost Grace. It follows that any rebel who succeeded in overthrowing the existing ruler and replacing him would be presumed to have *farr*, Divine Grace. In other words, there was no objective rule for succession, such as being the first son of the deceased ruler; and the legitimacy of a rebel was in effect measured simply by his success or failure.

All this meant that it was never clear who would accede to the throne after the death of a ruler. And that was why almost invariably there was conflict over the succession, sometimes resulting in civil war and chaos among different claimants. The revolt of Darius and his joint conspirators in 522 BC against Smerdis or

Gaumata, the magus who claimed to be a son of Cyrus the Great, is the first experience of the perennial problem of succession in written Persian history (see Chapter 1). The last example was in 1834 upon the death of Fath'ali Shah Qajar and the succession of his grandson and heir-designate, Mohammad Mirza, against whom some of his uncles and other princes rebelled and had to be put down by the use of force (see Chapter 6). After that, the succession of the Qajar heir-designates was guaranteed by Russian and British imperial powers who, at the time, enjoyed extraordinary influence in the country.

The fact that the state monopolized power did not necessarily mean that its administration was highly centralized. For example, the Arsacid (*Ashkani*) state was decentralized and for that reason the early post-Islamic Arab historians of Persia described its rulers as *muluk al-tawa'if*, which in Arabic literally means rulers of tribes or communities. Thus the Arsacid state was considerably less centralized than the Achaemenid (*Hakhamaneshi*) state before it or the Sasanian (*Sasani*) state after it. Likewise, the Qajar state was much less centralized than the earlier Safavid state and, especially, the Pahlavi state, which came after it.

Lack of administrative centralization in certain periods has been another reason for the belief that Iran was a feudal society. The Qajar system, as noted, was decentralized at least in part because of the absence of a reasonably viable transport system and the high cost of transport in what was an increasingly impoverished state. The system turned to virtual chaos during and after the Constitutional Revolution at the beginning of the twentieth century when the government was unable to maintain peace in many parts of the country (see Chapter 8). Iranian nationalists and modernists of the time who dreamed of a strong centralized government described that chaotic state as *muluk al-tawa'ifi*, using the term as the Persian translation for feudalism (see further Appendix).

The arbitrary power of the state in Iran – that is, a power not constrained by *independent* laws and social classes – would also become absolute in the hands of a strong ruler such as Shah Abbas, but unstable and divided in the case of weak rulers such as Shah Soltan-Hosein (see Chapter 5). Normally, it was not the strong and absolutist ruler who had to face serious rebellion, however harsh his rule might be, but the weak and incompetent, who was often confronted with the potentially dangerous actions and reactions of society. It was, after all, the former who were supposed to be 'just', since they could hold the peace, and the latter 'unjust', since they could not. Therefore, and precisely because of the nature of arbitrary government and the position of the shah over and above society by virtue of Grace, the shah's character and personality traits played an unusually important role in determining his fortunes and those of the country as a whole.

Absence of law of the kind which existed throughout the history of Europe did not mean that there were no rules and regulations. It meant, rather, that there were no long-term laws or firmly entrenched traditions by which the state was bound. Regarding judicial laws, for example, the *shari'a* supplied an extensive and elaborate civil and criminal code in Islamic times. The restrictive factor, however, was that the laws could be applied only insofar as they did not conflict with the wishes of the state. That is why the state could deal out such punishments against persons, families or whole towns which had no sanction in *shari'a* law; that is how the condemned could sometimes escape punishment if they could make the shah or the local ruler laugh at the right time.

Society, on the other hand, tended to be rebellious precisely because of its endemic rejection of the state, even though in each short-term situation there were methods of legitimation and bargaining between state and society. In a word, since the people had no independent or intrinsic rights, they did not accept any independent and intrinsic responsibility. They were not engaged in perpetual rebellion, which was not possible except on the occasions when the state was considerably weakened by domestic and/or foreign factors. But society did not normally regard the state's rule as legitimate and therefore often thought of it as an alien force. Society's voluntary cooperation with the state – as opposed to enforced submission – was a rare occurrence in Persian history.

Full-scale revolt occurred occasionally and resulted in total chaos. In such situations – as in the revolt of an Afghan tribe under the Safavid empire in the eighteenth century – the people either sided with the rebels or remained neutral at the crucial moment, though they regretted their lack of support for the state after experiencing the total chaos which normally followed the fall of the state. The reason why the people either welcomed the rebellion or remained neutral was precisely because they did not regard the state – certainly when it was already weak, divided and incapable of maintaining peace and stability – as inherently legitimate. This was essentially a consequence of the separation of state and society, which itself accounted for the general anti-state tendencies of the society.

Traditional Iranian revolutions aimed to remove an 'unjust' ruler and replace him with a 'just' one, whoever that might turn out to be, although they would begin to regard the new ruler as 'unjust' not long after celebrating the fall of the previous ruler. Therefore such revolutions were in practice much more focused on removing the existing ruler and state than finding an acceptable replacement, much less on the removal of the system of arbitrary rule, which, until the nineteenth century, was believed to be natural and therefore unavoidable. This latter became the central objective only at the turn of the twentieth century, in the Constitutional Revolution, and it was inspired by the realization in the nineteenth century that European governments were based in law (see Chapters 7 and 8). Iranians almost constantly hoped and prayed for change – the more drastic the better – but were almost always disappointed when change came, partly at least because it did not correspond to their expectations. Combining a highly idealistic outlook in public life with a very pragmatic attitude in private behaviour is an Iranian trait which is unlikely to be matched by many other people.

The state–society conflict had a number of important consequences for the lives of individuals and society as a whole. Because the state was not dependent on any social class, its power was extraordinary and not bound by any written or unwritten law or tradition. This does not mean that the ruler's power was unlimited and he could do whatever he wished – which is impossible at any time, anywhere. For example, he may not have been able to interfere in the internal affairs of a strong nomadic tribe since he lacked the appropriate means for so doing. But he could order the blinding or execution of his son, another prince, the chief minister or whoever, or could confiscate the wealth and property of other persons however high in society they might be. In other words, he could exercise coercive control to the full extent of his physical power and was not bound by any legal restraint. This being the case, there developed two possible instruments of restraint when the shah or governor ordered the execution (or beating and maiming) of a prince or an official. One was for the would-be victim to take *bast* or sanctuary in a sacred or respected place, even at times in the royal stables, because of their proximity. The other method was for influential people to intervene and beg for the withdrawal, commutation or reduction of the sentence. These methods were only sometimes effective.

However, it must be stated that none of the above arguments is 'ahistorical', with the implication that society remained the same throughout history. On the contrary, because of the short-term nature of society at any given time, change was more frequent than in European history. What persisted as the norm in Iranian history was the arbitrary nature of power.

THE SHORT-TERM SOCIETY

Thus the state's independence from society, which accounted for its extraordinary power, was also the main source of its weakness and vulnerability. It could seldom depend on the sympathy and support of the privileged classes in its hour of dire need, as happened twice in the twentieth century, in the Constitutional Revolution and the Revolution of 1979 seventy years later (see Chapters 8 and 12). And, as noted above, since the right of succession was not guaranteed in law or entrenched custom, any rebel could replace the reigning ruler if he overthrew (and usually killed) him.

All this resulted, to an unusual degree, in personal as well as social unpredictability and insecurity. On the one hand, the exercise of arbitrary power by the state made life insecure and unpredictable. On the other hand, the fact that, at least in practice, society did not regard the state as legitimate and would try to harm it anytime and in any way it could, made the state insecure and fearful of losing its grip. The shah did not kill or blind his son, a minister or other princes of the blood or officials for pleasure. He did so out of fear, when the slightest suspicion made him feel vulnerable. And he felt vulnerable precisely because he had no legal and social protection other than his own power, knowing that if the other side moved more quickly and succeeded there would be nothing that could prevent or mitigate his demise.

All this gave rise to the 'short-term society'. A shah was not sure that his favourite son would succeed him after his death. A minister, governor or other official knew that at any moment he may lose his post, often together with his property and sometimes his life as well. A rich man was not sure if he could hold on to some or all of his wealth vis-à-vis the ruler, governor or other powerful persons. Hardly anyone could be sure that his position and/or possessions would be passed on to his descendants, a minister's grandson becoming an important person and a merchant's a well-to-do man.

Hence seldom, if ever, were decisions made on the basis of long-term considerations. The Persian expression 'Six months from now, who dead, who alive?' summed up the general attitude towards time, prediction and planning. Officials knew that they could suddenly and unpredictably lose their posts and hence tried to enjoy the privileges of their positions as much as they could while they lasted, and this made them highly predatory and exploitative towards the people who were under their rule. Investment was typically short term, the investor looking to one or two years for the return of his capital plus profit, that is – putting it in formal terms – investment horizons did not normally go beyond two years.

Thus, although long and eventful, Iranian history has lacked long-term continuity. It has consisted of a series of connected short terms. Long-term accumulation of capital was impossible for the reasons discussed above, since even if a merchant made long-term investments, this would be interrupted by plunder, confiscation or division in his lifetime, after his death or not long after that. Post-Islamic laws of inheritance have sometimes been cited as the reason for the lack of concentration of wealth. The fact, however, is that wealth could be lost even in a person's lifetime by plunder and confiscation, and it was not at all certain that a rich person's estate would be inherited by his heirs or confiscated by the state in part or as a whole.

The short-term nature of society was also both a cause and an effect of the absence of a long-term aristocratic class. Institutions of learning, too, although they existed in every short run, and sometimes excelled in learning and academic achievement, did not continue over the long term but had to be renewed in the next short run. In general, there is a notable absence of long-term and continuous classes and institutions in Persian history.

THE IRANIAN PEOPLE

Originally, Iranians were more of a race than a nation, the Persians being only one people among many Iranians. Apart from the country that is today called Iran, Afghanistan and Tajikistan also belong to the wider Iranian entity in historical as well as cultural terms, and the Iranian cultural region is even wider than the sum of these three countries, extending to parts of north India, Uzbekistan, Turkmenistan, the Caucasus and Anatolia: this is now described as the Persianate world.

Persian is only one of the Iranian languages, there having been many others, of which Kurdish, Pashto, Ossetic and a few local languages in Iran still survive as living tongues; while other, non-Iranian, languages are also spoken in Iran, notably Turkish and Arabic. On the other hand, other varieties of Persian are spoken both in Afghanistan and Tajikistan, so that the people of these three countries can understand each other in conversation as well as literary communication. And many more Persian dialects are spoken in Iran.

No discussion of Iran's history, economy, society and polity may be sufficiently realistic and complete without taking full account of its nomads, beginning with the Persians who built its first empire to the Qajars who ruled until the twentieth century. Looking for greener pastures, a variety of Iranian as well as Turkish peoples of different origins were attracted to the region from the north, northeast and east, and once they were established they had to face the menace of other incoming or internal hordes. Aridity and/or the pressure of population in their own lands were a cause of their migration to Persia, and aridity in Iran was the cause of their internal movements from their winter to their summer quarters and back every year.

What gave them the advantage over sedentary people was that they were both martial and mobile, and more numerous than villages which they raided. It was also this martial and mobile quality that enabled a tribe or a federation of tribes to subdue the others and form a central state, which was therefore able to collect, directly or by proxy, the entire surplus agricultural product for its finance and become a colossal state, capable of policing, administering and defending vast territories of land. And it was precisely because of their nomadic nature and origins that most Iranian rulers were on the move for much of the time, so that the Achaemenids had three capitals, Susa, Persepolis and Ecbatana – four if Babylon is included (see Chapter 1). All Iranian states, from the beginning to the twentieth century, were founded by nomadic tribes which, after turning into a state, had to face the not infrequent challenge of other existing and incoming nomads.

Historically, Iran has been the crossroad between Asia and Europe, East and West. People, goods as well as beliefs and cultural norms and products have passed through it, usually, but not always, from east to west. The eastern influence was such that even much of ancient Iranian myths and legends originated in eastern Iranian lands (see Chapter 1), although Islam and the Arabs came from the opposite direction (see Chapter 3). This peculiar geographical location gave rise to what may be termed 'the cross-road effect', both destabilizing and enriching the country; both making its people hospitable and friendly towards individual foreign persons and highly self-conscious vis-à-vis foreigners in general; both making the acquisition of foreign ways, habits, techniques and fashions desirable, and making the fear of the foreigners' designs normal, although the tendency towards xenophobia and fear of foreign conspiracies was at least in part a product of arbitrary rule and the habitual alienation of society from the state.

One product of the cross-road effect is the fact that Iran now inhabits a variety of ethnic and linguistic communities which include those whose mother tongue is Persian, as well as Kurds, Turks, Arabs, Baluchis and so forth. Turkic-speakers are concentrated in the north-western region of Azerbaijan, now divided into several provinces, bordering Turkey and the Caucasus. Other Turkic-speaking peoples, such as the Turkamans of the central north-east, and tribal Turkic-speakers, such as the Qashqa'is in the south, are of Turkish extraction. But Turkic is spoken also in other parts of the country, not least in some of the villages in the central-north regions near Tehran. Kurds, the majority of whom are Sunni Muslims, are an Iranian people and their language is an Iranian language. They live in the Kurdistan region in western Iran, but there are people of Kurdish origin also in the north-east. Iranian Arabs are Shia and almost entirely located in Khuzistan next to the Iraqi border. The Baluchis, on the other hand, are Sunni and live in the south-east, on the Pakistani border. Their language is Iranian and their region is one of the least developed parts of the country. This does not exhaust the list of ethnic and linguistic Iranians, which includes small numbers of Armenian, Assyrian and Jewish peoples. Lors and Bakhtiyaris, for example, are still partly tribal.

IRANIAN IDENTITY AND THE IDEOLOGY OF
MODERN NATIONALISM

The rise of modern Iranian nationalism – that is, Aryanist and pan-Persian ideology – will be discussed later in the chapters on the history of the twentieth century (see Chapters 8–11). But briefly for our purpose here, the reinvention of an ancient pre-Islamic past in the light of modern European, especially German, nationalism for forging an entirely new, modern, identity was not successful because it was more a product of ideological fever and romantic dreams than a realistic view of the country's history and society. For a few decades it influenced the social and political consciousness of many, if not most, modern educated Iranians – not all of them ethnic Persians – despite the fact that many of them, such as the outstanding writer Sadeq Hedayat, were alienated from the Pahlavi state.

Thus the official claim throughout much of the twentieth century that Iranians were of pure Aryan race and spoke one language, namely Persian, was a myth, an even less realistic and credible product of the influence of extreme European nationalist ideologies. It led to ethnic resentment and conflict, the consequences of which are still felt in parts of the country. Indeed, conflict and antagonism over race, language and ethnicity in Iran were almost as new as the twentieth century itself, and were a product of the Aryanist and pan-Persian ideology which swept over the then-modern intellectual terrain and became the ideology of Pahlavi Iran. Iranian history, like that of other countries, saw significant conflicts over power, religion and creed, but ethnic or racial hatred or a sense of superiority and inferiority was not normally a significant factor in its make-up.

Few people realized as clearly as Seyyed Hasan Taqizadeh, a leading politician and scholar of the twentieth century, the ahistorical nature of this Aryanist nationalism and its dangerous implications for the national unity and territorial integrity of Iran. The nationalism that Taqizadeh denounced was not patriotism but the ideology which claimed inherent superiority for a race, nation and culture. In one of his official letters sent to Tehran in the 1940s when he was Iranian ambassador to London he attacked pan-Turanian nationalism or 'Pan Turkism', mentioning 'the extreme and aggressive cult of national worship, full of inflated self-glorification with no regard to history and historical facts, and the interpretation of every issue in the world on the basis of one's own cult of national worship, which is the attitude of some Turkish politics-mongers'. In a following letter he took up the same theme with equal force, and said that if Iran is ever 'struck by the hand of God and falls prey to [extremist] nationalist madness' it must sever some of its regions that house various ethnic and linguistic groups, and even perhaps expel as many clans of mediaeval Arab descent.

However, by the 1970s that ideology was so confined to official propaganda that – true to the natural antagonism of society towards the state – not only traditional Iranians but even the modern intelligentsia were now denying anything glorious or even worthy of respect in ancient Persia. In other words, precisely because official nationalism had identified the state with (reinvented) ancient glories, those who rejected the state also negated the glories with which the state identified itself. For a short while virtually the whole nation embraced the cultural norms of Islam as the main elements of its identity, precisely because this Islamic identity negated the identity and legitimacy of the state which it confronted. But although Iran remained a Muslim society, the *Islamist* identity did not survive much beyond the death of Ayatollah Khomeini (in 1989), even among the traditionals. Once again the conflict between society and state tended to downgrade the state's projected identity and raise the flag of ancient Persia. This was consistent also with the short-term nature of Iranian society.

To put a complex issue in simple terms, since the Constitutional Revolution of 1906, whenever the state was identified with Islam and traditionalism, society identified itself with a reinvented modern concept of pre-Islamic Persia; and whenever the state assumed the latter identity, society looked to Islam and Shia traditions. Thus the identity that Iranians assumed at any given point in time was largely a product of their conflict with the prevailing state and should not be taken as a cultural identity which they share independent of short-term political considerations. As a matter of sociological and historical – even psychological – fact, an Iranian is a product of centuries of Islamic social and cultural experience even though he or she may not be a believer; and likewise he or she cannot rid himself or herself of ancient Persia if only because it is the historical background to Islamic Iran and has considerably influenced it in cultural terms, so that, historically, Islam in Iran has been distinct from Islam elsewhere, in other Muslim countries. Not even the concept of 'bipolarity' (the country's identity being both Islamic and pre-Islamic), which is more realistic than the other two extremes, is adequate for describing Iranian identity because it implies that there is such a thing as Islamic Iran separate from its ancient historical roots. There could only have been an Islamic Iran independent from its past if Iranians had lost their pre-Islamic identity and effectively become Arabs, as did the Egyptians.

Moreover, not only does describing Iranians (and even native Persian-speakers) in terms of a single pure race fly in the face of historical as well as empirical facts but, more importantly, it ignores the Iranians' remarkable capacity and potential to receive, absorb and adapt foreign cultures from that of Babylon in the sixth century BC to that of America in the twentieth century. Indeed, this is the secret of the richness and continuity of Iranian culture and civilization.

IRANIANISM

Yet although ancient and mediaeval Iranian empires sometimes included even more diversity of peoples than present-day Iran, a quality and characteristic of Iranianism (Iranian-ness or *Iraniyat*) always distinguished the country from neighbouring lands and peoples. Iranian-ness was not nationalism in any modern sense of the term, but consciousness of a social and cultural collectivity which made the country and its peoples different and distinct from the Greeks, Romans, Arabs, Chinese and Indians. The same sense of togetherness in spite of diversity was perhaps even truer of India, which despite so many languages and religions prevailing in a much larger and much more populous land than Iran, was bound together by a general culture which was unmistakably Indian.

The factors which bound the peoples together and determined their shared identity of Iranian-ness have not been the same throughout the ages, although some have always played an important role, and three have been especially important since mediaeval times. One is the Persian language as the lingua franca and the medium of high literature and culture; this was often used beyond Iranian borders and even became the official and cultural language in other countries such as Mogul India. Another factor is Shii Islam, which is unique to Iran as a state, is followed by the great majority of Iranians and has aspects and implications that are deeply ingrained in Iranian culture since pre-Islamic times. The third factor is territoriality, the fact that despite territorial expansion and contraction through the ages, which across the centuries has led to the formation of several states in Iranian lands, there has been a distinct Iranian territory, at least as a cultural region.

Conclusive evidence for this broader Iranianism – which remained alive even during centuries of disunity, mainly through the media of Persian language and literature – is provided, not only by great chronicles and literary anthologies and works of criticism, but even by classical Persian literature in the narrower sense. Here are two examples of what may take volumes to document comprehensively.

The great twelfth-century Persian poet Khaqani, who is especially known for his lofty odes that rival Beethoven's symphonies in their Olympian thunder, was a native of Shirvan, in the Caucasus (now in the Republic of Azerbaijan), from a Christian, probably Armenian, mother, to whom he was exceptionally attached. When he received the news of the sacking of Outer Khorasan, which was then a part of the eastern Seljuk empire, and was about as far away from his native land as central Europe, he wrote two long and powerful odes mourning the catastrophe. The poems are in the form of elegies for Imam Mohammad Yahya, the revered religious leader whom the invaders had put to death by pouring dust into his mouth. Khaqani says in one of the poems: 'Heavens watched them pour dust into his mouth / Being aware that dust is not worthy of his mouth.'

The second example is from Sa'di, the great thirteenth-century poet, doctor and sage of Shiraz. He wrote in his *Golestan* that when he visited Kashghar, the Kwarazmian city now in western China, he met in the college there a youthful scholar who was reading a classic work on Arabic grammar. Sa'di quoted a short Arabic poem to the boy, who asked him to translate it into Persian so he could understand its meaning. When Sa'di told the boy that he came from Shiraz – the Persian city thousands of miles away – the boy asked him to quote something from Sa'di. Next day, when the poet was leaving the city, the boy learned that he was Sa'di himself, and there followed a moving farewell scene.

This Iranian-ness is not just cultural but also social and psychological, so that beyond all the ethnic and linguistic diversities which have been noted one may distinguish an Iranian persona and character. No foreign observer, however critical, has failed to acknowledge Iranian hospitality. *Ta'arof* is a form of 'ritual courtesy' or 'ritual politeness', well-known as an Iranian habit of being extremely polite or generous. It is difficult to hold the door to an Iranian or eat modestly as their guest. But its scope is wider than that and it is not always literally meant: it is also 'a certain linguistic behaviour in language communication' to which non-Iranians usually find it difficult to respond accordingly. Another general characteristic of Iranians is their pride, both as individuals and as a people, which sometimes assumes inflated proportions. Yet at the same time they are capable of a good deal of humility, sometimes even self-denigration, especially with reference to their country: Iranians can be both very proud of and very embarrassed by their country, depending on the mood, moment and situation.

An aspect of Iranian social psychology which has seldom escaped comment by foreign observers is the prevalence of *taqiyeh*, or dissimulation. It is the practice of hiding one's true beliefs, religious or otherwise, when necessary, and – in very difficult circumstances – even pretending to views which are not genuinely held. This quality is usually regarded as a maxim of the Shiite faith; but it runs deeper and is a product of the social and historical insecurity discussed above, which was due primarily to the arbitrary nature of the Iranian state and society and was further encouraged by frequent foreign invasions.

However, there is another side to the coin of Iranian dissimulation. When the Iranians decide to express their emotions they do so openly and strongly. A typical Iranian usually holds a strong position, both in thought and action. Compromise (*sazesh*), as distinct from putting up with an unpalatable situation, is normally looked upon as abandonment of principles, as sell-out. Therefore, in a situation of open conflict – such as occurred several times in the twentieth century – Iranians tended to risk total failure rather than accept a compromise solution. When Iranians let loose their passions, they cannot be easily appeased even though they may stand to lose rather than win. Moderation is not an Iranian virtue.

CONSPIRACY THEORY

Iranians seldom take things – events, phenomena, opinions, suggestions – at face value. On the contrary, they are more inclined to believe that appearances are deceptive and that the truth is hidden beneath them. This is most famously expressed and conspicuous in the conspiracy theory of politics, which is by no means exclusive to Iran and, in recent times, has even spread to some western societies, although in Iran and a few other eastern countries it tends to be deep-rooted, strong and widespread. A well-known example was (and to some extent still is) the tendency to see the hidden hand of Britain (of *Ingilis-ha*) sometimes in very insignificant events, a phenomenon which is normally held to be a conse-quence of modern western imperialism. But the habit is much older, and affects many individual and social phenomena. A Persian expression used to describe Iran as 'the country of possibilities' (*mamlekat-e emkanant*), but if anything could happen nothing would be predictable, and this is consistent with the logic of 'the short-term society'.

In the twentieth century, in particular, the belief that the slightest event in the country was caused and manipulated by the hidden hand of the British became so widespread that virtually everyone, from shah and minister to teacher and taxi-driver, felt that their country was little more than a pawn in the hands of *Ingilis-ha*, who masterfully – indeed magically – plotted and executed some of the minutest happenings affecting the least important issues in Iranian society. In some of Taqizadeh's official letters as ambassador to London in the 1940s he took up this theme. In one he wrote:

> I do not know why a general paranoia has inflicted many people of our country which is just like a melancholia epidemic. It is the general belief that the British are involved in every affair of the country just like fairies and *jinns* and – like kismet and destiny – all matters big and small, even the fate of individuals, the promotion of civil servants . . . and appointment of the mayor [of the village] of Joshaqan are subject to their will, and run on the tip of their fingers.

My Uncle Napoleon (*Da'i jan Napoleon*) is a famous satirical novel that has brilliantly portrayed the paranoia regarding the supernatural powers and actions of the British in Iran. But, as indicated above, the matter is in fact deep-seated and historical, not being simply a product of Iran's weakness vis-à-vis foreign powers in recent centuries, or just exclusive to Britain and other foreign countries. Many ordinary Iranians who supported the Constitutional Revolution of 1906 soon came to believe that it had been one big trick played by the British to reduce Tsarist Russia's influence in Iran (see Chapter 8). Many who seventy years later shouted slogans against the shah in the streets of Iranian cities, some-times even risking their lives, became convinced not long afterwards that the revolution of 1979 had been organized by the Americans, the British, or both, from start to finish (see Chapters 12 and 13). Many more even became certain that Iranian-American antagonism and confrontation of the later periods was just a show, that America herself was the real instigator of the hostage-taking of their diplomats in Tehran, and that they were behind Iranian efforts to develop a nuclear industry. When the son of Ayatollah Khomeini died in the 1990s, many firmly believed that he had been killed on the order of the Iranian president, who had subsequently arranged the murder of his doctor as well, as part of a cover-up – the fact that the doctor was shown on television to dampen down speculation was not helpful since rumour had it that this was old television footage. And when Iran's national football team unexpectedly lost a match to Bahrain, many were adamant that the team had been told by the country's spiritual leader to lose on purpose, so that the people would not take to the streets to celebrate their victory. The types and examples of such beliefs are innumerable, and are encountered on a daily basis.

PERSONALISM

Few foreign observers have failed to comment on what they describe as 'Iranian individualism'. While they refer to something special in Iranian attitudes and behaviour, this has never quite been defined clearly, and the term itself is misleading in a number of ways. In western tradition the term 'individualism' refers to the attitude and outlook advocated by the liberal thinkers – mainly of Britain and France – of the eighteenth and early nineteenth centuries. Such indi-vidualism was a reaction both to the corporate mercantile state with its strict regulation of trade and creation of monopolies and to the power of the Church in determining the modes of individual and communal living. And it was an attitude and policy which became gradually established in the West in the nineteenth and twentieth centuries, challenged only by the socialist movement which, in the democratic West, never lost its regard for the rights and freedoms of the indi-vidual. Thus, western individualism is a historically recent phenomenon and has special characteristics of its own.

Let us for the sake of convenience call the Iranian concept 'personalism' rather than 'individualism'. First, this is an age-old phenomenon and not a product of recent social and intellectual developments in Europe. It is true that something of individualism in the European sense has found its way to Iran since the turn of the twentieth century but that is simply a by-product of modernization or pseudo-modernism. Iranian personalism, on the other hand, is a historical phenomenon, has been part of Iranian social psychology and attitudes for centuries and affects modern and traditional Iranians alike.

There are two sides to this personalism. First, Iranians who are not related by family bond or friendship are unusually detached from one another: the sense of social cohesion and regard for *unknown individuals* among Iranians at large is not very strong. That is why collective activity, such as party politics, voluntary social institutions and so forth do not have strong roots in the country. That is also why Iranians have often been much better at individual sports such as wrestling and weightlifting than at football and basketball. Exceptions to this rule occur in rare circumstances such as a revolution, in which Iranians become passionately attached to each other even if they are perfect strangers, for the sake of the common objective of bringing down the state, which they believe will be followed by bliss. In such circumstances they behave and act as one big family.

This side of Iranian personalism is most readily and clearly observed in the Iranians' driving habits, where everyone behind the wheel is anonymous and virtually every driver cares little about traffic regulations and the rights of other drivers. Nor does any driver apparently care about the rights of pedestrians, even at designated pedestrian crossings. The feature may be also observed in urban architecture, where virtually every building is different from, and unusually out of harmony with, the others, to the extent that it is sometimes said that out of the million or so buildings in Tehran hardly any one resembles another. And it may be further observed in the fact that almost any building, however old or new, may be put to the axe by its owner or buyer, the building being commonly described as a 'pick-axe building' (*sakhteman-e kolangi*). This is also a glaring and frequently recurrent example of the short-term nature of society, for which reason 'the short-term society' may be alternatively described as 'the pick-axe society' (*jame'eh-ye kolangi*).

The second characteristic of personalism runs in the opposite direction and results in unusual care for and attachment to others. Iranians are unusually attached to members of their own family, extended family, clan and close friends, and will help, defend and even make sacrifices for them when they are in need. For example, they will make great sacrifices, if necessary, to give their children the best possible education, which apart from its instrumental use is held in high regard for its own sake; but the extent and scope of clan support may go well beyond that.

In a comparison with modern European individualism, the strong detachment from strangers and strong attachment to relatives and friends give rise to another observation. Iranians are not too conscious of the interests of society in the abstract, although they do display sympathy and support for strangers whom they know to be in trouble. However, when they are related and belong to the same community, not only do they care but sometimes even interfere in each other's lives. An Iranian is hardly ever alone when he or she is among or close to his or her relatives and friends.

In any realistic analysis of Iranian society it is vital to take into account this deep-seated personalism in all its manifestations, for it both results in and is reflected in an unusually strong sense of security and degree of protection within the clan and familiar community, and an unusually strong sense of insecurity and vulnerability outside it, among the strangers in society at large.

Iranians, as a people, are intelligent, inventive and artistic. They are versatile and adaptable to different situations. They love fun, gaiety and outdoor activity. They almost make an art of eating, and Persian cuisine is one of the best in the world. They enjoy fiction, tales, anecdotes, jokes and rumours. They tend to accept rumours and anecdotes spread against the state without question and are experts at making the funniest jokes at the expense of those who wield power and authority, especially the government. A leading modern poet once wrote the verse: 'Our life is Poetry, legend and myth'. And although there is much more to Iranian life, poetry, myth, legend, mysticism and religion form a substantial part of everyday living. Emotion has the upper hand among Iranians and reason takes a lower seat in forming opinions. An average Iranian is more likely to be convinced of the truth of a statement if it is justified by an anecdote, an appropriate verse or an extraordinary and extra-rational explanation than by mere logical argument or empirical evidence.

This, then, is the frame and skeleton of Iranian society and culture, which will be elaborated upon in the following pages, to tell the story of one of the most varied, volatile and fascinating civilizations of humankind, the story of a land and people who have seen all seasons and currently face a future that is predictably difficult to predict.

CHAPTER 1

Myths, Legends and Ancient History

This is what the Lord says to his anointed, to Cyrus, whose right hand
I take hold of to subdue nations before him and to strip kings of their
armour...

The Bible, Isaiah 45:1–3

IRAN IS MUCH OLDER than its three millennia of written history. There is
evidence of civilization in parts of the country that in some cases goes back
several thousand years. The Iranian nomads who were to give their name to the
country wandered into it more than a thousand years before one group among
them, the Persians, founded the first Persian empire in 550 BC. Rich, complex
and elaborate myths and legends developed in those earlier periods, before the
Medes founded the first Iranian empire, which in turn was overthrown and
replaced by the first great world empire, founded by the Iranian Persian Cyrus
the Great.

MYTHS AND LEGENDS

Ancient Iranian myths are vast, varied, rich and colourful. They originate
in ancient Indo-Iranian traditions which are themselves represented by ancient
Indo-Iranian cults. Later developments of Persian mythology have given rise to a
body of myth, legend and legendary history which is assumed to have been gathered in the *Khodaynamag* during the Sasanian period (AD 224–651). This has
been lost, but both written and oral post-Islamic accounts based on it contain the
whole or parts of ancient pre-Islamic myths and legends. Their best-known and
most complete source in New (post-Islamic) Persian is *Shahnameh* (The Book of
Kings), which exists in Ferdowsi's rendering of the book in Persian poetry.

Shahnameh is made up of three cycles, the Pishdadiyan, the Keyaniyan and
the Sasanian. The first, beginning with the dawn of man and the Pishdadiyan, is
pure mythology. The next cycle describes the Iranian kingdom of Keyaniyan, the
long story of a heroic age in which myth and legend combine to produce an
ancient epic. The first two cycles of *Shahnameh* are centred on eastern Persia
whereas the third cycle is centred on the south and west. It mixes history with

legend while providing an account of the history of the Sasanian monarchy, the last Persian dynasty before the Arab conquest.

THE DAWN OF MAN

Shahnameh's first cycle begins with the birth of Kiumars (Geyomard). According to Ferdowsi, he was the first world king, before Iran came into existence as a distinct country. He wore a leopard skin and ruled over humans and beasts alike. Other sources describe him as the human prototype created by the god of light and good, Ahura Mazda, but killed by the god of dark and evil, Ahriman, the first mortal man and woman being born from the seed of Kiumars. The next king, Siyamak, is therefore either the son of Kiumars, according to Ferdowsi, or the son of the first mortal man and woman, according to the other sources.

Jamshid, who descends from Siyamak, is one of the most well-known figures in Iranian mythology, most of all for the 'Cup of Jamshid', or *Jam-e Jam*, a poetical metaphor for a cosmic vision of the world, which is often used as such in classical Persian poetry. He possesses the *farr*, or Divine Grace, the proof of a just and legitimate ruler (see the Introduction). He rules over a happy and trouble-free society, being so successful that he overreaches himself and demands to be worshipped as God. Thus he loses Divine Grace – which, as noted in the Introduction – can be lost by a ruler if he becomes 'unjust', or claims divinity. And the loss of Grace enables Zahhak (Dahak) to attack, defeat and replace him as ruler of the world. Zahhak eventually finds Jamshid in the Sea of China, where he has taken refuge, and cuts him in two.

Zahhak also turns out to be unjust and rules oppressively for a thousand years. He has many young men killed and their brains fed to the two serpents that have grown on his shoulders. Resistance and revolt develop against Zahhak's rule, led by Fereydun (or Faridun) and Kaveh the Blacksmith, who has lost all but one of his sons to Zahhak's serpents. 'Blessed Fereydun' is born with the Divine Grace destined to destroy Zahhak, who dreams one night that a hero about to be born named Fereydun will overthrow him. Zahhak's men find the newborn's father, Abtin, and kill him. But the baby's mother, Faranak, the first Persian heroine, runs away with him. The story is comparable to that of the birth of baby Jesus in the shadow of the massacre of newborn babies by King Herod, who had had a similar dream about the birth of Christ.

Fereydun finally gathers a force, goes to the aid of the revolt led by Kaveh, who carries his leather apron on a stick as the popular banner which later, called the Kaviyani flag, became the Persian imperial standard. Eventually, they defeat the unjust ruler and Fereydun chains him on Mount Damavand. On their way to join battle with Zahhak, he and his force perform the supernatural feat of crossing the River Ervand safely, both mounted and on foot. In its basic aspects the story has features in common with many myths and legends of Iran and elsewhere in the Middle East, including walking on water, which has been claimed later for some legendary Sufis as well. The point to emphasize, however, is the role and significance of Divine Grace, which enables its holder to perform super-natural feats. This is repeated regularly in the mythological and legendary parts of *Shahnameh*. Grace plays a supernatural role even in the account of the rise of Ardeshir Babakan, the founder of the Sasanian empire, who was essentially a historical, not legendary, figure (see below).

Salm, Tur and Iraj

During his lifetime Fereydun divides his world empire among his three sons, Salm, Tur and Iraj, in order to prevent conflict after his death. He gives the west to Salm, the north and east to Tur and Iran, which is the centre of his world empire, to the youngest, Iraj. But the move does not result in harmony. Salm and Tur become jealous of Iraj, who has been given the most attractive realm of the lot, and so they attack and kill him. That launches the bitter and protracted feud between Iran and Turan, which continues for a very long time through Iranian myth and legend. From Kiumars to Jamshid to Fereydun the entire world, not just Iran, is ruled over by the Pishdadiyan and their forebears. But from now on the focus of mytholog-ical history is on Iran in relation to her neighbours.

This launches a long-standing feud between Iranians and Turanians. Iraj's grandson avenges his death on the Turanians; later, the Turanian ruler Afrasiyab attacks Iran and forces the Iranians to retreat. Both sides agree to peace and decide to settle the border dispute by letting Arash, the champion Iranian bowman, shoot an arrow to mark the border between the two realms. Putting his entire lifeforce into the act, Arash shoots eastwards from the top of Mount Damavand. The arrow flies from dawn until noon and lands by the River Oxus, which thenceforth becomes the frontier between the two countries.

In the meantime Zal is born to Sam, the local ruler of Sistan and the chief paladin of the realm. Zal is an albino and Sam, fearful of becoming the butt of ridicule, abandons him in the wilderness. The child is discovered by the magical bird, Simorgh, who takes him and brings him up along with its own young, and returns him, when he is grown up, to his father, who now regrets his abandonment of the boy and is looking for him following a prophecy revealed in a dream. Later, as we shall see, Simorgh plays an important role in the birth of Rostam and the tragedy of Esfandiyar. But Simorgh's fame has gone beyond the Iranian cultural region because of its symbolic use by Farid al-Din Attar, in the mystical poem Assembly of the Birds (*Mantiq al-Tair*).

Zal falls in love with and marries Rudabeh, another Persian heroine, daughter of the ruler of Kabul, who is a descendant of Zahhak. She bears him a son, Rostam, so big that he has to be delivered by cutting his mother's frame. This is done on Simorgh's advice and under its supervision, the first successful caesarean section. Rostam is the greatest hero of Iranian mythological and legendary history. He is the protagonist in many epic and tragic stories in *Shahnameh*, and saves the Iranian throne several times. He fights and kills his own son, Sohrab, born and brought up in his father's absence, the two recog-nizing each other only when it is too late. Rostam also kills the hero Esfandiyar, despite his best intentions. One of Rostam's most famous exploits is his passage through the Seven Trials (*Haft Khan*). The devil in human form seduces Key Kavus, the frivolous Keyani emperor of Iran, to go to Mazandaran and is there captured by the White Demon (*Div-e Sefid*). Rostam sets out to free the emperor on his matchless steed, Rakhsh (who also has mythological attributes), and on his way passes through seven life-threatening stages until he finds and kills the White Demon and frees Kavus.

Key Kavus is the son of Key Qobad (Key Kavad), who is thus the founder of the line of Keyanian – 'key' meaning chief or king – with whom *Shahnameh's* second cycle begins.

KEYANIYAN

Kavus is one of the most famous personages of Iranian mythological history, in whose long reign a great deal happens both in Iran and between Iran and Turan. He is far from a 'just ruler', even though he has to be such if he is to hold Divine Grace which alone qualifies him to hold that position (see the Introduction). This is an example of a basic anomaly between the theory of Divine Grace and the reality to which it refers.

The feud between Iran and Turan, led by Kavus and Afrasiyab, continues during Kavus' long rule, with losses and gains on both sides. On two occasions, however, it assumes the form of a full tragedy, the tragedy of Sohrab, son of Rostam, and the tragedy of Siyavosh, son of Key Kavus. The last great tragedy of Iranian mythological history is the tragedy of Esfandiyar, son of Goshtasp. Thus each of the three great tragedies results in the death of a young and noble prince and hero.

The tragedy of Rostam and Sohrab
The story of Rostam and Sohrab is the most moving tragedy of *Shahnameh*. In its opening verses Ferdowsi gives a personal commentary:

It is a story which keeps the eyes well watered.
It brings on Rostam the anger of the soft-hearted.
If a whirlwind blows from the Ganges
It would bring down unripe oranges . . .
Why should the young person feel free of care?
Death after all is not just due to old age.

One day, feeling unhappy, Rostam mounts his horse, Rakhsh, and goes out to hunt in the plain. After a while he reaches a hunting ground, kills an onager, roasts and eats it and goes to sleep while Rakhsh roams about the plain grazing. A group of Turanian horsemen find Rakhsh, catch him with great difficulty and take him with them. Rostam wakes up and is angry not to find his steed. Unhappy and distraught he walks to the city of Samangan, part of the land of Turan, where he is greeted by the king, who assures him that Rakhsh is too well known to be lost. That same night Rostam marries the king's daughter, Tahmineh, who has fallen in love with him. But Rakhsh is found the following morning and so Rostam leaves, after giving Tahmineh, the third heroine in Iranian myth, his jewel-studded armband, telling her that if she bears him a daughter she should wrap it around her hair, and if a son, around his arm. Nine months later the son Sohrab is born. Receiving the news, Rostam sends gold and jewels to be given to his son when he grows up. Sohrab grows rapidly in body and mind and quickly proves to be extraordinary in intelligence, physical prowess, strength of will, martial arts and leadership of men.

When Sohrab has barely come of age he challenges his mother to tell him the name of his father. She tells him that he is the son of Rostam, the world-famous hero, but stresses that the ruler of Turan, Afrasiyab, must not know – otherwise he may kill the son to avenge himself on the father. Sohrab says that such a thing cannot remain a secret and decides to take an army to Iran and look for his heroic father and bring down Kavus, then turn to Turan and destroy Afrasiyab: 'With Rostam the father and me the son / Crowns everywhere will be undone.' When Afrasiyab hears that Sohrab is crossing the water to Iran he sends a group of his most gallant knights to his aid but tells them that father and son must not recognize each other so that if Sohrab kills Rostam they could take over Iran and that if Rostam kills his son, he will be consumed with remorse and grief.

On his way Sohrab comes across the White Fortress, where an ageing warrior and his daughter, Gordafarid, another heroine of *Shahnameh*, live. He quickly captures Hazhir the veteran castellan and prepares to seize the castle. Gordafarid puts on a suit of armour, hides her hair in a helmet and rides out to meet Sohrab in combat. During the fight Sohrab snatches off the girl's helmet and her long hair falls down on her shoulders. Bedazzled by her beauty and courage, Sohrab begs her to desist. She agrees but does not deliver the castle to Sohrab as he expected. Next morning Sohrab arrives to storm the castle but finds the gate open and the fortress empty. Father and daughter as well as guards had left at night by a secret passage. The empty triumph and the departure of Gordafarid break Sohrab's heart.

Alarmed at Sohrab's lightning successes, Kavus sends the valiant general Giv to Sistan to seek Rostam's assistance. Rostam is not impressed, believing that comparisons of Sohrab with himself are exaggerated, and tells Giv that he has a son by the princess of Samangan but he is still too young to take to the field. Therefore he is in no hurry, and they spend a few days drinking and merry-making before going to Kavus' help. The shah is livid about their lax behaviour and clashes with Rostam, but they are quickly reconciled by the intervention of the nobles.

Rostam, Kavus and the Iranian army meet the Turanian army led by Soharab. Sohrab views the Iranian soldiers and heroes from his side of the field with the captive Hazhir next to him. He asks Hazhir to point out the Iranian champions and generals to him and especially asks him to identify Rostam. Hazhir lies, worried that by identifying Rostam he will put his life in danger. The Turanian knight and agent of Afrasiyab, who knows Rostam, also hides the truth from the youth, as instructed.

Father and son meet on the battleground in hand-to-hand combat. The first day neither of them succeeds in overpowering the other but both feel that they are facing their match. On the second day, and after a lengthy struggle, Sohrab manages to get the better of his father and is about to kill him when Rostam plays a trick and tells him that according to their custom they do not kill the combatant the first time they thrust him on the ground. While in combat, the young man repeatedly asks his father about Rostam, without revealing that he is his son, but Rostam is not drawn. Knowing that he is unable to defeat Sohrab, Rostam prays to God before the third combat to restore to him the strength of his youth. His prayers are answered and on the third day he manages to knock Sohrab down: 'Quickly he drew the dagger off his waist / And tore off his enlightened son's chest.'

Sohrab moans that it is not Rostam's fault but the irony of fate that has brought him to Iran in search of his father only to be killed without finding him:

Now if you become a fish in water
Or like night into darkness you enter
And if you rise up to the sky like stars
Abandoning the love of this earth of ours
My father will avenge my blood on you
When he sees me in my grave because of you
For among those heroes and champions
There will be one to take Rostam the news
That Sohrab was cut down and destroyed
While he was searching for you in void.

Rostam is shattered. Kavus has a panacea (*nushdaru*) that will save Sohrab's life, but, true to character, refuses to send it to Rostam, being worried that Sohrab's survival might spell doom for his rule. Rostam is about to ask Kavus personally for the medicine when he receives news of his son's death. Ferdowsi comments: 'The world is filled with everyone's destiny / Ironic roles like this it plays many.'

The tragedy of Siyavosh

Siyavosh is the young and exceptionally noble and chivalrous son of Key Kavus. Sudabeh, Kavus' beautiful wife, falls in love with her gallant stepson and tries to seduce him. When the young man turns down her advances she complains to Kavus that he has attempted to seduce her; but the king does not believe her. Sudabeh then hatches a plot, and they decide on trial by ordeal: Siyavosh agrees to ride through fire to prove his innocence. A huge fire is made through which the young prince rides on his black charger and out of which he emerges perfectly sound. Kavus, now convinced of his son's innocence, calls Sudabeh before him and denounces her wickedness. But he spares her life at Siyavosh's request, although later she returns to favour once again.

Shortly afterwards Afrasiyab invades Iran, and Siyavosh volunteers to lead a force against him. He is accompanied by Rostam as his lieutenant and guardian. The Turanian ruler meanwhile has an apocalyptic dream, panics, sends Siyavosh fabulous gifts and sues for peace. Siyavosh accepts his offer and sends Rostam to his father with a report of successful negotiations.

Kavus is angered by Siyavosh's settlement and tells Rostam that Siyavosh must throw the gifts on a fire, send the captives to him to be beheaded and make war on Afrasiyab. Rostam tries but does not succeed to dissuade Kavus from this course and unhappily leaves for his native Sistan. Siyavosh, finding his father's orders unreasonable and dishonourable, sends his army back to Iran and takes refuge in Turan. Afrasiyab receives him in great honour and gives him the hand of his daughter, Farangis (or Farigis), in marriage.

Siyavosh is held in high respect by Afrasiyab, but his great success arouses the jealousy of Afrasiyab's brother, Garsivaz, who incites the king against the Iranian prince, claiming that he is secretly in league with the Iranian court to commit an act of treachery. Afrasiyab is deceived and sends an army to arrest Siyavosh, who tries to flee, but is captured. The pleas and tears of Farangis, another of *Shahnameh*'s heroines, prove fruitless. Siyavosh's head is cut off and on the spot where his blood is spilt a plant grows, which is later called Blood of Siyavosh. Farangis curses her father on hearing the news of her husband's execution and Afrasiyab orders that she too be put to death, but she is saved when it is discovered that she is carrying the prince's child.

The news of the death of the young, valiant and innocent Siyavosh shakes the Iranian elites and nobles, who criticize his father, Key Kavus, for having driven him into seeking refuge in Turan. Savashun, the annual mourning for the blood of Siyavosh, continued to be held into the twentieth century, and in its forms and rituals sometimes closely resembled the mourning for Imam Hosein, giving the impression that, as the more ancient tradition, it probably influenced the style of mourning for Hosein's martyrdom (see Chapter 3). In a metaphorical reference to the tragedy of Siyavosh, Hafiz wrote: 'The king of the Turks accepts the detractors' words of blame / May the injustice of the blood of Siyavosh bring him shame.' In her well-known novel *Savashun*, Simin Daneshvar has used the theme to tell a modern story of political martyrdom.

In due course Farangis (or Farigis) gives birth to Key Khosraw, who is destined to become one of the most renowned shahs of ancient Iranian mythology. The young prince is carried off to the frontiers of China. The paladin Giv is then sent to find Key Khosraw, and together with his mother Farangis they set out to cross the Oxus to Iran. Upon hearing this news, Afrasiyab goes in their pursuit, but they manage to cross the wide and turbulent water on horseback, a miraculous feat which is made possible since Key Khosraw possesses the *farr*, or Divine Grace. And so his grandfather, Kavus, names him as his successor in preference to his son, Fariborz.

Key Khosraw becomes a very successful shah, an epitome of the Just Ruler. He fights his Turanian grandfather, Afrasiyab, defeats and eventually kills him as well as his brother, who had been the instigator of Siyavosh's death. This brings to an end the long feud between the two houses of Iran and Turan. But in the end Key Khosraw also decides to step down, and hands over to Lohrasp, a distant descendant of a former shah.

The advent of Zoroaster

Lohrasp, too, abdicates later in favour of his son Goshtasp (or Vishtasp) and withdraws to a temple to lead an ascetic life. It is in the latter's reign that Zoroaster begins to preach his new faith and converts the shah and his court. Arjasp, the Turanian ruler, regards this conversion as a betrayal of the 'old faith' and attacks Iran. What the old faith was is not clear. It was probably the Iranian cult that recognized Ahura Mazda, the god of light and good deeds, and Ahriman, the lord of dark and evil acts, before the cult was reformed and developed by Zoroaster. On the other hand, and as noted, this second cycle of *Shahnameh*, like the first, takes place in eastern Iran close to lands in which Buddhism flourished (see Chapter 2). Lohrasp himself seems to have entered a Buddhist temple, and the Turanians who condemned Goshtasp for abandoning 'the old faith' were central Asian people.

However that may be, a protracted war between the two countries results in the death of Lohrasp, until Esfandiyar, Goshtasp's son and heir apparent, defeats and kills Arjasp. At one point Goshtasp throws Esfandiyar into jail, but when he releases him to lead the war against Arjasp he promises him the throne if he wins the war.

The tragedy of Esfandiyar

But Goshtasp reneges on his promise. Esfandiyar complains to his mother, who advises him to accept his father's decision to remain at the helm. Esfandiyar then confronts his father, reminds him of all the hardship he has suffered in defeating Arjasp and demands the crown and the throne as the shah had promised. The cunning and cold-hearted Goshtasp then asks the advice of a sage, who reads the future and tells him that Esfandiyar is destined to be killed by Rostam. To rid himself of his son, Goshtasp summons him and tells him that Rostam has defied him and that he should go to Sistan and bring Rostam to the court in fetters, whereupon he will abdicate in Esfandiyar's favour. The young prince is suspicious of his father's motives, but he nevertheless sets out to subdue Rostam.

Arriving in Rostam's domain he tells him to submit and go with him to the court in chains. Rostam answers that no man will ever see him alive and in fetters: 'Who told you to go and tie Rostam's hands / Not even the high heavens could tie my hands.' The conflict eventually results in a series of combats.

During these Rostam notices that no amount of effort can shake Esfandiyar. He seeks the advice of the magical bird Simorgh, who tells him that Esfandiyar is invincible, except in his eye. He instructs Rostam to make a special arrow and use it if he must. In the next combat Rostam humbles himself to Esfandiyar more than before, and says he is prepared to give him boundless treasures and other gifts and go with him to the court. But Esfandiyar responds that there must be either fetters or war. At that point Rostam:

Put the tamarisk arrow in the bow
Just as Simorgh had told him to
He shot straight into Esfandiyar's eye
It turned the world dark in the champion's eye.

Rostam is killed not long afterwards through a plot hatched by the King of Kabul in which Rostam's half-brother Shaghad is a principal culprit. Before dying, Rostam kills Shaghad. Sometime later Goshtasp dies and leaves the throne to Esfandiyar's son, Bahman. Enthroned, Bahman attacks Sistan in revenge for the blood of his father, lays it waste and kills Rostam's son and brother. Bahman has a son by his daughter, Homay, whom he has married, incest being permitted not just in ancient Iranian myth but also in ancient Iranian society. Homay succeeds her father and husband, and is in turn succeeded by her son, Darab, while her brother, Sasan, wanders away. Darab is in turn succeeded by his son, Dara. It is during Dara's reign that Alexander attacks and conquers Iran. This ends the second cycle of *Shahnameh*, that of Keyanian.

After a short and fleeting reference to the Arsacids (*Ashkaniyan*) in *Shahnameh* comes the book's third cycle, the legendary history of the Sasanians, beginning with the founder of the dynasty, Ardeshir Babakan (see below and Chapter 2). The first two cycles, of the Pishdadiyan and the Keyanian, are set in the eastern parts of the Iranian plateau. The Sasanians, on the other hand, were concentrated in the south and west. Ferdowsi's *Shahnameh* does not mention the Seleucid period, when the Alexandrian Greeks ruled over Iranian lands. His reference to the Arsacids, who flourished for more than four centuries until they were overthrown by Ardeshir in AD 224, is passing although they are more extensively noted in other post-Islamic sources (see below and Chapter 2).

The greatest omission, however, is the absence of any reference to the Achaemenids, the founders of the first Persian empire, the last of whom, Darius III, was defeated by Alexander. In real history, they come first, are followed by the Greek Seleucids, who are replaced by the Iranian (Parthian) Arsacids, who in turn are succeeded by the Persian Sasanians. Thus in Iranian mythology the Keyanians have taken the place of the Achaemenids, who rose from Pars in the south, not the east, and who ruled the empire from the west and south, just as did the Sasanians later.

ANCIENT HISTORY: THE ACHAEMENIDS

In ancient history, Iran was known both as a land and a people, though it is not likely that the empire was known as such until the Sasanian period. Aryan tribes

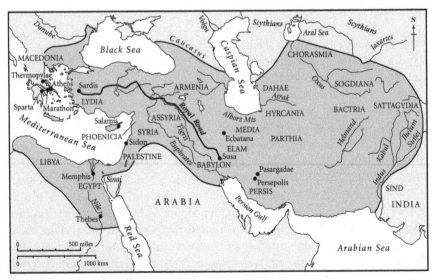

The Achaemenid Empire, 550–330 BC

arrived in the land in the third and second millennium BC, probably in more than one wave of immigration. Nomadic Iranian tribes settled across the Iranian plateau and by the first millennium BC, Medes, Persians, Bactrians and Parthians populated the western part, while the Iranian Pashtuns and Baluch began to settle on the eastern edge, on the mountainous frontier of north-western India and into what is now Baluchistan. There were still other Iranian peoples, such as the Scythian and Alan tribes, the former later harassing various Persian empires with their border raids.

Ancient Persian history begins with the creation of the first world empire by Cyrus the Great of the Achaemenids over two and half thousand years ago. This empire did not remain as glorious as it was under Cyrus and his successor once removed, Darius, but it was still the greatest world empire when it was defeated and conquered by Alexander the Great, characteristically within a short period of time in 330 BC. The Seleucid empire established after Alexander's death introduced aspects of Greek culture to Persian lands but not sufficiently deeply for them to take strong root in subsequent cultural developments. From 247 BC onwards Parthian Iranians of the north-east began to form a state, although it took another century for the Arsacid empire to come fully into its own. Nevertheless, a certain degree of Hellenism survived under the Arsacids, who were in turn overthrown in 224 AD by Ardeshir Babakan, founder of the Sasanian dynasty, once again with typical swiftness. The Sasanians were ethnically Persian and, having risen from Persis (*Pars*), tried to reconstruct the traditional Persian empire, though it was not as vast and powerful as that of the Achaemenids. More than four centuries later they were overthrown by Muslim Arabs, again in a relatively short time scale.

The reasons for the swift rise and fall of these empires were varied and numerous. But the arbitrary system of government which they all shared played a crucial role in hastening their downfall when faced with strong opposition. Such a system did not provide a social base for a state on whose loyalty and support it could depend in time of need for its defence and survival. Such was the case both in the demise of Darius III, the last of the Achaemenid emperors, in the fourth century BC and that of Mohammad Reza Shah in the twentieth century. The few historians who have taken note of this phenomenon have usually attributed it to the alienation of the *common* people from the state. Yet those states fell swiftly precisely because at the crucial moment they did not have the support of any of the social classes, and especially the upper classes which in a European-type class society would normally have defended the state against domestic trouble and foreign invasion (see Chapters 3, 6, 8 and 12).

MEDES AND PERSIANS

Of the various Iranian nomads who began to move into the Iranian lands from the north-east and north-west some time in the second millennium BC, the Medes and the Persians were destined to form, respectively, a local and a world empire. At the beginning of the eighth century BC the Iranian Median tribes united under the leadership of one of their chiefs, Dayukku, whom the Greeks called Deioces. He was thus the founder of the nascent Median state, which had to struggle for its survival with powerful neighbours such as Assyria, Urartu (later Armenia) and the Scythians, who were also of Iranian race. The capital city of the Medes was Ecbatana – meaning 'Place of Assembly' – which is now buried underneath the city of Hamadan. Dayukku's grandson, Cyaxares (Hovakhshatarah), was for a time a vassal of the Scythians but eventually consolidated his position by defeating them and annexing some of the regions around Lake Urmia in modern Azerbaijan.

Meanwhile, at some point in the eighth century the Iranian Persian tribes moved down from the north-west and settled in the central western Bakhtiyari Mountains. They were a vassal state of the Medians, and under Thiepes (Persian: Chishpish), king of the city of Anshan, extended their rule further towards the south-east at the expense of the Elamites, an old and indigenous civilization. The territory extracted from Elamite rule became known as Persis (Persian: Parsa; modern Fars) after its new occupants. Thiepes thus became King of Parsa as well as Anshan, but before his death in 640 BC he divided his kingdom between his two sons Cyrus (Persian: Kurosh) and Ariarnamnes (Ariarnamna). Cyrus became king of Anshan and Ariarnamnes, ruler of the south-eastern part of the territory of Persis proper. It was by the time of Cambyses (Kambujiyeh) I, king of Anshan and father of Cyrus the Great, that the two small Persian kingdoms were united. Cambyses was a vassal of the Median Cyaxares, who by this time had defeated the Assyrians and destroyed Nineveh for ever, and extended his empire from the Caspian littoral to Elam.

The Median empire, which had grown large and strong under Cyaxares, was not to last for long. The reign of Cyaxares's son, Astyages (Azhdahag, 584–550), was relatively peaceful until his empire was overthrown by Cyrus the Great, his own grandson by his daughter Mandana, who was married to the Persian king, Cambyses I. The revolt of Cyrus and his triumph over Astyages was characteristically short and decisive.

CYRUS THE GREAT

Cyrus (559–529) united the Medes and the Persians in 550 BC. Herodotus tells the legend that after the birth of Cyrus, Astyages had a dream which his magi interpreted to mean that his grandson would eventually overthrow him. He then ordered his steward to kill the infant boy. This the steward felt he could not do and so asked a herdsman to do it for him; but the latter kept the child and brought him up as his own. When Cyrus was ten years old, it appeared from his attitude and behaviour that he could not be a common man's son. His suspicions aroused, Astyages talked to the old steward, who confessed that he had not killed the boy. Angered, the king tricked him into eating his own son's flesh, but allowed Cyrus to return to his biological parents, Cambyses and Mandana. This is clearly a legend, the likes of which have been told about other legendary and historical figures, but may not be entirely without historical interest.

Cyrus succeeded his father to the throne of Anshan and Persis in 559. There are various legends about the causes of Cyrus' revolt in 553 against his grandfather and overlord. But the fact that the Medians of all ranks welcomed it and the Babylonians had broken their tie with the Medes played a crucial role. Having conquered the Medes, Cyrus then set out on a career of conquest, and by 530 or 529, the year of his death, he had created the first world empire. Next he attacked and conquered Lydia and much of Asia Minor, including some of its Greek cities. Traditionally the date of the conquest of Lydia was believed to be 547, but more recent scholarship has cast doubt on this. A few years later he turned his attention to the east to secure his eastern frontiers from nomadic incursion, conquering vast territories including Hyrcania, Parthia and Soghdiana up to the River Jaxartes (Seyhun or Syr Darya), which flows into the Aral Sea. Cyrus introduced agriculture in these regions and built fortress towns – of which the most famous now is the city of Samarkand in Uzbekistan – to defend the north-eastern part of his empire against the attacks of Central Asian nomads.

But the jewel in his imperial crown came with the conquest of Babylonia in 539, which was the oldest surviving civilization in the region and included Mesopotamia, Syria, Phoenicia and Palestine. The fairness and moderation with which Cyrus treated the conquered people is legendary. The Cyrus Cylinder, now in the British Museum, on which is proclaimed the freedom of his subject peoples in matters of religion and culture, is sometimes described as the first charter of human rights. While 'human rights' is a modern concept that is no more than two centuries old – dating back to the American and French Revolutions – the appellation may be relevant to the extent that it highlights moderation and toleration by a supreme overlord in a generally immoderate and intolerant age. Cyrus demonstrably respected the god Bel (Marduk) of the Babylonians, and famously released the Jews from captivity and ordered the temple at Jerusalem to be rebuilt.

When he began his conquests his capital was Anshan, making Ecbatana his second capital after he had extended his rule to Media. In another capital, Babylon, he was officially and ceremoniously invested as king, but he lived in all of these cities at different times. He founded his own new and entirely Persian capital, Pasargadae, which may have meant 'the camp of the Persians', some 150 kilometres north-east of the modern city of Shiraz. Its construction begun in 546 BC or later, and it was not yet finished when Cyrus died in 530 or 529, remaining the Persian capital until Darius began building another in Persepolis.

The archaeological site covers 1.6 square kilometres and includes the tomb of Cyrus, its greatest surviving monument, the fortress of Tall-e Takht sitting on top of a nearby hill and the remains of two royal palaces and gardens. Carved above the gate was a message in Old Persian, Elamite and Babylonian: 'I, Cyrus, the king, an Achaemenian'. The gardens are the earliest known example of the Persian *chahar bagh*, or fourfold garden design. Now in ruins, Pasargadae represented Persian art at its best in this period. Architectural and decorative borrowings from Babylonia, Egypt and other foreign lands were infused with indigenous Iranian art to produce a unique composite effect, an artistic wonder that some scholars have put above even the much more majestic and complete complex at Persepolis.

Traditions about how Cyrus died are varied. According to Herodotus, he was killed in battle as he rushed east to face intruding nomads of Iranian origin; Xenophon believed that he died of natural causes; and according to yet another tradition he was mortally wounded during an expedition to the Far East. He had already made his first son Cambyses (Kambujiyeh) king of Babylon and charged him with preparations for an invasion of Egypt, while his younger son, Bardiya, was in charge of the eastern provinces. Before setting out for Egypt in 525, Cambyses had his brother secretly murdered, apparently from the fear that he might revolt in his absence. He conquered Egypt and was believed to have displayed religious and cultural intolerance towards the Egyptians, although recent research has tended to modify that belief. Meanwhile, he heard that back in Persia an impostor had claimed to be Bardiya and had usurped the throne. It was while rushing back from Egypt that he died, perhaps by accidentally wounding himself with his own sword, deliberately committing suicide or in some other way.

HEYDAY OF THE EMPIRE

The usurper known as Gaumata (Greek: Smerdis) was a Median from the Magi tribe, who were generally religious figures although it is not clear if at that time they were Zoroastrian divines. He ruled for some three years until, in 522, Darius (Dariyush) and his fellow conspirators succeeded in destroying him. There is a colourful legend that to select the next King of Kings from among the conspirators they agreed to gather one morning in a meeting place and choose the person whose horse neighed first. This was the horse of Darius, as a result of a clever trick played by his groom.

The basis for this account of Gaumata and his demise is Darius' own spectacular inscriptions at Behistun (Bistun) near modern Kermanshah, and the much later writings of Herodotus. This account may be true. On the other hand it is not unreasonable to think of other possible scenarios. For example, 'the usurper' might in fact have been Bardiya, if the story of his assassination by Cambyses is untrue or indeed if he had survived the attempt. He might then have rebelled and declared himself king in the absence of his brother, which might have led to the latter's suicide or murder on his way back. In that case there would be two rebellions: Bardiya's against Cambyses and Darius' against Bardiya.

Whatever the truth, we shall note that fratricide, filicide and parricide were familiar features of Iranian history, resulting from the arbitrary nature of power and the fact that the success of a rebel was sufficient proof that he had the *farr* and his rule therefore legitimate (see the Introduction). And if the whole of Gaumata's story as received is true, it is important to observe that he was a religious figure and an apparently populist ruler who had abolished military service and remitted taxes for three years. Also characteristic of Persian history was the series of revolts that broke out after the fall of Gaumata, which Darius successfully suppressed. The death of a ruler nearly always led to chaos, at least for a while.

Darius (522–486) was an Achaemenid and a very able administrator who divided his vast empire into twenty satrapies, each with a governor, or satrap, and a military commander independent from him, both of whose activities were checked by a secret intelligence service – 'the shah's eyes and ears' – to forestall rebellion. Variations of this system survived in Iran until recent times, not least under the Pahlavis.

This did not stop revolts and rebellions breaking out in regions and provinces, which is not surprising in such a vast empire, made up of diverse peoples and run with the transport and technology of the age. There were revolts in Babylonia and elsewhere, but, in view of subsequent history, most important of all in Ionia, which led to defeat at Marathon a few years before Darius' death. Yet he extended the frontiers of the empire in the Caucusus, beyond the Caspian Sea and beyond the Oxus, which were inhabited by various Iranian and non-Iranian nomadic peoples.

The king's power was absolute and arbitrary, and the satraps, although largely autonomous in their domains, enjoyed the same kind of power in their satrapies as servants of the ruler. Justice meant that they and other state officials would not exercise their powers beyond what the king permitted as legitimate. Darius fixed the coinage and introduced the *Darik* or *Zarik* gold coins. The tax rate was standardized, though it varied from the richer to poorer satrapies. Each satrapy was assigned a gold and silver quota, which in some cases, such as Babylonia, was too heavy and led to economic decline. Another practice, which persisted in various forms down to the nineteenth century, was tax farming, whereby the province's revenues were contracted to a rich and powerful tax-farmer against a fixed annual payment by him to the state. This was then an efficient method of filling the state treasury but in effect delivered the people to the mercy of the tax-farmer.

Not only was Darius a very able civil and military ruler, but he was also a man of vision and grandeur, conscious of building monuments to his name and leaving his version of events to posterity. He began the building of the complex of palaces known as Persepolis some 70 kilometres north-east of Shiraz, buildings that redounded to his power and glory and to art. This was the new and most important capital of the empire, the others being at Babylon, Ecbatana and Susa, where he also built a monumental palace, of which unfortunately no part is still standing. Since he was usually on the move, the king and his retinue could winter in Susa, spend the spring in Persepolis and go to the cool elevations of Ecbatana during the summer.

Archaeological evidence suggests that the earliest remains of Persepolis date from around 518 BC, only four years after the accession of Darius. Some scholars have suggested that Cyrus chose the site of Persepolis, but it was Darius who built the terrace and the great palaces. He ordered the construction of Apadana Palace and the Debating Hall, the main imperial Treasury and its surroundings, which were completed during the reign of his son, Xerxes. Further construction continued until the downfall of the Achaemenid dynasty.

The greatest and most glorious palace at Persepolis was Apadana, used for the King of Kings' official audiences. The work began in 515 BC and was completed thirty years later. The palace had a grand hall in the shape of a square with seventy-two columns, thirteen of which still stand on the enormous platform in the surviving ruins of the city. The columns carried the weight of the vast and heavy ceiling. The columns' capitals were styled as animal sculptures, such as two-headed bulls, lions and eagles. The columns were joined to each other by oak and cedar beams. The walls were tiled and decorated with pictures of lions, bulls and flowers. Darius' name and the details of his empire were written in gold and silver on plates, which were placed in covered stone boxes in the foundations under the four corners of the palace. Two symmetrical stairways were built on the northern and eastern sides of Apadana. There were also two other stairways in the middle of the building. The external front views of the palace were covered with pictures of the Immortals, the kings' elite guards.

But perhaps no less spectacular as a feat of civil engineering was the construction of the royal road from Susa to Lydia, capital of Sardis. The road had 111 stations, was patrolled by army units, could be covered from end to end in three months, which was very fast for the time, and was used by the king's couriers to receive information and convey commands. Almost equally impressive was the construction of a canal in Egypt (already begun before the Persian conquest) from the Nile to the Red Sea, thus connecting the Mediterranean to the Indian Ocean.

In his inscriptions Darius addressed Ahura Mazda, the Zoroastrians' supreme deity, as the supreme lord to whom he owed his sovereignty on earth. This may be taken as evidence that he was a Zoroastrian but other evidence makes this unlikely. First, Zoroastrianism could not have been the state religion because, had this been the case, Darius, like Cyrus, would not have tolerated and sometimes even paid tribute to other people's cults and gods. Second, Zoroaster's name is not mentioned in any of the inscriptions. Third, the Achaemenid kings, including Darius, were buried in tombs, contrary to the strict Zoroastrian rule that the dead should be exposed to the elements. Fourth, Ahura Mazda was also one of the pre-Zoroastrian Iranian triad, Ahura Mazda-Mithra-Anahita. Besides, the cult of the entire Iranian pantheon flourished at this time and it is not even certain that ordinary Persians had yet fully absorbed Zoroastrianism (see Chapter 2).

Darius' war with Athens followed his subjugation of the Ionians and conquest of some Aegean islands and the suppression of the revolt of some Greek cities in Asia Minor that had been backed by Athens. The decisive battle was fought in Marathon in 490 in which the Persians were defeated. From the point of view of the Persian empire this was a relatively minor setback, but from the vantage point of Europe it was a historic event.

END OF EXPANSION

Xerxes (Khashayarsha, 486–465) had been viceroy of Babylon when his father died and he succeeded to the imperial throne. He possessed little of the genius of his father or Cyrus the Great. The Greek victory had led to a series of revolts in Asia Minor as well as Egypt which, typically of Iranian history, had been exacerbated on account of the death of the great shah. Xerxes' first task was to quell the rebellions. He was less inclined to campaigns for the expansion of his mighty empire than to court life and building palaces, including extensive additions to Persepolis. But there was pressure for punishing Athens and subduing the Greeks both from his own subordinates and from the Athenian exiles.

In 480 BC Xerxes, the Shahanshah, gathered the greatest army the world had yet seen – although the figure of a million men given in Greek sources is bound to be exaggerated – and crossed the Hellespont, secured Thessalay and Macedonia, broke the heroic resistance of the Spartans at Thermopylae, captured Athens and set fire to the Acropolis. Most of the Greek world in Asia, Africa and Europe was then in his possession. But the Greeks did not give up, concentrated their fleet on Salamis and defeated the King of King's forces at sea before his own eyes, watching as he was from his throne placed on the shore. The chance of Persian victory that yet remained was shattered by the shah's angry reaction, including the killing of his Phoenician admiral, which led to extensive desertions from his army and his withdrawal back to Persia. That ended the Persian ambitions for extending the empire to Europe.

Xerxes was an ill-tempered ruler with proclivities to impulsive and cruel behaviour. He was assassinated in a palace coup, the first of many of its kind in Iranian history if we discount the fate of Gaumata. In this case the assassin was the shah's own son.

GRADUAL DECLINE

The Achaemenid empire was to survive for more than 130 years after the death of Xerxes before it was conquered by Alexander the Great. But although the empire remained unrivalled in its vastness and power it had already passed its peak and was never to attain the glory that its founders had brought to it. The rest of Achaemenid rule was generally distinguished by court intrigues, assassinations and struggles for succession, with frequent rebellions often in more than one province at once. Bloodletting became virtually a regular feature of the court and the royal family, and some of the satrapies effectively passed out of the Great King's rule. There was a last-minute revival under Artaxerexes III, but the foundations had already been weakened beyond repair.

Artaxerexes I (Ardeshir, 465–424 BC) first had to put down the rebellion of his brother, the satrap of Bactria in the eastern reaches of the empire, which he followed by the slaughter of his remaining brothers. He then put down revolts in Egypt and Syria. His Greek policy was to use gold to play one local power against another. Thus he turned Sparta against Athens, but this enmity did not last and, reunited, they defeated the Great King in a war that resulted in the loss of some Greek cities and much of the aura of the Persians among the Greeks. There were also some territorial losses on the empire's eastern frontiers. The king's Babylonian policy was in the direction of Persianization, which caused dissent in that province. But he continued the friendly relations with the Jews.

Typically, there was a struggle for the succession after the death of Artaxerexes, his son Xerxes II quickly losing the throne to another member of the family who ruled as Darius II. His reign was riddled with intrigue and corruption. He continued to use Persian gold in his Greek foreign policy, with mixed results. Upon the revolt of the satrap of Sardis he sent a force that succeeded in suppressing the region, though the satrap's son continued his father's struggle. Egypt was perennially in revolt, and in 411 the Egyptians rose again, although rebellion subsided with the death of Darius later that same year.

Artaxerexes II succeeded his father, though his mother had preferred his younger brother, Cyrus, and had arranged for him to be satrap of Lydia and commander of the army in Asia Minor. Indeed, Younger Cyrus made an attempt on the life of his brother during the coronation ceremonies, but his mother saved him from punishment and he went back to his satrapy and command of troops in Asia Minor. Being brave and audacious he soon rose against his brother at the head of a strong army and almost won the battle before being struck down himself. It is sometimes believed that had he become shah he might have arrested the steady decline of the dynasty and empire. Artaxerexes famously could not prevent the 10,000 Greek mercenaries in Cyrus' army from marching back to Greece, the account of which has been colourfully told by Xenophon.

But he took back the towns of Ionia from the Greeks, if more with gold than with military action. Despite such successes the empire was in deep trouble. The Egyptians had been in revolt since the accession of Artaxerexes and attempts to subdue them did not succeed. A number of satraps revolted and in time all the countries west of the Euphrates, including Cyprus, were in revolt. Taxes had become oppressive. The rising of peasants and artisans who could barely feed themselves was put down, but was characteristic of the trend of events. The shah, tormented with continuing court intrigue, died after a long reign. He was remembered as a weak, unreliable and blood-thirsty monarch, influenced largely by his mother, a monarch who did not manage to maintain the frontiers of the empire.

Artaxerexes III (359–338 BC) mounted his father's throne and put his numerous brothers and sisters to death. He combined cruelty with an iron will which he applied to restore the empire's power and glory. He turned on the rebel satraps, as well as the Cadusians who had been in revolt for some time, with exemplary ruthlessness. Egypt was recaptured after two attempts and punished severely. Greece felt the pressure of the Persian reorganization – in fact, a determined leadership – and expansion. Campaigns for the unity of the Greeks and others who shared their culture did not get far. Meanwhile a fresh force from Macedonia, which was not Hellenic but was culturally Greek, began to enter the field. Philip, ruler of Macedon, who had annexed some Greek territories, began to be recognized as the leader they needed to stand up to the Persians. He moved cautiously, first concluding a peace treaty with the Great King. Not long afterwards, in 338 BC, Philip attacked Greece and put an end to Greek independence. The same year the strong Persian king was poisoned to death by his general, Bagoas.

This was the beginning of the end for the mighty Achaemenid empire. Bagoas also poisoned Artaxerexes' son just after he had acceded to the throne. It is not surprising that by then no obvious successor had survived, and it fell on the ill-fated Darius III (335–330), a family relative, to take over the realm. He, too, would have been poisoned by Bagoas had he not moved first and made the general drink his own medicine.

ALEXANDER AND THE FALL OF THE ACHAEMENIDS

Philip of Macedon had gathered a strong army when he fell victim to assassination. His successor, his young son Alexander, led an army of 40,000 men who met no resistance and liberated Persia's Greek colonies. The first clash came at Granicus, where the Persians were defeated. Darius had not taken Alexander seriously at first, but then led a large army and met him at Issus, where Alexander again defeated the Persian army, capturing Syria and being welcomed by Egypt. When Darius' peace offerings were rejected by Alexander, the final battle was fought in 331 at Gaugamela, among the foothills of the Assyrian mountains: here the Persian army broke and Darius fled to Ecbatana. This was tantamount to abdication, and, accordingly, Darius was soon killed by two of his satraps. The gateway to Susa and Persepolis was then open to Alexander's forces, but it is not clear whether Persepolis was burned intentionally or by accident. Alexander then traversed and subdued the eastern provinces, passing through Central Asia to India, and is said to have married a Bactrian noble girl called Roxanna (Roshanak). It is also reported that, back in Susa, he married a daughter of Darius named Statria, and likewise some of his generals and soldiers married Persian girls. However, the earlier view that Alexander had intended to unite Greece and Persia has been rejected by recent scholarship.

Thus the mighty Persian empire crumbled even more swiftly than it had been built.

Persian legends of Alexander

These legends are preserved in Ferdowsi's *Shahnameh*, Nezami's *Eskandar-nameh* (Book of Alexander) and some other sources, showing how Iranians adopted the conquerer as one of their own and raised him almost to the level of a sage. Philqus (a corruption of Philipus), King of Rum (= Greece), is a contemporary of the legendary Persian king Darab, son of Homay (see above). There is a war between them; Philqus sues for peace; Darab asks for the hand of his daughter Nahid, whom he joyfully marries. But later Darab loses interest in Nahid and sends her back to her father unaware that she is pregnant. She gives birth to a son whom she calls Sekandar (= Alexander). Philqus pretends this is his own son and makes him his heir. When Philqus dies Alexander becomes king of Rum. According to this legend, therefore, Alexander is half-Persian, of the line of Goshtasp and Bahman, and half-brother of Dara, his contemporary shah of Persia.

A philosopher called Arastatalis (= Aristotle) becomes Sekanadar's chief advisor in all matters. Dara sends an envoy to Sekandar to demand tribute from him. Sekandar refuses, and first attacks and conquers Egypt, then turns on Iran. The two armies meet at the River Euphrates. After a week's fighting a dust storm arises, blinding the Persians, who turn back – not through weakness but by a mysterious calamity. Sekandar's army captures Persepolis, the Persian capital, while Dara and his men retreat to Kerman. Dara's approaches to Sekandar are disregarded and Sekandar's forces rout the reluctant Persian army. At this, two of the shah's counsellors, believing that he is doomed, decide to kill him in the hope of receiving favours from Sekandar. They attack and mortally wound Dara and inform Sekandar of their deed. Sekandar asks them to lead him to the shah and tells Dara that he will return him to the Persian throne and exact terrible vengeance on his two assassins. Dara asks him to look after his children and kinsfolk and marry his daughter Roshanak (= Roxanna); Sekandar accepts.

Dara then dies. In the verse of Nezami's *Eskandar-nameh*: 'The acceptor rose, the requester slept.'

Sekandar declares himself the successor of Dara, pledges to carry out Dara's will and reassures everyone of their safety and security. Thus the Iranian legend turns defeat into triumph: Sekandar, son of Darab and half-brother of Dara, sits on the Persian throne in peace and prosperity. But the Persian legend of Sekandar or Eskandar does not end here. He leads campaigns against India and Egypt, visits the sacred Black Stone of Mecca and, being attracted by reports of Andalusia, visits that country incognito as his own ambassador, although he is recognized by the Andalusian queen who earlier has secretly had a portrait made of him.

The Alexandrian romances in Persian literature are varied and adventurous. The most fascinating and enduring – simplified versions of which were until recently a children's tale – is his pursuit of the Water of Life, the elixir of immortality. As told by Ferdowsi, in one of his adventures Sekandar comes across a city whose people, red-headed and pale-faced, are of enormous size. There he is told about the legend of a spring in the kingdom of darkness which they call the Water of Life and which immortalizes anyone who drinks from it. Sekandar chooses the best men of his troops and seeks out a guide, which he finds in the person of a prophet called Khezr ('the Greenman'). He gives Khezr one of the two rings in his possession which will shine like the sun at the sight of water and sends him in advance, keeping the other one himself to lead his troops in darkness. On the third day two different paths appear in the darkness, and then Sekandar disappears from Khezr's sight. Khezr alone reaches the stream of life, bathes in it, drinks from it and thus becomes immortal. It is interesting to note that the Persian legend of Alexander as told by post-Islamic writers includes such Islamic aspects as Mecca, the Black Stone and Khezr. Hafiz puts the myth of Alexander to another use: 'The Mirror of Sekandar is the chalice of wine, look / It will show you the kingdom of Dara like a book.'

◆ ◆ ◆

The Achaemenids built an empire and created a world civilization. Never before had such diverse and distant peoples and lands been brought under one rule, in spite of ethnic, religious, linguistic and cultural differences. The generally tolerant attitude of the state towards diverse cultures helped rather than hindered the development of a sense of community within the empire. The large scale of this society and economy resulted in the flourishing of agriculture and commerce, thanks to the extent of the market and the relative safety of roads and communications. The diversity of the peoples of the empire and their art, and the massive expenditure of central government on buildings, in addition to the luxury consumption of the upper classes, led to the emergence of a distinct Persian art in architecture, sculpture and decorative arts and crafts which even spread to foreign lands such as India.

There is no evidence of the scientific (other than astronomical/astrological) developments and philosophical speculation and historiography in which the contemporary Greeks excelled. But the freemen in Greece were citizens who were, within certain limits, free to indulge in such subjects without state interference. Absolute and arbitrary government had been the legacy of virtually all the subject peoples of the Persian empire, especially the old and more civilized of them, such as Babylonia and Assyria. This became a permanent feature of Iranian history although it did not arrest cultural and technological development: these could proceed from one short term to the next (see the Introduction), especially as the Persians were extremely good at adapting from other cultures.

The fall of the Achaemenids and the death of Alexander shortly afterwards led to the Hellenistic phase of Iranian history, when the country was ruled by the Seleucids, who were later driven out by the Parthian Iranians. Thus it took five centuries after the collapse of the first (Achaemenid) Persian empire for a second (Sasanian) Persian empire to take its place, the five centuries in which the Hellenic Seleucids and the Parthians ruled Iran.

CHAPTER 2

Greeks, Parthians and Persians

Zoroaster was ... the first to teach the doctrines of an individual judgement, Heaven and Hell, the future resurrection of the body, the General Last Judgement, and life everlasting for the united soul and body.

Mary Boyce

WITHIN TWENTY YEARS OF Alexander's death in 323 his vast empire was divided up between Macedonia (including Greece), the Macedonian Ptolemys of Egypt and the Seleucids of Iran. In the beginning the Seleucids held much of the old Achaemenid empire, excluding Egypt, southern Syria and parts of Asia Minor. Seleucus, one of Alexander the Great's officers and founder of the Seleucid dynasty, built two capitals: Seleucia, on the Tigris in Mesopotamia (modern Iraq), and Antioch, on the Orontes in Syria. The Seleucids adopted the basis of the Achaemenids' system of administration, and as heirs to the Achaemenids the state owned all the land. But they founded new cities and rebuilt some old ones under new names, which were run along the lines of the Greek *polis*, with its assembly of peoples, its council and its officials appointed annually.

Greek colonies were founded as far east as Bactria (Afghanistan), and aspects of Greek culture appeared in Iranian lands, including the Greek religion, which was practised along with other cults and religions. Greek, now the official language and the language of the upper classes, replaced Aramaic, which had been the official language under the Achaemenids. Greek was still spoken in Asiatic Greek cities under the Parthian Arsacids, surviving in their inscriptions and coins for a couple of centuries. It was not uncommon for Greeks and Macedonians to marry Persian women and settle in Persia. Thus Hellenization took place without compulsion or a designated official policy to promote it. Indeed, it was a two-way process, since the intermingling and intermarriage of the peoples also led to the Persianization of some Greeks, even in matters of religion.

Achaemenid art was inevitably interrupted because patronage passed on to the Seleucid court, the Greek settlers and colonies in Persia and the Hellenized Persian upper classes. The result was neither Greek nor Persian art but hybrid forms of both, which reflected a conscious or unconscious artistic compromise. There nevertheless existed both pure Greek art and pure Iranian art in addition to the hybrid forms, though from what little is known of the art of this period the Graeco-Iranian compromise tended to have greater currency.

The Seleucid empire was vast, stretching from the Mediterranean to Syr Darya (Jaxartes) and the Send (Indus), and was made up of various Iranian and non-Iranian peoples. Consequently, it proved more difficult to unite as one political body than the Achaemenid empire, if only because the latter's power was based on the Iranians of their empire whereas the Seleucid dynasty did not have such an Iranian base. By the middle of the third century BC the Seleucids had effectively lost control over Bactria and Parthia in the east, while the Romans were gradually advancing from the west. After losing Mesopotamia to the Parthians about a century later, they were reduced to little more than a monarchy made up of a couple of countries which were in effect largely independent. Shortly thereafter they were absorbed into the Roman empire, as were the rest of the Greek monarchies.

THE ARSACIDS

In 247 BC two brothers of Iranian Scythian origin dislodged the Seleucids in the north-east of their empire shortly after the Bactrian Greeks had declared independence from them. Arsaces (Arshak; Ashk) was a chief of the Parni tribe, one of the great Scythian (Saka) Dahae nomads from the region between the Caspian and Aral Seas. His rebellion led to the defeat of local Seleucid forces and the conquest of Parthia. The Parthians themselves had been originally a nomadic Iranian people who raided the eastern marches of the Achaemenid empire until they settled in Parthia and became subjects of that empire. At about the same time Arsaces' brother, Tiridates (Tirdad), wrested Hyrcania (Gorgan) from Seleucid hands. He built a strong defensive fortress and a new capital named after the founder of the dynasty, Arshak or Ashk (cf. the modern Ashgabat / Ashkabad, capital of Turkmenistan).

The Seleucids did not succeed against Tiridates in 228 because they had to withdraw their troops to face a revolt in Syria. By the time of his death in 211 Tiridates had extended his kingdom yet further at the expense of the Seleucids, and in the following, second, century BC the Arsacid kingdom regained all the Iranian lands, though they stopped well short of retrieving the whole of Achaemenid Persia. The true founder of the Parthian empire was Mithridates (Mehrdad) I, who between 160 and 140 BC conquered Media, Babylon and Seleucia, on the Tigris, and revived the Achaemenid title King of Kings. As the founder of the Parthian empire he is often compared to Cyrus the Great. He built a vast army camp outside Seleucia which later became Ctesiphon, capital of the empire.

The Parthians were semi-nomadic north-eastern strangers to the central and western Iranian lands that they conquered. They were therefore greeted with a good deal of hostility by their newly won Greek and Persian subjects, rather than being regarded as liberators. That is why the Seleucid emperor, when he led a major campaign to regain his losses, was welcomed by the peoples of many of the western provinces, although he was defeated and captured. The Greek Seleucids made a final attempt under Phraates (Farhad) II, and it looked as if all was lost by the Parthians. But they were lucky that the people of the reoccupied territories revolted against the Greek army's economic demands and so were able to counter-attack in 129 BC and drive the Seleucids back to Syria.

In the next few years fortune turned its back on the Arsacids. As so often happened in Iranian history, there was a massive nomadic invasion, from the east, this time by the Iranian Scythians (Sakas) of eastern Turkistan, which neither Phraates, who fell in battle, nor his uncle and successor, who also fell in battle, could stop. Meanwhile rebellions had broken out in the western provinces, including the Arab kingdom of Charecene (cf. Saracen). Once again it looked as if the Arsacid empire was threatened with annihilation when around 123 BC Mithridates II took over the realm. He has been compared with Darius I as the ruler who consolidated and rebuilt the Arsacid empire. But, before that, he first reasserted the Parthian grip in the west of the empire and only then turned to the east, where he pushed the nomads back to the far side of the River Oxus and turned their newly founded kingdom of Sakastan (later Sistan) into a vassal state. In the process, the Graeco-Bactrian kingdom was overrun, and by the beginning of the first century BC Saka kingdoms had taken its place.

It was under Mithridates that the Romans reached the Euphrates and for the first time became neighbours with the Parthians. He tried to woo them into an alliance against the kingdoms of Armenia and Asia Minor, which had successfully resisted Roman advances; but the famous Roman political and military leader Sulla, who knew little about the Parthians, responded with contempt. Therefore Mithridates, who felt slighted, himself entered into an alliance with those two kingdoms.

The foregoing has highlighted how the fortunes of Iranian history changed from one short term to the next. Typically, the death of the able and powerful Mithridates II in 88 BC was followed by almost three decades of decadence and decline. Armenia conquered as far south as Ecbatana (modern Hamedan) while the Armenian king was invited by the Seleucids to occupy the throne of Syria and called himself King of Kings. In this short term it looked as if the sun had completely set on the Arsacid empire, reducing them almost to the level of a vassal state. Yet the Romans, alarmed by the expansion of Armenia in Asia Minor, offered – or almost imposed – a treaty on Phraates III, who adhered to it with complete loyalty, though the Romans, not yet having shaken off their contempt of the Parthians, did not serve them well when they intervened in the settlement of the conflict between them and the Armenians.

In 58 BC Phraates was killed by his sons Mithridates III and Orodes (Orod) II, who then fought each other for the throne. Orodes won the contest and had his brother killed. A few years later, in 53 BC, Crassus, Roman triumvir and consul of Syria, decided to score a great victory over his fellow triumvirs (Julius Caesar

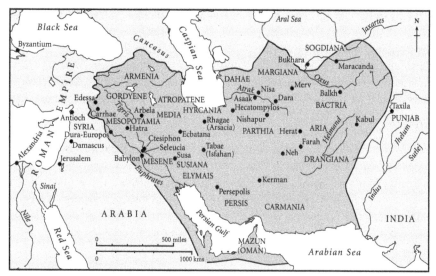

The Parthian Empire, 247 BC–AD 224

and Pompey) by attacking and inflicting a heavy defeat on the Parthians. This led to the battle of Carrhae (Haran), where the Parthian cavalry, led by the able Iranian general Sorena (Suren), broke Crassus' army, captured 10,000, killed and injured 20,000 more and sent Crassus' head to Orodes' court in Seleucia.

Once again there was a meteoric rise in the Iranians' fortunes. Some of this quickly turned, however, when Orodes decided to cash in on Crassus' defeat and march through Syria to the Mediterranean. It is true that the Parthians were usually better on the defensive than on the offensive, but at least some of the defeat of this campaign must have been due to the fact that Orodes had had the great general Sorena killed from fear and jealousy and put his own young and inexperienced son in command. Orodes in turn was killed by his son Phraates IV despite the fact that he had nominated him as his successor.

From then onwards the Parthians had to face the Romans in the west and deal with the perennial invasion of Iranian nomads from Outer Iran in the east. The campaigns of Mark Antony, a member of the second Roman triumvirate, did not pay off in the end and later he lost ground to Augustus. But the Romans adopted a friendly attitude towards the Parthians, realizing that their frequent palace coups and slaughter of royalty, quarrelling amongst the clans, the tendency towards provincial rebellion and frequent invasion from the east would prevent them from becoming a serious menace to the Roman empire. For the same reasons it was not difficult for Rome to interfere in the internal affairs of Parthian Iran.

The first major Roman invasion was led by the Emperor Trajan in AD 115 and resulted in the fall of Ctesiphon. For a while it looked as if Parthia was lost for ever, but, in the next short term, pressure from the forces in the north-east pushed the Romans back. Twice more was Ctesiphon to fall into Roman hands before the Parthians were replaced by the Sasanians. Under Vologases (Balash) III the Parthians went on the offensive and made some advances, but the Romans turned the tide against them and in AD 165 once again entered Ctesiphon. Though this victory was short-lived, still some of the western Iranian provinces had to be ceded to Rome, especially as the Parthians' continual struggle for succession to the throne resulted in feeble and divided leadership. This was what enabled Emperor Septimus Severus to attack and capture Ctesiphon again in AD 197. On the other hand, in AD 217 Artabanus (Ardevan)V defeated the Romans heavily and exacted a high price from them. But fortune had now permanently turned its back on the Parthians, for while Artabanus and his brother Vologases V were busy fighting each other for the throne the rebellion in Persis led to the downfall of the Parthians in AD 224.

The Parthian system of administration was loose and, by comparison with the Achaemenid system, decentralized. In fact it did not change much from the late Seleucid system when the vassal states had become stronger and largely autonomous. The Arsacids did not, and perhaps could not, change that system, partly because their own origin was nomadic and partly also because the old western provinces did not look up to them as culturally equal. Indeed, when there was a clash with the Seleucids and later the Romans the old countries of the empire often welcomed the invaders. That is why whenever the Arsacids were in dire trouble they tried to organize support from people of their own origin in the north-east, to the east of the Caspian Sea.

Nevertheless, in normal times they were in charge of the empire and the vassal states had to pay tributes and taxes and to contribute to the military forces whenever there was an external war. Hence the description of the Arsacids by early Islamic historians as *Muluk al-Tawa'if*, literally meaning 'Kings of Tribes' (see the Introduction). There were some differences with the Achaemenid system even at the centre, especially with the existence of two councils – one of the great nobles and one of the elders and magi – who advised the king. It is, however, unclear what the nature of these councils and their power was since events took place on a short-term basis and the element of continuity was lacking, but outside periods of weakness, decline and chaos, the emperor held full authority.

While there were always men under arms both at the centre and in the vassal states, there was no central army as such and, as noted above, levies would be called from across the empire at times of war. The cream of the army consisted of heavy and light cavalry, the latter consisting of mounted archers who were especially noted for their mobility and ease of manoeuvring.

Perhaps because they had succeeded the Greek Seleucid empire in Iran for centuries, the Arsacids continued to use the inscription 'Philhellene' on their coinage, indicating their positive attitude towards Greek culture, and in fact to Hellenistic Iran. Twentieth-century Iranian historians tended to interpret this as lack of nationalism. But the application of such modern ideologies to ancient times is anachronistic and inappropriate. In fact it is likely that the Parthians, as simple and undeveloped nomads, were themselves influenced by the Hellenized Persians of the Iranian hinterland. However, the first signs of a neo-Iranian cultural revival appeared under Vologases I in the first century AD. On the reverse side of his coinage a fire altar was depicted together with a sacrificing priest, and the money bore letters of the Arsacid Pahlavi (Parthavi/Parti) alphabet, the latter language evolving under the Parthians from Old Persian and later developing into Sasanian Middle Persian or Pahlavi.

Scholars disagree about the religion of the Arsacids. The cults of the old Iranian pantheon were certainly worshipped at this time, but it cannot be easily assumed that the Arsacids were Zoroastrian, since they tolerated Greek as well as Iranian cults, whose bloody sacrifices would be repugnant to Zoroastrians, and great temples flourished particularly dedicated to the worship of the old Iranian triad, Ahura Mazda-Mithra-Anahita (see below). It must be emphasized that in any case the religions of the common people were very likely mixed and varied.

The known literature of the period consists largely of religious hymns and traditions, which are likely to have remained mainly oral. The short Pahlavi story *Derakht-e Asurik* (Assyrian Tree), relating a debate between a goat and a palm tree, is likely to date from the Parthian period, though its origins are in ancient Sumerian culture. The ancient romance *Vis o Ramin*, which in some ways may be compared with the European Tristan and Isolde story and which has been rendered in Persian verse by the eleventh-century poet Fakhr al-Din As'ad Gorgani, is normally traced back to the Arsacid period, although it is no longer extant in the Parti-Pahlavi language.

Parthian art and architecture reflected the artistic eclecticism of the period. Most of the architectural remains lie in the west and are influenced by Achaemenid, Hellenistic and Mesopotamian forms, tempered by their own nomadic traditions. Some of the most important features of Sasanian and Islamic art, for example the *eyvan* (or *ivan,* the huge portal before the entrance) and stucco decoration, have their origin in the Arsacid period.

THE SASANIANS

The Sasanians ruled Persia for over four centuries between AD 224 and 651, when they were overthrown by Muslim Arabs. They ran an empire which at its greatest was as large as that of the Achaemenids, if one excludes Egypt, Syria and Asia Minor. Evidently they knew little of Achaemenid history, and yet the centuries of Hellenistic and Parthian rule had left a significant social and cultural

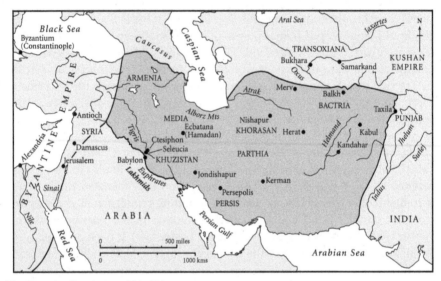

The Sasanian Empire, AD 224–651

impact on Iran. Persis, or Persia proper, had nevertheless retained certain traditional Persian characteristics and Zoroastrianism had flourished there more widely and strongly than elsewhere. Strangely enough, Iranian myths and legends gathered under Sasanian rule completely ignore the Achaemenids (see Chapter 1). But their disregard of the Arsacids is largely explained by the fact that they had defeated and destroyed them. This was a familiar feature of history writing, and not just in Iranian history: the Tudors were not very complimentary towards the Plantagenets, or the Bourbons towards the Valois.

The Sasanians' international problems arose from periodic conflicts in three of their frontiers: west, east and north. In the west they faced the Byzantine Romans – the Eastern Roman empire centred in Constantinople, which had come into existence in AD 395 upon the division of the Roman empire into the western and eastern empires – the objects of their conflicts often being Armenia and western Mesopotamia. In the east they faced the pressure, and sometimes downright power, of various eastern nomads. Some of them, notably the Kushans, racially of Iranian stock, and others of east-central Asian origin, notably the Hephthalites (or White Huns), established semi-nomadic states one after the other next to or inside the eastern marches of the Sasanian empire. They were later supplanted by Turks, who were destined to play epoch-making roles in Iran, western Asia and eastern Europe in centuries to come. In the north the Sasanians had to contend with the perennial raids of nomadic Huns, apart from the 'Armenian question', which was at once a separate problem and a bone of contention with Rome, or rather Byzantium.

But while the Sasanians' foreign problems and conflicts have been sufficiently described and discussed, less attention has been paid to their internal divisions and difficulties. In fact the age-old Iranian tendency towards conflict over the succession and chaos as a result of foreign or domestic weakness was also evident under Sasanian rule, so that there were many more years of near anarchy or weak government than of stability and firm rule. And, as part of that, the arbitrary killing and maiming of members of the royal family and the senior administration were not infrequent occurrences.

Only four Sasanian rulers ably defended or extended the empire's frontiers and maintained powerful and stable governments at home: in the third century AD, Ardeshir Babakan, founder of the empire, and his son Shapur I; in the fourth century, Shapur II; in the sixth century Chosroes (Khosraw) I, entitled Anushiravan. Bahram V (Wild Ass), in the fifth century, and Chosroes (Khosraw) II, Parviz, in the sixth to seventh centuries, are also famous, but that is due to the legendary romances based on their life and times rather than their ability and competence.

The Sasanian ruler was, like previous Iranian rulers, omnipotent and, as one such ruler described himself, 'companion of the stars and brother of the sun and moon'. His word was law. The grand vizier, or *vozorg farmandar* ('the great governor'), was the next most powerful in the land, more powerful than princes of the blood, but constantly in danger of losing everything including his property and life. The pattern remained the same throughout Iranian history.

According to historical tradition there were four main social classes in Sasanian society. These classes may have been further subdivided, but the most difficult problem regarding stratification is that the sources are thin and their interpretation by archaeological historians not always reliable. The four classes traditionally mentioned are priests, the armed forces (probably only higher officers), administrators or scribes and commoners, who are subdivided into peasants and artisans. Note that the first three classes were in fact professional groups in the pay of the state; their rank and composition were determined by their position in the state hierarchy, and they must have represented only a tiny percentage of the population, with peasants and craftsmen making up some 95 per cent.

The administration of the state was centralized along Achaemenid lines. A few vassal states remained, the remaining provinces being run not by satraps but by governors-general or *marzbans*, who played an important role, especially in the frontier provinces, in keeping the peace and managing their regions. Secretaries, administrators or scribes (*dabiran*) made up the heads of the bureaucracy and ran the *divans* or 'ministries', including matters regarding finance, justice and war. There were two principal taxes. The land tax or *kharaj* was levied on agricultural produce and varied from region to region according to yields. It consisted of at least one-third of the produce and could rise to as much as one-half.

This system was later taken over by the Arabs and those who replaced them, the term *kharaj* being retained. The other principal tax was the poll tax, or *gezit*, which every individual was obliged to pay. The Arabs later called this *jezieh* and applied it only to non-Muslims. Other revenues included the income from crown lands and the exploitation of mines, which, like all natural resources, were ultimately owned by the state. War booty was another source of revenue but losses were correspondingly made at times of defeat. Customs duties collected at the frontiers were another significant source of revenue. The trade routes remained more or less the same as before, Iran being the commercial link between East and West, a role she continued to play for centuries to come.

The official Sasanian language was Parsi or Middle Persian, later to be known as Pahlavi. It used a form of the Aramaic script, so complicated by the frequent use of *hozvaresh*, or ideograms, that only a small minority, largely scribes, are likely to have had it in their command: for example, the word *shahanshah* was written as the ideogram *malekan-maleka* but read *shahanshah*. Not much has survived of Sasanian literature and historiography, except for religious, mystical and mythological texts or their later renderings in post-Islamic literature. Some works may have been lost after the Arab conquest. Little of the *andarz* literature or formal counsels on manners and morals, 'mirrors for princes', and folklore survived beyond that time. Some texts, notably *Khodaynamag*, the main body of epic literature, were later translated into Arabic, although in this case both the original and the translation are now lost.

A text that is held up as an excellent example of Sasanian literature is the sixth-century translation of the Indian fable *Panchtantara*, which did survive in the Pahlavi language long enough for it to be translated into Arabic, and was later translated and adapted into New Persian, both in poetry and prose, as *Anvar-e Soheili* and *Kelileh o Demneh*. Sasanian poetry, mainly accentual, included the *sorud*, used for celebration and exaltation, the *chekameh*, a kind of narrative poetry, and the *taraneh*, or short poetical songs. *Ayadgar-e Zariran* (The Exploits of Zarir) described the exploits of the hero Zarir. Together with *Derakht-e Asurik* (The Assyrian Tree), mentioned above, this seems to have been translated from Parthian originals.

There is little trace of Sasanian philosophy or speculative sciences, and in fact it is unlikely that such disciplines existed in this period. Persian medicine, based on ancient Greek knowledge, developed and was taught and studied in a few medical academies, notably at the academy in Jondishapur. A famous Sasanian physician-cum-philosopher whose name has survived is Borzuyeh the Physician, the translator of *Kelileh o Demneh*. He added an autobiographical essay to his translation which has a certain charm but does not reflect any wide or deep scientific or philosophical knowledge.

The Sasanians formed the first Iranian state to have an official religion, Zoroastrianism; since then Iran has always had a state religion. Nevertheless, other cults and faiths had open or secret currency at this time, including Judaism, Christianity and Buddhism.

ZOROASTRIANISM

Zoroastrianism emerged from ancient Indo-Iranian cults. The Indo-Iranians were Indo-Europeans who lived as pastoral semi-nomads, probably in the southern steppes of Russia, east of the Volga and Central Asia. They forged a strong religious tradition, elements from which still survive in our time both in Zoroastrianism and Hinduism.

They held fire and water to be sacred and worshipped a pantheon of nature gods such as the Earth, Sky, Sun and so forth. They believed that the world was made up of seven regions, the biggest being that inhabited by human beings. *Asha* was the principle of natural law as well as order and truth. It was opposed by *drug*, disorder and lie. There were three principal gods: Varuna, the god of the oath and lord of the waters, Mithra, the god of the covenant and lord of fire, and Ahura Mazda, whose name in Avestan literally meant 'Lord Wisdom'. There were other gods, including Khavaarenah or Divine Grace (later *farr*), who supported kings, heroes and prophets but dropped them if they abandoned the right path.

Zoroaster

Zoroaster is the English name of the prophet Zarathushtra, who revolutionized the ancient Iranian cult and taught the first revealed religion of the world. There is much uncertainty about the time and place of his birth. He may have been born in Choresmia (Kwarazm, south of the Aral Sea), or in Sistan. His father was from Media, his mother probably from Rhaga, an ancient city in Central Asia, and he preached in the east, in Bactria, modern Afghanistan. Traditionally the prophet's lifetime was placed between the seventh and sixth centuries BC but more recent studies have pushed this back to between the fifteenth and eleventh centuries, 1400–1000 BC.

According to the *Gathas*, the seventeen hymns in verse which are his own works, Zoroaster was trained for the priesthood and probably became a priest at the age of fifteen. Zoroastrian tradition claims he was thirty when he received his call: he saw a shining divine being at the bank of a river which led him to the presence of Ahura Mazda, flanked by six other radiant beings. The six divine beings were the Amesha Spentas (Persian: Ameshaspendan), headed by the Supreme Being Ahura Mazda. It was there and then that the prophet received his revelation.

As noted above, the Indo-Iranian cult put Mazda on a par with two other ahuras. Zoroaster proclaimed Ahura Mazda – Spenta Mainyu (or the Holy Spirit) – as the one eternally existing god and supreme creator of all that was good, including all the beneficent divinities. Coexisting with Ahura Mazda was the lord of darkness, Ahriman – Angra Mainyu (the Hostile Spirit) – the equally uncreated god who is the supreme lord of everything bad, of 'non-life', in contrast to Ahura Mazda who is lord over all that is good, over 'life'. There are thus two supreme spirits in Zoroastrian theology, and nothing evil can be regarded as the creation of Ahura Mazda, the supreme god whom Zoroaster worshipped. The lord of darkness, Ahriman, not having been created by Ahura Mazda (later: Ormazd), Zoroastrianism appears to be a dualistic religion. In fact it is devotionally monotheistic since it recognizes and worships only one supreme beneficent god, its dualism being theological or metaphysical, and it ends with the inevitable triumph of good over evil, of Ahura Mazda over Ahriman.

The six beneficent divinities together with Ahura Mazda make up the holy Zoroastrian heptad which appeared to Zoroaster in his first revelation. All these lesser divinities (comparable with the archangels in the Abrahamic religions) emanated form Ahura Mazda, and together with him fashioned the seven creations which make up the world. These Amesha Spentas or Holy Immortals in their turn evoked other beneficent divinities who are in fact the beneficent (as opposed to malign) gods of the pre-Zoroastrian paganism, including Mithra, who is thus demoted from his high position of being one of the Ahuras. These lesser divinities are known as Yazatas (Persian: Izadan, Yazdan), who are often invoked by Zoroaster himself in his hymns.

Zoroaster assigned individual responsibility to human beings for clean living and care for others, summarized in the moral code 'good thoughts, good words, good deeds'.

Cosmic history
All beneficent life led by humans emanates from and is created by Ahura Mazda, who created the world of spirit and matter in two stages. This exposed the perfect static creation of Ahura Mazda to attack by Ahriman, and a furious war broke out between the forces of good and evil, light and darkness, which inaugurated the second phase of cosmic history, that of the Mixed State where good and evil exist side by side. This is the present world, the world known to mortal human beings in their history.

Once the war by Ahura Mazda, the Holy Immortals, the Yazatas and good human beings is won against the forces of darkness led by Ahriman then the third and last phase of the Zoroastrian cosmic history begins. The Mixed State thus comes to its end and is followed by the State of Separation. This is the state of permanent and everlasting bliss for holy spirits and human beings alike. Zoroastrian cosmic history thus consists of three cosmic cycles: Creation, the Mixed State and Separation.

All human beings, irrespective of rank and gender, will go to paradise (Old Persian: *pardis* = garden) if they are worthy. The deceased is met on the Bridge of the Separator by three angels who weigh up his or her worldly deeds on a scale. If the scale tips towards the good deeds the person is sent to paradise, if bad deeds, to hell, and if they just balance, to purgatory, a neutral state of neither bliss nor torment that lasts until the end of the world.

The soul's entry into paradise will not attain perfect bliss while the world is in the Mixed State, when the struggle between good and evil still goes on. Perfect bliss will prevail only at the end of that phase when evil is utterly and irreversibly defeated and all bodies are resurrected to join their respective souls in the other world. It is only from the onset of this third and last cycle that perfect bliss returns to all existence, as was the case in the first cycle, the cycle of Creation.

The saviour

Zoroaster seems to have taught that a saviour will come after him to lead the final war on evil and return peace, harmony and bliss to the world. His followers believe in the eventual advent of Saoshyant, who will be born of the sacred seed of the prophet himself, which is miraculously preserved at the bottom of a lake. When the time comes, a virgin will bathe in the lake and become pregnant with the prophet's seed, giving birth to a child who will thus become the saviour of humankind. According to Zoroastrian theology, though not Zoroaster's own direct teaching, the world will last six thousand years from beginning to end. Zoroaster's mission begins in the year 3000. At the end of each subsequent millennium there will rise a saviour who is defeated by Ahriman, except the third and last one, Saoshiyant, who will triumph and save humankind.

The popular belief in Iran and elsewhere that Zoroastrians are fire-worshippers is due to a misunderstanding. Zoroastrians did indeed hold fire sacred, as the symbol of light. The guardian of fire was Mithra (Persian: Mehr), one of the three Ahuras of the Indo-Iranian cult who became a lower divinity – one of the Yazatas – in Zoroastrianism. The original cult of Mithra migrated to the West and went through certain developments to give rise to the cult of Mithraism, which was popular with the Roman armies and reached as far as Scotland. Still today Iranians display awareness of the festival of Mehregan in the solar month Mehr, the autumnal equinox, and more actively celebrate the festival of Yalda on 21 December, winter solstice, the first day of winter and the longest night of the year. *Yalda* means birth in Aramaic and – although many modern Iranians are unaware of this – it is the ancient festival of the birth of Mithra. It is generally believed that Christmas, 25 December, has been influenced by *Yalda* since Mithraism was a popular cult in Syria and Palestine at the time of Christ's mission. Recent scholarship has gone further than that and traced influences of Mithraism in Christianity itself.

Thus, fire as a symbol of 'Asha' and the 'original light of God' holds a special place of esteem in the Zoroastrian religion. Prayers were normally held in front of a fire, and consecrated fires were kept perpetually burning in the major temples. Fire temples were built in all Sasanian lands where the faithful held their communal prayers and sang the sacred hymns in front of permanent fires. The site of some of Shii *Imamzadehs* that one finds in in virtually every Iranian village – scared places in which the believers say their ritual prayers and/or ask for intercession with God – might well have been fire temples dedicated to Mithra, Anahita, goddess of the waters, and other Yazatas.

Zoroastrians did not bury their dead, nor did they cremate them because they believed that such rites pollute earth and fire. Instead, they exposed them to the elements in *dakhmeh*s or towers of silence, so that nature would clean their bodies through time. This practice has now been abandoned among Iranian Zoroastrians in favour of burial.

The advent of Islam led to the gradual conversion of many Zoroastrians and persecution of others until it was firmly established that as a People of the Book (in this case *Avesta*) they should be allowed freedom of worship along with Jews and Christians, against the payment of a special tax. Many emigrated to India, where they were given refuge on condition that they did not proselytize. These Zoroastrians were the ancestors of the modern Parsi or Parsee community of India and elsewhere. But Zoroastrianism is still alive in Iran, centred mainly in the cities of Yazd, Keraman and Tehran, using various dialects of a language they call 'dari', not to be confused with the official name given to the Persian language as it is spoken in Afghanistan.

Zorvanism

The Zorvanite heresy appeared in the late Achaemenid period, and its influence and long survival is explained by the fact that Sasanian rulers and many nobles were themselves Zorvanites. Zorvan in Avestan means 'time'. The Zorvanites maintained that both Ahura Mazda (Ormazd) and Ahriman had been born of Zorvan (= Zurvan) and were thus brothers in perpetual conflict. Since Ahriman, the force of darkness, had thus been born of the remote absolute lord as well, they explained that he came into being as a result of a moment of doubt by Zorvan about his powers to beget a worthy son.

All subsequent creation was still made by Ahura Mazda, and all the power over this world had been entrusted to him by his 'father', Eternal Time, so that the rest of the Zoroastrian manner of worship and moral goals remained the same. On the other hand, Ahura Mazda was now a created god and, moreover, his being the brother of Ahriman destroyed the basic Zoroastrian principle of the total separation of good and evil. Zorvanism also opened the way for reflection and meditation upon the power of time and its influence on human lives and world events. It therefore led to the doctrine of fate and predestination, which ran contrary to the Zoroastrian principle of free will and personal responsibility. Some of the utter and intractable fatalism of later mystic and non-mystic Persian poets and thinkers such as Khayyam, Baba Taher, Sa'di and Hafiz may have its distant origins in Zorvanite doctrines. Their influence still persists in Persian language and literature through such words a *ruzegar, dahr* and *zamaneh*, all of which imply the absolute dominion of time over human destiny.

The legacy of Zoroastrianism

Despite its metaphysical dualism, Zoroastrianism is the first monotheistic and universal religion. Scholars have argued that until the end of the Jewish captivity in Babylon Yahweh was just a tribal god and that it was in consequence of their release by Cyrus the Great and their coming into contact with Zoroastrian teachings that in their later scriptures God assumes a universal and almighty quality. However that may be, it is likely that Zoroastrian teachings about world history, from the creation to the final judgement, predated those of the Jews, and therefore Christians and Muslims. The Zoroastrians seem to have been the first to give human beings moral choice and regard them as responsible for their actions, be they good or evil. Their concept of the saviour who will come and rid the world of all evil for ever was original. So were the ideas of heaven and hell, individual judgement after death and universal judgement at the end of the world. The late R.C. Zaehner, who held the Chair of Eastern Religions at Oxford University, wrote:

> from the moment the Jews first made contact with the Iranians they took over the typical Zoroastrian doctrine of an individual afterlife in which rewards are to be enjoyed and punishment endured. This Zoroastrian hope gained ever surer ground during the inter-testamentary period, and by the time of Christ it was upheld by the Pharisees, whose very name some scholars have interpreted as meaning Persian, that is, the sect most open to Persian influence.

According to the late Mary Boyce, a leading scholar of Zoroastrianism at London University:

> Zoroaster was . . . the first to teach the doctrines of an individual judgement, Heaven and Hell, the future resurrection of the body, the General Last Judgement, and life everlasting for the united soul and body. These doctrines were to become familiar articles of faith to much of mankind, through borrowings by Judaism, Christianity and Islam; yet it is in Zoroastrianism itself that they have their fullest logical consequence, since Zoroaster insisted both on the goodness of the material creation, and hence of the physical body, and on the unwavering impartiality of divine justice. According to him, salvation for the individual depended on the sum of his thoughts, words and deeds, and there could be no intervention, whether compassionate or capricious by any divine Being to alter this. With such a doctrine, belief in the Day of Judgement had its full awful significance, with each man having to bear the responsibility for the fate of the world.

Scholars of other religions may not entirely agree with the above assertions and assessments, but few would doubt that Zoroastrianism has been an original, innovative and comprehensive world religion.

ARDESHIR BABAKAN AND THE RISE OF
THE SASANIANS

As noted in Chapter 1, the Sasanians make up the third and last cycle of *Shahnameh*, but one which is not mythological and which mixes history with legend. In *Shahnameh* and other traditional sources Ardeshir descends directly from Bahman, grandson of the hero prince Esfandiyar and great-grandson of Goshtasp, who significantly was the first shah to convert to Zoroastrianism (see Chapter 1). His ancestor Sasan had become a shepherd through misfortune. His grandfather, also named Sasan, was, according to Ferdowsi, also a shepherd, marrying the daughter of a local king, Babak, who gave birth to Ardeshir; while according to the historian Tabari he was in charge of a fire temple in Pars and married the local king Barzangi's daughter, who gave birth to Babak the father of Ardeshir.

But most important of all Ardeshir has the *farr*, Divine Grace. When he is running away from the last Arsacid emperor, Ardevan (or Artabanus), and is being chased by him, the latter reaches a town through which the former has passed. He asks if Ardeshir had been seen there and, in Ferdowsi's verse, he is told that they had seen:

A ram galloping after a rider
More beautiful than fabulous pictures.

Ardevan's counsel then tells him it would be useless to go on chasing Ardeshir, because Grace in the form of the Ram is accompanying him. The rock relief at Naqsh-e Rostam shows Ardeshir's investiture, receiving the diadem from the god Ahura Mazda. Both man and god are shown mounted on horseback while Grace is being conferred. Trampled under the feet of their horses are Ahriman, the god of darkness and evil, and Ardevan, the fallen and perished Arsacid emperor.

In real history, Ardeshir was already ruler of Pars when he rebelled against his overlord Artabanus (Ardevan). He was son of Babak son of Sasan, who in his time had been the high priest of the temple in the city of Estakhr. After the death of Babak, Ardeshir was about to rebel against his elder brother, Shapur, who had replaced their father, when Shapur died before war broke out between them. Ardeshir reunited the kingdom of Pars under his rule and extended his authority to neighbouring provinces as well. Artabanus was alarmed and sent another of his vassals to fight Ardeshir. Ardeshir defeated him, took to the offensive and in the third successive battle in AD 224 finally defeated Artabanus, who lost his life.

Typical of Iranian history, however, Ardeshir's triumph led to the rebellion of other vassals and provinces, who wished to become independent and/or – as in the case of the king of Armenia – emperor themselves. They had the support of the Romans and northern Scythians (Sakas). Faced with Ardeshir's determined resistance they withdrew, but still it took Ardeshir ten years to stamp out the rebellion completely. At that point, direct conflict with Rome became inevitable, and after a series of defeats Ardeshir made some territorial gains at the expense of Rome.

SHAPUR I AND THE RISE OF MANICHAEISM

There is a legend in *Shahnameh* and other traditional sources about the birth of Shahpur I. In one of them, Shahpur's mother, the daughter of Ardevan, tries to poison Ardeshir, who had killed her father and married her; she is caught, and Ardeshir orders the high priest to put her to death. According to another source, Ardeshir orders his wife's death upon discovering that he has inadvertently married Ardevan's daughter, whose whole house he had vowed to destroy. But the girl is pregnant and the priest secretly keeps her at his own home, where she gives birth to a son. Years later when Ardeshir is unhappy about being childless the priest tells him the secret and he rejoices in having a son and heir.

It was in 240 upon Ardeshir's death or retirement that his son Shapur mounted the throne. First he attacked the Kushan empire, which had grown rich and powerful on the eastern marches of Persia, gaining considerable territory and reducing the Kushans to a small vassal state of Iran. It would not take very long before the Chionite Hephthalites (White Huns) would appear in the same region and menace not just the frontiers but at times the whole of the country. The perennial war with Rome extended Persian territories to the north and west. At one stage the Roman emperor Valerianus himself became a prisoner and died in captivity. A famous relief on the wall of Naqsh-e Rostam shows Shapur mounted while Valerianus is kneeling in front of his horse. Shapur also had to deal with the perennial menace from the north and north-east. He founded the city of Nev-Shapur, later Neishabur, in Khorasan.

Mani and Manichaeism

It was during Shapur's reign that Manichaeism made its first appearance. Mani was an Iranian born in 216 from noble Parthian descent eight years before Ardeshir Babakan founded the Sasanian monarchy. His father had joined an ascetic community in Babylonia, where Mani grew up to speak a Semitic language. Mani saw his mission as providing a synthesis of Zoroastrianism, Christianity and Buddhism, which both borrowed from and influenced Gnostic ideas and was also influenced by Hinduism and Babylonian beliefs. It was this eclecticism that made it possible for Manicheans to pass as heretics in various different religions.

Mani maintained all the basic tenets of Zoroastrianism: the belief in God and the devil, heaven and hell, the three States, individual judgement after death, the last judgement and so forth. But he taught a strict dualism of spirit and matter. This differed fundamentally from Zoroastrian dualism where in the First State, the cycle of creation, and before Ahriman's attack, spirit and mind had existed in a blissful union. And, unlike Zoroastrianism, his view of the present world, the Mixed State, was highly pessimistic, describing it as one in which spirit is imprisoned by and in matter, struggling to break free from it and return to the perfect state of pure light. He virtually identified Light with spirit and Darkness with matter, the mixture of which led to the domination of good by evil. It is not difficult to see the connection between this view and related Gnostic ideas with the attitude of the later Islamic mystics who advocated the destruction of *nafs*, the material self, to liberate the spirit and reunite it with its blissful origin. Thus Rumi wrote: 'Let me taste the wine of union so that, drunk / I break down the gate of the eternal prison.' And Hafiz: 'I am a bird of the celestial garden, not from earth / It is for a short while that they have put me in my body's cage.'

Mani saw nothing good arising from nature, physical existence and individual life in this world, and taught ascetic living, celibacy and vegetarianism. He was well received at first by Shapur I, but was denounced by the Zoroastrian priesthood, who saw him both as a heretic and as a threat to their power. Advised by Shapur to go into exile, he spent many years in Central Asia and western China, where he made many converts. Upon Shapur's death in 272 he returned to Iran and was welcomed by the new shah, Hormazd I, but the latter soon died and his successor, Bahram I, disliked Mani and his creed so much that he put him to a horrible death. Thenceforth the Manicheans, now spread also to Africa and Europe, were persecuted by Zoroastrians as well as Christians. They survived in various guises, even amongst the Cathars, who were a heretical Christian sect in south-west Europe, until the seventeenth century when all traces of them vanished both in East and West.

Despite its spiritual otherworldliness Manichaeism posed a threat to the arbitrary power of the state and the priesthood as a part of the state, which was perhaps the most important reason for its suppression, although it would have been virtually impossible for a faith as ascetic and pessimistic as Manichaeism to become or remain the state religion.

CHAOS AND RESTORATION

Shapur I's able and strong rule was typically followed by a period of weakness, rebellions, palace coups and short reigns. Between 272, the year of Shapur's death, and 309, the year of the accession of Shapur II, no fewer than six rulers reigned in Persia. The country had been in a state of anarchy when the chiefs agreed upon the succession of the little boy King Shapur II. His was once again a strong and successful rule.

The Kushans took advantage of the turmoil and rose while he was still a minor and reasserted themselves, even annexing some territories of Persia proper. Once Shapur reached his majority he took the first opportunity to lead a campaign against the Kushans, whose state was completely dissolved as a result, with only a part of it turned into a vassal state ruled by a king or governor sent from the centre.

Shapur then turned westwards, where considerable territory had been ceded to Rome following the weakness and instability of the intervening period. The war first went in favour of Rome, then Iran. It was interrupted when Chionite Hephthalites disturbed the eastern frontiers, leading to concessions from both sides. Shapur then continued the campaign against Rome and, after the death of the emperor Julian, succeeded in recovering the disputed territories, including Armenia. Shortly afterwards, and as a response to Roman intrigue, he put Armenia under military occupation and appointed a governor (*marzban*) to run it. Another frontier to which Shapur led his forces was that of the neighbouring Arabs, who had led incursions in this chaotic period. The Arabs nicknamed Shapur Shoulder Master (*Zu'laktaf*), apparently because he had ordered the shoulders of Arab prisoners to be pierced and ropes passed through them to tie them together.

An important event under Shapur II was the conversion of the emperor Constantine to Christianity, which later became the state religion in Rome. Armenia, too, was converted, and from then on the Armenian question acquired a whole new dimension and the attitude of the Sasanians towards their Christian subjects underwent a fundamental change. Christians were persecuted under Shapur II and perennially afterwards, except for Nestorian Christians escaping from Roman persecution into Iran. And just as the Christians had made common cause with the Zoroastrians against the Manicheans, so they did much the same later when the Mazdakites suffered persecution by the state and Zoroastrian priesthood.

Shapur II died in 379 after ruling Persia with an iron fist for almost seventy years. Once again, this was followed by a century of turmoil and mediocrity. There were periodic provincial rebellions, palace coups and even the intervention of Chionite Hepthalites in Persia's internal affairs. The Perso-Roman dispute over Armenia resulted in Armenia's partition in 398, the lion's share being placed under Persian suzerainty, and by 429 the remaining part fell under Roman – now effectively Byzantine – rule.

WILD ASS BAHRAM

The Christian question took an unusual turn under Yazdgerd I (399–421) who was well-disposed towards the Christian community. This dissatisfied the notables and Zoroastrian priesthood, who later described him as Yazdgerd the Sinner (*Bezehkar*). According to the legend in *Shahnameh* he was kicked to death by a mysterious – perhaps divine – horse, although it is more likely that, not unlike the wolf of Joseph, the horse has been accused of the work of others who somehow got rid of their 'sinful' ruler. Those in power put someone other than Yazdgerd's son on the throne, but Bahram V (421–38) managed to defeat the usurper and recover his throne with military aid from the Arab prince of Hira, a Sasanian vassal state west of the Euphrates, who had brought him up. It is he who, according to legend, took the crown from between two hungry lions and was known as Wild Ass, apparently because of his love of the chase and especially onager (wild ass) hunting, although the title may reflect what contemporaries thought of the man himself. He loved music, wine, women and the chase and has been widely romanticized in classical Persian literature, especially in Nezami Ganjavi's famous romance *Haft Peykar*. According to legend he was swallowed up in quicksand while hunting an onager, though it is not unlikely that he was in fact disposed of by conspiratorial techniques. Khayyam, playing on the word '*gur*', which means both 'wild ass' and 'grave', says in verse: 'Bahram who was hunting the *gur* all his life / Did you see how in the end the *gur* took him alive?'

QOBAD AND THE MAZDAKI MOVEMENT

Bahram curbed the Hepthalites in the east, though he was not as successful with Rome, and so Iranian Christians were allowed freedom of worship as a consequence. But this did not last for long and both Jews and Christians were persecuted once again under Bahram's successor, Yazdgerd II (438–59). Yazdgerd II was succeeded by Piruz (Firuz, 459–84). During his reign several years of famine were followed by defeat at the hands of the Hephthalites, who exacted a heavy tribute and kept Piruz' son, Qobad (Kavad), hostage as the price of setting himself free. He tried his luck again after a few years of peace but lost once again and was killed in the process. The Hephthalites then became so strong that they were able to impose a heavy annual tribute on Persia and began to interfere in its internal affairs. The throne was then occupied for four years by Qobad's younger brother, after which Qobad himself acceded, in 488. His subsequent deposition and imprisonment in 497 can only be explained by his conversion to Mazdakism and the consequent revolt against him, as we shall see below.

Mazdak and Mazdakism

Mazdakism emerged after fifty years of famine, defeat and chaos, which showed no sign of subsiding. The principal message of Mazdak's religion was social and economic reform, and so, unsurprisingly, it was a religion that attracted many converts, supporters and activists. Whether by choice or necessity Qobad converted while the priesthood and notables were concerned about the threat that Mazdakism posed to their social position.

Mazdak was a reforming Zoroastrian priest. Therefore in its cosmology and theology Mazdakism was based on Zoroastrianism, although it was also influenced by Manichaean ideas. It held on to the dualistic vision of existence, advocated an ascetic life, banned the eating of meat and enjoined private and public morality. But its outlook was not as pessimistic as Manichaeism: it envisaged the possibility of increasing good and reducing evil in this world by social action. That is what gave it its energy as a movement campaigning for social justice and equality, the reduction of the power of the priesthood and simplification of religious ritual and worship.

Virtually all our information about Mazdak and his movement are from hostile sources, according to which he also advocated the common ownership of property and women and demanded lower taxes for the common people, who then bore almost the entire burden of taxation; he even opened up state granaries to feed the needy. It was the popularity afforded by such measures that impelled the shah to support Mazdak. This led to a backlash on the part of the nobles and priests, which in turn led to Qobad's deposition in 497. When he returned to the throne later, with the help of the Hephthalites, he distanced himself from Mazdak and in due course made his third son, leader of the anti-Mazdakite forces, his heir.

Rather than advocating the common ownership of property, it is in fact probable that the Mazdakites were in favour of a more equal distribution of wealth, including the breaking up of the great estates, most of which were directly or indirectly owned by the state. As for women, by law they were owned by their male next of kin, and rich men kept large harems. Talking about Khosraw II (Parviz) decades later than Mazdak's time, Ferdowsi says in *Shahnameh* that he had 12,000 concubines in his 'golden harem' (*moshku-ye zarrin*). Even if 1 per cent of that number is true, it goes a long way to show that Mazdak had probably advocated the abolition of harems and the release of their inmates, who were owned by their men.

In 528, three years before his death, Qobad succumbed to the full force of Mazdak's enemies and allowed his third son and heir (later Khosraw I) to invite Mazdak to a banquet ostensibly in his honour: the feast ended in the slaughter of the man and his close followers, including the shah's first son. Mazdakites were then outlawed and massacred all over the country. Qobad, who willy-nilly had allowed events to develop as they did, sat on the fence and observed a massacre which seems to have been even more horrific and destructive than the massacre of St Bartholomew's day in Paris more than a thousand years later. Mazdakism did not survive for long after this, and was later absorbed into Central Asian Buddhism. Still later, some of its ideas influenced social movements in the Islamic era (see Chapter 3).

'JUST AND IMMORTAL'

On Qobad's death in AD 531, his third son Chosroes (Khosraw) I, later entitled Anushiravan, that is, one with an immortal soul, succeeded to Persia's throne. His full title was Anushiravan the Just, a title that in Iranian socio-historical culture was fully justified not only because he destroyed Mazdakism but especially because he finally put an end to almost a century of chaos, turmoil, foreign defeat, economic decline and weak government. He was therefore deemed to have held the *farr*, or Grace, more clearly than most other Sasanian rulers according to the theory or myth of *farr-e Izadi*. Apart from stamping out rebellion, he imposed the strong rule of the centre over the provinces, reformed taxation and restructured the administration of justice.

With a strong and stable Persia, war with Byzantium was virtually inevitable. At one stage Chosroes captured Antioch. But it was a protracted war with (usually minor) victories and defeats until after thirty years there was a return to the status quo, with the right of worship for Christians and Zoroastrians respectively in Persia and the Byzantine empire so long as they did not proselytize. Between 558 and 561 Chosroes finally overthrew the Hephthalite kingdom in the east, to which Iran had been paying tribute for a long time. That was made possible largely because the Central Asian Turks were pressing them from behind, replacing them as the new nomadic and semi-nomadic power on Persia's eastern frontiers, with far-reaching consequences for both Iran and Europe for centuries to come.

Chosroes' reign was also marked by cultural developments. The game of chess was introduced from India and the *Kelileh o Demneh* was translated into

Sasanian Pahlavi. As a quintessential example of a just Persian king, classical Persian literature abounds with legends and anecdotes about his life and times. Bozorgmehr, his legendary vizier, has been portrayed in that literature as the repository of wisdom and knowledge, although he has no known historical counterpart. There are anecdotes about him in Ferdowsi, Sa'di and many other classical poets and writers. According to one anecdote, he was a very early riser, saying 'Rise early and you will be in luck.' One day, the shah arranged for some thieves to rob him as he left home at the crack of dawn, taunting him that this proved he would not necessarily be in luck if he rose early. He replied that the thieves had risen earlier, and so they were luckier than him.

Sa'di says in his *Golestan* that, once on a hunting expedition, Anushiravan sent one of his guards to the nearby village for salt, emphasizing that he should buy it at the market price. When the guard pointed out that salt was not worth much, the shah replied: 'The foundation of injustice in the world was at first very small. Each person added something to it until it became so big.' In another anecdote, he says that, once in council with his ministers, various opinions were expressed on a subject and Bozorgmehr preferred the shah's own view. When he was asked later in confidence the reason for this, he replied: 'Because the consequences are not predictable, and everybody's opinion may turn out to be right or wrong. Therefore it is best to agree with the shah's view so that if it proves to be wrong, having followed him we will be immune from chastisement.'

DECLINE AND FALL

Hormazd (Hormoz) IV succeeded his father after the latter's death in 579. Typically, the country's stability and strength then began to crumble, and its underlying tendency towards weakness and chaos set in, leading several decades later to the defeat and dissolution of the Sasanian empire by Muslim Arabs. According to Ferdowsi, Hormazd killed all his father's counsellors and secretaries upon his accession. Sa'di wrote that he put them all in prison, and when asked why he explained that he was afraid of them since he sensed they were afraid of him.

Conflict with East and West continued, with little success on either side. There was domestic conflict and opposition too, when Bahram Chubin, an able general, rebelled and in 590, with the support of Hormazd's son Chosroes and his maternal uncles, deposed and killed him. Shortly afterwards Bahram also deposed Chosroes and declared himself shah, though this time his rebellion did not succeed and he lost his life.

Chosroes (Kohsraw) II, later entitled *Aparviz* (modern Persian: *Parviz*), meaning 'Victorious', for a time plastered over the crumbling structure of the Sasanian empire, although the rot had begun to set in since the death of his grandfather. Of all the rulers of ancient Persia he is the most romantically portrayed in classical Persian literature for his adventurous love affair with Shirin, his Armenian wife or concubine, other women, wine, music and horses, as described in *Shahnameh* and Nezami Ganjavi's long poetical romance *Khosraw o Shirin*. But his protracted wars with Byzantium, lasting some twenty-seven years, though at first successful, ended in crushing defeat and the country's material and moral ruin when the rebels, taking a leaf from his own book, supported his son Shiruy (or Shiruyeh), deposing, blinding and later killing him in 624.

Shiruy's turn came within six months when he died in mysterious circumstances. There followed about a dozen rulers one after the other in the midst of chaos, most of whom were killed or blinded until in 632 a son of Chosroes II was put on the throne as Yazdgerd III by the notables, who in fact dominated him. Thus, a great empire that had lasted for four centuries, and which had withstood great upheaval and changes of fortune, began to crumble fast. Many long- and short-term factors were responsible for its demise, including the long wars, both of Anushiravan and especially Khosraw II, and the subsequent chaos and loss of will in the face of a highly motivated and determined adversary. But most telling of all, perhaps, was the fact that the people did not regard the state as their own.

CHAPTER 3

Arabs, Islam and Persians

[A]ll the great jurists were Persians as is well known. . . . Only the Persians engaged in the task of preserving knowledge and writing systematic scholarly works.

Ibn Khaldun

THE FALL OF THE SASANIANS

IRANIAN HISTORY HAS BEEN punctuated by dramatic events of varying significance, hardly any century passing in which at least one major upheaval did not shake the foundations of the land. But the greatest of all these dramas – great even by the standards of Iranian history – were the Alexandrian conquest of the Achaemenid empire, the Arab conquest of the Sasanian empire and the Mongol invasions and conquests of the thirteenth century, all of which had profound consequences for the country's history and culture. If all these have one thing in common which makes them distinctly Iranian it is the fact that they were all short, sharp and decisive, taking place over only a few years and encountering little resistance.

MOHAMMAD

The Prophet of Islam was born in Mecca *c.*570 into a family of the Hashim clan of the great Quraish tribe. As a young man he became a merchant travelling to lands such as Syria and Palestine, earning the title of Amin (the Trustworthy) and at twenty-five marrying one of his employers, Khadija, who was then forty.

According to Islamic sources the Prophet was forty in about 610 when he received his first revelations in a cave, with the Angel Gabriel appearing to him and telling him to 'Read in the name of the Lord who created you'. Mecca was a centre of trade and a place of pilgrimage where the devout gathered every year in peace to exchange goods and enjoy the festival. The Ka'ba (as the name suggests, a cubic structure) was an object of pilgrimage which at the time housed idols worshipped by most people of Arabia. Mohammad's message, 'Say there is no god but the one God', was therefore dangerous from the start.

The first converts included Mohammad's wife, his cousin, son-in-law and ward Ali ibn Abi Talib and Abubakr, on whom the Prophet later bestowed the title of 'The Honest'. Further conversions led to division and persecution; one of Mohammad's uncles, Abu Lahab, joined his enemies, and another, Hamza, was converted. By 622 the persecution of Muslims in Mecca had reached a point that Mohammad responded to sympathetic calls from the town of Yathrib (later called Medina), to which he and his followers migrated. This is called *hijra* in Arabic and is the basis of the Islamic calendar.

Thenceforth a state of war existed between Muslims and Meccans, and so the Muslims began to raid caravans bound for Mecca. Three battles ensued. At Badr in 624 the Muslims won the day. The battle of Uhud in the following year went well for the Meccans though not well enough for them to pursue the Muslims into Medina. Two years later the Meccans marched in force against Medina but the town was defended by digging a dry moat around it, a tactic said to have been suggested by one of the Prophet's Companions known as Salman the Persian. In the meantime the Muslims were continuously growing in number and self-confidence, and in 628 Mohammad felt strong enough to lead them on pilgrimage to Mecca. The Meccans entered an agreement with him whereby he and his followers could go on pilgrimage the following year. This they did, but the Meccans broke the treaty in 630, whereupon Mohammad led a force of Muslims to Mecca, so strong and so determined that the Meccans surrendered without a fight. An amnesty was announced, but the idols in the Ka'ba were destroyed. Before his death in 632 Mohammad had united the whole of the Arabian peninsula as the *Umma*, or community of Muslims.

Muslims believe that one night when he first journeyed to Jerusalem Mohammad miraculously ascended to the heavens, and from there he made a tour of heaven and hell and met some of the earlier prophets. This is described as 'The Ascension'. It is believed that Mohammad got so close to the almighty that the Angel Gabriel who was accompanying him was left behind, since it was not his place to go there. In Sa'di's immortal verse:

One night he mounted up, traversed the universe
Surpassed the angels in place and status
Hot in his drive in the plain of closeness [to God]
At Sedreh he left Gabriel behind in that place.

In the opinion of some Muslim scholars 'The Ascension' was a spiritual, not physical experience.

ISLAM

Islam means submission to the will of God. The Koran, Islam's holy book, contains the revelations of God to the Prophet from his first investiture in the cave until his departure from this world. Abraham is seen as the first Muslim in the word's literal sense, the first person to become monotheist (*muwahhid*), the ancestor of the Arab (as well as Jewish) people and founder of the Ka'ba as the House of God. The Old and New Testaments are accepted in Islam as holy books of the Abrahamic tradition, with reservations about those parts that contradict the teachings of the Koran. For example, the Koran rejects the divinity of Christ – describing Christ as a great prophet – but accepts the virgin birth, explaining it as an expression of the will of almighty God: 'And when He decides upon a subject He says be and it will be.' Mohammad is the last ('the seal') of the long line of prophets from Abraham through Moses, Joseph, David, Solomon to Jesus.

The three pillars of Islam shared by all the Muslim sects are monotheism, prophethood and Resurrection on the Day of Judgement, to which the Shiites add divine justice (*adl*) and leadership of the community (imamate). Muslims are obliged to say ritual prayers (Arabic: *salat*, Persian: *namaz*) five times a day, go on pilgrimage to Mecca (hajj) at least once if they can afford it, enjoin the good and forbid the bad, give alms to the needy and so on. They are not to drink alcohol, eat pork, backbite and must avoid incest.

There is no celibacy in Islam; marriage is in fact encouraged. Men can marry up to four wives, although strict instructions were given in the Koran for the just and equal treatment of wives and their offspring (it should be noted that polygamy and harems had been familiar features of pre-Islamic Iran). Women had the right to inherit from their parents and siblings, but only half the amount inherited by the male heirs. *Hejab* – the Islamic dress code for women – did not include the covering of the face and hands, and women were in fact quite active in the community as witnessed by the careers of Fatima, daughter of Mohammad and wife of Imam Ali, Aisha, the Prophet's wife and daughter of Abubakr and Zeinab, the Prophet's granddaughter, daughter of Imam Ali and leader of the family after the martyrdom of her brother Imam Hosein (Hussein). Men had the right of divorce but women could ask for divorce on certain grounds. Considering that in the Persian empire women were owned by their next of kin, and that in other communities women did not have the right of property ownership – in Christendom until recent centuries – early Islam does not seem to have been too discriminatory towards women, although women patently did not enjoy equal status with men.

Heaven, hell, angels and Satan are all in line with the Jewish, Christian and, if in a different form, Zoroastrian traditions. 'God created the world in six days.' Adam and Eve were expelled from the Garden of Eden because they ate the forbidden fruit, which in the Koran is not an apple but wheat. The worst sin in Islam is to be unjust to other human beings. Helping the community is a highly rewarded deed. 'Muslims are brethren; make peace among your brothers.' There are moral obligations to oneself, one's relatives, society and God. Human beings are judged at death, and their good and bad deeds are weighed up to see whether they should go to heaven or hell. There will be universal judgement at the Resurrection when 'People rise [from the grave] in their totality.' God is merciful, compassionate, loving and forgiving, but he is also the ultimate judge and arbiter of right and wrong, and will reward and punish the righteous and the wrongdoers.

In the early days of Islam the sole source of faith, law and tradition was the Koran. Later, a body of *hadith* (the traditions of Mohammad, to which the Shia added the traditions of the Imams) were added to it, and still later extensive bodies of law and jurisprudence were developed on the basis of those sources by the ulama (Islamic divines and doctors of religious law) in various sects and schools of law.

ARABS AND ISLAM

The early Islamic conquests resulted in widespread revolution in lands which soon extended from the Indus to Spain. Not only parts of the Byzantine empire but the whole of the Persian empire succumbed to its onslaught within a short period after the death of the Prophet Mohammad in 632. In 636, only four years after Yazdgerd III's succession, at Qadesiyeh (= Qadisiyya) a small Arab force led by Sa'd ibn Waqqas defeated the mighty Persian army led by Rostam, son of Farrokh (Farrokhzad), its commander-in-chief, who himself fell in battle. Ctesiphon fell a couple of years later, followed by the rout of Yazdgerd's army at Nahavand in Persia proper. Thus in a matter of years the mighty Persian empire was defeated and conquered by Muslim Arabs.

The will to resist was not lost as a result of Qadesiyeh in 636, which was, after all, a local battle. It had been lost already, the country being in continuous chaos and – as has happened so many times in Iranian history – the people, both high and low, wishing for a saviour to bring forth the millennium. The war began first as an uprising of Sasanian Arab subjects in Mesopotamia who had converted to Islam, perhaps because of Islam's ideological appeal and as a means of liberating themselves from Sasanian rule. However, Sasanian imperial attempts to suppress the Arab rebellion helped widen the conflict and bring in the entire Muslim military capability. As we have seen, the Arabs won the battle of Qadesiyeh with incredible ease, and the battle of Nahavand was a foregone conclusion. Yazdgerd was abandoned even by his own military and civilian officials and had to flee eastwards as far as Marv (Merv, now ruins in Turkmenistan), where he met his death. According to the *Shahnameh*, he had to go so far because, as he marched eastwards, nowhere were they prepared to allow him to stay, let alone give him support. In the end he sought refuge with Mahuy Suri, governor of Marv, but even he was far from helpful, and was about to arrange for the Turks to seize the shah when he escaped and was killed by a miller who wanted to rob him of his precious possessions. Historians suspect that, unlike the legend, Yazdgerd was in fact killed by Suri himself.

The ideology of Islam was probably highly instrumental in motivating and energizing not only the conquerors but also the willing losers among the Iranians. But the almost inexplicably swift collapse of this great empire must be attributed to the lack of will to uphold or support the disintegrating and unpopular state. It has been repeatedly shown in Iranian history that when the state weakens because of domestic or foreign factors, society – which is normally opposed to the state – either supports its downfall or remains neutral. This happened in 651. The western and central provinces were captured quite quickly and it did not take long for Arab armies and tribes to reach as far as the eastern marches of Outer Khorasan in Central Asia. Only the Caspian provinces proved impregnable and resisted invasion for any length of time, thanks to the natural barrier of high and thickly forested mountain ranges and the fact that, for this same reason, they had always been out of the reach of the central state power.

If conquest was easy and swift, conversion to Islam took much longer. Occupation did not automatically lead to conversion, since conversion was voluntary – it took about two and a half centuries for all the Iranian lands and peoples to be converted. Indeed, in the beginning the Arabs preferred to collect the *jezyeh* (*jizya* in Arabic pronunciation), the poll tax paid by non-Muslims, rather than take converts who would then be exempt from this tax; but in time, non-Muslims began to appreciate the economic benefits of conversion both in avoiding *jezyeh* and in protecting their property.

Many of the Iranian Christians of Khuzistan were converted early, perhaps mainly on religious grounds, given the Abrahamic nature and background of the new religion. So did some Iranian Jews. But it took much longer for Persis, the Fars province which was the homeland of the Sasanians and Zoroastrianism, to become Muslim, despite the fact that it was invaded in the early days of the conquest. There were more converts in Khorasan, partly because Zoroastrianism did not have a strong hold in the east and partly because of the settlement of Arab warriors and their tribes and followers there to garrison the towns and protect the road to Central Asia and the Far East.

The region known as Jebal (Arabic: Jibal), roughly the area between Hamadan, Isfahan and Reyy, converted somewhat later. So did Azerbaijan and the Caucasus. But, as noted, the Caspian provinces were the last since they were protected by high mountains which the Arabs could not easily penetrate. The peoples of the Caspian provinces were converted largely by Shiite missionaries and other non-conformist Muslims who took refuge in Deylaman and Tabaristan, and were partly conquered later in the ninth century by other Iranians such as the Taherid rulers of Khorasan, who were Muslims. The rural areas converted much more slowly, but by the end of the ninth century most Iranians had accepted the Islamic faith.

It would be a great exaggeration to think that it was just the Persian and Iranian peoples and civilization that laid the foundations of Islamic society by virtue of their superiority in administration, culture, arts and historical imagination. But the modern Iranian nationalist conception of the first two centuries of Islam as a period of Iranian 'silence' and quietism flies even more blatantly in the face of the facts. It is true that there were no independent Iranian states in these two centuries and there is virtually no evidence of written literature in the various Persian and Iranian languages. But these languages were spoken by most Iranians, and if urban Iranians learned to speak Arabic, Arabs in Iran also learned to speak Persian.

From the beginning of the Arab conquest Iranians were involved in the new regime, whether as converted warriors, local administrators, scribes or later as viziers, linguists, poets, literati, intellectuals, rebels and eventually founders of new dynasties. But not until the fall of Umayyad rule in AD 749–50 by what was largely an Iranian army did Persian participation and influence become widespread. The loss of the Sasanian empire was not synonymous with the demise of the Iranians, who, even in the first two centuries after the conquest and before the foundation of Persian dynasties, played a decisive role in the internationalization of Islamic society and culture.

SHIISM VERSUS SUNNISM

Upon the Prophet's death, conflict had broken out over the succession. Both old Muslims, that is, the *mohajerin,* or immigrants (those who had migrated to Medina from Mecca), and the *ansar,* or 'supporters' (the converts of Medina), believed that one of their elders should succeed Mohammad. They gathered in a 'shed' (*saqifa*) where Sa'd ibn Ubada of the Supporters was nominated. But some of the close Companions of the Prophet nominated Abubakr (632–34), who was elected successor or *khalifa,* from which the word caliph originates.

The Bani Hashim clan were not pleased with this election. Among them were Abbas, the Prophet's uncle (from whom the long line of Abbasid caliphs would later descend), and the party of Ali, Mohammad's cousin, ward and son-in law, who had not been present at the election meeting. His followers made up Shia Ali (Shi'a Ali, literally 'the followers of Ali'); they would later form a sect of Islam and Iran's state religion.

Abubakr was followed as caliph by Omar (634–44), also a leading Companion, under whose rule Arab conquest of the Sasanian empire began. But Omar was assassinated by a slave believed to have been an Iranian Christian. Next came Osman (Arabic: Uthman, 644–56), who was married to two of the Prophet's daughters (at different times), hence his title 'Owner of Two Lights'. Osman was not an ascetic like the first two caliphs and was suspected of favouritism and nepotism. Opposition to his rule finally led to a rebellion that cost him his life.

Shia Ali believed that Ali should have succeeded the Prophet; some of them were among those who had risen against Osman. From this originates the rift between the Shia and Sunnis, although later developments added a good deal more to their differences. Ali succeeded Osman as the fourth caliph, but there was much civil strife during the five years of his rule, from 656 until 661. Aisha (Persian: Aisheh), Abubakr's daughter and Mohammad's favourite wife, together with two important Companions, rose against Ali, accusing him of complicity in the assassination of Osman, but they were defeated in the battle of the Camel. Much more serious was the opposition of Mu'awia (Persian: Mo'avieh), governor of Syria, a relative of Osman and head of the strong and influential Umayyad clan. He was based in Damascus while Ali ruled from Kufa, in Iraq.

When war failed to settle the conflict the matter was put to arbitration. Mu'awia won, since his representative cunningly outmanoeuvred Ali's. This led to a split in Ali's camp with the Kharejites (meaning 'seceders', Arabic: Khawarij) turning against their former leader. Their initial objection was to the fact that Ali had accepted the arbitration (though at first they themselves had apparently insisted on it), but they subsequently formed the more substantive opinion that anyone could be chosen as caliph and a caliph who did not lead the Muslim community satisfactorily should be deposed. Thenceforth they became a radical rebel sect that caused much trouble to the caliphate, not least in Iran. One of their zealots assassinated Ali in 661, barely five years after he had been elected caliph, thus ending the rule of the four great Companions, whom the Sunnis call *Rashidun* or Rightly Guided.

Contrary to the Sunnis, the Shia held that Ali was the rightful successor because, they believed, the succession was not an elective matter but had been preordained by God and confirmed in public by the Prophet before his death. Thus, much to the consternation of the Sunnis, they regarded the first three caliphs as usurpers, and revered Ali not just as a caliph but the real and rightful leader of the Muslims from the start, the imam who was sinless and infallible and (according to some interpretations) omniscient.

Shiism made a deep impression on Iranian Muslims but it was not until the sixteenth century that it became the majority sect and state religion in Iran (see Chapter 5).

Twelver Shias

Of the various differences in ritual and law between Sunnis and Shias the most fundamental difference concerns the imamate. The Twelver or Imami Shias believe that the Twelve Imams descending one after the other from Ali and Fatima have been the rightful, preordained, leaders of the Islamic community. None of the imams ever ruled the Islamic world, except in Ali's short period, but this did not put in doubt their true righteousness in any way and each in their time was regarded as spiritual leader of the Shia community. Four of these imams have the greatest significance. First is Ali, 'Lion of God' and 'Shah of Men'. Second is the Third Imam, Hosein, second son of Ali, who was martyred by the army of Yazid, son of Mu'awia, in the plain of Karbala (see below). Third is the Sixth Imam, Ja'far al-Sadiq, who is the founder of the Imami Shia school of law and jurisprudence. Fourth is the Twelfth Imam, Mohammad son of Hasan, entitled Al-Mahdi (the Guided One), the Hidden Imam, 'Lord of the Time' and 'Guardian of the Age', who disappeared from sight and then went into 'the greater occultation', being present but hidden all through time as the leader of the Twelver Shiites, who would eventually rise as the Saviour and rid the world of injustice and corruption.

The Shii imam is sinless, infallible, possibly all-knowing and capable of making miracles both alive and dead. Unquestioning obedience to Him is the duty of all the faithful, who must follow, 'emulate', him in every way. All except Ali are believed to have been martyred, directly or indirectly, by the Umayyad and Abbasid caliphs. Indeed, their martyrdom, too, had been preordained. This, as we shall see below, led to serious controversies among traditionalist and revisionist Shia theorists and activists. According to Ayatollah Khomeini, in his famous book on Islamic government, *Velayat-e Faqih*:

> It is one of the essential beliefs of our Shii school that no one can attain the spiritual status of the Imams, not even the cherubim or the prophets. In fact, according to the traditions that have been handed down to us, the Most Noble Messenger [Mohammad] and the Imams existed before the creation of the world in the form of lights situated beneath the divine throne; they were superior to other men even in the sperm from which they grew and in their physical composition.

The Shia Imamate is undoubtedly a product of Shia theory and history. But it closely resembles the myth of the Persian *shahanshahi* based on the possession of the *farr*, which, as has been noted, is bestowed by God and could be taken away by God alone, the people having no independent rights before the ruler and no independent power for removing him. He is God's viceregent on earth, anointed and – if he stops being just – dismissed by God alone. Ferdowsi has put forward an abstract model of not only the just but also the perfect ruler. The *perfect* just ruler not only possesses the *farr* but is also of pure seed, able to learn and correct his mistakes and has the wisdom to distinguish right from wrong, which is not very different from infallibility (see Introduction).

Some extreme Shia and Sufi sects go so far as regarding the imams as divine. There have certainly been some – known as the Ali Allahis – who have worshipped Ali as such. The great majority of the Shia ulama do not go to this extreme, but in practice the idea is not far from the attitude of the common Shia believer.

Ali and Mu'awia were still contesting the caliphate when, as noted above, Ali was assassinated by one of his former followers, a radical. His eldest son Hasan came to terms with Mu'awia and renounced his claim to leadership of the Muslim community, but upon Hasan's death his brother Hosein renewed the family's claim. The martyrdom of Imam Hosein, whom the Shia describe as Lord of the Martyrs (*Sayyid al-Shuhada*), is vital to the understanding both of the history of Shiism and of the structure of belief and religious psychology of the Shii masses. It happened in the plain of Karbala (in modern Iraq) on the 10th (Ashura) day of the Islamic lunar month of Muharram, AD 680. Hence the slogan: 'Every day is Ashura, every land is Karbala', which emphasizes the continuity of martyrdom as the ultimate route to salvation in this world.

After Mu'awia's death, his son Yazid took over as the ruler of the Muslims in Damascus. Hosein in Arabia was invited by Ali's old followers in Kufa in Iraq to pursue his claim. But when he reached Kufa the people deserted him, and he and his family and devotees, believed to have been seventy-two in all, fought against Yazid's army. All the fighting men lost their lives except Hosein's sick second son, Ali, known as Zain al-Abidin, who did not join the battle. The women and children became captives and were taken to Damascus, where they were bravely led by Zeinab, Hosein's sister. Zain al-Abidin later became the Fourth Imam; there is a legend, believed as fact by most Shias, that his mother was the daughter of Yazdgerd III, the last Sasanian king, called Shahrbanu.

In some ways Hosein's martyrdom recalls the Persian myth of the conception of the death of Siyavosh and the annual mourning commemorating it, described in Chapter 1. But, according to the Shia, Hosein saved Islam by sacrificing his own life. Therefore in its importance, intensity, function and the psychological bond between the martyr and his followers, the martyrdom at Karbala is reminiscent of the Crucifixion, except that the Shia ulama do not believe in the divinity of Hosein, and he is not the awaited Saviour.

Until the second half of the twentieth century the Shia ulama and faithful generally believed that Hosein's martyrdom had been preordained, and was therefore inevitable. But from the 1960s onwards, with the rise of militant Shiism, the view began to be actively canvassed (not least in Qom) that, like a revolutionary activist, Hosein had exercised his free will to fight and die for Islam. This led to a controversy among the ulama which has not yet been resolved, although the revision played a vital role in legitimizing militant action against unpopular rulers (see Chapter 12).

The juridical differences between Sunnis and Twelver Shias are not so great as to be the fundamental cause of schism. There are also differences in theology, Shia theology being more complex and esoteric, but, in Islam, religious philosophy has seldom been at the forefront of sectarian controversy. As noted, the fundamental and virtually irresolvable conflict is over the succession to Mohammad and, more significantly, the Shiite conception of the imam and imamate, to the point that some extreme Sunnis believe that the Shia are *mushrik*, or pantheistic, accusing them of regarding the imams as godheads.

Many Shias regard pilgrimage to the holy shrines where the imams and their close relatives are buried almost as obligatory and rewarding as hajj. They pray to imams to fulfil their wishes and believe that to do so in person at their shrines will be most effective. This is reminiscent of some pre-Islamic Persian practices, but in its Shia form it is called *tavassol*, that is, asking for the imam's intercession with God on their behalf, which is analogous to Roman Catholic attitudes towards the saints. The great shrines are few, therefore the Shia regularly visit the smaller shrines of other, lesser, holy persons – the *imamzadehs* – believed to have descended from the imams. There are a number of such shrines in Greater Tehran and four in the nearby town of Reyy, although two of the latter have been of great teachers rather than of descendants of the imams. However, many a village across the country has its own imamzadeh, which is the centre of religious rituals and ceremonies and the place for making wishes, and some of which are likely to be sites of pre-Islamic fire temples and temples of Mithra and Anahita.

The Shia, like Sunnis, observe the great Islamic festivals: the Festival of *Fetr* (Arabic pronunciation: *Fitr*), the end of Ramadan and fasting and *Adha*, or Sacrifice (Persian: *Eid-e Qorban*), which concludes the hajj rites. The Shia also celebrate *Ghadir*, the day on which Mohammad is believed to have nominated Ali as his successor. But their two greatest events are the commemorations of the martyrs of Karbala in the first Islamic lunar month, Muharram, and the birthday of the Mahdi (Persian: Mehdi), the Lord of the Time, in mid-Sha'ban, the eighth Islamic lunar month. The Twelfth Imam (b. 868) is believed to have hidden for some time in 'the Lesser Occultation', then disappeared completely in 'the Greater Occultation' until 'the end of time' when he rises and together with his followers rids the world of all evil. Before the rise of the Mahdi, the false Mahdi (*Dajjal*), comparable to the Anti-Christ, appears but fails in the end and gives way to the true Mahdi.

The commemoration of and mourning for the martyrs of Karbala takes place in the first ten days of Muharram. The rituals reach their climax on the 9th and 10th days, the eve and the day of martyrdom, with *ta'zieh*, a dramatic representation of the actual battle, which is normally staged in open air. There are long processions in which men beat their naked breasts with their hands and their shoulders with chains. There are also gatherings in mosques and private homes at midday when breast-beating is followed by a communal lunch. The mourners sometimes make superficial cuts in the skin on their heads to let blood pour down their faces, which looks horrible but is in fact not harmful. (The practice, now banned in Iran, has not totally disappeared.) Predictably the whole atmosphere is filled with personal and communal passion. The psychology is one of identification with the martyrs; the sociology, of being involved in the greatest event of the year as an actor, breast-beater, ordinary mourner, charitable organizer of group lunches and dinners and of congregations every evening in which officiating preachers recall aspects of the martyrdom to loud cries of the public.

During the absence of the Lord of the Time, the faithful pay their religious dues to the *mojtahed*s, doctors of Shia law and held as the imam's deputies, but not his representatives. The faithful also put their problems to the *mojtahed*, whom they choose to 'emulate', and ask questions regarding law and proper conduct. The great *mojtahed*s are called *maraje'-e taqlid* or 'source of emulation', a position which has evolved since the mid-nineteenth century. The *mojtahed*s and *marja'-e taqlid* have been addressed, respectively, as ayatollahs and grand ayatollahs since the early to mid-twentieth century. There is no organized church in Shiism but there are Shia colleges, mosques and other institutions which have been undergoing change since the Islamic Revolution. The Sunnis in Iran make up about 10 per cent of the population and are mainly concentrated in Kurdistan and Baluchistan.

Ismailis and Zeidis
These are the other main Shia sects apart from Twelver Shiis. At present, Zeidis are almost non-existent in Iran and Ismailis (Isam'ilis) make up a very small minority, but historically they played important roles in the country, as will be seen below and in Chapter 4. Zeidis are followers of Zeid son of Ali, the only son of Imam Hosein to survive Karbala thanks to his being sick on the day of the

battle. He rose up against the Umayyads, was defeated and killed in battle and has been followed by those Shias who regard him as the Fifth Imam, rather than his younger brother, who is the Fifth Imam of Twelvers and Ismailis. The Zeidis do not hold their imams, who have continued to lead them down to the present, to be as sacred and infallible as the Twelver Imams, and they are less censorious of the first three caliphs. They once ruled the Caspian province of Deylaman but now are largely concentrated in Yemen and have virtually no adherents in Iran.

Ismailis are Sevener Shias. They adhere to Isma'il, eldest son of the Sixth Imam and his descendants, whereas the Twelver's Seventh Imam is the younger son, Musa al-Kazim. Between the tenth and twelfth centuries they founded the successful Fatimid caliphate in Egypt and North Africa. Towards the end of their rule a schism arose over the succession. One section regarded al-Musta'li as the rightful imam, whereas the other sect adhered to his elder brother, Imam Nizar, from whom the Aga Khan, the present Ismaili leader, traces his descent. The seat of the Nizaris then moved to Iran, where they established themselves in a number of mountain fortifications and waged war against the Seljuk Turks, who were orthodox Sunnis. There are few Ismailis now left in Iran; most live in Central Asia, Pakistan, East Africa and the West.

These first two centuries (650–850) of Arab rule may be neatly divided into two. The first (650–750) began with the consolidation of the Arab conquest and ended with the fall of the Umayyad caliphate in 750. The second century (750–850) began with the establishment of the Abbasid caliphate and ended with the accession of the caliph al-Mutiwakkil (Persian: Motevakkel), which concluded the golden age of the Abbasids and saw the establishment of the Persian Taherid dynasty in Khorasan.

ARAB CALIPHATES

The Umayyad dynasty was founded by Mu'avieh, who defeated Ali, came to terms with his eldest son, Imam Hasan, after his death and nominated his own son, Yazid, for succession. This led to Imam Hosein's revolt and martyrdom in Karbala. The Umayyads ruled an empire from Damascus that was even greater than that of the Achaemenids, stretching from Spain to Central Asia and western India. Theirs was no longer a popular and egalitarian government, as had been under the *Rahsidun*, but an absolute and arbitrary rule, styled to some extent on the Sasanian and Byzantine monarchies, although it still retained some of its original tribal roots. Unlike their Abbasid successors they were not Iranophile, but nevertheless largely depended on Persian administrators, scribes, accountants and tax collectors in running their caliphate, especially in the east. Subjects of the caliphate were in general divided between Arab Muslims, non-Arab (including Persian) Muslims, who were known as *mawali* or clients, non-Muslims or *zemmis* (Arabic: *dhimmis*) and slaves.

The Umayyads have had a bad press in history, and especially in popular and religious history. But it is not clear to what extent they were more unjust or less pious than those who succeeded them. It is, however, true that they did not have a firm basis of legitimacy from the start, and became increasingly unpopular with their subjects, except for the short interlude of Omar II's benevolent rule (717–20). Nowhere were campaigns against them more potent and effective than in Persia, and particularly Khorasan, where underground Abbasid propagandists (*du'ats*) advocated the righteousness and legitimacy of 'the Prophet's family' in general and the House of Abbas in particular.

The movement chose Mohammad, a great-grandson of Abbas, the Prophet's uncle, as their leader, and upon his death at the hands of the Umayyads his son Ibrahim, who in 745 sent the Khorasani Persian Abu Muslim as his personal representative to Khorasan. Abu Muslim succeeded in creating a solid base of support and raised the standard of the Abbasids against the Umayyads in Marv two years later. The capture and death of Ibrahim in 748 could not halt the westward march of Abu Muslim's formidable army, which reached Iraq in 749 and declared Ibrahim's brother, Abu' l-Abbas, entitled al-Saffah, as caliph. The final battle was fought at the River Zab. The Umayyad caliph Marwan II was defeated; in 750 he was found and killed in Egypt.

PERSIANS

The Abbasids

The early Arab historian Jahiz described the Abbasids as Khorasani Persians. The Abbasids were themselves Arabs of course and there is no doubt that they had a considerable following among Arabs, especially Shia Arabs. The description of Jahiz, although an exaggeration, indicates both the degree to which the Abbasid victory depended on the Persians and the extent that Persian culture and peoples influenced their court, culture and government. That they were called Persians at all was the result of the fact that they maintained their Iranian identity by holding on to their language.

As we have seen, the hero of the revolt against the Umayyads was Abu Muslim, who both raised and led the pro-Abbasid army to victory. He had good relations with al-Saffah, the first Abbasid caliph, who died early in 754, being succeeded by his brother al-Mansur (Persian: Mansur). The latter was in fear of Abu Muslim's ability, power and popularity and had once advised his brother – who had also been somewhat wary of him – to have him killed. He posted Abu Muslim to Syria and Egypt in order to keep him away from Iran, his natural base and constituency. But their relations deteriorated further and Mansur tricked Abu Muslim to go to Baghdad to settle their differences. Once at court facing Mansur, he was attacked and killed by a number of assassins chosen by Mansur for the purpose even before he had arrived. Not only the killing but also the murder and treachery that this involved resulted in a highly negative reaction, especially in Khorasan where many believed that the hero was not dead and would return as a saviour. It was also followed by a number of revolts. Ungrateful and treacherous though the murder of Abu Muslim was, it was not unfamiliar in Iranian history for successful generals and viziers to fall victim to the fear or jealousy of their sovereigns: Abu Muslim himself had been involved in the killing of an able and loyal minister by al-Saffah.

It was under Mansur (754–75) that the Abbasid revolution was consolidated, renouncing the Shiite overtones of the movement and turning the caliphate into champions of orthodoxy, which helped them consolidate their hold over a cosmopolitan Muslim community (although from the early days Spain rejected their authority and went its own way). The seat of government was transferred from Syria to Iraq, then a largely Iranian province. And Baghdad (a Persian word meaning 'God's gift') near the old Ctesiphon, the Sasanian's imperial capital, was expanded to become the most important seat of Islamic culture, civilization, government and administration. Arabs no longer occupied a special place in the state or in society as they had done, if increasingly rarely, under the Umayyads. Men's importance was now determined by their relationship to the ruler, much as had been the case under the Sasanians and would remain so throughout Iranian history.

Under Mansur, Persian court etiquette was adopted and some Iranian offices and institutions revived. Nawruz, the Persian New Year, began to be celebrated. But most important of all the Persian office of vizier was reintroduced, headed by the Iranian Khaled (Arabic: Khalid) Barmaki, a very able administrator from Balkh whose father had converted to Islam, probably from Buddhism, since Barmak or Parmak implies guardianship of the famous Buddhist temple Nawbahar (= New Temple) in Khorasan. For more than three decades the Barmakis (Bermecides) were the pillar of government. Khaled, his son Yahya and his sons Ja'far and Fazl served the caliphate from Mansur through Mahdi (775–85), Hadi (785–6) to Harun al-Rahshid (786–809), the most celebrated Abbasid caliphs in the golden age. Then Harun ordered the massacre of the Barmakis, simply it seems because they had become too powerful and had the entire realm under their administrative command. This was the eighth century: as late as the nineteenth century Fath'ali Shah Qajar ordered the massacre of his able and loyal vizier and his family and relations for similar reasons (see Chapter 7).

Persianism during the early Abbasid period peaked under Ma'mun (Arabic: al-Ma'mun, 813–33) son of Harun al-Rashid. Ma'mun's mother had been a Persian slave and for that reason Harun had chosen his brother Amin (Arabic: al-Amin) to succeed him, since although younger, he had been born of a wife related to Harun. Ma'mun was made governor of Khorasan and Harun willed that he would be the successor to Amin. Amin did not observe this will and instead named his own son as his successor. This resulted in civil war, Ma'mun's army being led by the Persian Taher (Arabic: Tahir) ibn Hosein, who was entitled Ambidextrous, or Owner of Two Right Hands, because he used the sword in both his hands.

Taher was soon to begin a line which would lead to the establishment of the Taherids as an autonomous dynasty. It was he who defeated Amin's armies, conquered Baghdad and put Amin to death. Ma'mun preferred to rule in Khorasan with his seat in Marv until he was forced to return to Baghdad after a few years in the face of rising Arab discontent. Ma'mun's vizier was the Persian Fazl ibn Sahl. Both he and his vizier were sympathetic to the Shia, who had many adherents in Iran, and he named the Eighth Imam of the Twelver Shiites, Imam Reza (Arabic: Ali ibn Musa al-Ridha) as his successor. But the imam died in 818, the Shia firmly believing that he had been poisoned on the orders of Ma'mun.

Ma'mun launched a cultural renaissance at his court by gathering scientists and thinkers, Persian, Greek and others, to conduct discussion and debate on important intellectual subjects. But he particularly annoyed the orthodox community by his encouragement of the Mu'tazila school of thought. Rooted in Aristotelian rationalism, the Mu'tazila believed in the analysis and interpretation of the Koran as opposed to the general Muslim belief that the content of the holy book should be taken literally and at face value. They thus elevated esoteric exegeses and interpretations of the Koran and other holy texts which were familiar to the Shia, especially the Seveners or Ismailis.

The most important single tenet of Mu'tazili thought was their rejection of predestination and the advocacy of free will, in contrast with the Ash'ariya, who believed in strict determinism. Since this was a fundamental Zoroastrian belief, they were sometimes described by their detractors as Muslim Zoroastrians, although the Shia too believed in free will, for like the Mu'tazilis they believed in divine justice. According to the Mu'tazilis predestination meant that God is not just, since He punishes wrong-doers for behaving the way they were preordained to behave. The other important tenet of the Mu'tazilis which the orthodox found repugnant was their belief that the Koran had been created. They argued that if the holy book had been old and uncreated, then it would mean that it was on a par with God. Under Ma'mun, official pressure was applied to force the ulama to bend to Mu'tazili ideas, but some of them – notably Ahmad ibn Hanbal, the founder of the Hanbali legal school, the most orthodox of the four Sunni schools – resisted it.

The heyday of religious liberalism and cultural Persianism at the Abbasid court came to an end with the death of Ma'mun's grandson Wathiq (847). The accession of his brother al-Mutiwakkil (Persian: Motevakkel) saw the eclipse of the religious liberalism, cultural renaissance and Persian ascendancy which had developed since the rise of the Abbasid caliphate. There was a clampdown on the Shia and the Mu'tazila in a high tide of orthodoxy. The influence of the Persians was fast replaced by that of the Turkish soldiers whom the caliph al-Mu'tasim had imported to strengthen his military machine. Indeed al-Mutiwakkil himself was murdered by the Turks, who henceforth formed the real power at the centre of the caliphate, similar to the power formations characterizing the dynasties that rose in eastern Persia from the ninth to the eleventh centuries.

This brings us to the end of the second century of the Islamic conquest, the emergence of the Persian dynasties and with them the return of Persian as the court, administrative and literary language.

Persian contributions

Let us look briefly at the contributions the Iranians made to the development of international Islamic society in the two centuries of direct Arab rule. Ibn Khaldun, the great Arab historian and sociologist (before sociology) of the fourteenth century, wrote in his celebrated *Muqaddima*:

> Thus the founders of grammar were Sibawaih and after him, al-Farisi and Az-Zajjaj. All of them were of Persian descent . . . They invented rules of [Arabic] grammar . . . Furthermore all the great jurists were Persians as is well known . . . Only the Persians engaged in the task of preserving knowledge and writing systematic scholarly works. Thus the truth of the statement of the Prophet becomes apparent, 'If learning were suspended in the highest parts of heaven the Persians would attain it' . . . The intellectual sciences were also the preserve of the Persians, left alone by the Arabs, who did not cultivate them . . . as was the case with all crafts . . .

There may be some exaggeration in this, but it shows the extent of the contribution made by Iranians in all aspects of learning, from Arabic grammar to Islamic jurisprudence to arts and crafts. E.G. Browne once calculated that in this period thirteen out of forty-seven masters of high Arabic literature were of Persian extraction. They included the great grammarian Sibawaih, mentioned by Ibn Khaldun, and Ibn Moqaffa' (Arabic: Ibn al-Muqaffa'), who was not only a high-ranking administrator but a master both of Arabic and of Middle Persian (Pahlavi). His Persian name was Ruzbeh and he or his father had converted from Zoroastrianism to Islam. It was he who translated *Shahnameh* and *Kelileh o Demneh* from Pahlavi into Arabic, both of which are now lost, though the latter was later translated from Arabic into New Persian. Bashshar ibn Bord (Arabic: Burd) was a notable poet in Arabic and was executed – as was Ibn Moqaffa' – on charges of religious deviancy, although it is fairly certain that the charges were false in the latter's case; he fell victim to the usual court intrigues to which viziers and high civil servants were exposed. The leading poet and favourite of Ma'mun, Abu Nuwas, was also of Persian descent. The greatest jurist of Persian extraction perhaps was Abu Hanifa Nu'man ibn Thabet, the founder of one of the four Sunni schools of law, the Hanafi school, which has many adherents among Sunni Muslims. Ali ibn Hamza al-Kisa'i (Persian: Hamzeh Kesa'i) was a Persian grammarian whom Harun al-Rashid put in charge of the education of his two sons, Amin and Ma'mun. His pupil al-Farra was also a grammarian of Persian origin. The list is long.

Shu'ubiyya or the *Shu'ubi* movement began a controversy in the ninth century and beyond on whether Arabs or non-Arabs, and more specifically Persians, were superior one to the other. This was a literary and scholarly argument confined to a relatively small elite, all of whom were Muslim. It is interesting that there were also Persian writers who defended the Arabs against the claims of the Persians. The Persian historian Baladhuri and the Persian philologist Zammakhshari were among the Iranians who, in the controversy, expressed a high regard for the Arabs.

Shiism and other Islamic religious movements were Arab in origin, although they tended to be concentrated not in Arabia or Syria but in Iraq, which had been mainly an Iranian region and the centre of the Sasanian empire before the Arab conquest. Iranian Shiites were largely concentrated in Reyy, Qom and the Caspian provinces, but most Iranian Muslims, in the west as well as east, were orthodox Sunnis. From their midst arose such great jurists and theologians as Mohammad Bokhari (Arabic: al-Bukhari) from as far east as Bokhara (Bukhara, now in Uzbekistan), the author of a highly authoritative Sunni source, Sahih. At the time and for some time to come Persian authors of theological, jurisprudential, philosophical, medical and scientific works wrote in Arabic because they could then be read and discussed from Transoxiana to Spain.

The rise of Sufism, or Islamic mysticism, to which Persians made a significant contribution, initially owed perhaps more to Gnosticism, Manichaeism and Iranian Buddhism than to orthodox Islam. What is known about Ibrahim ibn Adham (d. 777) as the prince of Balkh who repudiated his worldly power and possessions to become a mystic, and of the beliefs and practices of his followers, is rather reminiscent of the life and works of the Buddha himself. Bayazid of Bastam (d. 875) was one of the first Islamic Sufis to contrast spirit with matter along Manichaean and Gnostic lines – matter being the source of all evil, spirit, of good – and advocate the annihilation of the self in seeking God to achieve mystical reunion. Both Ibrahim and Bayzid are pillars of Islamic mysticism, venerated not only by the great classical Sufi poet and writer Farid al-Din Attar, but even by Sa'di, who, despite his respect for the legendary Sufis, was not one himself. He quotes Bayazid as having been thankful for someone pouring a bucket of ash over him as he was leaving a public bath on the Festival of 'Id, because he felt that he deserved hell fire and had only received ashes.

In medicine, the Persians continued Sasanian traditions, as exemplified by the school at Jondishapur and the Bokhtishu' family of renowned physicians, who were Christian Iranians and acted as court physicians to a number of Abbasid caliphs. Sabur (Shapur) ibn Sahl wrote the first of many treatises on antidotes in medicine. Another author in medicine was Ali ibn Rabban al-Tabari, an Iranian Christian convert to Islam who flourished in the ninth century. There were also some outstanding Arab physicians in the earlier period, but with the passage of time the Persians excelled in the field of medicine, culminating in the careers of such great figures as Mohammad ibn Zakaria Razi (= al-Razi; Razes) and Abu Ali ibn Sina (= Avicenna), who flourished in the tenth and eleventh centuries. The latter two were also great rationalist philosophers who, having been preceded by Abu Nasr-e Farabi (= al-Farabi), continued and developed the application of Aristotelian and Neoplatonic philosophy to Islamic knowledge and learning.

Musa al-Kwarazmi (Persian: Kharazmi, c.780–c.850) is often regarded as the greatest or at least the most original mathematician of mediaeval history. His famous book al-Jabr wa'l Muqbabala offers the first systematic solution of linear and quadratic equations. The word algebra is derived from the title of this book, and the word algorithm is based on the Latin version of his name, Algoritmi, by which he had been known in the western world through the translation of his works. The contribution of Persian scientists to Islamic science was substantial in this period even before reaching its zenith in the works of men such as Abu Reyhan Biruni (= Al-Biruni) and Omar Khayyam in later centuries. The brothers Banu Musa, who translated scientific works from Greek and Pahlavi, flourished under the caliph Ma'mun in the early ninth century. Many other names may be mentioned from the earlier period, including Mahani and Neirizi.

The Iranian contribution to early Islamic civilization in matters of government and administration was, from a purely practical point of view, even more important than to the arts and sciences. Almost from the beginning the Arab administration had to depend largely on Sasanian models of managing the realm and on Persian administrators to apply them. Land tax, or *kharaj*, was retained and *amil*s (Persian: *amel*s), often Persian *dehqan*s, were appointed to collect them. In certain areas the tax was farmed out to nominal landlords who would pay a designated sum to the state and collect the revenue themselves – a practice which had had precedents in Iran as far back as the Achaemenids. Land assignment or a system of uncertain tenure was also applied whereby a general or other high servant of the state was rewarded for their services. Still, all land was in principle ultimately owned by the state.

The Persian *divan*s, or departments, whether of finance, army or postal services, came into being much earlier than did the office of vizier, although they became much more extensive and influential when the early Abbasids adopted the Sasanian model of administration, government and court etiquette almost entirely and appointed a vizier to head the administration. The heyday of the Barmakis mentioned above exemplifies this trend, although it did not disappear with their demise. It was a system which in its basic features continued in use to the twentieth century. The *dabiran*, scribes or secretaries, manned the *divan*s from the beginning, or rather went on to run its affairs more or less as they had done before the conquest. It took some time before Arabic replaced Pahlavi as the language of the administrators.

The imperial art of Sasanian Persia also had a large impact on the development of artistic culture in the centuries following the conquest. There had been no substantial architecture, decorative arts or crafts in Arabia before Islam, and the conquest of Persia, Syria and North Africa marked the beginning of Islamic art. Muslims were not in favour of images and icons, which in their view might mean or imply idol worship, the struggle against which had been the central issue of the Prophet Mohammad's campaigns. But unlike Byzantine art, Sasanian art was neither religious nor predominantly based on images. Thus the art of Persia, and more especially of western Persia, which had enjoyed direct court patronage, provided models for the development of Islamic art, crafts and architecture, including rich textile motifs and designs of objects made of gold and other precious metals, as well as jewellery.

It took the Persians two centuries to found Persian-speaking dynasties and produce written literature in New Persian (see Chapter 5). But they were otherwise very much engaged in creating the new international Islamic civilization.

PERSIAN REVOLTS

After the battle of Nahavand no serious attempt was made to reverse the fortunes and drive the Arabs completely out of Iran, although there was local resistance in certain places as the Arabs steadily advanced towards the eastern reaches of the Sasanian empire. The most serious of these was the force of 40,000 men led in Khorasan by the nobleman Qaren shortly after the death of Yazdgerd; however, the Arabs surprised and defeated this force.

Once the Umayyad caliphate had been established, it had to face perennial revolts, the most important of which were Arab in origin and religious in character, such as those by the Shiites and Kharejites, culminating in the successful revolt of Abu Muslim in the cause of 'the family of the Prophet' and more specifically the House of Abbas. Virtually all the major Persian revolts took place from the mid-eighth century, about one hundred years after the Islamic conquest. The nature, causes and motives of these revolts are far from certain, particularly since those who subsequently wrote about them, whether Arab or Persian, were hostile to them. These revolts are mainly attributed to religious motives although at least in some cases, as with the *Khorramis* or the followers of al-Muqanna', political and social motives may have been the real force behind them. None was, however, motivated by an overt or covert objective of restoring the Sasanian empire.

Revolts against the state had been a familiar feature of Iranian history. The most dangerous and widespread faced by both the Umayyads and the Abbasids were those rebellions motivated by religious dissent within Islam itself. The Umayyads experienced the uprising of Imam Hosein, followed by several other revolts of a religious and political nature, until they were overthrown by the Abbasids. The Abbasids faced the opposition of the Shiites and Kharejites, the former of whom were particularly angry as they felt they had been cheated by the Abbasids after the victory against the Umayyads. Later, an Ismaili Shiite movement led by Abdollah, son of Meimun, known as al-Qaddah, who was of Persian descent, eventually resulted in the establishment of the rival Fatimid caliphate in Egypt and North Africa. And another Ismaili movement known as Qarmatian (= Carmathians), after its founder Qarmat, caused serious trouble to the Abbasid state over a long period. At one stage they even took away the sacred Black Stone of Mecca, though they eventually returned it to its place.

Revolts against the state therefore were far from confined to Persians or non-Muslims. The revolt of Behafarid in mid-eighth century Neishabur (= Nishapur), however, seems to have been motivated by religious heresy within the Zoroastrian religion itself. It was not the Umayyads but Abu Muslim, then the strong man of Khorasan, who defeated Behafarid's revolt at the request of

Zoroastrian religious leaders in the region. Abu Muslim was not just the chief missionary of the Abbasids for organizing the revolt against the Umayyids but a highly popular and charismatic leader as well. His murder by the caliph Mansur was received very badly, especially in Khorasan, and triggered a number of revolts in eastern Persia. In the earlier revolts the claim was often made either that Abu Muslim was not dead but hidden somewhere (e.g. in Reyy) and would rise again soon or that he would return as the (Zoroastrian or Muslim) saviour who would rid the world of injustice and corruption.

Sinbad was one of the first to raise the flag of revolt in Neishabur after the death of Abu Muslim. He had been close to the dead leader, and his followers were made up of both Zoroastrians and Muslim heretics. The sources even include Mazdakites among his followers, but it is difficult to believe, as some of the sources claim, that his avowed aim was to invade Arabia and destroy the Ka'ba. He was eventually defeated by the caliph's army in Reyy in 755; he then fled north and was caught and executed by the Persian Espahbad of Tabaristan. Another man to rise virtually at the same time (755–7) as a follower of Abu Muslim was Eshaq the Turk, who was so called because he extended his mission to Transoxiana. He claimed that Abu Muslim was alive and hidden in the Alborz Mountains. His followers became known as the *Muslimiyya*, many of whom – if the sources are to be believed – were Zoroastrian, although his own name shows that he was a Muslim, and his revolt was a response to the murder of a Muslim leader.

More formidable still was the revolt of Ostad Sis in 766, still during the reign of Mansur, in the districts of Herat, Badghis and Sistan. He is likely to have been joined by the Kharejites, who at the time had a strong presence in Sistan. Claiming to be a prophet he led large numbers of his anti-Abbasid supporters to certain defeat. The sources speak of 300,000 men in arms fighting against the government forces and tens of thousands of them being executed after defeat. These figures are likely to be inflated, especially as they imply that similar, if not bigger, numbers made up the forces that defeated them.

More famous, more colourful and more dangerous was al-Muqanna', 'the veiled prophet of Khorasan', on whose career the nineteenth-century English poet Thomas Moore based his poem *Lala Rookh*. Muqanna', as his title implies, permanently wore a mask – according to his followers so he would not bedazzle the people by his shining face and according to his detractors to hide his hideous aspect. Biruni says he was born Hashem ibn Hakim in Marv, claimed to be God and applied the rules of Mazdakism. Apart from his mask he is best known for sending up a false moon – a shining spherical object – every night from a hole or well in Nakhshab, 'the Moon of Nakhshab', which later became a favourite metaphor in classical Persian literature. When in 786 he and his followers were finally surrounded by government forces and there was no hope of escape, it is said that he and (all of?) his followers set fire to themselves to avoid falling into the hands of his enemies and to create the legend that he was not dead but had disappeared to return some time in the future. The supporters of Muqanna' are sometimes known as *Sepid-Jamegan* ('The White-clad'), implying that they wore a white uniform.

There is even less certainty about the origins and beliefs of the movement known as the Khorramis, or Khorramdinan. They flourished and rebelled over a relatively long stretch of time which might date back to pre-Islamic Persia, and may have been made up of various types of heretics grouped together by historians under that general title. Nezam al-Molk claims that they had first been organized after Mazdak's death by his wife, and since she was called Khorram (= Happy) they became known as Khorramis. The most famous, powerful and influential of the Khorramis was Babak, who rebelled under the caliph Ma'mun and held out in Azerbaijan and western Iran for more than twenty years, from 816 to 838. His movement, too, is variously described as Mazkdakite and Zoroastrian. The historians of early Islam tended to describe such movements in purely religious terms. Religion might have been a motive, in some cases more, in others less. But one must not overlook the fact that these rebellions, and especially one such as Babak's, were revolts against the state, the state being the caliphate at the time. One traditional source claims that Babak introduced murder, conflict and cruelty into the Khorrami sect. He defeated several forces sent out against him until he in turn was defeated by the able and cunning Persian general Afshin, then in the service of the caliph Mu'tasim.

It was at about the same time that Maziyar, a local ruler in Tabaristan, was caught as a rebel. His rebellion was not rooted in religion and did not have a popular following; his had a more immediate cause, being a rebellion against Abdollah ibn Taher, the Persian Taherid ruler of Khorasan, who was nominally endorsed as governor by the caliph. Maziyar was sent to the caliph's court where he was executed. Afshin, who was accused of complicity with Maziyar, was also executed shortly afterwards.

PERSIAN DYNASTIES

Between the early ninth and eleventh centuries there arose Persian principalities and states, mainly in the east, with the vast region of greater Khorasan as their centre, except for one major Iranian dynasty, the Buyids, who ruled in the west, centre and south, including, for some time, Iraq and Baghdad. Such a development was not planned or consciously designed. Indeed, the dynasties that ruled in this period usually had the nominal approval of the caliph in Baghdad, who himself was often a puppet in the hands of his Turkish generals. The development was a natural consequence of the weakness of the caliphate at the centre and – as part of this – the growth of regional powers in the east, where genuine as opposed to nominal direct rule was no longer tenable. With Persians increasingly present in the military, administrative and literary spheres of the Abbasid caliphate, and with their involvement in regional government, especially in the east, it was only a matter of time for autonomous or independent powers to rise from their midst.

The Taherids

As noted above, Taher son of Hosein, entitled the Ambidextrous, led Ma'mun's armies against his brother, Amin, and secured the caliphate for him. His great-grandfather, Rozayq, had been in the service of the Arab governor of Sistan. Rozayq's son had joined the Abbasid movement and had been rewarded with the governorship of Poshang, near Hari Rud (in modern Afghanistan), where he was in turn replaced by his son, Hosein. Taher son of Hosein had once served in an army led by Ma'mun which the latter's father, Harun, had sent to put down a rebellion in the east. The death of Harun saw Ma'mun as the governor of Khorasan, centred in Marv, but when war broke out between him and his brother, the caliph Amin, he made Taher the commander of his army. Once Amin was defeated and killed, Ma'mun put Taher in charge of the army, the police and tax collection in northern Iraq.

In 820 Ma'mun gave Taher the highly important governorship of Khorasan, the first Persian ever to hold the post, while his son Abdollah replaced him in his former position. Once in Khorasn, Taher's relations with Ma'mun began to cool off, for reasons that are not quite clear. He minted coins on which the caliph's name was not mentioned and is said to have omitted Ma'mun's name from the Friday prayers, which would have been tantamount to rebellion or a declaration of full independence. What this might have led to we cannot know, since he died in 822; some early historians, notably Tabari, believe that Ma'mun had arranged for him to be poisoned.

Taher was succeeded by another son of his, Talha, who died in 828 and was replaced by his brother Abdollah as governor of Khorasan. Abdollah still owned land in Iraq and nominally held several official posts there including that of chief of the police in Baghdad. With the accession of Mu'tasim after Ma'mun relations cooled but remained correct, and Abdollah, though virtually independent, had the formal approval of the caliph to rule his territories. Abdollah was an able general who had displayed his military ability on missions as far away as Egypt before becoming governor of Khorasan. From his capital Neishabur he ruled a vast territory which later stretched as far as Kerman and eastwards to the borders of India. His vassals included Maziyar the Espahbad of Tabaristan, whose rebellion, as noted, he put down.

Abdollah thus established a large domain with the nominal endorsement of the caliph. He was nevertheless loyal to the caliphate and saw the interests of his dynasty as being tied with those of the Abbasids. He was a patron of art and culture, but he did not promote Persian literature, the poets in his service being all Arab. After his death in 845 the new caliph, with some hesitation, confirmed Abdollah's son Taher in his position. The family had now become quite extended and various Taherids acted as sub-governors and local governors, and not just in the east and north-east – the caliph appointed one of their number to the governorship of Iraq and Fars. As loyal supporters of the caliphate, however, they had to face the opposition of the Shiites in the north, such as periodic revolts in Qazvin, Reyy and Gorgan. In fact Hasan ibn Zeid, the Alid ruler of eastern Tabaristan who had been a vassal of the Taherids, shook off their dominion, and Mohammad son of Taher III was not able to stop him. Nor did he manage to put down the rebellion of the Kharejites in Sistan. But soon he had to face an enemy who would spell doom for Taherid rule. This was Ya'qub son of Leith the Coppersmith (*Saffar*).

The Saffarids

The Taherids had initially owed their power to the caliphate and went on ruling in Khorasan as the caliph's nominal representatives and real allies. Therefore the fact that they were virtually independent did not in practice threaten Abbasid interests in the east. Ya'qub and his brothers, on the other hand, who rose from Sistan to establish Saffarid rule, were common local people whose achievements were owed entirely to their own efforts, not to the appointment or endorsement of the caliph. They too tried to have peaceful relations with Baghdad most of the time, but they lacked the genuine loyalty of the Taherids whom, for a short period, they replaced as rulers of Khorasan.

Ya'qub was a coppersmith, and probably a Kharejite, who had been relatively strong in Sistan for a long time. What made him give up his trade and become a bandit leader is not known, but according to legend he, predating Robin Hood, robbed the rich and helped the poor. He and his two brothers then joined the commander Derham ibn Saleh, who chased the Taherids out of Zaranj and declared war on the Kharejites. The Kharejites were defeated and their leader killed by Ya'qub himself, but many of them then joined Ya'qub, who had replaced Saleh as the chief commander. Having been alarmed at his successes, Mohammad, the last Taherid, tried to keep him away by tempting him with the governorship of Kerman. Yet Ya'qub conquered Shirz as well and established good relations with Baghdad so that the caliph – who was not in fact happy with Ya'qub's conquests – appointed him to the governorship of Balkh and Tokharistan, further in the northeast. In 872 Ya'qub finally used a pretext to attack Neishabur and topple Taherid rule. Since the Taherids had been nominally governors of the caliph, Ya'qub's conquest of Neishabur was therefore not legitimate. The caliph ordered Ya'qub to restore the Taherids. But he refused, and in the long struggle that ensued he eventually led his army against Baghdad. The caliph, who was still facing the Zanj rebellion of Ethiopian slaves in Iraq, was trying to sue for peace when the old warrior died on the way.

Ya'qub was succeeded by his brother Amr, who immediately professed fealty to the caliph and was rewarded by being formally appointed to the governorship of Khorasan and Fars; but it took him time and effort before he could establish his authority in Khorasan. Later, and for unknown reasons, Amr's relationship with the caliph soured and he was twice defeated by the caliph's army, although eventually he was re-instated to the governorship of Khorasan. But he was not satisfied with that and tried to extend his rule to Transoxiana. Here he faced the able and competent Samanid ruler Isma'il, who in 900 finally defeated him and thus terminated the short span of Saffarid glory, although the Saffarids persisted as small princelings until the fifteenth century. Amr was no less a military commander than his more famous brother and was a fairer and more able administrator. In the war with Isma'il Baghdad had at first supported Amr and then changed sides with the reversal of fortunes. Isma'il sent the captured Amr to Baghdad, where he was put to death.

The Samanids

Isma'il was son of Ahmad, whose earliest known ancestor was called Saman Khoda, a *dehqan* in the district of Balkh who claimed to have descended from Bahram Chubin, the colourful rebel general of Khosrow II (Parviz; see Chapter 2). His brother Nasr had secured his rule in Bokhara when the caliph appointed him as governor for the whole of Transoxiana.

According to a tradition, the first distich or couplet in New Persian poetry had been written by Ya'qub's secretary. However that may be, it was under the Samanids that Persian literature and culture began to flourish, the foundations of classical Persian literature were laid and Persian science experienced a period of glory. With the rise of pan-Persian nationalist ideology in the twentieth century the Samanids were represented as modern Iranian nationalists who had consciously tried to shake off Arab rule and culture by promoting Persian language and literature. This overlooked the fact that the Samanids ruled from Transoxiana, were committed Sunni Muslims and loyal clients of the caliphate in Baghdad and promoted Arabic as well as Persian literature. There can be no doubt that New Persian literature flourished and developed under the Samanids, but this is no more proof of their being ideological nationalists than the Ghaznavids after them, who were even greater patrons of Persian literature.

Isma'il replaced his brother Nasr after his death in 892 as the ruler of Transoxiana. He was only nominally endorsed by the caliph, but was loyal to him. After defeating the Saffarids in Khorasan, Isma'il extended his conquests to the west as far as Reyy and Qazvin. On his return he had to face the intrusion of Central Asian Turks and other nomads. He managed to stem the Turkish tide for the time being but it would not be long before they overran not only Transoxiana but also Khorasan and beyond.

Nezami Aruzi, the famous classical essayist and chronicler, described Nasr ibn Ahmad, Isma'il's grandson, as 'the central medallion in the Samanid necklace'. He ruled for thirty years. Under him the Samanids reached the zenith of their power and glory, and their capital, Bokhara, was the centre of arts, letters and culture. Abu Abdollah Rudaki, the virtual founder of classical Persian poetry, as well as other poets enjoyed his patronage.

According to a legend related by Nezami Aruzi, Nasr ibn Ahmad had once been camping away from Bokhara (= Bukhara) and enjoying it so much that he prolonged his stay indefinitely. The officials accompanying him, missing their homes and families, begged Rudaki to try to persuade the amir to return to Bokhara. Rudaki composed a few simple but moving and nostalgic verses about Bokhara and sang them in the ruler's presence. Nasr ibn Ahmad was so moved that 'he mounted his horse with bare feet'.

Both Khorasan and Transoxiana were in turmoil and Nuh, Nasr's son, had to face the menace of the Turks both from outside and from within his realm. Just as had happened in the Abbasid court earlier, the Turkish slaves who had been purchased to serve as soldiers had gained power and influence in the Samanid court. One of these was Alptegin, who had risen from being a slave soldier to the headship of the army. Nuh's son became a pawn in his hands and the learned vizier Abu'ali Bal'ami – who is famous for his translation of a part of *Tarikh-e Tabari* into Persian – did not carry much weight beside him. Nuh's second son, Mansur, who succeeded his brother, sacked the meddlesome Turk from the governorship of Khorasan. Defeating in Balkh the force that Mansur had sent against him, Alptegin went to Ghazna and laid the foundations of the Ghaznavid empire.

The fortunes of the Samanids rapidly declined towards the end of the tenth century. They failed to suppress a rebellion in Sistan and were constantly under pressure from the Ilek-khanid Turks. One of them was in fact deposed and blinded by the Turks, and his successor, who appointed Saboktegin, Alptegin's son-in-law, to the governorship of Khorasan was later defied by the latter's son Mahmud and eventually killed by the Ilek-khanids in 999. Thus ended the illustrious Samanid rule.

Nezami Aruzi tells the remarkable legend of the treatment by Razes (Mohammad Zakariya Razi), the great physician, scientist and philosopher, of a less well-known Samanid ruler. This amir became paralysed in his legs and no amount of treatment had the slightest effect. In the end, he sent for Razes, who lived far away in Reyy but agreed to come. When they reached the Oxus, Razes, who had never seen such a great river, refused to board the boat, saying that if he drowned wise men would blame him for having taken the risk. When it proved impossible to change his mind, he was forced to board the boat.

The officials apologized to him once they left the boat on the other side, but he replied that he did not mind since if he had been drowned no one would have blamed him for it. However, his treatment also proved ineffective. In the end he said he had only one treatment left, but for this he and the amir must be left alone in a bath. Once in the bath, he took off the Amir's clothes and gave him some soothing medicines. Then he suddenly began to abuse the amir for his own enforced crossing of the river and drew his sword as if he wanted to strike him with it. In absolute terror, the amir stood up, passed out, and later rose fully recovered. Razes then left the bath and, together with the slave who was waiting for him, rushed back home. Whether or not this legend is true, it certainly shows that not only did the Iranians at the time know of hysterical paralysis as a psychological illness but also about the shock treatment necessary to cure it.

The rise of New Persian and classical literature

It used to be believed that Dari or New Persian – the classical form of modern Persian – evolved between the seventh and ninth centuries AD from the Sasanian Middle Persian language. According to more recent scholarly opinion, in fact there had been not one but three main languages before the fall of the Sasanian empire: Pahlavi, the Parthian language spoken in the north-west (ancient Media); Parsi or Middle Persian, spoken in the south; and Dari which had replaced Parthian in the north-east. It was this last language which was to spread after the Islamic conquest and gradually become the official court language of Islamic Persia.

One of the earliest Persian poets still remembered was Abu Hafs Soghdi from the early ninth century, the author of a single, simple but charming distich: 'How does the mountain gazelle run in the plain? / It is friendless, how can it live without a friend?' The Persians adapted Arabic quantitative metres to their own literary traditions, but in such a way that the Persian metres can nevertheless be distinguished from the Arabic. In the earlier part of the next century there came other, more mature poets such as Shahid-e Balkhi and Kesa'i Marvzi, both from greater Khorasan, who typically wrote short lyrics, laments and contemplative and didactic poetry. It was with Abu Adollah Rudaki, often described as the founder of classical Persian poetry, that New Persian poetry reached its early, youthful maturity. Another notable poet of the tenth century was Abu Mansur Daqiqi, who also flourished under the Samanids. His fame is mainly due to the fact that he was the first poet to put *Shahnameh* to verse, writing a thousand distiches on the advent of Zoroaster under Goshtasp Shah, which Ferdowsi later openly incorporated into his own complete poetical rendering of the book (see Chapter 2).

Buyids and Ziyarids

While the Samanids flourished in eastern and north-eastern Persia, two other dynasties were established in much of the rest of the country. Mardavijj ibn Ziyar was a local Caspian ruler who fought and defeated Makan, the governor of Gorgan who had rebelled against the Samanids. In this campaign Ali, governor of Reyy, and his two brothers Hasan and Ahmad joined the service of Mardavijj. They were sons of Buyeh or Buweyh from the northern mountainous region of Deilaman and displayed exceptional ability and courage. Mardavijj appointed Ali, the eldest brother, as governor in a town near Hamadan. He himself was assassinated by his Turkish soldiers apparently because of displaying excessive cruelty, and his brother Voshmgir replaced him as the head of the Ziyarid dynasty.

In the meantime the Buyids had reached as far as Kerman and Fars where Ali, now entitled Emad al-Dawleh by the caliph, ruled from Shiraz. The elder brother Hasan, entitled Rokn al-Dawleh, eventually occupied Isfahan and later Qom and Reyy after clashes with Voshmgir, who from then on was confined to rule in the western Caspian region, centred on Gorgan. The greatest Ziyarid was perhaps Qabus son of Voshmgir, who seems to have excelled in learning as well as cruelty. He spent eighteen years in jail and yet on return to power he continued in his old ways. Eventually he was deposed (and left to die of hypothermia) and was buried in the tomb tower of Gonbad-e Qabus which still stands near Gorgan, the first of its kind to be built since the Islamic conquest. In 1012 Qabus was replaced by his son Manuchehr, who ended up becoming a vassal of the Ghaznavid Mas'ud son of Mahumud (see below). He was the first patron of the great poet Manuchehri. The claim to fame of the last important prince of the Ziyarids, Keikavus ibn Eskandar, is his authorship of the famous *Qabusnameh*, a kind of 'mirror for princes' which he wrote for his son Gilanshah.

Much before that, the youngest Buyid brother – Ahmad, entitled Mo'ezz al-Dawleh – had entered Baghdad and turned the caliph into his pawn. There were then three Buyid rulers at the same time: Ali, the senior Buyid, with his centre in Shiraz; Hasan, based in Isfahan; and Ahmad in Baghdad. The Buyids were Shiites but were not intolerant; it would not have been in their interest to try and suppress the Sunnis or abolish the caliphate. Instead, for decades they ruled in Iraq and virtually appointed the caliphs. After Ali's death Hasan became the senior Buyid and his son Fana Khosraw, entitled Azod al-Dawleh, replaced his uncle in Shiraz. After the death of his father, he became the senior Buyid and was in command of all the Buyid lands, a powerful empire which flourished throughout his long rule. The reign of Azod al-Dawleh was the high point of Buyid rule. There was opulence and splendour, and he was the first post-Islamic ruler of Iran to assume the title of Shahanshah.

His death in 983 typically led to a struggle for succession which ended up by breaking the unity which Azod al-Dawleh had achieved and marking the beginning of the decline of Buyid fortunes. His brother Fakhr al-Dawleh continued to rule Reyy until his death in 997 at the close of the tenth century and the emergence of Ghaznavid power in the east. The latter's son, Majd al-Dawleh, was a minor and so his mother Seyyedeh ruled in his name. Nezam al-Molk Tusi tells the story that when the mighty Mahmud of Ghazna asked her to submit to him she refused, telling him that if Mahmud conquered her then they would say a mighty emperor had conquered an old woman and if he did not succeed they would say that he was defeated by an old woman. However that may be, Mahmud attacked Reyy and abolished Buyid rule – incidentally executing two hundred Shiite notables – after Seyyedeh's death.

The Ghaznavids
The century and a half which separates the rise of the Samanids from the fall of the Buyids is usually regarded as a Persian interlude between Arab and Turkish rule in Persia. It is, however, more realistic to include the early Ghaznavids – before they lost Khorasan and other Persian territories – in this Persian period. The founders of the Ghaznavid dynasty were Turkic but the Turks in their service were no more than those who served and eventually dominated the later Samanids. And, unlike the Seljuks, who later led hordes of Turkaman nomads into Persia and beyond, they were essentially an indigenous Iranian dynasty.

As we have noted above, Alptegin, once a slave soldier in the service of the Samanids, established himself in Khorasan in defiance of the Samanid ruler. Later his successor received help from the Samanids in restoring his authority in

Ghazna. The latter's death in 970 led to a period of chaos until Saboktegin, one of Alptegin's Turkish slaves who later rose high and became his son-in-law, defeated his opponents, established himself in Ghazna and extended his rule to a relatively vast territory, although he was nominally still a vassal of the Samanids. His death in 997 – the same year that Fakhr al-Dawleh of the Buyids died in Reyy – typically led to a struggle for the succession out of which his younger son Mahmud emerged victorious. Mahmud was recognized by the caliph in Baghdad and given the title Yamin al-Dawleh.

Mahmud was an able military leader as well as an empire builder. At the same time he was an orthodox Sunni who was dedicated both to the persecution of Shiites and the destruction of Hindu temples. Religious intolerance and love of riches were his principal motives for attacking Indian territories to the east of his domain, conquering Punjab and destroying and looting Hindu temples further beyond. He refused to recognize the last Samanid prince, who in any case was soon overrun by Ilek-khanid Turks, overthrew the Buyids and extended his rule to as far west as Isfahan. Thus he built an empire which extended in the south-east into India and covered much of central and northern Persia, with Khorasan as its main homeland. Turkish pressure was increasing steadily in Transoxiana and on the eastern borders of Khorasan, but Mahmud kept it at bay as long as he was alive.

Mahmud was not just an incorrigible warrior but also a dedicated patron of literature and science. There were many leading poets and scientists at his court, including such stars as Onsori, Farrokhi and Biruni. He also invited Avicenna to his court, but the latter declined his invitation and instead joined the small court of Qabus, the learned but unpopular Ziyarid ruler, and later the courts of the last Buyids. Ferdowsi dedicated his *Shahnameh* to Mahmud's name and wrote in his praise, although he had been writing the great epic before Mahmud, and he does not seem to have spent any length of time at his court.

According to a colourful legend told by Nezami Aruzi, Ferdowsi had been living at Mahmud's court and hoping for a substantial reward when the book was finished. But instead of gold, Mahmud sent him a much smaller reward in silver money. This angered the poet, who, upon receiving Mahmud's reward in the resting room of a public bath, 'had a drink of beer, and divided the silver between the brewer and the bath-keeper'. Anticipating the shah's punishment for this insult, he ran away, ended up in Mazandaran and wrote a long lampoon or *hajv-nameh* against Mahmud. In many of its details the story is unlikely to be true, but there can be little doubt that Ferdowsi was disappointed by Mahmud and ended his days in financial difficulty. He said in a verse towards the end of his life: 'Do not remain long in the world / It is a disaster to be poor and old.'

Mahmud's death in 1030 characteristically led to a struggle for succession between two of his sons, Mohammad, who had been his favourite, and Mas'ud, the elder son who was then governor of Isfahan. Beihaqi's account of these events is highly instructive in how chaos and conflict arose in Persia after the death of a great ruler, how quickly various parties shifted their positions to be on the winning side and how the vanquished lost everything, usually including their lives. In this case the highest state official to lose everything was Hasanak the Vizier, the full account of whose fall and execution Beihaqi recounts in his *History*.

Mahmud had nominated his younger son Mohammad instead of Mas'ud to succeed him, and Hasanak had done everything in his power to fulfil the shah's wish, both when he was still alive and after he died. Mas'ud, who had been dispatched as governor of Isfahan in honourable exile, rose, fought his way back with ease, dethroned and blinded his brother and took over the realm. He took revenge on many, but especially Hasanak, who was not only vizier but had defied him most effectively. Hasanak was accused of being a Carmathian Ismaili, his property was appropriated and it was ordered he should be stoned to death, though Beihaqi, who witnessed it all, says that he had already been strangled by the noose before the stoning commenced.

In 1035 Mas'ud was defeated by Seljuk Turks but made an agreement with them to rule certain areas with his approval on condition that they stem the tide of the Oghuz Turkamans, to which tribes the Seljuks themselves belonged. But the peace did not last. In his second war with the Seljuks Mas'ud was heavily and irreversibly defeated and withdrew from Khorasan. The Ghaznavids thereafter kept their possessions in India, but they still maintained a link with Persia through their official use of the Persian language and patronage of Persian literature. Such great poets as Sana'i Ghaznavi and Mas'ud-e Sa'd Salman belong to the latter period.

CHAPTER 4

Turks and Mongols

Persian-speaking Turks are donors of life.*

Hafiz

THE TURKS WERE A Central Asian people of various tribal groupings, apparently originating in the Altai Mountains. They moved into Transoxiana in the fourth to sixth centuries AD, raiding the eastern Sasanian frontiers. They began to cross the Oxus from Central Asia and move westwards into Persia's interior in the eleventh century, led by the Seljuk (the anglicized form of Saljuq) of the Oghuz or Ghozz tribes, a movement which eventually led to the creation of the Ottoman empire and modern Turkey. First they encountered the Ghaznavids, whom they chased out of Khorasan; then the gateway was open for conquering the Iranian hinterlands, Iraq, Syria and Anatolia.

As noted in earlier chapters, in the latter part of the Sasanian period, the Turks had replaced most of the troublesome nomads on the eastern reaches of the empire. The early Abbasids, recognizing the Turks' martial qualities, had used individual Turks as military (and to a lesser extent domestic) slaves. Within a short period these began to dominate the caliph and interfere with the affairs of the caliphate. Likewise, such eastern Persian states as the Samanids had later taken Turkish slaves into their (mainly military) employment. This too had in time led to the rise of individual Turks, such as Alptegin and Saboktegin, who founded the Ghaznavid empire. Yet none of this had been due to invasion or the mass migration of Turkish hordes into Persia and beyond. That privilege first went to Seljuk Turks, who prepared the ground for later migrations and invasions. Thus it was the steady and continuous migration of Turkish nomads for the centuries following the Seljuks that resulted in the considerable linguistic and ethnic impact of the Turkish people on Iranian civilization.

---

* Torkan-e Parsi-guy Bakhshandegan-e Omrand.

THE SELJUKS

Having moved westwards and converted to Islam, the Seljuks first made contact with the Samanids, and later with Mahmud of Ghazna: this did not end well. In the 1030s they moved into Khorasan and made peace with Mas'ud of Ghazna on condition that they would keep the Ghozz under control. But they routed Mas'ud's army in 1040. The Ghaznavids were thus pushed out of Khorasan, and though they still held on to Ghazna for some time, they were eventually reduced to a local power in western India.

Abolfazl Beihaqi, the Ghaznavid loyal state secretary and contemporary historian who witnessed these events, wrote in his famous *History* that the loss of Khorasan was due to the plundering and injustice of Ma'usd's governor-general in that province, who sent half of his loot to the court in Ghazna. He relates his conversation with a courier to whom Mas'ud had praised the governor-general as 'a good lackey', adding that if he had a couple of other lackeys like him his financial situation would be sound. The courtier told Beihaqi that he had confirmed Mas'ud's opinion, adding that he did not have 'the guts to tell him that it is the people of Khorasan, *high as well as low*, who must be asked as to how much suffering he must have caused them . . . and the future would show what the consequences of his action would be'. Beihaqi confirms that opinion and says that the Seljuks won in the end with the blessing and support of the people of Khorasan.

Early Seljuks

The Seljuk invaders were led by the brothers Toghrol Beg and Chaghri Beg. While the latter remained behind in Khorasan, Toghrol pushed westwards, captured Reyy, which he made his capital, overran the scattered Buyid principalities, entered Baghdad in 1055 and ended Buyid rule in Iraq. As noted in Chapter 3, the caliphate had already lost much of its executive power, first to individual Turkish generals, then to the Buyids, who had captured Baghdad. Thus the caliph conferred the title of sultan on Toghrol, since he was both the dominant ruler of the Abbasid domains and, contrary to the caliph's previous Buyid overlords, an orthodox Sunni. Until then, apart from the Ghaznavid territories in the east, Shiism had been the dominant power in much of the Muslim Middle East, with Buyid control of Iraq and western Persia, while Egypt and North Africa were in the hands of the Fatimid (Ismaili Shii) caliphate.

There has been a good deal of speculation on the implications of the title 'sultan' – which was used by subsequent Turkish rulers as well – for the relationship between the caliphate and the sultanate from this time onwards. Some have even interpreted it as a division along church/state or religious/secular lines. It is extremely unlikely that in conferring the title of sultan on Toghrol the caliph had anything of the kind in mind. The caliphate does not compare with the Christian church; the caliph did not have the doctrinal authority of the pope; and the new sultan's independent power vis-à-vis the caliph was not very different from that of the Buyids and the Ghaznavids before him.

In 1063 Toghrol died and was buried in a tower in Reyy which is still standing and bears his name. His brother Chaghri, who had been ruling Khorasan, was already dead. Since Toghrol did not have a male issue of his own, Chaghri's son Alp Arsalan succeeded to the sultanante. Typically, however, there was conflict and rebellion on Toghrol's death. Alp Arsalan's younger brother, Soleiman, had apparently been nominated by Toghrol for the succession and his vizier, Amid al-Molk Kondori, a very able and learned man, had backed his claim only to lose his own life, the incoming vizier, Nezam al-Molk, having encouraged the new sultan to have him killed.

The new sultan had to be constantly on the move to keep the peace in all his provinces. Having put down a rebellion by the Qarakhanid Turks in the east, he then led his troops to eastern Anatolia where the unruly Ghozz were engaged in plunder. The Byzantine emperor wrongly interpreted this as a threat to himself, led a large army to meet Alp Arsalan, was routed by Arsalan's much smaller army at Malazgerd and was himself taken prisoner. Central and western Anatolia were lost to Byzantium and though the west was recovered some time later, central Anatolia henceforth became the base for the Seljuks of Rum, which in later times led to the foundation of the Ottoman empire.

Having returned to the east to suppress a Qarakhanid rebellion once again, Arsalan was killed by a prisoner who had been brought before him for execution. There followed the familiar rebellions after the death of a ruler, which had to be put down by his son, Malekshah, who succeeded him. Malekshah also had to face revolt from a pretender, his uncle Qavort Beg, the first Seljuk king of Kerman, whom he defeated and killed as well as having his two sons blinded, although one of the latter continued to rule in Kerman.

Malekshah's able and learned vizier Nezam al-Molk Tusi noted in his treatise on the art of governance, *Siyasatnameh* (or *Siyar al-Muluk*), that the people's transgression against God would result

> in the disappearance of a good ruler (*padeshahi nik*), swords would be drawn, and much blood would be spilt – and whoever has more power would do whatever he pleases – until all those sinners would be destroyed amidst all the chaotic rebellions (*fetneh-ha*) and bloodlettings ... And in consequence of the bad omen created by these sinners many an innocent person would be destroyed in those chaotic rebellions.

This was part of the vizier's abstract and general observations on the cycle of arbitrary rule–chaos–arbitrary rule in Iranian history, based on observations in his own time.

The Seljuk empire at its peak

In Malekshah's reign the Seljuk empire reached its apogee both in extent (surpassing even the Sasanian empire), prosperity and glory: the empire stretched from Central Asia to the Mediterranean. The administration of the empire was in

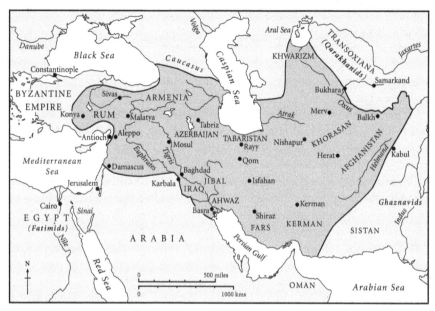

The Seljuk Empire at its peak, AD 1072–92

the hands of Nezam al-Molk, who had posted his twelve sons to various provinces to ensure loyalty and efficiency. From the beginnings of the Seljuk conquests the administration of the state was left in the hands of Persians, running a system which was broadly similar to that of the Ghaznavids and earlier periods, being based on *divan*s, secretaries, *mostawfis* (tax accountants) and the like, a system which in general served the country until the mid-nineteenth century when European influence introduced new forms.

Apart from the *divan*, there was also the sultan's *dargah*, the often mobile court held in tents in various parts of the country, where at least in theory any aggrieved person had the right to present a petition suing for justice. The army was run by the Turks. Apart from tribal levies there was a select professional army, under Arsalan, comprising ten to fifteen thousand men. This vast empire had been founded almost unintentionally over a very short period of time by an essentially nomadic people. Part of the reason for the court to be regularly on the move, even more than under the Ghaznavids, was the vastness of the empire and the nomadic culture of its rulers. For both these reasons provincial rulers and governors were appointed, although they were still under the command of the sultan and could be dismissed at his will so long as the centre had the physical strength to control its periphery, as was the case until the death of Malekshah.

Eqta' (Arabic: *iqta'*) was a form of land assignment which had been in use since the Arab conquest, itself modelled after the assignment systems which had prevailed before Islam. Later, under the Mongols, a similar assignment system called *soyurgal* came into existence and still later systems included *tiyul* under the Safavids and Qajars in the nineteenth century. The Seljuks made extensive use of the *eqta'* system in assigning lands and provinces to their relatives, their favourites and their military and administrative staff, to be run by them from the local revenues.

Under this system, the title to land was not hereditary nor was there security of tenure, the land-assignee retaining his post at the sultan's will. As noted in previous chapters, this was not a feudal society: there was no feudalism at any time in Iran. It is true that when the central authority was weak enough not to be able to remove an assignee even if it so wished, then he could retain his position until the state or anyone stronger could replace him. But such a position was not tenable in the long run, except in the case of rebels who effectively declared independence and became rulers of their province in their own right.

The supreme example of this unusual development under the Seljuks was the case of Khiveh (Khiva, Khwarazm). In 1077 Malekshah granted the *eqta'* of this eastern province to his favourite cup-bearer, Anushtegin, who was not a nobleman but a humble servant. The assignment was later confirmed in his line, until one of his descendants claimed independence from the then sultan, Sanjar. Eventually the Khwarazm-shahs as they styled themselves founded an empire over a brief period which was destroyed by the Mongols shortly afterwards. Thus, they were not from noble descent, and they managed to found a new state by rebelling against their masters, their independence lasting barely half a century.

Nezam al-Molk continued as Alp Arsalan's vizier virtually until the end of Malekshah's rule. He came from Tus in Khorasan, as had Ferdowsi before him and the great mystic theologian Abu Hamed Ghazali, who was his contemporary and for a few years taught in the Nezamiyeh College of Baghdad, which had been endowed by the vizier himself and bore his name. Nezam al-Molk built other mosques and *madresehs* (Anglicized: *madrasas*), his addition to the great Congressional Mosque (Masjed-e Jame') of Isfahan, then the capital, being regarded as a most notable architectural achievement of the period. Another of the great vizier's protégés was Omar Khayyam, from Neishabur, the famous poet who was much better known at the time as a mathematician and astronomer. He and other scientists were employed in the observatory founded by Malekshah to calculate the new Jalali Era, based on solar years, which was inaugurated from the *Nawruz* of 1079, 'Jalali' being an adjective of Jalal al-Din, Malekshah's title.

If Malekshah was a notable example of the just ruler along traditional Iranian lines, Nezam al-Molk was one of the most illustrious viziers in Iranian history. He was an accomplished man of letters (as most Persian viziers were in Iranian history) and is the author of the classic *Siyasatnameh* or *Siyar al-Muluk*, mentioned above, a book in the genre of 'mirrors for princes' on how to run the realm justly and successfully. As is characteristic of this genre, on every subject his advice is followed by anecdotes giving examples of the practice of past rulers, both Islamic and pre-Islamic, the probable authenticity or accuracy of which varies one to the other. In the chapter on the judges, law-enforcers and royal justice, he relates the following anecdote from the reign of Ibrahim (son of Mas'ud) of Ghazana, who had flourished not long before.

> Bread became short in the city; the poor sought justice (*tazallom*) at the court and accused the royal baker of hoarding wheat and flour. The king ordered the man to be trampled under an elephant's foot, and his dead body hung from its tusk, taking it around the town and crying that any baker who did not open his shop would receive the same treatment. By the evening there were fifty *man*s of surplus bread at each bakery and there was no demand for them.

This kind of justice or punishment by rulers and governors is quite familiar from Iranian history; in Qajar times the favourite method in similar circumstances was to throw the chief baker into a baking oven. It was the absence of established laws, coupled with real or suspected irresponsible behaviour, which resulted in such extreme and arbitrary measures.

Yet Nezam al-Molk did not escape the fate that befell most Iranian ministers before and after him. He was eighty when the sultan dismissed him, accusing him of arrogance to the point of pretending to partnership with himself, and worried by the extent to which his kindred were in charge of affairs. The vizier had committed the mortal sin of becoming rich and powerful, more than the sultan would tolerate. He was replaced by Taj al-Molk, a protégé of the sultan's favourite wife, Torkan Khatun. Shortly afterwards the disgraced vizier fell victim to the dagger of an Ismaili assassin, although it is very likely that Taj al-Molk had arranged the attack with the sultan's knowledge. Typically, fallen viziers did not survive their fall, as Abdolhosein Teymurtash was to learn even as late as the twentieth century (see Chapter 9).

Malekshah died at the age of thirty-seven, in 1092, three weeks after the death of the disgraced vizier, whose loyal supporters killed Taj al-Molk four months later. There followed the usual acts of fratricide and turmoil over the succession. Torkan Khatun proclaimed her young son Mahmud successor in Isfahan. The sultan's eldest son, Berkiyaroq, fled to Reyy where he was declared sultan. Rather than attacking Isfahan, he then went to Hamadan but soon had to face the rebellion of his maternal uncle, whom he defeated. Moving on to Baghdad, where he was proclaimed sultan, his paternal uncle rebelled, caught him and took him to Isfahan: here he was about to be blinded when his brother Mahmud died of smallpox and so he succeeded him. Another rebellious uncle was killed by his own slave, and meanwhile Torkan Khatun, Mahmud's mother, had been killed. In 1099 Berkiyaroq's younger brother Mohammad rose against him. Peace was reached in 1103–4 but in the meantime Mohammad had killed Berkiyaroq's mother, and

Berkiyaroq had killed his vizier, Mo'ayyed al-Molk. Shortly afterwards, Berkiyaroq died and was replaced by his five-year-old son Malekshah II, but he was caught and blinded, and Mohammad succeeded to the throne.

Soleiman Ravandi, the classical historian of the Seljuks, casually relates a story about Sultan Mohammad which is worth a brief mention. Zia al-Molk Ahmad, son of Nezam al-Molk and currently the sultan's vizier, had offered him money to put a very important man (who was also a seyyed – one of the Prophet Mohammad's descendants) 'at his disposal', and the sultan had agreed. Having got wind of the situation in time, the seyyed quickly saw the sultan, and offered him a greater amount so that he would put Zia al-Molk at his disposal instead, and the sultan agreed. This is how he made his bargain. He told the sultan:

> I have heard that Khajeh Ahmad [Zia al-Molk] has bought this slave of yours [i.e. himself] for five hundred thousand dinars. I wish that the Lord of the Universe [i. e. the sultan] shall not see fit to sell this descendent of the Prophet. I should raise the five hundred thousand dinars to eight hundred thousand on the condition that you would put *him* at my disposal.

Ravandi adds that 'the love of money proved stronger to the sultan than the preservation of the vizier. He agreed [to the offer] and delivered Khajeh Ahmad to the seyyed, who rightly took his revenge from him, and he [Ahmad] suffered everything he had thought of doing to Amir the Seyyed.' We shall come across the sale of state dignitaries to each other even in the nineteenth century.

The last great Seljuk

The glorious days of the Seljuk empire had already passed by the death of Malekshah towards the end of the eleventh century, but Sanjar's sixty years of wise and relatively stable government in the east kept the Seljuks of Iran under an overlord – 'the Great Sultan' – until the mid-twelfth century. In 1096 Sanjar was made governor of Khorasan by his brother Berkiyaroq and kept aloof from the ongoing bouts of Seljuk fratricide until young Mahmud, who succeeded his father Mohammad in Isfahan, declared war on him in 1119; and although his uncle Sanjar defeated him he forgave and reinstated him in his capital. From then onwards, given the growing fragmentation of the Seljuk possessions, Sanjar was recognized as the Great Sultan of the Iranian Seljuks (having been formally proclaimed king in Baghdad), the Seljuk Turks further west having completely gone their own way. Sanjar's greatest sources of worry were the unruly Ghozz and the rebellious Atsez, descendant of the cup-bearer Anushtegin, who succeeded to the governorship of Khiveh in 1127. Having learned of his ambitions, Sanjar fought and put him to flight in 1138, and replaced him by a new assignee or *eqta'*-holder. But after the sultan had returned to his capital in Marv, Atsez once again took over Khiveh. He incited the Qarakhataiyds (or Black Cathay, a Chinese kingdom) against the sultan, who in 1141 fought and heavily defeated him and took his wife captive.

But the great catastrophe came in 1153, when Sanjar finally lost control of the Ghozz, who defeated and took him into captivity, while at the same time subjecting Khorasan to slaughter and plunder. Khaqani Shirvani, the great contemporary poet, was on his way to Khorasan when in Reyy he received news of the catastrophe. He wrote two lofty as well as moving poems painfully lamenting these events. The opening of one observes: 'That Egypt of a kingdom which you saw was ruined / That Nile of chivalry of which you heard turned into a mirage' (see the Introduction).

Sanjar escaped after three years in captivity, but being both old and broken he died shortly afterwards, and with him the great Seljuk sultanate of Iran fell away. A Seljuk innovation had been to appoint child princes as provincial governors under the supervision of Turkish guardians, who were called Atabeg (Persian: Atabak) or chief lords. In time, when the central Seljuk authority loosened up, these Atabegs assumed independence and set up their own dynasties. One of the most famous of the Atabeg dynasties in Iran is that of the Solghorids (or Salghorids) of Fars, who began their line from around the middle of the twelfth century and lasted until the 1260s. Their fame rests largely on the fact that the last two great Atabegs of this dynasty were patrons of Sa'di (and from one of them, Sa'd ibn Zangi, the poet assumed his pen name.).

THE ISMAILIS

The Ismailis were the Sevener Shiites who, after the death of the Sixth Imam, Ja'far al-Sadiq, had adhered to his eldest son Ismai'l, contrary to the Twelvers, who regarded the younger son, Musa al-Kazim, as the Seventh Imam. Since then the Isamilis had advanced both in intellectual thought and in social power. They believed in an esoteric doctrine – a cyclical theory of history mystically revolving around the number seven – far removed not only from Sunni teachings but even from Twelver Shiite thought. From 909 their main branch had established its rule in North Africa and Egypt, and was finally overthrown by Saladin in 1171. They were known as the Fatimid caliphate because of their claim to descend from the Prophet's daughter Fatima, a claim denied by their opponents.

The most brilliant era of Fatimid rule was perhaps the long reign of Al-Mustansir (1035–94), which coincided almost exactly with the period from the rise of the Seljuks to the end of Malekshah's rule. It was at this time that Naser Khosraw, the great Persian poet and thinker, visited Cairo, was converted to the Ismaili cause and returned to Khorasan as a chief missionary (hojjat). The death of Mustansir led to schism because of the rival claims of his two sons, Musta'li and Nizar, to the succession. While Must'ali won the contest, his elder brother Nizar had a strong following, which within a short period concentrated itself in Iran.

Hasan Sabbah, the legendary Ismaili leader, had already been an astute and tireless campaigner for the Ismaili movement in Iran before these events. While Nezam al-Molk's men were on his trail, he had managed by a brilliant strategy to get hold of the mountain fortress of Alamut near Qazvin. That was in 1090, but when a few years later the Musta'li-Nizar schism occurred, Sabbah went over to the Nizari cause and in effect severed the Persian Ismaili movement from Cairo. In time the Persian Isamailis built or conquered other mountain strongholds, for example in Shahdezh near Isfahan and in the Khorasan region of Qohestan (which literally means 'mountain region'). And from their impregnable positions they struck terror into the hearts of rulers, governors and other important orthodox Sunnis by sending individuals or a small group of their devotees to assassinate them.

These devoted assassins usually had no hope of escaping after carrying out their mission and were often caught and killed in the most hideous manner. Being thus indifferent to death, a theory emerged for explaining their selfless devotion to their cause. It was claimed that under the influence of hashish they were shown scenes of paradise which they were told was a foretaste of what was to come in the event of their being caught and killed. This gave the Persian (and later Syrian) Isamailis the title *hashashin* (literally, heavy hashish users), from the corruption of which the European term 'assassin' was coined.

It is almost certain that there is no foundation in fact to this theory, although it was believed by many Muslims and Europeans until recent times. To understand the psychology of those selfless devotees it would be sufficient to be reminded of the Japanese kamikaze pilots and contemporary suicide bombers. Europe came into contact with the Assassins via Syria, where a branch of Iranian Nizaris was founded, and Europeans used to describe its leaders as the Old Man of the Mountain, which was apparently a translation of the Arabic *Shaykh al-Jabal*.

Although the Persian Ismailis were not a territorial state, they had a great deal of power and influence because of their successful raids and assassinations, striking virtually anywhere in the Iranian lands. They killed many a mighty person, including – as noted – Nezam al-Molk. In retaliation, apart from the individual assassins being caught and killed, there were periodic killings and massacres of the usually non-combatant Ismailis by the orthodox authorities. No amount of effort made it possible for the later Seljuks to bring the Assassins to heel or indeed conquer and destroy one of their fortifications. That was left to the Mongols, when they were a fresh force and the Assassins a declining power.

There is a legend, colourful but unfounded, that Omar Khayyam, Hasan Sabbah and Nezam al-Molk had been childhood schoolmates and had promised to support one another in adult life. Sabbah and Nezam al-Molk entered government service and, Sabbah being the more brilliant, Nezam al-Molk arranged for him to be unfairly represented and disgraced. This resulted in Sabbah's vow to avenge himself, joining the Ismailis, wreaking havoc on the Seljuks and ordering Nezam al-Molk's assassination.

The twelfth century was a period of great advancement in Persian literature, both poetry and prose. Khayyam, Naser Khosraw and Khaqani have already been briefly mentioned, though the latter was not at the court of a Seljuk ruler, nor was Nezami Ganjavi, his great contemporary. Still, Khorasan abounded with prominent poets, some of them, like Anvari, becoming a great figure; other major poets included Mo'ezzi, Sana'i, Mas'ud-e Sa'd, Adib-e Saber and Rashid-e Vatvat. Nezam al-Molk's *Siyasatnameh* has also been noted as a major work of prose, but there were other important works from this period, such as Keikavus ibn Eskandar's *Qabusnameh* and Qazi Hamid al-Din's *Maqamat*.

Art and architecture flourished in the Seljuk period despite the recurrent turmoil and instability. Seljuk art is known for combining Persian, Islamic and Central Asian elements, and thus gaining distinction in the Islamic world. The art of inlaying metal objects, whether copper, silver or gold, became prominent in Khorasan. The items were often decorated with Arabic inscriptions written in the 'animated script' in which the letters were transformed into human and animal figures. Ceramic arts also showed innovations in this period, and often carried patterns similar to those of metal objects. The art of the book was also important, but little has survived. Architecture flourished, of which the most glorious surviving examples are the additions commissioned by Nezam al-Molk and by his rival and successor Taj al-Molk to the old Congregational Mosque in Isfahan. Sanjar's Mausoleum is also extant, in Marv, now in Turkmenistan.

THE KHWARAZM-SHAHS

We have seen how Atsez, a descendant of Anushtegin, Malekshah's favourite servant to whom he had given the *eqta'* of Khiveh (Khwarazm), rose in Sanjar's time and eventually obtained his independence as Khwarazm-shah. He died in 1056 shortly before Sanjar and was succeeded by Il-Arsalan. From then onwards the Khwarazshahids quickly grew from being a provincial power into a major territorial state, rising above the fragmented Seljuk rulers, even those of Kerman. Yet much of the expansion took place under the last effective sultan of the Khwarazm-shahs, Ala' al-Din Mohammad (1200–1220), who for a brief period became ruler of a vast empire. He drove the Ghurids out of Afghanistan, who retreated to their Indian possessions, and conquered virtually the whole of central and eastern Persia.

Yet the foundations of this empire in the making were weak and the sultan himself was not an able or strong ruler. The Khwarzam-shahid sultanate had expanded too rapidly; it had been weakened by Mohammad's conquest of territories which, especially in the east, were vulnerable to a serious attack. The ruler's mother, Torkan Khatun, was an able and powerful intriguer who virtually acted as the rival power to his son, whom she had not favoured for succession to the throne. Mohammad's relations with the able and ambitious Abbasid caliph al-Nasir (Persian: Naser) were far from amiable, and this was damaging to his position at home and abroad. He even led an army towards Baghdad, which the unusually severe winter rendered futile.

Meanwhile Changiz (Anglicized: Genghis) Khan had united the Mongols, conquered parts of China and extended his vast empire to the neighbourhood of the Khwarazm-shahs. He was, unlike Mohammad, an accomplished military leader, an able organizer and an astute diplomat. It is likely that he had had designs for expansion in the west if only because the mere conquest of eastern and central Persia did not put an end to his and his descendants' expansionist ambitions. But the when and how of the catastrophic invasion was largely of Mohammad's own making.

THE MONGOLS

There were two Mongol invasions of Persian lands. The first, led by Changiz Khan, began in 1219 and subsided at his death in 1227. The second was led by Changiz's grandson, Holagu Khan, in 1253, which resulted in the foundation of the Mongol Ilkhan empire in Iran. There were Mongol incursions into Persian lands both between these invasions and after them. But the greatest disaster that befell Iran, greater by far than any other single event in Iranian history, was those two major invasions, and especially the first, which had no other motive than death, destruction and plunder. The Arab conquest had made a profound and lasting impact on Iran largely because of Islamic rule and the conversions that followed, but the level of destruction was no more than expected by any large-scale war at the time; specifically, the Arabs did not draw their swords on the civilian population and there was no wholesale destruction of towns and cities. The Turkish invasion of the Seljuks was even less dramatic, with comparatively little effect on the civilian population; the Seljuks' religious culture was already the same as the Iranians'.

Changiz was perhaps motivated by revenge and punishment as well as conquest, apart from the fact that the Mongols put little value on human life, and especially that of their enemies. There are near contemporary reports of the total destruction of cities and the massacre of their inhabitants, some with populations of more than a million, many of the cities being in Khorasan but also others beyond. The veracity of these reports has been doubted by some modern historians on a number of grounds. For example, it has been argued that the cities could not have had such large populations and that the contemporary historians may have been somewhat biased.

The most authoritative historians of these events are Ala' al-Din Joveini, author of *Tarikh-e Jahangosha* (History of the World Conqueror, i.e. Changiz) and Rashid al-Din Fazlollah, author of *Jami' al-Tawarikh* (The Complete History). Both these men were illustrious Mongol Ilkhan ministers and so they are unlikely to have exaggerated their accounts well beyond common belief, including that of their Mongol masters. One historian put the number of those killed in Holagu's massacre of Baghdad in 1258 at 800,000. Holagu himself in a letter to St Louis put it at above 200,000, that is, 25 per cent of 800,000. However, if we assume that 25 per cent of the figures quoted by contemporary historians for all the cities sacked by Changiz is an accurate figure, then we still have a holocaust of unparalleled proportions up to that time. No wonder that a contemporary historian said that the country would not recover from its impact even in a thousand years.

Changiz Khan

Changiz was a Mongol of noble descent who had united the Mongol tribes under his own leadership and had been 'elected' khan by their council. He was already fighting in China, which he regarded as the biggest prize, when he found himself a neighbour of Kwarazm-shah's empire. He sent a friendly message to Ala' al-Din Mohammad, offering peace and trade, although patronizingly he said that he thought of him as one of his own sons, which may not have been appreciated by the weak and arrogant shah. Next, Changiz sent a number of merchants from his Muslim subjects to Otrar on the Persian side of the border between the two countries. The town's governor apparently thought they were spies, had them killed and seized their goods. One of the merchants got away, however. When Changiz heard what had happened he fell into a rage and sent three envoys to the shah demanding that the governor in question be handed over to them. The shah killed one of the envoys and sent the other two back empty-handed. Upon receiving this news, and despite the fact that his troops were still fighting in China, Changiz mobilized the available troops and led them into Transoxiana. Mohammad lay idle, apparently thinking that the Mongols would halt before the Oxus. But when the Mongols poured into Khorasan wreaking untold havoc, apart from a brief and superficial victory, he retreated and fled to central north Persia as far as Qazvin, then turned back via Mazandaran and died in the Isle of Absgun, off the eastern coast of the Caspian Sea.

His son, Jalal al-Din Menkaborni, was made from a different fibre as regarded courage and prowess, but he was otherwise tactless and to some extent aimless, wasting time in drinking and merrymaking. He met the Mongols on several occasions in different parts of the country, managing to get away but without once inflicting a crushing defeat. In the last major battle, by the Indus, he fought bravely and when no hope was left jumped into the river together with some of his officers and crossed safely on horseback. According to legend, watching this feat of courage, Changiz told his sons that an army like his needed a general like Jalal al-Din, and a father like him deserved a son like that.

Having spent three years in India, Jalal al-Din then led his forces to Kerman and Fars, where there were no Mongol troops, married the daughter of the Atabeg of Fars and moved to Azerbaijan and Georgia, fighting secondary foes here and there, although he encountered the Mongols once again in Isfahan, inflicting heavy casualties but not winning the battle. Eventually, in 1231, he was ambushed by a Mongol force and fled to Kurdistan, where he was killed by Kurds. Yet he was and remained the hero of the time, for decades Iranians awaiting his return to rid them of the Mongols.

Holagu and the Mongol empire

Meanwhile, in 1227 Changiz had died. In 1251 his grandson, Mangu, became the Great Khan and two major expeditions were planned. The first was to China, led

by the renowned Qubilai (Kublai) Khan, who later became the Great Khan. The
second was to Persia, led by Holagu, who later became the Ilkhan. Both were
brothers of Mangu and grandsons of Changiz.

Holagu led his forces into Iran with the aim of overthrowing the two centres
of Islamic faith, the Ismailis in Iran and the Abbasids in Iraq, although his motive
was military rather than religious. Ismaili castles fell in 1256 and the head of the
community was killed despite his surrender and cooperation. Nasir al-Din Tusi,
the great Persian scientist and scholar resident at Alamut castle, accompanied
Holagu to Baghdad, which was sacked in 1258, the caliph being beaten to death.
Holagu's later invasion of Syria did not succeed. His troops were defeated by the
Egyptian ruler: this was the first check to the advance of the Mongols since the
beginning of their campaigns. Yet, as the Ilkhan, he was in possession of a vast
empire consisting of Persia, Iraq and parts of Anatolia, centred in Azerbaijan,
with Maragheh as the capital, though this was later moved to Tabriz by his
son Abaqa.

The Ilkhans ruled Iran for about eighty years, from 1260 to about 1340. Both
Sa'di and Rumi were contemporaries of Holagu, in their fifties, though this is not
evident from Rumi's works. Rumi in fact lived in Anatolia, in the safety of Seljuk
Rum. Sa'di left his native Shiraz in the wake of the first Mongol invasion. When
he returned thirty years later, in about 1255, he celebrated the peace – 'the leop-
ards had given up leopard-like behaviour' – little knowing that Holagu's troops
were on their way. He wrote two poignant elegies, one in Persian and one in
Arabic, on receiving the news of the sack of Baghdad: 'The sky would rightly
weep blood on the earth full / For the kingdom of Musta'sim, Commander of the
Faithful.' He was a friend and admirer of the brothers Shams al-Din and Ata
Malek Joveini, both of them Ilkhan viziers and great men of letters.According to
an account which is likely to be generally true, once the elder Joveini, Shams
al-Din, wrote Sa'di a letter in which he asked him three questions and made one
request. The first question was who were better, Alavis – that is, decandants of
the Prophet Mohammad through his daughter Fatima and son-in-law Ali – or
non-Alavis. Sa'di's answer was diplomatic. He wrote in a short poem that he had
never met an Alavi who drank alcohol and gambled. Therefore he was
concerned lest at Resurrection the Prophet would be so busy interceding on the
Alavis' behalf that he would not have time to defend 'us' non-Alavis. Thus he
does not say that the Alavis are better; merely that in his experience they did not
commit two Islamic sins.

The next question was whether Hajjis were better than non-Hajjis. Here Sa'di
made a very scathing remark about Hajjis without answering the question
directly:

Tell the Hajji who hurts the people
Him who viciously skins the people
You are not a Hajji; it is the camel
Which carries burdens and eats thistle.

The camel of course was used as the beast of burden by those who could afford to cross the desert to Mecca mounted.

The last question asks what Joveini should do with one of his enemies. The answer is much like Sa'di's fair as well as realistic approach to such questions and like his style of versification on such subjects:

First is advice and admonition,
Second is house arrest and prison,
Third is repentance and regret,
Fourth are oath and agreement,
Fifth behead the wicked man,
Who is begging for a bad fate.

The minister had also made a request. He had asked the poet to accept a gift of 500 dinars (silver coins) which he had sent along with the letter. The amount had not been mentioned in the letter out of courtesy, calling it a sum 'for feeding the chickens'. The courier from Tabriz to Shiraz decided to include himself among the chickens and invest 150 dinars of the money in Isfahan, especially as Sa'di had turned down previous gifts of money. Sa'di sensed that the 350 dinars were short of the total amount, accepted it and wrote the following verses in gratitude:

My lord you sent me gift and money
May your money grow and your enemy fall
May for every dinar you live one year
So you would live three-hundred and fifty years.

When the courier took back Sa'di's reply to Shams al-Din, the vizier asked him what he had done with the money. The courier explained the reason for his action. Ala' al-Din Ata Malek, Shams al-Din's brother and the other great vizier, was present. He wrote a letter of credit to a banker in Shiraz (whose name is mentioned in the text) instructing him to pay 10,000 dinars to Sa'di. When the letter reached Shiraz the banker was dead. Sa'di wrote back in verse thanking the vizier profusely, giving news of the banker's death and saying that he would not claim the money from his estate, thus leaving it for the banker's family. On reading the poet's reply the vizier ordered 50,000 drachmas (gold coins) to be sent to him, begging him to take the money and build a guesthouse with it in Shiraz for visitors to the city. Sa'di accepted and built the guesthouse.

The mystic poet Fakhr al-Din Araqi also flourished in the thirteenth century, while Hafiz in the fourteenth century was a contemporary of the late Ilkhans. There were many other notable poets and writers during the Mongol era, for example Obeid Zakani, Khaju-ye Kermani and Salman Savaji. The later Ilkhans undertook building projects, even a town, of which by far the greatest surviving example is the Oljaitu Mausoleum in Soltaniyeh near the city of Zanjan. In addition, calligraphy, miniature painting and the arts of the book continued to develop, though reaching a pinnacle of perfection only in the fifteenth century.

The adminstration of the realm was, as usual, in the hands of Persian viziers and ministers, who, also as usual, were constantly in danger of losing their lives and possessions. Of the nine grand viziers of the Ilkhans only one died a natural death; others, including great figures such as the Jovieinis and Rashid al-Din Fazlollah, were killed and expropriated, often together with their families, friends and relations. Military affairs, by contrast, were in the hands of Mongols.

The viziers' most important function was to raise finance through taxation. The early Ilkhans, being foreign as well as nomadic, hardly cared about the welfare of the sedentary population, and least of all the peasantry. Their attitude towards their Iranian subjects resembled that of an occupying force rather than an imperial power – they tried to milk their subjects as much as possible. The Iranian peasant was used to a heavy tax burden, but the early Ilkhans' taxation policies were so exploitative that they left little or no motivation for the people. With government policy being to kill the goose that lays the golden egg, frequent financial crises arose. The peasants fled and hid on seeing taxmen, envoys and other officers whom they were obliged to look after and who would often confiscate what little they had left.

Ilkhan rule may be reasonably divided into two: the period from Holagu to Ghazan (1258–95); and from Ghazan to Abu Sa'id (1295–1335). In the first period, except for a short while, they had not yet been converted to Islam, were therefore less integrated with their subjects and had a more predatory attitude towards them. But they had a tolerant religious policy, allowing freedom of worship even to the point of not charging the *jezyeh* tax on Christians, Jews and other religious minorities. Most of the early Iranian Mongols adhered to their native shamanist beliefs, although a few were converted to Buddhism, Christianity or Islam.

On the death of Holagu's first son, Abaqa (1265–82), his brother Tegudar became ruler after a power struggle in which he defeated his nephew, Arghun son of Abaqa. Tegudar converted to Islam – renaming himself Ahmad – and sent peace feelers to the Egyptian government, who were and remained the Ilkhan's traditional enemy. This was an unpopular move and was the main cause of a coup against him by Arghun and his supporters. The coup proved the age-old maxim of Iranian arbitrary rule that anyone capable of rebellion must be killed instantly to prevent them having the opportunity to rebel and overthrow the ruler. Having learned from his uncle Tegudar's mistake, Arghun (1282–91) put him and his leading supporters to death. Unlike most Ilkhan rulers Arghun did not drink himself to death but died of a poison which he took, thinking that it was the elixir of life. Shortly before this, he had put to death his able Jewish Persian vizier, Sa'd al-Dawleh.

He was succeeded by his brother Geikhatu (1291–5), who faced an economic crisis he was quite incapable of resolving. The increasing tax burden, the high state expenditure and a cattle epidemic combined to bring the state finances to near ruin. Geikhatu's vizier experimented with the introduction of paper currency on the contemporary Chinese model, but the policy was an abject failure because it was unacceptable to traders. Not being an able and efficient ruler, Geikhatu fell victim to his cousin Baidu's successful rebellion and lost his life. But his vizier was to survive him, only to be put to death later by Ghazan.

Ghazan Khan (1295–1304) had been Khorasan's governor under his uncle Geikhatu, and it was as ruler of that vast province that he had converted to Islam. Shortly after Baidu's coup against his uncle, Geikhatu, he fought, defeated and killed Baidu and became the new Ilkhan. Under Ghazan Islam once again became the state religion and thus the Mongols attained cultural conformity with the country they ruled, though how sincere the early converts were is a matter for speculation.

Ghazan's rule, although no more than nine years in duration, is generally regarded as the climax of the Ilkhan regime. He began by a significant amount of bloodletting of potential pretenders and rivals to secure and stabilize his power base, but also issued an important series of administrative and financial reforms. He showed awareness of the fact that plundering the peasantry would mean long-term financial bankruptcy for the state, and set out to reform taxation and to moderate the abuses to which the people were subject from travelling officials. He renewed the traditional policy of land assignment to pay the army, which would also bring the nomadic soldiery closer to settled agriculture. Such were Ghazan's edicts and intentions as detailed by his exceptionally able vizier, Rashid al-Din (who was killed under the later Ilkhans) in his *Complete History*. It is more difficult to know the extent to which the reforms were implemented, given that they required the cooperation of a large number of Mongol commanders and officials. Ghazan's notable achievement in foreign relations was his capture of Syria from the Egyptians, thus, contrary to Tegudar, continuing the policy of hostility towards Egypt despite his conversion to Islam. But his policies did not last long.

Ghazan's early death without a male issue led to the succession of his brother Oljaitu (1304–16), who is especially remembered for three things: his personal experiment with various religions; his capture of Gilan; and his building of the new capital, Soltaniyeh, near Zanjan, which had been started by Ghazan. Oljaitu converted to Christianity and Buddhism before he converted back to Islam and then oscillated between the Sunni and Shia sects. His Muslim name was Mohammad Khodabandeh (God's Slave). He was the first ever to conquer Gilan, since the natural barriers of high mountains and thick rain forests had made that province virtually impregnable through most of Iranian history. He transferred the capital from Tabriz to Soltaniyeh, where he built a magnificent mausoleum which still survives as the greatest architectural monument of the whole of the Mongol period. He also planned to transfer the remains of Imam Ali and Imam Hosein here, but abandoned the idea after Imam Ali told him in a dream to give it up. Instead it became his own mausoleum.

Typically, Oljaitu died early, probably from excessive alcohol consumption, and was succeeded by his eleven-year-old son, Abu Sa'id (1316–35). For the first eleven years of his rule the young Ilkhan was under the tutelage of the strong Mongol Amir Chopan, whose faction was opposed to that of Hasan Jalayer – both factions were to form separate kingdoms after the disintegration of the Ilkhanid empire. In 1327 Abu Sa'id killed Chopan's son and fought Chopan himself, who was killed in Herat, and took control of his own realm. He ruled effectively until he, too, died young, probably poisoned, at the age of twenty-nine.

It is sometimes believed that the factional struggles and fragmentation of the Ilkhanid empire after Abu Sa'id's death were largely due to the fact that he did not have a male issue. This is unlikely because a brother or cousin could well have succeeded instead of a direct male heir. Rather, the disintegration of the Ilkhanids falls into the pattern of Iran's short-term society. The Seljuk's primacy soon gave way to fragmentation. The Khwarazm-shahid empire did not survive even for half a century before the first Mongol invasion. The disintegration that followed was checked by the second Mongol invasion and the rise of the Ilkhans. They, in turn, survived for less than eighty years of crisis and turmoil which included the killing of numerous rulers, princes and viziers. The pattern was familiar.

It is difficult to credit the Mongol regime in Persia with much positive achievement. The greatness of Sa'di, Rumi and Hafiz, who lived on the fringes of their empire, cannot be attributed to their patronage of literature. The development of miniature painting would have proceeded without them. A few notable constructions such as Soltaniyeh and Holagu's observatory in Maragheh are hardly compensation for the losses they inflicted on the country. Hundreds of thousands (perhaps millions) were killed; towns were devastated; sedentary agriculture suffered tremendously from pillage, plunder and heavy taxes. Any brave attempt to find a balance for these disasters under Mongol rule would be reminiscent of Voltaire's poetical caricature of the pious belief that the earthquake of Lisbon had some beneficial effects such as the dogs being able to help themselves to the corpses of the dead.

FRAGMENTATION

The faction fighting that followed the death of Abu Sa'id in 1335 eventually led to the emergence of four main powers in various parts of Persia before they were abolished or made tributaries by yet another eastern conqueror, Amir Timur (Persian: Teymur). The Jalayerids defeated the Chopanids and established themselves in the west and north-west. The Mozaffarids, led by Mobarez al-Din Mohammad, took Kerman, Fars and eventually Isfahan but were finally overthrown by Timur. Mobarez al-Din Mohammad was the ruler who imposed the rule of arid piety on Shiraz which Hafiz so outspokenly decried in his poetry: 'Would that they open the Taverns' door / Un-knot our complicated life for sure?' Eventually, he was overthrown and blinded by his son Shah Shoja', Hafiz's beloved patron. Not surprisingly, there was much spilling of royal blood during the forty or so years of their rule.

In the east and north-east two other powers held sway between the fall of the Ilkhanids and the rise of Timur. The Karts had ruled Herat as a virtually autonomous line of rulers under Ilkhan suzerainty. With the disintegration of the Ilkhans they carried on to rule in the north-east of Khorasan until they were abolished and annexed by Timur. The other power was the enigmatic Sarbedars, centred on Sabzevar in the north-west of present-day Khorasan, who had risen to power by collective rebellion, a Shia movement without a dynastic line. Their background and power base remains obscure, but they certainly had their origin in a revolutionary movement. Sarbedar literally means 'head to the gallows', implying their readiness to be martyred for their cause. They became a tributary of Timur.

TIMUR AND HIS DESCENDANTS

Amir Timur's devastation of Persia and other lands was on a par with that of Changiz; some say it was even greater, except that perhaps the number of people killed was smaller. Yet the degree of cruelty which Timur displayed surpassed that of Changiz.

Timur was born a Muslim near Samarkand (in Transoxiana, now in Uzbekistan) in 1336 and began his career of continuous conquest when he was thirty-five. He had become lame in childhood and so was known as Timur the Lame (Persian: Teymur-e lang; classical English: Tamerlane). He claimed descent from Changiz through his son Chaghatai, but there are strong doubts about the veracity of this claim. He was later known as 'guregan' or 'son-in-law' when he married two women who descended from Changiz Khan. Having secured Transoxiana in 1370 he crossed the border to Khorasan in 1380, attacked Herat whose Kart ruler submitted and, as mentioned above, became a tributary of Timur for a decade before Timur overthrew him and ended the Kart dynasty. Having razed a few other towns and castles to their foundations in Khorasan and Mazandaran, he returned to Samarkand, but resumed his conquest of Iran in 1383, attacking Mazandaran again, conquering and massacring Sabzevar, followed by Sistan and Qandahar. But he was back in Mazandaran again in the following year, then moving to Azerbaijan in 1385, later to Loristan and still later again to Azerbaijan to suppress the Jalayerid ruler, who nevertheless escaped.

The pattern that emerges from the career of Timur is that he did not have – or perhaps did not want to have – a plan of conquest, but attacked, conquered and reconquered towns and regions several times, and that everywhere he went he caused wholesale death and destruction. In Isfahan alone, which had risen against his unbearable taxes, some 70,000 people were slaughtered. Until his death in 1405, he attacked, subdued or reduced vast territories as far apart as the Mongol Golden Horde in Russia, the Ottoman Turks in Anatolia and the Sultanate of Delhi. In 1405 he set out for the biggest prize, the conquest of China, then under the Ming dynasty, but died when he had reached the border town of Otrar and was buried in his beloved Samarkand. He was undoubtedly a military genius and a man of great courage and determination. He was also an agent of death and destruction, often in the cruellest possible manner, apparently having no other aim than his own greater glory and the suppression of all comers with any claim to power; but the irony is that he befriended and patronized Sufis and Sufi orders.

There is a legend about Timur's meeting with Hafiz, colourful but unlikely to be true. Hafiz has a famous poem, probably addressed to his beloved Shah Shoja', which begins with the following couplet:

If that Turk [= light-skinned boy] of Shiraz meets my wishes all
I will grant Samarkand and Bokhara for his Hindu [= black] mole.

According to the legend, Timur summoned Hafiz on entering Shiraz and told him: 'I fought hard to conquer these great cities, and a beggar like you claims to give them away for the mole of his beloved?' And the witty Hafiz replied: 'Sire, it is precisely because of such generosity that I am so poor.'

Timur's main constructive work was his adornment of Samarkand with beautiful suburbs and fine buildings where he stored some of the art and other treasures which he had plundered from the vanquished civilizations. His administration was in the hands of Persians but he did not have a great vizier, perhaps because of his tendency not to share significant amounts of power in his empire.

Typically, the death of Timur led to civil war, fratricide and killings of members of Timur's house and others. His youngest and only surviving son, Shahrokh, eventually emerged as his successor, although neither he nor any of the following Timurid rulers managed to hold on to the conqueror's empire intact. Timur himself had designated his grandson Pir Mohammad, Shahrokh's nephew, to replace him. But, as throughout much of Iranian history, the wish of the deceased ruler carried little influence in the struggle for power which followed his death. Pir Mohammad's claim was rejected by his cousin Khalil Soltan, who took Samarkand, though his behaviour led to a rebellion forcing him to flee to the east, to be eventually shaken off by Shahrokh a few years later. In the meantime Pir Mohammad was also killed, and Shahrokh began to consolidate his rule from his base in Herat, from where he had governed Khorasan under his father.

Shahrokh was far from a conqueror in his father's mould but he was a good military leader and managed to recapture Transoxiana and most of his father's possessions in Persia. For a time he even held Azerbaijan, but the west, including Anatolia, was now the competing ground for the Turkaman tribal confederations Qara Qoyunlu (Black Sheep) and Aq Qoyunlu (White Sheep), whom Timur had kept at bay but had not crushed.

Shahrokh's reign was, for the time and place, a peaceful period in which arts and letters flourished to the extent that the Timurid era may be regarded as a notable artistic era in Iranian history. Much of this can be attributed to the patronage of Shahrokh's wife, Gawharshad Begum, and his two sons, Ologh Beg and Baisonqor. Ologh Beg built an observatory in Samarkand and was himself involved in its activities. Baisonqor was a notable calligrapher and promoter of the arts of the book. Gawharshad developed urban architecture not only in Herat but also in Mashhad, her mosque in the latter city still standing as a great monument of the period.

Predictably, Shahrokh's death in 1447 was followed by a power struggle and royal bloodletting. It left his sensitive son Ologh Beg with a bout of depression, and before he could move to claim the throne others began to fight over it. Gawharshad supported Ologh Beg's son Abdollatif, but the latter was confronted by his three cousins, sons of Baisonqor, who likewise claimed the prize. Eventually Ologh Beg made a move and put them in their place, but rebellion did not completely cease. Some time later there was a revolt in Samarkand against Ologh Beg's younger son Abdol'aziz, and Abdollatif rose in Balkh against his father, defeated him and had both him and Abdol'aziz put to death. He himself was killed a year later.

Abdollatif was succeeded by Ologh Beg's nephew Abdollah, who ruled for a brief period but was successfully overthrown and killed in 1451 by his cousin Abu Sa'id with Uzbek support. Since the reign of Shahrokh the Uzbeks had been trying to penetrate Transoxiana and Ologh beg had had to try to resist their pressure in the east as well as that of the Qara Qoyunlu Turkamans in the west. The Uzbeks eventually conquered the whole of Transoxiana, thus anticipating the modern republic of Uzbekistan, which paradoxically upholds Amir Timur as its greatest historical hero.

Abu Sa'id had an unusual interest in promoting agriculture by building dams and reducing land tax, and was a patron of the arts. He took complete control of Herat only gradually, and in the process murdered Gawharshad, the aged and distinguished wife of Shahrokh. His reign coincided with the rise to power of the Qara Qoyunlu Turkamans. Under Shahrokh, their chief Jahanshah had been allowed to govern western and north-western Persia, but after Shakrokh's death Jahanshah defeated all Timirud claimants to the western territories and became completely independent. He conquered Isfahan and Khorasan and made Tabriz the capital, not far from which the fortunes of the Safavid movement, the devoted followers of the thirteenth-century Sufi Sheikh Safi al-Din, had begun to rise.

Meanwhile, the confederation of the Aq Qoyunlu Turkamans, who were based further west in Diarbekr, gradually expanded their territory in the north-west and west and came to blows with the Ottoman Turks who had recently captured Constantinople and overthrown what was left of Byzantium. Led by their able chieftain Uzun Hasan they fought and defeated the Qara Qoyunlu, who lost their leader in the battle. Having seen the demise of the Qara Qoyunlu, Abu Sa'id moved headlong to eliminate the Aq Qoyunlu before they replaced the Qara Qoyunlu empire in Iran. But he was soundly defeated and captured, and was delivered to a great-grandson of Gawharshad, who put him to death in revenge for her murder.

Once again there was chaos and civil war among the Timurids, with fighting for what was left of their empire in the east. The last Timurid ruler, who ruled little more than Herat, was Hosein Baiqara; in 1506 the Uzbeks eventually put an end to his rule. Although a relatively minor ruler, he is known in history for his notable patronage of the arts and the circle of illustrious men in his service. One such was Abdorrahman Jami, the greatest fifteenth-century Persian poet and writer. Another was Mir Alishir Nava'i, his chief administrator, who was both a littérateur and a patron of the literati. The great miniaturist Hosein Behzad and the distinguished historians Mirkhwand and Khwandmir were also at Hosein's court. Thus his rule was an agreeable epitaph for a regime which had been founded by wholesale death and destruction.

That was the end of the Timurids in Persia. But they were soon to found the so-called Mogul empire in India, which lasted until 1857. The language and culture of the Mogul court was Persian, and many of them were great patrons of the arts, especially Persian poetry.

TURKAMAN CONFEDERATIONS AND THE RISE OF THE SAFAVIDS

The Turkaman tribal confederations Qara Qoyunlu (Black Sheep) and Aq Qoyunlu (White Sheep) first made their appearance in western Persia, Iraq and Anatolia after the collapse of the Ilkhanid empire. The Black Sheep, who until their defeat in the late fifteenth century by the White Sheep, were the more important of the two confederations and were at first clients of Jalayerid Mongols; in the early fifteenth century, however, the Black Sheep defeated their former patrons, who had begun to decline. The White Sheep confederation made peace with Timur, but the Black Sheep fought and were defeated, though not destroyed. Shahrokh defeated the Black Sheep leader Jahanshah in 1421 but made him governor of the west and north-west. After Shahrokh's death Jahanshah declared independence and raised the Black Sheep's fortunes to their highest level. Meanwhile the Aq Qoyunlu had begun to emerge from the latest period of their habitual civil wars under an able leader, Uzun Hasan, who defeated Jahanshah and the Timurid Sultan Abu Sa'id in the late 1460s. For a while the Aq Qoyunlu empire extended into Persia's heartland, Khorasan and the parts of Transoxiana still in Timurid hands, while the Uzbeks had become the rising power in Transoxiana and began to interfere in Khorasan's affairs.

After the death of their great leader Uzun Hasan, the Aq Qoyunlu or White Sheep had to face the growing menace of the Safavids, who did not take long to topple and replace them. The Safavids descended from Sheikh Safi al-Din of Ardabil (1252–1334), who was a Sunni Sufi leader, probably of Kurdish descent, although the late fifteenth century Safavid movement that captured secular power had an unmistakably Turkaman character. For centuries it was believed, because of the propaganda put out by Safavid rulers, that Sheikh Safi had been a Shia leader and a descendant of the Seventh Shia Imam, Musa al-Kazim. But the twentieth century scholar Ahmad Kasravi showed that neither claim was in fact true. By the biographical accounts left of Sheikh Safi it appears that he was a venerable and influential Sufi leader presumed to have performed extraordinary feats.

After the death of Safi al-Din the order grew steadily and extended its wealth and property, but for more than a century it still remained an essentially Sunni Sufi order. By the mid-fifteenth century the fourth head of the order had died and been replaced by his brother – not his son Joneid, as later Safavid propaganda claimed. The conflict between Joneid and his uncle led to Joneid's expulsion from Ardabil, and he gathered a group of Turkaman devotees in Anatolia and Syria who, like Imam Ali, claimed divine attributes for him. He thus became head of an extremist militant movement and allied himself to Uzun Hasan of the White Sheep, who married him off to his sister. To demonstrate his religious zeal, Joneid moved to fight the Christians of the Caucasus, but while on his way crossed the Muslim Shirvanshah and was killed in battle.

His son Heidar was also to die in a like manner, trying to lead an expedition against the Christians of the Caucasus and being killed in battle by Shirvanshah, son of the Shirvanshah who had fought his father. This time, however, Shirvanshah received aid from Ya'qub, the White Sheep leader who had taken Uzun Hasan's place after his death, and was alarmed by the growth of Heidar's following. Heidar was not only a nephew of Uzun Hasan and brought up at his court but had also married his daughter from a Byzantine mother. Thus Heidar's son Shah Isma'il was variously related to Aq Qoyunlus and had a Byzantine grandmother. It is believed that it was Heidar who invented the famous Safavid headdress, the *taj*, a twelve-gored red hat which was worn by his followers, who therefore became known as *Qezelbash* or (in Turkish) Redheads. Heidar's elder son Soltan Ali replaced him as head of the movement but was imprisoned and eventually killed by Aq Qoyunlus in 1494, which made his seven-year-old brother Isma'il head of the movement. Isma'il found refuge in Gilan and was nurtured by Shii tutors, thus becoming probably the very first Safavid leader with a generally Shiite culture, although both he and his devotees saw him more as godhead than just a Shia leader. In 1499 the twelve-year-old warrior led his troops against Shirvanshah, his father's enemy, and later captured Tabriz. The Aq Qoyunlus were once again caught up in a civil war, which was one of the reasons Isma'il defeated them at the battle of Sharur in 1501, to become the first shah of Persia since the Arab invasion of Iran in the seventh century.

CHAPTER 5

Persian Empire Again

When this great prince [Abbas I] ceased to live, Persia ceased to prosper.
Jean Chardin

THE ANCIENT PERSIAN EMPIRE was restored by the Safavids as a Shia Muslim state. Persian society and culture had never died, as has been seen in the foregoing chapters. It had survived the Arab conquest without losing its cultural identity, and Persian influence in culture and administration had been considerable even under Arab rule. Many Iranian languages had survived the conquest: New Persian had become the language of the court, government and literature with the rise of independent states in Iranian lands. And it had so remained even under Turkish and Mongol rulers, in fact becoming the lingua franca for a vast region in western and Central Asia.

Yet it was the Safavids who restored the old Persian empire by reuniting virtually the entire Iranian lands as 'the Protected Kingdoms of Iran' under one standard, which bore the insignia of the lion holding a sword in its hand and carrying the sun on its back – a Muslim empire, but one which exclusively followed the Twelver Shia faith, once again giving Iran a distinct religious identity. However, contrary to some views, the Safavid empire was not built on a wave of modern Persian nationalist sentiment sweeping across the old Sasanian lands with the conscious intention of reuniting and reconstructing ancient Persia. The Safavids were themselves Turkamans of remote Kurdish descent who claimed (and convinced all) that they were direct descendants of the Seventh Twelver Shia Imam and therefore of Imam Ali and the Prophet Mohammad. Isma'il was the leader of a fanatical Sufi order, and both he and his disciples saw him as a divine being rather than an Iranian nationalist leader. And although the literary and administrative language remained Persian, the Safavids spoke Turkic at court and at home.

The Safavids (1501–1722) ruled Persia for more than two centuries, longer than any other dynasty since the Arab conquest, or indeed afterwards until today. But, as in the ancient past, even this apparent continuity was marked by short-term breaks, major crises and the probability on several occasions of the fall of the dynasty, perhaps even the breakdown of the empire. This in the end is what happened as a result of the fall of Isfahan and the abdication of Soltan-hosein at the hands of the

Ghalzeh Afghan tribe in 1722. A moment's reflection on the pattern of events during the long period of Safavid rule, perhaps more than many other periods of Iranian history, reveals the extent to which the personality of the ruler determined the course of history, and stability or disorder in state and society, precisely because in a system of arbitrary rule it was one person alone who, in the ultimate analysis, was the arbiter of life and death, ownership and dispossession, success and failure.

It cannot be assumed with any degree of certainty that if Isma'il had been killed at or before the battle of Tabriz in 1501 Iran would once again have been reunited and remained as one political entity. And it is highly unlikely that, had Abbas I been murdered young in the 1580s – as he was about to be shortly before he made his bid for the throne – the Safavid dynasty would have survived or indeed that Iran would have been saved from being dismembered. Domestic causes alone might well have caused the Safavid state and empire to have broken down on a number of occasions.

THE EMERGENCE OF THE NEW STATE

The coronation in Tabriz was only the beginning of the establishment of the new state. When in 1503 Isma'il defeated Morad Aq Qoyunlu in Hamadan he was at last free from any danger posed by his Turkaman relatives, and by 1507 extended

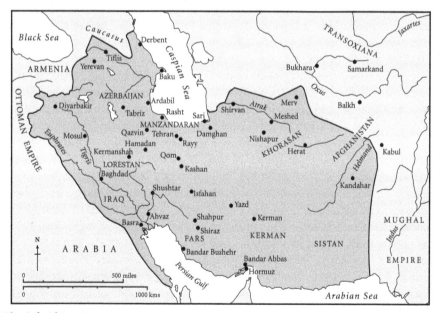

The Safavid Empire, AD 1501–1722

his rule to Diyarbekr. He captured Baghdad in 1508 and next overthrew the Musha'sha'iya in Khuzisatan, a line of heretical Shias who had ruled the region for many decades. Isma'il had by then inherited the Aq Qoyunlu empire and almost appeared as another ruler of a Turkaman empire like his maternal grandfather Uzun Hasan, but one who was ruthlessly imposing Shiism on many of its subjects. He did not yet have any possessions in eastern Persia.

Meanwhile the Timurids had lost their possessions in Khorasan to the expanding Uzbek empire, and the Uzbek ruler Mohammad Sheibani Khan ('Sheibak Khan') had begun to raid Kerman. Having received a rude reply from the Uzbek leader to his letter of protest against his offensive behaviour, Isma'il decided to act. He led his army to Khurasan and met Sheibak Khan's forces at Marv, winning the day after a pitched battle which claimed heavy casualties. Sheibak Khan was killed in the battle and Isma'il sent his head to his Sunni co-religionist, the Ottoman Sultan Bayazid, as a gruesome gift, an insult to which he received the full reply four years later at Chaldiran. Isma'il's later adventure in Transoxiana in supporting Babur, the future founder of the Mogul empire in India, to hold Samarkand did not pay off and the eastern borders of his empire were set at the Oxus, although Balkh was later to be lost to the Uzbeks.

With the capture of Khorasan Isma'il became the ruler of an empire which stretched from Diarbekr to the Oxus. Some of his western and eastern possessions were lost in later years but in its extent his empire resembled that of the Sasanians before the Islamic conquest. In personal allegiance his power base was also remarkable. The main body of Isma'il's devotees, commanders and soldiers consisted of the seven Turkaman Qezelbash tribes of Shamlu, Rumlu, Ostajlu, Afshar, Qajar and so forth, who worshipped him personally as a divine being. Isma'il's dubious claim of direct descent from the Shii Imams and through them the Prophet of Islam was believed by friend and foe alike for centuries to come. He was the Perfect Spiritual Guide (*Morshed-e Kamel*) of the Savfavid Sufi order, a movement which had had its roots firmly if embarrassingly in Sunni Islam. Yet outwardly to his subjects he was a fanatical Shia, who since the capture of Tabriz in 1501 had declared Shiism to be the official state religion and imposed it on his subjects on pain of death.

Shiism was already familiar in Persia. The Buyids had been Shia and the Ismailis, though not Twelver Shiites, had militantly held up the standard of Ali against the rule of Sunni orthodoxy. Iranian Sufi movements had generally been more inclined towards Shiism, and even those which were based on Sunni Islam venerated the Shii Imams, and especially Ali, whom many of them regarded as the perfect man, perhaps a godhead. And for centuries both sides of the Alborz range, the Caspian provinces and the region which included Reyy, Qom and Kashan, had adhered to Twelver Shiism. Above all perhaps, ancient Iranian religious and cultural traditions made the country susceptible to Shii thought, sentiments and culture.

Yet at the time Isma'il launched his revolution – and it was an authentic revolution in the Iranian tradition – the majority of the people were Sunni. When in 1501 in Tabriz the fourteen-year-old Safavid shah was told that at least two-thirds of the city's 200,000 inhabitants were Sunnis who would resist forced conversion, he said he would draw his sword and kill anyone who resisted his command to convert to Shiism. That indeed is largely how he imposed Shiism on the whole country, through fear, harsh punishment and persecution. The result was mass conversion, except in the impassable mountain regions of Kurdistan and Afghanistan, although it probably took one or two generations before the forced converts became true believers in Shiism. There must have been enough ground even as late as the 1570s for his grandson, Isma'il II, to be able to make an attempt to return to Sunni Islam, though in any case the latter did not live long enough for the results of his move to be known.

The minimum formal requirement for conversion was to bear witness that Ali was the *Vali* (Friend and/or Vicegerent) of God and to include both that witness and the command 'Rise up to good deed' in the *azan*, the call for prayer. These the Sunnis regarded as innovations, on the premise that they had not been observed in the Prophet's own time. Further, the convert had to publicly curse the first three caliphs, Abubakr, Omar and Osman, who are objects of great veneration in Sunni Islam. All this was sufficient to incense Isami'il's Sunni neighbours, the Ottomans in the west and the Uzbeks in the east. But the further implications of the Shii faith, the elevation of the imams to viceregents of God and devotion to their shrines and those of their descendants, were perhaps as repugnant, if not more so, to the religious sensitivities of orthodox Sunnis.

Some Persian and European historians, including Ahmad Kasravi, have interpreted Isma'il's imposition of Shiism as a shrewd and cynical political calculation, an ideological weapon against the Ottoman Turks. But this is a complex matter and it would be too simplistic to attribute it alone to conscious political motives before the event.

The conversion of large numbers of Ottoman subjects in Anatolia by Safavid religious propaganda was bound to lead to full-scale war between the two powers. As early as 1502 the Ottoman ruler Bayazid II ordered the deportation of large numbers of Shii Turkamans from Anatolia. In 1511 there was a widespread Shii revolt at Tekke on the eastern Mediterranean coast. In 1512 a Safavid force waged a campaign in eastern Anatolia. And when the relatively mild Sultan Bayazid died shortly afterwards, Isma'il tried to interfere in the Ottoman succession against Selim ('Selim the Grim'), who in fact succeeded to the throne. The Ottoman persecution of the Anatolian Shias culminated in a massacre which is said to have claimed 40,000 lives.

In 1514 Selim led a formidable army east to meet Isma'il in the field of battle. The figure of 200,000 has been quoted for the size of the force, although this may be somewhat inflated. To move such an army forward 1,000 miles was itself a great achievement in logistic and strategic terms, given contemporary standards and circumstances. The figure for the opposing army led by Isma'il himself has been quoted at 40,000, though this may be an underestimate. It is, however, virtually certain that the size of the Ottoman force was at least two and half times that of the Iranian. The battle was joined in Chaldiran, in eastern Anatolia, and despite Isma'il's great display of bravery his army was routed. Isma'il retreated, but Selim, thinking it was a ruse, did not pursue him.

Shortly afterwards the Ottomans occupied Tabriz, the Safavid capital no less. Selim planned to winter in the area and resume his campaign in the spring. His troops, however, wearied of the long winter with limited provisions, and so he had to withdraw. Isma'il re-entered Tabriz when Selim had left, but, having occupied eastern Anatolia, the Ottomans had now been settled dangerously close to the Safavid capital. This was later moved east to Qazvin, and later still to Isfahan, but not in Isma'il's lifetime.

Many historians, old and new, believed that the cause of the Ottoman victory at Chaldiran was their use of firearms, not only muskets but especially field artillery. A persistent myth held that firearms were unknown to the Safavids and that they acquired them only in the early seventeenth century when Abbas I led his armies to victory against the Ottomans. This myth has now been exploded by historical evidence. Firearms, including artillery, had been used in siege warfare before Isma'il, for example when his own father Heidar had laid siege to Shirvan. But historians have instead suggested that the Qezelbash did not use firearms in field warfare because they regarded them as unmanly and cowardly in comparison with their mounted archers.

There may be some truth in this, though it is not sufficiently clear why the use of firearms in siege warfare was not likewise thought to be unchivalrous. However that may be, the argument still assumes that Isma'il lost the battle of Chaldiran mainly because his men were not armed with firearms. Yet this theory has almost universally overlooked that Isma'il's army was at least two and half times smaller in size than its opponent. It is true that Isma'il had in earlier battles defeated armies larger than his own, but those armies were much smaller than the Ottomans', and the differences in their relative sizes had not been as great; whereas this time he had faced an excessively large army put in the field by the greatest war machine that the world of Islam had yet seen, the greatest military power perhaps even in western Asia and the whole of Europe. That, surely, was the main reason why Isma'il lost the battle of Chaldiran.

From the inauguration of the new monarchy Isma'il faced problems arising from the very nature of his revolution and the regime he was founding. He himself was regarded not just as shah but, more importantly, as a direct descendant of the Prophet and Imam Ali and the vicegerent of the Mahdi, the Hidden Imam. More than this, at least until the defeat in Chaldiran the Qezelbash went even further in their beliefs and thought of him as a divine being. He was the commander-in-chief of his army and, again until Chaldiran, personally led them to fields of battle. Also, as mentioned above, as the successor to his paternal forefathers he was the Perfect Spiritual Guide of the Safavid Order, and he had imposed fanatical Shiism on the land as his revolutionary ideology. Thus he seems to have combined the positions and functions of traditional rulers, executive caliphs and imams, spiritual guides, revolutionary leaders, ideological campaigners and supreme military commanders all at once.

European historians and commentators have sometimes applied the term and concept of 'theocracy' to define the nature of his regime. Nominally, theocracy refers to a system of government by the religious leadership, which combines both religious and secular authority but is still distinct from forms of government that have a state religion, are influenced by theological concepts or held 'by the Grace of God'. However, theocracy is a concept which has emerged from European history and society. It is difficult to compare Isma'il's rule with that of Jean Calvin in the sixteenth-century city-state of Geneva, or indeed that of the popes in the Papal States or later the Vatican. And, apart from Rashidun, who ruled for less than three decades at the dawn of Islam, it is not easy to describe the rule of the Umayyads and Abbassids as theocratic in its European sense, even before the Abbasids had been reduced to puppets of Persian and Turkish rulers. Isma'il's position therefore defies categorization in familiar terms, perhaps being most comparable with that of Ardeshir Babakan, founder of the Sasanian empire and an earlier revolutionary leader of Persia who combined royalty, spirituality and military power and prowess all at once (see Chapter 2). At any rate, since Iran is a short-term society, the so-called theocracy did not survive either Ardeshir or Isma'il.

Once the conversion to Shiism had been imposed, largely by force, it became clear that there were hardly any Shiite institutions and few Shia ulama in the country to continue the task of conversion and to spread the knowledge and practice of the new doctrine, its rites and its culture. To fill the gap a continuing stream of Shia ulama, teachers and jurists were imported from Shia lands, most frequently from the Syrian Jabal Amel, now in Lebanon. One of the most well-known divines of Safavid Persia, Baha' al-Din Mohammad Ameli, better known as Sheikh Baha'i, who even wrote poetry in Persian, belongs to the line of such spiritual immigrants. The contemporary Sadr family in Iran and Iraq, of whom the Iranian Imam Musa Sadr was the most famous and the Iraqi Muqtada al-Sadr is now a powerful Shiite leader, also descend from one such immigrant to Persia. Many Persian Sunni ulama also converted and joined the service, both to save their lives and to maintain their social and financial positions.

As we have observed, Isma'il himself had assumed a position which undermined the traditional Twelver Shia ulamas' claim to be deputies of the Mahdi during his absence, leading and guiding the community until the Hidden Imam's coming. This did not mean that Isma'il was in practice the head of the religious institution, and in any case the perception of him as the Imam's vicegerent did not pass on to his descendants, even if he himself continued to be so regarded after Chaldiran. But since he was the leader among other things of the Shiite revolution in Iran he naturally became the chief organizer of its hierarchy and institutions. He appointed a spiritual leader, described as *sadr*, as chief of the religious hierarchy, who managed and oversaw the affairs of the religious institution including the all-important *vaqf* (religious endowment) property. The office of *sadr* had existed before the Safavids but under them it assumed new functions and importance, especially as it was a political appointment made directly by the shah.

The position of *sadr* was normally given to Persian Iranians as opposed to Qezelbash Turkamans. But the supreme civil post was at first occupied by a Qezelbash, although later Persians were also appointed to the post. This was called *Vakil-e Nafs-e Nafis-e Homayun* (Deputy to His Majesty's Exquisite Person), later simply known as Vakil. As is clear from the title and description, this office was the highest civil position in the land, its holder (especially in the early years of Savafid rule) being the most powerful person after the shah himself. He deputized at once both for the spiritual and the bureaucratic positions of the shah. The office of the vizier, though it existed, was no longer as important as it had been for centuries.

Both of the two great army commanders were also Qezelbash, but it would be too simplistic to say that the Qezelbash Turkamans ran the army and the Persians led the civil administration. The first Vakil, as noted, was a Qezelbash. And in later years Persians and administrators, even judges, occasionally found themselves in military roles. Predictably, there was rivalry and even mutual antipathy between the Persians and Turkamans. The latter originally made up most of Isma'il's devotees and virtually the whole of his army. They were jealous of their status and did not wish Persian Iranians to compete with them in power, prestige and authority. Isma'il was aware of this, and being somewhat weary of the ambitions of his Qezelbash chiefs, tended to increase the influence of the Persians as time went by, and took measures to limit the Turkaman leaders' hold. Towards the end of his rule they went so far as to assassinate his Persian Vakil, whose position and influence they had resented for some time.

Isma'il died in 1524, ten years after Chaldiran, when he was barely thirty-seven. The myth of his invincibility having been broken at Chaldiran, he no longer impressed his devotees with as much divine effulgence as before. It is said that no one saw a smile on his face after Chaldiran. That cannot be literally true since in his remaining years he spent much of his time drinking and debauching in the company of 'rosy-cheeked' youths. But that itself indicates unhappiness and attempts at drowning his sorrow by reckless living. He certainly did not lead his army again into battle.

Still, from his early youth he had led a revolution and founded an empire which, after experiencing the vicissitudes of time, would lead to the physical and cultural boundaries of modern Iran. He was as intelligent perhaps as he was cruel, and as valiant, charming and charismatic as brutal; one contemporary observer compared his bloodthirstiness to Nero's. His remains were laid to rest in the Safavid ancestral mausoleum in Ardebil, which has attracted visitors to this day.

CHAOS–ABSOLUTE AND ARBITRARY RULE–CHAOS (1524–88)

It does not come as a surprise that the death of Isma'il was followed by chaos, as had been the normal pattern in Iranian history. As has been noted before, all Iranian rulers enjoyed arbitrary power. Some of them were strong and absolute rulers as well and were able to impose order, often by taking harsh measures and striking fear into the hearts of the people, especially soldiers, administrators and tribal and provincial chiefs and potentates. Weak rulers on the other hand presided over a semi-chaotic situation which could lead to further chaos and/or the emergence of a strong ruler who would then bring back order, discipline and security to society and, with it, normal social and economic activity, which in turn brought prosperity. This was the definition of 'the just ruler', who was normally disliked in his own time but missed and lamented when his disappearance once again led to chaos. Khosraw I (Anushiravan) had been the epitome of 'the just ruler' before the coming of Islam (see Chapter 2).

Tahmasp I was only ten years old when he succeeded his father in 1524. This fact alone was enough to result in conflict and faction fighting among the Qezelbash and even the collapse of the dynasty. It took Tahmasp nine years before he could assert his absolute power and stamp out domestic chaos. And though until the end of his natural life the country faced many foreign wars and domestic difficulties, chaos no longer prevailed. His death in 1576 was followed by renewed turmoil until his grandson, Abbas I ('The Great'), took the reins of power and imposed his 'just rule'. Had it not been for him, Safavid Persia might well have come to an end at the close of the sixteenth century. This shows once again the all-important historical role of the Iranian ruler's personality in determining the course of events and the destiny of the country.

On Tahmasp's succession a Qezelbash chief, Div Soltan of the Rumlu tribe, seized power and became the shah's guardian (*atabeg*) as well as commander-in-chief of the army. The result of an ensuing power struggle among the Qezelbash chiefs was the emergence of a triumvirate led by Div Soltan, which included a Tekkalu and an Ostajlu chief. The compromise did not last, however, and in 1526 civil war broke out when the Ostajlus were defeated and their triumvir chief was killed. The civil war weakened Khorasan's defence, giving the Uzbeks the chance of invading and occupying parts of the province. But the domestic faction fighting still continued and in 1526 the young shah himself shot and wounded the Rumlu *atabeg* with an arrow; he was then finished off by the royal guards. As the only surviving member of the triumvirate, Chuha Soltan Tekkalu took over the affairs of the state. In 1528 the battle of Jam was fought to drive the Uzbeks out of Khorasan. The young shah displayed courage but the same could not be said for the Tekkalu chief. Herat was under siege, but out of vindictiveness, Chuha Soltan would not send a relief force to help its governor, Hosein Khan Shamlu. Therefore the latter had little choice but to surrender the city to the Uzbeks, although he negotiated favourable terms, thus winning the shah's approval.

The chaos was to continue for some time. The Tekkalu–Shamlu feud led to mortal struggles in which the Tekkalus won the day and killed hundreds of the Shamlus, although Chuha Soltan himself was killed too. All this was happening not only in distant places but in and around the shah's camp; and it should therefore come as no surprise that during a struggle his crown was hit by two arrows. Finally, when a Tekkalu attempt was made to abduct the shah, the latter ordered the general slaughter of the Tekkalus. The massacre took place in 1530–1, when the shah was about seventeen years old. Yet even this was not yet the end of instability and turmoil. The fall of the Tekkalus resulted in the supremacy of the Shamlus, led by Hosein Khan, and it did not take long for the head of the Shamlu chief, who was the shah's own cousin, to roll. In 1533 he was suspected of plotting to bring down the shah and replace him with his brother, Sam Mirza, and getting into league with the Ottoman enemy. Whatever the truth of these accusations, Hosein Khan had 'to go' in order for Tahmasp to become an absolute and arbitrary ruler in his realm; and 'going' in such situations meant losing one's head, sometimes together with those of one's family and clan.

As can be imagined, the country's enemies in the east and the west had not failed to take advantage of almost ten years of discord, chaos and civil war. From 1524 to 1538 there were five major invasions of Khorasan by the Uzbeks, not including their almost continuous short-term raids. The Ottomans invaded Persia four times under Tahmasp, the last incursion in 1553, which led to a lasting peace two years later under the Amasya treaty. Not surprisingly, Tahmasp moved the country's capital from Tabriz to Qazvin, putting a reasonable distance between himself and the Ottoman camps across the border.

Both western observers and Persian sources have left an unfavourable impression of Tahmasp's character and personality. Much that they say was true of most Iranian shahs and virtually all the Safavids, including the proclivity to intemperance, love of the harem and a tendency to cruelty, although at least Tahmasp did not kill or blind his two brothers condemned for treason and rebellion, but merely had them incarcerated. He certainly was a bigot and tried to convert to Shiism any foreign dignitary with whom he came into contact. He led his expeditions to Georgia and Armenia in the name of religion, although the desire for booty, including pretty women and youths and other slaves to serve in the royal household and the army, is likely to have been an equally strong motive. He was also a miser, reluctant to spend and keen to accumulate riches. He was by no means as dashing and charismatic as his father, nor as intelligent, able and powerful as his grandson, Abbas. But he does not seem to have performed as modestly as would be expected from the traditional descriptions of his character: he put an end to the chaos, ruled single-handedly for more than forty years and held the country together despite some loss of territory, mainly to the Ottomans. He was also a patron of the arts, especially miniature painting and the arts of the book, which had flourished under the late Timurids in the previous century.

There were four expeditions against the Caucasian Christians between 1540 and 1553. The number of Georgian, Armenian and Circassian slaves taken in 1553 alone has been put at 30,000. This made a significant impact on the composition of the higher echelons of society and quite unintentionally introduced a new factor into domestic politics. Many of the slaves joined the military network, for the first time, as a force independent from if not rival to the Turkaman Qazelbash, thus breaking the virtual monopoly of the latter in military affairs. Others among the royal slaves (*Gholaman-e Khasseh*) became administrators, alongside Persian bureaucrats. At the same time, the women who were added to the shah's harem, and the new eunuchs created from young Caucasians, began to actively participate in court intrigue, even to the extent of pushing their own candidates – princes born of Caucasian slaves – for the succession. Thus, the higher echelons of Safavid society were now made up of Caucasians as well as Persians and Turkamans. The Caucasian factor became more important under Abbas, especially regarding his policy of reducing the military weight of the Qezelbash tribes.

It would have been against the logic and sociology of Iranian history if political turmoil had not broken out after Tahmasp's death in 1576. Already in 1574, when he was ill and was thought to be dying, chaos was emerging, aborted only by his recovery. There was a scramble for the succession after his death, and, one or two claimants having been killed in the process, Tahmasp's son Isma'il Mirza mounted the throne as Isma'il II. He had had a good start, becoming governor of Shirvan in 1547 and governor-general of Khorasan, a much more prestigious post, in 1556. Typically, however, he was suspected of plotting the downfall of his father, and Tahmasp had him put in the same remote prison where he had jailed his brothers. There he spent almost twenty years before succeeding his father amid turmoil and bloodletting. He put to death many of those who had supported other candidates and killed officials who had served under his father. Besides, he openly killed princes of the blood simply because they were in the line of succession. It was not the action itself but the extent of bloodletting within a few months which was relatively unusual, and may be explained by his extensive prison experience. More than fifty years later his great-grandnephew, Abbas's grandson, behaved in a similar fashion, perhaps in consequence of his confinement in the harem for many years.

Isma'il II also made an attempt to restore Sunnism, which supplies further evidence for his serious lack of judgement. In the end even many of those who had helped him take over the realm turned against him, not least his powerful sister, Pari Khan Khanom. Before his first year as shah was out he was found dead, probably poisoned and with the knowledge of his sister. The half-blind Mohammad Khodabandeh was the only one of his eight brothers whom he had not killed or blinded. The Qezelbash put this meek and mild prince on the throne, leaving it to his strong wife, Mahd-e Olia, and his equally strong sister, Pari Khan Khanom, to struggle for power behind the throne. In the end, the latter lost the game, together with her head; the queen was also to meet her death, though at the hands of the Qezelbash, because of her harsh and arbitrary rule. Neither her husband nor her favourite son, Hamzaeh Mirza, were able to save her or punish her assailants. A couple of years later the Qezelbash murdered the vizier as well. In 1586 Hamzaeh Mirza, the heir apparent, who had been directing the affairs of the state after the vizier's murder, was himself murdered while campaigning in Qarabagh.

The Ottomans and Uzbeks had not been idle in the face of all this turmoil and discord in Persia. The Uzbeks continued their raids with increasing vigour and success. In 1578 the Ottomans finally violated the Amasya peace treaty of 1555 by invading Azerbaijan; by 1585 they had captured Tabriz, where they remained for the next twenty years. Herat was the seat of the shah's youngest son, Abbas Mirza, a teenager who had miraculously survived through the chaos. In 1587 the Uzbeks mounted a massive attack on Khorasan and threatened to engulf the whole of the province. Morshed Qoli Khan, leader of the Ostajlu faction in Khorasan, decided to carry out a putsch by taking Abbas Mirza to Qazvin and forcing his father to abdicate in his favour. The ploy worked and the shah vacated the throne in favour of Abbas Mirza in October 1588. While this bold move succeeded, the country would not have been saved from chaos had it not been for the extraordinary personality of the fifteen-year-old youth who had acceded to the throne.

THE SAFAVID CLIMAX

In the twelve years since the death of Shah Tahmasp domestic chaos, strife, rebellion and civil war had left little or no central authority. Since the assassination of the queen, Mohammad Shah and his son Hamzeh Mirza had been no more than pawns in the hands of conflicting Qezelbash chiefs. The country's external weakness was a direct consequence of its internal discord and anarchy. The Ottomans had occupied considerable tracts of Persian territory in the north-west and west, including most of Azerbaijan. The Uzbeks had helped themselves to large territories in Khorasan and Sistan and were posed to occupy the whole of that province. Thus Abbas faced an enormous task of putting down domestic turmoil and recovering lost Persian territory. He began by reasserting his authority against rebellious and unruly Qezelbash chiefs, including reprisals against those responsible for the death of his brother, Hamzeh Mirza. At first he used the assistance of his mentor Morshed Qoli Khan, whom he had named as Vakil, but – and this was the refrain of Iranian history – soon had him killed because he did not want a man as powerful as Morshed Qoli Khan, in charge of the affairs of state, especially as he had proven himself to be a skilled coup-maker by bringing Abbas himself to the throne.

The long-term task of achieving domestic peace and stability required a significant reduction in the power and influence of the Qezelbash chiefs. That could be best achieved by creating a military countervailing power which would be permanently available and directly under the shah's own command. Apart from such small forces as royal guard detachments, Iran had not had a standing army during Islamic times, the bulk of the army being made up of provincial levies which, in Safavid times, the Qezelbash chiefs would raise from their tribes and governorates when required. But this was precisely the kind of force that was needed to strengthen the central state power and to keep the Qezelebash chiefs in their place. Shah Abbas set about systematically organizing a standing army from the Caucasian *gholams*, the Georgian, Armenian and Circassian military slaves who had been brought from the Caucasus or were of Caucasian extraction. As noted above, the process had begun in an unplanned and embryonic manner under Tahmasp, but under Abbas this was a conscious and highly organized developement.

The *gholam* regiments were equipped with muskets and artillery, and were commanded by their own generals. One of these was the famous Allahverdi Khan of the Georgian feudal house of Undiladze, who rose to become governor-general of Fars and commander-in-chief of the army and whose name is alternatively used for the attractive bridge in Isfahan known as '*Si-o-seh pol*', which he had built himself. His son Emamqoli Khan also became a rich and powerful man and governor-general of Fars before Shah Abbas's successor slaughtered him along with his family.

Funds were needed to maintain a standing army for which the existing crown and state revenues were far from adequate. Hitherto the Safavids had, with some modification, continued the policy of land assignment of their Ilkhan and Seljuk predecessors, except that the assignment system was now known as *tiyul* rather than the *siuyrghal* and *eqta'* of the former dynasties. In this system a province would be assigned to a Qezelbash chief. He was the governor and was responsible for running the province from the revenues extracted from it, the remainder being paid into the state treasury. In return, he was obliged to contribute the assigned levies when required by the shah.

As we have learnt from earlier chapters, there never was a feudal system in Iran. In principle, the state – and ultimately the shah – had the sole monopoly of the land. The assignees – governors, landlords or whoever – were not independent freeholders of the land assigned to them, and the state had the right to withdraw their title and give it to someone else or add it to the state or crown lands, which under the Safavids were known as *khasseh*. When the state was weak it may have been difficult for it to impose its will in practice, but as long as the state had the physical power to enforce its decisions the rule remained unchallengeable.

Shah Abbas had both the will and the ability to transfer some of the provinces to *khasseh* land, so that a large proportion of provincial revenues could be paid directly to the state; and by considerably increasing state revenues he was able to meet the financial requirements of his *gholam* army. Further than that, this policy reduced the wealth, weight and importance of the Qezelbash and at the same time enabled him to appoint *gholam*s to governorships of the reclaimed provinces, as in the case of Allahverdi Khan, thus extending his patronage to those whose loyalty was solely and directly to himself.

The shah took further measures to break the traditional power of the Qezelbash. He broke up some of their tribes into parts and moved and resettled them in different regions, the case of the Qajars being the most well known in view of their future history (see Chapter 6). He sometimes appointed as chief the chief of another tribe. He also organized a composite tribe, the Shahsevan, who, as their names suggests, loved and were loyal solely to the shah himself. By the time he had carried out all his domestic reforms he had become the supreme, absolute as well as arbitrary ruler, 'the just ruler', who put an end to chaos, crushed rebellious behaviour and brought peace and security to the land so that governors and state officials were not able to behave unjustly towards the people – that is, in a way that would not be approved by the shah himself.

Yet 'the just ruler' also had to maintain the country's traditional frontiers, if not extend them, and put its enemies in their place. Abbas was wise enough not to take any major steps in that direction before much of the domestic chaos had been dealt with and the military force had been put in a better shape. The very existence of the Safavid empire had come into question at his accession, when the Ottomans and Uzbeks were occupying large parts of the country in the west and east while virtual civil war was breaking out in the rest of the country and the city of Qandahar had been once again lost to Mogul India. Abbas knew that he could not win a war on two fronts and that the enemy in the east was the less formidable adversary. In 1590 he reached a humiliating agreement with the Turks whereby he ceded to them the territories they already occupied, much of Azerbaijan and the Caucasus, including the former Safavid capital Tabriz, as well as Iraq, Baghdad and the holy cities of the Shiites, Kurdistan and parts of Loristan.

The temporary peace in the west made it possible to take on the Uzbeks, who were still marauding in Khorasan in the 1590s. The death of Abdollah Khan, the able Uzbek leader, and the onset of discord among their chiefs in 1598 provided the first real opportunity for pushing back the Uzbeks and recovering Khorasan and Sistan. Herat was taken in that year, and by 1602–3 the Uzbeks had been sufficiently driven out of Persian territory for the shah to turn his attention to the Ottomans. Taking advantage of Uzbek disunity, Abbas succeeded in establishing useful alliances with Uzbek chiefs who were close to the frontier in order to ensure that the peace would be reasonably lasting.

In 1603 Abbas marched to Tabriz and took it from its Ottoman garrison. Intermittent clashes with the Ottomans continued until 1605, when the Ottomans suffered a crushing defeat at Sufiyan near Tabriz. Earlier, the battle of Van had led to brilliant victories led by Allahverdi Khan, but the shah himself demonstrated his exceptional talent as a commander at Sufiyan. By 1607 Iran had gained all the territory which it had owned at the time of the 1555 treaty of Amasya.

For one reason or another, attempts at peace negotiations did not succeed; sporadic skirmishes were followed by a lull until, in 1623, taking advantage of the Ottomans' internal conflict in Baghdad province, Abbas invaded the region and took the city of Baghdad. Meanwhile, Qandahar had been retaken from the Moguls in 1622, and the island of Hormuz from the Portuguese with English help. By the time of Abbas's death in 1629 Persia had once again reached the borders that had been established by Shah Isma'il at the peak of his reign.

Abbas encouraged domestic and international trade directly as well as through the construction of extensive infrastructures such as roads and caravansaries. Carpet weaving, which had begun to develop into a major industry under Tahmasp I, received a further boost under Abbas, so that the art of Persian carpet weaving reached a peak during the Safavid period. As part of his policy of economic development the shah transferred thousands of industrious Armenians from the northern city of Jolfa to the southern suburb of his new capital of Isfahan, which thenceforth was called New Jolfa or Jolfa of Isfahan.

Merchants from various European and Asian countries came to the Persian capital in pursuit of profitable trade. Although he displayed outward signs of piety, for example by his pilgrimages to Mashhad and other Shiite holy places, Abbas did not have the bigotry of his grandfather. His intolerance of Sunnism may be at least partly attributed to his hostility towards the Ottomans (and the Uzbeks), but, on the whole, he displayed a tolerant attitude towards his non-Muslim subjects, and was keen to establish political and trade links with European countries as potential allies against the Ottomans. Not many results were achieved by the missions he sent to or received from Europe, however, partly because of distances of place and time and partly as a consequence of the quarrels which often broke out among members of these missions.

Among the Europeans who came to Abbas's court were the two colourful English adventurers the brothers Sir Anthony and Sir Robert Sherley, at the head of a group of twenty-six Europeans. In due course Abbas sent Sir Anthony on a mission to European courts. This was far from successful since he picked one quarrel after another with his Persian and other companions, was arrested in Venice and was banned from returning to England. Sir Robert acted as a military advisor and was later also sent on a mission to England, which did not yield tangible results. Still, it was with the help of an English fleet that the shah recovered the island of Hormuz in 1622 from the Portuguese, who had occupied it with Isma'il's reluctant agreement since 1515. In the process, the Portuguese fortifications off the strait of Hormuz were also captured, the name of the place being changed from Gameron to Bandar Abbas, which became the main Iranian port on the Persian Gulf. Abbas had already expelled the Portuguese from Bahrain.

The change of capital from Qazvin to Isfahan enabled the shah to apply some of his energies to the conversion of his seat of government into a great world city. Isfahan was an ancient city and had flourished as a Seljuk capital when under Malekshah the great Congregational Mosque (*Masjed-e Jame'*) had been repaired and considerably extended. To this day it is probably the greatest single monument in that city, situated as it is in the heart of the old city and dating from more than twelve hundred years ago. Rather than demolishing and rebuilding the old city as was hitherto normal in Iranian history, the shah built a new city beside it, which through the Chahar Bagh parkway extended to the river, Zayandeh Rud, with the Armenian district being built on the left bank of the river.

Much of Shah Abbas's Isfahan has been destroyed, first by the Afghan invasion and devastation of the early eighteenth century. Fortunately, Meydan-e Naqsh-e Jahan, the great central piazza, has survived intact as a tribute to the architectural genius of the period and a symbol of the city built by Shah Abbas. To the south is situated the majestic Masjed-e Shah or Royal Mosque, sometimes known in the West as the Blue Mosque, indicating the dominant colour of its exquisitely decorated tiles and dome. The Palace of Aliqapu, the Exalted Porte, is located on the piazza's west side, facing the small but beautiful Mosque of Sheikh Lotfollah, an immigrant Lebanese divine whose daughter was in the shah's harem. In the north, opposite the Royal Mosque but at some distance away, is the entrance to the main bazaar.

It was not just architecture but other visual arts which flourished under Shah Abbas and some of his descendants, more even than they had under his grandfather Tahmasp I. Reza Abbasi perfected the art of manuscript illustration while Sadeq Beg Afshar, director of the royal library, introduced a new realism in his paintings which set the scene for the increasing realism of later periods. Apart from traditional manuscript illustration, large numbers of single-page paintings were also made under Shah Abbas, a genre which had little precedent in the earlier periods. Other arts related to manuscript production, such as calligraphy and *tazhib*, also flourished, reaching their peak in the art of Mir Emad Hassani, the great calligrapher of the reign of Shah Abbas II.

For all his positive achievements Shah Abbas was a cruel and brutal ruler. He blinded his half-blind father after deposing him. He killed his son on suspicion of plotting against him, and having got proof of his innocence too late he is said to have suffered so much that he ordered the executioner to kill his own son so that he would experience the same pain. He also blinded two of his sons on similar suspicions, one of whom committed suicide as a result. All this was of course due to the fact that, as noted before, royal legitimacy in Iran lacked a firm legal basis, so that virtually anyone who managed to seize and maintain power could become a legitimate ruler. The shah's mind must have been constantly alive not only to the murder of his brother, uncles and cousins and nearly himself in previous reigns but also to the fact that he himself had revolted and seized power from his father. He thus set the policy and precedent of immuring royal males in the harem, so they would be ignorant of the outside world and cut off from would-be plotters. It is not difficult to imagine what effect this had on the future Safavid shahs who emerged from the harem to rule the country.

Being ready to treat his own children in this way, it is not surprising that he was quite capable of ordering mass killings and deportations – the worst perhaps being the Georgian massacre of 1615, in which 100,000 were killed and 60,000 deported – and the infliction of hideous torture and punishment to death of individuals who incurred his wrath or suspicion.

Paradoxically, he may not have been a 'just ruler' according to the logic of Persian history had he not been so harsh and fearsome. It is quite probable that he may not have survived or been so successful had he been kinder towards his family, servants and subjects. After all, other shahs who were as harsh or cruel did not share his positive achievements and so were not 'just rulers'. Jean Chardin, the French jeweller who spent several years in Iran and ended his years in England and who understood the nature of the Iranian state and society as few other Europeans did, wrote in full knowledge of Abbas's positive as well as negative sides: 'When this great prince ceased to live, Persia ceased to prosper.' Such are the ironies of Iranian history.

THE LATER SAFAVIDS

The Safavid dynasty lasted for another century after Abbas I. This has been traditionally described as the 'decline and fall' of the Safavids both by Persian and western historians. While it is true that the Safavid empire never again experienced the power and glory of Abbas's reign, the pattern seems to be familiar from the whole of Iranian history. One could equally speak of 'decline and fall' after Darius I, Shapur I, Shapur II, Khosraw I, Mahmud of Ghazna, Malekshah and so forth. However, Abbas I's reign was more glorious not only than those which followed him but also than those which had preceded him.

There were four other Safavid shahs between the death of Abbas I in 1629 and the conquest of Isfahan by the Ghalzeh Afghan tribe in 1722. It is only after the death of Abbas II in 1666 that 'decline and fall' becomes an apt description. It may be argued that the seeds of this decline were sown in the previous periods; but this would perhaps be truer of Abbas I's reign than those immediately following it. While by turning some *mamaleks*, or state provinces, into *khassehs*, or crown provinces, he had managed to increase state revenues to pay for his *gholam* army and to centralize the state administration, he had at the same time reduced the military potential of the Qezelbash and the influence of their chiefs. Further, by introducing the policy of incarcerating royal males in the harem he had made it highly unlikely for a balanced, let alone able and efficient, ruler to accede to the throne. The exception was Abbas II, who was too young to have been corrupted and incapacitated by being cut off from the outside world amidst intriguing women and eunuchs.

Given the logic of Iranian history, the fact remains that much of the 'decline and fall' was due to the ineptness of the rulers, in this case the last two, Soleiman and Soltan-hosein. There is no reason why someone like Abbas I could not have prevented the decline such as he had done in extremely dangerous circumstances. Even though the reign of his namesake and great grandson Abbas II was not as glorious as his own, he was still able enough to reverse the tendency towards decline had opium, alcohol and promiscuity not limited his life to thirty-three years.

Abbas's grandson Sam Mirza emerged from the harem at eighteen to claim his grandfather's throne as Shah Safi. Not much could have been expected from someone who had been raised in the harem and witnessed his father being killed by his grandfather. He was usually inebriated when he indulged in many of his cruel acts. The massacre of Emamqoli Khan and his family, the Georgian *gholam*, son of Allahverdi Khan and 'conqueror of Hormuz', was only the most spectacular of such 'decisions', but the murder of powerful ministers and military chiefs, often together with their offspring, was and remained familiar in Iranian history. Familiar too was the murder of royal princes, in his case including his only surviving uncle, who had been blinded on the orders of his grandfather. It was his ineptness and lack of interest in the affairs of the state rather than cruelty and brutality that made him an unworthy ruler of the great empire he had inherited.

On the advice of his able chief minister, Saru Taqi, he continued the policy of converting state provinces into crown provinces, by far the most important being Fars. It was a continuation of Abbas's policy and contributed to military decline in later years. Sporadic clashes with the Ottomans continued until 1638 when Baghdad was retaken by the Turks; by the time of the peace treaty of 1639 the whole of Iraq had been ceded to them. It was a peace that was to last for almost ninety years, making seventeenth-century Persia a relatively peaceful country. Also in 1638, Qandahar was once again lost to the Moguls of India, though it was retaken again in the following reign. On the eastern frontiers predatory Uzbek raids continued as before, but there was no more Uzbek attempts at the conquest of Khorasan and therefore no full-scale war with them in the east. When Safi died in 1642 aged thirty-two, the country still looked in good shape despite some loss of territory.

Abbas II was barely nine when he succeeded his father. As mentioned above, this was perhaps a blessing since, unlike his father, his incarceration in the harem had not been sufficiently long to make a permanent mark on his character. He ruled the country for twenty-four years, dying early as a result of excessive indulgence in sex and drugs. He, too, was good at killing and blinding royal persons and notable men, which he did often when he was drunk. On the other hand, he had abilities resembling his namesake and great-grandfather. The peace with the Ottomans was maintained during his reign, but there were clashes with Mogul India over Qandahar, which Abbas retook in 1648, and he managed to repulse India's later attempts to take it back. Still, the army was not in better – perhaps even in worse – shape than it was under Safi, mainly because of lack of important foreign wars but partly also because of the continuation and extension of the policy of converting state provinces into crown provinces. This, as we have seen, was the policy of Saru Taqi, who had remained chief minister after Abbas's accession. Thus, parts of Azerbaijan, Gilan, Mazandaran, Kerman, Yazd and Qazvin, which were not on vulnerable frontiers, were added to *khasseh* lands.

This is likely to have led to discontent among those who lost their *tiyul* and the Qezelbash chiefs in general, but there is no reason to believe, as some have argued, that it had an adverse effect on the state's financial position. Saru Taqi at any rate was assassinated by a group of military and other notables who were unhappy with the concentration of power in his hands, little knowing that the youthful shah would have the moral courage to have them all executed in retribution.

Abbas II was a ruler of considerable ability who took charge of the administration and ruled over the mass of his subjects with an even-handedness reminiscent of his great-grandfather. He took an interest in agricultural development and tried to increase the supply of water in the Isfahan area from the Karun, though his attempts were frustrated by the fact that his plan was too ambitious for existing technology. On the whole, he pursued a policy of religious tolerance and would welcome European visitors to his court, the most notable being the French priest and mathematician Raphael du Mans, who supplied Colbert, the celebrated minister of Louis XIV, with a manual on Persia in 1660. He received diplomatic missions from France and Russia, neither of which was very successful; and in the case of the latter certain events led to the development of bad feelings on the part of Russia: the 800-strong Russian mission was suspected of trying to dodge customs duties, and in the quarrels that followed before their return home one of them was killed.

Painting and calligraphy flourished under Abbas II. Mohammad Zaman's studies in Italy led to his introduction of perspective into Persian miniature painting, but Mir Emad Hasani, one of the greatest calligraphers of all time, was killed, probably on the shah's orders.

Abbas added to the architectural monuments of Isfahan, notably by building the impressive Khwaju bridge and weir and completing the charming, if small, Palace of Chehel Sotun.

The real decline began from 1666 under Abbas's son and successor Safi, who later crowned himself again on an auspicious occasion as Soleiman. He, too, had emerged from the harem at eighteen to rule a vast empire and, like his grandfather, displayed all the symptoms of such an upbringing. Early in his reign Russia, though not declaring war, provoked trouble in Mazandaran in retaliation for the ill-feeling created in consequence of its failed mission under Abbas II by encouraging and helping a notorious marauder to lead 500 Cossacks to occupy an Iranian island in the Caspian Sea. This, coupled with his illness at the beginning of his reign, both of which he saw as bad omens, explains why the shah held a second coronation under a new name three years after his accession. According to a Safavid historian 'Shah Soleiman used to spend most of his time drinking and debauching, and apart from that, he killed military chiefs and leaders of the bureaucracy.' Like Shah Safi, he had little interest in running the state; and during his rule it was not able ministers like Saru Taqi but eunuchs and other members of the royal household who ran affairs while making sure to deprive the country of able and responsible leaders.

It was lucky for this shah, who had all the vices of his father and almost none of his virtues, that the Ottomans were busy fighting in Europe and the Uzbeks had given up the thought of conquering Khorasan. He did indeed receive word from Europe that he could open an eastern front against the Turks and recover lost territory, but he declined to violate the peace of 1639, perhaps wisely since in view of the country's declining military power it could well have led to defeat and further loss of territory.

It was during the latter part of his reign that the power of the *mojtaheds*, led by Mullah Mohammad Baqer Majlesi, began to rise and the persecution of religious minorities – not just Christians and Jews but equally Sunni Muslims and Sufis – was introduced.

On the death of Soleiman, his son Soltan-hosein left the harem to occupy the throne of the Safavid empire. Almost the only thing worthy of praise from his reign was the Madar-e Shah College in Chaharbagh Avenue of Isfahan. He was a pious and good-natured man of twenty-six, completely unsuited to the situation in Persia, not only in making a 'just ruler' but even in being able to hold the fort:

he was neither able nor ruthless. Although used to sexual promiscuity, he was not used to drinking before he came to power, but the court intriguers taught him this habit to make sure of their own dominion over the affairs of state. This time, however, a powerful new factor had entered the scene, that of the *mojtaheds* in general and Majlesi in particular. It became much more effective than before, especially in view of the shah's arid piety.

The persecution of Sufis as well as of religious minorities became widespread, resulting in growing discontent among the Sunni populations in Dagestan, Shirvan, Baluchistan and Afghanistan. In 1698 the government forces led by Gregory XI of Georgia successfully defeated the Baluch rebels and cleared them out of Kerman. Six years later Gregory, or Gorgin Khan, became governor of Qandahar, where the Ghalzeh Afghans had been subjected to injustice and religious persecution and were in a state of revolt. He set about dealing with the situation with an iron fist and sent off the Ghalzeh tribal chief Mirveis, the leader of the revolt, to Isfahan, describing him as a dangerous element. But Mirveis turned the table and endeared himself to the shah and notables, obtaining permission to go to hajj, where he also managed to obtain fatvas from Sunni ulama that it was incumbent on the Sunnis to revolt against Shia rule.

On return to Qandahar Mirveis surprised Gregory with another revolt, which led to Gregory's death and the massacre of his Georgian troops. Several expeditions sent against the Ghalzeh rebels failed, and so the rebels became effectively independent from the empire. Meanwhile, the Sunni Abdalis of Herat, who had also suffered persecution, learned their lesson from the Ghalzeh rebels. They too revolted against the state, and efforts by the government to suppress them did not succeed.

In the meantime Isfahan received a commercial mission from France followed by another from Russia. The latter caused some concern: it was thought that the real intention of Peter the Great was to test the ground for marching southwards into Iranian territory with the distant wish of having access to the Persian Gulf. In fact the mission sent seven years later, in 1715, had the secret agenda of collecting intelligence. By then the deteriorating situation in Iran was becoming obvious to its neighbours, Russian as well as Ottoman.

In 1719 the revolt of the Lezgis – an ethnic group who were settled predominantly in Dagestan, in the Caucasus – led to the fall of Shirvan and parts of Georgia. The governor of Georgia requested permission from the shah to lead a strong force against the rebels, but the shah declined and, in retaliation, the governor ignored his call for help three years later when Isfahan was under siege by the Afghans. In 1722 the Afghans triumphantly entered Isfahan, and the shah abdicated in favour of their chief. That was in effect the end of Safavid rule in Iran, although it took another fourteen years for it to be formally ended by Nader Shah Afshar.

The Safavids were not noted for their patronage of poetry. The poetry of the period is described as the Indian Style, partly because many of the Persian poets of the period were Indian and partly because a number of Iranian poets visited the Mogul court (and some lesser courts) in India, sometimes for long periods, because the Moguls were great patrons of Persian poetry. In his long visit to India, the seventeenth-century poet Saeb-e Tabizi wrote:

Our homeland has hurt our disillusioned heart
Our amber has a bloody heart from Yemen

The amber stones of Yemen were regarded as the best at the time. And again:

Do not sigh remembering your homeland for it is
The same homeland that gave not even a garment to Joseph.

Yet the so-called Indian Style itself was initiated and first evolved in Iran. It was a style that had been adumbrated in the fourteenth century in the works of Kamal Khojandi and (to a lesser extent) Khaju and Hafiz among others. The most well-known Iranian poets in this style are the fifteenth- to sixteenth-century Baba Faghani Shirzi, the sixteenth-century Orfi Shirazi and Vahshi Bafqi and the seventeenth-century Kalim-e Kashani and Saeb-e Tabrizi. Baba Faghani is sometimes credited as being the founder of the Indian Style movement, but that is an exaggeration since the movement evolved over a long period of time. Vahshi is more in the tradition of Baba Faghani, whereas Saeb's and Kalim's styles were more distinct. Saeb was the greatest of all Indian Style poets.

CHAPTER 6

Disintegration and Reunification

At night he was thinking of plunder and pillage
At dawn he was headless, and his head, crownless
At a turn of the deep blue sky
*Neither Nader remained nor a Naderite.**
Popular poem circulating after the assassination of Nader Shah

THE EIGHTEENTH CENTURY WAS a dark period in Iranian history. Apart from two decades of relative peace in parts of the country under Karim Khan Zand later in the century, it was a period when on many an occasion it looked as if the country would be broken up as badly as before, especially as the Ottomans and the Russians took advantage of the situation and occupied parts of Iranian territory. Long periods of death and destruction, even though less intense than during the time of the Mongol invasions five centuries earlier, meant that in some ways life for the people of the country was not much better than in the thirteenth century (see Chapter 4). A distinguished historian has observed that sedentary life became so insecure that nomadic living began to expand. Both high and low, mighty and meek, rich and poor suffered. The century began with growing turmoil and speedy decline resulting in the fall of the Safavids amidst catastrophic chaos, which was to continue in different forms until the Qajar peace of the end of the century brought not a time of great prosperity but certainly one of more security and tranquillity than before.

THE FALL OF ISFAHAN

Mirveis, the rebellious Sunni Afghan leader, had died and his son Mahmud had replaced him as the Ghalzeh chief in 1717. Next year Mahmud attacked and captured Kerman, but had to retreat to quell the rebellion that had broken out in his absence in Qandahar. Amidst a Baluchi rebellion he captured Kerman

---

* Sar-e shab beh del qasd-e taraj dasht / Sahargah nah tan sar nah sar taj dasht / Beh yek gardesh-e charkh-e nilufari / Nah Nader beh ja mand o nah Naderi.

once again and marched to Yazd, which he did not take, and went straight to Isfahan. A force of 42,000 men, vastly superior in numbers to that of Mahmud, was sent out of the capital to meet him but was defeated and the city was put under siege. The shah's appeal to the governor of Georgia, who might well have saved the situation, fell on deaf ears, in retaliation for his earlier refusal to grant him permission to suppress the Lezgis rebellion. Famine and plague finally brought the capital to heel. Mahmud triumphantly entered the city, the shah abdicated and the Afghan chief claimed the crown of Persia. These events were typical of Iranian history: the fall of a weak, unjust and incompetent arbitrary state, this time as a result of the revolt of some of its own people, while – as a nineteenth-century Iranian chief minister observed – hardly any of its subjects were prepared to defend it.

Meanwhile, chaos in Iran offered a golden opportunity for intervention by Russia and the Ottomans, both of which wished to extend their realms in the south and east. The forces of Peter the Great of Russia entered Darband in August 1722. They would have joined forces with the Georgians and conquered the whole of the Caucasus had it not been for an Ottoman ultimatum. Still, the Russians captured Baku and occupied parts of Gilan and Mazandaran. A little later the Ottomans also occupied extensive parts of Iran in the west and north-west.

While Isfahan was still under siege, Tahmasp Mirza, Soltan-hosein's third son, made a sortie and went to the former capital, Qazvin, where, after receiving the news of his father's abdication, he declared himself shah as Tahmasp II, although he spent more time on wine and sex than on mobilizing resistance to the Afghans. Thus the Ghalzeh troops attacked and captured Qazvin and forced him to flee to Tabriz, the original Safavid capital. But early in 1723 the people of Qazvin rose against the Afghans, killed many of them and drove the rest out of town.

Mahmud had at first tried to rule even-handedly, but the news of the uprising in Qazvin frightened him into ordering the slaughter of many royal persons and notables as well as 3,000 Qezelbash in Isfahan. In the summer of 1724 Shiraz fell to Mahmud. On the other hand, the Afghan forces on the way from Qandahar to Isfahan had a bloody reception before Yazd, and when Mahmud himself went to punish the people of Yazd, they defeated and almost captured him. Feeling highly vulnerable, he returned to Isfahan and ordered the slaughter of all but two of the princes. Soon after, he himself was killed in a coup led by his cousin Ashraf.

Declaring himself shah in April 1725, Ashraf was more balanced, more astute and more popular with his troops than Mahmud. He sent a mission to Constantinople to persuade the sultan to recognize him as the shah of Iran and withdraw his forces from the occupied Persian territories. Despite the play on Sunni fraternity, the attempt backfired and instead the Ottomans declared war. Ashraf's forces were at first defeated but the Turkish army was defeated by the Afghans when it moved from Hamadan to Isfahan. Ashraf made a favourable peace with the Ottomans, but his effort to drive the Russians out of Gilan was unsuccessful. Meanwhile, in response to a denigrating letter from the Turkish army commander, Ashraf had killed the unfortunate Soltan-hosein, fearing that he might still be regarded as the legitimate ruler of the country.

It was from the same motive that he sent troops after Tahmasp II, who was defeated near Tehran and fled north to Astrabad. Tahmasp had the support of the Qajar chief Fath'ali Khan, who for a time was virtually the commander-in-chief of his forces. At this point a new and highly important factor entered the scene in the person of Naderqoli Afshar, a Sunni of military genius, who joined the shah's forces at the head of his 2,000 Afshar tribal troops. The competition between the Afshar warrior and the Qajar chief led to the execution of the latter on Tahmasp's order in 1726.

Having completely gained Tahmasp's confidence and put down various attempts to dislodge him, Nader then attacked and defeated the rebel Abadali Afghans. On receiving this news, Ashraf realized that he had to reckon with a major power and rushed to meet it, but was defeated in a battle near Damghan. It was after the second defeat that Ashraf slaughtered 3,000 (virtually all the remaining) notables of Isfahan; but he himself was defeated in the third battle and fled to Shiraz. Nader then entered the dead and devastated city of Isfahan, followed by Tahmasp, and Safavid rule was apparently restored. Shortly afterwards, in the winter of 1729–30, Nader went in pursuit of Ashraf and defeated him in two more battles, whereupon Ashraf fled east and was killed on the way by a force that Mahmud's brother, the ruler of Qandahar, had sent to meet him.

THE RISE OF NADER

Large parts of the country were still under Ottoman and Russian occupation and the rest was in chaos and despair. Nader attacked and defeated the occupying Ottoman forces but had to postpone complete victory in order to turn his attention to the revolt of the Abdali Afghans in Herat, which he successfully quelled. While Nader was in Khorasan, Tahmasp, perhaps in an attempt to compete with Nader, violated the Perso-Ottoman ceasefire but was defeated and had to cede much of the territory which Nader had previously regained. Having returned to Isfahan in August 1732 Nader persuaded the army chiefs to replace Tahmasp by his infant son Abbas under his own vice-regency with the title of Vakil al-Dawleh (Deputy of the Crown).

The renewal of war with the Ottomans eventually led to full victory and the peace of late 1733 whereupon the Ottomans agreed to withdraw from all the occupied lands; and when, a couple of years later, they tried to renege on the agreement, they were once again defeated and thenceforth kept the peace. In the meantime Nader also drove the Russians out of Iran by the 1735 treaty of Rasht.

In 1736 when the country was totally cleared of domestic chaos and foreign occupation Nader called a meeting in Dasht-e Moghan of chiefs and notables from all over Iran, ostensibly to decide the country's regime but in fact to depose the Safavids and choose Nader himself as the shah of Persia. The conference participants knew their role well, but it would be a mistake to think that they took their decision merely or even mainly through fear and bribery. They offered Nader the crown, which he accepted on the condition that Iran revert to Sunnism, a wish which could not possibly be realized outside official formalities.

Nader was forty-seven and had he then settled down to a long period of reconstruction he would have been worthy of much of the praise that Iranian governments and historians bestowed on him in the twentieth century. He was portrayed as a modern Iranian nationalist, a hero who had not only saved Iran from chaos and foreign occupation but had also brought the country fabulous riches and glory. Nader was in fact an illiterate Sunni tribesman whose mother tongue was Turkish and who saw himself as an Asian conqueror in the style of Amir Timur. His reign saw little peace, and he was given to cruelty, enslavement, pillage and slaughter, both inside and outside Iran. He was far from another Abbas I, with whom he has been unrealistically compared.

The first major act of the new shah was to lead an expedition against Qandahar in 1736, despite the fact that its ruler had acknowledged his sovereignty. Much of his baggage and equipment was carried by peasants whom he had enslaved in Kerman just for that purpose. He defeated the force that the ruler of Qandahar had sent to meet him, but had to camp for a long siege, and the city did not fall before March 1738. Following that, Nader attacked Mogul India on some flimsy pretext.

He had two interrelated motives for attacking India. Firstly, his wars had emptied the treasury, despite the imposition of heavy taxes, and he needed substantial funds to maintain his growing army. Secondly, he was, as he showed until the very end of his career, an obsessive conqueror who had to be on the move virtually all the time. Kabul fell first and Peshawar not long afterwards, and the Indian army was defeated at Lahore after stiff resistance. Then the Mogul emperor Mohammad Shah himself left Delhi to meet Nader in combat. They met at Karnal in February 1739: the Indians were defeated and Mohammad Shah surrendered to Nader.

Nader's triumphal entry into Delhi was followed by an indiscriminate massacre of the population because some Indian soldiers still resisting had killed some of his troops. The number of those killed has been quoted as 20,000 and the massacre has been compared with that by Timur three and a half centuries earlier. Nader returned the Indian crown to Mohammad Shah and went back to Iran with a large quantity of fabulous jewels and with his army enhanced by a further 40,000 men. Meanwhile, Nader's eldest son and heir apparent, Rezaqoli Mirza, having received false intelligence that his father had been killed in battle in India, murdered Tahmasp and his two sons, who were being held at Sabzevar, fearing that they would become a focus for a Safavid restoration.

Before returning to the Persian hinterland, however, Nader led his army to Bokhara and Khwarazm, and having defeated the rulers of Turkistan he conquered the whole of Transoxiana, which had not been part of a unified Persian empire since the Achaemenids. On his return, he moved the capital from Isfahan to Mashhad, which was closer to his Central Asian empire.

In March 1741 Nader set out to punish the rebellious Lezgis of Dagestan (Daghistan), who had defeated and killed his brother. On the way there a shot was fired at him in Mazandaran. He believed that the attempt had been prompted by his son Rezaqoli, whom he therefore ordered to be blinded in both eyes. The campaign in Dagestan did not pay off. Two years of constant fighting yielded no victory, and Nader had to withdraw without having suppressed the rebels.

There was ebb and flow in Nader's relationship with the Ottomans. In the summer of 1743, not long after the failure in Dagestan, he laid siege to Mosul, but had to give up and send troops to suppress rebellions in Iran while he himself went for a visit to Imam Ali's shrine in Iraq. He suggested a religious settlement to the Ottomans whereby Iran would remain Sunni (as he believed was the case) and the Ottomans should accept the school of law of the Sixth Shia Imam, Ja'ar al-Sadiq, as valid as the four schools – Hanafi, Shafi'i, Maliki and Hanbali – to which the Sunnis adhered. In fact, this was no more acceptable to the Ottomans than the imposition of Sunnism to the Iranians.

Domestic rebellions having been suppressed, Nader reopened the war with the Ottomans, but in the end the 1746 treaty confirmed the settlement of the 1639 peace treaty regarding the frontiers between the two countries (see Chapter 5). Meanwhile, Nader's oppression and cruelty were increasing by the day. While on his way to suppress a rebellion in Sistan he showed signs of mental imbalance in Isfahan. Having crushed the revolt in Sistan, he went to Mashhad and became so fierce and unpredictable that even his family and others close to him were in fear of their lives. From there he led his forces to quell a rebellion in Khabushan (Quchan), and thinking that his life was in danger from the Persian commanders of his army, he ordered the Abdali Afghans, whom he trusted, to massacre them all. The order somehow leaked out and before it could be implemented some of his Persian military chiefs attacked and killed him in his tent in 1747. He died a universally feared and hated man.

Nader's nephew Aliqoli Khan quickly took the crown for himself. He took personal responsibility for the murder of his uncle and cancelled taxes for three years, knowing that both actions would bring him popularity. He ordered the slaughter of Nader's blind son and other Afsharid males of Nader's descent, and spared only his youthful grandson, Shahrokh. He then crowned himself as Alishah Adelshah (Alishah the Just), but was soon deposed and blinded by his brother Ebrahim, who in 1748 crowned himself in Tabriz. Ebrahim was even worse than his brother and unsuccessfully tried to capture and kill Shahrokh, but was soon killed by his own soldiers, his brother Alishah also dying in the process. In 1749 Shahrokh was declared shah in Mashhad, was deposed and blinded five months later on suspicion of wishing to restore Sunnism, but his supporters soon deposed and blinded the man who had deposed and blinded him, and restored him to the throne later in 1749. He was to rule in Khorasan until Aqa Mohammad Khan Qajar captured Mashhad in 1795 and tortured him to death.

KARIM KHAN AND THE ZANDS

Persia fell from Nader's organized chaos into lawlessness and disintegration. In June 1750 Alimardan Khan of the Bakhtiyari tribe captured Isfahan and appointed a descendant of Soltan-hosein as a puppet shah. Among his military chiefs was Karim Khan Zand, a Lor of humble origin who had been a commander in Nader's army. Alimardan Khan and Karim Khan Zand soon fell out with each other. The Bakhtiyari chief was killed by another khan and the Lor leader became the undisputed ruler of the south-west.

Ahmad Khan, leader of Nader's Abdali troops, had taken Qandahar, and with the title of Dorrani had declared himself shah of Afghanistan. He was thus the founder of the Dorrani dynasty in that country, which was overthrown in recent times. The north-west was in the hands of Azad Khan of the Afghan Ghalzeh tribe, who eventually lost to Karim Khan and submitted to him. In the north and north-east Karim Khan's most serious rival was Mohammad Hasan Khan Qajar, son of Fath'ali Khan, who had been put to death by Tahmasp in 1726.

The Qajars were a confederation of tribes in the Caucasus, originally part of the Central Asian Oghuz or Ghozz Turkamans (see Chapter 4). They were an important contingent in the Qezelbash confederacy, the Safavid military elite, two branches of whom were dispersed and relocated by Shah Abbas I, one to Marv and the other to the Gorgan area. The branch that was sent to Marv lost their identity through time. So did those who remained in Qarabagh in the Caucasus. But the branch settled in the Gorgan area and centred on Astrabad maintained their Qajar identity. The Astrabad Qajars were themselves divided into two tribal groupings: the Ashaqeh-bash, so-called because they occupied the lowland pastures, and the Yokhari-bash, the upstream settlers. The chief clan of the Ashaqeh-bash, from whom the Qajar royal family descended, was the Qoyunlu (flock keepers), that of Yokhari-bash, the Develu (camel herders). There was bitter feuding between the two tribes and their chief clans.

After his father's death, Mohammad Hasan Khan became the Qoyunlu chief and a contender for power, fighting Nader and the Afsharids and, following them, Karim Khan. In 1744 he had attacked and captured Astrabad, but was later defeated by the force that Nader sent against him. Following Nader Shah's death, Mohammad Hasan Khan tried again to capture Astrabad but was defeated by Nader's nephew, Adelshah, who captured his six-year-old son Mohammad and had him castrated after receiving pleas not to kill him.

However, Mohammad Hasan Khan remained a serious contender for power and at one stage, in 1756–7, he ruled much of north, north-west and central Persia. But his assault on Shiraz from Isfahan failed and, while in retreat, he was pursued by one of Karim Khan's ablest military commanders. Trying to reach Astrabad, he was betrayed by the Develu chief among his commanders and was killed while trying to escape. Some of his sons were confined to Qazvin while others, including the castrated Aqa Mohammad Khan and his full brother Hoseinqoli Khan, were taken hostage in Shiraz.

Karim Khan treated Aqa Mohammad Khan and his brothers well and sometimes sought the Aqa's counsel in dealing with matters of state, recognizing his intelligence and astuteness in assessing problems and situations. On his part, he did not waste the twenty years of his virtual captivity and, as well as gaining Karim Khan's confidence, familiarized himself with Zand chiefs and their open and hidden conflicts, partly with the help of an aunt who was in Karim Khan's harem. A decade after they had been made hostage, Karim Khan sent Hoseinqoli Khan as governor to Damghan. He set about seeking vengeance against his father's Develu enemies, with the result that he earned the title Jahansuz (World Burner) for burning down the Develu fortress, but was killed in the end, leaving a young son who became the future Fath'ali Shah. Had he survived he might have had a better claim for leading the Qajars, given that Aqa Mohammad Khan had been castrated.

With the death of Mohammad Hasan Khan, Karim Khan became the ruler of Iran, with the exception of Khorasan, which was being ruled by the blind Afsharid Shahrokh, and of course Afghanistan, which had in effect declared independence, although conflict over the possession of Herat was to continue until the mid-nineteenth century. Yet Karim Khan had to deal with intermittent Qajar revolts and was not the undisputed master of the Caspian provinces. He ruled from 1759 until his death in 1779, calling himself Vakil or Deputy and pretending to rule on behalf of the Safavid puppet, Isma'il III, who died in 1773. By all accounts he was a good-natured ruler and the two decades of his rule brought relative peace and security to those parts of the country which were in his possession. But all was not fair and even-handed, and some of his military chiefs, notably his half-brother Zaki Khan, behaved with memorable barbarity towards the conquered and vanquished.

Karim's foreign relations were relatively eventless. He allowed the British East India Company a monopoly of foreign trade from Bushehr, where they moved from Bandar Abbas. He also allowed the Dutch East India Company to move to Kharg Island from Basra, where they had got into conflict with the Ottoman authorities, but because of piratical operations against them they did not stay long on the island, and left the Persian Gulf for ever. The French East India Company obtained agreement to move from Basra to Kharg Island, but also failed to take advantage of it.

Relations with the country's Ottoman neighbours were fair until 1774 when a clash broke out between the two countries on two fronts. The Ottoman governor of Baghdad had tried to reduce Persia's influence in a part of Kurdistan, now in Iraq, while ignoring repeated Persian complaints about the mistreatment of Iranian pilgrims to Shiite shrines in Iraq. Karim Khan sent a force to Kurdistan and another to Basra, led by his brother Sadeq Khan, who captured the city after a long siege. Four years later, however, Sadeq Khan abandoned Basra and rushed back to Shiraz on hearing the news of Karim Khan's death.

A number of buildings and monuments remain in Shiraz from Karim Khan's time, of which the imposing royal citadel (the Arg), the Mosque of Vakil and the Bazaar of Vakil are the most prominent. He also built public utility buildings such as caravanserais and renovated others, including important shrines and tombs.

Karim Khan's death was followed by the usual chaos, scramble for succession and fratricide of the first order. After the first round of bloodshed, Zaki Khan took charge, and when his half-brother Sadeq Khan approached Shiraz with his army to press his claim, his army deserted him after Zaki Khan threatened reprisals on their families in the city. Meanwhile the Qajar hostage, Aqa Mohammad Khan, had fled north and Zaki Khan sent Alimorad Khan in pursuit. Alimorad Khan rebelled in Isfahan and when Zaki Khan led an army to suppress him he was killed by his own troops on the way. Taking advantage of the event Sadeq Khan returned and occupied Shiraz, but eight months later the city fell to Alimorad Khan, who had Sadeq Khan and all but one of his sons, Ja'far, murdered.

Thus in 1781 Alimorad Khan became the undisputed Zand ruler, basing himself in Isfahan and campaigning against Aqa Mohammad Qajar, who had meanwhile subdued the north, and later the south and the south-east, and become a great menace to Zand rule. By 1785 he had conquered much of the Persian hinterland, but Fars, the Persian Gulf littoral, Khorasan, parts of Azerbaijan and the Caucasus were still beyond his control. He made Tehran his capital in 1786, mainly for strategic reasons, and eventually subdued the whole of the country.

In 1785, while Alimorad Khan was campaigning in Mazandarn, Ja'far Khan, Sadeq Khan's surviving son, rebelled and took Isfahan. Rushing back to reclaim his capital Alimorad Khan died en route. Four years later Ja'far Khan, who had lost north and central Persia to Aqa Mohammad Khan, was killed by some of his own supporters, who had mutinied in response to his treacherous behaviour. He was succeeded by the young Lotf'ali Khan.

THE RISE OF QAJAR POWER

The last of the Zands, Lotf'ali Khan, was noted for his courage and chivalry but lacked the kind of ability and tact which was needed for dealing with the able, fearless, cunning and pitiless Qajar chief. He lost support rapidly in a series of typically short confrontations, which ended in his defeat and tragic death in 1794. A crucial factor was the defection of his chief ally, Hajji Ebrahim Kalantar, 'Mayor' of Shiraz – later entitled E'temad al-Dawleh – to the Qajar chief, mainly perhaps because he saw the writing on the wall for his master.

Lotf'ali Khan's last stand was in the ancient city of Kerman, whose inhabitants paid a terrifying price by standing firm against Aqa Mohammad's long siege and even taunting him personally by regularly shouting 'Aqa Mohammad Khan-e Akhteh' ('the Castrated') from the city's keeps. Reports vary about the number of Kermani people who were killed, blinded and taken into slavery after the fall of the city through treachery. But they all run into tens of thousands. It took more than a century for the town to recover from the consequences of Aqa Mohammad Khan's wrath and barbarity.

Aqa Mohammad Khan subdued his opponents both within the Qajars and across the country with efficiency, ruthlessness and cruelty, but was welcomed for bringing peace and stability, which after all was the most important component of the Iranian concept of 'justice' and 'the just ruler' under arbitrary rule. He suppressed his rivals and opponents among the Qajars – he even killed his brother and comrade-in-arms Ja'far Qoli. But at the same time he used tact and diplomacy in trying to integrate the Qajar chiefs into the new kingdom by rewarding those who rallied to his side and encouraging intermarriage between the Qoyunlus and the Develus. He married off his nephew and heir-designate Baba Khan Jahanbani, later Fath'ali Shah, to a daughter of the powerful Develu chief, Mohammad Khan Beglerbegi, who in turn married off his own heir-designate, Abbas Mirza, to another daughter of the same khan. There is a legend that, before Aqa Mohammad's rise to power, the Beglerbegi had declined the offer by his tribe of becoming the Qajar leader in favour of Aqa Mohammad; hence the fact that his descendants adopted the surname Tajbakhsh ('Donor of the Crown') in the twentieth century. However that may be, these measures did not quite remove the old feud between Qoyunlus and Develus, and it was to flare up again under Mohammad Shah.

Thus the Qajar khan reunited the country and put an end to widespread marauding and pillage. He also began the process of making the roads safer, the peasants less liable to suffer regular looting, towns more immune from chaos and normal productive and commercial activities less hazardous, which was to continue under his nephew and successor. He put down all claimants to autonomous power and recaptured Khorsan from its blind Afsharid ruler, Shahrokh, whom he tortured savagely so that he would reveal the hiding place of his treasures; but Shahrokh died from the ordeal, having given up his secrets.

Aqa Mohammad Khan's last great military campaign was in Georgia, which had in effect slipped out of Persian suzerainty since the death of Nader. The campaign ended in the massacre, in 1795, of the people of Tiflis after the town was captured, and 15,000 souls were taken into slavery. Aqa Mohammad Khan was crowned in Tehran the next year. During his last campaign in the Caucasus, in 1797, he was assassinated by three of his slaves whom he had vowed to have executed the next day. The three were later found and cut into small pieces.

ENCOUNTERS WITH MODERNITY

Baba Khan, who was crowned as Fath'ali Shah, was the son of the late shah's brother, the aforementioned Hoseinqoli Khan, known as Jahansuz on account of his burning down a whole fortress of tribal enemies with the inhabitants inside before meeting his death in another battle. If the father was 'the World Burner', the son was 'the World Founder (Jahanbani)'. Predictably, the death of Aqa Mohammad Khan resulted in turmoil among his troops and in the north-western provinces. Aqa Mohammad Khan's brother Aliqoli rebelled and proclaimed himself shah, but within a short period he fell into Fath'ali's hands, and was then blinded. Shaqaqi Kurds occupied parts of Azerbaijan, but their leader later surrendered and was pardoned after returning the late shah's jewels, which he had taken after his murder. Yet by traditional Iranian standards this chaos and conflict over the succession was relatively limited and soon contained. An important role was played in this by the tact and alertness of Hajji Ebrahim Kalantar, now known as E'temad al-Dawleh ('Confidence of the Crown'), in holding the fort while Fath'ali moved up north from Shiraz. Perhaps inevitably, Hajji Ebrahim and his family later fell victims to one of Fath'ali's purges, partly in consequence of the former's astuteness; the shah is quoted as saying that as long as the vizier was around, his own authority would be contingent.

Aqa Mohammad Khan's and Fath'ali Shah's achievements in state building had had no match since the Safavids. Despite the fact that the Qajar eunuch was a fierce and relentless worrier, he, like his father, had aspired to building up a kingdom and dynasty comparable to the Safavids', and had the foresight and ruthlessness to remove the potential barriers to its achievement. Following his death, his nephew Fath'ali Shah went on to revive ancient traditions of court splendour and protocol. He was pleasure-seeking, unheroic and avaricious, but it was partly due to fundamental changes in global and regional circumstances that his reign was not a glorious one. He was quite capable of cruelty when he was sufficiently frightened or angered, but was not a cruel ruler by the standards of previous history.

Fath'ali Shah was in fact a poet (and has a published *Divan*), and in encouraging and patronizing poets and poetry he followed the traditions of pre-Safavid rulers and royal courts. According to an anecdote, in a poetry reading session at the court the shah recited a piece by himself and asked the leading court poet's opinion of it. The court poet was not very impressed, so the shah became angry and ordered him to be held in the royal stables for a while. Some time later, at another poetry reading, the shah once again read one of his poem and asked the court poet what he thought. The latter quietly rose and began to walk towards the door. When the shah wondered what he was doing, he replied: 'Sire I am going to the royal stables.'

It can be argued that Iran entered the modern era from the accession of Fath'ali Shah, although it took another century before movements for modernization began to attract popular appeal. Iran's encounters with modernity began with her perennial military conflicts with Russia, which also led to closer contacts with Britain and – to a lesser extent – other European powers. Iran was thus introduced to modern techniques of warfare, modern technology and, above all, the European systems of law and government which it tried to adopt with little material success, although it was inevitably affected by the actions and reactions involved in the process. In the first half of the nineteenth century, however, before the reign of Naser al-Din Shah, the impact of modern technology was most keenly felt in military techniques and organization. Seen by contemporary observers, whether Iranian or non-Iranian, Persia was still as deeply traditional as it had been in previous centuries.

The reign of Fath'ali Shah saw the emergence and rivalry of two powerful European empires, those of Britain and Russia, in Iran and the inauguration of the great imperial game, which was to continue in various forms for the next one hundred and fifty years. The Russo-Persian wars first broke out in 1804. At first, British contact was intended mainly to contain Napoleon's influence in Iran. With Napoleon out of the way and Britain's power emerging in the Persian Gulf, British policy focused on the maintenance of the status quo. Britain was also anxious to forestall Russian expansion, which would have resulted from a state of chaos in Iran, and to seal off Afghanistan from Qajar rule, since in Britain's view Russian advance towards India might be assisted by the cooperation of the Qajar court. It may be tempting to think that, had the Iranians grasped the issues sufficiently well, they could have played a better diplomatic game in defending their interests, but at least some of Iran's growing dependence on the two empires was in the circumstances unavoidable.

According to some twentieth-century Iranian historians the decline of Iran in the nineteenth century was simply due to lack of intelligence and wisdom on the part of her rulers as well as corruption, caprice and lack of patriotism. This view over-looks the very fundamental problem of Iranian society since ancient times. Structurally, as has been noted, Iran lacked the long-term stability and predictability which was necessary for a stable and loyal administrative system. Long before Iran became categorically unequal with her imperial neighbours, the shah's principal concern had been to maintain his power and authority in the face of the endemic danger of being undermined by disloyalty and rebellion; and the concern of the vizier and governors was the permanent threat of deadly intrigue by their rivals, subordinates and retainers. It was a short-term society, and the country was now facing foreign powers which it could not overcome, compete with or neutralize, and could only try to play one against the other in the hope of moderating their power and influence.

And it was traditional fear for their lives and property, rather than any lack of patriotism or 'treachery' in its post-Constitutional (European) sense, which drove some Iranian officials to court the favour and protection of British and Russian diplomats in their country, some of them even placing themselves under their protection to secure their lives, although their property still remained insecure. From ancient times, such insecurity and unpredictability of life and fortune had also been the source of the Iranian conspiracy theory of politics and other social events and phenomena, when nothing was believed to be quite as it appeared to be and every phenomenon had to have a hidden, 'true', explanation (see Introduction). This conspiratorial instinct was simply necessary for survival, affording protection via the art of striking first at the slightest suspicion. From the mid-nineteenth century the conspiracy theory was most frequently applied to interpreting the actions and motives of the great powers, largely because they were, or rather they were perceived to be, the most powerful players in the Iranian game.

As noted in the foregoing chapter, there had been brushes with the emerging Russian empire since the reign of Peter the Great, putting aside the traditional intrusions of Russian and other raiders across Iran's northern borders. After the fall of the Safavids the Russians had occupied some of the north-western provinces, even at times the north-central Caspian provinces. Nader Shah put an end to that. But it had become Russia's policy to extend its rule to the Caucasus. Georgia, a Christian principality with a sizeable Muslim minority, had been a vassal state of Iran under the Safavids. With the expansion of the Russian empire Georgian rulers preferred to be under Russian protection.

The Russian empress Catherine the Great would have taken action against Aqa Mohammad's assault on Tiflis had she not had her hands tied with other foreign conflicts; and though she died shortly afterwards, late in 1799 Russian troops entered Tiflis, abolished the Georgian principality and annexed the territory. The Iranians were alarmed and began to woo Britain and France for support. The latter countries were themselves involved in conflict, sometimes with and sometimes against Russia. Various French and British missions came, but eventually it was Britain which became Iran's countervailing power to Russia, first because Napoleon changed course after the Franco-Russian treaty of Tilsit (1807) and then because he lost the European war.

In 1802 Prince Tsitsianov became Russian commissioner for the Caucasus. He regarded the Persians as 'Asiatic', Muslims and inferior people, although his own behaviour was far from civilized even by the then European standards. The subsequent Russian commanders in the region, Yermolov and Paskevich, were perhaps a little less arrogant but no less aggressive. Tsitsianov's deliberate encroachment on Iranian territory led to war in 1804. Protracted war continued until the Iranians sued for peace via British mediation and signed the Golestan treaty in 1813. Most of the Caucasus was ceded to Russia, and only the Russians could keep a fleet in the Caspian Sea.

The Golestan treaty humiliated the shah and his heir-designate Abbas Mirza, Prince Regent and governor-general of Azerbaijan, who led the Persian armies and conducted the negotiations on the spot. It also hurt the feelings of the people and the ulama, because of the subjugation of the Caucasian Muslims by a Christian power and reports of their harsh treatment under the Russian generals. Abbas Mirza perhaps did not regard the 1813 peace as more than a truce. His rival brothers and others jealous of him tried to blame him for defeat. In particular, the shah's eldest son, Mohammad Ali Mirza Dawlatshah, governor-general of the western regions, who displayed personal characteristics of great courage and ruthlessness resembling Aqa Mohammad, both led military expeditions against the Ottomans (even without authority from Tehran) to prove his superiority and levelled charges of ineptitude and spinelessness against Abbas Mirza. Mohammad Ali Mirza died in 1821 of cholera, but pressure for the renewal of hostilities remained.

Abbas Mirza led the campaign in 1826. His attitude towards the renewal of war seems to have been ambivalent, but his able and trusted minister Mirza Abolqasem Qa'em-Maqam was opposed to the conflict. On the other hand, his maternal uncle and the shah's son-in-law, the powerful Develu chief Allahyar

Khan Asef al-Dawleh, was in favour of war and led an army into the Caucasus. Russian encroachment along the uncertain border had continued, and persecuted Muslims were pouring across the border, asking the ulama, both in the *atabat* holy shrines in Iraq and in Iran, to intervene. And so they did, with great vigour. Helped by British officers, Abbas Mirza organized a new army, *Nezam-e Jadid*, along European lines. The Persians were also banking on direct help from Britain on the basis of the Anglo-Persian treaty of 1814, but it did not materialize.

The campaign ended in disastrous defeat. The Russians entered Tabriz in the wake of a popular uprising in the town against the same Allahyar Khan who had fallen back and become governor of Tabriz: this was an example of the people rising against the government at any opportunity that promised success. Allahyar Khan did not resist and was captured while trying to escape, a lack of gallantry which Qa'em-Maqam noted in a scathing poem as 'That disrupter of peace and runner from war' (*an solh beh ham barzan o az jang beh dar zan*). Negotiations for peace led to the signing of the treaty of Turkamanchai in 1828, by which the whole of the Caucasus was permanently ceded to Russia, this time including the khanates of Nakhchivan and Erivan (Yerevan), and an indemnity of one million roubles was paid. The capitulation agreement gave Russia extra-territorial rights in Iran for the voluntary repatriation and legal protection of its subjects as well as former subjects of the Russian empire. In compensation to Abbas Mirza, Russia endorsed his succession to the throne. This was a further setback for Persian sovereignty; but it was consistent with the historical fact that rulers could not guarantee the succession of their heir-designates. In time, capitulation rights were also granted to Britain. The decline of Persia as an independent state began from 1828.

Fath'ali Shah's death in 1834 ended a reign which had seen Iran's first encounter with and responses to the consequences of modernization and industrialization in Europe. The experience was all the more extraordinary because nothing in Iranian tradition could make sense of the sources, the origins and the logic of the new phenomenon. Never before had Iranian rulers faced a power which it apparently could never match either in open conflict or through peaceful diplomacy. At first they regarded the problem at its most obvious level, the difference in military technology, structure and organization. Hence Abbas Mirza's well-intentioned rush to raise his new army, a fashion which was copied to a more limited extent by his father and his two rival brothers, Mohammad Ali Mirza in Kermanshah and Hosein'ali Mirza in Fars. It proved ineffective, partly because of insufficient funds and partly for lack of experience. Besides, since the death of Aqa Mohammad Khan, there was a general decline in the country's military power, which was to continue throughout the nineteenth century.

It has even been suggested that Abbas Mirza's force proved to be less effective in its modern form when facing the Russians, because the traditional tribal levies and provincial militias were much better at the less formal and disciplined tactics and manoeuvres. However that may be, it is true that such partial changes could not be of much consequence unless there were corresponding changes in other key aspects of society. Put simply, it would not be easy to have an orderly, disciplined and efficient army in a functionally disorderly, undisciplined and inefficient system. It took half a century for some leading intellectual and administrative figures in Qajar society to see the problem and begin to advocate change in the direction of lawful government and orderly society. The climax was the Constitutional Revolution, followed by a century of modernization, reform and revolution, but the central, fundamental, goal of law-based government and orderly society had yet to be realized.

The Russian humiliation of the Persians met its match in 1829 by the massacre of Alexander Griboyedov and his suite. A very promising writer, Griboyedov had been implicated in the Russian Decembrist Plot of 1825 but acquitted afterwards. He had been Russian chargé in Tabriz and diplomatic advisor in Tiflis before he arrived in Tehran as minister plenipotentiary. His immediate task was the implementation of the Treaty of Turkamanchai, notably the collection of the war indemnity and repatriation of subjects of territories now in Russian hands who wished to return. The mission had behaved badly on its way from Tabriz to Tehran, extorting goods and money from villagers and behaving arbitrarily towards Persians with Christian wives, sometimes trying to forcibly divorce and repatriate Armenian and Georgian women who had married Iranian Muslims.

Griboyedov had barely arrived in Tehran when Mirza Ya'qub, a converted Armenian eunuch at the royal court, asked to be repatriated. The problem was compounded when two Armenian women were removed from Allahyar Khan Asef al-Dawleh's house to decide whether or not they too wished to be repatriated. They were removed by none other than the man who in fact had arrested and humiliated Allahyar Khan in Tabriz. It was, however, not just the shah's and Allahyar Khan's honour and pride that had been gravely hurt. The incident was the first test in Tehran of the results of the capitulation agreement in the Treaty of Turkamanchai. In public eyes, not only had Griboyedov and his staff violated the harems of the shah and his son-in-law but they had also attacked the integrity of Islam and the Muslim community. They demanded the intervention of the ulama, and the latter eventually responded. But Griboyedov was still adamant that the letter of the treaty had to be observed.

A large mob gathered outside the Russian legation and demanded that Ya'qub and the women be handed over. Ya'qub was delivered and hacked to death, and the women were released. The violence would have ended there had it not been for the bullet of a Cossack shooting from a rooftop which hit and killed a youth of sixteen. Jihad was declared and the mob went on the offensive. More than forty Russians and eighty Iranians lost their lives in the conflict, only one member of the Russian mission surviving to tell the story.

The government had in fact felt helpless in stopping the mob but it appeared as if it had been behind the attack, or had acquiesced in it once it had begun. Yet the spectacle of an Iranian ruler, however strong, feeling helpless before an urban revolt, and especially one driven by religious and national feelings, is a familiar story in Iranian history both before and after this event, at least in the short period in which the rebels are angry and united over a single purpose.

After the attack had died down there were retributions against some of its perpetrators, which included the execution of a few civilians and the banishment of a
leading Tehran *mojtahed*. The shah sent a high-level delegation to St Petersburg to
offer fabulous gifts and profuse apologies for the incident. Tsar Nicholas I obliged
and the matter was relegated 'to eternal oblivion'. Griboyedov became a hero later
in Russian history in no small part because of his promise of a great literary future
which he did not live to fulfil. Many Russian and Soviet historians, followed by
Iranians, claimed that the whole incident had been instigated by the British to give
a bloody nose to their Russian rivals. But such theories are familiar both in Russian
and Iranian history.

There were clashes with other, less powerful, neighbours as well, with more
honourable results. In 1820, following a few border clashes and intrusions, war
was formally declared between Iran and Turkey, the shah's sons Abbas Mirz and
Mohammad Ali Mirza invading Ottoman territory from Tabriz and Kermanshah.
The latter died of cholera in the meantime, but Abbas Mirza repelled the Ottoman
counter-attack in May 1822, when a cholera epidemic raging in his army made
him opt for peace, which was signed two months later. In 1818 another of the
shah's sons, who was prince governor of Khorasan, defeated an Afghan force in
Toprak Qal'eh.

As noted above, despite the defeats and humiliations in foreign wars and relations, Fath'ali Shah's reign was one of the most peaceful and stable since the fall of
the Safavids. His court's splendour and strict protocol was such that they
impressed even some of his English visitors, who were used to high standards in
both London and Delhi. He patronized poetry and painting, in part because of his
appreciation of literature and the arts and in part to satisfy his vanity by having
himself praised in portraits, paintings and panegyrics. He had bas-reliefs of
himself and his sons made in rocks near Tehran and in Persepolis in the style of
ancient Sasanian rulers. There were significant developments in poetry and prose
in relation to the previous century. Both European-style and Persian miniature
painting flourished, though no outstanding masters emerged in either discipline.
Much that survives of the architecture of the period in fact consists of the royal
mosques in Tehran and other cities, much of the royal compound (the Golestan
Palace) having been demolished in the Pahlavi era.

Fath'ali Shah patronized religious institutions, seyyeds and *mojtaheds*, and his
reign saw the rise of the autonomous power of the Shia ulama, first in the *atabat*
then in Isfahan, Tehran and elsewhere. The ulama often benefited from the state
and even intermarried with the Qajar nobility and higher state officials; some of
them, the Imam Jom'ehs and sheikholeslams in particular, were semi-official religious dignitaries. Nevertheless, they were seen by the people as the countervailing power to the state, as leaders of the people (*ro'asa-ye mellat*) as opposed
to chief officers of the state (*ro'asa-ye dawlat*), and they used their power as inter-
mediaries between the people and their rulers.

The ulama regarded the state essentially as usurping the kingdom of God,
which could be legitimately ruled only by the sinless Imam. This was old Shia

theory, but it was also consistent with the ancient Iranian tradition of the people regarding state power as illegitimate. Their ambivalent relationship with the state was not due to hatred of the Qajars, as some historians have believed, nor to any special sense of social fairness of the ulama as such. In any case, their relationship with the public was two-sided: in their turn, the urban populace, especially the merchant and bazaar community, provided a social base for the ulama, paying them their religious dues and giving them support whenever they confronted the state. The novelty was that the ulama in the nineteenth century enjoyed a degree and level of autonomous power that they had never quite experienced before.

The origins of the rise of the power of the ulama is not easy to discern. On the theoretical plane, the triumph of the Osulis over the Akhbaris was certainly instrumental. The Akhbaris maintained that the principal source of guidance was the tradition of sinless imams, as received through *akhbar*, the traditional body of knowledge on their thoughts and actions. The Oslulis by contrast advocated the necessity of *ejtehad* (rational interpretations of *fiqh*, the religious law) by the ulama and of *taqlid*, the emulation by the faithful of such interpretations and pronouncements issued by a *mojtahed*, that is a *faqih* recognized by his learning and piety. Thus the Osuli view placed the ulama in a pivotal position, providing them with legitimate authority to pronounce opinions which might even conflict with the rules, ordinances and decisions of the state. But it was recognized that one *mojtahed*'s opinion may be different from, even sometimes conflict with, another *mojtahed*'s, the opinions of each being incumbent upon his own followers or *moqalled*s among the Shia community.

The Osuli–Akhbari conflict had its origins in the centuries before the rise of the Qajars, but its sharpening in the eighteenth century and the ultimate triumph of the Osulis was not entirely incidental. The Safavids had had a claim to Shia legitimacy both because of the belief that they descended from the Seventh Imam and because of their establishment of Shiism as the majority and state religion. The ulama were largely dependent on the state both for finance and for public authority, and there could be no question of actual, let alone active, autonomy from the state, though, as noted, their influence substantially increased towards the end of the Safavid rule. It was therefore no mere accident that the Osulis began to gain ground during the post-Safavid interregnum and rapidly rose to supremacy towards the end of the eighteenth century, led by Aqa Mohammad Baqer Behbahni (d. 1791) and his son Mirza Mohammad (d. 1801), who were based in Najaf.

In part this was due to the virtual autonomy of the Shia cities under the Ottomans, where the *hawzeh* of Najaf grew powerful as a result of the decline of Isfahan, itself a consequence of the long-standing chaos in the eighteenth century; in part it was a product of Aqa Mohammad Khan's and Fath'ali Shah's deference to religious institutions and dignitaries and need for their support, unsuspecting that this would lead to the creation of a rival authority to the state. From Mohammad Shah (Fath'ali Shah's successor) onwards the ulama's power

became too entrenched to be dislodged, and all successive rulers and governments could do was to try to contain their power, usually by favours and
ultimately by force. The ulamas' ascent culminated in their leadership of the
Tobacco Revolt of 1891–2, the triumph of which raised their power and
authority to levels not experienced before (see Chapters 7 and 8).

The administrative system created by Fath'ali Shah was highly decentralized.
Provincial governors virtually had a free hand in their seats of power so long as
they observed the various requirements of the central authority, whether explicit
or implicit. Government was absolute and arbitrary both in the centre and in the
provinces. The difference was that all power was vested in the centre, in the
person of the shah, by whom the governors were appointed and sacked at will,
despite the large amount of freedom they enjoyed while they remained in the
shah's favour. On one or two occasions the prince governors came to blows with
each other, sometimes to the amusement of their royal father. Virtually all of
them were the shah's own sons (and later grandsons), the many who were born
to different wives and concubines, those under age being accompanied by a tutor
or minister to help him run his office. The decentralization therefore was not one
of power but of administration, unlike the situation in feudal Europe, where the
power of the barons in their domains was largely independent of the king's.

State officials and their functions were similar to what they had been under the
Safavids and before them. Fath'ali Shah had five chief ministers, the first being Hajji
Ebrahim, whom, as we have seen, he had killed together with his family. Of the
remaining four, two were generally men of learning and ability, though none was
outstanding. The third was Allahyar Khan Asef al-Dawleh, whose appointment
was unusual because he was both noble and a military commander, the fourth
being the colourful, pragmatic, desolate and amoral Mirza Abolhasan Khan Ilchi,
who had been an ambassador to London and provided the model for James
Morier's *Hajji Baba of Isfahan*. The most outstanding civil servants of the period
were Mirza Isa and, even more, his son Mirza Abolqsem, both entitled Qa'em-
Maqam, who served as Abbas Mirza's minister in succession. The financial administration was run by *mostawfi*s or auditors headed by Mostawfi al-Mamalek, the
chief auditor. The position of *mostawfi*s involved longer and more secure tenure
than was enjoyed by most other servants of the state because of the particular skill
involved, which required long training and experience.

It must be pointed out that the peace and stability gained under Fath'ali Shah
was relative, measured against Iranian conditions and especially the chaos of the
eighteenth century. Otherwise there seldom was a year which did not see one or
more revolt and rebellion, the last major disturbances occurring in the north-east:
this was put down severely by Abbas Mirza, who had been made governor-general
of Khorasan but who died in Tehran shortly afterwards, having ordered his son
Mohammad Mirza in Mashhad to prepare for an expedition against Herat. The
shah went to Isfahan three times to forestall rebellions in the southern and central
provinces, in which his son Hosein'ali Mirza Farmanfarma, prince governor of Fars
had been suspected of complicity. He died there on his third visit, in 1834.

MOHAMMAD SHAH'S INTERREGNUM

Fath'ali Shah's death was followed by the familiar struggle over the succession. Early in 1834 he had appointed as heir-designate Mohammad Mirza, the eldest son of Abbas Mirza, who had died the year before aged forty-four. This was partly consistent with Aqa Mohammad Khan's original design that the dynasty should pass on to the family of Abbas Mirza, whose mother as well as wife had been Develu; partly in recognition of Abbas Mirza's contributions and untimely death; and partly in keeping with the Turkamanchai treaty. Nevertheless, Fath'ali Shah's death brought the revolt of Alishah Zel al-Soltan, Mohammad's uncle and governor of Tehran, who literally proposed to him to divide the country between them; but he surrendered after his nephew's triumphant march from Tabriz with the support of the British and Russian envoys. At the same time Fath'ali Shah's senior son and long-standing aspirer to the throne, Hosein'ali Mirza Farmanfarma, governor-general of Fars, proclaimed himself shah, aided by his full brother Hasan'ali Mirza Shoja' al-Saltaneh, governor-general of Isfahan. They were defeated in the ensuing civil war. The former died (probably killed) soon in captivity; the latter was blinded together with another of the shah's uncles, the handsome Khosraw Mirza, who together with all other rebels and suspects were imprisoned in the Ardebil citadel. Apart from that, and as usual, the mere news of the shah's death, which was announced only after his body was rushed from Isfahan to Qom, where it was put to rest, led to regional insurgencies, the worst of which shook the western regions for some time.

In putting down these typical *fetnehs* after a shah's death, the able but unpopular chief minister, Qa'em Maqam, played a very important role. But it did not take long for Mohammad Shah to feel threatened by the power of the vizier and have him put to death, despite the fact that he was a mild and meek ruler and inclined towards Sufism. There is a gruesome, but significant, legend that the shah had the vizier strangled to death, because before Mohammad's succession, they had sworn an oath that neither would 'spill the other's blood'. The significance is, first, in the need for such oaths, usually by both parties holding the Koran as witness; second, the fact that they were easily broken, even though in this case the letter of the oath was observed. The shah's tutor and mentor Hajji Mirza Aghasi and his wife Malak Jahan Khanom were also instrumental in the demise of the vizier.

The fourteen years of Mohammad Shah's rule may almost be described as an interregnum. It was volatile as regards court intrigue, foreign relations and provincial chaos, but otherwise almost static. There was a shift of emphasis in foreign relations to greater reliance on Russia than Britain now that Russian territorial ambitions towards Iran had been satisfied, but Britain was determined to thwart Iranian ambitions towards Afghan lands. Russia encouraged Iran to reach an entente with Kabul and Qandahar and to assert her traditional sovereignty over Herat. Mohammad Shah's siege of Herat in 1837 was abandoned in the following year as a result of intense pressure by the British. The envoys of both powers were regularly involved in the usual court intrigues, not least regarding the question of the succession.

Naser al-Din Mirza, the shah's eldest son by the wilful Malak Jahan Khanom (later entitled Mahd-e Olya), his first wife of Qoyunlu descent, was heir apparent and governor-general of Azebaijan. The shah's full brothers, Qahreman Mirza (d. 1839) and Bahman Mirza (d. 1884 in exile) were favoured by the imperial envoys as regents and possibly successors in the event of the shah's death. Hajji Mirza Aghasi, who had succeeded Qae'm-Maqam as chief minister, courted the shah's favourite son, Abbas Mirza, the little boy whom the shah had named after his father and given the latter's title of Prince Regent. As chief minister Hajji was bound to be unpopular. But his most powerful detractors at court were Malak Jahan Khanom, who was concerned about her son's succession, and Allahyar Khan Asef al-Dawleh, the Develu chief and shah's uncle who had once been chief minister and still aspired to that office. As governor-general of Khorasan, Allahyar Khan was restless and scornful, and this led to his honourable exile to *atabat,* from which he never returned. His son Hasan Khan Salar later rebelled before the shah's death, and was put down by Amir Kabir afterwards (see above and Chapter 7).

By the time of Mohammad Shah's succession the ulama had acquired a large degree of independent authority. But because of Fath'ali Shah's normally good relations with them, this did not lead to ongoing tension between ulama and state. On the other hand, Mohammad Shah's spiritual leanings were very much influenced by his strong Sufi beliefs and loyalty to his mentor and chief minister Hajji Mirza Aghasi, who was likewise a Sufi. Theirs was a firm religious and Islamic form of Sufism, but inevitably there was some shift in state patronage from the ulama and colleges to the Sufis and *khaneqahs,* and this was one important factor in clouding the relationship between the ulama and the state. Thus, while the ulama had been suspicious of Mohammad Shah's father Abbas Mirza on account of his apparent adoption of European ways, they were also critical of the son, who was pious but an adherent of Sufism. Another factor which influenced the ulama's attitude was the widespread unpopularity of Hajji Mirza Aghasi, who as a vizier was almost bound to be unpopular.

The strongest and longest example of state–ulama conflict found expression in the attitude and behaviour in the 1830s of the extremely rich and powerful *mojtahed* Seyyed Mohammad Baqer Shafti in Isfahan. He became virtual ruler of the province, running the city with the aid of the *luti* (ruffian) community. This was a glaring example of chaos in the midst of arbitrary rule. The shah's personal expedition to the city did not alter the situation; after his return, the seyyed's power and autonomy grew even greater. It weakened only upon the appointment of the tough and ruthless Manuchehr Khan (Mo'tamed al-Dawleh), known as Gorji, the Armenian eunuch who in 1834 had stamped out the rebellion of Farmanfarma and his brother with exemplary severity. The seyyed himself was left unmolested, a fact that still bore witness to the exceptional position of the ulama within the state.

Mohammad Shah's rule also saw the rise of the Babi movement. Sheikh Ahmad Ahsa'i was the founder of the Shia doctrine and sect which later became known as

Sheikhi. He preached that although the Twelfth Imam, the messiah or Mahdi (Mehdi) of the Twelver Shiites, was hidden from the material world, his essence was always present in a living person. This is what, centuries earlier, Seyyed Mohammad Mosha'sha' – the founder of the Mosha'sha'iyeh dynasty in Khuzistan – had claimed for himself. Ahsa'i further argued that apart from General Deputyship (*Niyabat-e 'Amm*) of the Imam held by ordinary *mojtaheds*, there would or could also be *Niyabat-e Kass* or Special Deputyship, a *Bab* or door between Him and the Shia community. Sheikh Ahmad was succeeded by Seyyed Kazem Rashti, who advanced similar views.

After Seyyed Kazem Rashti's death the Sheikhi movement divided along three lines. Karim Khan Kermani, the Qajar khan (not of the royal line) and follower of Seyyed Kazem, founded the Karim Khani line. Mirza Shafi' Tabrizi founded another movement, which retained the appellation Sheikhi. The constitutionalist leader, Seqat al-Islam Tabrizi, whom the Russians hanged in Tabriz in 1911 or 1912 in the wake of the fall of the second Majlis (see Chapter 8), was a direct descendant of this Mirza Shafi' and the last prominent leader of the Sheikhis of Tabriz. But the third, the Babi movement, became the most popular of the three. It ended up in confrontation both with the ulama and the state, and its mainstream became a completely new faith: the Baha'i movement.

This was the movement of Seyyed Ali Mohammad Shirazi, known as the Bab, since he declared himself to be the intermediary between the Hidden Imam and the Shia faithful, later saying further that he was the Hidden Imam himself. It was the Bab's appeal to relatively large numbers of people that, in the first place, caused concern both to ulama and state, although the movement also attracted sympathy and support from some members of the ulama, mainly of the lower ranks but including a few *mojtaheds*. Eventually, the Bab was arrested in Shiraz, to be taken to Tehran, but Manuchehr Khan Gorji kept and protected him in Isfahan when the Bab and his captors reached that city on their way. Manuchehr Khan died about six months later and the Bab was taken to Tehran on the request of the Isfahan ulama and on the orders of Hajji Mirza Aghasi, and thence sent off to Tabriz, the seat of Naser al-Din Mirza, the youthful heir apparent. It was there that, according to the letter sent by the prince to his father, the Bab was questioned in front of three leading Tabriz ulama and severely flogged. He was executed in 1850 in the wake of the Babi revolt (see Chapter 7).

The premature death of the lethargic and mystical Mohammad Shah, the inevitable fall of his lacklustre vizier and the succession of the young and dashing Naser al-Din Mirza with the chancellorship of Amir Kabir heralded a hopeful new age; but these hopes were soon shattered.

CHAPTER 7

The Dilemma of Reform and Modernization

All the order and progress ... in Europe ... is due to the existence of law. Therefore, we too have made up our mind to introduce a law and act according to it.

Naser al-Din Shah (1889)

THE PREMATURE DEATH IN 1848 of the ailing Mohammad Shah once again threw the centre into chaos. Hajji Mirza Aghasi, the unpopular chief minister, was in fear of his life. He failed in his bid to maintain his authority and his troops were routed, but he escaped by the skin of his teeth, being allowed safe passage to the *atabat* while forfeiting his large fortune as a matter of course. Tehran was divided between a group of notables who had the support of the queen, Malak Jahan Khanom, and another opposed to them. Each side styled itself as a ruling council, but the arrival of the heir apparent Naser al-Din Mirza from Tabriz put an end to the uncertainty.

Naser al-Din Mirza's triumphant march from Tabriz, organized by his able minister Mirza Taqi Khan Amir Nezam, later entitled Amir Kabir, and supported by the Russian and British envoys, was reminiscent of his father's, led by Qae'm-Maqam, fourteen years before. It ended the chaos in Tehran and inaugurated the long and eventful reign of the new shah. The shah's nine-year-old half-brother, Abbas Mirza, the dead shah's favourite son, would have been blinded had it not been for the intervention of Amir Nezam and the imperial envoys. The boy's house and property, however, were looted.

NASER AL-DIN SHAH: PHASE I (1848–58)

Between 1848 and 1852 Amir Kabir, first Vazir Nezam then Amir Nezam, ruled the country in the shah's name. The shah was young, intelligent, somewhat shy and hopeful. Over time, he became vain and pleasure-seeking but still wishing to make the country stronger through basic administrative reform, the building up of institutions and modernization. Still later, he lost heart in reform and progress and became resigned to a life of hunting and lust for money and women. But he was able, authoritative and self-respecting at home as well as abroad; and he held the country together in such a way that neither his father nor his son could have done had they been in power in the latter half of the nineteenth century. In better times he might even have made a 'just ruler' in the traditional Iranian sense, but the times were decidedly not good for Iran.

Amir Kabir was brilliant as a civil and military administrator, in certain respects comparable with Reza Khan in the twentieth century, although he was highly educated and with a greater imagination, and his hands were considerably tied by the absence of a wide measure of support for state building and modernization. He depended almost entirely on his own ability and the goodwill of the shah, while making powerful enemies among the elite, the ulama as well as large segments of the public. His dependency on the shah as his sole power base is comparable to that of Abdolhosein Teymurtash on Reza Shah, and so when the shah turned against him he had no one to turn to for support (see Chapter 9). Being the most powerful man in the land, the habitual opposition of Iranian society to the state was directed against him while he was in power, although, also characteristically for Iranian society, he became popular, and later was even idolized, after he had fallen and been destroyed.

Son of the head cook of Mirza Isa, Qae'm-Maqam I, he attracted his master's attention as a child and was educated under his care to become an official in the court of the heir apparent in Tabriz. He first came to public notice as a delegate in the long negotiations under Mohammad Shah with the Ottomans over border disputes, which eventually led to the treaty of Erzerum. By the time of the young shah's succession Amir Kabir had his full confidence as well as loyalty, and became chief minister and Atabak, in charge of both civil and military administration.

His vision in so far as it may be discerned from his actions was to stamp out actual or potential revolt and rebellion with an iron fist and centralize the state both horizontally and vertically, that is, both across the country and at the centre.[1] Thus, in 1850, he not only stamped out the Develu Qajar chief Hasan Khan Salar's ongoing rebellion in Khorasan and had him and his brother executed despite the promise of pardon upon their surrender[2] but also suppressed with great severity the revolt of the Bab's followers in Mazandaran, Zanjan and Fars.[3] And he set out to reduce all autonomous power, be it of the provincial magnates, of the ulama, of the court nobility or of dignitaries and officials. The latter, notably Aqa Khan Nuri and Hajji Ali Farrash-bashi (Hajeb al-Dawleh), in time gathered around the shah's mother, now entitled Mahd-e Olya, who, despite Amir Kabir's marriage to her young daughter (Ezzat al-Dawleh), led a deadly campaign against him. According to a legend repeated as fact by Mokhber al-Saltaneh (Mehdiqoli Hedayat), Amir Kabir in turn was trying to prompt the shah to get rid of his mother by a contrived accident.[4] There is also a legend that upon his decision to stop the tradition of taking sanctuary (bast) by those whose life was in danger (usually officials who had fallen out of favour) he was advised to leave at least one sanctuary in which one day he himself might need to take refuge.

Amir Kabir tried to continue Abbas Mirza's military reforms with greater vigour and intensity. Apart from reorganizing the tribal levies, he introduced the *bonicheh* system, whereby every district was obliged to make a contribution to military recruitment. The Dar al-Fonun, which was opened after his demise, had been planned along the lines of the renowned French *ecoles polytechniques*, where European (many of them Austrian) teachers taught military, medical and other sciences as well as modern languages. The impact of Amir Kabir's administrative reforms was felt mainly in the short term and for as long as he was at the helm. They could not have long-term and cumulative effect in a fundamental way so long as they were applied in a short-term, arbitrary state and society. Whether or not he was aware of the necessity of reforming the arbitrary nature of power and introducing government based on law is virtually impossible to know. He certainly did not have the chance to take any steps in that direction – a task much greater and more essential than all of his reforms put together – before he fell victim to court intrigue in 1852. He died with few friends either in government or among the people. It was some time later that be began to emerge as a legendary hero, and – typically – a victim of foreign intrigue.

Shortly after the dismissal and killing of Amir Kabir, a group of Tehran Babis made an unsuccessful attempt on the shah's life. The result was a hideous backlash, such that, in Ahmad Kasravi's words, Tehran had not seen such atrocity before. Scores of leading and activist Babis were handed over to various groups who killed them by extremely cruel methods such as making holes in their bodies and filling them with lighted candles (*sham' ajin*).[5] This was followed by the exile of leaders and activists of the Babi movement to Ottoman territory, where conflict between the two leading figures, the brothers Mirza Hosein'ali Baha'ullah and Mirza Yahya Sobh-e Azal, led to schism and split, the Baha'is founding a completely new religion and emerging as the main body of the movement and the Azalis remaining a minority, actively supporting the Constitutional Revolution and dwindling into insignificance by the 1920s.

Russian and British rivalry and interference in Iranian affairs, which Amir Kabir had intended to curb, continued and intensified as the century advanced. Not only did the Russians and the British demand and generally obtain various trading concessions but they were constantly engaged in a political game of chess, especially as regarded the appointment of top officials, and in efforts to enlist their cooperation. Imperial interference in the country's affairs sometimes went as far as the court and the harem. Towards the end of the century almost all important state decisions had to have the approval of at least one of the two great powers. Sometimes a decision approved by one power was withdrawn as a result of pressure from the other. The rivalry almost certainly saved the country from direct colonization by either of the two powers; on the other hand, Iran was no longer a fully independent country.

Russian and British influence had at least one positive result in tempering certain features of arbitrary rule. For example, without their support Mohammad Shah's accession would have involved more conflict and chaos, and Naser al-Din

Shah's would have been less smooth than it was. Their strong protest against the killing of Amir Kabir (which the British foreign secretary described as an uncivilized act[6]) introduced a new factor for stopping the arbitrary killing of nobles and high officials by the shah, although it did not go as far as saving their property from confiscation.

The case of Abbas Mirza, the shah's brother and a boy of thirteen, is a good example. As noted above, he would have been blinded at the age of nine on the shah's accession had it not been for the intervention of Amir Kabir and the foreign envoys. Now the shah was thinking of killing him for fear that he might become the centre of sedition by some unknown rebels. Normally he would have carried out his decision, but in the new circumstances he felt that he should test the opinion of the British and Russian envoys to stop them from protesting after the event. This he did through Mirza Aqa Khan Nuri, his chief minister, who was told by the two envoys that they should not kill or blind the boy without his being charged with an offence. In his reply to the British minister, Nuri did no more than reveal the logic of such behaviour under arbitrary rule, namely that whoever moved more quickly would win the game; and that was so because legitimacy and succession were not firmly rooted in any law or entrenched tradition. He wrote that he had reported the British minister's letter to the shah. The shah had agreed that the minister meant well, but added that:

> Your excellency must pay attention to some peculiar Iranian customs and traditions and realize that, in Iran, the things that your excellency has in mind will not work, and one cannot be immune from the evil intent of seditious and rebellious people. If the leaders of the Iranian state wish to act on the basis of fairness and justice to maintain order and security for all their subjects, *they would have no choice but at the slightest thought, imagination or supposition of rebellion, irrespective of who it might be, to try to put it down forthwith and not to hesitate even for a moment.*[7]

In the end, the boy was exiled to Ottoman Iraq.[8]

Thenceforth considerations of European opinion became an important factor in such decisions. For example, decades later when Rokn al-Dawleh, governor-general of Fars, bastinadoed Qavam al-Molk, one of the most powerful magnates and grandees of Fars, and threw him in jail, he then asked the shah to 'sell' Qavam to him for money. And according to E'temad al-Saltaneh, minister of publications and the shah's private secretary, he did not 'buy Qavam', partly because of probable adverse European opinion:

> After entering Shiraz, Rokn al-Dawleh had had [Qavam al-Molk] bastinadoed and imprisoned, and then wrote a letter to Tehran saying that he would pay 100,000 tomans to the Shah and 30,000 to [the chief minister] Amin al-Soltan to sell Qavam to him, that is, for him to have the life and property of Qavam at his disposal. But he did not manage to buy Qavam, since he is a nephew of

Sahab-Divan, and, besides, this is not like the age of Fath'ali Shah to be possible to buy and sell the magnates and notables; the Europeans would make a fuss. He did not manage to buy Qavam . . .[9]

The reference to the sale of important people by Fath'ali Shah is not spurious, for Amin al-Dawleh writes in his memoirs quite independently:

[Fath'ali]Shah even used to sell the court officials and state dignitaries to each other . . . [since], as Iranian sycophants keep repeating, life and private posses-sions were the rightful property of the Shahanshah.[10]

Selling notables to each other for money had had other precedents in Iranian history (see Chapter 4).

Mirza Aqa Khan Nuri, who replaced Amir Kabir, had been a senior official under Mohammad Shah. He had been bastinadoed and banished to Kashan by Hajji Mirza Aghasi and returned to Tehran only after the latter's fall. He survived longer in office and was, just like most other officials, a time server, but when he fell in 1858 he might well have lost his life had it not been for the shah's sensi-tivity towards adverse European opinion. He lost all his property, however, was banished to the edge of the great desert and was only allowed towards the end of his life to go to Qom, which at the time was but a little shrine town in the desert. He once indirectly sent a message to the shah, saying, 'if you are a butcher kill me, if you are a [slave] merchant sell me and if you are a ruler forgive me'. But his plea did not help.

Unlike Amir Kabir, Mirza Aqa Khan resumed normal Iranian 'politics', that is, doing his best to stay alive and in power. He openly placed himself under British protection at least as a life insurance policy, but he was good at changing with both internal and foreign winds, just like the shah's last chief minister Amin al-Soltan in the 1880s, 1890s and even afterwards until his assassination by leftist constitution-alists in 1907. For example, despite his dependence on the British, Mirza Aqa Khan remained in position during the capture of Herat, which the Russians endorsed and the British fought against. In the same way, while he owed his post as much to the shah's mother as to anyone else, when the shah fell madly in love with the beautiful and intelligent peasant girl Jeiran, elevating her above all the women of the harem including his redoubtable mother and designating her son, the boy Amir Qasem Khan as his heir, Nuri was good in moving forward with the wind. However, this did not in the end serve him well, as both Amir Qasem and his mother died soon, leaving the shah's mother and the other intriguers to catch Nuri in the wings.[11] It was all a familiar story in traditional Iranian 'politics', of life at the top in the short-term society.

The loss of Herat in 1857 was also an indirect cause of the fall of Mirza Aqa Khan. The young shah had wished to pursue Iran's long-standing claim to sover-eignty over Herat and score a heroic point in the process. The military expedi-tion was successful and Herat fell to the shah's forces. The British were alarmed because of their belief that this would, or at least could, open the gateway for the Russians towards India, given that Herat's strategic location made it virtually the only passable route for a large army to cross the Afghan lands into the Subcontinent. They landed troops in southern Iran in a bid to force the shah to withdraw from Herat. The Iranians withdrew, and in the peace treaty which Farrokh Khan Amin al-Dawleh Kashi negotiated in Paris through the good offices of Napoleon III, Iran gave up her claim on Herat and perforce the rest of Afghan lands, this being the origin of the international recognition of Afghanistan as an independent state.[12]

PHASE II (1858–73)

The Herat campaign was a monumental failure for Naser al-Din Shah, reminiscent of his grandfather's and great-grandfather's humiliations in the two Russo-Persian wars and his father's involuntary lifting of the siege of Herat twenty years before. Not only did it fail to turn him into the hero he had aspired to but it led to the end of Iran's claim of sovereignty over a land which had been part of the Iranian empire until not so long ago. And, once again, the failure was not a consequence of a traditional local war but a conflict with the wishes of a modern power thousands of miles away which it seemed impossible to thwart in spite of decades of haphazard measures for military and technological modernization.

It became clear that partial attempts to acquire European technology and science had been far from effective. This was seen in the fall and execution of Amir Kabir at a clap of the hands in 1851, the demise, without any ceremony, of the most powerful chief minister and military commander the country had seen for decades and the founder of an *école polytechnique*, a man who was fast becoming a legend and who had already engaged some of the country's most intelligent and forward-looking minds over the same question. For the first time in Iranian history they struck upon the most ancient and fundamental problem of the state and society, that is, arbitrary rule (*estebdad*), which revealed the *differentia specifica* between Iran and Europe: in the latter, lawful government and orderly society had been the rule rather than the exception.

Young Malkam Khan, son of an Armenian convert to Islam, who had spent about ten years as a student in Paris, became the chief theorist of constitutional and responsible government. Views of Malkam's personal attributes have varied, some critical, some full of praise, but it cannot be disputed that his ideas formed the strongest single impact on the psyche of upper- and middle-class campaigners for reform. Regarding the negative comments on Malkam's personality, one is reminded of Ablofazl Beihaqi, the great eleventh-century historian, who, in passing severe judgement on a leading minister, added that, nevertheless, 'intellectual excellence has its own place'.

In about 1860 Malkam submitted his long and comprehensive constitutional proposal to Naser al-Din Shah, apparently at the shah's own bidding, shortly after the collapse of the siege of Herat and the resulting Paris peace treaty, which exposed Iran's weakness vis-à-vis Europe once again following the Russo-Iranian wars. This was the first draft constitution ever written in Iranian history. Its most striking feature is the distinction Malkam makes between absolute monarchy and arbitrary rule. There were two types of monarchy, he said at the outset: absolute monarchy, such as those of the Russian and Austrian empires, and moderate monarchy, such as in England and France. He then distinguished between two types of absolute monarchy, one of which he called 'organized and orderly absolute monarchies' (i.e. European despotism, as in Russia and Austria). The other type of absolute monarchy he described as 'disorganized and disorderly absolute monarchies'. He gave no example of this, though it was obvious that he had Iran's regime in mind. He said that moderate monarchy – by which he meant one that was both lawful and representative – was irrelevant to the case of Iran. What was needed was an *orderly* absolute monarchy, that is, one that was based in law: an absolute monarchy in which the crown laid down the law, which was observed and executed by an organized, disciplined and responsible administration.[13]

It was an extremely clever scheme, given that it had been intended for constitutional reform from above by an arbitrary ruler. It made the fundamental distinction between absolute government and arbitrary rule, arguing that absolute government is in reality more powerful than arbitrary rule. When it came to the legislative and executive functions of the state, however, he proposed the formation of a legislative and an executive council to which the shah would delegate his absolute powers for the legislation and application of the law.

There then followed a comprehensive draft constitution which required all state and religious laws to be organized and written by the legislative council. Ministers were to be independent and responsible. Administrative regulations were to be consistent with the law. No one could be arrested except by order of the law. Nothing could be taken from anyone except by order of the law. No one's home could be entered into without the authority of the law. Taxes were to be collected on a basis laid down by the law. And, in the reassuring guise of 'orderly absolute monarchy', he even managed to slip in the rule that 'the people of Iran would enjoy freedom of thought'. This is a large and elaborate document, and the articles not mentioned here follow from these basic precepts and principles.[14]

It was also with the shah's knowledge that Malkam and a few other advanced men of note, including Jalal al-Din Mirza, a son of Fath'ali Shah who was a forerunner of modern Iranian nationalism, set up the *Farmush-khaneh* (House of Oblivion). This was modelled after European Masonic lodges both in its name and in its aura of secrecy, although contrary to popular belief it was not an official Masonic lodge. It was the first modern society for political discourse, and its deliberate though superficial resemblance to Freemasonry stemmed from the important role of Freemasonry in the French Revolution and the mystique with which it was held even in Europe, which in Iran amounted to no less than real magical powers.

In a country where suspicion and conspiracy in matters of state had been an ancient preoccupation, these developments were bound to alarm many a powerful person in society, not least some of the ulama, especially given that its trimmings appeared to be foreign and Christian. Indeed, in a letter addressed to the shah, the rich and powerful Tehran *mojtahed* Hajj Mullah Ali Kani attacked those who spread 'the pernicious concept of liberty', bearing in mind that the word *azadi* had been traditionally equated with licence and chaos (as opposed to *azadegi*, which referred to contentment and otherworldliness). The shah himself might have been concerned at the danger of licentious ideas being discussed behind his back, but pressure from the secret society's opponents must also have been instrumental in his order that it should disband itself. He went further than that, and honourably dispatched Malkam to the Persian embassy in Istanbul, though this is more likely to have been intended to silence his enemies. There Malkam joined the staff of Hajj Mirza Hosein Khan Moshir al-Dawleh, who was to lead the shah's second reformist ministry after Amir Kabir.

In the meantime, the coming of the telegraph to Iran, the single most important technical advance in the nineteenth century, had increased the central government's grip on the provinces insofar as information could now be received and orders dispatched much more cheaply and quickly. It was later to prove to be an equally effective instrument for organizing countrywide protest and revolution.

The administrative system under Naser al-Din Shah was relatively decentralized as before, but the shah was still the ultimate arbiter and decision taker, and had the power to enforce his arbitrary decisions far and wide through governors, financial auditors and other officials. This did not mean that the shah could enforce any and all decisions as he liked. For, apart from financial constraints, it was not possible to interfere in the internal affairs of nomadic tribes, and there were occasional revolts in the provinces, though these were infrequent, and major rebellions such as that led by Sheikh Obeidollah in Kurdistan were exceptional.

The army continued to decline in men, equipment, discipline and leadership. It was lucky that the country did not experience an important war at this time, except perhaps the war in Herat, which was quickly conceded to the British, and the attempt by a large army to teach a lesson to Yamut Turkamans, which was routed. Later on, the only relatively disciplined and effective force was the Cossack Brigade, which was commanded and run by Russian officers. The Persian Cossacks were a gift of the Tsar to the shah as his personal guards, an outcome of his second visit to Europe in 1878, and in time became an instrument of Russian policy in the country.

There were also other constraints to the shah's power, such as the need to keep the ulama contented, to allow people in fear of their lives to take *bast* or occasionally to accept the intervention of favourite notables to spare a person's life. Still, as throughout Iranian history, the shah's power was not constrained by any law or entrenched tradition.

Moshir al-Dawleh, Iran's ambassador to the Ottomans, was a maternal cousin of the shah, although his grandfather had been a bath assistant in Qazvin. Having been impressed with modern European developments and the Ottoman *tanziamat* (administrative reforms and reorganization), Moshir al-Dawleh wished to promote both political and technological reform in Iran. He had accompanied the shah on his visit to Ottoman Iraq, and had impressed the shah both with the idea of progress and with his own personal ability. Since the downfall of Mirza Aqa Kahn Nuri, no chief minister had been appointed, the conservative chief revenue official, Mirza Yusef Khan Mostawfi al-Mamalek, having been generally in charge of the administration as well. It was in 1871 that Malkam's reform theories received a chance of being tested in a mild and pragmatic though no less important form when the shah finally agreed to the formation of a cabinet run by ministers with defined duties, having decision-making powers as well as individual and collective responsibility. Moshir al-Dawleh, now entitled Sepahsalar, was made chief minister as well as army commander-in-chief – the only man apart from Amir Kabir to combine both those positions under Naser al-Din Shah – and thus he led Iran's first-ever cabinet government. Malkam was Sepahsalar's principal advisor in matters regarding administrative reform and economic development.

Significantly, this came after another loss of territory. In 1869, the Iranians had acknowledged without a fuss Russian sovereignty over some of the Turkaman territory to which they had had traditional claim. When Sepahsalar put forward the reform programme at the shah's bidding, the shah wrote underneath it:

> Jenab-e Sadr-e A'zam, I very much approve of this account which you have written concerning the Council of Ministers. With God's blessings make the necessary arrangements and put it into action soon, since any delay would mean a loss to the state.[15]

But the shah's commitment to administrative reform proved to be half-hearted, and the opponents of reform, many of them from purely personal motives but some also from principled opposition, as effective as ever. The ulama were unhappy not just for fear of Europeanization but also because they were inherently opposed to a strong central administration, as they had been to Amir Kabir's and as they would be to the modernizing government of Mirza Ali Kahn Amin al-Dawleh, early under Mozaffar al-Din Shah. They saw such an administration as a threat to their own authority, especially as it was in a crypto-European form and as the new cabinet had avowedly modernizing aims. There were others in government and among the notables who felt threatened by the programme of a reformist administration. It was fairly typical of Iranian history that various, at times conflicting, elements combined to achieve a certain objective, in this case the downfall of Moshir al-Dawleh and his reforms.

Moshir al-Dawleh hoped for substantial and far-reaching investment projects to exploit Iranian minerals, coal as well as metals, construct a railway network for creating a modern transport system and, in the process, mobilize the unused domestic labour force, which went to waste on account of over-manning. With such highly ambitious projects in mind he convinced the shah to grant a concession to Baron Julius de Reuter, a naturalized British subject of German origin, a leading European entrepreneur and the founder of the news agency, to provide the necessary capital, technology and skill. Reactions were sharp and strong when in 1872 the Reuter concession was finally approved. The ulama attacked the decision for reasons mentioned above. So did the opponents of Sepahsalar's government and virtually everyone else with power and influence who felt they had been left out of the game. The Russians were against the scheme because it gave far-reaching concessions for exploration, exploitation and construction, including a railway network, to a British subject. Moshir al-Dawelh (Sepahsalar) hoped to have Britain's backing for the Reuter concession to counter Russian opposition, but, strange as it may look, the British government was not forthcoming, partly at least to avoid offending the Russians over a scheme in which they were not involved. With no powerful party in favour of the scheme, it collapsed and the concession was withdrawn.

The Reuter concession has remained controversial down to the present-day. Even an old-school imperialist such as Lord Curzon expressed surprise at the granting of such extensive concessions to a foreign firm when he commented on it, though he is unlikely to have held that view had the British government supported the scheme.[16]

E'temad al-Saltaneh was later to put in writing the allegation that Reuter had paid Moshir al-Dawleh, Malkam and some other officials handsomely for arranging the concession.[17] Malkam was apparently paid a commission but there is no evidence that Moshir al-Dawleh also received a subsidy for arranging the concession. However that may be, the payment of commissions on such transactions was normal at the time; it was a practice that continued even in the twentieth century, if then usually covered up.

Perhaps in view of the vigorous domestic and foreign campaign against the Reuter concession the writing was already on the wall for Sepahsalar (Moshir al-Dawleh)'s government. But he and Malkam did not yet give up. In 1873, they persuaded a willing and curious shah to go on his first tour of Europe, hoping that the spectacle of modern societies would strengthen his resolve to continue with modernization and reform. The idea boomeranged. The shah went on the tour from Russia to England and was much impressed with European industrial and social developments, as the Europeans were also fascinated by this seemingly mediaeval ruler who was nevertheless both intelligent and highly self-confident. He was accompanied by Sepahsalar and a large retinue, but barely had they returned than he sacked the hapless Sepahsalar on arrival in Rasht. For all his hopes of legal reform, the man had to take sanctuary in the stables in fear of his life, although the shah later showed that his decision had been due to pressure from all sides. An immediate factor behind Sephasalar's dismissal was the campaign of the shah's favourite and influential wife, Anis al-Dawleh, against him. She and a few other women of the harem initially had accompanied the shah's party but the difficulty in Russia of presenting totally veiled women, segregated from the male company and the hosts and hostesses, led to the decision to send them back to Tehran. Anis al-Dawleh was deeply disappointed and blamed Sepahsalar for their return despite his denial of having initiated that decision.[18]

That, at any rate, was the end of any serious reform from above, although the shah did return to the issue of government by law after his third and final visit to European countries. Meanwhile, the Reuter concession was cancelled, in compensation for which another concession was later obtained. Sepahsalar was given other posts and eventually made governor-general of Khorasan, where he died shortly after assuming his new office, rumours spreading that he had been poisoned on the shah's order. Whether or not this was a false rumour, it was widely believed because such had been the fate of fallen chief ministers until the time of Amir Kabir – Mirza Aqa Khan's treatment was only slightly better – especially now that the open killing of fallen viziers was no longer an option for fear of European backlash. The fact that the shah appropriated the dead man's estate was virtually routine and had no bearing on his sentiments towards him.

PHASE III (1873–96)

Thus ended the second phase of Naser al-Din's rule. In the remaining twenty-three years of his life he contented himself with maintaining his own authority at home, managing foreign relations as best he could and continuing to enjoy hunting and women. To this was added extensive European tours, another in 1878 and a third in 1889. He watched over the country's decline if not stoically then with a cynicism reminiscent of the saying attributed to Louis XV of France, 'After me the flood', although he still toyed with the idea of introducing law and responsible government in the country. On his return from his third European visit, as we have seen, he returned to the question of government by law instead of fiat – which he, like the reformists, believed was the key to the secret of European success – and ordered state luminaries to set up a council of state. His brother Abbas Mirza Molk Ara, who was present at that fruitless meeting, even quotes him as saying:

> All the order and progress which we observed in Europe in our recent visit is due to the existence of law. Therefore, we too have made up our mind to introduce a law and act according to it.[19]

After some kind of a council was set up, he sent Amin al-Dawleh with a message to the council to advise him on what to do 'so the people are content and the affairs of the state truly orderly'. Their unanimous reply was that the shah was 'the wisest of all beings', and any change would be up to his 'majestic will': if in his opinion the existing situation is good he can confirm it; if not, he can change it.[20] Power was still arbitrary, that is, unconstrained by an independent body of law. But government was decentralized, state interference in the lives of ordinary people was limited and many decisions were reached through a bargaining process.[21]

The shah's last important vizier was the young Mirza Ali Asghar Khan Amin al-Soltan, who was only twenty-six when he first became chief minister. He was the eldest son of Aqa Ebrahim of the same title, a semi-educated man who had typically risen from humble origins to become Head of the Household Staff

(*Abdar Bashi*) at the court and whose cleverness and cunning had enabled him to have a disproportionate influence on the shah and perforce on government affairs. A close friend of Hajj Mohammad Hasan Amin al-Zarb, the great merchant and Master of the Mint, who was accused of flooding the market with black pennies (*pul-e-siyah*), thus devaluing the currency and adding fuel to rampant inflation,[22] the younger Amin al-Soltan, later entitled Atabak, was an intelligent, able and educated man on whom the shah became increasingly dependent for running the administration and dealing with foreign envoys.

Cunning and duplicitous, attributes that were necessary for success in an arbitrary society, he was very good at building up support among the court and the notables and dealing with Russia and Britain in a self-serving and pragmatic way. He was not a paid agent of Russia or Britain (or both) as was then and later believed, but played the game of survival in regard to domestic and foreign affairs, the principal secret of which was to be on the right side at the right moment, whether London or St Petersburg, whether Tehran or Tabriz.[23]

His greatest feat of survivalist performance was perhaps when he switched sides from Britain before the Tobacco Revolt to Russia afterwards. Throughout the 1880s various trading concessions were granted to Russian and, especially, British companies. In 1888 the shah opened up the River Karun for navigation, which could only benefit Britain, not Russia. Next year, the year of the shah's third and last visit to Europe, the British actively canvassed and obtained the concession for the Imperial Bank of Persia to facilitate compensation for the cancellation of the Reuter concession. The bank was granted the exclusive right for issuing banknotes as well as extensive privileges for mineral exploitation. This hurt and angered the merchants and traders who already had their own forms of note in limited circulation. In turn the Russians also obtained a concession for the creation of the Discount Bank of Russia.

The concession policy reached its climax, then anti-climax, when in 1890 the shah granted a concession to the British firm Talbot for the monopoly of production, sale and export of Iranian tobacco. Its scope was more limited than the ill-fated Reuter concession before it, but, unlike Reuter's, it was of little or no consequence for economic development, only for lining the shah's and ministers' pockets with royalties and commissions. Besides, the Reuter concession involved investments in railways, mining and so on, in which there was little or no existing domestic activity, whereas the tobacco concession excluded existing domestic production and trading. The Russians were naturally opposed to it. So were tobacco merchants, who were joined by other merchant guilds. The ulama were drawn in because of their role as 'protectors of the people's interests' and because of fear of growing European domination. In turn, their opposition encouraged other urban groups to protest.

The merchants and traders were upset partly on account of the direct interest of those of them involved in the tobacco industry, but also because of their own collective interests, since this concession could open the door to foreign concessions being granted in other profitable areas of trade. The fact that the Talbot concession covered domestic trade and production was particularly alarming.

Most of the ulama accepted the call of the protestors for support, and this came to its climax when a fatva by Hajj Mirza Hasan Shirazi, the senior Marja', who lived in Samerra, a Shia holy city in Iraq, was published equating the consumption of tobacco with waging war against the Hidden Imam. It simply read:

> As from today, consumption of tobacco and smoking the water-pipe (*qalian*) is forbidden (*haram*) and tantamount to waging war against the Imam of the Time.

It was doubted even then whether the fatva had indeed been issued by the Marja' himself. Its importance lay, first, in the fact that it was in line with the people's wishes, and, secondly, that it was subsequently acclaimed by the highly respected divine. The people responded with full vigour and boycotted the use of tobacco. This was a blow to the shah and his chief minister, Amin al-Soltan, in particular. The shah tried to save part of the deal by offering to withdraw the concession for domestic trade, but to no avail.

When he began to back down, he wrote in his first letter to Hajj Mirza Hasan Ashtiyani, the leading *mojtahed* and the movement's leader in Tehran:

> As for the tobacco question, no one is infallible, and – among human beings – perfect knowledge belongs to the pure person of our prophet, peace be unto him. There are times when one takes a decision which he later regrets. Just on this tobacco business I had already thought of withdrawing the domestic monopoly . . . such that they [Talbot] would not be able to complain and ask for a large compensation while, at the same time, the people be rid of the European monopoly of internal trade which was truly harmful. We were about to take action when the edict (*hokm*) of Mirza-ye Shirazi . . . was published in Isfahan and gradually reached Tehran. . . . Would it not have been better if you had petitioned us – either individually or collectively – to withdraw the monopoly . . . without all the noise and the stopping (*tark*) of *qalian*?[24]

However, Ashtiyani and the public insisted on the cancellation of the entire concession, and the conflict reached its climax in the bloodshed that followed public demonstrations outside the royal compound. In the end, the shah cancelled the entire concession. Not only did the hoped-for royalties not materialize but the shah had to pay a £500,000 cancellation fee facilitated by the Imperial Bank of Persia[25]

The tobacco concession was obviously against the economic interest of merchants and traders, who were more active than any other social class in the revolt. Yet the matter went well beyond this particular context, since it provided an important focus for all the discontented groups, reformist or other. Most of the ulama supported the cause, which incidentally gave it a religious aspect, especially as it was against a concession given to non-Muslim foreigners.

This was an unprecedented event in Iranian history. For the first time the public had revolted peacefully, and for a clear and well-defined purpose. For the first time also, the arbitrary state had given in to a public demand rather than either suppressing it or being overthrown violently. It was perhaps the nearest thing to the European practice of politics that had ever been experienced in Iranian history. Fifteen years later the Constitutional Revolution also started and succeeded peacefully at first, although subsequent developments led to violent confrontation and civil war (see Chapter 9).

The shah, his third son Kamran Mirza, governor of Tehran, and Atabak tried but could not stem the tide of mass revolt. The telegraph, which had helped integrate the country and make central government more effective, also proved helpful in creating efficient, countrywide mobilization against the state. It was a case of the people versus the state, a familiar state of affairs in Iranian social history. The great difference was that the campaign was entirely civil and urban – as opposed to military and nomadic – and it was centred on a clear and specific demand, which triumphed without the collapse of the entire state or the plunging of the country into its traditional chaos. Thus it was the first *political* campaign in the country's history, as the term is understood from European history and experience.

Apart from Shirazi and Ashtiyani, two figures who played important roles in the campaign against the concession, albeit less directly, were Malkam Khan and Seyyed Jamal al-Din Asadabadi, known as Afghani. Malkam, who was Persian minister in London during the shah's visit there in 1889 fell out of favour and was sacked shortly afterwards over a conflict that was fomented by his enemy, Atabak. He had sold the Persian lottery concession to a firm in the City of London which the shah had authorized but later withdrawn, having been egged on by Atabak that Malkam was cheating him out of considerable royalties. Atabak also mobilized the ulama to declare that the lottery was tantamount to gambling and against the *sharia*. Malkam cashed the £40,000 worth of royalties and moved into open opposition, commencing the publication of the newspaper *Qanun* (Law). The paper advocated the establishment of government by law as opposed to arbitrary rule, and emphasized that this was consistent with Islam, thus trying to enlist the support of the ulama to the cause of constitutional government. It became very popular among the reformist elite through secret circulation.[26]

Jamal al-Din, a charismatic and enigmatic religious figure posed in Sunni countries and in the West as a Sunni – hence his pretence to be an Afghan from Kabul. He travelled far and wide, impressing both reforming Muslim thinkers such as Mohammad 'Abduh of Egypt and European intellectuals such as Ernest Renan.[27] He had been to various courts, including the Ottoman Porte, and had been invited by Naser al-Din Shah to the rival 'Caliphate' of Tehran. His first visit did not bear fruit, and on his second the shah saw him as a subversive element and had him arrested and expelled from the country with indignity.[28] This act would cost the shah his life (see Chapter 8).[29] In the four years or so that separated the end of the Tobacco Revolt from the shah's death, the ulama's power grew further than it had ever done before. Some of this new-found authority was spent on inter-personal rivalries, in increasing their own and their clients' fortunes and in illicit interference with the affairs of the state.

Naser al-Din Shah was an arbitrary ruler just like all Persian rulers in history, but by no means one of the worst. It may even be argued that, allowing for the steady decline in the country's position in the nineteenth century, he was personally the best ruler that Iran had had since Karim Khan. Although occasionally he ordered harsh punishment he cannot be described as cruel by the standards of Iranian history. He managed to keep the peace at home and did not cede much important territory except for Herat, which was beyond his power to regain.

He carried out some construction and developments, notably in Tehran, including the remapping of the city, building various gates, the collection of rubbish and the installation of street lighting. His two most interesting additions to the palace complex were the Shams al-Emareh, which still survives, and the Tekyeh-ye Dawlat, designed mainly for official religious congregations and services, which, while perfectly sound, was demolished (or 'pick-axed') in 1946 to enable the building of Bank Melli's bazaar branch on the site.

Literature flourished in the nineteenth century, although no truly outstanding figure emerged in that field. Traditionally, scholars divided the history of Persian poetry into three periods. That from the tenth to the sixteenth century was called the period of Classical Literature; the sixteenth to the nineteenth century was described as a period of 'decadence' (*Enhetat*); and the nineteenth century was held to be the period of *Bazgasht* or 'restoration', that is, the period of return to the tenth- to sixteenth-century styles. However, from the standpoint of the twenty-first century all these three periods together are classical and may be respectively described as Classical, Indian Style and Neoclassical. Decadence had set in only in the eighteenth century, and the reaction to it resulted in the nineteenth-century Restoration, when poets like Poet-Laureate Saba, Qa'em-Maqam, Qa'ani Shirazi and Forughi Bastami along with many others reverted to classical styles and wrote lyrics, panegyrics, epics and mystical poetry in the style of the great classics. They did not reach the standards of the great classics, but the twentieth-century view of their work as merely imitative and void of originality is not entirely fair, just as the latter's description of Safavid poetry as decadent is unreasonable.

Calligraphy, lacquerwork, miniature and especially western-style painting grew both in quantity and quality. The greatest painters of the period were Kamal al-Molk, Sani' al-Molk and Mahmud Khan Malek al-Sho'ara (all of them from Kashan), the first of whom became especially famous, but recent critical opinion puts greater value on the work of the latter two. Mirza Gholamreza Isfahani was perhaps the best calligraphic artist of the period, original and innovative. Printing, though still limited, became more widespread than before, and newspapers, virtually all of them official and semi-official, came into circulation.

THE ECONOMY

Three phases may be distinguished for the study of Iranian economy in the nineteenth century: 1800–50, 1850–70 and 1870–1900. As noted above, the first half of the nineteenth century was a period of relative stability as compared with the chaos of the eighteenth. The heavy taxation and extortion of this age – 'the fleecing of the flock' – was no different from normal periods of arbitrary rule. But it was a definite improvement on the previous state of chaos, disorder and constant plunder. The second half of the century may be divided into two parts with respect to the economic situation. The period 1850–70 was probably the happiest economic phase of the nineteenth century. By contrast, there was noticeable deterioration in the last phase (1870–1900), when foreign debts accumulated, the balance of payments deficit kept rising and there was a sustained and accelerating decline in the value of money.

There is a general consensus that the population grew from around 6–7 million at the beginning of the century to about 8–9 million at its close. The nomadic population remained virtually constant throughout the century, roughly at 2.5 million, since the process of re-nomadization had ceased because of greater security. This meant that the settled population grew by about 2 million, or 30 per cent over the whole of the nineteenth century, implying a very modest average annual growth rate, which was nevertheless quite significant for its time. Population growth may be secular (long-term), cyclical or – quite often – both. There may have been a secular trend for modest population growth, though it is not easy to discern the factors behind this. But there were undoubtedly cyclical tendencies for both the growth and the decline of population, for example as a result of the rise in the birth rate after the end of chaos and a subsequent decline of the death rate thanks to better health conditions, loss of territory, especially in the more densely populated north-west of the country, and occasional famines.

Taxes consisted mainly of the land tax, the poll tax, various other taxes on productive activities and customs duties; but land tax was by far the biggest source of central and provincial revenues, to which must be added both regular and irregular extortion and official plunder of output and property. Other non-fiscal methods of raising revenues – such as sales of trade concessions to foreigners, sales of public offices and direct foreign loans – became more significant in the last decades of the century, though this does not imply an easing off of taxes on the agricultural sector. The rate of land tax varied according to the productivity of the land, and it generally increased by about one-third in the last decades, mainly because of a further rise in fleecing and exploitation, since land tax was mostly collected in kind, and its rate cannot have been raised merely or mainly in response to the rampant inflation.

There were inflationary pressures throughout the century, but they became much stronger between 1870 and 1900. The causes of inflation were the official and unofficial debasements of the currency, the dramatic fall in the international price of silver – on which the Iranian currency was based – and the structural balance of payments deficit. The fall in silver prices and the deterioration of the balance of payments was most dramatic in the last three decades, and so was the rise in the rate of inflation. The increasing balance of payments deficit was due to the growing gap between imports and exports. The favourable tariff treaties of no more than 5 per cent imposed by the European powers played an important role in increasing imports, largely for minority consumption. The growth of exports was far short of imports, and hence the balance of trade went on deteriorating.

Since domestic hand-made commodities, such as textile materials, were generally dearer and less fashionable than European machine-made products, there was a relative decline in the demand for them in the home market and an absolute decline in the foreign (i.e. export) markets. On the other hand, much of the growth of Iranian exports was due to the shift from secondary to primary products, and particularly to the two main cash crops, opium and cotton. The figures indicate that, in the 1850s, the share of primary products in total exports was less than 20 per cent, but in the 1880s it had risen to 60 per cent, with a corresponding decline in the export of secondary products. The rise in cash crop production was largely at the expense of food production, and this raised food prices further (in addition to other inflationary factors), thus pushing the bare subsistence of the vast majority of the people to still lower limits.

It is clear from the above that the large increase in the volume of trade was, first, due to increasing European imports and, second, to the shift from food crops, such as corn, to cash crops, such as opium and cotton, for exports to European countries. It was not due to the growth, much less development, of the Iranian economy, which might possibly have led to greater saving and investment and the growth of employment and income, though it did enrich merchants involved in foreign trade, swelling the wealth and importance of the most successful among them, such as Amin al-Zarb and Malek al-Tojjar.

Barring the telegraph there was no significant technical progress in the economic sense of the term in either industry or agriculture. One could even observe economic regress in the sense of loss of traditional know-how, refined over centuries, without the acquisition of a suitable substitute which in economic terms would be at least as useful and productive as the older techniques. The 'technical progress' to which political historians usually point largely refers to the minority consumption of products of modern European technology. Likewise, there was no significant increase in the accumulation of financial capital and rise in the stock of physical capital.

Foreign trade grew and was the main force behind the concentration and centralization of financial capital; it represented shifts between different trade sectors as well as between individual merchants. Trade with Europe benefited the big merchants, and by increasing their personal fortunes it increased their potential political power at the expense of the state. European trade also played an important role in weakening the arbitrary system in a number of indirect ways. First, the growing role of imperial powers exposed the weakness of the Iranian state and robbed it of the traditional public belief in its omnipotence, thus prompting Naser al-Din Shah to tell E'temad al-Saltaneh that 'the people's eyes and ears had not yet been opened' under Fath'ali Shah. Second, their payments for various concessions and privileges to the shah and state officials helped weaken the structure of arbitrary rule from within. Third, the greater specialization in the production and export of raw materials, the relative decline of manufacturing, the use of the telegraph as a modern means of communication, the endemically rising inflation, the crippling deficit in foreign payments and the resulting accumulation of foreign debt led to a structural disequilibrium in the economy which the traditional state apparatus could not comprehend, let alone cope with. The turmoil that followed the death of Naser al-Din Shah led to further deterioration of the economy.[30]

CHAPTER 8

The Revolution for Law

*People! Nothing would develop your country other than subjection to law, obser-
vation of law, preservation of law, respect for law, implementation of the law,
and again law, and once again law.*

Seyyed Jamal al-Din Isfahani (1906)

NASER AL-DIN SHAH WAS preparing for the celebration of his golden
jubilee – the fiftieth anniversary of his accession according to the lunar
calendar – when Mirza Reza Kermani shot him dead in May 1896 as he
was visiting the shrine of Hazrat-e Abdl'azim near Tehran. Whether or not
Mirza Reza was instructed to assassinate the shah by Seyyed Jamal al-Din
Afghani, whose devoted disciple he was, his strongest motive was to avenge the
shah's ill-treatment of his mentor, although he himself had also experienced
torture and jail. Fearing the usual outbreak of chaos upon the news of the shah's
death, while the body was being transferred to Tehran and for a while afterwards
the chief minister pretended that the shah had just been slightly wounded. Naser
al-Din Shah's assassination was a modern phenomenon. Regicide was an age-old
method of changing the government in Iran, but there was no precedent for a
middle class trader-cum-intellectual such as Mirza Reza to assassinate a ruler
such as Naser al-Din Shah, and, moreover, to do so in the name of law, justice and
political reform. The death of Naser al-Din Shah quickly plunged the country into
chaos. This was not because of a conflict over the succession, which had become
less of an issue since Naser al-Din Mirza's own succession due to the recognition
of the heir-designate by Russia and Britain (although the shah himself had once
contemplated the disestablishment of his heir-designate Mozaffar al-Din Mirza
and the sale of the position to his eldest surviving son, the tough and very
ambitious Zel al-Soltan).[1]

In this instance, the chaos was essentially the result of the disappearance from
power of an authoritative ruler, which had been foreshadowed by the continuing
weakness and decline in the early 1890s. The new shah, Mozaffar al-Din, who
had been the increasingly frustrated prince governor of Azerbaijan for decades,
was weak, simple and harmless. And precisely for those reasons power fell into
the hands of warring officials and courtiers of both the Tabriz and Tehran courts

in the centre and into the hands of governors-general and local khans and magnates in the provinces. Non-canonical taxes and plain looting, both by government officials and by magnates and nomads, were on the increase. Every week there were complaints from one or another province of plunder, rape and enslavement of ordinary people, especially women and girls, many of whom were subsequently sold.

At first Amin al-Soltan remained chief minister, but, apart from his usual opponents at the centre, he now had to reckon with enemies from the shah's Tabriz entourage, 'the hungry men' as they were called on account of their years of awaiting the new shah's accession and their insatiable appetite for riches, which they stole from the treasury, as attested by the writings of Mokhber al-Saltaneh, who was then a high senior civil servant and later became a leading moderate constitutionalist and, still later, prime minister under Reza Shah.[2] One of 'the hungry men' was Majid Mirza Ein al-Dawleh, a grandson of Fath'ali Shah and a long-standing servant of Mozaffar al-Din Mirza in Tabriz. Another was Mirza Mahmud Khan Hakim al-Molk, who is quoted as saying that the Tabriz party had waited forty years for the accession of the new shah and had only four years to take what they could.[3] A third was Amir Bahador-e Jang, who was a simple, direct and openly reactionary servant of the shah. There were many other hungry men in the new regime.

Other opponents of the chief minister were the loyal pro-reform party, led and symbolized by Mirza Ali Khan Amin al-Dawleh, himself son of an earlier reformer and grandfather of Ali Amini, the reforming and loyal prime minister of Mohammad Reza Shah whom the latter disliked as well as distrusted (see Chapters 10–12). Amin al-Dawleh and other reformers were considered to be pro-British, just as Atabak (Amin al-Soltan) was believed to be pro-Russian. Thus there were three main 'parties' at the time of the new shah's accession: Amin al-Soltan, the existing chief minister and his supporters; Amin al-Dawleh and his reforming group; and the shah's Tabriz entourage, of whom Ein al-Dawleh was the most prominent. Atabak was hated by reformers and especially the radicals. Amin al-Dawleh was an able and educated man who wished to reform the government of corruption and inefficiency. He replaced Atabak as chief minister in 1897, but the latter went on campaigning and eventually supplanted him. Atabak in turn was toppled and replaced by Ein al-Dawleh and his Tabriz group. Ein al-Dawleh took over in September 1903 and remained in office until he was sacked on the insistence of the constitutionalists at the point of their triumph in August 1906.

CHAOS

To show the extent of the confusion, chaos and inability to deal with day-to-day matters within the state and government itself we shall cite below a few examples from two important contemporary sources, both by the same author, a notable historian of the time. They were published in one volume for the first time in the late 1980s, and report on daily events between Mozaffar al-Din Shah's succession in 1896 and 1906, in the middle of the campaign for constitutional government. These are the *Mer'at al-Vaqaye'-e Mozaffari* and the *Diaries* of Malek al-Movarrekhin, who was far from a revolutionary activist and formally presented the first book to the shah himself.

Aziz Mirza is a Qajar nobleman and 'one of the noblest ruffians of Tehran'. Together with his band he causes a great public mischief, and the governor of Tehran has the soles of his feet beaten with a stick. While the governor is watching the beating, Aziz Mirza pulls a 'revolver' out of his pocket and fires a bullet, which misses him. The governor reports the incident to the shah and the latter orders them to cut off Aziz Mirza's hand. This causes unrest among other young *shazdeh*s [Qajar noblemen], the shah sacks the governor and orders him to pay 600 tomans compensation to the mutilated man. He also orders the expulsion from town of the officer who had arrested him.[4] . . .

Early in 1899 bread is short in Tabriz. The landlords are suspected of hoarding, there are riots in the city, shops strike, and many people take *bast* at a shrine. Enemies of Nezam al-Ulama – a leading landlord and religious figure – declare him to be the main culprit. A mob attacks his house and there are a few deaths and injuries. The able and respected Hasan Ali Khan Garrusi, Amir Nezam, twice intervenes and humours the mob and public to relent. Nezam al-Ulama leaves for Tehran. Next day, 'the hooligans and ruffians' attack his house again, and loot and set fire to it. They also attack and loot the homes of his brother and his nephew, the latter of whom is *chef-de-cabinet* to the heir designate and governor of Azerbaijan.[5] . . .

In April 1903, Ein al-Dawleh, Tehran's governor, receives a regular bribe of about 1,000 tomans a day from the bakers and butchers. Bread as well as meat are scarce and expensive. Some women stop the shah's and the governor's carriages and complain. The governor orders them to be beaten up. There is an ongoing struggle between the chief minister, Amin al-Soltan, and the shah's personal 'lackeys'.

In the same month, Salar al-Dawleh, one of the shah's sons and governor of Borujerd and Arabistan (later Khuzistan), is behaving very unjustly towards the people and families there, and rapes the women. A brother of the shah who rules Kashan has behaved so unjustly that the people have taken *bast* in Qom's shrine. When Atabak (Amin al-Soltan) is told that money is so short and injustice so great that the state is about to fall, he answers that he is so busy defending his own position that he has no time to see to these problems. In the following month 'the shah's Turkish lackeys [i.e. his Azerbaijani entourage]' together with Ein al-Dawleh are agitating against Atabak. There is a great shortage of bread in Khorasan and Kashan.[6] . . .

In May 1903, the governor of Mashhad, a grandson of Fath'ali Shah, has angered the people so much that they strike and go on the rampage. The governor runs away. The shah sends in 300 troops without success. Then the shah backs down and sacks the governor. This does not satisfy the people, who set fire to the grave of the governor's father. The Russians send word that unless the government quells the unrest they will send troops to protect their subjects. The shah is frightened, but Atabak says he is unable to act successfully unless he is given real power. The shah agrees. This happens just at the time when thirty men closest to the shah have conspired against the chief minister, and he is about to fall. Next month one of the shah's sons who was governor of Araq, Golpaigan and Khansar is removed because he has done grave injustice to the people, taking their money, raping their women, and accumulating 100,000 tomans over a short period.[7] . . .

In June 1903 there are riots in Azerbaijan. They say there should be no Armenians in Tabriz, and the heads of post and customs offices should be Muslim. The ulama of Tabriz are behind 'the rabble'. The governor of Gilan, Mirza Mahmud Khan Hakim al-Molk, has died. Some say he has been poisoned. He was a favourite of the shah and an enemy of the chief minister. Within a short period he made two and a half million tomans. After his death the government orders his house to be sealed off on 'the pretext that his accounts would have to be investigated'.[8]

Still in the same month the governor of Fars summons the Qashqa'i chiefs. They refuse, and say if it is for taxes someone should be sent to them and they would pay up. The governor is angered and sends troops against them. They shoot forty of the troops down, and the government is now helpless against the Qashqa'is.[9] The Bakhtiyaris refuse to pay their tax. Mounted troops are sent from Tehran to collect it. The Bakhtiyaris kill a few of them and the rest run away.[10] . . .

The chief minister Amin al-Soltan is dismissed (in September 1903), and four months later Ein al-Dawleh replaces him.[11] . . .

December 1904: a note on a grandson of Fath'ali Shah who has just died. When he was governor of Astrabad (later Gorgan) he subdued the rebel Turkamans, and then killed and looted the property of the loyal Turkamans who had helped him subdue the rebels. As governor of Khamseh he also killed and looted the property of many innocent people. Although the shah had been told of all this he was made head of the armed forces and took much of their pay for himself. They say his estate is worth five million tomans.[12] . . .

July 1905: a prominent Qajar nobleman quarrels with a merchant over property and seeks the help of Seyyed Abdollah Behbahani, a leading *mojtahed*, whose students beat up the police (*farrash*), and the nobleman in question breaks the rib of one of them. The heir designate, Mohammad Ali Mirza who is acting as regent in the absence of his father in Europe has the nobleman brought before him, personally beats him, orders that the soles of his feet be heavily beaten by a stick, and throws him into jail. Next morning he orders his release, apologizes to him, and gives him a ring.[13] It is years now that the Lor nomads around Behbahan have looted the townspeople's property, raped their women and sold the men into slavery at lucrative prices.[14]

The people of Quchan run away to Akhal over the Russian border to escape from the injustices of local rulers and, being destitute, sell their daughters to Turkamans.[15] [This became a famous scandal and a subject of loud protests by the constitutionalists.[16]] . . .

November 1905: Political agitation begins in mosques. The sermons of Seyyed Jamal al-Din Isfahani and the activities of Seyyed Mohammad Tabataba'i and Seyyed Abdollah Behbahani are noted.[17] The Russian Revolution of 1905 is also noted, as is the decision of the Tsar to grant constitutional government. It is described as *hokumat-e mashruteh* in Persian.[18] . . .

December 1905: Vazir Nezam 'takes for himself' one toman of the pay of every soldier under him. The soldiers get together and give him a good hiding. The shah dismisses him and gives his regiment to someone else.[19] The Imam Jom'eh gives the home of a dead prostitute to a prayer leader. The relatives of the deceased complain to Ala al-Dawleh, the governor of Tehran. The governor sends for the prayer leader, swears at him as well as Imam Jom'eh, and restores the property to the beneficiaries of the dead woman. Sheikh Fazlollah Nuri intervenes, but the governor sends him a message full of invective, saying that he has no authority, is neither the shah nor the chief minister, and even if the latter likes him he does not.[20] . . .

Bread is in short supply and expensive in Tehran. The chief baker (*Nanva-bashi*) is ordered to be brought before the chief minister, Ein al-Dawleh, and the governor, Ala al-Dawleh. To frighten the *Nanva-bashi*, the minister tells the executioner 'to tear off his belly', but the governor pretends to intervene on his behalf. Instead, they have the soles of his feet heavily beaten and obtain a pledge that he will solve the bread problem. Next day the price of bread rises even further.[21] [See Chapter 4 on the punishment of bakers at times of bread shortage.]

Three days later, on 11 December 1905, comes the famous heavy flogging of the sugar merchants (see below).[22]

Malek al-Movarrekhin's *Diaries* come to a sudden end with his note on the meeting in 1906 of the royal council convened on the shah's orders to set up an independent judiciary. In it, Ehtesham al-Saltaneh, a non-royal Qajar notable and former head of Iran's legation in Berlin, famously attacks Amir Bahador-e Jang for opposing legal justice, because this signifies that the son of the shah and the greengrocer would be treated equally.[23] The revolutionary process has begun.

REVOLUTION

In 1906 a constitution laid down the rules and procedures for government based in law. It was the first time in Iranian history that government was 'conditioned' (*mashrut*) to a set of fundamental laws which defined the limits of executive power and detailed the rights and obligations of the state and society. No such revolution had ever happened in Europe, because, as a rule, there had always been legal limits to the exercise of power in European societies, however powerful the government might be and however narrow, limited and unequal the scope of the law in defining the relationship between the state and society and among the social classes. In Europe, the law had often been unfair to the majority of the people, but even in the four centuries of absolutism or despotism which reigned over the Continent from England to Russia – the only country in which absolutism survived for so long – there had been limits to the exercise of state power, though such limits were considerably less in Russia than in the West. Revolts and revolutions in Europe had never been fought for law as such, but for changing the existing law to extend and increase its scope of application and to make it fairer.

It is not surprising then that, as noted in Chapter 7, when in 1889 Malkam Khan was sacked as Iranian minister in London he began to publish a highly effective newspaper, *Qanun* (Law), while his disciple Mirza Yusef Mostashar al-Dawleh wrote a book entitled One Word (*Yek Kalameh*), the one word which would solve all the country's main ills was thus dramatically revealed to be LAW.[24] When he was discovered to be the author of *Yek Kalameh* he was put in chains, his home looted, his property confiscated and his pension stopped.[25] This shows the extent of Naser al-Din Shah's awareness of the degree of subversion implied by the word 'law' within the Iranian social and historical context, despite the fact that he himself had occasionally expressed the wish to establish government based in law (see Chapter 7).

In an editorial in the first issue of *Qanun*, Malkam emphasized the essential need for lawful as opposed to arbitrary government if there was to be any progress in Iran at all:

Iran is full of divine gifts. What has left all of these gifts unused is the absence of law. No one in Iran owns anything, because there is no law.

We appoint rulers without law. We remove officers without law. We sell what rightfully belongs to the government, without law. We imprison God's subjects without law. We tear open bellies without law.

And he went on to add:

There is no one who knows what amounts to an offence and what constitutes a service. What law did they use to exile such and such a *mojtahed*? What law did they use to stop such and such an officer's salary?

What law was the basis of the removal of such and such a minister?

What law was the basis of the title that was given to such and such an idiot?

There is not a single governor or prince who can feel secure about his condi-tions of life as much as the foreign [i.e. European] ambassadors' slaves.[26]

Other intellectuals discussed the uses of law and freedom in theory as well as fiction. Mirza Fath'ali Akhundzadeh (d. 1878), social, religious and literary critic, whose ideas were to make a deep impact on the rise of nationalist modernism, was an influential contemporary and close friend of Malkam. He campaigned both against arbitrary government and for westernization. His later disciples, Mirza Aqa Khan Kermani and Sheikh Ahmad Ruhi – who once converted to Azali Babism but later became free thinkers – were more moderate than him in tone though not much in ideas. Zeinol'abedin Maragheh'i advanced constitutional and patriotic thoughts through his highly influential novel *The Travelogue of Ebarhim Beg*. But perhaps the politically most sophisticated of them all was Abdorrahim Talebof Tabrizi, who was both an educationalist and a novelist.[27]

As we have seen, the accession of Mozaffar al-Din shah was followed by chaos both at the centre and in the provinces. The new shah was a well-meaning but feeble and weak man, easily manipulated by his entourage, especially those close to him. Revolutions normally occur when the state is weak, even though the revolutionary ideas and agenda may have been advanced over a period of time. In Iranian history, at any rate, weakness of the state always opened the risk of rebellion. As explained in previous chapters, the aim of traditional Iranian rebellions was to overthrow an 'unjust' ruler and replace him with a 'just' one, since otherwise arbitrary government was regarded as a natural, both a necessary and inevitable, phenomenon.[28] But this time the window of Europe had offered the very attractive alternative of *lawful and responsible government* running *an orderly society*. It was such that Prince Zel al-Soltan, the shah's elder brother who was not at all noted for democratic sentiments, wrote, after visiting Paris:

> Although they say there is freedom and republic, and there is absolute licence (har keh har keh ast), this is not the case ... In this country, it looks as if everyone – whether king or beggar, rich, master or lackey – has the book of law under his arm and before his eyes, and he knows that there is no escaping from the claws of the law ... The power of the police must be seen; it cannot be gauged from the description of others.[29]

This was the other side of the coin. Lawful government was not just the opposite of arbitrary rule, but the opposite of chaos as well. Chaos had always been seen as the natural alternative to arbitrary rule, just as absolute and arbitrary rule had been regarded as the only alternative to chaos. Arbitrary rule (*estebdad*) was identified with stability, and chaos – *fetneh, ashub, enqelabat* and so forth – with generalized lawlessness. Now it looked as if there was a magic wand – and it was seen as a magic wand, except by the very few most sophisticated intellectuals – that was certain to rid the country of its traditional habits, arbitrary rule and chaos, at a stroke. And especially now that chaos had become widespread, many of the intellectual reformists were as concerned with stamping out chaos as they were with the abolition of arbitrary rule. They believed that once government based in law was established it could bring order to society.

A glimpse at widespread disorder in the reign of Mozaffar al-Din Shah was shown above through the diary notes of Malek al-Movarrekhin. That was informal history. At the formal level, Atabak (Amin al-Soltan) took two large government loans from the Russians during the five years (1897–1903) that he ran the government after Amin al-Dawleh. The loans were partly used to finance the shah's costly and wasteful tours in Europe, but they were also helpful to save the state from bankruptcy, although many people believed that they had been entirely squandered, for which Atabak took much of the blame. He also took the blame for the rising resentment against the operations of the new team of Belgian officials who were employed to run Iran's customs. There were campaigns against him especially in Tehran, Tabriz and Isfahan

The Belgian customs officials were led by Joseph Naus, director and later minister of customs. The rescaling of tariffs by the Belgians led to the charge that they were biased in favour of the Russians and against both the British and the Iranians. The charges were fairly well founded, and though the government took some steps to redress British grievances, the resentment of Iranian merchants turned into hatred, not least for Atabak, who was seen as little more than a Russian puppet. On the eve of the revolution in 1905 the discovery of a fancy-dress party photograph which showed Naus and other Belgians in the mullahs' attire, though it belonged to two years earlier, added fuel to an anger which had essentially political and economic roots.

Some important religious dignitaries began to support the merchants, and the great ulama in Najaf provided further encouragement. In the ongoing campaign for the overthrow of Atabak, a letter of his excommunication attributed to the *maraje'* in Najaf played an important role. The document turned out to be a forgery, although it is true that the ulama in question were opposed to Atabak. Another fatva from Najaf was also forged in Tabriz, which led to the expulsion of the head of customs there, though, upon discovering the fabrication, a leading *mojtahed* who had been suspected of being involved was driven out of the city. The anti-Babi 'pogroms' or *Babi-koshi*s in Isfahan and Yazd, with 120 killed in Yazd alone, was in part aimed at Atabak, though there were religious motives behind them as well. Atabak fell in September 1903; Ein al-Dawleh replaced him within a couple of months.[30]

A deadly 'competition' arose between Ein al-Dawleh and Amin al-Soltan (the title of Atabak was now bestowed on his rival and successor). Even after the latter was sacked and went on a journey round the world, his party was still quite active against Ein al-Dawleh. Given the highly decentralized nature of the Shia institutions, vigorous competition and/or destructive conflict among the ulama was a familiar tradition. After the death of Mirza Hasan Ashtiyani, who had been the most prominent *mojtahed* and leader of the Tobacco Revolt in Tehran (see Chapter 7), both Sheikh Fazlollah Nuri and Seyyed Abdollah Behbahani wished to be recognized as the chief *mojtahed* in the city. Nuri, Imam Jom'eh and a few other important divines tended to support Ein al-Dawleh. He was opposed by Behbahani's circle and the somewhat otherwoldy Seyyed Mohammad Tabatab'i. Some of the conflict concerned who was to have control of certain colleges, especially Madreseh-ye Marvi in Tehran.[31]

The personal rivalry between Nuri and Behbahani began to take shape along political lines, although Nuri acted in concert with other ulama at the crucial moments before the campaign for the constitution bore fruit. Ein al-Dawleh's first major friction with Behbahani was in fact as governor of Tehran in 1901, when Behbahani had intervened to save some seminary students (*talabehs*) from being banished for a misdeed which they had committed against himself. But the governor had replied with contempt, saying that the men had not been arrested for Behbahani's sake so that they could be set free by his intervention.

Two international events which played important psychological roles in strengthening the cause of constitutionalism and emboldening its partisans in Iran must be given the emphasis they deserve. First was the defeat of Russia in the Russo-Japanese war of 1904–5. Iranian constitutionalists literally believed that 'Japan defeated Russia, because the former was a constitutionalist regime, the latter a despotic one'. The outbreak of the 1905 revolution in Russia, itself encouraged by that defeat and humiliation, was even more potent, both in providing a model from the dreaded big bear itself and by spreading radical ideas and campaign methods – sometimes embodied in activists arriving from the Caucasus – especially among the modern intellectuals, many of whom, such as Taqizadeh, Dawlat-Abadi and Mosavat, were still in religious attire. Young radicals, democrats and social democrats, particularly in Tehran, Tabriz, Gilan and Mashhad, had begun to form groups and launch campaigns for radical revolutionary programmes.[32]

As noted above, there had been constant reports, from the four corners of the country, of tyrannical behaviour by governors-general. More recently, there had been reports of injustice to the people of Fars by the governor-general Sho'a' al-Saltaneh, one of the shah's important sons, and by the governor-general of Kerman. Although in the latter case matters were a good deal more complicated and the sources of blame numerous, nevertheless the news in Tehran put the whole of the blame on the government. On the other hand, Sho'a' al-Saltaneh, who was the shah's second son and a favourite of Ein al-Dawleh for the succession after his ailing father, had definitely been confiscating the people's property in Fars.[33]

What triggered off the first explosion was the increase in the price of sugar. The governor of Tehran, Ala al-Dawleh, suspected the sugar merchants of hoarding, and had the soles of the feet of a few of them – including an old and much respected Seyyed – heavily beaten, as we have seen. Next day the bazaar shut down, and large numbers of merchants, ulama and others joined a congregation in the central Royal Mosque to protest against the governor's arbitrary behaviour. A leading preacher and radical constitutionalist, Seyyed Jamal al-Din Isfahani, attacked the government from the pulpit while Imam Jom'eh, who was a friend of the chief minister, denounced him: the meeting was broken up and the gathering ended in confusion, fear and flight.[34]

The event led to the departure of many ulama, students, merchants and shop-keepers to the shrine of Hazrat-e Abdol'azim, south of Tehran, in a traditional demonstration of anger against the government. The *bast*, or sit-in, also called 'migration', took place in December 1905, and was led by Behbahani, Tabataba'i and a few other important divines, whom Nuri joined a couple of days later. The *bast* was financed by various sources, especially merchants and traders, but also by some important enemies of Ein al-Dawleh who otherwise cared little for lawful government. They included Mohammad Ali Mirza, the heir designate, and his unbalanced and pitiless brother, Salar al-Dawleh, sons of the shah who later were to fight against constitutionalism for as long as they could. This demonstrates in a particularly clear and unambiguous way the discordant and intrigue-ridden nature of the arbitrary state, where, seen from the angle of the European tradition, some of the biggest pillars of the establishment were apparently joining with those who wished to bring it down. Phillippe d'Orléans ('Phillippe Égalité') had played a similar role in the French Revolution, but, rather like Zel al-Soltan in this case, he had been a pretender to the throne, not an heir. And further than that, although a few enlightened members of the aristocracy (such as the Marquis de Condorcet, not to mention Lafayette) supported the French Revolution in its earlier stages, there was no onrush of the nobility, high or low, to abandon ship in the way that Orléans had done, to the disgust or disapproval of almost all the French peers. But this was not a feudal aristocratic system such as France under the Bourbons. It was the ancient Iranian arbitrary state and society where considerations of short-term personal gain had the better of long-term class interest.

It may be necessary at this point to make a few remarks about the old theory that the Constitutional Revolution was a bourgeois revolution. The alternative theory that it was plotted and organized by Britain merely to weaken Russian influence in Iran is no longer in fashion, although some Islamist historians still adhere to it.

Marx's concept of bourgeois revolutions is a product of his theory of (European) history or his historical sociology (of Europe). Marx argued that, in their conception of social reality, people were strongly influenced not only by their personal history and self-interest but notably by their social history and class interest. Here he had in mind the independent, functional classes of European society, long-established classes which were independent from the state, from and into which movement in and out was rare and unusual – they were solid, not malleable, social entities. He saw European history as a process of struggle between social classes – masters and slaves, patricians and plebeians, feudal lords and serfs, the nobility and the bourgeoisie, industrial capitalists and the proletariat – and their various subdivisions.

It was against solid, empirical and historical evidence *from European history and society* that Marx put forward the above sociology of history. He expressly excluded Asiatic societies from this theory of European history because he realized that both the sociology and the pattern of historical change in Asian societies, including Iran, had been fundamentally different from the experience of Europe. In this, of course, he had been long anticipated, from classical Greeks to Montesquieu, Adam Smith, James Mill and Hegel among others.

Marxist analyses of the Constitutional Revolution have run along the following lines. Economic development in the nineteenth century led to the growth of an urban bourgeoisie which could not be accommodated within the existing feudal system. The resulting conflict eventually manifested itself in a political upheaval for the establishment of a new (and historically relevant) institutional framework. This is a brief and basic statement of a familiar model, for the original formulation of which the French Revolution had supplied much of the empirical data. Explicitly or implicitly, it has been used by many historians and sociologists of Iran, although in a few cases with some qualifications.[35]

However, contrary to European experience, the Constitutional Revolution in Iran was not instigated by the less privileged classes of society against the ruling classes. It was a revolt of society against the state in line with Iran's own age-old historical experience, except that this time it was not directed just against an 'unjust' ruler in the hope of replacing him with a 'just' one. It was a revolution for law and against arbitrary rule itself. Thus when Seyyed Jamal al-Din Isfahani asked his audience in a sermon what the country needed most, there were calls for 'unity', 'patriotism' and so on. Admitting the desirability of all of these, the Seyyed emphasized that first and foremost there was need for law, QANUN. And in the traditional style of teachers trying to teach the Persian alphabet to little children, he began to spell out each letter, then two letters together – Q, A, QA – and asked the entire audience to repeat after him. He then launched into the following, which must be the most intensive single eulogy ever sung in praise of LAW in the annals of the Constitutional Revolution:

> People! Nothing would develop your country other than subjection to law, observation of law, preservation of law, respect for law, implementation of the law, and again law, and once again law. Children must from childhood read and learn at schools that no sin in religion and the *shari'a* is worse than opposing the law ... Observing religion means law, religion means law, Islam, the Koran, mean God's law. My dear man, *qanun, qanun*. Children must understand, women must understand, that the ruler is law and law alone, and no one's rule is valid but that of the law. The parliament is the protector of law ... The legislative assembly and legislature is the assembly which makes law, the sultan is the head of the executive which implements the law. The soldier is defender of the law, the police is defender of the law, justice means law, riches means implementing the law, the independence of the monarchy means rules of the law. In a word, the development of the country, the foundation of every nationality, and the solidarity of every nation arises from the implementation of the law.[36]

The nature of any revolution may be discerned by an examination of its *aims*, its *supporters*, its *opponents* and its *results*. Here, the central objective – indeed the very desideratum and password – was *mashruteh* or '*qonstitusiyun*', that is, government conditioned by law. That was also its principal result. There was not a single social class as such that opposed it. And it was supported by virtually the whole of (urban) society, including landlords who in fact were an urban social class and who benefited most from the revolution.

Religious dignitaries, too, wholeheartedly embraced the movement, even such exalted divines as Hajj Mirza Hosein Tehrani, Akhund Mullah Kazem Khorasani and Sheikh Abdollah Mazandarani, who in terms of rank and influence were even higher than cardinal archbishops. Provincial magnates and tribal leaders as great as Sepahdar-e (later, Sepahsalar-e) Tonokaboni, Fathollah Khan Akbar, Aliqoli Khan Sardar As'ad and Najafqoli Khan Samsam al-Saltaneh, who ruled their own territories with more authority than the average European duke, marquis or count, led the revolutionary forces in the military campaigns which resulted in their capture of Tehran. High mandarins who were running the government apparatus such as Mokhber al-Salataneh and Vosuq al-Dawleh joined the movement. The ranks and leadership of the revolution were packed with royals, royals' relatives and other Qajar clansmen like Farmnafarma, Ehtesham al-Saltaneh, Abolhasan Mirza (Sheikh al-Ra'is) and so forth, some of whom openly denounced the system of arbitrary rule.[37]

By January 1906 the protesters had returned from their *bast* to Tehran on the shah's agreement to meet their demands, including the central one of instituting independent judicial courts, which they called *Edalat-khaneh*. Prior to this, the most dramatic attempt to try to persuade them to return was the mission of Amir Bahador-e Jang, the simple-minded devotee of the shah and of arbitrary rule, who was sent by Ein al-Dawleh both to plead with them and to intimidate them into breaking sanctuary; but, if anything, this backfired.[38]

The triumphal return of the *basti*s strengthened the cause of the opponents of the chief minister and the campaigners for the constitution. As of this time the Persianized term *qonstitusiyun* still had a strong currency, although, certainly since the Russo-Japanese war, *mashruteh* was also being used for constitutional government. This is worth mentioning because later Mohammad Ali Shah would argue that he and his father had not agreed to *mashruteh*, simply to *qonstitusiyun*. It was a play on words and Mokhber al-Saltaneh warned him that the implications of the latter could be even more radical.[39]

Ein al-Dawleh resorted to familiar tactics: stalling, bribery and intimidation. But the point had been reached that such tactics would not work. In June 'the two seyyeds', Behbahani and Tabatab'i, held congregations almost every night in different mosques, which thus became the main popular assemblies of the movement. It was early in the following month[40] that Ein al-Dawleh ordered the arrest of Sheikh Mohammad Va'ez, a leading constitutionalist preacher who relentlessly attacked him from the pulpit. Attempts by seminary students (*talabeh*s) and others to rescue the sheikh led to the death of one of the *talabeh*s, whom the campaigners saw as the first martyr to the cause. Shops went on strike and the people and ulama gathered in the Friday Mosque, also in the bazaar just behind the Royal Mosque. Troops were sent in to disperse them, resulting in more bloodshed, especially when the leaders replied to Ein al-Dawleh's message that not only must there be '*majlis-e adl*' (House of Justice) but that he himself must go. The *bast* ended when the ulama were given safe conduct to leave town. The ulama, together with many of their adherents, 'migrated' again, this time to Qom, where, a few days later, they were joined by Sheikh Fazlollah Nuri, despite Ein al-Dawleh's efforts to dissuade him.

Public agitation in Tehran spread further and resulted in large numbers of people led by the wealthier merchants taking *bast* in the British legation compound. At the same time, Mohammad Ali Mirza, the heir-designate seated in Tabriz (who, as noted, opposed the chief minister), encouraged that city's religious dignitaries to appeal to the shah, attacking 'arbitrary' and 'traitorous' ministers and supporting the cause of the ulama of Tehran. The pressure was such that the shah, who personally had no stomach at all for the prolongation of the conflict, agreed both to the demand – this time clearly – for a constitution creating an independent legislature and judiciary and for the dismissal of Ein al-Dawleh, who, upon further public pressure, was sent off to Khorasan.

This was August 1906, and the constitution which was hurriedly written to ensure it would be completed in time to be signed by the shah and the heir-designate (since there were rumours that the former was unwell) was signed late in December. Five days later the shah died and was succeeded by his son, whom certainly the younger, radical and modernist intellectuals of the movement both disliked and distrusted.[41]

The first Majlis, as it came to be known, represented the six classes of people defined for this particular purpose: the ulama, men of royal descent (*shazdehs*), notables (*a'yan*), merchants, ordinary traders and artisans, but not peasants or women, the latter of whom at the time had not been granted the right to vote in almost any western country. Its first and foremost task was the preparation and approval of the constitution that was later endorsed by the shah and Mohammad Ali Mirza. Many of the future Iranian politicians found their way to this Majlis, including Vosuq al-Dawleh, Taqizadeh, members of the Hedayat clan, Amin al-Zarb and others. Mosaddeq, who was destined to nationalize Iranian oil decades later, was elected but could not meet the mandatory minimum age qualification.

This Majlis soon came into increasingly destructive conflict both with the new shah and with Nuri and his followers, who were critical of what they saw as Europeanizing policies and legislation. There was also serious conflict between constitutionalist moderates and radicals, but this did not come into full light until after the shah and Nuri had been defeated.[42]

Perhaps the victory of 1906 had been too easily won and further conflict and confrontation were inevitable. But beyond that and beyond the mere personality traits of the chief antagonists (which were obviously important) was the more or less impersonal, structural logic of the situation, the state–society conflict and the tendency to chaos after the fall of the arbitrary state.

In the Constitutional Revolution, Mohammad Ali Shah and his close advisors, if not hoping to reverse the clock completely, wished to retain as much executive power as possible. The Majlis in general did not trust the shah, and insisted on exercising much of the executive functions as well. It saw itself as the House of the People (*Khaneh-ye Mellat*), as opposed to the state. In other words, although a constitution had apparently removed the traditional antagonism between *mellat* (the people or society) and *dawlat* (the state), it still survived in actual attitudes and relationships. Historically, when the state was beaten, society came out on top, with the chaotic consequences that have been noted. Now, for the first time, law had been established to define and regulate the relationship between the state and the people. But neither the state (or what was left of it) nor society had sufficiently absorbed the fundamental novelty of the situation. Therefore, both society and state were still trying to eliminate each other as a political force and to hold the reins of power exclusively to themselves.

Apart from that, the constitution itself had granted too much power to the legislature. Indeed, it was a more democratic constitution than that of Russia, Germany, the Austrian empire and, in certain respects, even more democratic than that of Britain at the time, for example, in its later provision of unqualified and universal male suffrage and the absence of a hereditary parliamentary chamber. And yet there were no real parliamentary parties which might have negotiated with each other and the shah in an attempt to manage conflict. Finally, the revolutionary radicals – who were especially influential in some of the official and unofficial *anjomans* (leagues or associations) – were not in the mood for compromise. Not only did they insist on virtually unlimited people's power, but, at the same time, they were impatient to apply European modernization as quickly as they could.

This was the sharpest end of the conflict in so far as the religious traditionalists were concerned. It certainly is true that Nuri, regarding himself as the most learned *mojtahed* in Tehran – perhaps everywhere outside the *Atabat* – felt slighted by the ascendancy of Behbahani as the chief religious leader of the revolution. But the fears and forebodings of Nuri and some other *mojtaheds*, particularly Sheikh Mohammad Amoli, Mirza Hasan Tabrizi, Seyyed Ahmad Tabataba'i (brother of the great Tabtaba'i), the Imam Jom'ehs of Tehran and Tabriz and Hajj Aqa Mohsen Araqi, were not just limited to private self-interest. And, in any case, they tried to make a public case for their opposition, as will be noted below, although eventually they sided with the shah against constitutional government.

The first test was the government of Amin al-Soltan. As we have seen, he had been very unpopular as chief minister both before and after the death of Naser al-Din Shah, and had left the country after his fall in September 1903. Now it looked as if someone as able, pragmatic and wily as he could work a compromise. He had the support of Behbahani and other moderate constitutionalists, but both the radicals and the shah distrusted him, for apart from purely personal considerations his success would have reduced the chances of total triumph either by the shah or by the radicals, especially as it was likely to have the support of Russia and Britain. Amin al-Soltan's assassination at the end of August 1907 was a consequence of such fears by those opposite forces. Lengthy discussions and debates have taken place about whether the shah or the Democrats arranged the assassination. The balance of the argument shows that Abbas Aqa, a young radical activist from Tabriz, had shot the fatal bullet, but there is very little doubt that the shah's party received the news with a sigh of relief and even that they themselves were busy plotting when they were relieved of the task by the other side.

Perhaps the fate of Naser al-Molk's cabinet demonstrates the problem of the moderate, compromise-seeking parties in a less ambiguous way. Atabak's assassination had been followed by a ministry led by Mirza Ahmad Khan Moshir al-Saltaneh, a man of the shah's party. Predictably, his term of office was short-lived, giving way to Naser al-Molk's, which was largely made up of politically moderate and sophisticated and financially honest constitutionalists such as the brothers Mirza Hasan Khan Moshir al-Dawleh and Mirza Hosein Khan Mo'tamen al-Molk. This lasted only a few weeks, while the shah was preparing his first open assault on the Majlis, and the radical newspapers *Ruh al-Qodos* and *Mosavat* would not even stop short of publishing invectives against the person of the shah and his mother.[43]

In mid-December, large numbers of ruffians organized by the shah's party took to the streets shouting slogans against constitutional government: 'We follow the Koran, we do not want *mashruteh*; we want the Prophet's faith, we do not want *mashruteh*.' It is little known that the Jewish community was forced to join the demonstrations, but – being distinct in their community attire – they explained that it would look farcical for them to shout, 'We want the Prophet's faith.' Hence they were told to follow the Muslim crowd shouting, 'On behalf of the Muslims we do not want *mashruteh*.' At the same time as the mob set up tents in Artillery Square (not far from Baharistan, the parliament square), the shah summoned, beat up, dismissed and arrested his ministers, threatening to kill Naser al-Molk (the first Iranian educated at Oxford), who was saved by the intervention of the British legation on the condition that he left Iran, as he duly did the next morning. This shows clearly how the moderates were caught between the radicals of both right and left.[44]

As things turned out, the shah was not yet ready to go the whole way against the Majlis. His hesitation, in fact, helped to turn the situation, and he himself had to sue for reconciliation, however flimsy it in fact was. But, in retrospect, it is clear that Naser al-Molk's ministry was the last chance for a compromise, if a compromise were at all possible in a situation where most of those concerned did not want one.

The shah was more determined and better prepared next time round, but he went into action after an unsuccessful attempt on his life: a bomb was thrown at his carriage and a leading radical, Heidar Khan Amoqli, was arrested on suspicion of organizing the attack, but the Majlis stopped him from being prosecuted. There followed the coup of June 1908 in which the shah's Cossack Brigade led by Russian officers bombarded the Majlis, attacked and looted the homes of constitutionalists and their sympathizers and arrested a large number of younger leaders and activists, which included some Qajar noblemen. Among them, Seyyed Hasan Taqizadeh and Ali Akbar Dehkhoda took refuge in the British legation compound and later obtained safe conduct to go abroad. Others, such as Jahangir Khan, the joint editor of *Sur-e Esrafil*, and Malek al-Motekallemin, a popular preacher, were killed on the shah's order. So was Seyyed Jamal al-Din Isfahani, whom they caught on the run. These were disgraceful acts by a deceitful arbitrary ruler. But the part of the radical constitutionalists in helping him bring about the situation was not lost on an old leader with such impeccable credentials as Abdorrahim Talebof, who wrote to Dehkhoda in exile condemning zealous and excessive behaviour by the idealists and unruly alike.[45] The coup led to numbness at first, but the people of Tabriz rose and took over their town and through heroic resistance led by the legendary folk leader Sattar Khan held the revolutionary fort until other provinces – Gilan, Isfahan, Fars, in particular – also began to move against the shah's unlawful government. The government laid siege to Tabriz, and almost brought it to its knees by blocking food supplies. At one stage there was a real scare that Russian troops would go to the help of the government forces on the excuse of protecting European lives. The threat was there most of the time, but when in the end they did go (in April 1909), they went to relieve the town from certain famine and the government had to lift the siege.

Meanwhile, Britain and Russia had realigned in regard to their semi-colonial polcy in Iran. On 31 August 1907 the Anglo-Russian Convention, subsequently known as the 1907 agreement, was signed in St Petersburg to put an end to the long and intense rivalry in Iran between the two imperial powers. This had been actively canvassed and brokered by the French, anticipating the 'Triple Entente' between the three countries when World War I broke out. It divided Iran into three parts, Russian and British spheres of influence and a neutral zone, although it made the usual, but largely spurious, profession of respecting Iran's independence and integrity. This was a deliberate come-down by Britain from her position in Iran in anticipation of a European war which everyone expected. Yet while it visibly reduced the level of official British sympathy for the constitutionalists, it later became known that Sir Edward Grey, the Foreign Secretary, had played a role in discouraging the Russians from overt intervention on the shah's behalf. This was largely due to pressure brought from within the British government and politics by those, headed by Lord Curzon, who were opposed to the 1907 agreement.[46]

Therefore, as the shah continued to behave tactlessly and inconsistently and lose support in the country, even the Russians began to lose confidence in him, so that in the end the two great powers publicly demanded that he restore a form of constitutional government and sue for compromise.[47] They did not wish to help bring down his government, but their joint statement was helpful in boosting the morale of the revolutionaries, who had believed that the Russians would defend the shah to the bitter end.

Strangely enough, the turn of events was somewhat similar to those of the revolution in 1979, when the shah was constantly a step or two behind events, not taking the right step at the right time, acting indecisively and thus emboldening his radical opposition and losing the confidence of western powers, who, though they did not wish his downfall, would not encourage him to apply an 'iron fist' policy (see Chapter 12). It is difficult to know whether it would have been possible for the opposition to sell to the people a peaceful settlement with Mohammad Ali Shah or, if that was possible, for the settlement to be long-lasting in view of the shah's duplicitous and untrustworthy character, rather reminiscent of Charles I of England. Yet it is instructive that, of all the people, Taqizadeh, the then intellectual tribune of the radical revolutionaries, expressed profound regret, in his old age, to a close friend for his total rejection of the shah's offer of a return to constitutional regime short of his deposition.[48]

Nevertheless, if the constitutional restoration had led to a relatively peaceful and cohesive system resulting in gradual developments in politics, society and the economy, only die-hard reactionaries would have harked back to the *ancien régime*. It was because the ideals of political development were quickly lost that hope gave way to despair and harsh government came to be valued over persistent chaos, a change of attitude which has occurred in similar situations everywhere (see below and Chapter 9).

In July 1909 the forces of Gilan were led by Mohammad-Vali Khan Tonokaboni, entitled Sepahdar (later elevated to the higher title of Sepahsalar), and Fathollah Khan Akbar, entitled Sardar Mansur (later Sepahdar). Neither was a radical, though unlike Sardar Mansur, the former had a fiery temper. But their armies included a notable contingent of militiamen from the southern Caucasus – especially Baku – almost all of whom were radical democrats or social democrats. The most able single military leader of the Gilan *mojaheds* was Yephrem Khan, the Persianized revolutionary leader from Armenia and probably a military genius. Morgan Shuster wrote of Yephrem that 'he was the real head and shoulders of the expedition from Resht [Gilan]'.[49]

The forces of Isfahan were made up largely, but not entirely, of Bakhtiyari riflemen, led by their khans headed by Aliqoli Khan Sardar As'ad (II). Earlier, and in his absence in Europe, his brother Najafqoli Khan Samsam al-Saltaneh had already captured Isfahan.

Having joined forces, the revolutionary fighters then approached Tehran and fought a battle outside its gates with the shah's Cossacks before entering Tehran and quickly securing the city. In a recently published letter to the shah from his uncle and father-in-law, Kamran Mirza, while fighting was still going on in Tehran, the latter numbers the revolutionary forces at 10,000, explains that the royal forces were in dismay and retreat and says that, in response to his pleas for help, the Russian *chargé d'affaires* had told him that their forces were three days away from Tehran and that, in any case, their intervention would not be in the interest of the monarchy.[50]

The shah and his entourage took refuge in the Russian embassy compound in the north of Tehran and they were given safe conduct to cross the Caspain Sea for Russia. The battles outside and inside Tehran neither took long nor heavy casualties; nor were vindictive measures taken against supporters of the shah's regime, largely because of the moderating influence of Britain and Russia. But a couple of executions were allowed, including that of Sheikh Fazlollah Nuri. This would not have been possible without the approval of Behbahani and Tabataba'i in Tehran and Khorasani and Mazandarani in Najaf, suggested by the fact that they did not object to it after the event. For Nuri, by his actions more than his beliefs, had deeply hurt the feelings of the constitutionalists – and especially the leading among them – so that, in the process of the conflict, the three constitutionalist ulama in Najaf publicly condemned him as a *mofsed*, the Koranic term which in Islamic *shari'a* describes a capital offence.[51]

After the establishment of the first Majils in 1907, Nuri had felt slighted by Behbahani's ascendancy, but the criticisms by him and his circle of constitutional government revealed fears that secularization and modernization along European lines would destroy the authority of Islam as they knew it. They attacked the view that private money destined for religious congregations should be diverted for investment in modern industry and objected to clapping and cheering on festive occasions because these were European habits. Nuri and his supporters interpreted liberty as little more than licence. In the leaflets they were putting out from the shrine of Hazrat-e Abdol'azim, where Nuri had taken *bast* against the first Majlis, they described the constitutionalists as free thinkers, Babis, nihilists, anarchists and socialists and as advocates of licentious and irreligious agendas.[52] Hence they insisted that they were not opposed to *mashruteh*, only it had to be *mashru'eh* as well, that is, consistent with Islamic law as they interpreted it. But after the shah's coup, their leaders, including Nuri and Imam Jom'eh, addressed a letter to the shah condemning constitutionalism without qualification, thus endorsing the shah's restoration of arbitrary rule, which after its fall became known as the Lesser Arbitrary Rule (*estebdad-e saghir*). It must, however, be pointed out that the upholders of *mashru'eh* (just like those of *mashruteh*) were not an entirely homogeneous group, those in Isfahan in particular following their own distinct course.[53]

Rebutting Nuri and his group, the ulama in Najaf, Khorasani, Mazndarani and Tehrani (who died in 1908), had supported the Majlis against the claims both of the shah and of Nuri, and after the coup threw all their power behind the movement. It is difficult to see how the movement might have succeeded the way it did if the Najaf ulama had wavered in their support or, indeed, doubted the legitimacy of constitutionalism. On the contrary, they joined battle on the theoretical issue as well, arguing that arbitrary rule was not legitimate in Islam and that constitutional government was not a government of licence and chaos but one based in law, in which the government was responsible to the public and the people were equal before the law.[54] Their interpretation of constitutional government was sound, but that is not the spirit in which the country, even most of its leaders, responded to the new regime. The second decade of the twentieth century was a period of growing licence rather than rising liberty.

However, at the moment of the onslaught of Mohammad Ali Shah's Cossack force on the Majlis with Nuri's open support in 1908, a European observer (the young British diplomat Walter Smart, though his identity is not revealed in the source), who described himself as being 'no friend of religion', wrote of the part played by constitutionalist religious leaders and community that

> in Persia religion has, by force of circumstances, perhaps, found itself on the side of Liberty, and it has not been found wanting. Seldom has a prouder or a stranger duty fallen to the lot of any Church than that of leading a democracy in the throes of revolution, so that [the religious leadership] threw the whole weight of its authority and learning on the side of liberty and progress, and made possible the regeneration of Persia in the way of constitutional Liberty.[55]

Smart's surprise was quite understandable from the vantage point of European history, where revolutions were led by the lower classes and the underprivileged against the upper and privileged classes, including the established clergy, who were generally on the latter's side. It was very difficult from that standpoint to imagine religious pontiffs fighting the state on behalf of the people, although this was a typical scenario in the Iranian state–society conflict.

It was during the constitutionalist movement that the modern public sphere, to use Habermas's special conception of civil society, emerged in Iran. According to Habermas, the public sphere, as a sphere of critical association and discussion which is autonomous both from the state and the private sphere, emerged in eighteenth-century Europe, although the origins of this may be traced to late seventeenth-century England. In this sense, the modern public sphere, or something resembling it, emerged in Iran at the turn of the twentieth century in the form of independent and critical newspapers and journals, as well as rapidly increasing voluntary associations and societies.[56] Indeed, it could be argued that the Majlis itself formed a part of the public sphere rather than a part of the state, since it saw itself as the tribune of the people as opposed to the state.

The modern revolutionary press, poetry and publications gave a tremendous boost to the development of prose, literature and journalism, but they also played an important role in promoting destructive conflict and licentious speech. Of the newspapers which were remarkable for their libellous and intolerant expression, *Ruh al-Qodos* (The Holy Spirit) and *Mosavat* (Equality) headed the list. *Sur-e Esrafil* (The Trumpet of Esrafil) was a more sophisticated newspaper, though it, too, sometimes overstepped the mark.[57] This was co-edited by Mirza Jahangir Khan, who was executed on the shah's order after the coup, assisted by Dehkhoda who, as noted, would have met with a similar fate had he not managed to escape arrest after the coup.

Dehkhoda's prose, especially in his satirical column, has become standard reference for the model and origin of modern Persian prose, both in its use of simple language and in its application of common expressions. Naturally there were forerunners, ranging from Fath'ali Akhundzadeh through Talebof, Mirza

Habib Isfahani, Sheikh Ahmad Ruhi, Mirza Aqa Khan Kermani and others. But anyone who has read the works of Malkam Khan, written from the late 1850s onwards, would not fail to notice how distinctly modern his prose was in relation to his time and how clear its influence was on subsequent developments, including Dehkhoda's prose. Poetry also underwent change, both in form and content. Seyyed Ashraf al-Din, the owner-editor of *Nasim-e Shomal*, produced almost the exact counterpart of Dehkhoda's prose in journalistic, revolutionary poetry, which was humorous and even more colloquial than Dehkhoda's prose, although he too occasionally wrote poetry, notably his moving *mosammat* in memory of his murdered friend and colleague Jahangir Khan. Another rising young literary talent of the revolution was Poet Laureate Bahar.

Yet the triumph of 1909 did not and could not turn the country into paradise on earth overnight, as had been hoped by many. The revolution did not result in a bourgeois government, democratic or dictatorial. It resulted in greater legal security of private property in land as well as capital and a government led by landlords and merchants which quickly turned to chaos (as we shall see below).[58] It could possibly have led to gradual reforms and developments resulting in long-lasting achievement; but the old habits of discord and lack of social cohesion and cooperation and the attitude of total gain or total loss – in short, the politics of elimination – was too ingrained to make that possible. Clearly, then, this was a revolution that answered to virtually all the features of traditional Iranian revolts as a revolt of society against the state. The only unusual trait was that it aimed to establish the rule of law and was against arbitrary rule rather than mere injustice, and it used modern European forms and devices in trying to achieve its goals.

DISILLUSIONMENT

It took only a short while for constitutionalism to lose its popular appeal. Many would describe reports of killing and looting by saying 'there was constitutionalism' (*mashruteh shod*); and anyone who had made good through fraud and duplicity was said to have 'made it to his constitutionalism' (*beh mashruteh-ash resid*).

The logic of the growing chaos which followed the triumph of the revolution was similar to the familiar pattern we have discussed several times in this study when the state collapsed due to a combination of its own weakness and the onslaught of rebellious forces. The form was inevitably different, at least on the surface, since this time the revolt had been led in the name of law, liberty, constitutional government and – in the case of secular nationalists – modernism. In terms of constitutional theory, the lack of cooperation between the parliament and the government may be described as a confusion between the *separation* of powers and the *confrontation* of powers, especially as Iranians, then as now, set a high store by Montesquieu's doctrine of the separation of powers. Ahmad Matin Daftari, prime minister and minister of justice in the 1930s, reflecting on the post-Reza Shah chaos, recalled the post-constitutional chaos. He wrote in 1945:

What has remained in our memory from those [post-constitutionalist] years is that, as regards social life, we are immature and have not yet graduated from the elementary school. I cannot forget that in that period of democracy, our players sewed so much division, and displayed so much extremism and childishness, and, in a word, dried the roots of liberty to such an extent that the whirlwind of events suddenly uprooted it.[59]

Another important contributory factor was the traditional impetus towards autonomy, rebellion and pillage in the provinces and border regions, which normally happened only when the centre itself was weak or in chaos. This process, as noted above, had already begun under Mozaffar al-Din Shah's feeble government. Yet the most fundamental cause of chaos was confrontation rather than competition *in the centre*, which was most clearly manifested in political assassinations. For it was characteristic of the whole of Iranian history that, in the midst of prolonged chaos, unified and determined authority could suddenly establish order within an incredibly short period of time. Reza Khan did in two years what had seemed to be impossible to achieve for years or even decades to come. It is typical of Iran's history that whoever has the centre also has the periphery.

THE ONSET OF CHAOS

It took a few months after the fall of Tehran to constitutionalist armies for a permanent government to be formed. At first a High Commission was appointed to settle such matters as the deposition of the shah, his replacement by the heir apparent Ahmad Mirza and the second Majlis elections. The High Commission was then replaced by a 'Directory' or governing committee (cf. the *Directoire* after the Thermidor in the French Revolution), but shortly afterwards Sepahdar (now entitled Sepahsalar)-e Tonokaboni formed the first permanent ministry. This was early in October 1909.

By mid-July 1910 the ministry had fallen, because of the opposition of the Democrats, who were backed by the Bakhtiyaris, the other and better-organized military leaders of the revolution. Mirza Hasan Khan Mostawfi al-Mamalek then became prime minister. He was a relatively young man, very rich, pro-Democrat, popular with the political public, not very effective but honest in all matters. In late September Naser al-Molk was elected Regent by the Majlis, the position having become vacant upon the death of Alireza Khan Qajar (Azod al-Molk). Naser al-Molk was a constitutionalist of moderate views who had a realistic understanding of the country's capacity and resources and believed in gradual political development, and was therefore in the minority.

Mostawfi al-Mamalek's government of the summer of 1910 lasted until March 1911, and Sepahdar (Sepahsalar) returned once more. He was seen as the conservatives' candidate, and fell in mid-July on suspicion of being in league with the deposed shah in the latter's return to Iran in a desperate gamble to retake power. This time Samsam al-Saltaneh, the Bakhtiyari chief himself, became prime minister with the Democrats' backing, though in the imminent Shuster crisis they would regard him as an ogre.

Destructive conflict had already begun during Sepahsalar's first ministry in 1910 when, in the summer of 1911, Mohammad Ali Shah, aided by his brother Malek Mansur Sho'a' al-Saltaneh, decided to give his luck another run and try to stage a come-back. At about the same time, their unstable half-brother, Salar al-Dawleh, plunged into Iranian Kurdish territory from the west.

Both the regent (Naser al-Molk) and the prime minister (Samsam al-Saltaneh) organized the defence against the former shah's invasion with loyalty and commitment, as was witnessed by the young American Morgan Shuster. The Russians were already unhappy about the Majlis' appointment of Shuster as Iran's Treasurer-General with sweeping powers which went beyond the authority of the cabinet. Before the Anglo-Russian Convention of 1907, the constitutionalists had sought sympathy and support from Britain. After their triumph in 1909 they increasingly began to look elsewhere for help. The new Iranian regime often recruited military and civilian personnel from smaller European powers, especially Sweden and Belgium. This time they went for a young, efficient and reckless American. In his *The Strangling of Persia* Shuster makes it abundantly clear that he was opposed to old-school imperialism and felt much in sympathy with Iran in her relationship with her two imperialist neighbours. It is also clear that as a young liberal American he had little understanding of the traditional methods of bargaining and exchange with which things were somehow managed in Iran. He set out to create an island of efficiency and propriety in a traditional ocean which was still going through a revolutionary storm and was virtually dominated by Russia and Britain. Under the powers given to him by the Majlis, he organized the treasury gendarmerie as an instrument for collecting overdue and other revenues.

Predictably, he began to make powerful Iranian enemies as well as Russia, but he still had the support of the Majlis and the public. For example, he clashed with Ala al-Dawleh over his overdue tax payments. The latter had Shuster's men beaten up and turned away. Following a public outcry Ala al-Dawleh was gunned down outside his house by unknown assailants.[60]

Matters came to a head when the Majlis backed Shuster's decision to confiscate Sho'a' al-Saltaneh's property in compensation for unpaid taxes and retribution for his rebellion. This led to a clash with the Russians, who were claiming that Sho'a's property was the collateral for his debt to the Discount Bank of Russia. Shuster believed that at first the Russian consul had acted on his own initiative but that later St Petersburg had decided to back his policy.[61] That may have been so, but the Russians did not like Shuster and inevitably had been humiliated over the failure of the deposed shah's bid to return.

The triumphalism of the Majlis and the people had added insult to injury for the highly arrogant imperialist power. In any case, Shuster and the Majlis ignored the Russian claims as well as the advice of the cabinet to retreat. The battle of wills reached its climax when the Russians moved their troops in the north and delivered an ultimatum to the government that they would occupy

Tehran unless Shuster was dismissed and Iran promised not to employ any other advisor without the agreement of the Russian and British governments.

The Majlis overwhelmingly rejected the Russian ultimatum,[62] and the people took to the streets shouting 'Death or independence'. This made a face-saving compromise impossible and led to total surrender. The originally pro-Democrat government of Samsam al-Saltaneh then sent troops headed by the revolutionary hero Yephrem Khan to clear the Majlis, which, in any case, was close to the end of its mandatory dissolution. Iran accepted the ultimatum and Shuster was dismissed. The Russians occupied Tabriz, massacred some respectable community leaders, including the leader of the Sheikhi sect, and installed a pitiless Iranian governor of their own to run the province. This was December 1911, which is now normally regarded as the end of the Constitutional Revolution.[63]

Samsam's government eventually fell in early December 1912, because of pressure both from the Democrats, who were campaigning for Majlis elections, and conservatives, who had a new candidate for his post. Ala al-Saltaneh was a more acceptable conservative candidate to radicals and Democrats, although his ministry lasted only until mid-August 1913, and he was replaced by Mostawfi. By the time World War I broke out in August 1914, Ala had replaced Mostawfi and had been once again replaced by him. Thus nine ministries were formed in less than five years.

WORLD WAR I AND AFTER

In the summer of 1914 the young shah came of age and elections for the third Majlis were held. This was when World War I broke out. The war had been expected for at least ten years, and there were many long- and short-term causes. As soon as the Turks declared war on the Entente (Britain, France and Russia), the war was brought to Iranian borders. Iranians were generally pro-German and thereby pro-Turk. Mostawfi's government declared Iran neutral, but the Turks would not recognize the neutrality while Russian troops still occupied the northwestern province of Azerbaijan, which bordered on Turkey.

Russia's forces were in Iran, and Russia herself was as arrogant and moody as ever. Britain, who disembarked troops in Bahrain and Abadan to meet the Turkish threat, was also present, now with greater emphasis on her alliance with Russia. The Germans were trying to contact the Afghans and use them against British India, while at the same time fomenting religious and nationalist sentiments in Iran, India and elsewhere in the region. They therefore helped to organize Taqizadeh's National Committee in Berlin,[64] began to contact other Iranian nationalists and Democrats and sent agents to nomadic chieftains and other magnates in the southern Iranian regions.[65]

In March, the ulama in the *atabat* sent the shah a formal fatva against the Entente,[66] while the expulsion of German diplomats from the Russian sphere of influence had driven yet another hole into Iran's profession of neutrality.[67] Mostawfi's government fell under Entente pressure and the more flexible Moshir al-Dawleh formed a ministry that, nevertheless, did not satisfy either Russia and Britain or the pro-Germans of the third Majlis. There followed a typical example of rift in the very centre of politics until Mostawfi returned after a couple of others had become or had been nominated to become prime minister.

Bushehr, Iran's major port near the Abadan oilfields, had been put under British occupation as a result of a raid by local tribesmen apparently organized by Wassmuss, the legendary German agent, which had led to the death of two British officers.[68] Shiraz, the seat of the governor-general of Fars, was in turmoil, with both British and German consulates involved, though the Germans had public sympathy on their side. All the four warring parties were violating Iran's neutrality, but, in general, the Iranians saw the Russians and British as the aggressors, while the Germans and (less) Turks were seen, if not as liberators, then as merely responding to Anglo-Russian intervention.

In November 1915 the Russians moved their considerable troops in Qazvin towards Tehran. Panic spread and there was talk of the capital being moved to Isfahan, where the Entente position was less strong and outside Russia's sphere of influence. About half of the Majlis deputies moved to Qom, thus causing that body to cease to function, and set up the National Defence Committee led by Soleiman Mirza (later Eskandari), the Democrat leader. The young shah was determined to move the capital but he was dissuaded from this, and in December Farmanfarma became prime minister, with British backing.[69]

The Russian show of force had apparently secured Tehran for the Entente. When Russian troops took Qom and the *melliyun* fell back on Kashan and then Isfahan, Nezam al-Saltaneh (Rezaqoli Khan Mafi), governor-general of the south-western provinces, threw in his lot with them. He attacked and took Kermanshah and formed the Provisional Government, which, unlike the government in Tehran, was allied to the Central Powers, in which both Soleiman Mirza and Seyyed Hasan Modarres took part.[70]

It was in the same period that the British South Persia Rifles were organized in Fars and the *Jangal* Movement, led by Kuchik Khan and his followers in Gilan, declared its affiliation to the Union of Islam movement, just launched by the Turks to boost their popularity in Muslim countries.[71] Farmanfarma's government was later replaced by Sepahdar's and his by Vosuq al-Dawleh's (who was seen as a British candidate), but the Entente did not manage to obtain any significant concessions from them.

The February 1917 revolution in Russia, followed by the October revolution, looked little short of a miracle for Iran. The Russian yoke, the greatest weight set against Iran's independence, was suddenly taken off, but the country was otherwise in a state of collapse. Several other cabinets came and went until 1918, when the defeat of the Central Powers was in sight and – with active British backing – Vosuq formed an eventful government. Thus between 1914 and 1918 there were twelve premierships and between 1910 and 1918 twenty ministries with an average life of five months. The same pattern was to be repeated in the period 1941–51, when chaotic trends re-emerged after the fall of Reza Shah.

Vosuq's 1918 government was to last longer than any other between 1906 and 1926, except Reza Khan's cabinet of 1923-5. In retrospect, it was the last chance that the Iranians had for reaching a workable political settlement along the rules established by the constitution of 1906. The alternatives were disintegration or the establishment of a dictatorial regime, which could easily and quickly turn into arbitrary government. This in fact was what happened.

THE RISE OF IRANIAN NATIONALISM

The origins of much that happened in Iran in the decades following the Constitutional Revolution lay in two distinct but closely related features of state and society since 1909: domestic chaos and foreign intervention. A third factor that became entangled with the other two was the conflict over modernization and, especially, how, in what sense and at what speed modernization might be achieved. Almost all Iranian politics in the twentieth century – conservative, constitutionalist, democratic, nationalist, Marxist-Leninist and Islamist – had their roots in these problems, which intermittently produced chaotic trends and arbitrary governments.

There had been no 'nation' in Iran before the Constitutional Revolution, just as there had been none in Europe *before they were built* between the Renaissance and the Reformation and the 1848 revolutions, although there had always been a sense of communal identity and belonging among various peoples everywhere in the world.

Since the latter part of Naser al-Din Shah's reign modern concepts of nationhood and nationalism had begun to emerge among a very small elite. These were men of whom Fath'ali Akhundzadeh and Mirza Aqa Khan Kermani were probably quintessential examples, in two successive generations.[72] It is sometimes thought that an Iranian nationalism had existed before the Islamic conquest, for which *Shahnameh* is given as evidence. In fact there is as little substance to that claim as there was to the Nazis' claim that located the origins of their ideas and sentiments in the pagan, Teutonic age. The Persians, Greeks, Romans and Chinese were certainly proud of their civilizations and often belittled the outsider; but they cannot be described as nationalists in any sense conveyed by that term in modern times.

The emerging modern nationalists believed in Iran's superiority, not only on account of its real and imagined ancient glories but even more so because, as an Aryan people, it belonged to the western European race which had created the great social and scientific civilization that was contemporary Europe. And the frustration, not to say depression, of fervent nationalist intellectuals was the greater because of the glaring contrast between Iran's current backwardness and Europe's modern achievements, which they believed their country had failed to realize, mainly – if not solely – because of Arabs (later also Turks) and Islam.[73]

The most outspoken and a most sincere poet to express this ideology of Iranian nationalism was Aref-e Qazvini, whose passionate songs and poems are, ironically, in the genres and styles of traditional mourning for religious tragedies and martyrs, thus reflecting their hidden cultural and psychological affinities. He was either for sudden and miraculous delivery or total destruction and death:

> Naught but death would relieve my pain,
> Alas that which would relieve my pain did not arrive
> I am mourning Alexander's adventure in Iran,
> You wonder why at the Spring of Life he did not arrive . . .
> When the Arabs found their way into Iran and since,
> A word of happiness from the land of Sasan did not arrive . . .
> That is why Aref has arrived wondering
> Why the news of the total destruction of Tehran did not arrive.[74]

The Turks were soon to go down the same path in Aref's nationalist poetry, although the provocation came from their own quarters when Turkish writers and journalists began to claim that most Iranians were Turks and that Iranian culture had a 'Turkish spirit'. Reacting angrily, Aref wrote:

> The Turkish tongue is good for pulling out,
> It must be cut out of this country.[75]

This new ideology of modern Iranian nationalism was to deeply influence the official attitude and policy in the Pahlavi era, and even dominate the psyche of many Iranian intellectuals who were opposed to the Pahlavi regime.[76]

POSITIVE ACHIEVEMENTS

The Constitutional Revolution was indeed followed by chaos and disorder but it was not as if there had been all losses and no gains. The revolution had two main objectives, which were somewhat related to each other. First and foremost were the abolition of arbitrary rule and the establishment of a government by law as opposed to fiat, the goal that was unexceptionably espoused by all the forces supporting the revolution. Second, was the centralization of the state, the modernization of the administrative machinery and the introduction of modern education, modern transport facilities and so forth. The hopes and aspirations of the small modernist elite were more ambitious and amounted to an earnest wish to turn the whole country into a modern western European society within a short space of time.

Regarding the first objective of the Constitutional Revolution, we have shown above that little was achieved in terms of creating a constitutional state, because destructive conflict among the constitutionalists themselves made normal governance extremely difficult. In the absence of such distrust and conflict, slow but real long-term political progress would have been made. Nevertheless, the fact that a written constitution and forms of representative government, notably the

Majlis, had been established was by itself no mean achievement, even though they were often violated later in the century.

Regarding the second major objective of the revolution, that is state-building and modernization, there was perhaps more lasting progress, partly because there was greater consensus in the centre of politics and among the leading political elites. A body of civil servants and its corresponding institutions came into being who began to learn the modern methods of running a country. The police and the gendarmerie – both of them organized and led by Swedish officers – were definite improvements on what had existed before. Judicial courts became organized and were more accessible to larger numbers of people. There was a rapid and contin- uous development of a modern legal profession, including judges, lawyers and notaries public. Modern schools that had begun to appear before the revolution mainly through private and civic effort increased in number and capacity, and a growing number of middle-class families paid serious attention to the education of girls as well as boys.

Such achievements provided the basis for further and more rapid develop- ments under Reza Khan and Reza Shah, in part because (as before) there was little conflict over their desirability but mainly because both the concentration and the centralization of power made it much easier to pursue these aims with relative speed.

THE FAILURE OF THE 1919 AGREEMENT

There was not just chaos and fear of disintegration when Vosuq formed his cabinet but severe countrywide famine and the world influenza epidemic, which was taking a terrible toll of the population.[77] The two revolutions in Russia had saved Iran from the tyranny of Russian imperialism and the likely partition of the country between Russia and Britain after an Entente victory. And Bolshevism was so popular with nationalist modernists that Aref was singing its praises in his poetry.[78]

Britain, now the sole remaining power in the region, had to confront the situ- ation; and as the Iranian government was in dire financial straits for its daily needs, Britain was paying a monthly subsidy to keep the civil administration and the Cossack Division afloat. The evidence shows that, until some time after the 1919 Agreement was signed, Britain's primary motive was not to encircle revo- lutionary Russia since it believed that Russia would soon 'recover from her present madness'.[79]

Lord Curzon, the British policymaker who shortly became Foreign Secretary, saw his chance of bringing Iran into the fold of Britain's sphere of influence in the Middle East. The evidence shows that he did not intend to turn Iran into a British protectorate as the opponents of the 1919 Agreement universally believed, and even if he had he would have needed a mandate from the League of Nations rather than an agreement with the Iranian government. Curzon hoped to make Iran not a protectorate but a client state of Britain and no other great power, as she had been before the fall of Tsarist Russia, unsuspecting that the opposition of other great powers to his scheme would reinforce the greatest fears of Iranians about his intentions.[80]

The government of British India was well aware of the upsurge of modern Iranian nationalism. Their alternative to the Agreement was almost entirely consistent with the views of popular constitutionalist leaders.[81] But they were overruled by Curzon. The rumour, and later discovery, of the payment of money – despite Curzon's great reluctance to approve it – left little doubt in the minds of the Iranian public that their country had been 'sold' to Britain.[82] Mirzadeh Eshqi proclaimed in a verse: 'O' Vosuq al-Dawleh Iran wasn't your daddy's estate' – and much worse.[83]

The main terms of the Agreement were for Britain to provide advisors for organizing Iran's disintegrating financial and military organizations and to give Iran a long-term loan of £2 million, at 7 per cent interest. The more long-term perspective was British assistance for the development of Iran's transport system, other infrastructural concerns and modern manufacturing.[84] The whole affair made America, France and Russia hostile to the Agreement, and their belief that the country's independence had been compromised left little room for argument with the country's modern nationalists, radicals and pro-Bolsheviks. The more emphatically Curzon and Vosuq's government repeated that this was not the case, the more firmly the Agreement's opponents in and out of the country believed that it was.[85]

There was another upsurge of revolutionary activity in Gilan led by Kuchik Khan and his *Jangal* Movement, which, despite Vosuq's own tactful approach, the injustice, greed and incompetence of government officials and the Cossack Division did nothing to moderate.[86] In March 1920 Sheikh Mohammad Khiyabani led the revolt of the Tabriz Democrats and, for a few months, became the virtual ruler of Azerbaijan. Recent evidence has shown that, despite long-held views, Khiyabani's revolt was neither separatist nor pro-Bolshevik nor a reaction to the Agreement. He too understood the logic and despised the consequences of chaos, and hoped to bring order, at least to Azerbaijan, under his own leadership. Yet the revolt was generally believed (both then and since) to have been a move against the Agreement.[87]

The first major crack in the Agreement was caused by the Bolshevik landing of May 1920 at Anzali (on the Caspian Sea), and could probably have been avoided if Curzon had not in effect stopped Vosuq from talking directly to Moscow. The Bolsheviks had apparently come with the intention of recovering White Russian navy warships at Anzali. Both the War Office and the British cabinet wished to avoid a long and protracted conflict with Bolshevik Russia in Iran. The British North Persian Force (Norperforce), which was stationed in Qazvin with garrisons in Anzali and Rasht, had been ordered to evacuate Anzali if attacked by the Bolsheviks.[88] When the attack came in May 1920, the further withdrawal from Rasht – which seems to have been entirely unnecessary – sealed the fate of the Agreement. It lost Britain a great deal of prestige, emboldened opposition to them and the Agreement, further weakened Vosuq's position and led to the coalition of Kuchik and the Iranian Bolsheviks, backed by their Soviet allies, in launching the Gilan Socialist Republic. The coalition did not last, but until the 1921 coup Tehran was in fear of the Gilan Bolsheviks marching to the capital the minute Norperforce was withdrawn from Iran.

Thus Vosuq's cabinet fell in June 1920. Moshir al-Dawleh's government, which succeeded Vosuq's, faced many, almost insurmountable, difficulties, but it had public goodwill on its side, which is how he split Kuchik from the Gilan Bolsheviks and put down Khiyabani's revolt without difficulty. However, all that Curzon was interested in was that the Majlis should be convened without delay and the fate of his cherished Agreement be decided.[89]

THE *COUP D'ÉTAT* OF 1921

The War Office was weary of Curzon's pressure to keep their forces in Iran. They sent Major General Sir Edmund Ironside, a tough soldier and an expert in dealing with critical situations, to command Norperforce. At the time, Herbert Norman was the British minister in Tehran, 'minister' then being the title of an envoy and head of the diplomatic legation, lower in standing than 'ambassador', when full diplomatic relations did not exist between the respective countries. Ironside quickly toppled the Russian commander of the Cossack Division with Norman's support and the shah's acquiescence. This led to the resignation of the government of Moshir al-Dawleh at the end of October 1920, which was opposed to putting the Cossacks under British officers.[90]

The Iranian Cossacks had been a creation of the late nineteenth century. As we have seen, in 1878 the Tsar had agreed to Naser al-Din Shah's personal request to create a force similar to his own Cossack army, financed by Russia and led by Russian officers, as a favour to the shah and a useful instrument of Russian influence in the country. Once the Bolsheviks repudiated Tsarist interests and privileges in Iran, Britain began to pay a monthly subsidy towards the upkeep of the force, now upgraded to a division. Just before the fall of Moshir's government the Cossacks had suffered a humiliating defeat at the hands of the Gilan insurgents (following an initial victory) and were settled at the village of Aqababa near Qazvin under the watchful eyes of Norperforce and its new commander, General Ironside.[91]

Ironside felt that a military dictatorship might save the situation from chaos and/or 'Bolshevism', along with British honour.[92] On the other hand, Seyyed Zia (a leading journalist and political activist who had close relations with British diplomats in Tehran) and his Committee of Iron were looking for an opportunity to bring on a strong government, preferably their own.[93] Together they decided to bring the Cossacks to Tehran for a putsch before Norperforce's departure, which was set for April 1921.

They looked for a commander to lead the coup, and approached Amir Movassaq (later General Mohammad Nakhjavan), the most senior Cossack field officer, who turned them down.[94] They then settled on Colonel (*mirpanj*) Reza Khan.[95] In February, Ironside was suddenly summoned to a conference in Cairo and felt he had to act before leaving. He saw the shah with Norman and asked him to bring Reza Khan to 'a position of power', which the shah refused to do.[96] He then told Norman of his plan, which Norman did not endorse. However, when it became clear that the Cossacks were definitely coming, Norman was persuaded by his diplomatic and military colleagues in Tehran to cooperate. That is how the coup succeeded without a fight and Zia became prime minister.[97]

Within a couple of weeks the Foreign Office, which had neither known about nor approved of the coup, had a fairly accurate picture of what had happened, even though in his correspondence Norman denied any role by Ironside, himself or any other British officer or diplomat in organizing the coup.[98] But Curzon did not have the slightest interest in the new government; it had been brought about by a coup which had taken place behind his back, and Zia had committed the unforgivable sin of abrogating the 1919 Agreement. Curzon gave them precisely nothing.[99]

When in April 1921 Norperforce departed, Norman was left with no power, either moral or material, with which to defend Zia's government. Reza Khan was aware of this, and Zia's arrogance and tactlessness had left him with little domestic support, only the goodwill of the nationalist intellectual elite, which was of little help in sustaining him in power. On the other hand, the astute and manipulative Reza Khan posed as the loyal servant of the shah and the country who had no political ambitions. He persuaded the shah to dismiss Zia, and Norman, although he tried, was unable to prevent the dismissal.

Thus the tide began to turn again, from chaos towards arbitrary rule, a pattern entirely familiar in the country's ancient history.

CHAPTER 9

Modern Arbitrary Rule

Every country has a certain type of regime. Ours is a one-person regime.

Reza Shah

(quoted by Mehdiqoli Hedayat in *Khaterat va Khatarat*, p. 386)

IN THE PERIOD 1921–41 Reza Khan consolidated his power, built up the armed forces, put an end to chaos both in the provinces and the centre, thus establishing domestic order and stability, overthrew the Qajars and replaced them with his own monarchy, advanced the pan-Persian nationalist ideology which was already widespread among the nationalist modernist elite and pursued policies of modernization in line with the aspirations of that elite. What was remarkable but historically familiar was the speed with which the chaos was brought to an end and a period of dictatorial government later turned into arbitrary rule, begun with modern techniques and in a post-constitutional framework. Yet this, too, proved to be a short-term experience, quickly overturned as soon as Reza Shah abdicated and left the country.

Reza Khan was an intelligent, hard-working, forthright and ruthless soldier, with an astonishingly powerful memory and a high degree of self-confidence that, coupled with success, turned into arrogance. He was a pan-Persian nationalist and a pure pragmatist who would use whatever methods he thought were necessary to achieve personal and national goals.

Vested interests have portrayed Reza Khan's background, on the one hand, as being poor and uneducated and, on the other, as that of a thriving middle-class family of the time.[1] Whatever his family background, the evidence shows that even when he was a high-ranking Cossack officer he was not very literate and belonged to a lower culture, as did a number of Iranian Cossack officers.[2] His literacy and knowledge of the world improved significantly as he moved to higher positions, and he successfully assumed a royal stature after becoming shah. But certain deeply rooted cultural limitations remained with him all his life. His official date of birth was March 1878 but it is likely he was born before then.[3] He became known as Reza Maxim when, as an NCO, he distinguished himself in using a machine gun of that name. He fought against the constitutionalists as a Cossack soldier; he later fought with the constitutionalist armies against the rebels; still later, he fought with the Cossacks on the side of the Russians and against the forces of the popular pro-German provisional Government in World War I.[4]

Reza Khan was quick to learn and to adapt, and was a man of physical and psychological courage. In 1941, when he believed he had no choice but to abdicate, he did so with courage and resolution, even though the public who had lived in fear of him saw it as cowardice.[5] His self-confidence at first served him well, but easy success – together with the absolute power of the ruler and the extraordinary subservience and sycophancy of the ruled – later turned into self-delusion.

Reza Khan was a nationalist of the new cut, inspired by the Aryanist and pan-Persian ideology which had increasingly gripped modern Iranians since the end of World War I. He was tutored in that ideology by the younger politicians and intellectuals who gathered around him, notably his chef-de-cabinet, Farajollah Khan Bahrami, whom he later dismissed and banished. The principles of his reform programme – modernization, centralization and secularization – had already been laid down by the pan-Persian nationalist elite since the rise of constitutionalism, and especially the end of the Great War. They believed in the use of dictatorial powers to establish a unified army, stamp out chaos, build a modern nation-state, reassert national sovereignty, separate religion from politics, extend modern secular education, promote modern industry, impose a uniform dress code, impose the Persian language on the linguistic minorities and improve the status of women, all of which they hoped would turn Iran into a western European type of society within a short space of time, an attitude which has been described as pseudo-modernism.[6] What they did not anticipate was the likelihood of the dictatorship turning into arbitrary rule and in time turning against themselves.

THE END OF CHAOS

Reza Khan had begun to emerge as the country's military dictator at least as soon as Seyyed Zia had been dismissed and driven out of the country. Nevertheless, it took five years of power struggles before he could defeat all opposition and establish his own dynasty. The Bolshevik insurgency in Gilan with which Kuchik Khan once again joined forces was still in place, but in a little time Reza Khan led his troops and put it down.[7] This became politically possible when, shortly after the 1921 coup, Seyyed Zia signed the new Iranian-Soviet treaty which had been negotiated months before the coup, thus removing Soviet support for Gilan Bolsheviks. The young modern intellectuals saw the dismissal of Seyyed Zia and his replacement by Qavam al-Saltaneh, a conservative constitutionalist, as a reactionary move. Qavam was a brother of Vosuq, a wealthy landlord and a principled but pragamatic and not very scrupulous politician, a rare species among Iranian politicians in strength of character, coolness and lack of regard for popularity. The young nationalist Colonel Moahammad Taqi Khan Pesyan, the popular gendarmerie chief of Khorasan who had been pro-Zia and anti-Qavam, revolted, but he was killed in action before Reza Kahn could take any steps against him.[8]

The shah at first trusted Reza Khan, but it did not take long for him to become suspicious of his ambitions. Reza Khan had virtually a free hand in organizing the new army by uniting the old Cossack and gendarmerie forces under one command, expanding the armed forces and reforming their hierarchy, chain of command and uniforms whilst equipping them with more and better weaponry.[9] There was in the process a minor rebellion by Abolqasem Lahuti, the radical gendarmerie major and poet, which was swiftly put down, and Lahuti crossed the border to the Soviet Union.[10] Disorder in most provinces was eliminated even before Reza Khan became Reza Shah, once again demonstrating the ease with which prolonged and seemingly never-ending periods of chaos could be brought to an end by the existence of will in the centre. Other rebellions which surged up later – the most important being the tribal uprising of 1929 in the south – were often provoked by oppressive anti-nomadic policies and the harsh attitude and behaviour of the military and civilian administrators in the area. In the first few years after 1921, not only the ruthless suppression of rebellion and brigandry but also the subjugation of regional magnates and notables was very popular with the urban public, and certainly with the modernist nationalist elite.

The imposition of order and discipline was extremely urgent. There had been so much turmoil for so long, causing such social insecurity and economic damage and putting the very existence of the country in doubt, that suppressing it was the only achievement of Reza Khan and Reza Shah to be admired by well-wishers and critics alike. In October 1925, in their speeches in the Majlis against the motion for making Reza Khan head of state, both Taqizadeh and Mosaddeq praised his success in putting an end to the semi-anarchic situation.[11]

As noted in Chapter 8, chaotic trends had begun almost immediately after the death of Naser al-Din Shah, so that one of the main objectives of the reformers and later revolutionaries had been to establish order and centralize government. The constitutionalists had hoped that the establishment of the rule of law would almost automatically bring order as well, whereas in practice 'law', which was seen as freedom from arbitrary power, was also regarded as freedom from the state, and thus even greater disorder followed the triumph of the constitutionalists. Therefore although there was some criticism even earlier in Reza Khan's career of attempts by the army divisions to dominate provincial life, they were still mostly muted and few and far between. The operations of General Amir Ahamadi against Lor tribes in the west and south-west were numerous and became notorious for their ruthlessness. Amir Ahmadi says in his memoirs that his replacement, Hosein Aqa Khaza'i (or Khoza'i), executed twelve innocent chieftains in Loristan, although the local sources put the number at nine.[12]

As noted, these measures, even including those which were conducted with excessive force and ruthlessness, were in the first few years generally popular with the ruling elites and urban middle classes, and were seen to be necessary to bring the country to order.

REZA KHAN BECOMES REZA SHAH

It is unlikely that Reza Khan at first thought of establishing his own dynasty in place of the Qajars, but from May 1921 when he toppled Seyyed Zia there is little doubt that he aimed at becoming a dictator. His strategy consisted of organizing and expanding the armed forces under his own personal command, befriending and pacifying both Britain and the Soviet Union, winning the Majlis majority and gaining the support of the nationalist and modernist elites and intellectuals.

It took only two years and a few months, from June 1921 to November 1923, for Reza Khan to become prime minister while retaining the posts of minister of war and chief of the army, which he had held throughout that period. Interim events were typical of both conservative and popular politicians of the old school, even though many of them were becoming increasingly alarmed at the growing autonomy of Reza Khan – now entitled Sardar Sepah – and his army: there were no fewer than five cabinets in that period, which roughly covered the duration of the fourth Majils.

Qavam al-Saltaneh (later Ahmad Qavam) held office from June 1921 until February 1922. His government was followed by that of Moshir al-Dawleh only until May 1922, that is, less than four months. Qavam became prime minister once again, from June 1922 to January 1923. His cabinet fell and was replaced by that of Mostawfi al-Mamalek, who led the government until June 1923, just before the end of the fourth Majlis and the beginning of the elections for the fifth. At that point Modarres tried, but did not succeed, to form a majority for Qavam as a strong politician who could stand up to the rising power of Reza Khan. In the event, Moshir formed a ministry as a compromise candidate.

During these two years there were four main tendencies among politicians and Majlis deputies. Modarres, the astute if tactless *mojtahed*-politician who usually led the Majlis majority, soon became fearful of Reza Khan's dictatorial aspirations and tried to promote Qavam as the alternative to him. The popular constitutionalists were in favour of Moshir and Mostawfi, but appreciated Reza Khan's services in bringing order to the country. Democrats and Socialists were increasingly impressed, especially with Reza Khan's success both for that and for his attempts at military and administrative centralization and his aspirations for secularization and modernization. Radical nationalists regarded Modarres, Qavam and the conservatives as reactionary and subservient to Britain, and the popular politicians as totally incapable of dealing with the country's problems. Thus the latter two groups increasingly came to view Reza Khan as their man and the 'saviour' (*naji*) of the country. In time, some younger conservatives, notably Firuz Mirza Nosrat al-Dawleh, broke rank and actively began to promote Reza Khan.

Reza Khan established good relations both with the British and Soviet envoys. Sir Percy Loraine was most impressed with his attempts to bring order and discipline to the country and declared him as 'the winning horse' to the Foreign Office, although at no point did the Foreign Office display a high degree of enthusiasm for Reza Khan; it merely refrained from interference and in effect sat on the fence. Reza Khan also impressed the Soviet envoys, Rotstein and Shumiatsky, who regarded him as a bourgeois nationalist leader trying to combat feudal reactionaries and agents of imperialism. In fact there was little difference in substance between the assessment of the British, the Soviets and the Iranian modernists, except that the British government (as distinct from their Tehran envoy) was not as enthusiastic about Reza Khan as the rest of them. And when he made his bid for the throne in 1925 the British and Soviet envoys as well as the Iranian modernists still hoped that he would declare a republic.[13]

In October 1923 Sardar Entesar (later Mozaffar A'lam) apparently voluntarily made a long confession to the police that two years earlier Qavam had tried to conspire with him to have Reza Khan assassinated.[14] The charge is unlikely to have been true if only because not only was Entesar pardoned but he went on to enjoy important official posts throughout Reza Khan/Reza Shah's rule, whereas Reza Shah would have been very unlikely to forgive or forget less important offences. At any rate, Reza Khan used the story to hit four targets with one blow. Moshir's government resigned, Qavam went into voluntary exile, the shah left for a visit to Europe (from which he was never to return) and Reza Khan became prime minister.

By this time there had been many defections from the Modarres faction in the fifth Majlis, and the majority had turned in favour of Reza Khan. Shortly before Reza Khan became prime minister, a group of established politicians, including Seyyed Mohammad Tadayyon aided by younger intellectuals and journalists including Zeinol'abedin Rahnema, launched a new political grouping called Independent Democrats of Iran. They were staunch supporters of Reza Khan to the point of adulation, and began to woo Soleiman Mirza's Socialists for an alliance. At the same time, Ali Akbar Davar, the future minister of justice and finance, was organizing young nationalist radicals such as Ali Akbar Siyasi and Mahmud Afshar, who, like Davar himself, had recently returned from Europe and were full of nationalist aspirations for a radical change in Iran. These young men set up the Young Iran Club (*Kolub-e Iran-e Javan*) to promote their ideas and support Reza Khan, but the latter advised them to close it, promising personally to fulfil all their aspirations.[15]

The Independent Democrats carried much more weight. Their parliamentary group, the Modernization Faction (*Feraksion-e Tajaddod*)[16] soon became the most effective instrument in managing Reza Khan's supporters in the Majlis. Increasingly, they attracted the cooperation of old Democrats and Socialists. It was also from about the inception of the fifth Majlis and the election to premiership of Reza Khan that a growing number of younger journalists and intellectuals openly began to advocate the virtues of dictatorship. In fact dictatorship became the fashionable ideal among Iranian intellectuals both in Tehran and in Europe. At one stage Reza Khan's chef de cabinet, Farajollah Bahrami, in his capacity as a writer and intellectual, invited his fellow intellectuals to describe their ideal publicly in newspapers, it being clear that the expected response was the advocacy of a modern nationalist dictatorship. The only prominent intellectual to disappoint him openly was the nationalist poet Mirzadeh Eshqi, who became a victim of official assassination not long afterwards, although not for that reason.[17] The bitter fruit of chaos which had ripened in the name of constitutionalism had become so unpalatable that it was now chic to openly campaign for dictatorship. Davar, the honest, upright and Swiss-educated lawyer and nationalist, was proudly advocating such a system in his newspaper *Mard-e Azad*. It was being advocated in other journals as well, including the journal *Farangestan*, published by a group of Iranian students and intellectuals in Berlin.

There was no doubt in the minds of the advocates of dictatorship who the dictator was going to be. Therefore, only a few months after Reza Khan became prime minister a campaign, organized by modern intellectuals, Democrats and Socialists in the centre and the army divisions in the provinces, was launched to abolish the monarchy and establish a republic. Press campaigns, meetings, public speeches and petitions all contributed.

By March 1924, when the campaign was launched, Reza Khan had the army, the Majlis, the modern middle classes and the young nationalists behind him, and there was no fundamental reason why they should not have succeeded in abolishing the monarchy. The shah was still in Europe anxiously communicating with his brother the Prince Regent in Tehran. Apart from the royal court and their dwindling conservative supporters, there was little sympathy for the Qajars in wider political circles. And the religious establishment did not make any visible move against the republican campaign, however anxious some of them might have been that the new republic might promote secularism along the lines that was being promoted by Ataturk in Turkey. But the opposition were afraid that this would be the first step towards Reza Khan becoming shah and arbitrary ruler. For example, Poet Laureate Bahar, a leading Modarres supporter in the Majlis, wrote in one of his poems against the campaign for a republic:

In the guise of a republic he is knocking at the door of kingship
We are ignorant and the greedy enemy is canny.[18]

However, the campaign failed on this occasion. The leaders were in a hurry and not well prepared and, as the head of the Majlis opposition, Modarres played his hand well. On the day that the motion was to be debated, a huge crowd gathered outside the Majlis, not in Reza Kahn's support, as he had hoped, but in favour of Modarres. He ordered the Majlis guards to attack the crowd and as a result was severely chastised by the Majils speaker, the popular Mo'tamen al-Molk. The whole event was a failure for Reza Khan, who was consequently dismissed by a heartened Ahmad Shah from Europe. But a new Majlis majority soon reinstated Reza Khan to the premiership after threats were issued by some provincial army commanders that they would otherwise march on Tehran.[19]

It was only then that Reza Khan realized the value of having the religious establishment's active support. He met in Qom with Hajj Sheikh Abdolkarim Ha'eri Yazdi (who was soon to found the *hawzeh* in Qom and become the sole *marja'* in

Iran), Seyyed Abolhasan Isfahani and Hajj Mirza Hosein Na'ini, the Najaf *maraje'*
who were about to return from a visit to Qom. These ulama advised Reza Khan
against the establishment of a republican regime but in effect told him that they
would not oppose an attempt by him to become a constitutional monarch.[20] It
took another year and a half for Reza Khan to overthrow the Qajars and accede
to the throne. During that period he made visible demonstrations of religious
commitment, especially in organizing and leading mourning processions by the
army for the martyrs of Karbala. In turn, he received public acclamations by
the religious establishment, which sent him gifts from the treasuries of the *Atabat*
shrines.[21]

The campaign for the republic collapsed in March 1924. In July, anti-Reza Khan
demonstrations in Tehran (in the course of an anti-Babi outburst) led to the
lynching of the American vice-consul Robert Imbrie by a mob, and was followed
by Reza Khan's declaration of martial law. The royal court is likely to have had a
hand in this, although the killing of the vice-consul could not have been planned
in advance.[22] In the following October a movement organized in the south and led
by Khaz'al Khan, the Sheikh of Mohammara (later Khorramshahr), describing
itself as the Committee of Rising for [the country's] Happiness sent telegrams to
the Majlis and issued public statements against dictatorship and in defence of
constitutional government. Khaz'al had 25,000 troops at his disposal in Khuzistan
and could have received considerable support from Lor and Arab tribes as well. He
was virtually the autonomous ruler of Khuzistan and had enjoyed British support
since the beginning of the Great War. But the Qajar court in Tehran did not have
the courage to back him up publicly, and his hopes that Britain would support his
move were unfounded. Reza Khan led his troops to Khuzistan, and Khaz'al surrendered without a fight. He was later arrested and brought as a prisoner to Tehran,
where he was murdered in the 1930s.[23]

Late in October 1925 officially inspired petitions were sent to the Majlis
demanding the abolition of the Qajar monarchy. Shortly before, in a bread riot in
Tehran likely to have been organized by Reza Khan's supporters, demonstrators
had shouted the slogan 'We want bread, we don't want the shah.' In the absence of
the shah, the royal court was virtually helpless, particularly as the shah's prolonged
stay in Europe itself was a main cause of his unpopularity. He tried to test the
opinion of the British government but they remained neutral.[24] This confirmed
his unwarranted suspicions that the British were behind the move to oust him,
which was sufficient for him to take it as fate. Modarres and his dwindling Majlis
opposition tried to put up resistance, but it was a hopeless task.

Meanwhile, a motion was planned to be tabled in the Majlis which demanded the
deposition of the Qajars and the appointment of Reza Khan as temporary head of
state, pending the decision of a constituent assembly to establish a new regime. The
night before the motion was presented in the Majlis, Davar invited most of the
deputies to a meeting at Reza Khan's house where they gave a written pledge to
support the motion.[25] On the next day, 31 October 1925, Modarres tried a stalling
tactic; when it failed he stormed out of the Majlis shouting that the whole thing

was illegal. Four Independents, including Mosaddeq and Taqizadeh, spoke against the motion. None of them defended the Qajars or opposed Reza Khan but they argued that proper constitutional procedures must be observed, and Mosaddeq specifically warned that the election of Reza Khan as an executive monarch would mean the end of constitutional government. The Majlis overwhelmingly voted in favour of the motion.[26]

The constituent assembly which subsequently established the Pahlavi dynasty had not been elected freely but it did represent the top echelons of society. It included many khans and provincial magnates, some prominent religious leaders, former leaders and figures of the Constitutional Revolution, important bazaar merchants, representatives of religious minorities and even some members of the former Majlis opposition who had lately defected to Reza Kahn's camp. The assembly's deliberations were open and much discussion took place, though only Soleiman Mirza, the socialist leader, refused to vote for the motion, solely because he was in favour of making Reza Khan shah for life rather than establishing a new dynasty.[27] This was comparable to the wide support that Nader had organized and obtained for himself in the Moghan conference 190 years earlier (see Chapter 6). In many ways Reza Khan was a comparable figure to Nader Shah for his time, both in his success and in his failure.

ARBITRARY RULE, SECULARIZATION AND MODERNIZATION

Reza Khan believed and even told a group of his advisors that he had been brought to power by the British government.[28] This reinforced in him the conspiracy theory held by many Iranians that foreign powers and especially the British were behind sometimes even the most unlikely event in the country. Therefore, he regarded anyone else's contact with them, and later with other European embassies as well, virtually as an act of treason, punishable by imprisonment. It did not take him long, according to Mokhber al-Saltaneh (Mehdiqoli Hedayat) – his longest-serving prime minister – to come to expect 'to be worshipped'.[29] The shah himself once said to the cabinet that 'every country has a certain type of regime. Ours is a one-person regime.'[30] It was these characteristics, added to the effects of absolute and arbitrary power, that later led to his persecution of not only his opponents and critics but also those who had helped him to gain power and served him loyally.

Unlike the old-school politicians, he appeared to be open and forthright in his attitude, partly because he was not expected to observe the norms of the old social and political culture and partly also because he became too successful to be bound by it. Otherwise he could be highly duplicitous, both to foreigners and Iranians. For example, he ordered the arrest and later murder in jail of Ja'farqoli Khan Sardar As'ad, his devoted personal friend and minister of war, the day after they had played a game of cards together in good spirits.[31] Firuz, the minister of finance, was suddenly arrested when he was leaving a public meeting in the company of the shah himself.[32]

Reza Shah has often been compared to Mustapha Kemal Ataturk, whom he both admired and tried to emulate. The comparison is understandable but misleading since there were some fundamental differences between the two men and their roles in Iran and Turkey.[33] Ataturk was a modern dictator who tried to modernize Turkish politics along with his general nationalist and modernist drive, allowing for limited participation and consultation in political decision-making. He was not an arbitrary ruler like traditional Ottoman sultans and caliphs, he was not financially corrupt and neither he nor his army and bureaucracy liberally took other peoples' lives and properties.

Reza Khan also began as a modern dictator, and had he remained so subsequent Iranian history would have turned out very differently. But within a few years after his accession he became an absolute and arbitrary ruler and, just like traditional Iranian rulers before the Constitutional Revolution, increasingly looked upon his subjects and their property, indeed the whole of the country, as his own possession. Before the twentieth century, Reza Shah might have been viewed as a 'just ruler', that is, a strong reforming arbitrary ruler who brought stability, peace and relative prosperity to the country. In former times such an arbitrary ruler would have been regarded as natural, and his financial transgressions likewise as normal. The fact that his regime had been established after a revolution for law and against arbitrary rule was the most important reason behind his later unpopularity and even the false accustation that he was an agent of Britain, which the Iranians almost universally believed until recent times. If Reza Shah had remained a dictator along the lines of Ataturk, he would have been viewed much more favourably both in his own time and especially later.

Thus, the fundamental contradiction in Reza Shah was not that he was a dictator like Ataturk or Mussolini, it was the fact of his being a post-Constitutional ruler with strong claims to a nationalist and modernist agenda who nevertheless abolished politics altogether and violated the laws protecting life and property whenever it suited him. As early as 1929 the Secretary of the American legation in Tehran pointed out this fundamental feature of Reza Shah's rule in his report to the Department of State:

> [B]y incarcerating prominent persons without trial, and by forever silencing troublemakers without the due process of law, the Shah's reactionary tendencies are made visible . . . It may be doubted whether a nation is benefited by such a disregard for law and justice . . . As long as the army is controlled by the Shah, he can consolidate his power and brook no opposition; but reforms applied by force of arms are inclined to be ephemeral. Unless the people can feel confidence in the legal establishment of their country, they will have no confidence in their Shah and his reforms, and no lasting good will be accomplished.[34]

Thus Ataturk established a long-term socio-political paradigm for his country which has been largely respected, as he himself is, by generations of Turks of various social and political persuasions. But although some of Reza Shah's achievements also had long-term consequences, his era was no more than another Iranian short term which ended with his abdication and was followed by chaos.

In 1926 Reza Khan was at the height of his popularity and had the largest social base of his career, although even then his popularity was largely confined to the country's elites. He was in direct control of the army, which was his own creation, and he enjoyed its complete loyalty. He had the Majlis majority and most of the newspapers on his side, and the support of many of them was genuine. Many middle and upper class people were looking forward to a period of peace, prosperity and modernization. He was almost idolized by the young nationalist elite. Leading Qajar noblemen either actually supported and joined the regime or passively submitted to it. Many Tehran ulama and others from the provinces supported the change. Popular politicians such as Mostawfi and Moshir were worried about the growth of dictatorship but were not opposed to Reza Khan personally. Indeed, Mostawfi formed the new shah's first ministry after Mohammad Ali Forughi's caretaker cabinet. Yet by the time he left the country in 1941, Reza Shah had hardly any friends left in the country in consequence of his arbitrary and fearsome rule, especially in the 1930s.

Had Reza Shah maintained his 1926 power base and led the country as a strong ruler (even a dictator) there would have been a good chance for the country to enjoy long-term political development. The sixth Majlis (1926–8) was still alive, and sometimes even lively, and opposition deputies, notably Mosaddeq, had the freedom to oppose government bills. After the new dynasty was founded, Modarres and his supporters decided to try a new course of political compromise. His negotiations with the shah led to the formation of Mostawfi's government. Bahar was later to write that Modarres had told them that they should now accept the new regime and try to work with it.[35] He was thus hoping that the shah would keep the army and have a large say in civil administration but that he would leave some role for the Majlis and independent politicians. The shah, however, showed that his earlier response had been tactical and that he would wish to have absolute power. An assassination attempt was made against Modarres, which was generally believed to have been organized with the shah's knowledge, but he continued to support the government until Mosawfi resigned from the premiership in 1927 at his own insistence since he felt he could not work with the shah, and Mehdiqoli Hedayat (Mokhber al-Saltaneh) replaced him. Modarres was arrested shortly afterwards and banished to a prison citadel in the eastern desert, and nine years later murdered by a special police death squad sent from the capital.[36]

From the seventh until the thirteenth Majlis, before the fall of Reza Shah, elections were totally controlled, and from the eighth session (1930–2) the Majlis became no more than a rubber stamp. In 1927 Abdolhosein Teymurtash, minister of the royal court, attempted to launch a nationalist-modernist party (the *Iran-e Naw* or New Iran party) to provide a political base for the new regime, but even this project had to be abandoned because the shah was not in favour of party politics.[37]

After Modarres' arrest, it was not the new premier, Hedayat, but the very able and energetic Teymurtash who wielded real political power. While the shah spent much of his time on military organization and activities, Teymurtash almost had a free rein in running the civilian administration and foreign relations, with the shah's knowledge and approval. Meanwhile, many figures, both civilian and military, who had been instrumental in the shah's rise to power and the modernization of the state and the economy, were jailed, disgraced or dismissed from state service. In 1929 the minister of finance Firuz Mirza Firuz was convicted of trumped-up charges of financial corruption and served his sentence, but was later rearrested and strangled in a provincial police station in 1937. Ali Akbar Davar, the very able and honest justice and finance minister – the architect of the new judicial system and *étatiste* (state-dominated) political economy – took his own life shortly after Firuz's arrest but before his murder rather than be disgraced and possibly murdered like the others. Teymurtash himself fell in 1932 and was subsequently killed while in jail.

Hedayat remained in office for six years until 1933, and was replaced by the loyal and learned Forughi. He in turn was dismissed and disgraced in 1935 when he tried unsuccessfully to intervene with the shah to save the life of his son-in-law's father, Mohammad Vali Asadi, the trustee of the Mashhad shrine, an appointee and loyal servant of the shah himself who had been suspected of having encouraged the protests against the imposition of the European hat (see below). From 1935 to the Allied invasion in 1941, there were three other prime ministers, one of whom, the relatively young Ahmad Matin-Daftari (1939–40), was arrested without charge while in office (later rumours circulated that this was to appease Britain because of his pro-German stance, but this is unlikely because the shah himself was pro-German and his attitude towards Britain was far from friendly). After Matin-Daftari's arrest, Mohammad Mosaddeq, his father-in-law who had been out of politics and living in his rural estate since 1928, was also arrested without charge and banished to a prison-citadel in Khorasan.

Reza Shah's arbitrary rule was different from the traditional Iranian experience in three important respects. First, unlike traditional arbitrary rule, even of a relatively strong ruler such as Naser al-Din Qajar, the state had both the intention and the ability – born of European ideology and modern technology and bureaucracy – to interfere in the lives of the people at large and extend its direct control to all corners of the country. There was a modern standing army and gendarmerie, as well as a rapidly expanding bureaucracy and a modern police force all at the shah's command. The second important difference was that his arbitrary rule had been re-established after the Constitutional Revolution. There was a seemingly constitutional framework, even a parliament through which the business of government was usually conducted, although the parliament had no independent power and the state took arbitrary decisions and violated any and all laws when it suited it. The third important difference was that there was no longer any recognized facility for mediation and cooling-off such as taking *bast* in a holy place or even the royal stables (see the Introduction). In 1935, for example, when unarmed protesters in Mashhad took refuge in an old mosque adjacent to the holy shrine, they were gunned down on direct orders from Tehran.

It was in this atmosphere that the face of Iran changed within two decades of modernization, secularization and nation-state building, although, as noted, the first decade was one of growing dictatorship rather than sultanistic rule[38] and therefore was marked with a certain, even though declining, amount of optimism and participation. There was rapid social, economic and cultural change, expansion in modern education, industry and services, construction of roads and railways, centralization and concentration of the army and bureaucracy, reform of the judicial system and the administrative, civil and criminal codes, centralized registration of births, deaths, marriages and title deeds, greater social participation of women, forced removal of chadors and scarves, introduction of modern banking and so on. Much of this affected only a small percentage of the population and economic and cultural activities, but its historical importance was that it opened the way to developments which, despite social and political upheavals, still continue.

THE ARMY

Reorganization and the rapid expansion of the army was Reza Khan's first priority. As early as December 1921, he merged the Cossack Division with the state gendarmerie. The Swedish officers of the latter force were replaced by Iranians, and the Cossack officers became dominant in the new unified army, or *qoshun*. By 1926, Reza Shah had 40,000 soldiers and a small air force at his command. In 1941, the army had grown threefold to more than 120,000. To finance his ambitious plans for the expansion of the army he began to use any legal and illegal means, including use of funds from the revenue-bearing civilian offices, until 1922, when the American financial advisor Dr Arthur Millspaugh took over the country's financial administration and began to provide him with funds by budgetary allocation. In 1928, the year after Millspaugh's mission ended, the budget of the ministry of war was 122 million rials; by 1941, it had increased almost fivefold to 593 million rials.[39] Over the period 1928–41 one-third of the total regular budget was claimed by the war ministry.[40] Besides, almost all the oil revenues, which accounted for 13 per cent of total government receipts, were spent on the purchase of military hardware.[41] The shah and the army also used other means, including the confiscation of private wealth and property, to augment military finance. Even when Reza Khan was minister of war he 'consistently refused to submit the accounts of the ministry of war to examination . . ., although he was being criticized for amassing a large personal fortune out of the military budget'.[42]

Much of the army recruiting in the early 1920s was on the basis of the traditional *bonicheh* system of contributions by the settled agricultural population as well as tribal levies. One of the basic aspirations of the modernists and nationalists had been the introduction of a comprehensive system of conscription. Reza

Khan's 1923 conscription bill met with little opposition in the fourth Majlis, drawing support even from Modarres (who was much more of a politician than a traditional religious leader), but it took another two years for the bill to be finally passed by the fifth Majlis when Reza Khan himself was prime minister.[43] Neither landowners, the religious establishment nor the commercial sector was happy about the measure, although religious figures and seminary students had initially been exempted from the service. In 1928, an attempt to fully implement the national service law led to resistance from the ulama, some of whom gathered in Qom and demanded the abolition of the law.[44] There was also unrest in Tabriz over the issue.[45] The shah was cautious, but Teymurtash was talking about the bombardment of Qom.[46]

As a devoutly religious man, Prime Minister Hedayat defended the law from the standpoint of the Koran. The organized protests melted away but strong feelings against recruitment remained across the country, especially among the peasantry and the nomads, since the measure took away some of their young family hands (sometimes for good) and the returning conscripts brought modern ideas and attitudes to the village and the tribe. 'The annual visits of the draft boards to the village and tribal areas were generally a dreaded occasion,'[47] and 'fear of recruiting commissions was an important factor in the major tribal revolts of 1929'.[48] The family of every army officer was assigned one or more conscripts at home and used them as common domestic servants without pay.

A few army officers had been trained at French military schools, notably St Cyr, and more were sent by the state in the 1920s, although, due to the conservatism of the senior officers, the returning officers did not at first manage to influence military organization to a significant extent. Much of the officer training in the later years took place in the new military high school and military academy, which were largely manned by the officers trained in France. Increasingly, the army became a privileged class. Military officers could break the law each according to his rank, and senior officers grew rich by legal and illegal means. On the other hand, an atmosphere of suspicion and insecurity prevailed, especially among the higher echelons of the army and officers personally known to the shah. Many generals were dismissed and imprisoned, for example General Amanollah Mirza Jahanbani, then Director-General of Industry, who was dismissed in 1937 and subsequently jailed, apparently because he had had lunch at the French embassy.[49]

As early as 1926 Colonel Mahmud Puladin, the shah's able aide-de-camp, was arrested together with other officers on the charge of plotting a coup. There was in fact no case to answer, and at first he was given a prison sentence, but later in 1928 he was condemned to death at the shah's insistence. He was executed despite the fact that General Habibollah Sheibani, the army chief of staff, resigned rather than sign his death warrant. Three years later, having returned to active service in the meantime, Sheibani was dismissed, court-martialled and jailed. He eventually 'went insane' and left Iran never to return.[50] General Amir-Ahmadi, the highest-ranking army general, who had conducted the court-martial, had told Sheibani

بازخورد رستم دستان سپید
به گفت کار نزدنده هیل بلند
منزو اسب رنده بنیان نبرد
زدگ کنتر بدمیان نشد
بدو گفت زال ای خداوندگر
چو اکنون سود ز بارباک چمر
کنام ملکان و شیر کرگ کنند
نختاندر لفرزراه بیسگ
همان مرغ مرخشن زال او بنود
چورستم بدفرزند بالاید
چرارزم جشربا سنذیار
هیم شم انو و خسرو در کناز
کرایده وزنکه رستم نکرد در رز
کجاخواهم اهم اندر جهان قار
نشکوفکنده این تختما رین
کشف مهر جم ابراهیمه از یه آید مرگ
ازوهشته ملکان بیرون تیگ
بنقاراز ان خسگی زجم کلیبک

1 The mythical bird Simorgh attending to the wounded Rostam and his horse, from Ferdowsi's *Shahnameh*

2 Persepolis today, an aerial view

3 Bas-relief in Palace of Xerxes, Persepolis

4 Alexander holding the dying Dara in his arms while the latter's murderers stand bound, awaiting execution, from Ferdowsi's *Shahnameh*

5 Coins representing the Arsacid king Mithridates II

6 The Emperor Valerian kneels before Shapur I (bas-relief, Naqsh-e Rostam)

7 Abbasid Mosque, Samarra

8 Amir Timur (Tamerlane) holding court beside a pile of skulls after the battle of Baghdad in 1401

9 Painting of the battle with the Uzbeks, Chehel Sotun Palace, Isfahan

10 Naqsh-e Jahan Square, Isfahan

11 Painting of the Banquet of
Shah Abbas, Chehel Sotun, Isfahan

12 Fath'ali Shah receiving the
homage of his son, Abbas Mirza,
early 19th century

THE ILLUSTRATED LONDON NEWS.

REGISTERED AT THE GENERAL POST-OFFICE FOR TRANSMISSION ABROAD.

No. 2621.—VOL. XCV.　　SATURDAY, JULY 13, 1889.　　WITH EXTRA SUPPLEMENT　SIXPENCE. By Post, 6½d.

13 Naser al-Din Shah being greeted by Queen Victoria on his visit to England, as depicted in the *Illustrated London News*, July 1889

14 Constitutional Revolution: the bast at the British legation, 1906

روز افتتاح مجلس مقدس شورای ملی ایران در اطاق نظام

15 Constitutional Revolution: the opening of the first Majlis, 1907

16 Reza Khan with two of his daughters, and the future Mohammad Reza Shah on his lap, *c.* 1922

17 Reza Shah on the Peacock Throne at his coronation, April 1926

18 Upper-class Iranian women in Western clothing, *c.* 1936

19 Reza Shah and Prince Mohammad Reza at the former's abdication, September 1941

20 Mosaddeq lifted onto shoulders of the crowd outside the Majlis, delivering the speech which the opposition had not allowed him to deliver in the House, September 1951

21 The Shah and Queen Farah during their coronation in November 1967

22 The Shah, President Carter, Queen Farah and the First Lady on the White House lawn, wiping their eyes from the effect of tear gas used by the police to disperse the Shah's opponents demonstrating nearby, November 1977

23 Ayatollah Khomeini descending from the plane in Tehran airport, February 1979

24 Iranian revolutionaries burning US flag, November 1979

25 Modern Iranian women protesting against the suggestion that hejab should become compulsory, July 1980

26 Mourning Khomeini at his official commemoration, June 1989; (*left to right*) Ayatollah Khameini, Ayatollah Pasandideh, Ahmad Khomeini and Speaker Rafsanjani

27 Mohammad Khatami, reformist leader and president 1997–2005, shown here with President Chirac of France, April 2005

28 Modern Tehran

that the court was powerless. He himself was subjected to frequent dismissal, police harassment and official humiliation.[51]

TRIBAL POLICY

The armed forces' principal task was to bring order to the tribes and provinces. As with almost every other social, economic and cultural policy which he adopted and pursued, Reza Shah's tribal policy was determined by the pan-Persian nationalist and centralizing sentiments which had been developing since the Constitutional Revolution and, especially, World War I. This ideology did not just envisage the imposition of law and order in tribal areas but the total destruction of tribal life and culture. In the early 1920s, the immediate task was the ending of chaos. The Bakhtiyari resistance was quickly brought to an end. The killing of many government troops near Shalil in Loristan was blamed on the Bakhtiyaris, whose khans denied any knowledge and involvement but nevertheless compensated the families of the victims.[52] In fact, the cooperation of the great khans (as well as the feud amongst themselves) was more effective than military force in ending rebellion and resistance. Sawlat al-Dawleh, the paramount chief of the Qashqa'is, and Qavam al-Molk, the titular head of the Khamseh tribes (both in the province of Fars), also submitted and even supported Reza Khan. The campaigns of the early 1920s in Loristan and Kurdistan were effective largely because Lor and Kurdish nomads were not organized into great tribal confederations.[53] The Shahsevans in the north-west submitted peacefully, although later they became bitter about the government's harsh forced settlement policy.[54]

An important part of the military and political campaign to impose order in the tribal areas of the south, west, north-west and north-east was the policy of disarming the tribes – this had never happened before in Iran's history. Traditional regimes might well have wished to do the same but they did not have the modern military and technological means at their disposal to try it. Beyond the disarming policy, the policy of forced settlement or sedentarization of the nomads, however, was largely a product of the psychology of pseudo-modernism. The nationalist ideologists saw nomadic life and culture as evidence of backwardness and felt highly embarrassed by it when dealing with the Europeans, since a great deal of nationalist and pseudo-modernist policy and attitudes was influenced by what they thought the Europeans might think of them and their country. Reza Shah himself was extremely sensitive to European opinion even though this did not temper his style of government. Sedentarization could never be justified on rational grounds, as it led to widespread death, destruction and hardship, while at the same time it was economically harmful since it led to a sharp decline in the country's livestock production, comparable to the effects of Stalin's forced collectivization of Soviet agriculture in the same period.

The tribal uprising of 1929 in the south was a consequence of grievances arising mainly from the policy of sedentarization, the confiscation of tribal properties, military conscription, the punitive taxes imposed by the state monopoly of tea,

sugar and tobacco, the compulsory European dress code and the repressive attitude and behaviour of the military forces. Ultimately, the revolt was put down
more by political than military means, with the support of the great tribal khans
who lived in the capital.[55]

In 1932 a civilian office was set up for the forced settlement of the tribes. This
applied the policy systematically and with much harshness. 'This programme of
forced sedentarization . . . took a very brutal and, in some cases, genocidal form.
In a short period of time the tribal life of Iran was transformed . . . through coercive and violent methods that virtually wiped out a large segment of the tribal
population of Iran.'[56] After the shah's abdication in 1941, virtually all settled
nomads returned to nomadic life, and the bitterness of their treatment in that
period was to have serious consequences for their relations with the state.

ADMINISTRATIVE AND LEGAL REFORMS

At the same time as the central government's grip over the provinces was established, administrative reforms extended the hands of the bureaucracy both
horizontally and vertically. Horizontally, the provinces were governed by a
governor-general sent from Tehran as before, but the number of offices expanded
and the extent of their interference in local affairs continued to increase. There
was also a military force (usually a division) in each province, led by a general
who was directly appointed by and was responsible to the shah. Governors and
mayors of towns and cities were also appointed by the ministry of the interior in
Tehran. Many of them were actually sent from the capital to the provinces, and
almost all of them were Persian-speakers, even in the Turkish-, Kurdish- and
Arabic-speaking provinces. In the late 1930s the traditional *velayat* system was
abolished. Instead the county was divided into ten *ostan*s, numbered one to ten.[57]
In some cases the provinces were remapped to change their strong identification
with a particular ethnic group, and in all cases the number of the *ostan* replaced
the traditional name of the province (e.g. Gilan, Mazandaran etc.) in official
usage. The domination from Tehran was a source of complaint in all the
provinces, but the ethnic provinces felt particularly downgraded and humiliated.

The vertical growth of bureaucratization was a consequence of state-building,
the rapid expansion and proliferation of government offices regarding home
affairs, police, public finance, education and culture, customs, law courts, registration of personal matters (births, deaths etc.) and title deeds and municipal
government. Administrative modernization had begun in 1910 after the triumph
of the Constitutional Revolution. But it rapidly grew in the 1920s and 1930s. The
new civil service extended job opportunities to various layers of urban society, but
especially to both traditional and modern middle classes, who increasingly filled
the higher bureaucratic offices. They were better trained and more responsible
than the traditional bureaucrats. Nepotism in appointments now extended to a
larger social group than before, and although there was still much corruption, it
was less obvious than before.

Law reform came in various guises. Modern administrative, civil and criminal codes were introduced, largely based on French law, although the criminal and, especially civil, codes were strongly influenced by the Islamic *shari'a*. At the same time, Davar introduced his judicial reforms, also almost entirely based on the French judicial system, including courts of examining magistrates (*Dadsara*) and of the first, second and final instance. Many of the judges in the new system, as also notary publics who conducted the registration of private contracts, marriage and divorce, were clerics or former clerics (now observing the newly imposed European dress code), but both the new laws and new courts secularized the legal system and largely abolished the role of the ulama in judicial processes. A *shari'a* court was at first retained, but that too was abolished in the late 1930s.

Judicial reform was partly justified according to the argument that without it European powers would resist the abolition of the capitulation agreements which had given their citizens immunity from Iranian law courts. The capitulation agreements were abolished almost at the same time, in 1927 and 1928, but in fact judicial secularization was a firm policy objective in its own right.[58] The new law courts and justice system were one of the most important reforms of the period. However, like most of the reforms and developments of the period they affected only a tiny minority. The system was expensive and complicated and could serve perhaps no more than 5 per cent of the population among the upper and middle classes.

EDUCATION

Apart from Dar al-Fonun, the polytechnic founded by Amir Kabir in the mid-nineteenth century, some beginnings had been made with the introduction of modern secular education before the Constitutional Revolution, notably the establishment of missionary and 'progressive' (*roshdiyeh*) schools.[59] Early constitutional governments had tried to speed up the process by opening new schools and sending students abroad, but the process was slow and was disrupted by World War I. More modern schools began to be founded under Vosuq's government after the war, but were limited by financial constraints.[60] Modernizing education was high on the list of nationalist priorities and became an important government policy from the 1920s. Between 1928 and 1941, the education budget was, on average, 6.2 per cent of the total, which is considerably higher than the 4 per cent figure quoted in most secondary sources.[61] In the 1920s and 1930s primary and secondary schools for both boys and girls expanded, but the available statistics are not consistent. For example, Bharier puts the total number of schools in 1940 at less than 2,700, whereas Banani's figure is more than 8,200.[62] Different sources also give sometimes considerably different figures for the total number of pupils.[63] According to a recent study the total number of pupils increased from 44,819 in 1922–3 to 315,355 in 1941–2, a sevenfold increase. In 1922–3, 83.1 per cent of pupils were boys and 16.9 per cent girls; in 1941–2, the figures had changed to 72 and 28 respectively.

Therefore, although there were still fewer girl pupils than boys, they had experienced a higher rate of growth and improved their share in the total.[64]

Modern education was extended and expanded at other levels as well. Sending students to Europe had begun in the nineteenth century. Most such visits were privately financed by the students' families, but after the Constitutional Revolution a number of state students were sent abroad.[65] This continued in the early 1920s and included officer cadets, virtually all of whom were sent to military schools in France. In 1928 a law required the government to send a hundred students abroad every year for a university education. Most were sent to France, others to Belgium and Germany (and, later, America). On return, the graduates joined the civil service and state industrial establishments, and some of them began to teach at the University of Tehran.

Tehran University, founded in 1934, brought together a number of already existing schools and colleges of higher education, such as the medical school and school of law and political science, with some new faculties on a new campus. It admitted women as well as men. So did the two teacher training colleges (Daneshsara-ye Moqaddamati and Daneshsara-ye 'Ali) modelled on the French écoles normales, founded to train teachers respectively for primary and secondary schools and replacing the existing teacher training school, Dar al-Mo'allemin, which had admitted only male students.[66] Other schools for training primary schoolteachers were established in the provinces later in the 1930s.[67] An agricultural college also came into being in the 1930s and adult education schemes were introduced in the same period.[68] A military cadet school for teenage boys and a military academy were established to train army officers.

As noted, the secularization of education had made a beginning even before the Constitutional Revolution, though it was extended and grew much faster under Reza Shah. But it nevertheless occupied only a small part of educational instruction, which, especially in rural areas, was the domain of the village mullahs. Regarding the pseudo-modernist nature of the educational policy, Banani concludes his otherwise favourable account of educational reforms in the period by noting that 'the very cultural identity that the ardent nationalists sought to preserve was steadily weakened by an aimless imitation of the more superficial aspects of Western Civilization'.[69]

It was an elitist policy, favouring the children of upper and middle classes,[70] although it was open to all who had the means wherever modern schools had been founded. History and literature were taught at all levels in a propagandist style, romantically glorifying ancient Persia, denigrating and castigating Arabs and Turks, ignoring the numerous Iranian ethnic groups (including Turkish, Kurdish, Arab and other peoples) and pretending that Persian was the only language spoken in Iran. There was a great emphasis on academic education as opposed to practical and professional training. Examinations were little more than tests of memory. There was almost no encouragement of critical interpretation and analysis. This general outlook towards educational policy also continued later under Mohammad Reza Shah, but at a somewhat more sophisticated level, which reflected the greater competence of teachers and educational establishments than any change in state ideology.

Much of this was probably difficult to avoid in the Reza Shah period, given that the reform of education was still at an experimental stage and that pan-Persian zeal was widespread among the military and administrative elites, including most educated people and educationalists. The greatest criticism that can be levelled at the educational policy is that it created a very high-cost system, ignoring the country's needs for the growth of literacy and elementary knowledge. By the time Reza Shah abdicated in 1941, 90 per cent of Iranians, including virtually the whole of the rural community, were illiterate.[71]

SOCIO-CULTURAL CHANGE

This too was much influenced by prevailing nationalist sentiments as well as deference to European or, rather, imagined European opinion. As early as 1922, when Reza Khan was minister of war, the National Heritage Society (*Anjoman-e Asar-e Melli*) was founded by leading political and cultural figures including Teymurtash, Forughi and Firuz.[72] Western scholars such as the American Arthur Pope, the German Ernst Herzfeld and the French André Godard in various capacities took part in the study, preservation and resurrection of ancient art, architecture, history and culture. The erection of a modern mausoleum for Ferdowsi was high on the agenda. It was modelled after the tomb of Cyrus the Great in Pasargadae and, in 1934, Forughi as prime minister did more than most to bring it to completion. This was formally opened by the shah at Tus, near Mashhad, where two hundred Iranian and western scholars and politicians had travelled after attending the conference of 'Ferdowsi's millennium' (*Hezarhe-ye Ferdowsi*) in Tehran.[73] On their way they visited Khayyam's grave at Neishabur, which had been quickly repaired and rebuilt specifically so that the western visitors would not be disappointed by the sight of the existing tomb.[74]

The Iranian Academy (*Farhangestan-e Iran*) was founded in 1935, mainly in order to purge the Persian language of words of Arabic root or origin. In its wider objective it was bound to fail, as would any effort to purge English of Latin and French loan words. In some cases reasonable alternative words were coined, but in general the idea was an affront to the cultural sensibilities of educated people, including some of its own members, who coined the new terms and sent them forward to the court for the shah's approval. Taqizadeh wrote an article from Berlin, where he had gone after he was sacked as the head of the Iranian legation in Paris, and criticized the interference of 'the sword with the pen'. The shah's wrath and suspicion in response meant that Taqizadeh decided not to return to Iran.[75]

In the same year the Iranian government demanded that in the European usage of the country's name, 'Iran' must replace the historic term 'Persia'. This was to emphasize the Aryan, Iranian origin of the country, with no thought that it would rob the country of all its historical, cultural and literary connotations in western societies at least for decades to come. On the contrary, the government believed it would enhance the status of Iran in the West. The idea had been suggested by proto-Nazi German officials to Iranian diplomats in Berlin, who had passed it on to Tehran. Forughi said at the time that 'it turned a definite noun into an indefinite noun', and Isa Sadiq, another loyal servant of the regime, was to write decades later that the official replacement of 'Iran' for 'Persia' had led in the West to the confusion of Iran with 'one of the new countries which had emerged from the fall of the Ottoman empire [apparently meaning Iraq]'.[76]

The official imposition of new dress codes, and even the forced removal of the *hejab*, was based on another cherished nationalist modernist policy. The law of December 1928 made it compulsory for all Iranian men to wear European dress[77] (short jackets and trousers) and the 'Pahlavi hat', which was a variation of the French kepi. 'Looking like Europeans' was probably the strongest motive behind this law, although it was also part of the policy of nation-building, centralization and secularization.[78] By and large the ulama, preachers and seminary students were allowed to keep their attire and headgear; ironically, this helped to turn them into a distinct professional class: many non-professionals had worn a form of religious garb before the European dress code was imposed.[79] In fact some religious types who had joined the (mainly legal and academic) professions had to abandon their turbans and cloaks because everyone on the government payroll had to observe the modern dress code. Others abandoned their state employment, and a few preferred to stay indoors rather than change their sartorial habits.

Evidence of the strength of the psychological motive behind the compulsory dress code was the decree of 1935 that all men should replace the Pahlavi hat with the European chapeau or bowler hat. Clearly, this was not necessary for standardization, secularization and nation-building, since a uniform dress code and hat already existed. It was a product of the shah's recent visit to Turkey and his determination, on his return to Tehran, to make Iranian men look entirely like the Europeans. Indeed, shortly after the bloody suppression of the protesters in Mashhad who had taken *bast* in the Mosque of Goharshad adjacent to the shrine of Imam Reza, the shah told a sceptical Mokhber al-Saltaneh (Mehdiqoli Hedyat), the former prime minister, that through this action he intended to stop Europeans ridiculing us:

> In an audience the shah took my [chapeau] hat off my head and said, 'Now what do you think of this?' I said it certainly protects one from the sun and the rain, but that [Pahlavi] hat which we had before had a better name. Agitated, his majesty paced up and down and said, 'All I am trying to do is for us to look like [the Europeans] so they do not ridicule us'.[80]

The compulsory dress code was welcomed by the modernist nationalist elite but resented by the ulama and ordinary people and, as noted, was a main grievance of the nomadic tribes. However, public resistance focused on the imposition of the European chapeau (which most people had not even seen before) when the peaceful demonstrations in Mashhad were put down by force of arms.[81] The execution of Asadi and the fall of Forughi followed, as noted above.[82]

The shah's sudden decree for the removal of women's *hejab* (i.e. face veil, chador as well as scarf) which followed a few months later, in January 1936, was not openly resisted, coming so soon after the events in Mashhad over the European hat, but it left scars much deeper even than that of Reza Shah's tribal policy.[83] Criticisms of the *hejab* went back to the turn of the twentieth century, and had entered the realm of wider public discussion at least since the end of World War I among the modern middle and upper classes. Eshqi wrote the long poem entitled 'The Black Shroud' (*kafan-e siyah*, alluding to the chador), which ended with the verse 'As long as women live in shrouds / Half of the Iranian people are not alive.'[84] Iraj, the leading satirical poet, wrote against the *hejab* and blind marriage arrangements and emphasized that the covering of hands and faces by women was contrary to the teaching of the Koran.[85]

Women activists and self-help organizers such as Dorrat al-Mo'ali and Sediqeh Dawlat-Abadi began to campaign for women's rights. The women's journal *Alam-e Nesvan* (Women's World, 1920–34) was the longest-running journal of its kind over the period. Its owner-editor was Navvabeh Khanom Safavi, who wrote in the September 1921 issue's editorial entitled 'No one will scratch my back except my own fingernail' that women should not just hope for men to help their cause but take action themselves.[86]

Yet despite ardent and enthusiastic support for Reza Shah's reforms, the government banned the journal even before the official banning of the *hejab*. Other women's journals had been banned before it, the reason being that the shah would not tolerate any independent journal or organization even if it fully supported his regime. They were replaced by the official *Kanun-e Banuan* (Ladies' Centre).[87]

All the anti-*hejab* campaigners were opposed to the face veil, which some women had already abandoned in the 1920s. The more radical of them also opposed the chador, the long cloak which covered the woman's head and body. But they were not against scarves, which they would have welcomed as a great improvement on the chador, and hardly any of them believed that all women should be forced to remove their veils. They advocated the right of those women who wished to remove their *hejab* voluntarily to be recognized and protected. It therefore came as a great shock to the masses of urban women when the shah decreed that all of them must take off their chadors or face police harassment and arrest. Not even the wearing of scarves was allowed. As Mokhber al-Saltaneh (Hedayat) wrote in his memoirs in his typically telegraphic style, 'The police were ordered to pull the scarf off women's heads. The scarves were torn off or, if valuable, confiscated. The struggle between women and the police continued for some time.'[88] Reza Shah's visit to Turkey is often cited as the immediate cause of his decision to speed up the pace of modernization in Iran, yet Ataturk had not forced Turkish women to unveil.[89]

Compulsory unveiling was received very badly by the large majority of women. It was tantamount to a decree in Europe at that time that would have forced women to go topless in public. Some women remained at home for as long as the shah was in power and the ban was in force, and had to go to the public baths through the rooftops of the neighbouring houses that connected their homes to the bath. In 1936, orders were given for government departments and the municipalities to oblige their members, employees and the local middle class residents to attend social parties in the company of their wives.[90] Some men took temporary wives to accompany them to the party. A few committed suicide.[91]

The policy affected urban women alone, since those in rural society (probably 80 per cent or more of the country's female population) were not veiled; rural women wore peasant dress which included a scarf, and worked in the fields and carpet workshops. Reza Shah's speeches and the public propaganda which represented the forced unveiling as necessary to allow women's participation in the labour market was at best relevant to the urban community. Even then, some ordinary urban women already worked in textile workshops or as servants and seamstresses. The modernizing policies of the period had relatively little immediate effect on employment for modern middle and upper class women. Nevertheless, more women joined the work force over the period and there were greater opportunities for training as teachers, nurses and midwives. By 1941 there were even a couple of women university professors, mainly in foreign languages. There can be little doubt that the 1930s prepared the ground for the subsequent increase in the emancipation and participation of women in society. If arbitrary force had not been used in the process, the results would have been far more positive both in the short and the long run.

ECONOMIC DEVELOPMENTS AND POLICIES

The 1919 Agreement had intended to reform and reorganize the Iranian army, administration and financial system. The cancellation of that treaty after the coup led to the departure of the British financial advisors. In 1922, Hosein Ala, Iran's minister in Washington, employed a team of American advisors led by Dr Arthur Millspaugh. As we have seen, he was given extensive powers and in fact became the financial dictator of Iran. He did, however, establish a working relationship with Reza Khan, providing funds for the war ministry in exchange for a free hand to reform a financial system which was on the verge of collapse. Nevertheless, his contract was terminated in 1927, since Reza Shah would not tolerate another man (least of all a foreigner) enjoying independent power.[92] Millspaugh was partially replaced by a German advisor, Dr Kurt Lindenblatt, who helped organize Bank Melli, a commercial as well as a central bank, for which modern Iranians had been dreaming since the Constitutional Revolution when the British-owned Imperial Bank of Persia had the monopoly of note issue and the Discount Bank of Russia was the only other modern bank which operated in the country. This was in 1927. In 1933, Lindenblatt was convicted of embezzlement, but in the meantime the monopoly of note issue had been transferred from the Imperial Bank to Bank Melli.[93]

Government revenue, apart from oil, consisted of the traditional land tax, customs revenue and indirect taxation. The tax structure did not change much in the 1920s, though in the 1930s an income tax law came into being. Millspaugh's reform mainly concerned increasing the efficiency of tax collection, and Belgian advisors were also instrumental in the reform and growth of customs revenues. Customs duties were almost entirely revenue tariffs, seldom used for protective purposes. Indirect taxes were heavy as well as relatively easy to collect, the worst example being the crippling tax on tea and sugar, a part of the staple diet of the masses of the population, to pay for railway construction.[94]

The balance of trade, excluding oil, was in deficit throughout the period, but from 1922 onwards the balance, including oil, was permanently in surplus.[95] The crash of 1929 and the resulting slump in the world economy and trade had adverse effects for Iran as well, and the fall of the price of silver in the international market worsened matters since the Persian currency was still based on silver. These events may have quickened and intensified the trade monopoly acts of 1930 and 1931, which turned trade in some important domestic products (such as wheat) and the whole of foreign transactions into a government monopoly, but the measures themselves were perfectly in line with the general policy of state control of society, the polity and the economy.[96] In practice the state became obliged to issue licences for merchants to carry out much of the foreign trade, but it retained its tight control, and the state monopoly companies which came into being added to the complexity and inefficiency of the process. There were even internal tariffs on domestic trade, duties being collected outside towns and cities. And to leave town, people had to obtain an internal passport from the police department.

The D'Arcy concession for oil exploration and exploitation, granted by Mozaffar al-Din Shah in 1901, had led to the discovery of oil in 1908 and the formation of the Anglo-Persian Oil Company (APOC). Oil was by far the country's largest modern industry in this period, the largest industrial employer and the biggest export industry and foreign exchange earner, an industrial enclave owned and run by the Anglo-Persian (later Anglo-Iranian) Oil Company, 51 per cent of whose shares were owned by the British government. Attempts in the early 1920s to involve American oil companies (Sinclair and Standard Oil) in north Iran oil did not succeed, partly at least as a result of opposition by APOC.[97] Relations between the government and APOC were not very friendly, since Iran's share of the company's income was small; it paid its taxes (usually several times Iran's oil revenues) to the British government; it did not show its accounts to the Iranian government; it effectively controlled the province of Khuzistan; and it paid low wages to the local labour force.

Reza Shah hoped to increase Iran's oil revenues substantially for financing his military and industrial projects. Long drawn-out negotiations in the late 1920s and early 1930s with APOC to renegotiate the D'Arcy concession did not result in any agreement.[98] Suddenly, in 1932, the company declared Iran's revenue to be a quarter of the previous year. The shah saw this as a personal affront as much as a great loss of finance and foreign exchange, and ordered the cabinet to cancel the D'Arcy concession.[99] Britain took the matter to the League of Nations, and the subsequent negotiations between Iran and APOC resulted in the 1933 oil agreement. This included better terms than before but extended the concessionary period for another thirty years. Taqizadeh, who signed the agreement ex officio as Iran's finance minister, later explained that he had signed on the shah's order and against his own wishes, but he pointed out that the shah had also tried to resist the extension of the concessionary period.[100] The thirty-year extension was highly unpopular and deeply resented. It led to the Iranians' erroneous belief that the whole thing had been a conspiracy in which the shah had been a willing party; and it laid the foundation for the 1951 oil nationalization.[101]

Modern manufacturing expanded from the mid-1920s, ninety-two new factories with more than ten workers being built between 1926 and 1941. The state was the main investor and owner in modern industry, mainly light manufacturing such as sugar, textiles, matches, cement and soap. State investment was necessary because landowners were not interested in investing in modern manufacturing and merchants by and large preferred commerce and traditional industry. The new industries did not come into being on the basis of rational economic criteria, and so some of them failed while some others ran at a loss. The purpose of industrialization was modernization and self-sufficiency rather than profitability and employment creation,[102] although between 1934 and 1938, the highest growth years, the number of industrial workers rose at a high rate. Wages were low for a sixty-hour week or more. The wage rate in the cotton industry, for example, was a quarter of the rate in India.[103]

Extensive road construction (as well as security on the roads) resulted in a dramatic decline in the cost of transport, which in turn reduced production costs. Between 1923 and 1938 almost 13,500 miles of new roads were constructed.[104] This was the most beneficial and least wasteful single modernization project carried out under Reza Shah. The trans-Iranian railway, joining the Caspian Sea to the Persian Gulf, on the other hand, was a wasteful investment. The then colossal amount of $150 million was spent on a project which had little economic or social consequence for years to come. American, Scandinavian and German firms were involved in the design and construction at various stages. It had been a dream project of modern Iranians from the nineteenth century, the shah himself being passionately attached to it. Both he and the modernist nationalist elite believed that it would be a sure sign that the country had become 'civilized'. But, as we have seen, since there was a total aversion to foreign borrowing for fear of becoming dependent on European powers, the project was financed by the crippling tax on tea and sugar, paid by the mass of the people, who were least likely to benefit by it. The huge amount of money thus spent could have been used in useful economic and social projects, including more road construction, which was cheap in terms of domestic money and much cheaper in foreign exchange and which would have brought a lot more benefit to the economy and society.

Nothing was done to help agriculture, despite the fact that about 85 per cent of the population lived and worked as landless peasants. Agriculture therefore remained technologically backward, and the great majority of peasants stayed on the breadline, their lives being at the mercy of their landlords as well as the gendarmes, the new exploitative agents. Landowners benefited by the lack of state protection for peasants and the absence of any effective policy to regulate the land-lord–peasant relationship. From the mid-1920s the state began to sell some of its agricultural estates to raise cash, the policy accelerating in the next decade. These estates were sold not to peasants or local tenants but almost exclusively to large landowners, army officers, higher bureaucrats and big merchants.[105] Landlords also benefited by cheaper and more secure roads. But they (and the peasants) lost money by the state trade monopolies, which kept domestic agricultural prices down, while the overvaluation of the Iranian currency heavily cut the competitive-ness of agricultural exports. Landlords also felt insecure because of the shah's policy of confiscating or forcing them to sell the choicest estates to himself at nominal prices and encroachment generally upon their property (as well as merchant money) by the military and administrative departments.

Urban renewal and modernization took two forms, the expansion of towns and cities, notably Tehran, and the demolition of old structures to give way for wider streets in the old quarters of towns. The new quarters were modern in appearance, the streets were lit by electric lamps and trees were planted on either side. By 1941, many Iranian cities looked more modern, were cleaner and were environmentally more pleasant than before. There were some important draw-backs, however, to the modernization policies. The shah and his appointed mayor of Tehran (General Karmi Aqa Buzarjomehri) believed that the streets of Europe were not only wider but also in perfectly straight lines. They therefore ordered the demolition of any and all buildings which were in the way, destroying historic monuments instead of bypassing them. They also believed that Europeans held old gates and city walls to be symbols of backwardness. That is why the eighteen old gates of Tehran and the wall of Isfahan were pulled down. In Tehran much of the Qajar royal compound was demolished, to some extent perhaps as part of the general onslaught on the legacy of the Qajar era but also because their architecture was traditional.

There was considerable improvement in public health in this period, with growth in the number of doctors, nurses and hospitals, a cleaner environment in towns and cities and measures to combat endemic diseases such as smallpox, although many others, such as malaria and the most infectious diseases respon-sible for infant mortality, were left until a later date to be effectively combated. Improved health care, like virtually every other reform, benefited largely the urban upper and middle classes; but they were nevertheless important as far as they went and laid the foundations for future improvements.[106]

DOMESTIC AND FOREIGN POLITICS

The outline of domestic politics must by now be clear from the foregoing. The dictatorship of the 1920s rapidly turned into absolute and arbitrary rule, so that by the early 1937, when Davar committed suicide (and Firuz was killed while in police custody), there was no man of substance left in the shah's service from among those who had passionately and energetically campaigned for his cause twelve years before and were responsible for most of the reforms and developments that had since taken place. Thus the shah was virtually on his own when the Allies invaded Iran.

First began the process whereby politics was entirely divorced from society. No independent political party or other grouping (such as the pro-Reza Shah, women's and young people's organizations) was allowed. The Communist Party of Iran and workers unions had been banned in practice when a law of 1931 defined membership of any organization with a 'collectivist ideology' as tantamount to a revolt against the constitution. It was on the basis of this law that, in 1937, the group of young men subsequently known as the Fifty-Three (who did not belong to any organization and most of whom knew nothing about Marxism before being converted in prison) were given jail sentences of between three and ten years. By 1930 all independent newspapers, even though most of them were committed to the new regime, were banned and the public sphere that had emerged since the beginning of the constitutional movement was abolished. After imprisonment and banishment to Isfahan, despite the fact that he had gone over to the new regime, Poet Laureate Bahar presented little in public except the occasional panegyric for the shah to keep out of harm's way, expressing his real sentiments in the poems that he published only after the shah's abdication.[107] Sadeq Hedayat, Iran's greatest writer of the twentieth century, had to give a pledge not to publish again, and when he published his famous classic *The Blind Owl* in Bombay (Mumbai) in 1936, he added a note that it was not for sale or distribution in Iran, fearing that he might be prosecuted even though the book had been published abroad.[108] His friend the leading writer Bozorg Alavi went to jail as one of the Fifty-Three and secretly wrote short stories on various scraps of paper which he later published as *Prison Scrap Notes*.[109] Nima Yushij, the founder of modernist Persian poetry characteristically did not publish, and Jamalzadeh, the founder of modern Persian fiction (living in Berlin and Geneva), did not publish for almost twenty years after the publication of his masterpiece *Once Upon a Time* in 1921.[110]

Thus politics ceased to exist for many, but the matter went further than that, and in time any critical opinion or advice uttered, however well intentioned, could be used to arrest the person and confiscate his property. The notorious police chiefs generals Ayrom (who cheated the shah and fled the country) and Mokhtari were even keener in applying the system of repression and, in Ali Dashti's word, supplied a head whenever the shah asked for a hat. 'As soon as anyone so much as mentioned the shah's name they would grab him and ask him what he meant', wrote Mokhber al-Saltaneh (Hedayat) for six years Reza Shah's prime minister.[111]

From the seventh Majlis elections (1928) onwards all the Majils deputies were in practice appointed by the state, and by 1931 it was not possible for the deputies to engage in any political discussion. The immunity of any deputy suspected of the slightest disloyalty was removed and he would be arrested; he might even die in custody. Many Majlis deputies were landlords as before, but they no longer had a will of their own or any political power as a class. The landowners, and especially major landlords, benefited from the ending of chaos and the maintenance of their dominion over the peasants but were unhappy about the loss of political power and the low administrative prices government monopolies charged for the purchase of their products (see above).

Worse from their point of view was the shah's policy, noted above, of either confiscating or forcing them to sell their best estates to him at nominal prices in their lifetime or after their death. The shah's example was followed at a lower level both by military and bureaucratic departments and, sometimes, by senior army officers. Merchants too, although benefiting from peace and security, were unhappy about a lack of political power, the government monopolies and the official threat to their property. When Reza Shah abdicated there was not a single social class that regretted his departure, although the rise and persistence of chaos after him later made some of them change their mind.[112]

An ardent admirer and upholder of Reza Shah and the Pahlavi regime was to conclude:

> Unfortunately Reza Shah's self-dedication to the advancement of Iran was complicated by his increasing interest in accumulating a vast personal fortune and by unwillingness to delegate authority. Large sums of money and titles to villages, farm land, and forest came into his hands. In the realm of administration he exercised stern personal control, and Parliament, losing all spirit of initiative, passed every measure proposed by the government. At his orders the army used severe measures in suppressing disorder among the nomadic tribes. Government officials avoided assumption of initiative or responsibility, and presented only optimistic and favourable reports of the internal situation and of relations with foreign countries . . . Freedom of speech and of the press were nonexistent, and the government set up an office for guiding public opinion [The Office of Education of Minds]. The opportunity to develop capable administrators and public leaders among the rising educated generation was neglected. In general there was a weakening of moral stamina and a pervading atmosphere of resignation and helplessness.[113]

The modernists and nationalists who supported Reza Shah and provided him with an official ideology were ardent supporters of secularization on the French model, in the sense of a complete separation of religion and politics. Reza Shah's educational policy, the new judicial system, the imposition of a uniform dress code – which, inter alia, made it impossible for anyone wearing a turban to be a judge, a schoolteacher, a Majlis deputy or a bureaucrat – all served to remove religious and community leaders from important spheres of social and political action. State control of the owqaf, or publicly endowed religious property, further limited the religious establishment's sphere of action.

The religious community was particularly aggrieved by the conscription law, the dress code and financial restraints, but did not take any action, save for the protest against conscription, which was resolved peacefully, and the peaceful demonstrations in Mashhad against the imposition of the European hat, which were localized. The religious establishment became quietist both in Qom and in Tehran, and even in Najaf, where the hand of Reza Shah did not reach. Thus the attack on religious rites and worship was neither needed for secularization nor was it a reaction to resistance. The banning of processions and commemorative congregations for the martyrs of Karbala was therefore designed purely with an eye to imagined critical European opinion, to show that the country was not backward.

While the European 'other' exerted such an enormous influence on the psyche of the shah and the nationalist modernists, their relationship with Europeans and Americans took different turns. On the whole, there was little difference in the attitude and sentiments towards western powers between the shah and the wider political public. They feared Britain and regarded it with deep suspicion. They disliked the Russians for their past arrogant and repressive behaviour in Iran, and – as far as the mass of the people were concerned – the new Soviet regime did not fare any better, being officially atheist and – as they literally believed – forcing husbands to share their wives with other men. They loved France, which had had long-standing cultural ties with Iran without being a colonial power in the region. They thought of America as an anti-imperialist power which treated other countries with selfless benevolence. They looked up to Germany, which they had dearly wished to win the Great War, and when from the mid-1930s it began to show muscles and teeth again, it increasingly became the focus of admiration by state and society alike.

After the 1921 coup, which pronounced the bankruptcy of Lord Curzon's Persian policy, the new British minister Sir Percy Loraine managed by time and effort to bring the British government round to accepting the status quo and Reza Khan as the only one who could put an end to the disorder. Thus Britain was neutral during the power struggles which led to the fall of the Qajars, and by the time Reza Khan became shah, the British effectively saw Iran as a buffer state, putting aside their great oil interest in Khuzistan.[114]

The shah, on the other hand, who himself believed the British had 'brought [him] to power' in 1921,[115] and whom the people increasingly regarded as a British hireling, especially after the 1933 oil agreement, was an Anglophobe and saw British hands almost in every adverse event. For example, in 1936 he ordered Iranian officials in Europe not to return his son the Crown Prince from Switzerland to Iran via Beirut and Baghdad (whose government was under British influence), saying, 'You don't know who my enemies are; bring him back by way of Russia'.[116] And when, as finance minister Taqizadeh purchased a large amount of gold bullion to be shipped via Marseilles, the shah was certain that the British would confiscate it before it arrived safely in Persian waters.[117] Taqizadeh says that the shah was even suspicious that his son Mohammad Reza was in league with the British.[118] He persecuted and turned into a nonentity his highest-ranking general, Amir-Ahmadi, simply because he had once had a meeting with Loraine, the British minister.[119] In the early 1920s, Britain had been Iran's major trading partner; by the late 1930s, Britain had been replaced by Germany, followed by the Soviet Union.[120]

As noted above, the Soviet Russians had greeted Reza Khan's ascendancy with a positive note and hailed him as an anti-feudal, anti-imperialist, bourgeois-democratic dictator. The honeymoon did not last long after Reza Khan became shah, however, but relations remained cordial. Teymurtash, as long as he was the second-strongest man in the country, toyed with the idea of using the Soviets as a counter-vailing power to the British, especially as regarded the ongoing Anglo-Iranian argument over oil. Legends that spread after his downfall that he was the Russians' candidate for replacing the shah are bound to be fanciful, but it is quite possible that the shah's suspicions were the main instrument of Teymurtash's destruction. It is said that the Soviets interceded with the shah to save Temurtash's life, but if true this was enough to seal his fate. The Soviets clearly did not see the persecution of Iranian communists, socialists and trade unionists in a favourable light, but were satisfied both with the decline in British influence and modernist policies such as secularization and *étatsime* (i.e. a highly state-dominated economy), which in some ways resembled their own regime. Both Iran and the Soviets played their hands cautiously until June 1941, when Germany attacked Russia.

France and America, favourably though they were regarded by state and society alike, were not significant powers in the region. The legend of Morgan Shuster in 1911 had left a very good impression of America and Americans, which itself was the motive behind inviting Millspaugh's mission. This too had left a good impression in the country after Millspaugh's departure in 1927. Hopes for substantial American aid or investment did not, however, materialize, partly at least because of America's policy of isolationism between the wars. In 1937 the shah's extreme sensitivity to criticism in the western press led him to break off diplomatic ties with America.[121]

The same kind of sensitivity to press criticism, in this case a satirical journal, resulted in the rupture of relations with France at the end of 1938, to the point that even Iranian students were brought back home.[122] Most Iranian students in the west, both state and private, had until this time studied in France, and the French military schools alone had trained Iranian officers in the 1920s. There was even a French-style Pasteur Institute in Tehran, initially headed by a Frenchman. The 1938 rupture had had a precedent, though on that occasion the shah did not feel sufficiently grand to break off relations. In 1934 Taqizadeh was Iran's envoy in Paris, where the shah fell under press criticism and demanded that the papers in question should be punished. Taqizadeh made some official representation but explained to Tehran that the newspapers in question could not be censored. That cost him his job and he ended up as a lecturer in the University of London.[123]

Germany, as we have seen, was highly favoured by Iranians, and so trade and other relations with Germany began to improve during the Weimar Republic, including the employment of German banking experts. With the rise of the Nazis to power, political and economic relations became increasingly close. The year 1933 saw both the conclusion of the hated 1933 British oil agreement and the election of Hitler as German chancellor. Within a few years Germany turned again into the greatest European power, the British policy of appeasement tending to enhance its prestige among the eastern nations. With the facts and legends of British and Russian imperialism in mind, the Iranians saw Germany once more as their potential protector and saviour. The shah and the pan-Iranist elite were further enchanted by Nazi propaganda about the superiority of the Aryan race, to which they thought they belonged. These were the various factors that brought the shah's foreign relations and international trade close to Germany and prepared the way for the Allied invasion of 1941, which inevitably resulted in a major upheaval, followed by the return of chaos for many years.

CHAPTER 10

Occupation, Oil Nationalization and Dictatorship

The essence of civilization is that the people are mature, and the clearest sign of their maturity is that they observe the law.

Forughi (radio broadcast, 1941)

OCCUPATION AND ABDICATION

IN THE FIRST YEARS of the Second World War, Iran was formally neutral but sentimentally pro-German. For Britain, which relied on Iranian oil supplies to fuel the Royal Navy, this was a source of considerable anxiety, but as long as Soviet Russia collaborated with Germany there was nothing Britain could do.

Then, on 22 June 1941, Germany attacked the Soviet Union, utterly transforming the situation. A German advance through the Caucasus, which looked likely at the time, would have been welcomed by the shah and the Iranians and have exposed Russia from the rear, not to mention threatening the oil supplies. Now that Britain and the Soviet Union were allied, the trans-Iranian railways and road networks formed potentially the best route for British war supplies to reach the beleaguered Soviets, although the subsequent description of Iran as 'the bridge of victory' on this account is an exaggeration. The Allies also objected to the existence of several hundred German technical advisors and businessmen (describing them as agents of the German war machine, which some of them were) and demanded their expulsion from Iran.

Throughout July and August 1941, there was mounting Anglo-Soviet pressure on Iran to expel the Germans and allow the Allies to use the railways. But Reza Shah refused all the Allies' demands, totally failing to understand the gravity of the situation. And if anyone else did appreciate the real possibility of an Anglo-Soviet invasion, they would never have dared to point it out to the shah in a political situation so insecure and unfree that, as an upper class correspondent of Taqizadeh was to write later, even the upper classes 'were afraid of seeing their own relatives'.[1]

Reza Shah was therefore caught by complete surprise when Prime Minister Ali Mansur woke him up early on the morning of 25 August to inform him that British and Soviet forces had invaded Iran. By all accounts he kept his nerve, but to his horror the army by which he prided himself so much and on which he had lavished so much money and privilege behaved in such an undignified way that many believed that military officers had run away from the invaders wearing a chador to cover their uniform.[2] Enraged, the shah physically assaulted the minister of war and the chief of staff so hard that he hurt his own hand.[3] At first a war cabinet was formed to direct the defence but quickly it became obvious that resistance would be much more costly than surrender. By the time the shah abdicated in mid-September he had dismissed Mansur and appointed the loyal and respectable Foroughi as prime minister.

It has now become commonplace to say that the Allies forced Reza Shah to abdicate. In some platitudinous sense this may be true, but it calls for two important qualifications. According to Sir Reader Bullard, the British envoy in Tehran, the Allies never formally made such a demand, and there is no other evidence to contradict this, though he admitted that the news of the movement of the Russian forces from Qazvin towards Tehran had made the shah nervous.[4] According to Abbasqoli Golshah'iyan, then minister of finance, the Russian ambassador had denied the news. During the 1921 coup, British diplomats and officers had accompanied Iranian officials to Mehrabad, ostensibly to dissuade Reza Khan's Cossacks from marching to Tehran, which became a fruitless exercise (see Chapter 8). Now, by an irony of history, the military attachés of both Russia and Britain had left for Qazvin ostensibly to prevent such a move, but later the news came that the Russians were approaching Karaj.[5] However, Golshia'iyan is explicit that it was the cabinet that asked Foroughi to tell the shah to abdicate and that Foroughi, having said he personally believed that that was the wish of the Allies, saw the shah and told him so.[6]

The other qualification to the view that the Allies forced the shah to abdicate is that the shah had to abdicate simply because he had nothing to stand on. Virtually the whole of society was against him. Had he had a reasonable social base, with at least the upper classes behind him, he would not have had to abdicate and the Allies would not have insisted on that course of action now that he had agreed to cooperate with them.[7] Instead, even before he abdicated, the Majlis deputies, who had been in effect appointed by him, were implying that he had misappropriated some of the crown jewels,[8] and when he did abdicate they led scathing attacks on his violation of lives and private property, among other things.[9] Shortly after the abdication, court cases began to be brought against the shah by those whose relatives had been murdered in jail and/or their properties had been confiscated.[10] Golsha'iyan says in his contemporary diaries that, since the shah was so unpopular, those in government posts had been worried about what might happen to them (as a result of the public backlash) if he died or was assassinated, and almost rejoices in the fact that he had to abdicate while the Allies occupied the country and kept the peace.[11]

After the abdication, the Allies, and especially the British, were not keen to keep the Pahlavi dynasty in place. They suggested to Foroughi to become acting head of state[12] and to Mohammad Sa'ed (a senior career diplomat and ambassador to

Russia) to become president.[13] Both turned down the offer. The British even briefly toyed with the idea of restoring the Qajars but quickly gave up when they failed to find a suitable candidate.[14] Forughi moved fast and took Crown Prince Mohammad Reza to the Majlis for investiture as the new shah, and the Allies raised no objection.

Historians usually divide the period of Mohammad Reza Shah's rule into two parts: 1941–53, the period of turmoil and democratic experiment which ended with the 1953 coup, and the period 1953–79, which they normally describe as the period of Mohammad Reza Shah's dictatorship, ending with the revolution of February 1979. In fact, this second period can also be divided into two, with the cut-off point in 1963. In the first twelve years of his reign (1941–53), Mohammad Reza Shah was a constitutional monarch; in the next decade (1953–63) he was a dictator; but in the remainder of his reign, until the revolution, he was an absolute and arbitrary ruler.

On his accession, the shah was a young man of about twenty-two, inexperienced, shy and anxious about the country and his own position. As a child, he had attended Le Rosey, an exclusive Swiss boarding school, but his father had returned him to Iran when he was sixteen. He was then entered in the military academy in Tehran, from which he graduated in 1939. He suffered from a basic lack of self-confidence, which in bad times resulted in paralysis and in good times gave him a false sense of security and supreme self-assurance (see below and Chapters 11 and 12). He was a modernist and an Aryanist nationalist, highly embarrassed about Iran's underdevelopment and entertaining lofty dreams for her rapid modernization, of which a large and strong military under his direct command would be a main component. His pro-German sentiments, which he had shared with most Iranians, were within a short period of time replaced by a strong fascination and admiration for the United States, and he soon wished that it would become the country's patron for financial and military assistance and for countervailing power against both Britain and the Soviet Union. He was able in some respects and had a powerful memory, but lacked knowledge and experience and had a limited intellectual capacity. Dominated as he then was by older statesmen and political magnates, he was nevertheless skilful at political intrigue and manoeuvring and wished to have a strong say in civil government as well as the army, which in effect he controlled.

THE 1940s: THE POLITICS OF CHAOS

Chaos began to return to Iranian politics even before Reza Shah had begun his exile, first in Mauritius, then in Johannesburg, where he died in 1944. Thus his abdication meant the collapse of the strong regime, which led to renewed chaos, so that, as early as October 1941, a British diplomat in Tehran remarked that 'in the chaotic conditions inevitable in the sudden change-over from pure despotism to an alleged constitutional and democratic regime there was a general scramble for the fruits, though not for the responsibilities, of privilege and office.'[15] The phase '*pure* despotism' was no doubt intended to describe absolute and arbitrary rule, for which there was no term and concept in European history.

Some responsible politicians and observers saw the fundamental ills of the country in the state's perpetuation of arbitrary rule and society's licentious behaviour. Forughi's experience of the decade of chaos after the Constitutional Revolution, and the decade of absolute and arbitrary rule under Reza Shah, had given him an acute insight which is clear from his long radio broadcast to the nation three weeks after the shah's abdication. He began by defining freedom and the conditions for its existence:

> I hope that you will have learned from the pain and suffering which you have endured in the past few decades, and have realized how to cherish the blessings of liberty. You will therefore know that freedom does not mean that the people should be licentious and behave in an arbitrary fashion, but that it also involves certain limits, since if there are no constraints no one will be free, and the strong will enslave the weak.

He then went straight to the heart of the matter, that is, the meaning and implications of the rule of law:

> The limits set to arbitrary behaviour are none other than those defined by law, so everyone will know his own rights and will not go beyond them. It follows that in a country where there is no law, or the law is not observed, the people will not be free and will not enjoy security ... Therefore, the first thing ... which I would suggest to you is to note that a free people is one whose affairs are based in law, so that whoever ignores or violates the law is an enemy of freedom ...

This was followed by his careful distinction between modernization and pseudo-modernism. Forughi asked what the difference was between 'civilized' and 'uncivilized' nations:

> I suspect that some of you would say 'A civilized nation is one that has railways, modern industry, organized army, tank, aircraft, etc., and an uncivilized nation is one that does not possess such things.' Or you would say that a civilized nation is one whose cities ... have wide and paved streets, with multi-storey buildings, and so on.' Civilized nations, of course, do have such things, but I submit that these are products of civilization, not its essence. *The essence of civilization is that the people are mature, and the clearest sign of their maturity is that they observe the law.*[16]

The above allusions to the pseudo-modernist attitude towards social and economic development could not have been made more obvious. But, at the time, the most immediate problem was that of destructive conflict and chaos. That is why Forughi emphasized that the most important aspect of modernization – indeed, he said civilization – was that both state and society should observe the law.

Renewed chaos naturally had its own specific aspects arising from contemporary realities. Had Reza Shah fallen without direct foreign intervention the public reaction would have been much stronger and the consequences far-reaching, as was to be seen after the fall of his son's regime in 1979. It was in their own interests for the Allies to keep the peace. Accordingly, the British legation communicated directly with the Iranian government and various political circles and communities, and used their power and influence to ensure that the Allies' basic requirements were met. Outside that, the field was wide open for Iranian politicians, Majlis deputies, journalists, tribal leaders, provincial magnates and popular movements to be involved in destructive conflict rather than constructive competition. Between 1941 and 1946 as many as nine governments were formed amid faction fighting in the 13th and 14th sessions of the Majlis.

In January 1942 the young shah signed the Tri-Partite Alliance with Britain and Soviet Russia, under which Iran agreed to provide non-military assistance to the Allies, and the Allies – emphasizing Iran's independence and territorial integrity – pledged themselves to withdraw their forces no later than six months after the end of the war, a pledge that the Soviet Union did not keep. In September 1943 Iran declared war on Germany (and later Japan), and so became a member of the United Nations. In the following November, at the Tehran Conference, the Allied heads – Joseph Stalin, Franklin Roosevelt and Winston Churchill – reaffirmed their commitment to Iranian independence and territorial integrity. Thus almost from the start, the Allies did not treat Iran as an occupied country to be run by themselves, although they did indirectly interfere in Iranian politics to serve their collective as well as individual interests in the country. Apart from that, the British and Americans effectively controlled Iran's transport and communications system and even more. As the British minister reported to the Foreign Office, 'the compelling need to save shipping also forced us into a considerable degree of interference in local affairs.'[17]

Apart from safeguarding the oil supplies, the biggest help to the Allies' war effort was the so-called Persian Corridor, using the trans-Iranian railways as well as motor roads to supply some 5 million tons of war material to the beleaguered Soviet Union and another 2 million tons to the British forces in the Middle East. Having declared non-interference in the country's domestic affairs, the Allies nevertheless made important demands on the country which Iranian governments had little choice but to meet as long as the Allied troops remained in Iran. The rial (the Iranian unit of currency) was devalued to less than half of its rate of exchange. This meant that, in terms of gold and foreign exchange, Allied purchases of Iranian goods and services cost them less than half the price they had paid hitherto, and Iranian import of their products cost Iran more than twice as much as previously. Iranian paper money was expanded in order to extend credit to the Allies for their expenditure in Iran, to be paid back after the war was ended. Between 1941 and 1944 there was more than a threefold increase in the money supply.[18] These policies, added to the hoarding and speculation which they encouraged, led to rampant inflation, scarcity of goods (especially bread) and greater pauperization in the country at large.[19] In 1941 the wholesale price index was at 20.7; by 1944 it had risen to 61.9. In the same period, the general cost of living index rose from 16 to 67.9 and the index for food from 18.5 to 75.8.[20]

Yet at the same time, Allied diplomats and representatives in Iran kept pressing various Iranian authorities for social reform aimed at a better deal for the majority of the population; they met with little success. Predictably, after Reza Shah's abdication the social and political power of the numerically small landowning elite had been considerably enhanced. Under Reza Shah the power of the landlord vis-à-vis the peasantry had remained intact, but in other respects this social group too had been subject to arbitrary rule, having no political power as a class and their property rights being at the mercy of the almighty state. They had now stepped into the power vacuum created by the fall of Reza Shah, enjoying the privileges of wealth and political power but displaying little sense of responsibility towards their peasantry and society at large. In 1943, the British minister Bullard regarded the Tudeh party's reform programme as being 'mild in comparison with the conditions of the poor classes'.[21]

POLITICAL PARTIES AND GROUPS

The Tudeh Party was founded shortly after Reza Shah's abdication. Later developments turned it into an authentic Communist Party, but in the beginning and for most of the 1940s it was similar to European popular fronts, the anti-fascist movements of the 1930s and 1940s, consisting of various leftist and democratic tendencies with a broadly reformist programme. It was led mainly by Marxist intellectuals known as the Fifty-Three, who had been released from jail after Reza Shah's abdication, although its symbolic head and titular founder was Soleiman Mirza Eskandari, the old Democrat, later Socialist leader who was well known for his strict observance of religious duties.

The party pledged itself to constitutional monarchy and parliamentary government and put forward a policy framework (it was too general to be called a programme) for extensive social reform. The party was clearly inclined towards the Soviet Union, but that was not unusual before 1946, when the Soviet Union was popular in Iran as well as in the West, and the anti-Nazi alliance was still strong. In the early 1940s many educated people below the age of forty were either members, sympathizers or fellow travellers of the party. In the 1943 elections to the fourteenth Majlis – the first to be held since Reza Shah's abdication – the party managed to send eight deputies to parliament, mainly elected from northern constituencies which were under Soviet occupation, although the Tudeh Party itself was particularly popular in the northern, central and north-western regions. At the time, it was the only well-organized political party with a clear political outlook and which enjoyed popular support.[22]

Alongside the emergence of the Tudeh Party as the main voice of intellectuals and the modern educated elite, a religious movement began to grow and spread which, although virtually ignored by the modern Iranian community, was to anticipate the religious and Islamist movements of the 1960s and 1970s which, for a few crucial years before the Iranian revolution, impressed and influenced the moderns as well. Apart from the Society of the Devotees of Islam (*Jam'iyat-e Fada'iyan-e Islam*), a small but highly vociferous and militant political group which will be discussed further below, the other Islamist organizations which came into being in the 1940s focused their activities against the Baha'i community, 'materialism' and Ahmad Kasravi, a leading critic of Shiism as well as Baha'ism who was nevertheless instrumental in the formation of their new religious outlook (see Chapter 12).

None of these organizations aimed at overthrowing the existing regime and replacing it with an Islamist state. In fact, some of them tried and to some extent succeeded in using the royal court and various members of the political and religious establishments to help their cause, promoting religious studies in schools, removing known Baha'is from government employment and strengthening religious rites and duties. One of the most active of these new organizations was The Islamic Propaganda Society (*Anjoman-e Tablighat-e Eslami*), set up by Ata'ollah Shahabpur, an Aryanist and anti-Semitic campaigner of the 1930s who had turned into an Islamic propagandist of the new cut.[23] While in its broader outlook the Society antedated the political Islamists of the later periods, its focus on the Baha'is anticipated the anti-Baha'i but apolitical Islamic messianic society (*Hojjatiyeh*) of the 1950s and beyond.

The Society for Islamic Instructions (*Anjoman-e Ta'limat-e Eslami*) was founded in 1943 to spread formal religious instructions 'without intervening in current politics', and by 1947 it had set up sixty-one Islamic schools, sixteen day schools and forty-five evening schools. Other religious societies also came into being, both in the capital and in provincial centres. Alongside these religious organizations there appeared a number of Islamic journals, including *Parcham-e Eslam* (The Standard of Islam), *Donya-ye Eslam* (The World of Islam) and Fada'iyan's *Nabard-e Mellat* (Battle of the People), which, with different degrees of emphasis, advanced religious ideas and political views. Fada'iyan, as noted above, were militant and ideological, but the other societies, movements and campaigners were quite effective in pushing piecemeal Islamist objectives in less overt ways.[24]

Among the various political groupings and factions that came into being after the abdication – many of them small in number and short-lived – three of the most important were the Iran Party, Seyyed Zia's National Will (*Eradeh-ye Melli*) and Qavam's Democrat Party. The Iran Party, with its liberal and social democratic tendencies, was set up by a number of relatively young Iranian technocrats, many of whom had been educated in Europe. It believed in social democracy, was opposed to foreign domination and (along with many such individuals and groupings at the time) was sympathetic towards the Tudeh Party. It was relatively small in terms of organization, activity and publications but compensated for this by the fact that its top members were some of the country's best technocrats and university professors, holding what were then highly privileged and prestigious positions. Three of them became well known in the history of twentieth-century Iran: Allahyar Saleh, the party leader who later joined Qavam's coalition government with the Tudeh Party as minister of justice, becoming minister of the interior and ambassador to the United States under Mosaddeq and a leading figure of the second National Front; Karim Sanjabi, who became minister of education and Majlis deputy under Mosaddeq and ended up as the leader of the fourth National Front during the revolution of February 1979; and Shapur Bakhtiar, deputy minister of labour under Mosaddeq, who became the party leader during the revolution but was expelled when he accepted the shah's offer of premiership. The party became one of the main political organizations during the oil nationalization movement under Mosaddeq.[25]

National Will was the party organized and led by Seyyed Zia, who had been a joint leader, together with Reza Khan, of the 1921 coup and shortly afterwards had been dismissed as prime minister and exiled from the country (see Chapters 8 and 9). He returned to Iran in September 1943 after his long exile in Palestine, and was favoured by the British embassy as a candidate for the premiership.[26] At first the shah suspected his motives, thinking that he might attempt to overthrow or sideline him, but the Seyyed's reassuring attitude and their mutual opposition to the Tudeh Party helped improve his relations with the shah, although the latter never seriously considered him as a candidate for premiership, since he was anxious that, with British support, he might be too strong and independent of him.

Seyyed Zia was no longer the young harbinger of romantic nationalism and radical social reform that he had been in his short period of premiership in 1921. He was now a conservative politician who put much emphasis on 'popular traditions' (an'anat-e melli), symbolically wearing a traditional Persian karakul hat in public. He was universally believed to be an 'agent of Britain', a charge that was untrue but, in the eyes of his detractors, tended to be confirmed by his openly Anglophile views and inclinations. His National Will Party was largely a one-person affair; it was not a mass movement and did not include any other leading figure in its leadership, but apart from the British embassy, it also had the support of some landlords, big merchants and other religious and traditionalist groups. From the moment of his arrival back in the country, the Tudeh Party marked him as their greatest enemy and the reactionary-in-chief, more so at the time than the shah himself.

The Seyyed was elected to the 14th Majlis for Yazd, and Mosaddeq elected the first deputy for Tehran, unsuccessfully opposed his letter of credence because of his role in the 1921 coup.[27] Seyyed Zia was still hopeful until the mid-1950s but later gave up his efforts and concentrated on his chicken farming business, although little was left of his party after Qavam put him in jail in 1946.

Apart from the Tudeh Party and Mosaddeq, Zia's main enemy and rival was Ahmad Qavam, whom Zia had jailed after the 1921 coup but who had succeeded Zia after his dismissal and exile (see Chapter 9). Qavam had already been prime minister once in the 1940s, before Zia's return from Palestine. He was a strong personality and an independent politician, pragmatic but not unprincipled. He was prepared to deal with the great powers but was not a client of any of them, although since his two premierships in the early 1920s he had hoped to attract American investment and foreign aid to Iran. At different times he was accused of being an agent of America, of Russia and of Britain, but such accusations were unfounded.[28] It was he who invited Arthur Millspaugh's first mission to reform Iran's financial administration in 1922, and his second mission in 1942. In this second mission, Millspaugh was much less successful than before, one important reason being the greater ability and higher self-confidence of Iranian politicians and civil servants, for example, Abolhasan Ebtehaj, the able governor of Bank Melli whom he tried to but did not succeed in removing from his post.[29] More successful and lasting was the role of the American military, headed by Colonel Norman Schwarzkopf, who was put in charge of the Iranian gendarmerie, reforming and reorganizing the paramilitary rural police force.

As after the Constitutional Revolution, once again the Majlis became all-powerful, confronting weak and shaky cabinets which they changed every few months. As noted in Chapter 8, the constitutionalist principle of *separation* of powers was interpreted to mean *confrontation* of powers. Even then, the Majlis acted as a collective body only when they wished to confront the ministers; otherwise factional groupings and individual deputies would try to bargain directly with ministers in exchange for supporting even some of the most basic governmental decisions. It is telling that from 1941 until 1952 no government succeeded in passing an annual budget through parliament. Mohammad Sa'ed, the veteran diplomat and now foreign minister, wrote to Taqizadeh, who had become head of the Iranian legation in London after Reza Shah's fall:

The Majlis does nothing other than being involved in internal conflict and every few months appointing a new prime minister. There does not exist the kind of cooperative and sincere spirit that is needed at the present. To render any service over a length of time, the prime minister has to spend most of his time negotiating and bargaining with the deputies such that I can say there does not remain the slightest time for the head of government to see to the fundamental affairs of the country.[30]

This letter was written in July 1943, almost two years after the old shah's abdication. In 1948, George Allen, the US ambassador, wrote on the role of the Majlis that it was an almost entirely negative body with no apparent ability to take positive action. 'During six months of present Majlis it has passed only two laws ... It has two or three short sessions a week and spends most times debating members credentials ... Much positive action is required of Majlis if Iran is to improve, since executive in Iran has almost no authority to do anything under constitution as now drawn.'[31]

The pattern was to continue until oil was nationalized and Mosaddeq took over the government in 1951, but even then, as will be seen below, turmoil and chaos did not cease.

In the following years Taqizadeh wrote a number of letters from London to members of the cabinet in which he discussed the country's basic problems arising from arbitrary rule, chaos, official (romantic) nationalism and the conspiracy theory of politics.[32] Talking about chaos, which was then the most acute problem facing the country, he wrote:

> If licence is given rein in the name of democracy and . . . everybody objects to and opposes everything, and poor government officials, just like a cat cornered by a dog or a lion, constantly have to respond to criticism and defamation, then nothing will stand . . . and the country would certainly face destruction . . . The country may survive under an unjust and coercive ruler, but will certainly fall as a result of chaos, licence or 'extremism in freedom'.[33]

In a parliamentary speech in the 14th Majlis (1943–5), Mosaddeq took up the theme of turmoil following the fall of arbitrary rule:

> No nation ever got anywhere under arbitrary rule (*estebdad*). It would be a mistake to compare the present situation – when we have only just heard the name of freedom – unfavourably with the [Reza Shah] period. For one would still need many more years to get rid of the [destructive but unavoidable] reactions to the events of that period . . .[34]

There were almost continuous incidents of turmoil and rebellion up and down the country. Some of these were widespread and historic, such as the major revolts in Azerbaijan, Kurdistan and the south. Some were less spectacular but recurrent, monthly, weekly if not daily occurrences. A certain amount of disorder in certain provinces after the fall of Reza Shah was inevitable, both in reaction to his centralist and pan-Persian policies and because of the temptation for some provincial leaders or grandees to take advantage of the situation. Yet the turmoil would not have been so intense, so frequent and so difficult to settle quickly and satisfactorily if in the centre itself conflict had not been as destructive and chaotic as in fact it was. One notable example of the ongoing destructive conflict in the very centre and at the highest level of politics was that between the shah and Ahmad Qavam during the short period of Qavam's premiership between August 1942 and March 1943. There were many reasons for this conflict, including the fact that Qavam was a proud, strong and wily politician and that the shah did not have much confidence in himself, was afraid of being marginalized and was anxious to have personal control of the situation as much as he could. But perhaps his strongest fear at the time was kindled by Qavam's view that he, the prime minister, should be ultimately responsible for the army and the ministry of war. Ten years later the same problem was to become a major source of conflict between the shah and Mosaddeq.

The bitter conflict eventually led to the bread riots of 8 and 9 December 1942, when the mob occupied the Majlis, looted the shops and ransacked Qavam's house and set fire to it. During these disorders, a general close to the young shah asked the Soviet ambassador what his reaction would be if the shah and the army took over the government for a period. Later, when the matter leaked out, the shah said that the general had asked that question casually and without his knowledge. But, as the British envoy reported to the British Foreign Secretary shortly afterwards, this was not believed. On the contrary, most of the domestic politicians and foreign diplomats had little doubt that the shah had had a direct hand in the riots.[35]

THE AZERBAIJAN REVOLT AND CONFLICTS OVER OIL

When the war ended, Iran was facing all the difficulties mentioned above, to which the revolt in Azerbaijan was now added. There were many strands to the revolt in Azerbaijan. The Azerbaijanis had been oppressed and humiliated under Reza Shah. They aspired to a dignified status and, as everywhere in the northern provinces of Iran, were influenced by leftist ideas and demanded social and economic reform. The Soviet Union (more specifically the Communist Party chief of Soviet Azerbaijan) supported the reconstituted Azerbaijan Democrat Party, led by an old communist, Ja'far Pishevari, and hoped to fish in troubled waters. The Soviet army was still occupying the province and the access areas to it (contrary to their formal commitment to leave after the end of the war), making it impossible for the Iranian central army to move up to the province and unrealistic for the provincial army division to try to suppress the rebellion of the Democrats when they declared autonomy in December 1945.[36]

Pishevari's letter of credence had been turned down not only in the 14th Majlis in 1943 but by the first Tudeh Party conference as well. There was not much love lost between Pishevari and the Tudeh leaders, who had treated Pishevari with contempt while they had been in the same prison ward with him under Reza Shah.[37] Nevertheless, under Soviet pressure, the Tudeh uncritically backed the Azerbaijan revolt and even allowed its own party organization in Tabriz to be merged with that of the Democrats under Pishevari's leadership. Through 1946, the initial sympathy of many in Tehran for the Azerbaijan Democrats began to melt away as fears grew of a plan to separate the province from Iran and join it to the Soviet Union. The rebellion in Kurdistan and the formation of the Kurdish 'republic' of Mahabad in January 1946, also with Soviet support, made those in Tehran fearful, even those who had sympathy for the Kurds' and Azerbaijanis' legitimate grievances.

Qavam formed his second ministry of the 1940s in January 1946 with Soviet support in the wake of the revolt in Azerbaijan. The shah reluctantly agreed to Qavam's premiership because he had the ability to deal with the situation and was acceptable to the Russians. Although Qavam was not very keen on the idea, Iran complained to the UN Security Council against the Soviet Union's refusal to withdraw its forces, contrary to its firm commitment through the Tri-Partite Agreement. This received strong support from the United States. In March 1946 America issued strong notes of protest to the Soviet Union (although historians have cast doubt on President Truman's later claim that he had actually issued a formal ultimatum to the Soviets on the issue). Qavam's negotiations in Moscow did not yield immediate fruit, but the continuation of the negotiations with Sadchikov, the Soviet ambassador to Tehran, eventually resulted in agreement: the Soviets would withdraw their troops; the Iranian government would settle the Azerbaijan crisis amicably through negotiations with Pishevari's autonomous government; and the Iranian government would grant a concession for north Iranian oil to the Soviet Union subject to the approval of the Majlis, which at the time was in recess.

Qavam's negotiations with Pishevari in Tehran led to a large measure of agreement. In the meantime he formed his Democrat Party, which was intended to compete with the Tudeh Party (and with the Azerbaijan Democrats), putting forward a programme of social reform not much less radical than theirs: the Azerbaijan Democrats had distributed state lands and the property of absentee landlords among the peasants, founded a university at Tabriz and dropped Persian in favour of Azerbaijani Turkic in primary schools. The formation of a party with a radical reform programme was a prelude to the canny Qavam's invitation to the Tudeh Party for a short-lived coalition government. The coalition lasted no more than three months, during which there was a rebellion by southern tribes led by Naser Khan Qashqa'i, which was intended to counter the Tudeh and the Azerbaijan Democrats. There is no evidence that the British plotted or supported this rebellion, but, in view of the apparent rise of pro-Soviet power in the north, they kept their options open. It has even been suggested that the southern revolt had Qavam's tacit approval to enable him to shake off the Tudeh coalition and abolish the Azerbaijan and Kurdish autonomies. That is unlikely, but he certainly tried to turn it to his own advantage as much as possible.[38]

There was a peaceful settlement with the southern rebels shortly before the coalition with the Tudeh collapsed, following which Qavam sent troops to Azerbaijan ostensibly to ensure the freedom of the impending Majlis elections. With Russia having abandoned Pishevari's government and the Soviet troops having already departed, Azerbaijan resistance collapsed in December 1946, a year after the revolt, and most of its civilian and military leaders and officers crossed the border to the Soviet Union. The central army meted out a terrible punishment both to combatants and non-combatants, Azerbaijani as well as Kurdish, whose 'republic' likewise fell to pieces. This left Britain as the strongest great power in Iran until October 1952.

The ensuing 15th Majlis elections were manipulated by Qavam's party – the Tudeh having boycotted them largely because of its demoralization over the Azerbaijan fiasco – resulting in the overwhelming electoral victory of his Democrat Party and his return to office. But the appearance of parliamentary strength was deceptive: since the revolts and threats of disintegration had subsided, politics returned to its normal chaotic trends, with Democrat Party deputies splitting into pro-Qavam and anti-Qavam factions. This was encouraged by the shah, who was also busy trying to turn the British and American envoys against a strong, independent and triumphant prime minister. For example, the shah won the support of Reza Hekmat, chairman of the central committee of the Democrat Party, against Qavam, by paying off his gambling debts.[39] The shah's strong and interfering twin sister, Princess Ashraf, also played an active role in toppling Qavam's government. Before his government fell in December 1947, Qavam took the bill for the Soviet concession of north Iranian oil to the Majlis in October, virtually certain that it would be defeated, as in fact it was, adding to Soviet and Tudeh anger and delighting the Anglo-American powers.

The Soviet demand for north Iranian oil dated back to 1944 when, following earlier approaches by British and American companies, the Soviets demanded a concession for Iran's northern provinces. However, what they were in fact demanding in the guise of an oil concession – as Sergei Kaftaradze, the Russian deputy foreign minister, had intimated to Prime Minister Mohammad Sa'ed – was recognition of northern Iran as the Soviet sphere of influence.[40] Sa'ed and the conservatives resisted this demand and the Tudeh vociferously supported it, and this resulted in some internal party criticism.[41] Eventually, Mosaddeq submitted a bill to the Majlis forbidding the granting of any foreign concession without the approval of the Majlis, which passed overwhelmingly despite the Tudeh deputies' vote against it. That was why Qavam's subsequent proposal had had to be submitted to the Majlis. In his speech proposing the bill, Mosaddeq had incidentally attacked the 1933 oil agreement with the Anglo-Iranian Oil Company (AIOC) and the attitude and behaviour of the company in Iran.[42]

The AIOC had not even adhered faithfully to the 1933 agreement. It behaved like a colonial power in the Khuzistan oil province and suffered from bad labour relations. In 1944 a local workers' strike was settled as a result of government intervention, but in July 1946 a full stoppage ended in bloodshed. In order to maintain British goodwill Qavam sent two ministers together with two Tudeh leaders who were about to enter his coalition government to break the strike.[43] The Tudeh Party then had influence among the oil workers (which it was later to lose to Mosaddeq) as well as the textile workers' union in Isfahan and the workers unions in Tehran, which were affiliated to them.[44] The two consecutive ministries of Qavam from January 1946 to December 1947 – a long period by the standards of the 1940s – offered an opportunity for ending the politics of chaos and the establishment of long-term constitutional government. As noted, however, the politics of chaos proved stronger after the immediate threat of disintegration had subsided. After the abortive governments (December 1947–November 1948) of Ebrahim Hakimi and Abdolhosein Hazhir – the latter was an able but unpopular politician and a close favourite of Princess Ashraf's – it fell to Mohammad Sae'd's second premiership (November 1948–March 1950) to try to renegotiate the 1933 agreement with the AIOC.

The shah was anxious to curb the influence of the Tudeh Party, extend his own power and reduce parliamentary licence. The opportunity for banning the Tudeh Party and amending the constitution to enable him to dissolve the Majlis arose after an abortive attempt on his life on 4 February 1949. Nureddin Kiyanuri, a Tudeh leader later to become its first secretary under the Islamic Republic, was involved in the assassination plan, but the party as a whole did not have prior knowledge of it.[45] Many, including Saed, believed that General Ali Razmara, the chief of staff, had had a hand in the plot, despite the fact that the general himself arranged for the arrest of a number of suspects and the exile of Ayatollah Seyyed Abolqsem Kashani – a Tehran *mojtahed* and political campaigner – to Lebanon.[46]

Many of the original Tudeh Party members had left the party at three successive stages as it became more and more radicalized and exclusively identified with the Soviet Union: at the revolt of Azerbaijan in 1945–6; at the party split of January 1948; and after the banning of the party in February 1949. After this last event the party went underground and, in all but name, quickly became a solid and monolithic Communist Party of the kind that existed everywhere in Stalin's years, even to the point of resorting to the assassination of its own dissident members.

The constituent assembly met in the following April. It provided for the establishment of an upper house, a senate, half of whose members would be directly appointed by the shah, and the other half by an electoral college; more important than that, it empowered the shah to dissolve parliament. But this did not go without challenge: a few deputies censured the government; Qavam wrote a letter to the shah and strongly criticized the move, to the latter's annoyance; Kashani objected from his exile; and Mosaddeq (a few months later) made critical remarks about it.[47] The amendments, however, did little to improve the situation, which could only change by the use of military force, as it in fact did after the 1953 coup.

A seven-year-plan bill for economic development passed through the Majlis under Saed in 1949. It was due to be financed mainly by oil revenues and borrowing from the Intenational Bank for Reconstruction and Development, later known as the World Bank;[48] therefore, it became largely inoperative as a result of the 1951–3 oil crisis, which led to the boycott of Iranian oil. The plan was part of the aspiration for reform and development which were deemed necessary both to improve the general standard of living and to better the living conditions of the majority of people, although this was hard to achieve in the circumstances of the 1940s. The large majority of the peasantry were still landless sharecroppers, lucky to extract a bare subsistence. In 1947, a law passed by Qavam increased the the peasants' share of the crop by 15 per cent, but this became a dead letter, especially given that his government did not last long enough to begin to implement it.[49] The conditions of the urban poor and proletariat had slightly improved since the early 1940s mainly due to the slowing down of the rate of inflation and fewer food shortages, but they were still pitiful in most cases. Increasingly, hopes began to be pinned on a better deal from the AIOC to improve Iran's share of the oil revenues.

Qavam was still prime minister when the Majlis instructed the government to open negotiations with the AIOC after rejecting the north Iranian oil concession to the Soviet Union. A deal was eventually negotiated under Sa'ed, known as the Gass-Golsha'iyan or the supplemental agreement, the most important provision of which was to increase Iran's royalties from 4 to 6 shillings per ton of crude. The Majlis would have passed the corresponding bill had it not been for the vociferous opposition and filibustering of a small opposition group, backed by the press and the public outside parliament, in July 1949, only a few days before the life of the 15th Majlis came to an end.[50] In the meantime, Taqizadeh, who as Reza Shah's finance minister had signed the 1933 oil agreement, said in a Majlis speech that he had signed it under duress, and his statement seriously put in doubt the legality of the agreement (see Chapter 9).[51]

In October 1949 the National Front was formed. Elections for the 16th Majlis had been largely rigged in the provinces, and now the battle lines were drawn for the Tehran elections. Mozaffar Baqa'i and Hosein Makki, who had led the opposition to the supplemental agreement in the previous Majlis, had brought out Mosaddeq from his self-declared 'political retirement' to lead the campaign for free elections and against the supplemental agreement.

They accused General Razmara of manipulating the elections, and twenty of the protesters outside the shah's palace, led by Mosaddeq, were allowed to take *bast* in the palace. They broke the *bast* a few days later but, gathering at Mosaddeq's home, they declared the formation of the National Front.[52]

Mohammad Mosaddeq (1882–1967) had been born into a privileged family; his father was a high government official, his mother a Qajar princess. He was elected to the 1st Majlis in 1907, but did not pass the age qualification and later went to France and Switzerland, where he obtained a doctorate in law. Returning to Iran shortly before World War I, he taught law and was deputy minister, and later minister, of finance, provincial governor-general and foreign minister before becoming a deputy in the 5th Majlis (1923–5), when he opposed Reza Khan's successful bid to become shah. He left politics under Reza Shah but was nevertheless arrested in 1940 for unknown reasons, later to be released through the intervention of the then Prince Mohammad Reza and put under house arrest until the shah's abdication in 1941. He came back to politics as the first deputy for Tehran in the 14th Majlis, but having unsuccessfully campaigned in the 15th Majlis elections, he declared his 'political retirement', until 1949 when Makki and Baqa'i encouraged him to return to politics. He was an honest, upright and patriotic democrat with social democratic tendencies but was somewhat abrasive and, like most of his contemporaries, prone to the conspiracy theory of politics. All his life he suffered from a frailty of the nerves which manifested itself in various ways, such as fits of fainting.[53]

The formation of the National Front was announced on 23 October.[54] On the same day, the Tudeh Party's official organ described its leaders as agents of imperialism and the royal court. Ten days later, a member of the Fada'iyan-e Islam shot and killed the royal court minister Hazhir, on suspicion of being involved in ballot rigging and being an 'agent of Britain'. Hazhir's assassin had in 1946 assassinated Ahmad Kasravi, the outstanding scholar and critic of Shiism and Shii ulama (see Chapter 12), and had got away with it partly with Hazhir's help. The government took some measures against Mosaddeq and some other Front leaders after Hazhir's assassination, but they did not pursue the matter for long.[55]

The growing popularity of Mosaddeq and the Front, and the impression gained by the shah that America was unhappy about the election results, led to a second round of elections in Tehran in which six Front leaders, led by Mosaddeq – the first deputy yet again – were elected to the 16th Majlis, in addition to Ayatollah Kashani, still in exile in Lebanon. The National Front thus had been formed as a result of struggles for the freedom of parliamentary elections in the middle of the ongoing argument with AIOC, and quickly assumed the leadership of a movement for democracy within and independence without the country, which became focused on the oil issue. They saw Saed as an irredeemably pro-British prime minister with whom there could be no deal.

On the other hand, Razmara was waiting in the wings, although the shah had more reason to fear him than Mosaddeq. Thus Saed's new ministry fell shortly after it was formed and was replaced by Ali Mansur's, which lasted barely four months before it was replaced by Razmara's cabinet. In the meantime, an ad hoc oil committee of the Majlis chaired by Mosaddeq had been set up to deal with the oil question. The National Front faction in the Majlis was small but carried much authority because of Mosaddeq's charismatic leadership of a countrywide movement, which became known as the Popular Movement (*Nehzat-e Melli*) of Iran and in whose rise the increasingly bitter confrontation with Razmara acted as the catalyst.

Razmara was an exceptionally able general and an astute politician, both physically and psychologically strong, and popular within the ranks of the army. He had Britain, America and the Soviet Union on his side – which was why the shah consented to his premiership, despite his fear and jealousy of him: in the short period that the general was prime minister before falling victim to assassination, the shah secretly canvassed Mosaddeq for premiership since at the time he regarded Razmara as the more dangerous of the two, but Mosaddeq turned him down.[56]

Razmara supported the supplemental agreement bill and had friendly relations with the British embassy; he attracted America's support as a strong leader who would save Iran from communism; he also made a commercial treaty with the Soviet Union and had secret relations with the banned Tudeh Party. Through his long and bitter confrontation with Mosaddeq, the AIOC eventually offered Razmara a 50–50 deal after it became clear that the Majlis would not approve the supplemental agreement.[57] For unknown reasons he did not make this offer public before he was assassinated in the Royal Mosque on 7 March 1951, although it has been speculated that he was planning a coup and was keeping the offer up his sleeve as a prize. Razamara's self-confessed assassin was a member of the Fada'iyan of Islam; yet almost as soon as the news broke it was believed that the shah had had a hand in his assassination.[58] However that may be, it is virtually certain that the shah did not receive the news of the general's death with regret, since he firmly believed that Razmara had been planning a military coup.[59]

Shortly after Razmara's assassination, the Majlis unanimously passed Mosaddeq's oil nationalization bill, the only domestic political force which publicly opposed it at the time being the Tudeh Party, which believed the bill was a plot to deliver Iranian oil to America and was unhappy that the nationalization act covered northern Iran, for which the Soviet Union still had hope of an oil concession.[60] Hosein Ala's caretaker government lasted only for two months and, in extraordinary circumstances, Mosaddeq became prime minister on 29 April 1951.

MOSADDEQ AND THE POPULAR MOVEMENT (1950–53)

Mosaddeq's and the Popular Movement's declared aim was to strengthen constitutional and democratic government. Political parties and groups were free: this included the Tudeh Party, although not quite overtly because it had been banned by an act of the Majlis in 1949. The press was so free that, in part, it may be described as licentious. The courts were independent, and all other military and special courts were abolished. Yet the politics of chaos and elimination continued: the other main political forces neither believed in democracy nor observed the rules of the game, and the government would not use the law to bring them to book. In fact, political turmoil became more intense, because both the internal and external stakes were considerably higher than before.

There was a fierce struggle by the Left as well as Right, each wanting to bring down Mosaddeq's government and eliminate the other as a political force. Eventually, the Right succeeded in achieving this goal with the indispensable aid of America and Britain. The experiment of 1951–3 might possibly have led either to a stable democracy or to a dictatorship. For reasons explained below, it is not surprising that dictatorship ultimately won the day.

While the shah and conservatives saw themselves as the natural clients or allies of Britain and (later) America, and the Tudeh of the Soviet Union, Mosaddeq pursued a non-aligned foreign policy which, since the early 1940s, he had described as the policy of 'passive balance'. He saw the nationalization of Iranian oil as a necessary step towards the achievement of full independence and democracy. The strongest motive behind oil nationalization was thus political rather than economic, although the priority given to political development did not mean that the economic importance of the oil industry was ignored.

THE OIL DISPUTE AND DOMESTIC POWER STRUGGLES

Mosaddeq and the Popular Movement leaders argued that as long as a large and powerful foreign company owned the country's biggest modern industry, in effect controlled one of its provinces and interfered in its politics to defend and promote its own interest, it would not be possible to establish either sovereign or democratic government. They agreed to compensate the AIOC on similar terms to the nationalization of private industries in Europe, for example, the British coal industry, which the Labour government had recently nationalized. But they would not consider settlements involving a new concession, which they thought would mean the return of the company in a different guise.

Britain was unhappy with a Mosaddeq government from the start. As early as May 1951, when Mosaddeq became prime minister, Britain was actively canvassing Mosaddeq's conservative opponents to bring him down by a vote of no confidence in the Majlis. British documents show that the shah and the conservatives were receptive to British suggestions, putting forward proposals for weakening Mosaddeq's government: they even said that oil exports should be suspended forthwith so that there would be no prospect of revenues; Mosaddeq must not be made to look as if he had won, they insisted.[61] At first replacing Mosaddeq looked like an easy task because the conservatives had the majority in the Majlis and the Senate, but it proved almost impossible, mainly because of Mosaddeq's great popularity – especially as the issue at stake had a strong anti-imperialist overtone, shaking the resolve of many conservative Majlis deputies to vote against Mosaddeq. Besides, the absence of organized parliamentary parties made the control of factions extremely difficult.

Still, in the summer of 1951 Britain sent a government minister, Richard Stokes, to Tehran to try to negotiate a settlement. Stokes's proposals might have resulted in something similar to but considerably better than the Consortium Agreement of 1954, which was signed shortly after the 1953 coup. But the thought of giving another concession to the oil company amidst the excitement of the oil nationalization was difficult to entertain at the time.

There followed Iran's repossession of the oil operations in September 1951 amid a highly charged political atmosphere and passionately expressed public emotions. Troops were sent to Abadan, the oil capital, and oil workers enthusiastically marched and erected the Iranian flag at the top of the Abadan refinery, at the time the biggest in the world. The repossession led to the boycott of Iranian oil by the main international companies (known as the Seven Sisters), backed by the Royal Navy in the Persian Gulf and beyond. Thus, Iran's principal source of public revenue and foreign exchange was cut off, while it had to pay the labour and maintenance costs of a virtually idle industry.

Britain had obtained an injunction from the International Court of Justice at The Hague to stop Iran from repossessing the oil industry. Iran ignored this on the argument that, since the 1933 agreement had been signed between the Iranian government and a private company (APOC, later AIOC), only Iranian courts had jurisdiction in the matter, a position the International Court eventually upheld in July 1952. Britain then took the matter to the UN Security Council, but did not gain support. While Mosaddeq was in the United Sates in October 1951 at the head of Iran's delegation to the Security Council, the Americans offered him a solution to the oil dispute, which he accepted. But when they put it to the British government the latter turned it down.[62]

At the same time the World Bank offered to mediate by restoring and operating the production and export of Iranian oil for two years. This would have reduced considerably the scale of confrontation between Britain and Iran and might well have led to a permanent settlement of the dispute. Mosaddeq was receptive at first, but some of his advisors insisted that the letter of the agreement should describe the World Bank as acting on behalf of the Iranian government, to refute the charge by their Tudeh and other opponents that the government was selling out to western powers. The agreement fell through because Britain would clearly not have agreed to the mediation of the World Bank if it were acting as the agent of the Iranian government.

Both the Tudeh and the Right were claiming that the nationalization of oil was a device to deliver Iranian oil to the Americans, and took the World Bank intervention as evidence for their claim. On the other hand, the bank's proposal was the best guarantee for the survival of Mosaddeq's government, especially as at the time – winter 1951 – it was at the peak of its unity and strength and carried a great deal of authority both inside and outside the country. Furthermore, accepting the solution would have maintained American goodwill. When the bank's attempt failed, the government embarked upon a policy of 'non-oil economics', which in the circumstances it managed well by adopting realistic, albeit unpopular, measures. Clearly, non-oil economics could not promote social welfare and economic development. On the contrary, it was regarded as a relatively short-term measure in the hope that a solution to the dispute would be found soon.[63]

Domestic and international conflict, added to the loss of oil revenues, made it virtually impossible for the government to take major reformist decisions demanded by some of their supporters, notably Khalil Maleki and the Third Force party, such as land reform and the enfranchisement of women. The religious establishment's open opposition resulted in shelving the plan for giving the vote to women. Regarding rural reform, a law was passed that obliged the landlords to give 10 per cent of their share of the output to the peasants and another 10 per cent into a rural development fund, though the government did not last long enough to see it through. Mosaddeq was more successful with his legal and financial reforms, including the reorganization of the judiciary, the abolition of all special (notably military) courts and the reform of the armed forces and of tax law.[64]

Mosaddeq still hoped to reach an agreement with Britain via direct negotiations. But the British Conservative government, which was elected in October 1951, rejected direct negotiations, preferred not to reach a settlement with him and went on looking for a suitable successor. Thus the British embassy continued its campaign against Mosaddeq even in the summer of 1951 when Stokes's mission was busy negotiating with Mosaddeq for a settlement.[65] Later, they tried to replace Mosaddeq with Ahmad Qavam, having reached the conclusion that Seyyed Zia was too unpopular for the task.

Still, the fact that Britain preferred not to settle the oil dispute with Mosaddeq does not mean that it would or could have refused to settle in any and all conditions. More specifically, if in 1952 a solution had been found that would have looked fair and reasonable to the US government, Britain would have had little choice but to accept it. And this would have been possible if the Iranians had been prepared to settle for less than the ideal, that is, payment of no more compensation than for the value of AOIC's property. Meanwhile, the 16th Majlis having finished its term, parliamentary elections were held for the 17th Majlis, which had to be stopped in some places because of the degree of conflict and bloodshed due to political gang warfare. The number of government deputies rose from seven to about thirty, which made them the strongest minority faction in the new Majlis, while Mosaddeq also continued to obtain votes of confidence from other parliamentary factions for continuing in office. But the shah, Britain and Iranian conservatives were still looking for an opportunity to bring down his government by peaceful means.

As we have seen, since the initial attempts at rallying Majlis conservatives to bring down the government had failed, Ahmad Qavam began to emerge as a viable alternative to Mosaddeq. The opportunity arose shortly after the opening of the 17th Majlis, when Mosaddeq began to form a new cabinet. He had just returned from The Hague, where the International Court was hearing the British case against Iran. Being convinced that the court would rule in favour of Britain, he had decided to resign and spend the rest of his life abroad.[66] Mosaddeq was in such a pessimistic mood when discussing his new cabinet with the shah that they clashed over which one of the two should appoint the minister of war (later renamed 'minister of national defence' by Mosaddeq).

It had become a convention for the shah to appoint a general to that ministry, although this was not the constitutional position. When the shah insisted on making the appointment himself, Mosaddeq resigned without a fuss and disappeared from public view. The shah appointed Qavam prime minister and, quite uncharacteristically, the latter made a tactical blunder by making a speech which threatened repression. A popular uprising broke out on 21 July 1952, led by Ayatollah Kashani, the Popular Movement faction of the Majlis and pro-Mosaddeq parties.[67]

Mosaddeq returned to office just at the time when the International Court ruled in Iran's favour. The court rejected the British case, confirming that only Iranian courts had jurisdiction in the AIOC's dispute with Iran, unless the Iranians were also to ask for the court's arbitration. There followed the Truman–Churchill proposal, still stopping short of direct negotiations. Its fundamental point was that Iran should consent to the International Court's arbitration. Iran's fundamental counter-proposal was that she would so consent provided that the AIOC's compensation was determined on the basis of the market value of its property at the time of nationalization. Britain rejected this, claiming that the company should be compensated for its loss of profits until 1990, when the period of the 1933 concession would have come to an end.

To put the British position simply and briefly, they demanded one of the two following terms of settlement: either Iran should give another concession along the lines suggested by Richard Stokes (something more than that later granted in the post-coup consortium agreement) or it should compensate the company for all the oil that the company would have exported until 1990 if Iranian oil had not been nationalized.

The final Anglo-American proposal – presented by the American ambassador to Iran and named the Henderson proposal – did not succeed, essentially over full compensation for the AIOC's loss of profit until 1990. It was an improvement on the Truman–Churchill proposal, but it still demanded compensation for loss of operations until 1990. Mosaddeq went one step forward and agreed to the International Court's arbitration on that basis, on the condition that Britain would declare its maximum compensation demand from the outset. This was a significant retreat from his previous position that AIOC should be compensated purely for the market value of its property. Britain turned this down, and the proposal failed.

Neither of the two alternative British demands – another concession or compensation for loss of operations until 1990 – would have been made, let alone succeeded, if the dispute had been with Holland, Sweden or any other small European country. It was clear that Iran's position was weak, not on legal grounds but in terms of relative world power. But precisely for that reason the Popular Movement would not have succeeded without a settlement of the oil dispute that was tolerable to Britain and America. That is why some of the less idealistic of Mosaddeq's advisors, such as Mohammad Soruri and Khalil Maleki, believed that he should settle for something less than the ideal, so as to save the movement and his own government. On the other hand, many more of his advisors were afraid of cries of 'sell-out' the minute he began to reach such a settlement. Their fears of the fickleness of the Iranian people might have been exaggerated, but were not unrealistic.[68]

CRACKS AND SCHISMS IN THE POPULAR MOVEMENT

Ironically, the July 1952 uprising was also a turning point against the movement's fortunes. Soon afterwards, Kashani, as well as Baqa'i, Makki and Abolhasan Hayerizadeh – three leading figures in the Popular Movement's parliamentary faction – began to fall out with Mosaddeq and the rest of the movement. Many of the differences had their roots in personality conflicts and rivalries, and they went back a long way, although they had not surfaced in public before.[69] An early public warning of the schism was the split in the Zahmatkeshan (or Toilers') Party in October 1952, because the majority faction led by Khalil Maleki did not accept Baqa'i's proposal for a policy of confrontation with Mosaddeq.[70]

On 13 October, shortly after the split in the Toilers' party, Generals Zahedi and Hejazi were suspected (rightly, as the recent CIA history of the 1953 coup has shown) of plotting the overthrow of the government with the help of the British embassy and its Iranian agents, the Rashidian brothers. Hejazi was arrested but released shortly afterwards. Zahedi, who was known to be in contact with Baqa'i, could not be arrested because, as a senator, he enjoyed parliamentary immunity. Three days later, Mosaddeq broke off diplomatic relations with Britain on the grounds that it was interfering in internal Iranian affairs.

When he formed his second government after the July revolt, Mosaddeq had asked and obtained some delegated powers (*ekhtiyarat*) from the parliament, that is, the Senate as well as the Majlis, to which the shah had duly assented. This enabled him to enact a number of bills, notably for financial, judicial and social reform. These bills were then to be put in operation for six months before submitting them to parliament. Without these powers Mosaddeq would not have been able to run the country in the circumstances, and – as he made plain – he would have resigned. But the parliament remained open, there were daily debates about all matters of political interest and it gave Mosaddeq a vote of confidence each time he asked for it.

The delegated powers bill had had the support of Baqa'i and Kashani and had passed through both houses of parliament almost unopposed. The Majlis continued its increasingly lively debates, not least when cracks began to show within the leadership of the Popular Movement and its parliamentary faction. The delegated powers became a serious bone of contention when, in January 1953, the act fell due for renewal. Both Ayatollah Kashani, who was Majlis speaker but hardly ever attended its sessions, and Baqa'i, Makki and Hayerizadeh energetically campaigned against its renewal.

From the outset, there had been three distinct approaches towards the Popular Movement among religious leaders and activists. The conservatives, who dominated the religious establishment in Qom, Tehran and elsewhere, did not display much enthusiasm for oil nationalization, and even less for the Popular Movement and Mosaddeq's premiership. They are often described as 'quietists', although this may be misleading: if they looked apolitical, it was because, at the time, their politics were generally in line with the conservative political establishment. Therefore, as relations between the shah and Mosaddeq deteriorated and at the same time the Anglo-Iranian oil dispute reached a deadlock, their lack of enthusiasm towards Mosaddeq and the movement turned into more active opposition, though this was often communicated through informal channels. Ayatollah Seyyed Mohammad Behbahani generally represented them in the capital; and he in turn was represented most by Mohammad Taqi Falsafi among the leading preachers.

The second tendency among the religious leadership and community was pro-constitutional and anti-imperialist. Ayatollah Kashani, who strongly supported oil nationalization and Mosaddeq's premiership, was its supreme leader until the time – especially after the events of 28 February 1953 – when he openly joined Mosaddeq's opposition. But there were others both inside and outside the Majlis (though not of his rank) who remained loyal to Mosaddeq and the movement until the end.

The militant group of Fada'iyan-e Islam was the third distinct tendency, though they did not compare either in rank, number or popular base with the first two tendencies, their fame being due to their emotional activism, which included political assassination. As noted above, they were a group of young men who campaigned for the creation of an Islamic state, and they supported the Popular Movement until Mosaddeq became prime minister. But, almost immediately, they fell out with Mosaddeq, Kashani and the entire movement because they had hoped for an Islamic government, which neither of the two leaders had promised. Within a short period, they became mortal enemies of the movement and their leaders, and so, in 1952, they shot and permanently wounded Hosein Fatemi, a leading journalist and Majlis deputy who later became foreign minister. They supported the 1953 coup, but eventually fell out with the post-coup regime: their leading members were executed.[71]

The events of 28 February 1953 brought all the three religious groups together for the first time, not in any open or tacit coalition but insofar as all of them demonstrated explicit and active hostility towards Mosaddeq and his government. A few days earlier, the shah had sent word to Mosaddeq that he and Queen Soraya wished to go to Europe for treatment of suspected infertility, emphasizing that the matter must be kept secret until he had left the country lest it create public concern. Mosaddeq had counselled against it, but agreed to cooperate. He was therefore puzzled to discover on the day of the shah's departure – 28 February 1953 – that the matter had become public knowledge despite the shah's initial insistence on secrecy. Ayatollah Behbahni was first to make this known to Mosaddeq. Later, the Ayatollah visited the shah to dissuade him from leaving, and addressed an anti-Mosaddeq crowd outside the palace. Kashani appealed to the public to stop the move, saying that 'if the shah goes, all that we have will go with him'.

Mosaddeq, on the other hand, was certain that the shah's proposed journey had been designed just to start the riots to bring him down and/or kill him in the process. Certainly the mob went on to attack Mosaddeq's home after he had managed to escape from the royal palace through a backdoor. This time, too, he was lucky to go over the wall and make it to the Majlis, which was in emergency session.[72]

THE 1953 COUP

The next episode was the kidnapping and murder of the country's police chief, General Mahmud Afshartus, the following April; apparently, the plotters had intended to force Mosaddeq's resignation by kidnapping a number of important officials and dignitaries. Afshartus was first on the list if only because he headed the entire civilian police and security apparatus. In the event, police investigations quickly pointed to the likely perpetrators, who immediately killed Afshartus in the cave where he was being held. Four generals and a couple of junior officers confessed to having been involved in the plot, and they implicated Baqa'i. Whether or not the shah himself was implicated is not known.[73]

It thus became clear that the government's right-wing opposition were now prepared to resort to violent as well as peaceful methods to bring down the government. They had been receiving increasing encouragement – at different levels and with growing firmness and intensity – from the American and British governments via their diplomatic and intelligence staff and agents in Iran.[74] Yet the shah still suspected that the British were behind Mosaddeq, as he told the American ambassador in May.[75]

Previously, he had once told Senator Ali Dashti that in his view the British themselves had told Mosaddeq to nationalize Iranian oil. And when Dashti (who was no friend of Mosaddeq) had disagreed, the shah told him that it was obvious, because a brother of Hosein Fatemi, Mosaddeq's foreign minister, had gone to the British missionary school in Isfahan.[76]

The *coup d'état* of August 1953 has now been studied in detail.[77] It is important to emphasize, however, that the coup was a product of the close collaboration between Mosaddeq's domestic as well as foreign opponents, even though the role of foreign governments, especially the United States, in organizing and financing it was indispensable. The coup was eventually carried out by Mosaddeq's Iranian opponents, but they were too divided and too unsure of themselves and each other to organize and act in unison. As noted, some of them, including the shah, even suspected that the British were secretly behind Mosaddeq, and so were hesitant to commit themselves.[78]

In July, Mosaddeq, fearing that he was about to be given a vote of no confidence in the Majlis, decided to dissolve the 17th Majlis by referendum and hold fresh elections. The recent CIA evidence now shows that in June 1953 the Americans had been planning to buy off some Majlis deputies to topple the government.[79] On the other hand, the dissolution of the Majils through a controversial referendum would have made it much easier to bring down the government by force, backed up by the notice of Mosaddeq's dismissal, which the Americans eventually obtained from the shah, only after the referendum. Many if not most of Mosaddeq's close colleagues and supporters opposed the referendum for fear of some such development. As it happened, most of the Majlis deputies resigned on Mosaddeq's recommendation to justify the referendum.

The first CIA plan – laid out in 'the London Draft', which had been outlined long before the decision to hold the referendum – had envisaged that the shah would appoint General Zahedi as chief of the army, who would then proceed to complete the coup with the help of religious groups and some Majlis deputies. In the plan that was actually implemented – after the referendum and in the absence of the Majlis – the CIA team helped by the British agent Asadollah Rashidian succeeded in obtaining Mosaddeq's dismissal notice from a wavering shah and a notice of appointment to the premiership for Zahedi. This is exactly what Mosaddeq's advisors had feared. The coups of 16 and 19 August 1953 followed, overthrowing Mosaddeq's government.

Once the shah signed the decrees in his hunting lodge on the Caspian Sea, the CIA team assigned Colonel Ne'matollah Nasiri, commander of the Imperial Guards, the task of delivering Mosaddeq's notice of dismissal and arresting him. This was inexplicably delayed by one day: Nasiri delivered the notice on the night of 15–16 August. On the same day Mossadeq's government learned about the imminent coup from a variety of sources and took measures to stop it. While the military network involved in the coup were arresting a number of Mosaddeq aides and associates (including Chief of Staff Riyahi, who gave them the slip, and Foreign Minister Fatemi), taking over the telephone exchange and so forth, Nasiri was arrested at Mosaddeq's home, and the loyal troops in Tehran seized the army headquarters and disarmed the Imperial Guards. At dawn the news of the failed coup was announced on the radio. The shah fled to Baghdad and shortly afterwards arrived in Rome, apparently intending to go to the United States.

In the next two days growing turmoil and disorder beset the capital and some provincial cities. The CIA headquarters advised the team in Iran to stop operations and leave the country, but both they and the local British agents decided to persist.

The meetings and demonstrations denouncing the shah on 16 August were followed by a riotous situation the next day. The burning and looting of supposedly anti-shah rioters were largely carried out and led by 'black crowds' paid by the coup-makers and their associates. To spread panic among the ordinary public they chanted slogans for a 'democratic republic' and attacked and brought down the statues of the shah and his father. Tudeh and other activists also joined the demonstrations, until Mosaddeq ordered the security forces to attack the rioters on 18 August and advised the political parties loyal to him to keep their members off the streets on the fateful day of 19 August. On that day the rent-a-crowd demonstrators changed their slogans in favour of the shah and against Mosaddeq and began to attack public buildings as well as Tudeh and pro-Mosaddeq party premises. They were backed by the police and army units which were still loyal to the shah. With incredible speed the radio station was secured and Mosaddeq's home was attacked and sacked after a few hours of resistance by his guards. By the evening of 19 August it was all over.[80]

The fall of Mosaddeq's government was not inevitable. It would have had a good chance of survival if Mosaddeq had settled the oil dispute and at the same time used the law to contain the lawless right- and left-wing forces which were active against the government with impunity.[81]

DICTATORSHIP (1953–63)

The decade following the 1953 coup was a dictatorship comparable to that of the decade following Reza Khan's coup in 1921. The coup did not quickly result in personal and arbitrary rule, although within a couple of years – certainly after his dismissal of Zahedi – the shah became by far the most powerful player in the country. Apart from its foreign sponsors, the coup had been the product of a coalition of social and political forces. Therefore, all the shah's allies shared in the power – although at a decreasing rate – until the revolt of 1963 when the shah inaugurated his final phase, the period of absolute and arbitrary rule. Three phases may be distinguished. 1953–5 was the period of consolidation of power and elimination of both the Popular Movement and the Tudeh Party from politics. 1955–60 saw the concentration of power and a rising economic boom, which collapsed. This was followed by economic depression and power struggles between 1960 and 1963.

Zahedi headed the first cabinet after the coup. He was an influential army leader, an old hand and briefly Mosaddeq's minister of the interior in his first cabinet. Ali Amini, a strong, loyal but independent politician, and a member of one of Mosaddeq's cabinets, was minister of finance. Abdollah Entezam, a respected politician of similar views to Amini, was foreign minister. They were loyal to the shah but were not his clients. The 18th Majlis elections (1954–6) were not free, and this was even truer of the 19th Majlis elections (1956–60). Nevertheless, the deputies were largely made up of landlords or their representatives and other established or independent politicians. They had not been handpicked by a central machine, and a few of them such as the teachers' leader Mohammad Derakhshesh were independent with important constituencies of their own.

Thus the influential social classes had an independent share in the power of the state. The Constitutional Revolution had greatly enhanced the political and economic power of landlords and, to a lesser extent, merchants and traders. These classes had lost their independent power under Reza Shah, but they regained it after his abdication, although the disorders of the 1940s and the power struggles of the early 1950s had provided a check on their potential ability to run the state. This explains the relatively strong position of these classes after the 1953 coup, and also the relatively strong resistance which, ten years later, they offered to the shah's White Revolution and his successful bid for total power.

Between 1953 and 1955 Mosaddeq was tried and convicted in military courts and sentenced to three years in solitary confinement, although after his release he was forced to live on his estate in the west of Tehran until his death in 1967. The Popular Movement parties were banned and their leaders and activists jailed for some time, except Foreign Minister Fatemi, who was executed. There was an attack on the Tudeh Party, many of whose activists were jailed, others forced to make public recantations; and the discovery and destruction of its military network of more than 450 army officers dealt it a devastating blow, ending with the execution of more than twenty of its members. Many government employees and journalists with National Front and Tudeh affiliations or known sympathies were dismissed or forced to recant, and the press came under state control.

Relations with Britain were restored in 1954, following which negotiations over the oil dispute led to the consortium agreement. Receiving 40 per cent of its shares, Britain lost its monopoly of Iranian oil, with American companies getting another 40 per cent of the shares and French and Dutch companies the remaining 20 per cent. It was a 50–50 agreement for a period of twenty-five years, better than the AIOC's erstwhile offer to Razmara but worse than Stokes's to Mosaddeq. As Ali Amini, Iran's finance minister and chief negotiator, admitted both then and later, the agreement left much to be desired but it was the only one available in the post-coup circumstances.[82] Before the conclusion of the consortium agreement and the consequent lifting of the British oil boycott, substantial amounts of American aid were provided to keep Zahedi's government afloat. US aid continued throughout the 1950s even after earnings from oil were restored.

In his first move to consolidate his own power, the shah dismissed Zahedi in April 1955 and in all but appearance sent him in exile to his villa in Switzerland, where he died in the 1960s. He appointed the mild, meek and loyal Hosein Ala, minister of the royal court, to the premiership, his government lasting for a year until he was replaced by Manuchehr Eqbal. Eqbal was not just loyal but totally submissive to the shah, to the extent that he once described himself as the shah's 'house-born slave'. His government lasted until August 1960, when economic and political crisis had made it necessary to find major scapegoats. The tendency towards the concentration of power in the shah's hands could be clearly detected from the time he toppled Zahedi. But the landlords dominating the Majlis could still have an independent voice, though not necessarily a progressive one. The 18th Majlis (1954–6) virtually abolished Mosaddeq's law which obliged landlords to give 20 per cent of their share of the crop to peasants and into a rural development fund; in 1960, a bill, submitted by Eqbal and backed by the shah, limiting the size of agricultural holdings, was passed by the 19th Majlis (1956–60) with great reluctance, but became a dead letter.[83]

The conflict between the shah and Abolhasan Ebtehaj was symbolic of the tendency towards the concentration of power. Ebtehaj was an exceptionally able and honest technocrat and loyal to the shah, governor of Bank Melli Iran in the 1940s, later a senior member of the World Bank who, in 1954, had agreed to return to Iran to reorganize and lead the Plan Organization as the chief agency for economic development. Within a short period he ran into serious conflict with Zahedi, whose approach to politics was much in line with the old bureaucracy. After Zahedi's dismissal, and especially after Ebtehaj's old friend Hosein Ala gave way to Eqbal, Ebtehaj's relations with the shah began to be tested because he was firmly dedicated to financial honesty and the use of oil revenues for development projects rather than military expansion. Matters came to a head when, contrary to all techno-economic considerations, it was decided to construct Iran's first fertilizer plant, contracted by the ministry of industries and mines, in Shiraz rather than a port on the Persian Gulf. Corruption and high-level contacts had been behind this decision, and the shah backed the minister instead of Ebtehaj.[84]

In 1959 Ebtehaj resigned, indignant, and shortly afterwards founded his own Bank Iranian (*Bank-e Iraniyan*). But in 1961 he spent a period in jail for incurring the wrath of the shah, after he had criticized aid-giving to corrupt governments at a world development conference held in San Francisco.[85] Meanwhile, the shah, who at the time advocated the ideology of 'positive nationalism', had launched a two-party system. The *Melliyun* (purported to mean Nationalist) Party was headed by Prime Minister Eqbal; the *Mardom* (People's) Party was led by the shah's closest confidant and minister of the interior, Asadollah Alam. It was no more than a window-dressing exercise.

The religious establishment had been behind the new regime, as it had played a significant role in the coup and its legitimization. Kashani, who had supported the regime at first, fell out with it largely over its restoration of diplomatic relations with Britain and the consortium agreement. But the religious establishment remained quiet until the revolt of 1963, although it had already begun to become increasingly dissatisfied with the situation from the late 1950s. The shah's good relations with the religious establishment peaked during the anti-Baha'i campaign shortly after Zahedi's fall in 1955. The officially approved campaign began with a series of anti-Baha'i sermons by the leading preacher Mohammad Taqi Falsafi, mentioned above, during the month of Ramadan. These were broadcast live from the state radio and led to the confiscation and occupation of Hazirat al-Qods, the Bahai's' religious and administrative centre in Tehran. Its dome was symbolically demolished by the chief of staff, and it was turned into the office of Martial Law Administration. Ayatollah Behbahani met the shah and thanked him for the campaign,[86] and Grand-Ayatollah Borujerdi communicated his appreciation to the shah.[87] Fada'iyan-e Islam's newspaper *Nabard-e Mellat* lent it vocal support, describing the new martial law office as 'the office of Islamic propaganda'.

Yet, the Fada'iyan made an unsuccessful attempt on Hosein Ala's life the following November. Five of them, including their leader Navvab Safavi, were arrested, tried and executed, but the religious establishment did not rally to their support.[88]

After the 1953 coup British influence in Iran began to assume second place to that of America. Within a relatively short period a client–patron relationship was built up between Iran and the United States. American aid was crucial in the first two years before oil revenues could once again become a significant source of state revenue and foreign exchange. The aid was to continue throughout the 1950s in the form of financial and military grants and, later, public loans. Between 1955 and 1959 American aid supplied, on average, 31 per cent of Iranian public expenditure;[89] between 1955 and 1962, foreign aid was responsible for 37.5 per cent of total financial capital available in foreign exchange.[90]

Iran dropped its policy of neutrality and non-alliance. In 1955, with strong US support, it joined a military pact with Britain, Turkey, Iraq and Pakistan, first described as the Baghdad pact, later the Central Treaty Organization (CENTO) after the 1958 coup in Iraq when that country left the pact. The flow of American military grants and advisors helped expand and reorganize the Iranian army. This was both to strengthen the shah's government against internal opposition and to provide a first line of resistance to the Soviet Union in case of the outbreak of a local or global war. In 1957 the CIA sent a five-man advisory group to Tehran, which in the course of the next four years helped organize and train an internal security organization which became known as SAVAK. The principal function of this organization – which in time expanded and gained a notorious reputation – was to identify, control and persecute political opposition of any kind. In the late 1960s and 1970s SAVAK extended its functions to the suppression of any and all dissident views, however mild, unorganized and even loyal. It also assumed a counter-intelligence function, although the army intelligence and counter-intelligence continued to exist as parallel organizations focusing on the military side.

The Soviet Union did not at first react as sourly as might have been expected to the American-sponsored coup, the suppression of the Tudeh Party and Iran's alliance with the West. Indeed, it even paid to Iran its long-standing war debt (known as 'Iran's gold'), which they had refused to pay Mosaddeq's government despite its dire need of finance and foreign exchange. It invited both the shah and Princess Ashraf on official state visits, which were conducted with pomp and circumstance. But the Soviets became increasingly concerned about American influence and use of Iranian military facilities for intelligence gathering and the establishment of air bases along the Soviet border with Iran.

However, Soviet concern turned into public indignation and anti-shah propaganda in 1959, when the shah entered a mutual defence pact with the United States. While negotiating the pact with America, the shah had also entered negotiations with the Soviet Union for a non-aggression treaty. This had fallen through partly due to disagreement on what constituted a military base, but mainly perhaps because the Americans had sweetened their offer with a promise of greater aid.[91] From 1963 there was to be a thaw in the two countries' relations, following the decline of the Cold War and the shah's victory in the domestic power struggles of 1960–3 (see Chapter 11).

The flow of oil and foreign aid brought the economy out of the stagnant state of non-oil economics, with increasing consumption and imports, benefiting mainly the upper and middle classes. As stated above, in 1949 an ad hoc planning body had been set up which drafted a list of state investment projects entitled the Seven Year Plan but which had been rendered ineffective in consequence of the oil dispute. In 1955 the Plan Organization was turned into a large permanent body, charged with the preparation and execution of the Second Seven Year Plan (1955–62).

At the outset, 80 per cent of the annual oil revenues were earmarked for development expenditure, but this proportion declined in the later parts of the plan period, mainly because of the diversion of funds for military expenditure, which, as noted, was a main source of conflict between Ebtehaj, the Plan Organization chief, and the shah, the former being accused by Eqbal of 'creating a state within a state'. Total expenditure for the period came to about 70 billion rials. Some 48 per cent of this was spent on infrastructure – transport, telecommunications, public utilities and so forth – 22 per cent on agricultural projects, 14 per cent on regional development, 8 per cent on industry and mines and 7.7 per cent on unanticipated costs.[92] Thus, industry took very much a low profile, in accordance with prevailing attitudes towards third-world development at the time.

Meanwhile, the government of Eqbal followed an economic policy of high domestic consumption expenditure and liberal imports. Cheap money in the hands of the upper classes and speculators led to a thriving movement in urban land speculation, hiking up urban land and property prices and putting pressure

on the housing market, to the extent that the government felt obliged to acknowledge its existence and declare a policy for combating it (described as *zamin-khari*,
'land-eating'), which in practice was of little consequence. And despite growing oil
revenues and foreign aid, the balance of payments, even including oil revenues,
began to show a rising deficit. In 1955, the balance, including oil, was $11 million,
and, excluding oil, –$37 million; in 1960 the figures had respectively fallen to –
$219 and –$583 million.[93] There followed almost three years of economic depression and political power struggles, from which the shah emerged triumphant.

In 1960 the shah faced serious problems in both domestic and international
spheres. There was high inflation and the bubble of the previous years' consumer
boom was about to burst and turn into bust. Criticism of his dictatorship
mounted, not just among the democratic and leftist opposition but also within
the establishment: in 1958 he had foiled a suspected coup by General Qarani, the
army intelligence chief, who had made wide contacts with critics both in and out
of the establishment.[94] The American embassy had been aware of Qarani's activities, and Ali Amini, then Iranian ambassador to Washington, was dismissed on
suspicion of being involved in his plot. In 1960, Senator John F. Kennedy, a
severe critic of corruption and waste of American aid in Iran and similar countries, was elected president. The Soviet Union was still angry, conducting a
scathing radio propaganda campaign against the shah and the royal family.

The shah's declaration that the oncoming elections of the 20th Majlis would be
free was largely to appease Kennedy, just as his liberalization of 1977 was mainly a
response to the election of President Carter. The opposition saw this as a green
light from America and began to organize themselves. Amini declared his candidacy and put out a manifesto which included land reform. The second National
Front, Khalil Maleki's Socialist League and, later, Mehdi Bazargan's Freedom
Movement came into being. General Teymur Bakhtiyar, the head of SAVAK, began
to discover the virtues of freedom and was dismissed by the shah. The elections
were in fact rigged and, under pressure, the shah blamed events on Eqbal,
dismissing him from office, advising those elected to resign their seats (which they
duly did) and appointing Ja'far Sharif-Emami – a subservient minister, not yet well
known and unpopular – as prime minister.

The second Majlis elections, in winter 1961, were also rigged, but they allowed
a few democrats and reformists, notably the second National Front's Allahyar
Saleh, to get in. University students had been in revolt and the bazaar, that is, the
traditional business community, was restless, campaigning for free elections.
What broke the camel's back was the teachers' strike in April, when in the course
of a massive but peaceful demonstration a teacher was shot dead by the police.
The shah dismissed Sharif-Emami and sent for Amini, whom he believed was
America's candidate for the premiership. Amini accepted the offer on the condition that the shah, using his powers under the 1949 constitutional amendments,
should dismiss the parliament, knowing that the Majlis was packed with landlords and the shah's appointees who could bring him down any moment and
would certainly not support his land reform policy.[95]

The shah disliked Amini almost as much as Qavam and Mosaddeq because, although loyal, he was both independent and able and wanted to trim some of the shah's dictatorial powers. The shah was also afraid that Amini's moderately liberal approach and his land reform policy could help him steal the show both with the public and the Americans. The Rashidian brothers (who had helped to overthrow Mosaddeq) and other pro-shah and anti-reformist elements began to campaign against Amini. And to Amini's chagrin, the second National Front also led a relentless campaign against him and concentrated all their efforts on toppling his government. In January 1962, the Front was implicated in a plot to force Amini's resignation in which both the shah and General Bakhtiyar had had a hand.[96]

In January 1962, the Land Reform Law, described as the first stage of the reform, was passed and ultimately affected 14,000 villages or 30 per cent of the total (excluding hamlets) or 520,000 peasant households.[97] The logic behind Amini's land reform programme was to create a wider and more secure base for the regime and enable and encourage public participation in economic and social development. Hasan Arsanjani, the able minister of agriculture, was in charge of the planning and execution of the programme. He and Amini believed that comprehensive land reform with compensation to landlords, creating small-scale peasant ownership, would win the support of the peasantry and make agricultural development possible, while it would both persuade former landlords to invest (or lend to others to invest) in the urban sector and encourage the urban bourgeoisie to invest in modern industry (see further Chapter 11).

In this way, so Amini and his advisors believed, the regime would be turned into a moderately constitutional (though not necessarily democratic) system that would be widely based on the support of the urban middle classes and independent farmers. Although the shah did not have much love for the landlords, who had claimed a share of power since 1941, he had no wish to allow other, larger and more modern social classes to replace them and share in political power. He also resented Arsanjani's popularity among the peasantry, which listened with growing enthusiasm to the minister's daily radio broadcasts.

By July 1962, when Amini fell, he had no political force to depend on: the shah, the landlords, the National Front (to whom the urban middle classes still listened) and the Tudeh supporters (who believed he was an agent of America) were all against him. In a recent visit to America the shah had been reassured that he could dismiss Amini if he so wished. Following that, in a disagreement with the shah over the size of the military budget, Amini resigned[98] and was almost arrested.[99] He was replaced by the shah's close confidant, Asadollah Alam. This marked the beginning of the shah's direct and personal rule.

In January 1963, the shah took many, including his democratic and leftist opposition, by surprise when he put a six-point reform programme, described as the White Revolution, to referendum, which predictably returned a 99 per cent 'yes' vote: it included land reform; nationalization of woods and forests; women's suffrage; creation of a literacy corps to combat illiteracy; industrial profit sharing; and denationalization of some state industries (to finance the land reform programme). In different ways, the most important and controversial of these points were land reform (which had already begun under Amini a year before) and women's suffrage.[100] As noted, Mosaddeq's hope to enfranchise women had been frustrated by the opposition of the religious establishment, and this time there was similar opposition by many if not most religious leaders. In practice, election results were determined by the state, and voters, both men and women, in so far as they bothered to vote at all, had no role to play. Nevertheless, extending voting rights to women and sending a few of them to the Majlis and the Senate had an important symbolic social value, and could encourage greater emancipation and participation of women – in fact, upper and modern middle class women – in society.

There were several reasons why land reform was the most controversial point of the White Revolution. It was well known that the shah was opposed to Amini; therefore, the landlords and religious establishment, who had provided the strongest social base of the regime after the 1953 coup, expected a shift of emphasis from Amini's land reform policy after his fall. Many, though not all, of the higher ulama opposed land reform in the name of the defence of private property, both in response to the landlords' appeal to them for support and because they were anxious about its consequence for the *owqaf*, the religious endowments, which was an important source of revenue for religious institutions. In practice, the land distribution programme was diluted when it moved to its new 'second stage', but this was not apparent from the general policy principle in the shah's referendum.

At least as worrying for the landlords and the religious establishment was the fact that, in the long parliamentary recess, the shah had assumed personal rule and effectively abandoned his old allies. He brushed aside personal representations by pillars of the establishment such as Ayatollah Behbahani, Qa'em-maqam al-Molk (Reza Rafi'), Abdollah Entezam and Sardar Fakher (Reza Hekamat) and even sacked the loyal Hosein Ala, former prime minister and now minister of the royal court, for offering him unpalatable advice.[101]

It is highly instructive that at this time Taqizadeh, who was both strongly in favour of land reform and the vote for women and who had not made any notable political pronouncement for more than a decade, drafted a letter addressed to the shah complaining about the parliamentary recess and violations of the constitutional law. He intended the letter to be signed by a number of elder statesmen, but it was not eventually sent. There is no reference to land reform or women's vote. It shows the deep concern of the political establishment for the shah's assumption of arbitrary power, as opposed to mere dictatorship in which they had acquiesced since 1953. Its language is extremely polite and respectful, but its content is openly critical. It begins:

We the undersigned, on the basis of our patriotic duty to uphold the country's interest have the utmost loyalty to the exalted office of the crown and your own blessed person, and at the same time to the Iranian constitution which is the basis for the rights of the people and the crown, and for the protection of which both us and the person of your Majesty have repeatedly sworn to Almighty God and to the Heavenly Book.

Therefore [we feel obliged] to bring to your blessed attention the existing irregularity, which is contrary to basic principles and in violation of the constitution. We would also like to submit that the suspension of the constitution and parliament, and the violation of the freedom of speech and the press, and imposition of acute censorship contrary to the constitution, and the imprisonment of members of the public without proving their guilt on the basis of the law . . . and the illegal dominion of the security forces over the lives and property of Iranian people are contrary to the interests of the very person of the head of state, and would result in the loss of confidence of members of the public.[102]

The statement continued in the same tone and tenor, and ended by asking, in extremely polite terms, for 'completely free parliamentary elections' and 'the complete restoration of the freedoms allowed by the law, so that our country would be absolved of the charge of being a police state, which has been laid against it'.[103]

Likewise, the modern middle classes were not opposed to the principles of land reform. They were, however, opposed to dictatorship and were nostalgic about the freedoms enjoyed under Mosaddeq, who by this time had assumed an almost mythological status among most of the political public. The second National Front was not an effective political organization and did not have a clear social programme. Nevertheless, it reflected the attitude of its pro-Mosaddeq constituency when in a statement in response to the shah's referendum they advised them to say 'yes' to land reform but 'no' to dictatorship, which led to their arrest and imprisonment.

The strongest challenge was offered by the ulama and the religious community in general. Ayatollah Khomeini, in particular, came to public notice for the first time, and quickly became a national figure, though he was already well known in Qom and among the specialist circles. Since the late 1950s there had been a growing critical tendency among some of the ulama and the religious community against the concentration of power in an atmosphere which encouraged modernism, Americanism and good relations with Israel. Such criticism grew and become more vocal after the death, in March 1961, of Ayatollah Borujerdi, the symbol of the ulama's political 'quietism' and sole *Marja' al-Taqlid* in Iran. The shah's referendum provided a focal point for the religious opposition when, in a strongly worded statement, Khomeini opposed and denounced it. The shah responded strongly by visiting Qom and, flanked by his officers and troops, delivered a vehemently defiant speech denouncing 'a bunch of bearded idiots'. Agitation continued, arrests were made and the stage was set for the revolt of June 1963.

On 3 June (Ashura, the tenth day of the lunar Islamic month of Moharram) the day of the martyrdom of Imam Hosein and his followers, demonstrators carried portraits of Khomeini and chanted pro-Khomeini and anti-shah slogans. The government had forbidden speeches and sermons in Qom, and a strict security watch was maintained in Tehran. Defying government orders, Khomeini delivered a powerful sermon in a theological college in Qom, strongly attacking the shah himself. His arrest early next morning led to the eruption of riots, which reached a peak the following day, 5 June, the 15th of Khordad.[104] The riots were violently suppressed, with heavy loss of life, which the government put at ninety and the opposition at several thousands. A clampdown on the religious community followed, especially in Qom and Tehran. Khomeini was later put under house arrest and released after eight months. Still later, he was arrested and exiled to Turkey, and eventually allowed to live in the holy city of Najaf, in Iraq. This happened when he broke silence and delivered a long and stinging sermon against a new law which granted immunity from prosecution in Iranian courts to American technical and military advisors and personnel in Iran, a highly unpopular law which was reminiscent of the capitulation agreements under the Qajars (see Chapter 7). Khomeini said in the sermon:

> If some American's servant, some American's cook, assassinated your *maraje'* [grand ayatollahs] in the middle of the bazaar, or ran him over, the Iranian police would not have the right to apprehend him. The dossier must be sent to America so that our masters there can decide what is to be done . . . They have reduced the Iranian people to a level lower than that of an American dog. If someone runs over a dog belonging to an American he will be prosecuted. Even if the shah himself were to run over a dog belonging to an American he would be prosecuted. But if an American cook runs over the shah, the head of state, no one will have the right to interfere with him.
>
> Gentlemen, I warn you of danger!
> Iranian army, I warn you of danger!
> Iranian politicians, I warn you of danger!
> Iranian merchants, I warn you of danger!
> Ulama of Iran, *maraje'* of Islam, I warn you of danger! . . .[105]

The revolt of June 1963 marked a watershed in the relationship between state and society and inaugurated a new era which ended with the revolution of February 1979.

CHAPTER 11

⸰⸰⸰⸰

The White Revolution

*'The great civilization towards which we are now moving is not just a chapter in
the history of this land. It is its greatest chapter.'*
The Shah, *Towards the Great Civilization*, 1975, p. 252

THE SHAH PERSONALLY RULED Iran between 1963 and 1978. He tried to combine
the role of a traditional, arbitrary ruler with that of a modern revolutionary
leader. In a brilliant observation made to close friends (which belies his reputation
for naivety), Senator Hasan Akbar remarked as early as 1964: 'His Majesty is trying
to become both Xerxes and Fidel Castro; but this is impossible.' And his ultimate
tragedy was in the fact that he failed in both those ambitious roles, neither
succeeding as a strong arbitrary ruler nor as a popular revolutionary modernizer:
the revolution of 1979 was a revolt by the whole of Iranian society against both his
arbitrary rule and his modernist westernism (see Chapters 12 and 13).

Like his father before him, the shah was an Aryanist nationalist of the modern
breed, not the stooge of western imperialism virtually all his subjects believed
him to be. He had an Aryanist and pan-Persian view of Iranian history and
society like many modern Iranians who had grown up after World War I (see the
Introduction and Chapters 8 and 9). And, in common with many of them, he saw
social and economic development as an attempt to resemble western Europe and
later America as quickly as possible rather than as a fundamental, long-term
transformation that would run deep and result in irreversible progress. He was
embarrassed by Iran's status as a poor and underdeveloped country and sought
pomp and glory for himself as well as Iran without wishing to involve the Iranian
people in the process. He did not see himself as another Xerxes but as a modern
Cyrus the Great. Addressing Cyrus at his tomb during the fabulous international
celebrations which he hosted in 1971 for the 2,500th anniversary of the foundation of the Persian empire, he famously said: 'Sleep well, Cyrus, for we are awake.'

OIL, STATE AND ARBITRARY GOVERNMENT

From the mid-1960s Iran began a process of rapid economic and social change.
The most important single factor in determining both the pattern and the speed

of economic change and industrialization was oil revenue. Almost concurrent with the suppression of all opposition in 1963–4, oil revenues began to rise steeply as a result of a continuous growth in exports. From the early 1970s, the increase in revenue was explosive both because of export levels and especially because of the great increase in real oil prices. Oil revenues are by nature a form of economic rent: the cost of production of crude oil is small compared with the revenues that proceed from it, rather like the income of pop singers, which bears little relation to the amount of work they do, or the rent received by an individual on an inherited building. The revenues accrued to the state, and it was their disbursement that determined the direction, pattern, pace, indeed the whole character of industrialization and social change.[1]

Therefore, the combination of oil and state played the key role in determining the course of events. Yet this need not have resulted in the same *pattern* of events, nor the same (or a similar) *outcome*, had there not been an arbitrary government neither subject to legal restraints nor open to independent advice and mediation.

The failure of long-term development in the period concerned was neither for want of economic resources nor even because of political *dictatorship*. Indeed, there are very few examples in history of social and economic development having been achieved in a democratic environment as we know it, even in England, the founder of democratic traditions and the home of the first industrial revolution. Neither Georgian England nor – a century later – Meiji Japan may be described as democratic by any criteria recognized from the mid-nineteenth century onwards.

The failure of the shah's model is often blamed on 'dictatorship'. Dictatorships do allow for politics. They are based in law, even if the law may be unfair and discriminating. They have a social base either among the privileged or some sections of 'the masses' or among both, as in some fascist and populist regimes. The government is not democratic, but nor is it subject to the personal whim and will of one individual. As noted in the previous chapter, Iran had already been a dictatorship since 1953. But from 1964 onwards, it was not so much that there was no political development but more a case that politics itself began to disappear from the public sphere.

The regime lost its social base among the landlords, provincial grandees and religious establishment without replacing it (or wishing to replace it) with other existing and/or emerging social classes. In fact, the greatest sense of rift and social alienation was felt by the *emerging* and *growing* social groups (see Chapter 12). Even as early as 1964, when the state had beaten all opposition, substantially improved its foreign relations and was looking forward to economic growth and prosperity, its fundamental failure was not missed by some – albeit very few – realistic observers, of whom Martin Herz had the opportunity to record his exceptionally intelligent analysis for posterity.

Herz was then the political secretary at the American embassy in Tehran, and sent his long and prophetically insightful dispatch – countersigned as it was by the American ambassador – to the US Department of State as early as 1964. Most significantly, it was entitled 'Some Intangible Factors in Iranian Politics'. He pointed out that the shah was thoroughly successful in the recent power struggles against the second National Front, the Amini group and the religious leadership, yet he observed that not only did his rule lack a social base but that, much more importantly, it lacked a firm basis even among its loyal beneficiaries:

> Since the opposition is weak, divided and dispirited, the regime ought to be feeling happy and secure, particularly as it has important political assets in its favour. *But one of the remarkable intangible factors in the present situation is that the regime has so few convinced supporters.*

He then continued to enumerate all the social and professional groups who were the regime's greatest beneficiaries, including those who were running its affairs, as being alienated and bewildered by it:

> Evidence of this is to be found at every turn: prominent members of the New Iran party who express the belief, privately and quietly, that their party is a sham and a fraud and that no political party can be expected to do useful work as long as the Shah's heavy hand rests on the decision-making process; hand-picked Majlis members who deplore 'American support' for a regime which they call a travesty of democracy; civil adjutants of the Shah, who belong to his most devoted supporters, yet who express the belief that Iran will never be able to solve its problems so long as there is no freedom of expression, no delegation of authority, and so little selection of personnel for merit; prominent judges who declare with surprising lack of circumspection, that the anti-corruption campaign cannot get anywhere as long as it is known that certain people are immune from prosecution; military officers who tip off the [second] National Front regarding actions planned against its demonstrations; Foreign Ministry officials who privately advise against courses of action they are officially urging on the US with respect to the treatment of opposition spokesmen in the United States.

Herz then proceeded to emphasize that the people he was citing were loyal members of the regime:

> These are not members of the opposition. They are members of the Establishment who, even while loyal to the Shah, are suffering from a profound malaise, from lack of conviction in what they are doing, from doubts about whether the regime deserves to endure.

He then summed up succinctly the implications of his observations for the political framework which he was observing and analysing:

> Here, and not in particular activities of the exponents of the opposition, lies the real weakness of the regime, for even a militant minority in charge of the

apparatus of government could create respect in the rest of the country . . . Even when ample allowance is made for the ungovernable nature of the Iranian middle class . . . there remains the fact that the Shah's regime is a highly unpopular dictatorship, not only by its opponents, but far more significantly, by its proponents as well.[2]

It is clear that what Herz meant by 'a highly unpopular dictatorship' was precisely arbitrary government, for which he neither had the concept nor the terminology. That is why he wrote that the regime did not enjoy the kind of 'respect' that 'even a militant minority in charge of the apparatus of the state' – such as a Latin American military junta – 'could create in the rest of the country'.

What was true in 1964 was scarcely less true in 1977, when a limited opening of the political sphere by the regime quickly led to rebellion and revolution, which in turn would not have taken the course it did if civil servants, judges, university professors, schoolteachers, radio, television and newspaper journalists, and writers and poets – among almost all other social groups – had not actively supported the revolutionary movement (see Chapter 12).

THE EVIDENCE OF ALAM'S DIARIES

Much of this had been dreaded, if not anticipated, by the shah's most loyal servant, minister of the royal court and close confidant Asadollah Alam. Alam's confidential diaries, covering the period 1969–77, provide a first-hand account of the nature of the regime, its real weaknesses in the face of apparent success and, indirectly, the psychology of the man who was in complete command of all the key domestic and foreign policies.

When the diaries were published in 1991 (long after both Alam and the shah had passed away), Iranians – friend as well as foe – were especially struck by the degree of independence from foreign powers, notably the United States and Britain, the diaries revealed in the shah's words as well as deeds. This is hardly surprising because not only had all those opposed to him believed that he was virtually in the pocket of the West (and especially America) but even his few friends – whose number had grown in the 1980s – considered that this had been so because he had had no choice. To put the matter simply, whereas Iranians had almost universally believed that the fundamental factor against political development in their country was western imperialism, the Alam diaries show that the crucial factor was in fact arbitrary government combined with superficial modernism, in both of which the shah's persona played an important, indeed decisive part.

The shah had not always been as independent from the great powers as he became later in the 1960s and 1970s. It was the rapid and substantial increases in the country's oil fortune that made him increasingly independent of foreign aid, which could be (and had been) used as a lever to influence his policies, both domestic and international; Iran's oil revenues made him a powerful world figure, not least because of the country's ability to spend in foreign (eastern as well as western) markets; and it made Iran attractive to foreign investors.

The shah was certainly pro-American (though he was always suspicious of British motives), not only in terms of world politics but also as a model of industrial, military and perhaps even cultural excellence.[3] Yet Alam's diaries amply demonstrate that he saw America as his chosen great (and admired) partner rather than the master to whom he was slavishly bound by money or power. For example, in an entry for as early as March 1969:

> I made my report and mentioned complaints I have received from the American ambassador. HIM [His Imperial Majesty] has given an interview to the *New York Times* in which he announced his determination to prevent the American Navy, who have a temporary base at Bahrain, from replacing the British as Bahrain's protectors. Moreover, he declared that if America fails to come up with the arms he asked for, Iran will turn to Soviets for assistance. When I mentioned the ambassador's objections to these remarks, HIM [the shah] remarked that he had meant exactly what he had said and that the Americans should take careful note of our opposition to foreign intervention in the Gulf. America must be made to realize that we are an independent sovereign power and will make way for no one.[4]

In July 1972, Alam implies that the American ambassador, a Nixon partisan, asked the shah, through Alam, for financial contributions to his presidential campaign. This has not been spelt out in the text of the Alam diaries, but there can be little doubt that that is its meaning: 'Whilst I dare not set down his request in black and white, I can say that it demonstrates the extent to which Nixon is willing to rely on HIM.'[5] Alam reports further messages from Nixon regarding this matter.[6]

Early in 1973, when there was conflict between the shah and the oil consortium, Nixon intervened by writing a letter directly to the shah in very cordial terms, expressing 'the hope that you might defer any unilateral action until I can study the issue and put my consideration before you'. The shah replied in friendly terms but did not budge. He also instructed Alam to ask the American ambassador 'what makes ours such a "special" relationship, when it can be jeopardised merely by the complaint of an oil company?' Later he told Alam: 'Nixon has the audacity to tell me to do nothing in the interest of my country until he dictates where that interest lies. At the same time he threatens me that failure to follow his so-called advice will be to jeopardize the special relations between our two countries. I say to hell with special relations.' And having heard Nixon's inaugural address next day, he cited the latter's confirmation of the principle of non-interference in other countries' internal affairs, adding 'And yet the blasted man has the audacity to write such a letter.'[7]

In fact, the shah was far from accommodating western interests in respect to the oil price rises of the early 1970s. Before the Arab-Israeli (Yom Kippur) war of

October 1973, he had already played the hawk in pushing up oil prices. He pointed to the fact that the price of Iran's imports from western countries was rising due to inflation in the West, and this meant a real drain on Iran's resources if oil prices did not rise.[8] He did not join the Arab oil embargo against western countries and Japan which followed the Arab-Israeli war. Instead, he auctioned off non-consortium Iranian oil at prices of more than five times the going price, which played a decisive role in the fourfold price increase that almost immediately followed. In December 1973, in the wake of the 'oil shock', Nixon wrote another, much more urgent, letter to the shah urging moderation. On 22 December 1973 the shah chaired the meeting of the Organization of Petroleum Exporting Countries (OPEC), of which Iran had been a founding member in 1960. Next day the fourfold oil price increase was announced. A week later, the American ambassador handed a letter from Nixon to the shah which expressed 'great concern' over the Tehran oil price increase and 'strongly urged' that:

> The recent decisions in Tehran be reconsidered;
>   Steps be initiated to hold the kind of consultations that we believe most consumer and producer countries endorse . . .[9]

This the shah did not accept. Further to Nixon's letter, however, the American ambassador confided to Alam that some of the Arab representatives of OPEC – and specifically Saudi Arabia's Sheikh Zaki Yamani – had said that if it had not been for the shah, they would have settled for a lower price. Alam replied that 'if the Arabs turn out to be telling the truth, there is nothing for us to be ashamed of. The price revolution was a simple common sense.'[10]

Having thus dismissed the age-old theory that the shah was merely carrying out the wishes of America or Britain, the real motives behind his policies must now be examined. Before doing so, however, it would be useful to show the extent of the shah's belief in the conspiracy theory of international politics, since this comes through openly and without qualification in his conversations with the loyal Alam. The irony is that his people also subscribed to such theories, while regarding him as a pawn in international politics.

The shah believed that Baathist Iraq was a British creation. Alam noted in his entry for 19 September 1972:

> [The shah] is still inclined to believe that for all their lip-service and growing dependence on Moscow, the Iraqis are secretly manipulated by the British. All in all his suspicions of the British are quite incredible; he tends to see their secret hand behind virtually every international incident.[11]

Next day the shah repeated to Alam that 'the Iraq president, Al-Bakr, is an agent of the British'.[12] Two years before, Iran's plot to topple the Iraqi regime by organizing a domestic coup against it had failed. The shah had then told Alam that 'it was the British that betrayed us. They came to hear of our plan and tipped off the President of Iraq. Hasan al-Bakr may pose as an Anglophobe but in reality he's a lackey of the British.'[13]

Yet the shah's conspiratorial view of international politics did not stop at the British, and encompassed other powers as well. He even once said to his court minister that the United States is run by a 'hidden force': 'I feel sure that the country is guided by a hidden force; an organization working secretly, powerful enough to dispose of the Kennedys and of anyone else who gets in the way; so far I believe it has claimed upwards of thirty victims; people who had somehow come to guess of its existence'.[14]

In 1971, when the shah was supporting OPEC for a moderate oil price increase, he thought that Britain and America 'may harbour some delusion that by spending a few million dollars they can topple me and my regime', but he added that 'the days when that sort of thing was possible have vanished for ever'.[15] He was certainly thinking of a military coup, but he thought that the army was loyal to him, and in any case the generals were 'too much at one another's throat to constitute a threat'.[16] In December 1973, he thought it likely that America was behind the Arab oil boycott because it would stand to lose much less than western Europe and Japan.[17] Ironically, that was precisely the argument of those multitudes of Iranians who believed that the shah had helped promote the oil price revolution on the order of America.

On one occasion the shah felt that America and the Soviet Union might have devised some scheme to divide the world between them.[18] Certain BBC reports and commentaries particularly angered him, and he persisted in believing that there was a sinister political motive behind them somewhere within the British establishment.[19] Alam was petrified when once he heard that the BBC had said a few good things about his family. In the end he decided to report it personally to the shah, suggesting that he might seek out 'whatever idiot is responsible for the broadcast'. 'I am by no means sure', he added in his diary, that 'this allayed his Majesty's suspicions.'[20]

In 1965, the shah gave himself the title *Arya Mehr*, meaning 'the Aryan Sun', or 'Light of Aryans', just as his father had been entitled 'His Fate-making Majesty' (*A'lahazrat-e Qadar Qodrat*) in the absolute and arbitrary period of his rule. Like his father in the 1930s, the shah's deep pan-Persian feelings were much affected by a personal identification with the land, its culture and its history as he understood them. They both saw Iran as their personal property. Before the Constitutional Revolution, of course, the country had been universally regarded as the ruler's possession. But that was merely the possession of the land and (ultimately) its people in the physical sense of the term. Now, modern nationalism had added a large, abstract and imponderable dimension, the profound subjective and emotional involvement with the object. Hence the shah's extreme sensitivity not only to his own external image but to that of Iran and its importance to the world. Innumerable examples of this can be given. He once ordered the banishment to a distant province of the editor of the English edition of *Kayhan* daily newspaper because he had written a critical article on the problems of living in

Tehran. Alam was apparently touched by the fact that when he presented the title deeds of the newly built palace on Kish Island, the shah turned them down, protesting: 'The whole nation is mine without my having to stake some petty private claim. Everything is at the disposal of a ruler of strength, title deeds and all such trifles will avail me not one jot.'[21]

Before this, the clearest evidence of the shah's pan-Persian feelings and aspirations had been manifested in October 1971, in the famous 2,500th anniversary of the Persian empire. No expense was spared in organizing a series of festivities which culminated in a top-heavy international festival held in the ruins of Persepolis, where a large tent city was created to house the illustrious guests from sixty-nine countries. The shah was annoyed that Queen Elizabeth II did not attend, being represented by Prince Philip and Princess Anne; and he was angry by the fact that the French president, Georges Pompidou, withdrew his decision to attend in the face of serious criticism at home from human rights organizations, and so the French prime minister attended instead. The event was deeply resented by the great majority of the Iranian people, who saw it as a colossal waste of resources in what was still a relatively poor country, symbolizing the restoration of 'nezam-e shahanshahi', 'the imperial system'. Alam's diaries have now shown that one great domestic critic of that episode was no less a loyal and intimate person in relation to the shah than Queen Farah, now entitled Shahbanu:

> Asked HMQ [the queen] at the airport whether I might take the Crown Prince to the premiere of the film documentary about last year's monarchy celebrations ... 'For goodness sake, leave alone,' she said. 'I want our names to be utterly dissociated from those ghastly celebrations ...' But to my amazement she then said, 'HIM [the shah] and I see eye to eye on nothing; almost invariably I disagree with him.'[22]

Soon after the quadrupling of oil prices late in 1973, Alam told the shah that 'every one of his dreams seems to have come true, and HIM is now unrivalled amongst Middle Eastern statesmen': 'But I have so many more aspirations,' he replied. 'To be first in the Middle East is not enough. We must raise ourselves to the level of a great world power. Such a goal is by no means unattainable.'[23]

This is important evidence for the shah's vision, which directly affected both the state and society since he was the country's sole decision-maker. The same vision was later systematically expounded in the shah's last book before the revolution of 1979, Besu-ye Tamaddon-e Bozorg (Towards the Great Civilization). The book consists of three parts, and appears to be a comprehensive manifesto. Part One discusses 'the fundamental problems of the contemporary world', 'the crisis of civilization' and finally 'the way forward'. Part Two, 'Iran in the Age of [the White] Revolution', covers a number of subjects, including land reform, education, health, 'the extension of democracy' and 'The National Resurgence Party of the Iranian Nation'. Part Three, 'On the Way to the Great Civilization', expounds the ideological vision of the book. The shah wrote:

To take the Iranian nation to the age of 'the great civilization' is my greatest wish
... The goal which I have determined for my own nation is undoubtedly highly
ambitious and lofty, but it is not one that would be impossible for the nation, given
its plentiful material and spiritual possibilities, and its abundant mental and moral
resources. If such a goal looks beyond the normal limit, it is because to try and
achieve a lesser ideal is essentially not worthy of our nation.[24]

The shah then argued that the emergence of the Iranian empire (*shahanshahi*)
two and a half millennia before had opened the way to a new age in the development of human civilization, and so there was no reason why it should not try to
create the great civilization of tomorrow as the correct answer to the need which
is deeply felt by our anxious world.[25]

A century and a half before, Chateaubriand had written that 'when in the
history of the world we arrive at the Age of Persia, we feel to have stepped into
the stage of great history'. Why then should we not try to make this same country
and this same nation step into 'the great civilization' at the dawn of the third
millennium?

The shah saw this goal, which he believed to be within the country's grasp
over the next one or two decades, not simply as a return to the ancient glory but
as the very zenith of the country's history:

The great civilization towards which we are now moving is not just a chapter in
the history of this land. It is its greatest chapter; an ideal with which thousands
of years of Iran's development must inevitably end up, and which in turn must
be the dawn of a new era in our national life.[26]

Addressing the question 'What is the great civilization', he described it in
familiar utopian terms:

It is the civilization in which the best elements of human knowledge and
thought are employed in order to secure the highest level of material and spiritual living for every member of the society. A civilization which would be
founded on creativity and humanity, and where every human being, while
benefiting from complete material welfare, would likewise enjoy maximum
social security as well as spiritual and moral abundance.[27]

In April 1974, only a few days after the shah had told Alam that Iran should
become a world power and a year before the shah's book on the 'Great
Civilization' was written, the loyal Alam noted in his diary, after chairing a
meeting of the board of governors of the Rural Cultural Centres:

To my chagrin it was announced that so far only 1 per cent of our villages have
been supplied with clean piped drinking water, though the problem is not as
serious as it might appear, since most of the others can draw clean water from

their wells or *qanats*. Far more shameful is the fact that only one in twenty five villages has electricity, a ludicrous figure given the rate of national development.[28]

As noted in the previous chapter, with the launch of the White Revolution and the suppression of the revolt of June 1963, the shah in effect disenfranchised the upper and influential classes of the limited amount of power, influence and political participation which they had enjoyed since the 1953 coup. That is how he came personally to monopolize all power. Thus, politics was abolished just as it had been in the latter part of Reza Shah's rule, the difference being that now there were many more people with aspirations to participation in the political processes and the country was much more integrated into a world that was experiencing decolonization, socio-political development and revolutionary struggle (see Chapter 12).

The 21st Majlis that the shah opened late in 1963 was described as 'classless'. This was true in the sense that now the state could pick and choose whoever it wished from whatever social class and declare that he or she had been elected as a Majlis deputy, the deputies knowing that they could discuss only such matters as would be allowed by the shah and the state. This remained the pattern until 1978.

As noted in Chapter 10, after sacking Ali Amini in 1962, the shah appointed Alam as prime minister. Early in 1964, after the 21st Majlis had been established, the shah appointed the relatively young Hasan Ali Mansur prime minister and Alam minister of the royal court. It was a young and new cabinet, hardly any member of which had held a ministerial post before. This was consistent with the shah's new revolutionary phase, which continued until shortly before his downfall, to completely disown and discard old-school politicians and replace them with young and largely western-educated aspirants to high office. This was part of the new and 'classless' regime. It provided opportunities for co-opting actual or potential critics and dissidents into the regime and using them as administrators and technicians without granting them any real power of decision-making.

Mansur was assassinated in 1965 by a young Islamist in reaction to the grant of extra-territorial judicial rights to American personnel in Iran. He was replaced by Amir Abbas Hoveyda, a western-educated intellectual who had had leftist sympathies as a young man, had become a diplomat and had later joined the National Iranian Oil Company before being made minister of finance in Mansur's cabinet. He was upright himself but tolerated corruption by others and was subservient to the shah. Hoveyda remained in office until August 1977, when – in response to growing public unrest – the shah removed him and made him minister of the royal court. Still later in 1978, and in the midst of the revolutionary movement, the shah had him arrested along with some other high officials in an attempt to satisfy public anger. Shortly after the revolution he was 'tried' in a revolutionary court and shot to death (see Chapter 14).[29]

Many of the shah's subordinates were dissatisfied with their lack of independence, even regarding the most mundane matters of government policy, but Alam was the only one who both had the insight and courage to voice the need, not for democracy, but for politics to the shah. For example, in a conversation with the shah in 1972, he told him of the need for 'popular participation in the game of politics':

> For example, why does the government continue to meddle in local [municipal] elections. Leave the public to fight their own political contests and to choose whatever local representatives they prefer. Parliamentary elections may still require a degree of management, but surely this is untrue of elections in the municipalities. Why not allow the people free discussion of their local care and concern? What harm could it possibly do?

The shah thought that that would be harmful because the people would then want to talk about such matters as inflation:

> 'What are you talking about; of course it would be harmful ... they'd begin moaning about inflation or some such rot'. 'Sadly,' I replied, 'what they say about inflation is all too true. But even assuming it to be nonsense, why not open a safety valve and allow them to talk nonsense freely, amongst themselves?' 'Precisely the reason I've allowed the opposition party to continue in existence', he replied. 'Yes', I said, 'but an opposition deprived of free discussion is surely no opposition at all?' At this point he asked why the people pay so little attention to the progress we have made. 'Because,' I told him, 'our propaganda is applied in quite the wrong directions. So much of our self-advertisement is patently untrue, and for the rest it's mixed up with the adulation of Your Majesty's own person that the public grows tired of it'.[30]

By 'the opposition' the shah meant the People's (*Mardom*) party, which along with the Nationalist (*Melliyun*) party he had launched in the 1950s largely for western consumption (see Chapter 10). That is why, in their moments of heated debate, the party leaders usually accused one another not so much of implementing wrong policies but of not carrying out 'His Majesty's true intentions' (*manviyat-e molukaneh*) sufficiently well. After the White Revolution, the Melliyun gave way to the completely new New Iran (*Iran-e Novin*) party. This, too, was established at the shah's suggestion but its founders were young technocrats who were seen as the backbone of the shah's new reformist course. After the assassination of Hasan Ali Mansur, prime minister between 1964 and 1965, and his replacement with the cultured but submissive Amir Abbas Hoveyda, the party failed to play a political role. Most ministers, deputies and high state officials were obliged to join it, but it never attracted any public participation. Its most important function, perhaps, was to act as the administrative machinery for the selection of Majlis deputies.[31] As noted, *Mardom* was still retained as 'the opposition party', but was quickly censured on the rare occasions that it tried to play the role of a loyal opposition.

For example, in 1972 the party leader Alinaqi Kani was critical of Hoveyda's government and said that if the elections were not rigged, his party would win the vote. This threw the shah into a rage. He shouted to Alam, 'What on earth is the bloody man on about . . . He's got about as much hope of winning the election as of teaching a pig to fly!'[32] Later, a by-election took place in the northern city of Shahsavar (now Tonokabon). Backed by the new party secretary Naser Ameri, the *Mardom* party nominee acted like a genuine loyal opposition candidate, heavily criticized Hoveyda's administration and was elected by an overwhelming majority. But the government declared its own candidate as the winner. Ameri publicly denounced this as fraud, resigned his post some time later and was killed in a road accident shortly afterwards.[33]

DOMESTIC RULE

In March 1974, shortly after the fourfold increase in oil prices, official party politics took a dramatic turn. At a suddenly called press conference, the shah, who had once written that he would never institute a single party because that was what the communists and Hitler had done,[34] disbanded *Mardom* and *Iran-e Novin* and replaced them with the single *Rastakhiz-e Melli* (National Resurgence) party. Membership of the new party was in effect made mandatory for all Iranians. In a famous speech, the shah classified his subjects into three groups: the great majority who, he said, were behind the regime; those who were passive and neutral and should therefore 'expect nothing from us'; and dissidents and critics, for whom there was no room in the country and who were free to apply for passports and leave Iran.

Membership books were sent to all state offices, including universities, to be signed, and their members were told to join or face punitive action. Abolhasan Ebtehaj, the country's first and most able technocrat, who, having resigned as the head of the Plan Organization, had founded his own private bank, later recalled:

> the shah founded a single party and warned that whoever disagreed must leave [the country] . . . I telephoned Hoveyda, who was the party's general secretary. I said 'this means that I have to join the party, because I can't leave Iran'. 'Yes' he said. I said 'what should I do?' he said he would send me a piece of paper to sign. They sent a piece of paper which I signed, meaning that I had become a party member. That's all, just a signature . . . This warning was official, meaning whoever remained [in the country] and did not become a party member should not expect any help if anything happened to him. That meant that if someone out in the street beat me up violently and hurt me, if I raised my voice I would be told 'We told you so?' This is what had become of Iran, an Iran which enjoyed the support of two democratic western states. Isn't this shameful?[35]

The shah, as a trained military officer, had an even firmer grip on the armed forces and security networks than on the civil administration. The power and privileges of military officers went considerably beyond their good pay and conditions. Their military uniform, which they regularly wore in public, conferred extraordinary authority, and they could intimidate ordinary people in their contact with the public. Military organizations could also violate private property (especially urban land) whenever it suited their purpose. All this served to cause a great deal of public resentment against military officers and networks.

Yet as powerful as the military personnel and organizations were in relation to the ordinary public, they were completely powerless regarding their own professional tasks and activities. The shah was personally in charge of all arms purchases, made all the appointments and promotions of the senior and general staff, and heads of services, departments and operations had to report directly to him.

General Fereydun Jam, the honest and sophisticated chief of staff (1969–71) and former brother-in-law of the shah, found it virtually impossible to function in circumstances where

> none of the commanders had any power in his field of command which stems from responsibility; that is, they were all responsible without having power . . . Not even the army commander had the right to use more than a company in his area. In Tehran, they had to obtain [the shah's] prior permission even for nightly operations . . . It is clear that such an army which in normal times would have to seek permission to breathe, will have no one to lead in a crisis, and will disintegrate . . . exactly as it in fact did.[36]

General Jam, General Hasan Toufanian (Tufaniyan) and Admiral Amir Abbas Ramzi Atai are all at one in emphasizing the lack of coordination between various military establishments and the requirement that all the service chiefs both report directly to the shah and obtain permission from him for the slightest decision. As a result, said Jam, uncoordinated reports used to be sent to the shah, and similarly 'uncoordinated, illogical, and ill-prepared orders were sent down'.[37] According to Toufanian, the shah 'had created an ineffective ministry of war, and a general staff . . . which was even more ineffective, and we were all in it'.[38] Ramzi Atai remembered twice having asked Prime Minister Hoveyda why he did not throw his weight about, and on both occasions the prime minister had replied 'with embarrassment' that he in fact was 'no more than a chef-de-cabinet'. He added: 'You see, ministers would go straight to the shah. As the navy chief I would take my work directly to His Majesty. As a result, the prime minister was bypassed; the chief of general staff was bypassed – hierarchy was not observed.'[39]

Jam complained that the shah decided, and Toufanian executed, the army's purchase orders, but there was no logic or coordination so that 'every day they would order some [military] equipment and then say, "Do something with it". The general staff had no knowledge at all what was being purchased and for what purpose.'[40] Toufanian complained about the shah's interference in every little detail: 'After all we used to call the shah the supreme commander, and even the officers' leaves had to be reported [to him] – appointments, everything, everything. Therefore, officers were used to a certain system, [and] when the system's head went away, I believe it was almost bound to disintegrate.'[41]

Jam related an astonishing story about Iraq's ultimatum to Iran over the use of the Shatt al-Arab waterway in 1969. The border through the great river that divides Iranian and Iraqi territory had been disputed for some time, but the Iraqis were now claiming full control of the river up to the Iranian shore and threatening to attack Iranian shipping carried out without their permission. As the chief of staff Jam merely heard a rumour that such an ultimatum had been received by the foreign ministry. The ministry confirmed the rumour to him, but it turned out that the prime minister had not been told of the ultimatum, which had been received a few days before, because the foreign minister (Ardeshir Zahedi, who, on account of personal relations with the shah, was more powerful than Hoveyda) was on bad terms with him. Jam had to raise the alarm, and he and the prime minister between them took the necessary steps to deal with the situation while the shah was on a state visit to Tunisia. And yet when the shah returned to Iran the prime minister asked Jam whether he had packed his bags for both of them to go to prison because they had taken those decisions on their own.[42] The quick collapse of the shah's regime in 1979 had many long- and short-term causes, one of which was precisely that every decision depended on one person alone in an otherwise complex and expanding society.

SAVAK, founded in 1957, was the shah's secret police. There were other security and intelligence-gathering networks, each one watching the others and all of them under the shah's direct control: the special bureau, army intelligence, army counter-intelligence, the imperial inspectorate, the imperial commission and so on. There was intense, often destructive, rivalry between them. General Hasan Alavi-Kia, an acting SAVAK chief, said he had once jokingly told the shah that the competition between security organizations might have been the consequence of the shah's own policy of 'divide and rule'.[43] The shah once told Alam that his generals were 'too much at one another's throat to constitute a threat'. Jam confirms that the army had little or no contact with the general staff, was directly in touch with the shah and spent some of its time and energy fighting off other para-military and security organizations.

SAVAK was a large and ruthless security organization whose power, influence and sphere of operations grew from the mid-1960s in consequence of the interrelated growth of the shah's arbitrary power and the steady, and later explosive, increases in the oil revenues. It did not only suppress political dissidence and urban guerrilla movements but also struck widespread fear into the hearts of high and low alike in an attempt to obliterate any word of criticism, however harmless, even in private. This played an important role in spreading anger and frustration against the regime because of the fear and humiliation it created. In this way, SAVAK politicized large numbers of people, apparently to stop them from talking politics. This serves to explain the wide discrepancy between the official figures and estimates by international human rights organizations of the number of political prisoners before the revolution. The official figures (about 2,500) referred to those who had been convicted and sentenced in military courts, whereas the figures quoted by Amnesty International and similar organizations (70,000 or more) were based on the number of all political detainees, many of whom would spend months in jail without trial as punishment for minor misdemeanours and then be released.

FOREIGN POLICY

From 1963 onwards the shah personally conducted his own, largely successful, foreign policy with the help of some able and experienced diplomats at the foreign ministry. Armin Meyer, American Ambassador to Iran between 1965 and 1969, recalled that after his audiences with the shah, the foreign minister would 'pick my brains to educate himself as to what was on the Shah's mind'.[44] In a modest political programme, the second National Front had described its foreign policy as 'independent national policy' instead of its traditional commitment to non-alignment. In the new atmosphere of both domestic and international politics, the shah adopted the same slogan for his foreign policy.

Most important in the field of Iranian foreign relations were the United States (and Britain), the Soviet Union (and the eastern European countries) and the Arab (and Islamic) world. In the period of absolute rule the shah maintained and enhanced the support of America and Britain, established friendly relations with the Soviet Union and east European countries, was on good terms with Arab kingdoms, maintained friendly relations with Israel and even reached an accord with Mao's China.

As noted in Chapter 10, the Kennedy administration adopted a somewhat critical attitude towards the shah's regime following complaints both in Iran and America about the country's lack of freedom as well as corruption and economic mismanagement. Following that, President Johnson's administrations (1963–9) also expressed reservations, along similar lines. But from 1963 onwards such criticism did not amount to much, although it irritated the shah from time to time.[45] Both the Kennedy and Johnson administrations supported the shah's White Revolution, which they saw as an antidote to the influence of communism in Iran, but they were concerned about his massive spending on arms purchases. In 1962 President Kennedy cut US financial assistance to Iran, and by 1964 the Johnson administration, convinced that with rising oil revenues Iran no longer needed military grants from the United States, switched all grants to credits with which Iran was to purchase military equipment from America.

The shah's American card became much stronger upon Richard Nixon's assumption of the presidency (1969–74); the shah had contributed to Nixon's campaign fund. Nixon almost gave him a carte blanche for ordering arms from the United States, and openly asked him to keep the peace in the Persian Gulf on behalf of America. As noted above, however, the shah's relations with Nixon were far from slavish. Relations remained unchanged under Gerald Ford (1974–6), but they took a new turn on the election of President Carter, whose more liberal international policy and public espousal of human rights the shah feared. In the end the shah came to believe that America (perhaps together with Britain) organized the Iranian revolution; or at least that is what he publicly professed.[46]

Relations with the Soviet Union improved and were normalized in the 1960s and 1970s, although not to the extent of disturbing Iran's alliance with the West. Early in the 1960s, relations between America and the Soviet Union began to improve in relation to the height of the Cold War in the mid-1950s, while the Sino-Soviet dispute came out in the open and China increasingly assumed the leadership of third world revolutionary movements. The Soviet Union had adopted an openly hostile attitude towards the shah since the signing of the Iranian-American defence treaty in March 1959 (see Chapter 10). That was the reason for the considerable increase in Soviet popularity in Iran. In September 1962 the shah reassured the Soviet Union that he would not allow any military bases to be established on Iranian soil. The Soviets accepted his pledge, partly in line with their new foreign policy line of peaceful coexistence and partly because the shah had just emerged from Iran's power struggles as the sole victor. By trying to improve his relations with Soviet Russia, the shah meant to assert a degree of independence in his foreign policy now that the Soviets had abandoned the general policy of encouraging revolutionary movements and advocated 'peaceful coexistence' with the West.

The shah was encouraged in this new course by the mildly critical attitude of the Kennedy and Johnson administrations towards his regime. He also hoped to stem the negative impact of Soviet hostility on his popularity at home, although the result was a decline in Soviet popularity among Iranians and their increasingly warm feelings towards China, until that too was frustrated by the Sino-Iranian rapprochement of the 1970s. The normalization of relations with the Soviet Union resulted in better trade and economic relations between the two countries. For example, various agreements led to the Soviet construction of Iran's first modern steel plant in Isfahan, a machine tools factory in Arak and the gas pipelines which exported Iran's natural gas to the Soviet Union, as well as to purchases of arms and military equipment from Russia and some east European countries.[47]

Iran was becoming a regional player from the mid-1950s, about the time that Gamal Abd al-Nasser of Egypt began to emerge as the leader of the Arab nationalist movement. After the Suez crisis, Nasser's popularity surged not only among Arab counties but also in the countries of the third world, including Iran, where he was regarded as a non-aligned leader inspired by Mosaddeq. Thus a clash between the shah's Iran and Nasser's Egypt was almost inevitable, and when in 1960 the shah reaffirmed Iran's de facto recognition of Israel, Egypt broke off diplomatic relations with Iran. Relations were later to improve after Egypt's defeat in the six-day war of June 1967, and in the 1970s became friendly under President Sadat.

As noted in Chapter 10, in 1955 Iran entered the mutual defence alliance, the Baghdad Pact, with Iraq, Turkey, Pakistan and Britain. The 1958 coup in Iraq led to Iraq's withdrawal from the Baghdad pact (which was renamed CENTO) and a deterioration of Iran–Iraq relations. The further radicalization of Iraqi politics in the 1960s and the rise of the Baathist regime in Iraq were bound to increase tension between the two countries. However, the specific cause of conflict was the age-old dispute over Iran's rights in the Shatt al-Arab waterway. Iraq welcomed General Teymur Bakhtiyar, the founding SAVAK chief who had fallen out with the shah and was leading a campaign against him, but he was killed by an Iranian undercover agent in 1970.

Meanwhile, Iran had successfully called Iraq's bluff in its ultimatum of 1969 (see above). In 1971–2, Iraq resorted to the persecution and mass expulsion of Iraqi Shiites of Iranian origin. In this context, the upsurge of the Kurdish revolt in Iraq provided the shah with an excellent opportunity to retaliate and try to stem Iraqi hostility by providing effective support for the Kurdish insurgents. The tactic worked, and in 1975 at a summit of the Islamic countries in Algiers, Saddam Hussein capitulated and made peace with the shah.[48] The dictatorial Iraqi regime was very popular with the Iranian people – and not least with intellectuals – simply because of its confrontation with the shah's regime, and this was further proof of the fundamental conflict between state and society in Iran, especially when the state was strong and repressive.

The most sensitive question facing the shah in his relations with both Britain and his Arab neighbours in the Persian Gulf (which, following Egypt's lead in the 1960s, the Arabs had begun to call the Arab Gulf) was the question of Bahrain's independence after British withdrawal from the Gulf. Iran had a historical claim to Bahrain, as well as the islands of Abu Musa and the Greater and Lesser Tunbs, which are virtually uninhabited but are strategically located in the Strait of Hormuz and to which the then Trucial States in the south of the Persian Gulf also lay claim. The shah did not want to go to war with Britain and/or the Arabs over Bahrain, whose population was overwhelmingly Arab. But having previously declared Bahrain Iran's fourteenth province, he was mindful of Iranian nationalist feelings and did not wish to be seen as giving way to the secession of Iranian territory.

In the end, long and protracted negotiations with Britain led to Iran's recognition of Bahrain in 1971 following the report of a UN mission that the people of Bahrain wished their country to become fully independent after British withdrawal. The British did not formally agree to deliver the other three islands to Iran as a price for her cooperation over Bahrain, but informally let the Iranians know that they would not take any action if Iran occupied those islands after they withdrew from the Persian Gulf. This Iran did the day after the British withdrawal. The departure of Britain, combined with the election of President Nixon and the end of Iraq's confrontation with Iran, meant that by the mid-1970s Iran had become the foremost player in the Persian Gulf.[49]

Thus by the time the protest movement began in 1977, the shah's regional and international policy had been so successful that his only enemy was Colonel

Gaddafi of Libya – despite his belief that the revolution against him had been engineered by America and Britain.[50]

THE WHITE REVOLUTION

In 1979 Iran was incomparably richer than it had been fifteen years earlier, let alone before that. The population had almost doubled since 1955, but much of its growth had occurred after 1963. Rural-urban migration had been high, and by 1977 employment in industry had almost caught up with agriculture. Both state and private investment in industry and services had been growing. Construction, manufacturing and services grew at high rates, and new technologies were imported together with the machinery and equipment which they embodied. Education expanded rapidly at all levels, and large and growing numbers of people received higher education abroad, mainly in western Europe and America, most of them returning to fill ever-increasing vacancies in state as well as business posts and enterprises. Never before in modern and recent times had Iran been so rich, urbanized, industrial and educated.

None of this would have been possible without the steady growth, and later explosion, of oil revenues. In 1963 these were $300 million; in 1977 they had risen to $24 *billion*, that is, they had increased eightyfold over the period. Oil was the independent variable of the whole system. As noted above, it accrued largely as an economic rent, a gift or manna from heaven, because the cost of production of crude was minimal: in 1978 the share of oil revenues in national output was almost 35 per cent, whereas its share in total employment was as little as 0.6 per cent. Oil was therefore the engine of growth, of substantial improvement in general living standards; but by virtue of the fact that it was in the nature of a free gift and that its revenues were directly received by the state, it also had some negative impacts on political, economic and social development.[51]

In the crucial years following the restoration of arbitrary rule, it was increasing oil revenues that sustained and enhanced the power of the state. Increasingly, it made the state free from the need for foreign aid and credit and, therefore, the leverage that this could have afforded to the West for influencing its foreign and, especially, domestic policies. Likewise, these revenues made it largely independent from the domestic economy so that by 1977 oil contributed almost 77 per cent of state revenue, which was received in foreign exchange. It was state expenditure that determined the course and strategy of social and economic change, and the state sector grew much more rapidly than the private sector, although the growth of the latter was itself mainly due to state expenditure. Between 1962 and 1977, private consumption expenditure rose more than sixfold, but in the same period state consumption expenditure increased by more than twenty-four times.[52]

In this way, all social classes became directly or indirectly dependent upon the state: the higher the class the more benefit it received from the state and was therefore the more dependent on it. This was a familiar pattern under arbitrary rule, when the upper classes enjoyed their income and status largely by virtue of the privileges and benefits granted or confirmed to them by the state. But now that large amounts of oil revenues were flowing in, the population was growing fast and there was a high rate of urban expansion. A large and growing urban class emerged, best described as the state's clientele, whose welfare increasingly depended on state expenditure and who, in their own words, came to see their privileges as 'their share of the oil revenues'. This did not stop them from joining mass demonstrations in 1978. Far from it, they played a crucial role in the revolution by providing it with a modern middle class base (see Chapters 12 and 13).

The principles of the White Revolution were later gradually extended to include other measures without further referendums. For example, a health corps was created for medical graduates, who would spend part of their national service to provide medical assistance in rural and provincial areas. In the late 1960s the principle of 'educational revolution' (*enqelab-e amuzeshi*) was added to the list. Education was expanding at a fast rate at all levels during the whole period, but the educational revolution largely consisted of an overhaul of existing universities by retiring many of their academic staff and changing their structure from one based on the French to the American system. Other points, such as 'the administrative revolution' were later added to the principles of the White Revolution, some of which had little practical effect. Whereas the original principles had been submitted to referendums (however nominally), these new points were added to the list by fiat. The arbitrariness and lack of predictability which this involved increased the public's sense of general insecurity to the extent that by 1977 many believed that the next principle of the White Revolution would declare the nationalization of all urban property apart from personal dwellings (see Chapter 12).

As noted in Chapter 11, the implementation of the first stage of the land reform which had been enacted by Amini's government had led to the distribution of one-third of village lands (excluding hamlets) to the peasants, or so-called cultivators. Cultivators were defined as *nasaq*-holders, that is, those with existing rights of cultivation. This excluded the *khoshneshins* or landless peasants, who provided agricultural hands, petty trade and other services or owned and rented one or two oxen. Thus about 35 per cent of the peasantry were excluded from the reform. This was probably intended to keep the average farm size at a reasonable level, but it compounded employment and welfare problems in the rural as well as the urban sector.

The second stage of the land reform enacted and implemented after the White Revolution was more diluted than the first with respect to land distribution. The landlords were allowed to choose between five options: tenancy, sale to peasants, division of the land between the landowner and the peasant according to their existing sharecropping agreement, the formation of 'an agricultural unit' by the landowner and peasant to run the property and the purchase by the landowner of the peasants' rights.[53] Mechanized farms were exempted from the reform and could be kept by the landowner, but the definition of mechanized farms was so loose that, according to one acute observer, it enabled 'unscrupulous landowners to place their lands outside the operation of the land reform by ploughing it once by tractor, and declaring the peasants to be agricultural labourers'.[54] The second stage affected many more villages and peasants than the first. Unlike the first stage, however, most peasants did not receive land, only tenancy agreements with security of tenure.[55]

Hasan Arsanjani, the architect of the original first stage, believed firmly in the need for rural cooperative societies for the successful operation of the land reform. Membership of cooperatives therefore became mandatory for peasants who were affected by the reform policy. Arsanjani wanted a relatively autonomous cooperative movement run by the peasantry, but the shah later opted for a system that was bureaucratically controlled.[56] Furthermore, with new ideas regarding the third and fourth stages of land reform and the turn against small-scale peasant farming, the cooperatives nowhere received the amount of state credit which they needed for effective operation.

The third and fourth stages could not be realistically described as land reform. They were more in the nature of strategies to effect radical changes in agriculture and rural society, and they harmed rather than helped agriculture and the peasantry. The shah's vision was to turn Iran into a modern industrial society within a short period of time. That is why by the mid-1970s official propaganda was promising that Iran had become the 'Japan of the Middle East' and would soon be 'the fifth most industrial state in the world'. For reasons discussed below, the country could not yet be described as developed, let alone industrial. However, the rapid growth and later explosion of the oil revenues made it appear that a large agricultural sector was no longer needed to supply food and raw materials for urban development or foreign exchange to pay for the import of machinery and consumption goods, which could all be met by imports paid for by the oil revenues. This was in effect a case of 'oil versus agriculture', which would waste both of these resources.[57] But the consequences of this agricultural policy were even more dire since peasant agriculture is not just an economic sector but the home and livelihood of rural society as a whole. In 1973, when the rural population was over 17 million or 56 per cent of the total population, the shah claimed that by 1980 Iran's rural population would have declined to 2 million.[58] Clearly, this was beyond the realm of possibility, no matter how drastic a policy was pursued to reduce agriculture and the rural population. But it shows the vision that led to the third and fourth stages of official agricultural policy.

The third stage was the formation of large agricultural corporations made up of a number of villages. This turned peasant property into paper shares of the large corporations, with the prospect of the small shareholders selling up their shares to the big proprietors and over time themselves becoming ordinary farm labourers. It also brought the state bureaucracy into the management of the corporation and the lives of the peasantry while removing the boundary of the village, which had been the unit of rural production since time immemorial.[59] Between 1968 and 1975 the state credit extended to farm corporations was twenty times more than the credit given to the peasant cooperatives, whereas the number of households in the peasant sector was 98.8 per cent of the total, and in farm corporations just 1.2 per cent.[60] Furthermore, the credit given to the cooperatives was short term, but that of the corporations was long term. Yet a close study of the performance of the two systems showed that peasant farms performed better than the corporations.[61]

The fourth stage of agricultural policy was even more destructive and less relevant than the third stage. It was a policy of creating giant agri-business companies in some of the most fertile areas of arable production, described as 'the poles of land and water resources'. The peasants were forced to sell their lands as well as their homes at administrative prices, become landless farm labourers on daily wages and live in substandard housing estates, which lacked the communal environment of the village. In one case in the Khuzistan province fifty-eight villages were destroyed to give way to one agri-business company. Yet, as in the case of the farm corporations, the agri-businesses performed less efficiently than the existing agricultural systems.[62]

In the fifteen-year period between 1962 and 1977 covering the four stages of agricultural policy and the rapid growth of the oil and urban sectors, agricultural output also grew, but at a much lower rate than the rest of the economy. And although agricultural welfare as a whole also improved over the period, the gap between rural and urban society in regard to all the indices of material well-being widened enormously. In 1962 urban consumption per head was less than twice the rural; by 1977 it had increased to more than five times the rural figure. Putting it the other way around, rural consumption per head had fallen from a half of the urban in 1962 to one-fifth in 1977.[63]

This period also saw the continuing decline of the nomadic population and nomadic production. After putting down the revolt of the Qashqa'is in Fars province, and with rapid increases in the military and security networks of the state, the back of the nomadic tribal population was broken, and the government continued its policies of their forced settlement. The nomads were regarded as an embarrassment; it was thought that in western eyes they were evidence of the country's backwardness. Nor would the state tolerate the nomads' relative autonomy. The state's policy was both highly demoralizing to the nomadic people and harmful in regard to livestock production, in which the nomads were particularly engaged.[64]

Educational policy was much more successful. Education had always been valued highly in Iran, in part in consequence of the absence of a European-type class system that would have conferred continuing status and income on the privileged classes while at the same time limiting social mobility. Thus education became a major channel for the less privileged members of society who had intelligence and ability to (sometimes tremendously) improve their situation. The sword and the pen had been more certain instruments of social mobility than birth into a privileged family, although a combination of all three would have helped to ensure success. In time, culture and education came to be highly valued and respected for their own sakes as well as for conferring social prestige and material benefits. But now that oil revenues were flowing in, the economy was expanding rapidly and incomes were rising, and there were therefore increasing job opportunities for educated men and women. The demand for increased and higher education also expanded rapidly, with more and more social classes expecting their children to be educated at the highest levels. In purely material terms, the great expansion of education, especially at the primary and secondary levels, was due to the rapid increase in population and the fast growth of oil revenues.

New schools came into being all over the country, though Tehran did better than most of the provinces, and the urban sector was greatly favoured in comparison with the rural sector. The number of primary school students increased more than threefold between 1962 and 1977.[65] The growth of secondary education was even more impressive; there was more than an eightfold increase between 1962 and 1978.[66] Iran had been well behind Turkey and Egypt in its primary and secondary school population in 1960, but by 1975 it had left both those countries behind it. For example, in 1960 in Turkey only 46 per cent of children of school age had attended school, and in 1974, 66 per cent. The corresponding figures for Iran had grown from 29 per cent in 1960 to 70 per cent in 1975.[67]

There was a rapid rise in the number of schoolchildren of both sexes, although the population of boys going to school was and remained considerably higher: in 1960, 39 per cent of boys of primary and secondary school age were registered at schools, the figure rising to 87 per cent in 1975; in the case of girls, the figures were respectively 18 per cent in 1960 and 53 per cent in 1975.[68] But by 1975 Iran had almost caught up with Turkey regarding the female population at primary and secondary schools.[69]

Yet the philosophy, style, quality and results of secondary education proved embarrassing, with its traditional emphasis on a broad humanistic education, its insufficient provision for science and technology, especially applied science, and its emphasis on memorizing rather than acquiring a critical faculty. There was a good deal of complaint about such issues from both domestic and international observers. As a scholar of the subject has reported: 'All the veteran professors interviewed asserted that there was definitely a continual decline in the academic level of the freshmen in their departments since the early 1960s.'[70]

Higher education also expanded rapidly both at home and abroad. Following 'the educational revolution' in the late 1960s the state decided to expand universities and colleges rapidly despite its earlier reluctance due to students' tendency to get involved in politics. Between 1962 and 1967, the number of university students went up by about 6,000, from 21,000 to 27,000, but by 1975 it had more than doubled to 58,000, and in 1977 it was almost 69,000.[71] Yet because of the high growth rate of the population and the phenomenal growth of secondary school leavers, the ratio of university entrants to school leavers fell from 36 per cent in 1962 to 12 per cent in 1979.[72]

A number of new universities were founded over the period, and some colleges of further education were upgraded to university status. The downsides were that academic standards at the universities fell, and academic research and publications were also weak. An award-winning Iranian academic said that 'at the universities as well as "social circles" appreciation for research was still lacking [and] that his colleagues made no effort to publish in scientific journals or to participate in international conferences'.[73]

The number of colleges, some of which – unlike universities – were funded privately, grew at an even more rapid pace. These were institutions which offered first degrees in humanities, liberal studies or technical and vocational subjects. Since demand was very high and their entrance requirements were lower than the universities, these institutions grew fast in number and student population. In 1962, the number of college students was 1,700; by 1977 it had risen to 85,000. This meant that between those two years the ratio of university students to total students in higher education fell from 92.4 to 44.5, due to the much more rapid growth of college students.[74]

Thus although there was, perhaps inevitably, a general fall in the quality of higher education, the numbers taught grew at a very high rate, and – at least in relative terms – it was an area in which the state's policy proved to be successful. Yet true to the sharp conflict between society and state in periods of absolute as well as arbitrary rule, not only higher education and secondary school students but eventually even primary schoolchildren joined the demonstrations in 1978 and 1979 (see Chapters 12 and 13).

The growth of oil revenues and, therefore, middle class incomes, the increasing demand for higher education and the higher prestige and income prospects attached to western education – all these combined to lead to a rapid growth of students studying in western Europe and the United States. Having begun with probably no more than 15,000 in 1962, the number of Iranian students abroad was estimated to be 40,000 by 1977, a growth of more than 250 per cent, most of which occurred in the 1970s, especially after the quadrupling of oil revenues in 1973.[75] From the late 1960s western universities became hotbeds of activity on the part of their Iranian students protesting against the shah and the Iranian regime, led by the Confederation of Iranian Students and its later offshoots (see Chapter 12).

Just as the number of girls at schools increased, so there was also a corresponding increase in the number of women attending colleges and universities, and even women students going abroad. This, together with a more open attitude on the part of state and society towards female employment and the introduction of modern means of birth control, led to the growth of female employment in the modern economic sectors and the professions. By 1977 there were a number of women Majlis deputies, senators, ministers and higher civil servants. The law still discriminated against women, however, regarding divorce, inheritance, custody of children and so forth, but there was a growing tendency for women to obtain the right of divorce in their marriage contracts. Furthermore, the Family Protection Law of 1967 made it possible for women to apply to an appropriate court for divorce on certain grounds; and while it did not abolish polygamy, it applied certain restrictions to it.[76] In general, the 1960s and 1970s saw significant advances in the position and status of (mainly upper and middle class) women.

As we have seen, the economy expanded fast thanks to the oil revenues which were received and disbursed by the state: in 1975, oil contributed more than 84 per cent of government revenues, only less than 16 per cent being received from other sources, including direct and indirect taxes, customs, income from government property and so on.[77] The population also grew rapidly in this period, at an average annual rate of about 2.7 per cent in consequence of falling death rates and rising birth rates, both of which were directly or indirectly influenced by rising living standards.

The growing oil revenues, accruing as they did in foreign exchange, made possible the import of modern technology and machinery, leading to high levels of investment in modern manufacturing, services and construction. Yet while modern economic sectors expanded, economic development did not proceed in any long-term and self-sustaining sense. Rising oil revenues by themselves were clearly helpful to growth and expansion; indeed, they were almost indispensable if the high rates of expansion were to be realized. But the strategies pursued by the state were unhelpful to the objectives of long-term economic development.

In particular, the import-substitution strategy chosen for industrial development did not allow the emergence of modern industries and sectors which would have gradually supplemented and eventually replaced oil as the main export earners. Therefore, if at any moment Iran's foreign exchange receipts from the oil sector had drastically declined for reasons of depletion or a collapse in the oil price, modern industrial activity would also have faced serious difficulties. In other words, the economy was permanently dependent on oil, a depletable resource that was not created by domestic means of production and was unpredictable in its earnings. The decline of agriculture made matters worse. Agriculture ceased to be a net export-earning sector because, among other problems noted above, Iran's currency was overvalued, and this made her agricultural products expensive in the international market: throughout this period, the exchange rate kept to between 70 and 75 rials to the American dollar because the shah attached prestige value to a high rate of exchange.

Successful long-term economic development has everywhere depended on the support of a domestic export sector to supply foreign exchange for the import of modern technology and necessary consumer products. This did not happen in the case of Iran, so that, in spite of the high growth rate and considerable expansion of the economy, the country had not achieved self-sustaining development at the time of the revolution, nor had it in 2008, almost thirty years afterwards. Another basic requirement for long-term development is a reasonable saving rate – not less than 12 per cent of the national income – in the domestic productive sectors, to pay for investment and the accumulation of capital. Once again, the non-oil saving rate – that is, the saving rate from non-oil output – was usually negative, with oil revenues being the sole domestic source of investment: it was –1.3 in 1962, –4.2 in 1967 and +2 per cent in 1977.[78] This meant that total consumption was usually higher than the (non-oil) output produced by domestic economic sectors.

Economic growth, although high, was very uneven. Apart from oil, it was services rather than manufacturing that had the highest share in the national output. In 1977 the share of industry (i.e. modern as well as traditional manufacturing, construction and water and power) in non-oil output was 29.7 per cent whereas the share of services was 55.6 per cent; agriculture, on which about half the population depended, claimed the remaining 14.7 per cent. The share of oil and services put together was almost 70 per cent of total national output.[79]

While national income grew in all sectors of the economy, its distribution was highly unequal. This was partly due to the different rates at which the economic sectors grew and partly a consequence of state expenditure policies. In particular, the continuing relative decline of agriculture and the urbanization policies of the state meant that rural society was constantly losing in income and welfare in relation to the towns. In 1977, while the rural population made up about 55 per cent of the total, its share of total consumption was almost one-third of urban consumption.[80] This led to an increasing rate of rural-urban migration, creating problems for urban employment, urban housing and so forth.[81]

The shah's strategy of economic development led to constraints, bottlenecks, inflationary pressures and, above all, the frustration of expectations despite the fact that almost all sections of the population had in absolute terms gained in welfare over the period 1963–77. It thus contributed to social discontent and revolutionary trends. But it was by no means the economic factors alone or even primarily that determined the fundamental causes of the revolution of February 1979; for this was a time when the whole of society, rich as well as poor, high as well as low, burst out in a historic revolt against the state.[82]

CHAPTER 12

The Revolution of February 1979

I too heard the message of the revolution of you people of Iran . . . I guarantee that, in the future, Iranian government will be based on the constitution, social justice and popular will, and free from arbitrary rule, injustice and corruption.
The Shah (November 1978)

THE SHAH BELIEVED THAT he was highly popular with his own people,[1] an illusion due both to the rapid increase in the standard of living and the fact that his system did not allow any criticism, least of all of his policies, to be made by anyone, however highly placed in society. He therefore gauged his relationship with the people from sycophantic reports and stage-managed demonstrations of public support on certain occasions. His greatest tragedy, thus, was that he became a victim of his own propaganda.

THE POLITICS OF ELIMINATION

The politics of elimination had begun with the 1953 coup. Within two years after that coup, the Tudeh Party and the National Front had been eliminated from Iranian politics. The relatively gentle elimination of some of the loyal but independent-minded members of the regime in the 1950s – Zahedi, Amini, Ebtehaj, for example – did not amount to a major change in the nature of the regime although it indicated the trend towards further concentration of power. This was also true of the increasing coolness of the relationship between the shah and the religious establishment from the late 1950s. The power struggles of 1960–3 could have led in one of two directions, resulting in either a less dictatorial government within the existing system (if Amini or the second National Front had got the upper hand) or in absolute and arbitrary government (if the shah had managed to outwit them, as he in fact did). The shah then jettisoned any vestige of independent, though still very loyal, advice by men like Ala, Entezam, Qa'em Maqam al-Molk – indeed the whole of the conservative establishment who had given him support through and after the 1953 coup and who had ties with the religious establishment in Qom, Tehran, Mashahd and elsewhere. It was not land reform alone that led to the deep disenchantment of these groups since the first stage, passed by Amini's land reform law, had not led to any open confrontation, despite being less in the landlords' favour than the second stage. Much more provocative than land reform was the shah's assumption of total power and the elimination of the political establishment from politics in the wake of his White Revolution (see Chapters 10 and 11).

The bazaar and the urban crowd had a far greater role than the landowning class in the revolt of June 1963, even though land reform did not threaten their interests in any way. Even students joined the demonstrations. Indeed, in a published statement Ali Amini, who was no friend of landlords, condemned the way the revolt of June 1963 had been suppressed: this led to a government order confining him to the city of Tehran.

The second National Front had not been an effective movement despite the widespread support that it had enjoyed at the time of its formation in mid-1960, largely as a result of public goodwill towards Mosaddeq. By 1964 it had completely run out of steam and was under heavy criticism from its own members, including the university students' movement and other Popular Movement organizations, notably the Freedom Movement, led by Mehdi Bazargan, and the Socialist League, led by Khalil Maleki. The *coup de grâce* was delivered by Mosaddeq himself, who was drawn into the controversy by the critics; and from his country residence, to which he was forcibly confined by the government, he wrote highly critical letters about the Front's ineptitude. The Front leaders, Allahyar Saleh, Karim Sanjabi, Shapur Bakhtiar and so on, many of whom were leaders of the small but top-heavy Iran Party, resigned en masse and Mosaddeq gave the green light for the formation of the third National Front. This organization eventually came into being in 1965, and was made up of Bazargan's Freedom Movement, Maleki's Socialist League and Daryush Foruhar's People of Iran (*Mellat-e Iran*) and Kazem Sami's Iranian People (*Mardom-e Iran*) parties.[2] Times, however, had changed, and the shah would no longer tolerate so much as the existence of such moderate, open and peaceful organizations, which henceforth could do little more than publish critical leaflets and hold private meetings at their homes. From now on there had to be no word of opposition of any kind.

The Freedom Movement could best be described as a party of Muslim democrats who were in the tradition of Mosaddeq and the Popular Movement with the principal aim of establishing a parliamentary democracy. They were practising Muslims who did not see any basic conflict between modernity and Islam, but their ultimate aim was not the foundation of an Islamist regime. They were led by Mehdi Bazargan, a former dean of the University of Tehran's engineering school and chairman of the provisional board of directors of the National Iranian Oil Company under Mosaddeq; Yadollah Sahabi, a highly respected scientist and professor of the University of Tehran; and Seyyed Mahmud (later Ayatollah) Taleqani, who was destined to become a leading figure of the 1979 revolution with a moderate voice. Together with a few of the Movement's activists, they were tried in military courts on the familiar charge of 'revolting against constitutional monarchy' and condemned to several years of imprisonment. Prophetically, they said in court that they would be the last group to try to engage in a peaceful dialogue with the regime and that it would soon have to face armed struggle.[3]

Khalil Maleki and other leaders of the Socialist League suffered the same fate. Since the Tudeh Party split of 1948 Maleki had provided the most effective intellectual alternative to the Tudeh Party (see Chapter 10). Since the *coup d'état* of 1953 he had been subject to a barrage of criticism by friend and foe alike within the opposition for advocating critical dialogue with the regime. Yet according to the official report of his arrest, he was charged with 'spreading Marxist and collectivist [*eshteraki*] ideas, poisoning the people's minds and taking action against the security of the country'.[4] He and his colleagues were tried and convicted in a military court. Daryush Foruhar, Kazem Sami and others of the Popular Movement parties were likewise put in jail, and the third National Front collapsed even before taking off.

The politics of elimination thus spelt doom for open, liberal and democratic movements, which, beside the Tudeh Party, had occupied the sphere of political opposition since Mosaddeq. In this way the field became wide open for guerrilla campaigns, which began to take shape almost immediately after the onslaught against the democratic parties. Indeed the fiery and idealistic young people – mostly university students and graduates – who began to turn to violent solutions started by putting the blame for failure on democratic leaders themselves for choosing peaceful rather than violent tactics in their political struggles. For example, one of the three young members of the Freedom Movement who formed the nucleus of the Peoples' Mojahedin organization wrote:

The June [1963] uprising was a turning point in Iranian history. It revealed not only the political awareness of the masses but also the political bankruptcy of the old organizations that had tried to resist the regime and its imperial patrons through unarmed struggle ... After June 1963, militants – *irrespective of ideology* – realized that one cannot fight tanks and artillery with bare hands. Thus we had to ask ourselves the question, 'What is to be done?' Our answer was straightforward: 'Armed struggle.'[5]

SOCIETY VERSUS THE STATE

The politics of elimination had a dialectical effect. While it led to the elimination of conservatives, liberals and democrats from politics, it encouraged the development of its opposites, namely beliefs, ideologies and movements which, one way or the other, aimed at the overthrow of the regime and the elimination of the shah himself. Early in 1965, a few young engineering graduates of British universities – former Tudeh sympathizers who had recently turned to Maoism – were arrested on the charge of plotting to assassinate the shah. They were accused of conspiring with the young conscript who had been killed during his unsuccessful attempt on the shah's life in the grounds of Marble Palace. The charge was not true, but papers had been found in the possession of the young men, who were led by Parviz

Nikkhah, showing that they had formed a group for clandestine political activity. Significantly, the would-be assassin had been a former member of the second National Front, and Nikkhah and his associates had been members of the Confederation of Iranian Students (based in Europe and America), which until then had been involved in legal opposition and had not yet begun its campaign for the overthrow of the regime.

At his trial Nikkhah put up a bold and uncompromising defence, and suddenly found himself idolized by young and old, modern and traditional, who, while benefiting from the oil bonanza and economic growth, were becoming increasingly alienated from the state. Thus the historical state–society conflict began to reach its highest peak, paradoxically just as the shah believed that he was enjoying great popularity on account of rising incomes, the White Revolution, Iran's enhanced position as a regional player and greater recognition by the world community. Typically, jokes, anecdotes and rumours began to pour out, castigating the shah, his family and the whole regime in various ways and at different levels.

A rumour started that the young Crown Prince Reza had been born dumb and speechless. When he was shown on television playing with his friends, the public claimed that his speech had been dubbed. The shah's belated but magnificent coronation in 1967 led to rumours that the Queen Mother was dead and her body had been put in a morgue so as not to interrupt the celebrations. And when she was shown on television welcoming the royal family and others to the banquet which she had thrown on the night of the coronation, the rumour-mongers claimed that she had been represented by a mechanical doll to deceive the public. In his speech at the tomb of Cyrus the Great launching the unpopular and extravagant international celebrations marking the 2,500th anniversary of the Iranian empire, the shah famously had said 'Sleep well, Cyrus, for we are awake'. On the following day the joke circulated that a man, upon discovering another man in bed with his wife, had asked him, 'Who the hell are you?' and had been given the reply 'I am Cyrus'. 'Ah', he responded, 'in that case sleep well for we are awake.'

Such negative or hostile rumours and anecdotes in themselves may be quite normal in any society with a high degree of conflict. What made them reveal the degree of society's hostility towards the state at this time in Iran was their frequency, their persistence, their intensity and – most of all – their popularity among all classes of society. By the 1970s hostility had reached such proportions that society would simply not acknowledge any service to it rendered by the state. Far from it; they systematically represented every achievement of the state as another failure. The state was thus held to be inherently incapable of doing any good for society. The growing welfare, higher consumption, greater employment opportunities and rapid expansion of education, which were almost entirely due to direct and indirect state expenditure, were not only taken for granted but were dismissed as insignificant and no more than devices consciously set up for enriching the few and promoting corruption.

Such groundless charges reached their peak on two particular occasions. As noted in the previous chapter, long and protracted negotiations with Britain had led to Iran's recognition of Bahrain in 1971 upon the report of a UN mission that the people of Bahrain wished their country to become fully independent after British withdrawal. Following that, Iranian naval forces occupied the other three islands – the two Tunbs and Abu Musa – to which Iranians also had a historical claim. In the circumstances this was no mean achievement. Yet the Iranian people simply regarded the occupation as a product of a conspiracy between the regime and its 'British masters'. Not only that, they even coined a contemptuous title for the shah, describing him as the Conqueror of Underpants (*Fateh-e Tunban*) since *tunban*, the Persian plural of *tunb*, also meant 'underpants'.

The other occasion, also noted above, was the historic 'oil price revolution', the quadrupling of oil prices in which the shah played a significant role. Seen purely from a material viewpoint, this was a remarkable achievement. But Iranians at large saw little in it other than the shah acting on the order of his 'American masters'.

Iranian intellectuals and the intelligentsia had for decades blamed the state for social and economic underdevelopment and had been highly critical of the regime's association with the religious establishment, demanding a greater degree of secularism. It was a common jibe at the state that 'this country even has to import its needles', pointing to the absence of a modern steel industry in the country. They had been demanding modernization, industrialization, social and economic development and western-style standards of material and cultural consumption. But no sooner did the state begin to break its ties with the religious and traditional forces, invest in modern industry and encourage western culture than the intelligentsia began to turn their positions and shift to the opposite side. It was not development they argued, but dependency on western imperialism, promoted by the 'comprador bourgeoisie' and other capitalists dependent on the West and serving western interests. Land reform had been carried out on the orders of American imperialism, in part to forestall the danger of a socialist revolution and in part to provide a better market for western consumer goods.

Many of the most secular intellectuals – virtually all leftists, and most of them Marxist-Leninists – began to discover the virtues of the county's religious culture and traditions, decry Weststruckness, and advocate cultural authenticity and 'nativism'.[6] The terms *gharbzadegi* and *gharbzadeh* (variously translated, respectively, into 'Westoxication' and 'Westoxicated', 'Weststruckness' and 'Weststruck'), which Jalal Al-e Ahmad had used to attack the cultural and politico-economic influence of the West, became everyday words used by members of virtually all classes to denounce state projects and decisions as well as anyone or anything they did not like. When in 1970 in Paris, an Iranian economist disagreed with an Iranian physicist who argued that British economic problems showed that Britain had turned into an underdeveloped county, she responded by shouting 'Don't be Weststruck!' (*gharbzadeh nashaw!*). It is highly symbolic that the modernist writer and intellectual Sadeq Hedayat was almost forgotten by the 1970s; yet until the early 1960s a correct or incorrect quotation from him was sufficient to put an end to any argument. He had been replaced by Jalal Al-e

Ahmad – or, as all called him, 'Jalal' – who likewise was regarded virtually as infallible until after the revolution.

The history of these developments will be outlined below. The brief note above was intended to emphasize the rising intensity of an all-embracing society–state conflict and the changing places of the state and the intellectuals regarding Europeanism, modernization, tradition and authenticity. For opposition to the state to continue – even to intensify in the face of the change from dictatorship to absolute and arbitrary rule – the intellectuals had to shift from the advocacy of modernization and development to the advocacy of authenticity, religion and a return to self and to see no real conflict between that and the requirements of Marxist-Leninist ideology, which most of them now espoused or sympathized with.[7]

The search for authenticity and critique of the uncritical conversion to Europeanism went back at least to the 1920s and 1930s with the spread of pseudo-modernism among the upper classes and within the state apparatus. In the 1960s, however, it began to make a serious impact on intellectuals and the modern middle classes, mainly because of the shah's highly arbitrary rule, Americanism and Aryanist nationalism in his last phase. But it was helped by regional and international factors as well. The recent policy of peaceful coexistence between the American and Soviet blocs had greatly diminished the hope of third world countries, and not least those of the Middle East, of being 'saved' through communism and the Soviet Union, when even the Syrian and Iraqi dictatorships were clients of the Soviet Union.

The Maoist challenge, though influential among third world leftist elites, could not quite replace the faith that many had put in Soviet liberation. In the Arab countries which had had a background of Islamic movements, such as Egypt's Muslim Brotherhood, the two panaceas of communism and nationalism – both being essentially products of modern European history – quietly but increasingly gave way to Islamic politics, to the extent that by the end of the 1960s the Palestinian issue had become at least as much an Islamic as an Arab question. That is certainly how it was seen by the majority of Iranians. When in 1968, the Iranian national team beat its Israeli counterpart in the football final of the Asian Cup, there were not only spontaneous demonstrations and jubilation in the streets of Tehran, with many taxis and private cars turning on their lights, but, more significantly, many political and anti-Israeli slogans were shouted in the streets. In Iran such regional and international factors shaped not only the attitudes of committed Muslims but also those of the intellectuals and modernisers, who began to trade places with the state, reject westernism and look for authenticity in their own culture, most of all in Islam.

AUTHENTICITY, RETURN TO ROOTS AND SELF

Earlier developments

Almost as soon as the movement for modernization and westernization had begun in the early twentieth century, it had found its critics among various modern as well as traditional middle class writers, scholars, intellectuals and activists. Sheikh Fazlollah Nuri's almost total rejection of modern ideas and institutions, even including the publication of newspapers, did not take root, although his foreboding about the ascendancy of European civilization remained not only among traditionalist clerics and critics of his own cut but also in the midst of modern critics, whether turbaned or not.

Ahmad Kasravi, a former religious scholar and preacher who had left that profession and become a lawyer and a vociferous critic of Shiism and the Shia clerics, was one of the first modern critics of the rise of Europeanism and modernism in Iran. He was a staunch constitutionalist and an anti-clerical campaigner who had nevertheless been influenced by the ideas of Seyyed Jamal al-Din Asadabadi (Afghani) as well as Malkam Khan and Mirza Aqa Khan Kermani (see Chapters 7 and 8) and his friend and contemporary intellectual, Hosein Kazemzadeh, who published the intellectual journal *Iranshahr* in Berlin between 1922 and 1927. His argument was simple and clear: modern technology and secularism had led to irreligion and immorality everywhere, and while Iran should acquire what was necessary for her defence from modern European products it should reject 'Europeanism' (*orupa'i-gari*). His argument resembled those of Jean-Jacques Rousseau, who, simply put, believed that the march of material and scientific progress had led to the decline of morality rather than greater happiness and fulfilment of the human race.

Writing in the early 1930s, Kasravi's discourse was global: there was no basic moral difference between East and West, except that the European machine age had led to moral decline and unhappy living. 'Have modern European inventions added to human happiness?', asked Kasravi. 'Sadly not!' he replied:

In fact, such inventions and the inevitable changes which they have brought with them have caused increasing trouble to human beings ... We ourselves remember well what a peaceful life we used to enjoy until twenty years ago when we still had our own eastern mode of living, and know what difficulties we face now that we have been polluted by western style of living. And this is just the beginning ...'[8]

He continued:

Europe claims that the machine reduces human suffering ... This benefit of the machine cannot be denied. But the damages which these instruments have caused to the world are also numerous. One must say that if the machine has relieved hands a hundred times, it has added to the suffering of hearts a thousand times.[9]

He went on to argue that ever since Europe had begun to invent machines, it had risen against religion: 'lack of faith is now one of the gifts that people of the East bring for their fellow citizens from Europe'[10]:

They will ask, 'What is to be done?' We say, 'we must turn our eyes off Europe and return to our old eastern living. Governments will have to watch Europe and be aware of the intentions of the Europeans about the East so that they can protect their countries. And they should acquire war materials which are newly invented and whatever is useful for government and administration, and enact the laws which are necessary for it. But people must turn their eyes off Europe.'[11]

Kasravi began to publish his critical views in the 1930s. A critique of Iranian Europeanism by Seyyed Fakhreddin Shadman – a Europe-educated intellectual and politician with moderately religious views – was published in the 1940s, condemning Iran's 'conquest' by European civilization, but this was more of a project of 'self-renewal', which involved 'a dialogical engagement with the contemporary European civilization'.[12]

While Kasravi's criticisms of fundamentalist secularism and modernism were based on his own code of ethics and reformed religion, the views of Shia reformers and activists – who were both offended and influenced by Kasravi's ideas – were firmly based on a commitment to conventional Shiism and its traditional leadership. Writing in the 1940s after Reza Shah's abdication, the new religious reformists in Qom, Tehran and elsewhere argued that Islam was fully compatible with modernity, science and technology, so that there was no need for Muslim people to imitate European modes of ethics and social behaviour for the sake of modernization and development (see Chapter 10). This, they emphasized, was the difference between Islam and the Christian churches, which had had to give way to secular modes of belief and conduct in the West. Furthermore, they argued, Islam had all the necessary means at its disposal of forming and running a modern system of government and administration. But they stopped short of claiming that an Islamic government should be run by Shia clerics themselves. Ayatollah Khomeini, who was teaching at the Qom seminary, was involved in this process – not least in the polemics against Kasravi – but did not yet advocate the creation of an Islamist government.

A prominent advocate of the compatibility of Islam and modern scientific achievements was Mehdi Bazargan, a distinguished graduate of the Paris Ecole Polytechnique and professor of the University of Tehran, who not only believed in the possibility and desirability of modern Islamic government but further argued that Islam was fully compatible with democracy. As we have seen, he was a leading supporter of Mohammad Mosaddeq, the leader of the religious as well as Mosaddeqite Freedom Movement, and a leader of the third National Front, which led to his military trial and imprisonment in the 1960s.

Al-e Ahmad
It was against this background that Jalal Al-e Ahmad's *Gharbzadegi* or Weststruckness was published in 1962, although in its authorship, timing and

specific conception it was quite novel and within a few years began to make the kind of impact on the psyche of both intellectuals and the public at large which was briefly noted above. Al-e Ahmad had been born into a clerical family. He visited Najaf at the age of twenty and almost became a clerical scholar, but returned to Tehran and became an Islamic activist for a brief period, then joined Ahmad Kasravi's circle and ended up in the Tudeh Party, aged twenty-three. He was a leading actor in the Tudeh Party split of 1948, later joining the pro-Mosaddeq Toilers and Third Force party, led by Khalil Maleki, but gave up political activism after the 1953 coup. A schoolteacher by profession, he was already a well-known writer and intellectual journalist when he published *Gharbzadegi* at the age of forty.[13]

The book was published a year before the revolt of June 1963, when (especially since the death of Grand Ayatollah Borujerdi in 1961) louder critical voices had begun to be heard from some religious quarters about the social and political situation. It was not just the timing but also the position of the author as a leading secular leftist intellectual well-versed in European culture – a translator of Albert Camus, Jean-Paul Sartre and André Gide – that accounted for its extraordinary success among the religious and secular alike.

Al-e Ahmad began his essay by likening Weststruckness to a disease, an approach already familiar from both religious and secular social criticism which Mohamad Tavakoli-Targhi has described as the medicalization of critical discourse:[14] 'I say that *gharbzadegi* is like a cholera . . . this *gharbzadegi* has two heads. One is the West, the other is ourselves who are Weststruck.'[15] It was precisely Al-e Ahmad's varied social and cultural background and inclination, resulting in different and sometimes contradictory arguments in the essay, which at the same time accounted for its widespread appeal across the social and political spectrum. He both attacked Iranian Weststruckness and cited Nabokov's *Lolita* and Ingmar Bergman's Seventh Seal – both of them recently published and screened – as evidence of similar problems within the West itself, leaving the critical reader (of whom there were not many) to wonder whether he was discussing a specific Iranian affliction or the general problem of alienation in modern society. When I pointed out to him in his 1962 visit to London that in the book he attacked modern technology or the dominance of 'the machine', he denied it completely and said that he was almost in love with his Hillman Minx motor-car. I replied that in that case he must accompany every copy of his book to explain to the reader what he had just told me. It is true that somewhere in the essay, his criticism of 'the machine' had turned out to be the well-worn anti-imperialist argument that third world countries suffered from the fact that they were consumers of modern technology without being its producers:

> *Gharbzadegi* is therefore a characteristic of an era in which we haven't yet obtained machines and don't understand the mysteries of their structure and construction. *Gharbzadegi* is a characteristic of a period of time when we have not become familiar with the prerequisites of the machines – meaning the new

sciences and technology. *Gharbzadegi* is a characteristic of a time in our history when we're compelled to use machines because of the market and economic constraints on us to use machines and because of the incoming and outgoing petroleum. What brought on this era?[16]

Unlike Kasravi, Al-e Ahmad's discourse was neither religious nor moral. And unlike Bazargan, Shariati and Khomeini, he was not advocating one or another form of Islamic or Islamically inspired government. But he did argue that the intellectuals and other modern dissidents had to have the active support of the religious leadership and community to be able to bring about radical political change, which he believed had been the secret of success of both the Constitutional Revolution and Mosaddeq's Popular Movement. He both criticized the secularist, if not anticlerical, trends among the intellectuals and the tendency towards 'quietism' in the mainstream of the religious establishment, arguing prophetically that if they acted in unison they would be able to effect fundamental change in society. And in a following book on the 'services and betrayals of the intellectuals', he applauded Ayatollah Khomeini's leadership of the 1963 revolt and his later activities, which had landed him in exile – although he gently dismissed the Ayatollah's advocacy of *hejab*.[17]

Al-e Ahmad died of a severe heart attack in 1968 at the age of forty-five. Despite an eyewitness account of his death from his wife – the leading woman writer Simin Daneshvar – it was firmly believed and widely propagated that he was killed by SAVAK. Such a rumour was a familiar story, also to be repeated after the revolution. Already, the death of the popular and dissident wrestling champion Gholamreza Takhti had been (incorrectly) attributed to the same source and firmly believed by the public.[18]

Shariati

Ali Shariati (Shari'ati), who also made a deep impact among the young activists, did not share Al-e Ahmad's faith in the religious leadership. Indeed, he almost believed in an Islam and a Shiism without clerics. Although his influence was substantial – to the point that, not quite accurately, he is sometimes described as the ideologue of the Iranian revolution – unlike Al-e Ahmad's he appealed much less to the secularists than to the traditionalists. Shariati's social and intellectual background had certain points in common with Al-e Ahmad's. His grandfather had been a cleric, his father (whom he highly revered) had been a respected teacher of religious values and morals and both he and his father were pro-Mosaddeq activists. On the other hand, he had had no taste for involvement in leftist politics, was not a secular intellectual with important literary and journalistic credentials and was a practising Muslim.

Originally from the village of Mazinan in Khorasan, he was born in 1933. As a youth he became involved in pro-Mosaddeq political activities, for which he was briefly interned on a couple of occasions after the coup. He obtained a bachelor's degree from the University of Mashhad in 1955 before going to the

University of Paris on a state scholarship, where he obtained a doctorate in Persian literature. However, he took advantage of his years in Paris, reading widely in the philosophy of religion and sociology and attending courses on such subjects. He was particularly influenced by Louis Massignon (in Islamic studies), George Gurvitch (in sociology as well as anti-colonialism and human rights), Franz Fanon (in third-worldism and return to roots) and Jean-Paul Sartre (in existentialism). While in Europe, he was also briefly involved with the Confederation of Iranian Students as well as the European organizations of the second National Front and Freedom Movement, run by Iranian students.

Returning to Iran in 1963, he became a university teacher and a popular and charismatic speaker, especially when he joined *Hoseiniyeh-ye Ershad*, a highly popular forum for innovative and unorthodox religious studies and worship in Tehran, which included Mehdi Bazargan and Ayatollah Motahhari (a leading former student and supporter of Khomeini) among its patrons. In and out of jail in the 1970s, in 1976 Shariati finally managed to go to Britain, where he had friends and family; he died in Southampton of a severe heart attack in June 1977. Typically, however, it was widely believed that he had been murdered by SAVAK.[19]

Shariati's works, mainly transcripts of recordings of his talks and lectures, run into tens of volumes. He was a prolific and eclectic thinker in the style of religious reformers and prophets. He argued that Islam could and should be turned into an ideological weapon capable of successfully competing with modern ideologies in order to bring about radical change in Islamic societies. Since the popular ideology in the 1960s and 1970s among young people both in Iran and elsewhere was various strands of Marxism, it is not surprising that while trying to provide an alternative to this ideology Shariati felt impelled to employ its concepts and categories and address the political sentiments arising from them, though in his own fashion. He went so far as to say that 'the socio-economic order of Islam is scientific socialism based on the worship of God'.[20] And he used dialectical analysis to explain the course of human history within a moral and spiritual framework. That is probably why, according to a critic of his works, Shariati was influenced by Marx's social science as opposed to his philosophy and politics.[21] Yet, as his biographer explains:

> As much as Shari'ati presented a contemporary, progressive and socialist version of Islam, he was competing with a well established ideology, also engaged in armed struggle ... The formulation of a radical Islamic ideology, Shariati believed, was the first and most important step towards effecting social change.[22]

The publication of anti-Marxist material under his name in the Tehran press shortly before he left for England may have been an expedient move, as some critics have tended to believe, but there is little in their substance that is contradictory either with his ideas or his politics.[23] In his view, 'Islam, especially Shi'i

Islam, was a radical ideology that could outdo Marxism in championing revolution and the class struggle as well as in opposing feudalism, capitalism, and
imperialism'.[24]

It was not so much Shariati's ideological analysis as his simple discourse on
Islam, society and social change which was most effective in attracting young
men and women to his cause. Most of them were born into traditional religious
families; they were influenced by the modern secular environment in Iran and
elsewhere and were trying to hold on to their religious sentiments while at the
same time pursuing a modern, progressive line of thought and action. He casti-
gated conservative religious leaders, spoke of 'two different Islams' and distinguished between Alid Shiism (*Tashayyo'-e Alavi*) and Safavid Shiism (*Tashayyo'-e
Safavi*), identifying the latter with the established Shiism of his time, which he
held to be false and reactionary.[25]

Thus it was that he contrasted his version of revolutionary Islam to the Islam
of Shia clerics. On the other hand, and contrary to the prevailing official nationalism which emphasized Iran's pre-Islamic past, 'return to the self' meant
returning to pure Shia and Islamic roots:

> When we say 'return to one's roots', we are really saying return to one's cultural
> roots which in the case of Iran is not a return to pre-Islamic Iran, by which the
> masses of Iranians are not moved. Consequently, for us to return to our roots
> means not a rediscovery of pre-Islamic Iran but to a return to our Islamic
> roots.[26]

In sum, Shariati advocated a revolutionary Islam with a modern face which
involved a return to an idealized early Shia culture and tradition – a Shiism
virtually without the ulama – but which was influenced by European intellectual
and political developments of his time. Above all, it was his polemical, adver-
sarial and action-orientated style which most influenced his young followers. He
said, for example, in one of his innumerable addresses:

> I . . . am expecting . . . a revolution in which I must play a part; a revolution
> which does not come about with prayers . . . but with a banner and a sword,
> with a holy war involving all responsible believers. I believe that this movement
> shall naturally triumph.[27]

Khomeini

By the time religious and Islamist views and sentiments began to spread in the late
1960s and 1970s, Ayatollah Ruhollah Khomeini had already been established as a
leading national figure in opposition to the shah's regime (see Chapter 10).
Born in 1900 to a middle-class clerical family, he was orphaned as a child, went
to a traditional school in his native Khomein (about 300 kilometres south of
Tehran) and later studied in Arak and Qom, becoming a *mojtahed* and teacher
in the Qom seminary. He was a serious and principled but flexible person

whom time and circumstance were to turn into an austere patriarchal figure, but one who always spoke and acted as he thought was expedient. Time was to show that he would be prepared to say and do whatever he believed to be in the interest of Islam, regardless of its cost to himself and others.

He not only taught traditional subjects such as Islamic law and jurisprudence but also Islamic philosophy and mysticism, the teaching of which was not approved by the more orthodox seminarians.[28] He was not overtly active in politics when the Qom seminary was under the leadership of the 'quietist' *maraje'* Hajj Sheikh Abdlokarim Ha'eri and Grand Aytollah Borujerdi. But there is evidence that even in the 1940s he was not a quietist himself and was quite conscious of the importance of the political dimension for the religious leadership and community. Rather like some of the religious reformists of the 1940s (mentioned above and in Chapter 10), his critique of secularism had a modern ring to it. This is particularly evident from his *Kashf al-Asrar* (Discovering the Secrets, 1943), a critique of a tract by a critical disciple of Ahmad Kasravi, where, although not yet advocating direct rule by the ulama, he maintained that Islam was quite capable of running a modern state.[29]

From his exile in Najaf, Khomeini maintained close contact with his devoted former students such as Morteza (later, Ayatollah) Motahhari and Hosein'ali (now Grand Ayatollah) Montazeri as well as a growing number of other disciples and devotees in Iran, answering their letters and religious and political questions and encouraging them to struggle against the regime however they could.

As early as April 1967, Khomeini addressed a highly critical letter to Prime Minister Hoveyda which was distributed fairly widely among his followers by hand. He accused Hoveyda of creating 'the worst tyrannical and arbitrary government', acting against Islam and keeping the country 'in a state of backwardness'. 'Do you deny the abominations and uncivilized acts you have committed in preparing for the twenty-five hundredth anniversary [of the Iranian empire] celebrations?' he asked. The letter was concluded by an appeal to the United Nations and humanitarian groups, and ended with the warning that 'perhaps . . . the ruling class and tyrannical regime will come to their senses before it is too late.'[30]

While it was such letters, contacts and messages which had the strongest influence among Khomeini's disciples and well-wishers in Iran, what made the profoundest impact in the long run both on Iranian politics and on Shiism was Khomeini's theory of *Velayat-e Faqih* or Guardianship of Jurisconsult, which he formulated in his years of exile in Najaf. The traditional Shia theory of the state maintained that true and legitimate government belonged to the imam alone, holding all worldly government as unjust and based on usurpation. Not only the quietists but even the activists – such as Sheikh Fazlollah Nuri and the 1940s advocates of Islamic government – believed that the ulama should stay away from direct involvement in government. Ultimate salvation was in the advent of the Mahdi (Mehdi), Imam of the Time and Guardian of the Age, in whose absence the ulama were bound to teach and guide the faithful, and the whole of the Shia community had to wait and pray for his rise to rid the world of corruption and injustice.

Against this background, Ayatollah Khomeini's new theory was nothing short of revolutionary, in politics as well as religion. He argued that, in the absence of the imam, there could and should be Islamic government led by the ulama, just as the Prophet had ruled the Islamic community of his own time.[31] It was clear that this was not just Islamic government within the existing political framework but a novel institution:

> Islamic government does not correspond to any of the existing forms of government. For example, it is not a tyranny, where the head of state can deal arbitrarily with the property and lives of the people ... putting to death anyone he wishes, and enriching anyone he wishes by granting landed estates and distributing the property and holdings of the people ... Islamic government is neither tyrannical nor absolute, but constitutional.

He emphasized, however, that Islamic government was 'not constitutional in the current sense of the word, that is, based on the approval of laws in accordance with the opinion of the majority. It is constitutional in the sense that the rulers are subject to a certain set of conditions that are set forth in the Noble Qur'an and the Sunna [traditions] of the Most Noble Messenger.'[32]

Identifying the system of monarchy and *nezam-e shahanshahi* with arbitrary rule, he went on to add:

> Islamic government is not a form of monarchy, especially not an imperial system. In that type of government, the rulers are empowered over the property and persons of those they rule and may dispose of them entirely as they wish. Islam has not the slightest connection with this form and method of government.[33]

On the other hand, sovereignty in an Islamic state belongs to God, and Islamic law has absolute dominion over people and government alike:

> Islamic government is a government of law. In this form of government, sovereignty belongs to God alone and law is His decree and command. The law of Islam, divine command, has absolute authority over all individuals and Islamic government.[34]

Khomeini further argued that the view that the governmental powers of the Prophet and the imams were greater than those of the *faqih* (Islamic jurisprudence) is false. Their superiority with respect to spiritual matters does not confer increased governmental powers, and the *faqih* has the same powers and authority as them in matters of government:[35]

Now that we are in the time of the Occultation of the Imam . . . it is necessary that the ordinance of Islam relating to government be preserved and maintained, and that anarchy be prevented. Therefore, the establishment of [Islamic] government is still a necessity.[36]

Addressing the ulama, he said that it was their most important duty to preserve Islam, more important even than prayer and fasting. It is for the sake of fulfilling this duty that 'blood must sometimes be shed'. To be true successors to the Prophet, it was not enough to teach Islam to the people: 'Do not say "we will wait until the coming of the Imam of the Age". Would you consider postponing your prayer until the coming of the Imam?'[37]

Islamic government could only be brought about by taking direct action. Here the message goes well beyond the Shiite world and extends to the whole world of Islam:

In order to attain the unity and freedom of the Islamic peoples we must overthrow the oppressive governments installed by the imperialists and bring into existence an Islamic government of justice that will be in the service of the people.[38]

This manifesto was little known outside the Ayatollah's circle of disciples before the revolution. As noted, however, it both advocated revolution and Islamist government boldly and in an open and unambiguous way.

Khomeini's followers in Iran were active in seminaries, mosques, Islamic societies, Koran studies groups and, more widely, bazaars and other traditional business communities. One of the early Islamist political organizations was the Coalition of Islamist Organizations (*Hey'at-ha-ye Mo'talefeh-ye Eslami*), some of whose members and activists later became prominent figures in the Islamic Republic. Some clerical followers of Khomeini, such as Ayatollah Motahhari, were engaged in teaching and publications and in the proceedings of the aforementioned *Hoseiniyeh-ye Ershad* – an innovative place of congregation and discussion though not an exclusively Islamist haunt, its outlook being closer to the ideas of Bazargan's Freedom Movement. Others of Khomeini's clerical followers, such as Ayatollah Montazeri, Ali Akbar (now Ayatollah) Hashemi Rafsanjani and Seyyed Ali (now Grand Ayatollah) Khamenei, while teaching and preaching as well, were more militant and often found themselves in jail.

Two lower ulama made a significant impact in totally different ways, one after the other, in 1970. One of them, Seyyed Mohammad Reza Sa'idi, was a devotee of Khomeini and an angry and militant preacher in a traditional quarter of Tehran. He and his congregation had been under SAVAK surveillance for some time. But it was his death in a SAVAK prison which made a significant political impact on the opponents of the regime and enhanced the prestige of the Islamist movement. The opposition and human rights activists both in Iran and the West were convinced that he had died under torture, while SAVAK's internal report maintained that he had committed suicide.[39]

The other lower cleric's significant religious and political impact was made not by militant action but by radical thought. As a sign of leftist and religious opposition drawing close to each other, not just in practice but in some of their slogans and terminology, a saying attributed to Imam Hosein to the effect that life is none other than having principles and fighting for them (*Inn al-hayat 'aqidatun wa jihad*) was already widespread in the articles and public statements of both religious and leftist militants. It was in the atmosphere of rising Islamist and leftist militancy against the background of revolutionary ideas and events in various parts of the world that the religious scholar Salehi Najafabadi argued that, far from it being a merely preordained event, Hosein's historic martyrdom in Karbala had been the result of the imam's revolutionary decision to rise up against an illegitimate and unjust regime. He wrote in abstract summary:

> Apart from its divine and celestial aspect, the action of the Lord of the Martyrs, God's peace be upon him, was also necessary and inevitable from the standpoint of rational traditions and laws of society, and even if we put aside the aspect of his imamate, as an experienced and intelligent politician his movement would also be regarded as the wisest and most realistic movement . . . And as Imam Hosein himself said 'In this struggle my action will be your model.' Therefore Muslims must understand and follow his practical agenda.[40]

This interpretation of Karbala offended the traditionalist ulama mainly for professional reasons, although some of the refutations published against it might also have been prompted by conservative political motives. It was an invitation to revolutionary action whose implications were not lost on the militant, including leftist, opposition. Thus Khosrow Golesorkhi, the bold and defiant Marxist-Leninist journalist and poet who was killed by firing squad in 1974 after a military trial, proclaimed in the court:

> The life of Mawla Hoseyn is an example of our present days when, risking our life for the dispossessed of our country, we are tried in this court. He was in a minority while Yazid had the royal court, the armies . . . [Hoseyn] resisted and was martyred . . . The [path] that nations have followed and continue to follow is the way of Mawla Hoseyn. It is in this way that, in a Marxist society, real Islam can be justified as a superstructure, and we too approve of such an Islam, the Islam of Mawla Hoseyn and Mawla Ali.[41]

No wonder that Marxist-Leninists and Islamists joined in united action against the Pahlavi regime before their virtually inevitable clash after the revolution.

LEFTIST MOVEMENTS AND IDEAS

The most important causes of discontent, opposition and militancy were domestic, even in the case of those who literally believed that the shah was little more than an agent of the United States, receiving his daily orders and acting accordingly. Nevertheless, international revolutionary movements and ideas had a significant impact, not just in spreading hopes and aspirations for political change but also in hardening attitudes and influencing their forms and intensity. In 1949 the peasant revolution in China, then an underdeveloped country, had gained power. This was followed by the officially inspired Cultural Revolution of the 1960s. In the late 1950s Nasserism had triumphantly defied British and French power. The Algerians won their war of independence from France in 1962. The Cuban revolution succeeded in 1959 through open guerrilla warfare, and quickly led to confrontation with the United States. At about the same time, America began to commit itself to a long and painful war in Vietnam, which it effectively lost in 1975. The six-day war of 1967 between Israel and its Arab neighbours led to the rise of a new militancy among the Palestinian people, and greatly enhanced the popularity of their cause among Iranians. At the same time, guerrilla campaigns were going on in Latin America, when, after his death in action in 1967, Ernesto Che Guevara became a great icon for radical youth the world over, so much so that a young Iranian Muslim revolutionary compared him to Imam Hosein. All this had a large impact on the post-war generation of western Europe and America, leading to the revolt of French students in May 1968 and the rebellion of young Americans in the late 1960s and 1970s, all of which in turn enticed and encouraged young Iranians to seek and support revolutionary ideas and actions.

On the other hand, Soviet suppression of the Hungarian revolution in 1956 and the Warsaw Pact invasion of Czechoslovakia and overthrow of its legitimate and popular government in 1968 hardly drew any negative responses from ordinary, and almost none from radical, Iranians. The patent absence of individual liberties and the considerably lower standards of living in the Soviet bloc compared to the West were dismissed as western propaganda, not just by Marxist-Leninists but by the large majority of the political public. The simple reason was that, as in the other cases noted above, America was held responsible for the shah's regime. It would have been the other way around had Iran been in the Soviet camp. The Soviet Union lost much of its popularity in Iran in the 1960s when it established normal relations with the Iranian regime, and this is what happened also to China in the 1970s. But their loss of popularity was no gain for America, which was still held totally responsible for the absolute and arbitrary government in Iran.

In the 1960s and much of the 1970s the Iranian left, including the Muslim leftist Mojahedin, was in the forefront of publicity against the Iranian regime. But, at least in hindsight, there was a clear difference between the leftist movements in the country and those in the West: the Diasporic movements were dominated by Maoism and third-worldism, whereas domestic organizations largely held to the classical Marxist-Leninist approaches and attitudes. Nevertheless, they were both anti-shah and in favour of the dictatorship of the proletariat.

By then, the Tudeh Party had lost credibility except among some of its diehard supporters, a number of whom even worked with SAVAK while they were still emotionally attached to the Party and Russia. The most immediate reason for this was the Soviet rapprochement with Iran, which the party had little choice but to applaud with enthusiasm. At the same time, the Sino-Soviet dispute broke out into the open, offering the Maoist alternative to those of its members – mainly Iranian students in the West – to remain revolutionary Marxist-Leninists without having to support the new Iranian-Soviet friendship. In 1962 internal Tudeh Party disputes began in earnest in eastern Europe, with a few leading figures such as Ahmad Qasemi displaying Stalinist-Maoist tendencies while Khrushchev still ruled in Russia. At the same time, many of the young party members and fellow travellers in western Europe, led by able student activists such as Parviz Nikkhah, began to question the party leadership and contact the Chinese Communist Party. The ground was ready when, as a result of Nikkhah's arrest in Tehran and becoming a political icon through his defiant defence in the military court, the Tudeh Party Maoists broke away and launched the Revolutionary Organization of the Tudeh Party of Iran (*Sazman-e Enqelabi-ye Hezb-e Tudeh-ye Iran*).

This was early 1965. Almost at the same time the second National Front suffered its death agony in Iran and efforts were being made to launch the third National Front; but, as noted above, this was quickly suppressed by the regime inside Iran. Nor did it enjoy a wide base in the West, partly because most of the erstwhile Front supporters there did not belong to the parties of which it was made and partly because – given the world revolutionary ethos of the time described above – it had now become fashionable to become Marxist. Here again developments were facilitated by the rising international Maoist movement: it was possible to be Marxist-Leninist, anti-Tudeh and anti-Soviet and love Mosaddeq too, all at the same time. Both the emerging National Front Maoists and Tudeh revolutionary Maoists, though not in the same organizations, found their home and main base of activity in the Confederation of Iranian Students.

The rise of Iranian students' societies in European countries in the 1950s had led to the creation of the Confederation of Iranian Students in Europe in 1959. In its second annual conference, which took place in Paris in 1961, the Iranian students' body in America also joined the movement, which changed its name to the Worldwide Confederation of Iranian Students. At the same time as the CIS was created in Paris, there was a rift in the movement, since the Tudeh students felt that they would be in a permanent minority vis-à-vis the National Front and other pro-Mosaddeq organizations. The rift was patched up in the 1962 conference in Lausanne. By the time the fourth conference was held in London in December 1963, the White Revolution and the revolt of June 1963 had taken place, highly radicalizing the political atmosphere both inside and outside Iran. Thus from 1964 the Confederation, which had been mainly a students' union with a significant interest in political matters, began to function almost as a political organization. Not long afterwards came the Maoist split from the Tudeh

Party and the collapse of the second National Front, leading to the emergence of National Front Maoists, both of which, as we have seen, made the Confederation their main home. Soon the Confederation became an ideological organization: by the early 1970s, when it was banned by the Iranian government, it was virtually unknown for anyone to be a member of the Confederation without being a professed Marxist-Leninist of one denomination or another. It broke up into different organizations in the 1970s but all of them remained ideologically Marxist-Leninist.[42]

The Confederation was highly active and well organized. Its activities ranged from organizing talks, conferences, press reports and interviews, and publications to marches, demonstrations, sit-ins and even, occasionally, occupations of Iranian consulates in western countries. They contacted political parties, students' unions and human rights organizations in their host countries across Europe and the United States, feeding them with news of political activities, military trials, tortures and other human rights abuses and soliciting from them material as well as social and organizational support. Their publicity campaigns were highly influential in encouraging the concern and intervention of effective human rights groups such as Amnesty International, the Bertrand Russell Peace Foundation, Jean-Paul Sartre's human rights group and so on in matters regarding the absence of political liberties and human rights abuses in Iran. Further than that, they provided the background of adverse publicity for the regime among the western media – which was far from helped by the shah's own interviews with such leading journalists as Oriana Fallaci, Eric Rouleau of *Le Monde* and Philip Short of the BBC – ready to be exploited once the Iranian public took to the streets in 1977: he told Fallaci in 1976 that women were not equal in ability to men and had 'produced nothing great, nothing!'[43] He attacked Jean-Paul Sartre personally in an interview with Rouleau in 1968 because of his opposition to the celebrations of the 2,500th anniversary of the Iranian empire. He told Philip Short in an interview for the peak BBC programme *Panorama* that a person's guilt was proven when he was caught 'red-handed'.[44]

In the meantime, two armed guerrilla movements had emerged inside Iran: the People's Mojahedin (*Mojahedin-e Khalq*) and the People's Fada'is (*Fada'iyan-e Khalq*). The Mojahedin came into existence first in the mid-1960s. Their original founders were three young university graduates who had been active student members of Bazargan's Freedom Movement, led by Mohammad Hanifnezhad. After the arrest and military trial of their leaders, and especially in consequence of the military suppression of the revolt of June 1963, they, like some other young dissidents in Iran and the West, reached the view that the only avenue open to them was armed struggle.

However, they were raided by SAVAK and almost all their leaders and members were arrested in 1971, before they had taken any effective action. They had spent the first five years of their clandestine activity largely in theoretical and organizational preparation, trying to square their Muslim and pro-Mosaddeq background with modern revolutionary ideas and methods, which almost invariably involved some kind of Marxist analysis. The regime described them as Islamic Marxists, which may have been an exaggeration, but their outlook did combine faith in Islam with analytical and ideological tools borrowed from Marxist ideas. It was only after their mass arrest in 1971, resulting in the execution of many of their leaders, that the remaining body went into guerrilla action, mainly resorting to assassination. In fact, the Mojahedin have claimed that they were 'forced into action ... against their will and before they were ready' as a result of the Siyahkal operation and the emergence of the Fada'i guerrillas in 1971.[45] In 1975 ideological conflict led to internal disputes and assassinations when many if not most of the Mojahedin outside prison became fully fledged Marxist-Leninists and later renamed themselves as *Peykar bara-ye Azadi-ye Tabaqeh-ye Kargar-e Iran* (Struggle for the Liberation of the Iranian Working Class). In 1979 Mas'ud Rajavi, a survivor of the early arrests, was released from jail to assume the leadership of the Mojahedin.[46]

The Fada'i guerrillas organization was formed in 1971 and became the main movement for armed struggle in the 1970s. In February 1971 the *Jangal*, or 'Forest', guerrilla group attacked a gendarmerie post in Siyahkal, in the forested northern province of Gilan, which led to the arrest, trial and execution of most of those involved. Shortly afterwards the Fada'i guerrilla organization was launched under the leadership of Mas'ud Ahmadzadeh and Amir Praviz Puyan. It included the remnants of a group led by Bizhan Jazani who by then had been in jail for three years. Unlike most of the Diasporic Iranian Marxist-Leninists, they were not Maoist or third-worldist. Their basic ideological framework was similar to that of the Tudeh Party. They were pro-Soviet but independent, and although critical of the Tudeh Party's past leadership, they nevertheless considered it as the original Marxist-Leninist organization of Iran.[47] This was largely the background to the ideas of Jazani, who, despite differences on some theoretical details, became a main theorist of the Fada'i guerrillas and – posthumously – their chief ideological mentor.

In retrospect Bizhan Jazani was probably the most influential Iranian Marxist-Leninist theorist of his time, especially as his ideas were developed before Maoism and leftist third-worldism had taken root among Iranian students and activists outside Iran. The other principal Marxist theorist of the time was the anti-Soviet and anti-Lenin Mostafa Shoa'iyan, but his ideas did not enjoy widespread support before he died in a street battle with SAVAK officers in 1976.[48]

Jazani was born in 1937. His father was a gendarmerie officer who had fought in the Azerbaijan autonomous government's army and upon its collapse in 1946 had fled to the Soviet Union (see Chapter 11). His mother and uncles were all members of the Tudeh Party, and he became a member of the Tudeh youth organization as early as the age of ten. He was a student and (a pro-Tudeh) second National Front activist in the early 1960s, when he served several short jail sentences. Graduating in philosophy with distinction, he founded a successful advertising firm with friends and relatives, while at the same time organizing a secret organization with aspirations to launching an armed struggle. In 1968 he was arrested together with a few of his associates, notably Hasan Zia-Zarifi, without yet having taken any action, and since he defended himself boldly and with conviction, he was condemned by a military court to fifteen years' imprisonment.[49] In 1975 Jazani, Zia-Zarifi and seven other prisoners, five of them Marxist-Leninist Fada'is and two Mojaheds, were killed by SAVAK officers in jail in an attempt to cow the guerrilla activists at large.[50] In 1977 the Fada'i Guerrilla Organization declared that thenceforth their activities would be based on Jazani's teachings.[51]

Jazani was pro-Soviet but independent. Although he was critical of the Tudeh leadership, he described fundamental critics of Russia and the Tudeh Party such as Khalil Maleki as 'American Marxists', who wished to substitute the 'comprador bourgeoisie' and American imperialism for feudalism and British imperialism.[52] According to Jazani, in the period 1953–63 an alliance of the feudal and comprador classes had been in power, the latter of which had absorbed and overcome the national bourgeoisie. After the shah's White Revolution, the compradors had outmanoeuvred the feudal class, and Iran's regime had turned into a 'dependent capitalist system' sustained with the support of American imperialism. There were five different comprador groups, he asserted: commercial, industrial, financial, agrarian and bureaucratic.[53]

Notwithstanding such contrived, and almost mandatory, class analyses, Jazani was essentially a leftist activist who thought armed struggle was necessitated by the absence of alternative avenues for political action. Yet, unlike Ahmadzadeh, his main theoretical rival among Marxist-Leninist guerrillas, he did not regard the shah as merely an American puppet and did not believe that a general revolutionary situation existed in Iran in the early 1970s requiring a general armed uprising.

It would be apt to close this section with a note on Samad Behrangi. A leftist literary figure who became an idol of all the young – but particularly Marxist-Leninist – revolutionaries, he was essentially a young writer of children's stories, though he was also an essayist and translator from Persian into Azeri Turkic. Posthumously dubbed the Hans Christian Andersen of Iran, Behrangi's largest claim to fame was his brilliant children's tale 'The Little Black Fish', the story of the brave and determined little fish which made its way from its stream to the sea by taking great risks, a story which was given a revolutionary interpretation after his untimely death. An Azerbaijani himself, when his body was washed up in the River Aras in 1967, everyone was convinced that he had been drowned by SAVAK, though in fact this was not the case. He thus became the second of the four popular figures of the 1960s and 1970s: the wrestling champion Gholamreza Takhti, Behrangi, Jalal Al-e Ahmad and Ali Shariati, who were universally believed to have been martyred in the cause of freedom by the regime. It is important to note that of these, Takhti was a Mosaddeqite, Al-e Ahmad a leading secular intellectual and close friend of Khalil Maleki, Behrangi a Marxist writer and Shariati an ideologue of the Islamic revolution – a spectrum which represented the opposition of the various social classes to the state.

GENERAL DISCONTENT

The revolution had many long- and short-term causes, although it would not have turned into the revolt of the whole of society against the state had the state enjoyed a reasonable amount of legitimacy and social base among some (at least the propertied and/or modern and secular) social classes.

A major consequence of high, sustained and steady economic growth rates generated by increasing oil revenues was the rise of new social classes amid a high population growth rate. These new classes were from the lower and traditional strata of society. They would not have grown so rapidly in number and social significance had it not been for the continuing general rise in the standard of living. They were made up of small merchants and traders, the lower urban middle classes, recent migrants from smaller towns into the capital and other larger cities and the better-off peasants, both those still in their villages and those who had migrated to the towns. Besides the expansion of their population, many or most of them began to take part and participate in the modern social processes, which they had not done before. They sent their children to secondary school, and a growing number found their way to university and, in some cases, obtained state scholarships for further education in the West.

Yet they not only lacked a sense of obligation and gratitude to the state but were also discontented and rebellious on many grounds. They, like the rest of society, including the clientele of the state, believed that the rise in their standard of living was simply due to the growth of the oil revenues, for which they did not give any credit to the state. On the contrary, they pointed to the much greater rise in the fortunes of the state's clientele, the widening gap between the wealth and luxury consumption of the state and the small minority compared with the large majority, the existence of absolute poverty and growing numbers of people living below the poverty line as evidence of injustice and corruption.

They were also alienated from the state and modern Iranian society on cultural and religious grounds. Unlike in the latter part of Reza Shah's rule, the state did not suppress religious activities such as the holding of passion plays and congregations for the martyrs of Karbala and did not ban the wearing of *hejab*. On the other hand, the growth of such things as bars, night clubs and cabarets and the sartorial habits of the growing number of modern women wearing mini-skirts and the like was an affront to the sensibilities of the religious and traditional classes, both men and women. Most modern hotels and restaurants would not admit women wearing a chador. Further, television, which large numbers of people could now afford, mostly represented western values, standards and habits in its programmes and shows. This led to an increasing number of clerics advising their followers that it was sinful to watch television.

There thus developed a large community of traditional classes with good or reasonable standards of living, a modern education and a new sense of social confidence which regarded the state as alien and oppressive. And large numbers of their young people adopted revolutionary attitudes, joining, supporting or at least applauding guerrilla activities and any other action against the regime. They believed, as did virtually all other opposition groups, that the regime was in the pocket of the West, and therefore extended their anger against it to western countries, especially America, which was the state's strongest ally and had a considerable presence in the country.

However, the state's biggest failure from the point of view of its own interest was that it alienated the modern social classes as well, at least some of which should have formed its social base. That would have been the case if the regime had been a dictatorship instead of a one-person rule (*estebdad*) since it would have involved the participation of a political establishment in the running of the country, with the dual advantage of the regime benefiting from critical discussion and advice and the opposition not being uniform and comprehensive. Apart from that, the opposition would have faced not just one person but a whole spectrum of ruling people who, when the chips were down, would have rallied round and defended the regime in their own interest.

Increasingly, not only the traditional propertied classes or the growing middle class professionals and middle-income groups but even the modern propertied classes, who owed much of their fortunes to oil and the state, were alienated from the regime. They did not have any independent economic and political power and were critical of some of the economic policies of the state without there being a forum or channel for airing their views. No criticism of the regime, however mild and well-intentioned, would be tolerated, even if expressed in private. This was the greatest single grievance of intellectuals, writers, poets and journalists against the regime. Not only was censorship strong but even verbal criticism, if reported, would also be duly punished.

The oil revenue explosion of 1973–4 ironically had highly negative consequences for the regime. It greatly enhanced its sense of self-confidence and led to greater repression and a more arrogant attitude and behaviour towards the public. More than that, the economic consequences of the new oil bonanza and the political decisions to which it led resulted in widespread public indignation. The quadrupling of oil prices almost immediately led to a massive increase in public expenditure, including the doubling of the expenditure estimates for the fifth economic plan. As both state and private incomes rose sharply, so did consumption and investment expenditure, fuelling demand-push inflation. At the same time, since the increase in demand for many products – ranging from fresh meat to cement – could not be supplied by domestic sources, supply shortages developed in the midst of financial plenty. Imports could not relieve the situation adequately partly because of the delivery time involved, partly because in some cases, such as the supply of fresh local meat, imports were out of the question but mainly because of limits to storage and transport facilities, which could only be extended in the long term.

One area in which rising inflation was deeply felt far and wide was housing, especially in Tehran and the provincial capitals. Rapidly rising prices affected virtually all but a very small minority, albeit at different levels. Many of those with moderate amounts of excess liquidity put their money into urban land and property, which added to the market pressures for housing and inflated property prices. On the other hand, higher incomes increased the demand for housing, further increasing prices and rents, which particularly hit the young middle classes. To relieve the situation, the government issued orders that empty accommodation must be let on pain of confiscation; this did not happen in practice but it spread fear and anger among property owners. By 1977, rumours circulated that the next principle of the White Revolution to be announced soon would nationalize urban property. This was probably false, but it was feared by many middle-class people to be true, adding to their sense of insecurity.

However, the worst element of the housing situation was the rapid growth of shanty towns and 'out-of-bounds' housing estates. As in many other third world countries, the shanty towns were populated by the lowest marginal strata of the urban community, many being recent immigrants from rural areas. But from a political point of view, the 'out-of-bounds' estates were far more damaging. These were poor and humble dwellings built by their owners outside the city's official boundaries (*kharej az mahdudeh*), established precisely in order to contain the rapid expansion of poor districts in towns. Their occupants were often people with regular employment, such as taxi drivers, who could not afford dwellings in the existing slums. Being outside the city boundaries meant that water, electricity and other services were not extended to these estates. Yet many of them somehow managed to hold out, and this led to the policy of sending demolition workers to actually raze the dwellings to the ground, thus turning them into battlegrounds.[54]

The general rise in prices had other consequences, spreading anger among important social classes such as traders, merchants and business people. While, as noted, excessive state spending was the principal cause of rising inflation, the state blamed inflation on hoarding and profiteering on the part of producers, wholesalers and retailers. The prices of a number of commodities were reduced by fiat. A public campaign was launched against 'profiteering' (*geranforushi*) involving thousands of young men as agents of the official Rastakhiz Party who were sent to the bazaars, shops and other business premises to find the culprits and take swift administrative measures against them. Hundreds of merchants and traders, including one or two leading businessmen, were arrested. Others were fined. Shops were closed down and trading licences were cancelled. This did little to relieve inflationary pressures, but it spread and intensified anger among the business community, both traditional and modern. Nor did it satisfy the ordinary public, who came to see merchants and businessmen as scapegoats for the state's arbitrary policies.[55]

Given the state and scale of discontent among the various classes and communities of society briefly described above, it is not surprising that the revolution proved to be so widespread when it came. Still, the protest movement would not necessarily have resulted in a full-scale revolution had the state responded to its earlier stages differently.

THE PROTEST MOVEMENT

It is always difficult to discover with certainty the origins of any revolution. The origin of the February 1979 Revolution is sometimes put as far back as the *coup d'état* of August 1953. But in fact many things might or might not have happened between 1953 and 1979 which could have prevented the revolution, the larger factors being the revolt of June 1963, the rise of the shah's arbitrary rule and the quadrupling of oil prices in 1973–4, which further enhanced the arbitrary power of the state and led to misguided economic policies. Thus the long-term origins of the revolution may be said to go back to the 1960s, when the upper and modern middle classes were eliminated from politics; and the short-term factors stemmed from the explosion of oil revenues, with the result that virtually the whole of society became alienated from the state.

Ironically, it was President Carter's election in November 1976 and the Iranian regime's quick response to it which helped to launch the protest movement. As we have seen, for a decade already evidence of severe human rights violations – especially torture in SAVAK prisons, arbitrary arrest and imprisonment and the non-judicial nature of proceedings in the military courts – had been slowly building up in the reports of such important western human rights organizations as Amnesty International as well as the press and media. The murder in jail of the Jazani group in 1975 resulted in intense adverse publicity against the regime. The arrest and torture of prominent intellectuals – such as the leading author and playwright Gholamhosein Saedi – known in the West had also tarnished the regime's reputation among liberal groups there.[56]

Amnesty's first major report on Iran, which closely documented widespread legal violations and human rights abuses, was published in the same month that Jimmy Carter was elected president.[57] In February 1976 a detailed article on torture in Iran appeared in the London-based *Index on Censorship*; and through the reproduction of excerpts from this in the *New York Times*, the article had a significant impact on wider political circles in America. A major foreign policy point of Carter's campaign was his emphasis on human rights. The main targets were the Soviet Union and other socialist countries but also some Latin American countries, such as Nicaragua, whose illiberal regimes had been traditionally backed by US administrations. However, Carter did not pass any public comments on the human rights situation in Iran, either then or when he became president. The shah, on the other, hand, did not have good memories of Democratic presidents such as Kennedy and – to a lesser extent – Johnson and generally regarded Democratic administrations as being critical of his regime.

The inauguration of President Kennedy in 1961 had prompted the shah to allow for a certain amount of liberalization: this was followed by the power struggles of 1960–3, ending with his assumption of total power (see Chapter 10). His immediate response to Carter was similar. Early in 1977 he announced the end of torture in Iran, and by August of that year he had pardoned 357 political prisoners, allowed the International Committee of the Red Cross to visit Iranian jails and ordered changes in the procedures of military courts, including the right of civilian defendants to choose civilian lawyers.[58] And although censorship of the press was still very strong, it became possible to publish on certain subjects, for example, on the difficulties faced by Iranian agriculture.

The opposition saw all this as a sign of the shah's weakness, almost literally believing that he had been ordered by Carter to relax his regime, though their analyses of the possible causes were varied and typically fanciful. They talked about 'the change in the international atmosphere', meaning the attitude of America towards the shah's regime. Thus emboldened, on 13 June 1977 the Writers' Association, which had never had the right to function fully, issued an open letter demanding basic rights. Signed by forty writers, poets and critics, it was addressed to Prime Minister Hoveyda and asked for official permission to open a public office. This was followed on 19 July by another open letter on the same theme, signed by ninety-nine authors. Eight days before, a group of prominent advocates had signed a public statement demanding the return of judicial power and status to the law courts.

Within a couple of months a number of political and professional associations were reconstituted or came into being. These included the Freedom Movement, led by Mehdi Bazargan, the new National Front, led by Karim Sanjabi, the Iranian Committee for the Defence of Freedom and Human Rights and the National Organization of University Teachers, among others. Almost all these organizations had liberal-democratic tendencies, asking for freedom of expression, the enforcement of the county's constitution, the return of judicial processes and so forth. They included both leftist elements (for example in the Writers' Association) and Islamic views (as in the Freedom Movement), but until after the 'Poetry Nights' of November 1977, the far left and the Islamist movement – which later set the goal of overthrowing the regime – were still in the background.

Feeling the pressure from without and within, in August the shah dismissed Prime Minister Hoveyda and replaced him with Jamshid Amuzegar, a top minister and oil spokesman in all Hoveyda's cabinets, making Hoveyda minister of the royal court in place of Alam, who was suffering from terminal cancer. This appeared to be an old tactic: in 1960, being seemingly in similar trouble, the shah had replaced Eqbal with Sharif-Emami to weather the storm of domestic and foreign difficulties. In fact this had not paid off, forcing the shah to appoint the independent Ali Amini to office contrary to his own wishes. By now, times had changed since this, in 1977, was the end, not the beginning, of the process which had begun in 1963. Still, if the shah had replaced Hoveyda with someone like Amini, it is unlikely that there would have been a full-scale revolution resulting in the downfall of the regime. But instead of that, officially inspired articles were attributing the protest movement to an American plot, of which Amini was the leading agent.

Meanwhile, there had been a series of demonstrations and strikes at universities throughout the country, which was to increase in extent and frequency as the movement continued. The campaign for freedom and human rights, still short of a general call for the overthrow of the regime, peaked during the ten nights of poetry reading sessions held in November at the German cultural centre, the Goethe Institute, and Aryamehr technical university. Attended by thousands of people, they were organized by the Writers' Association and became known as the 'Poetry Nights', until the tenth night, when they were broken up by the police.[59]

Also in November, the shah paid a state visit to the United States, and while he was being welcomed by President Carter on the lawns of the White House, Iranian students demonstrating against him clashed with a small number of well-wishers, and when the police fired tear gas, the shah, Carter and their suite appeared to be weeping live on television. Viewers also heard the slogan 'Death to the shah' for the first time, shouted by the demonstrators outside the White House, before it became a regular slogan in the streets of Iranian cities less than a year later. The shah returned to a warm but officially organized welcome, and a few weeks later Carter celebrated the New Year as the shah's guest in Tehran. Both in Washington and in Tehran, the president was fully supportive of the shah, emphasizing Iranian-American friendship and cooperation. Shortly after the shah's return, a peaceful meeting of about 1,000 National Front supporters, held in a large garden outside Tehran and intended to unite the secular democratic opposition, was attacked by thugs sent by SAVAK.[60] Many were injured in the attack, including Shapur Bakhtiar, a Front leader who was destined to be the shah's last prime minister.

REVOLUTION

As noted above, until now the campaign resembled a protest or reform move-ment, although there certainly were revolutionary forces ready to come forward at the right moment. The first such opportunity was offered by the official vilifi-cation of Ayatollah Khomeini in the press. Earlier, the Ayatollah had issued a statement from his place of exile in Najaf (Iraq) attacking the shah, calling the shah a servant of America and saying that the Iranian people would not rest in their struggle against his regime. The article against Khomeini had been ordered by the shah and organized by Hoveyda, who had instructed the ministry of information and tourism to arrange publication. Signed under a pseudonym, it was published on 7 January 1978 in the leading semi-official daily, *Ettela'at*, against the best judgement of its editor, who feared a strong public reaction. It described Khomeini as an agent of both Black (i.e. British) and Red (i.e. Soviet) imperialism, 'an adventurous cleric, subservient to centres of colonialism':

A man with an unknown past, attached to the most dogmatic and most reac-tionary agents of colonialism, who had failed . . . to achieve a place amongst the country's high-ranking clerics, and was looking for an opportunity to enter political adventures at any costs and make a name for himself. Ruhollah Khomeini was a suitable person for this objective, and Red and Black reac-tions found him the most appropriate person for confronting Iran's [White] Revolution . . .

Describing Khomeini as an 'Indian Seyyed' who had 'lived in India for a while and had established links with British colonialist centres', the article went on to add that the Ayatollah was

> the instigator of the riots of 5 June [1963], the person who rose against the Iranian [White] Revolution with the intention of implementing the programme of Red and Black reaction . . ., showing that there still were people ready to make themselves available to conspirators and anti-patriotic elements.[61]

The reaction in Qom was swift and angry. Copies of the newspaper in which the article had been published were torn and burnt. The religious colleges and the bazaar were shut down. There were public clashes with the security forces, and an attack on 9 January on the headquarters of the official *Rastakhiz* (Resurgence) party led to civilian casualties, the official figure being two dead, the opposition figures, 70 dead and 500 injured.

This was a major turning point. Khomeini's direct and open attack on the shah made him popular, not just with his religious followers but with a wide spectrum of people, simply because this was what they wished to hear and he was the only person who could and would do it. The reaction in Qom showed his popularity among the religious classes and their willingness to risk their lives for him. Equally important, it put the spotlight on the other leading ayatollahs, who felt obliged to issue statements condemning the attack on Khomeini, as did other opposition groups and parties. The bloodshed in Qom opened a new chapter in the protest movement, hardened public attitudes, radicalized the political environment, undermined moderate and reformist views and encouraged riots and confrontations with police and (later) the army. It turned Ayatollah Khomeini into the incontestable leader of the revolution, and – as part of that – religion and (later) its Islamist interpretation became the most widespread ideology of the movement.

On 19 February 1978, the ritual fortieth day of mourning for those killed in Qom, there were vast demonstrations in Tabriz, most of whose people were followers of the moderate Grand Ayatollah Shariatmadari, the senior *marja'* in Qom. Once again, clashes with the security forces led to bloodshed: widely differing figures for the dead and wounded were quoted by the government and the opposition. In turn, the fortieth day of the dead of Tabriz resulted in demonstrations and bloodshed in various cities, and thus the forty-day cycle became a familiar event in the revolutionary process.

Qom, then, was the first major turning point. It was followed by two other major turning points: a fire which set a cinema in Abadan ablaze in August and the firing of live bullets into a crowd of demonstrators by the army. Meanwhile, the new technocratic government led by Amuzegar took measures that added to the rising public anger against the regime. For several years, there had been an economic boom – big even by Iranian standards at this time – with easy access to cheap credit for many middle-class people with some influence to start their own businesses. There had been a rush to invest in small businesses, which could survive only if the state's liberal monetary policy continued at the same level. In taking a longer view of economic policy the new cabinet decided to scale down this oil-based boom, especially in view of the fact that there had been a moderate decline in revenues compared with the previous year. But they applied the brakes too fast, with the consequence that many of the new investors went bust and joined the ranks of the revolutionaries. Further than that, the new government decided to cut down or reduce the hand-outs which in various guises were made to a large number of people, for example, many journalists who at the same time were on the payroll of various government departments. Such measures, while strictly correct in terms of economic policy, served to swell the ranks of the revolutionaries with more modern middle-class people – people who, had they chosen to support the regime instead, could well have prevented it from falling in the way it did.

The second major turning point of the revolution occurred on 19 August 1978. The Cinema Rex at Abadan, Iran's oil capital, was set ablaze by unknown arsonists, resulting in the death of more than 400 people inside. The crime was never fully investigated either before or after the revolution and it is still not known who the culprits were. But the state was blamed, partly as a matter of course and partly because it had been putting out propaganda that the opposition were utter reactionaries, opposed to all things modern, including cinemas. The public then believed that the arson attack was instigated by the state to blame it on the opposition and prove their point. Later, at least some came to believe that this had been undertaken by a gang of revolutionaries precisely in order to implicate the state.

Within a few days the shah dismissed Amuzegar's cabinet and appointed Ja'far Sharif-Emami prime minister. As we have seen, Sharif-Emami had been the shah's caretaker prime minister in 1960 when, feeling obliged to dismiss Eqbal, he had hoped to avoid appointing an independent prime minister such as Amini. Things were vastly different now, when virtually the whole of society was in revolt. Sharif-Emami's previous role as chairman of the Senate and head of the shah's business concern, the Pahlavi Foundation, for many years and, rightly or wrongly, his having been tainted with major financial corruption meant that he had virtually no credit left with any part of the population. No wonder that he said at his first press conference that he was no longer the Sharif-Emami of twenty days before. He even urged the media to disseminate the news truthfully or, he said, the BBC would do it for them. This showed the degree of the shah's unawareness of the scale, gravity and urgency of the revolt, offering the last chance for appointing an independent cabinet to save the situation, though inevitably involving some loss of his own power.

The third major turning point came on 8 September, subsequently dubbed Black Friday. Four days before, the great Islamic festival of *Fitr*, concluding the month of fasting, had been celebrated by tens of thousands of people in a mass prayer held in the streets of Tehran, led by a revolutionary cleric. This was followed the next day by a demonstration of a crowd of more than 100,000 people, who for the first time shouted 'Say death to the shah'. A huge rally was called for on Friday 8 September in Tehran's Zhaleh Square (Friday being the weekend in Iran) but the night before, martial law was declared in Tehran and twelve other cities and all public meetings were banned. It is likely that, as was said at the time, the public did not receive the news of the new measures in time. At any rate, the anticipated huge crowd gathered in Zhaleh Square at the appointed time and were told by the general administrator of martial law to disperse. When they refused, and after a round of warning shots in the air, the soldiers fired into the crowd. There were clashes elsewhere in Tehran as well as in other cities. Inevitably, estimates of casualties varied widely between government and opposition, ranging from less than 100 to more than 4,000. But the losses were doubtlessly heavy, and further inflamed public anger, which was especially directed at the shah.

There was a lull for a few days but street clashes often resulting in bloodshed soon broke out again, massive demonstrations (sometimes by one or two million people) were organized and there were political strikes by industrial workers, oil company workers and employees, the press, National Bank and other government employees, eventually embracing virtually every profession. At one point judges and the whole of the department of justice also went on strike. As an example of the deep involvement of well-placed government employees in revolutionary activities, the employees of the Central Bank of Iran published a list of prominent individuals whom they claimed had recently transferred a total of more than $2 billion out of the country.[62]

Meanwhile, Ayatollah Khomeini had been issuing written and spoken statements and, in line with the wishes of most people, insisting on the overthrow of the regime. In the face of official censorship, the widespread use of photocopying facilities and cassette tapes played a crucial role in disseminating political news, statements and propaganda throughout the revolution.[63]

The government, acutely aware of the uncompromising role played by Khomeini in Iraq in the absence of political restraint, brought pressure on the Iraqi government to restrict his activities. The ayatollah decided to move to Kuwait but the Kuwait government refused him leave of entry. It was at this point, on 6 October, that he responded to the call of a group of supporters in France to take the unlikely decision to fly to Paris. As things turned out, this decision played a major role in boosting revolutionary morale and turning the ayatollah into the undisputed leader and charismatic mentor of the revolution.

Once in Paris, he became the focus of attention of the western press and media and the object of pilgrimage for thousands of Iranians in Europe, America and Iran itself. He was given the title of Imam, an extraordinary and therefore highly honorific one for a Shia leader outside the twelve sinless Imams. Not long afterwards, the rumour spread that Khomeini's image could be seen on the moon, a rumour believed by most Iranians, including some of the educated and modern, many of whom would testify to have seen it themselves.

On 5 November the people of Tehran ran riot, attacked public buildings and set fire to banks, liquor shops and cinemas, the army standing aside apparently in order to show the gravity of the situation. A BBC television reporter was puzzled when he pointed to a man in an expensive suit and Pierre Cardin tie dancing around a burning tire and shouting revolutionary slogans.

At the same time, following a meeting with Khomeini, Karim Sanjabi, the National Front leader, issued a public statement in Paris attacking 'the illegal monarchical regime' and announcing the formation of 'the national Islamic movement of Iran'. Although the National Front was no longer a mass movement, the position taken up by its leader, a former leading colleague of Mosaddeq, sent a strong message both to the modern middle classes in Iran and to policymakers in the West of the relative standing of the shah and Khomeini among the bulk of Iranian society. It was seen as the submission of old Mosaddeqites to Khomeini's leadership.[64]

The shah was by now fully alert to the gravity of the situation and hoped to replace Sharif-Emami's cabinet by a liberal national government led by Sanjabi; but Sanjabi's Paris statement made it clear that he would not be drawn.[65] The shah then appointed a military government headed by the dovish General Azhari, chief of the general staff, although many members of his cabinet were civilian. Large numbers of both secular and religious people began to shout the religious slogan *Allaho Akbar* (God is the Greatest) from their rooftops every night. Azhari said in a press conference that the slogans issued from cassette tapes and had not been shouted by the people. Next day the people were shouting in a massive demonstration: 'Miserable Azhari! / Four-star donkey! / Keep saying it's tapes / But tapes have no legs.'[66]

On 6 November, the day Azhari took office, there took place one of the most remarkable events in the Iranian revolution: the shah's television broadcast to the 'dear people of Iran' in a most humble manner, acknowledging their revolution, promising full and fundamental reform, the removal of injustice and corruption, together with free elections and democratic government; and begging them to restore peace and order to make it possible to proceed with these reforms:

In the open political space which has been created gradually over the last two years, you people of Iran rose up against injustice and corruption. The revolution of the people of Iran cannot be disapproved by me as the shah of Iran as well as an Iranian individual. Unfortunately, alongside this revolution, the conspiracy and abuse of others of your anger and emotions led to chaos, anarchy and rebellion. Also, the strikes, many of which were legitimate, recently changed direction so that the wheels of the country's economy and the people's daily life will be stopped, and even the flow of oil on which the country's life depends be cut off . . . The unfortunate events that yesterday put the capital on fire cannot any longer go on and be tolerated by the country and the people.

He went on to explain that because his hope of forming a 'coalition govern-ment' had been dashed, he was left with no choice but to appoint a 'provisional government'. But this did not mean that the call for peace and order would be used as a pretext for returning to injustice, corruption and 'suffocation':

> I realize that some may feel that, using the pretext of the national interest and the country's progress, and [by] the application of pressure, the danger still exists that the unholy alliance of financial corruption and political corruption may be repeated. But in the name of your monarch, having sworn to protect the country's territorial integrity, national unity and Twelver Shia religion, once again I repeat my oath in front of the people of Iran and make a pledge that past mistakes will not be repeated. I further pledge that past mistakes will also be remedied in every way. I pledge that, after the restoration of order and peace, as soon as possible, a popular government for the establishment of fundamental liberties and holding free elections will come into being so that the constitution which is the price of the blood spilt in the Constitutional Revolution will come into full application. I too heard the message of the revolution of you people of Iran ... I guarantee that, in the future, Iranian government will be based on the constitution, social justice and popular will, and free from arbitrary rule (*estebdad*), injustice and corruption.

He then beseeched the religious leaders and intellectuals – the two main pillars of public opinion – to cooperate to bring about peace and order:

> At this point I request of the exalted ayatollahs and most learned ulama who are the religious and spiritual leaders of society and upholders of Islam, and the Shia religion in particular, to try to protect this sole Shia country in the world by guiding the people and asking them to maintain peace and order.
>
> I ask the intellectual leaders of the young people to help pave the way for a genuine struggle for the creation for a real democracy, by asking them to main-tain peace and order.

He ended this totally unexpected and apparently uncharacteristic message with the following plea:

> Let us all think of Iran together, and know that in the revolution of the people of Iran against colonialism, injustice and corruption I am at your side, and will be with you for the protection of the country's territorial integrity, national unity and Islamic principles, and the establishment of fundamental liberties and the realization of the demands and ideals of the Iranian people.[67]

Had the shah made and carried out even a tenth of such pledges six months before, this would have gone a long way to defuse the situation. But now it was seen as a sign of weakness, an act of duplicity to deceive the public and buy time for a come-back. Besides, public feelings were running very high, and the thought of revenge had a great deal more potency than the idea of compromise, as in 1909 when, before the conquest of Tehran by the revolutionary army, Mohammad Ali Shah had unsuccessfully pleaded for compromise and reconciliation (see Chapter 8). The political leaders and activists outside the Islamist and Marxist-Leninist forces, who hoped if not for dialogue and compromise, then at least for the orderly transfer of power, were increasingly pushed into the margin by the force of popular anger and indignation: the most popular slogan was 'Let *him* [the shah] go, and let there be flood afterwards'.

The shah's lack of a consistent policy is sometimes blamed on his illness. Some years earlier he had been diagnosed with a form of cancer, which only the queen knew about, he himself being apparently as yet unaware of the nature of his illness. At the time it was still well under control, and it is unlikely that it would have led to his death as early as July 1980 had it not been for the toll that the revolution and his subsequent exile took of him.[68] The illness might have possibly contributed to his bewilderment, but he had always been hesitant and indecisive in a crisis, as witnessed by his attitude and behaviour before and during the 1953 coup (see Chapter 10). Given his personality, he would have benefited from firm and consistent support and advice if he had tolerated the existence of a political establishment in the country. But then if such a socio-political force had existed, it would have been very unlikely for a full-scale revolution to have taken place.

On 10 December, during the annual mourning for the martyrs of Karbala, millions of people took part in massive demonstrations throughout the country, demanding the fall of the shah and confirming Khomeini's leadership. Having tried and failed to persuade Sanjabi to form a cabinet,[69] the shah turned to Gholamhosein Sadiqi, leading sociology professor and deputy prime minister under Mosaddeq who had served several jail sentences since the 1953 coup. Sadiqi came under extreme pressure, not least by his fellow Mosaddeqites, to decline the shah's offer of the premiership. Nevertheless he agreed to accept office on the condition that the shah would stay in the country but remain aloof from government, including the army. The shah might have agreed to go on a foreign trip, but he refused to stay in the country and have no say in matters civilian or military.[70] Sadiqi withdrew from the scene. Meanwhile, a number of unpopular people, including former Prime Minister Hoveyda and the SAVAK chief General Nasiri, had been arrested to placate public feelings. Some of them managed to escape later when, in the wake of the collapse of the regime, people broke into prisons and army barracks, but many were arrested and executed by the new revolutionary regime, including Hoveyda himself (see Chapter 13).

All the while America and Britain, the two most influential western powers in Iran, had been watching events with growing concern, especially since the start and spread of the strikes. The shah did not trust Britain and believed that it was working against him. He pointed to the faithful reporting of events by the BBC Persian service as evidence, but given his deeply ingrained general distrust of Britain he is unlikely to have thought otherwise in any case (see Chapters 10 and 11). And although he saw and sought the advice of the British ambassador regularly, he later showed in his memoirs that he did not trust the ambassador, despite the fact that each time the ambassador had emphasized that he was expressing his own personal opinion. As the ambassador explains in his own memoirs, the British government had given him a free hand to use his own judgement in a rapidly changing situation, and had never contradicted him upon receiving his reports of the situation.[71]

But by far the most significant western power was the United States, which the shah regarded as his most important foreign friend and mentor, and on which he was psychologically dependent. Although the Carter administration would not give blanket public support to the shah on matters regarding human rights and the sale of American arms, no one in that administration wished the shah's downfall. But the shah wanted more from America than goodwill and the expression of public and private support which he regularly received from them. He wanted a firm, clear and unambiguous directive on what he should do. He might have employed the 'iron fist' policy – their euphemism for a massive military repression – had he been told by America that that was what they wanted him to do. The American ambassador explained to him that while he as the shah of Iran was free to take any decision he deemed necessary, America was not prepared to take responsibility for it.[72] But American opinion was divided and, in particular, Zbigniew Brzezinski, the President's National Security Adviser, was prepared to go further than that,[73] while Secretary of State Cyrus Vance tended more towards the ambassador's view[74] and President Carter tried to steer a middle course.[75] By then, two of the popular slogans chanted in the massive street demonstrations were 'God's help and imminent victory / Shame on this deceitful monarchy'[76] and 'Until the shah wears a shroud / This will not become a proper homeland'.[77]

The final act of the great drama was played by Shapur Bakhtiar (Bakhtiyar), deputy leader of the National Front, who accepted the shah's invitation to form a cabinet. He was the son of a Bakhtiyari chieftain executed under Reza Shah, and had received his secondary and university education in France. Bakhtiar had been a leading member of the Iran Party and deputy minister of labour in Mosaddeq's last cabinet, and had been briefly jailed a couple of times after the 1953 coup (see Chapter 11). The shah agreed to go on a trip abroad, and Bakhtiar presented his cabinet on 6 January 1979. He emphasized his past association with Mosaddeq, promised parliamentary democracy and early elections and lifted the press censorship, which resulted in the ending of the two-month-long strike by the Journalists' Syndicate. Still staying near Paris, Khomeini declared Bakhtiar's government illegal and advised the strikers other than the journalists not to return to work.[78] At the same time, he appointed a secret revolutionary council, which included Ayatollahs Beheshti, Taleqani, Motahhari and Mahdavi Kani and Hojjatolesalms Bahonar, Rafsanjani and Khamenei as well as Bazargan and Sahabi of the Freedom Movement.

Bakhtiar's government was totally rejected by all the opposition parties as well as the general public, and not least by his own National Front, who expelled him from their ranks and leadership, partly on the argument that he had not had their approval to accept office.[79] Thus, despite his hopes of bringing some of the revolutionary forces to his side, the only force he could depend on was the army, and as events were to prove, the army could not act independently when its only effective head had left the country. Before leaving, the shah had set up a royal council to oversee the Crown's duties in his absence, but shortly after his departure from Iran the council's chair flew to Paris and tendered his resignation to Khomeini.[80]

The shah, accompanied by Queen Farah, left the country with tears in his eyes (captured by photographers at Tehran airport) on 16 January, which proved to be a journey without return. Ten days later, Khomeini returned to Tehran to a tumultuous welcome. Shortly afterwards, he asked Mehdi Bazargan to form a provisional government. Bazargan was a Muslim democrat and leader of the Freedom Movement who regularly wore a tie and had been Bakhtiar's colleague in the previous National Fronts, a close friend of the moderate Ayatollah Taleqani – an old Mosaddeqite and former colleague of Bazargan in the leadership of the Freedom Movement – who was the most revered leader of the revolution after Khomeini himself. Bazargan was not keen to accept office and agreed only on the condition that he would have a free hand (a condition that later proved not to be binding; see Chapter 13).[81] Immediately, large crowds of demonstrators began to shout the slogans 'Bakhtiar, lackey with no power'[82] and 'Bazargan, prime minster of Iran', but Bazargan himself did not adopt a belligerent attitude towards Bakhtiar. Before Khomeini's return to Tehran, Bakhtiar had decided to see Khomeini in Paris but Khomeini had declared that he would see him only if he first resigned from the premiership.[83]

By that time, not only judges and top civil servants but even some ex-ministers, royal court officials and others related to the royal family had begun to support the revolution, so that the only force still maintaining the regime was the army. But the army itself was not a uniform and homogeneous entity. The general staff were divided between a majority of 'doves' and a minority of 'hawks'. Facing the soldiers in the streets, the people were shouting 'Army brother, why kill your brother'[84] and putting flowers into the barrel of their guns. There was real fear of insubordination in the army ranks, especially given the religious aspects of the revolution. The lower ranks of the air force publicly supported the revolution, with a number of them appearing in street demonstrations in full uniform. Early in January, President Carter had sent General Robert Huyser to Iran to try to make sure that the army remain united and backed Bakhtiar's government.[85] But, as it often happens in such situation, an unpredictable event resulted in the army's collapse.

The units still zealously committed to the shah were the elite Imperial and Immortal Guards. On 5 February, a troop of the guards decided to teach a lesson to air force personnel – who were watching the tape recording of Ayatollah Khomeini's return to Iran, the live coverage of which had been stopped by the government – and attacked their barracks in Tehran. The airmen put up opposition and began to fight, while at the same time appealing to the people for help. Large numbers of people, led by young guerrillas, went to their aid and attacked the guards from the rear. Quickly, the situation got out of the control of both revolutionary leaders and the government. Fearing civil war, on 11 February the army declared neutrality and withdrew to their barracks. The government thus collapsed and Bakhtiar went into hiding, only to appear in Paris some time later. But despite appeals by the provisional government for calm, the people went on to attack the main prisons and military barracks, almost all of which surrendered without a fight.

It was now the turn of the revolutionaries to turn on each other, which resulted in the complete triumph of the Islamic revolution.

CHAPTER 13

The Islamic Republic

The 2,500 years of arbitrary rule (estebdad) ... *which has penetrated the whole of our life, culture and psyche is itself the strongest factor for ... the change [that took place] in the revolution.*

Mehdi Bazargan
The Iranian Revolution in Two Moves (1984)

THE REVOLUTION THAT 'SHOULD NOT HAVE HAPPENED'

IN SOME OF ITS basic characteristics, the Iranian revolution did not conform to the usual norms of western revolutions, and especially the French and Russian revolutions with which it was compared in the West while it was taking place. This became a puzzle, resulting in disappointment and disillusionment among western commentators within the first few years of the revolution's triumph. For them, as much as for a growing number of modern Iranians who themselves had swelled the street crowds shouting 'My dear Khomeini / Tell me to spill blood',[1] the revolution became 'enigmatic', 'bizarre', 'unthinkable'. In the words of one western scholar, the revolution was 'deviant' because it established an Islamic republic and deviant also since 'according to social-scientific explanations for revolution, it should not have happened at all, or when it did'.[2] That is why large numbers of disillusioned Iranians began to add their voice to the shah and the small remnants of his regime in putting forward conspiracy theories, chiefly and plainly that America (and/or Britain) had been behind the revolution in order to stop the shah pushing for higher oil prices. Incredible as it may sound, it was even said that the West had been afraid that economic development under the shah would soon rob it of its markets.

Before the triumph of the revolution, this puzzle was somewhat hidden from the eyes of western liberals and leftists, who at the time wielded considerable influence in western governments, societies and the media. But even western conservatives did not suspect the revolution would turn out as it did. All the signs had been there but they were largely glossed over by the huge peaceful processions, the solidarity and virtual unanimity of society in wishing to over-throw the state, the blood sacrifice and the phenomenon of Ayatollah Khomeini.

He was pictured sitting under an apple tree near Paris with a smile on his face; and every one of his words was received as divine inspiration by the great majority of Iranians – secular as well as religious – and he was the object of pilgrimage under the watchful eyes of the western media, which made him a permanent feature on television screens the world over.

At the time, the revolution was seen as a widespread revolt for freedom, independence, democracy and social justice – depending on the inclinations of the observer – and against oppression, corruption, social inequality and foreign domination. The anti-western overtones of the movement were merely put down to 'anti-imperialism' and 'nationalism' (the words being applied almost interchangeably) and were justified against the background of the 1953 coup, in ignorance that some of the domestic Iranian forces involved in that coup were prominently represented in the revolution. The widespread and deeply felt anger against the West and all things western by the great majority of Iranians – both traditional and modern, both lay and intellectual – in which the word *gharbzadegi* (Weststruckness) was used by everyone to condemn everyone and everything they did not like, was thus viewed lightly as no more than a manifestation of such a nationalism and anti-imperialism.

Certainly the revolution could not be fully explained 'according to social-scientific explanations for revolution' for the simple reason that such explanations are based on the characteristics of *western* revolutions, which themselves have in their background *western society, history and traditions*. It is possible to make sense of Iranian revolutions by the application of the tools and methods of the same social sciences which have been used in explaining western revolutions, but explanations which are based on *western history* inevitably result in confusion and contradiction. The most obvious point of contrast is that in western revolutions, society was divided: in the West it was the underprivileged classes that revolted against the privileged classes, who were represented by the state; whereas in Iranian revolutions it was society as a whole that revolted against the state, with no social class and no political organization standing against it, since the state was defended by its coercive apparatus and nothing else.[3] The Iranian example was stark evidence against Euro-centric universalist theories of history. As Karl Popper once observed, there is no such thing as History; there are *histories*.[4]

From western perspectives, it would certainly have made no sense for some of the richest (mainly traditional) classes of the society to finance and organize the movement, while a few of the others (mainly modern) were sitting on the fence. Similarly, it would have made no sense by western criteria for the entire state apparatus (except the military, who quit in the end) to go on an indefinite general strike, providing the most potent weapon for the success of the revolution. Nor would it have made sense for almost the entire intellectual community and all modern educated groups to rally behind Khomeini and his call for Islamic government. This was not a bourgeois capitalist revolution; it was not a liberal-democratic revolution; it was not a socialist revolution. Various ideologies were represented, of which the most dominant were the Islamic tendencies: Islamist,

Marxist-Islamic and democratic-Islamic, and Marxist-Leninist tendencies: Fada'i, Tudeh, Maoist, Trotskyist and others.

The conflict within the Islamic tendencies and the Marxist-Leninist tendencies themselves was probably no less intense than that between the two tendencies taken as a whole. Yet they were all united in the overriding objective of bringing down the shah and overthrowing the state. More importantly, the mass of the population, who ideologically speaking did not fit into any of these tendencies – and of whom the modern middle classes were qualitatively the most important – were solidly behind the single objective of removing the shah. Any suggestion of a compromise would have been dismissed as treason. Moreover, if any settlement had been reached, however peaceful and democratic, short of the overthrow of the monarchy, legends would have grown as to how the 'liberal bourgeoisie' had stabbed the revolution in the back on the order of their 'foreign (i.e. American and British) masters'.

Gholamhosein Saedi, a leading intellectual, writer and playwright as well as psychiatrist, who participated in the revolution but later fell out with the Islamic regime and died prematurely in his Paris exile in 1985, wrote in Paris in 1984:

> The whirlwind which . . . in 1977–1979 blew and whirled throughout Iran and overturned everything in its wake was at first the great revolt of all the masses, the solid and united action against a regime that had been insulting them for years. In those days if a stranger roamed around the city and just looked at the walls, he would know what was going on. The walls of all towns and cities were covered with writings which had only one motivation and one objective, and that was the overthrow of the royal regime.[5]

It was thus a revolution of society (*mellat*) against the sate (*dawlat*). What bound the revolutionaries together was the determination to remove one man, the shah, at all costs. The most widespread slogan which united the various revolutionary parties and their supporters regardless of party and programme was 'Let *him* [the shah] go and let there be flood afterwards'. Many changed their minds in the following years but nothing was likely to make them see things differently at the time. Thirty years later, Ebrahim Yazdi, a leading aide of Ayatollah Khomeini in Paris and later foreign minister in the provisional government after the revolution, was reported as speaking 'candidly of how his revolutionary generation had failed to see past the short-term goal of removing the shah'.[6]

Those who lost their lives in various towns and cities throughout the revolution certainly played a major part in the process. But the outcome would have been significantly different if the commercial and financial classes, who had reaped such great benefits from the oil bonanza, had not financed the revolution and, more especially, if the National Iranian Oil Company employees, civil servants, judges, lawyers, university professors, intellectuals, journalists, schoolteachers and students had not joined in a general strike or if the masses of the young and old, the modern and traditional, men and women, had not swelled the crowds or if the military had united and resolved to crush the movement.[7]

The revolutions of 1977–9 and 1906–9 look poles apart in many respects. Yet they were quite similar with regard to some of their basic characteristics, which may also help explain many of the divergences between them. Both were revolts of society against the state, and as such cannot be easily explained with reference to western traditions. Merchants, traders, intellectuals and the urban masses played a vital role in the Constitutional Revolution. But so did leading ulama and powerful landlords, without whose active support the triumph of 1909 would have been difficult to envisage, as if 'the church' and 'the feudal-aristocratic class' were leading a 'bourgeois democratic revolution'! In that revolution, too, various political movements and agendas were represented, but they were all united in the aim of overthrowing the arbitrary state (and ultimately Mohammad Ali Shah), which stood for traditionalism, so that, willy nilly, most of the religious forces also rallied behind the modernist cause.[8] It is worth repeating Walter Smart's remarks on this apparently strange behaviour, quoted before in Chapter 8, that

in Persia religion has, by force of circumstances, perhaps, found itself on the side of Liberty, and it has not been found wanting. Seldom has a prouder or a stranger duty fallen to the lot of any Church than that of leading a democracy in the throes of revolution, so that [the religious leadership] threw the whole weight of its authority and learning on the side of liberty and progress, and made possible the regeneration of Persia in the way of constitutional Liberty.

It was equally puzzling for the BBC correspondent, as noted in Chapter 12, to watch a man in an expensive suit and Pierre Cardin tie in November 1978 in Tehran, dancing around a burning tyre and shouting anti-shah and pro-Khomeini slogans. Many of the traditional forces backing the Constitutional Revolution regretted it *after the event*, as did many of the moderns who participated in the revolution of February 1979, when the outcomes of those revolutions ran contrary to their own best hopes and wishes. But no argument would have made them change their minds before the collapse of the respective regimes. There were those in both revolutions who saw that total revolutionary triumph would make some, perhaps many, of the revolutionaries regret the results afterwards, but very few of them dared to step forward. In the one case they were represented by Sheikh Fazlollah; in the other by Shahpur Bakhtiar. However, they were both doomed because they had no social base or, in other words, they were seen as having joined the side of the state, however hard they protested that they had the best of intentions. It is a rule in a revolt against an arbitrary state that whoever wants anything short of its removal is branded a traitor. That is the logic of the slogan 'Let *him* go and let there be flood afterwards!'[9]

THE ISLAMIC REVOLUTION

The Iranian revolution did not stop after February 1979, any more than the French Revolution had stopped after July 1789 or August 1792 or the Russian Revolution had concluded in February or October 1917. Even the Chinese revolution turned on its own children with delayed action in the 1960s and 1970s. The single unifying aim of overthrowing the shah and the state having been achieved, it was now time for each party to try not to share but to grab as much as possible of the spoils of the revolution. Apart from the virtually powerless liberal groups, headed by Bazargan's provisional government, most of the players were highly suspicious of one another's motives, hoping to eliminate their rivals as best they could from the realm of political power. Apart from the liberals no one was interested in *sazesh* (compromise), the dirty word of Iranian politics.

First and foremost in the minds of Ayatollah Khomeini and his lieutenants was the formal declaration of an Islamic republic. While in Paris, and in countless audiences he gave to his devoted pilgrims of almost all social classes, as well as public statements and interviews with the western media, Khomeini had often said that there was room for all shades of opinion, but he had never tired of emphasizing that his aim was to establish an Islamic government and pointing out that an Islamic republic is a republic based on Islamic law.

In a referendum held on 31 March the overwhelming majority of Iranians – both men and women, both modern and traditional, both rich and poor – voted for the creation of an Islamic republic; the official figure of 98.2 per cent was probably close to reality. There were a few dissenting voices, because the nature of the republic had not yet been defined, and the only alternative offered to voters was the monarchy which they had so actively rejected. Bazargan was much criticized by the Islamists when at the polls he emphasized that he was voting for a *democratic* Islamic republic.[10]

ISLAMIC REPUBLIC

One thing on which all the revolutionaries and their supporters other than the liberals were at first united was a systematic attempt to punish those associated with the former regime and to dismantle, as far as possible, the state's military and civilian apparatus. Very few had any objections to the unleashing of revolutionary anger on former officials and others who had had business and other dealings with the state. *Taghuti* was everyone's favourite term for describing the hated associates of the fallen state. Khomeini had used the Koranic term *taghut* (false god, applied to the Pharaoh) in his derisive description of the shah, and now *taghuti* was being used as an attribute of anyone or anything who or which was somehow perceived as related to the former regime. A very rich person who had had no connection with the state was *not* a *taghuti*, and his or her person and property were respected and protected. But any middle-ranking or senior civil servant, however conscientious and even if living on a relatively moderate income, would be in danger of being described as a *taghuti*, being dismissed from his post and having his property confiscated, as happened to many in the end.

In general, and putting aside the case of a few top generals and high officials, guilt or innocence, wealth and income had little to do with determining the fate of such people; it was their connection to the state. The only 'crimes' cited for executing General Nader Jahanbani were that he was blue-eyed (his mother was Russian) and had four horses which he kept on fitted carpets. It was not widely publicized that his youngest brother Khosrow was married to the shah's alienated daughter Shahnaz (by his first marriage to Princess Fawziya of Egypt), both of whom had been living in the safety of Switzerland for many years. But the chief revolutionary judge at the time, Hojjatoleslam Sadeq Khalkhali, did hint at this in an interview when he explained his own reason for ordering Jahanbani's execution:

> [General Jahanbani] was at the peak of power and could have protested [against the regime's injustices], since he was almost a relative of the shah and among his entourage, but for the sake of maintaining his parasitic living [he did not protest].[11]

Four generals, including the SAVAK chief Nasiri, were executed first with minimal judicial ceremony. There then followed the trial and execution of many military and civilian officials, including Prime Minister Hoveyda, chairman of the Senate Abdollah Riyazi and the Majils speaker, Javad Sa'id.[12] The charges often included 'waging war against God' and 'waging war against the Imam of the Time [the Hidden Imam]'. The standard of the judicial procedures applied may be gauged from the interview given at the time by Judge Sadeq Khalkhali:

> In *shari'a* law and the Islamic model we have no [rule] for someone to appoint a lawyer for himself unless he is dumb. [But] those whom we are trying are not dumb, and their faculty of reason also works sufficiently for them to be able to answer our questions, since, in any case, we do not ask any questions which they may be incapable of answering.[13]

For some time to come this and anti-Americanism was as much as the radicals of all sides and their supporters could agree on, some of them unsuspecting that their own turn for being condemned as counter-revolutionaries and foreign agents would in time arrive. There was continuing verbal and physical conflict, attacks on the press for not being sufficiently loyal to Islam or the revolution and almost daily clashes in the streets between leftist militants and Islamist gangs described as Hezbollah (party of God). While attacking their opponents with clubs and heavy chains they would shout: 'Party, only the party of God/Leader, only the Spirit of God',[14] 'Ruhollah', Khomeini's first name, literally meaning the 'spirit of God', an Islamic attribute for Jesus Christ. Street clashes later became common also between Hezbollah and the Hojattiyeh Society supporters, the latter pre-dating the revolution as an anti-Baha'i movement which concentrated on praying for the advent of the Hidden Imam and so regarded clerical rule as a usurpation of His government. Hojjatiyeh groups shouting in the streets 'Come Mehdi, come Mehdi, for burying the martyrs'[15] were confronted by the Hezbollah, who would shout back 'O God, O God / Keep Khomeini / Until the Mehdi's revolution / And even by the Mehdi's side.'[16]

The first intra-revolutionary assassinations were carried out by the shadowy Forqan terrorist gang, their most important victims being Ayatollah Motahhari, Khomeini's former student, close lieutenant and chairman of the High Council of the Revolution, Hojjatoleslam Mofatteh, a leading figure in the emerging Islamic Republic Party and General Qarani, the first chief of the military staff appointed by Bazargan, who had lately been set aside under pressure from both Islamist and leftist radicals. Given its name, which is an attribute of the Koran, the Forqan was posing as a radical Islamic gang which believed in 'Islam without the clerics',[17] although they were never discovered since they did not continue their terrorism, at least under that name. By far the most important of their victims was Motahhari, who had much influence with Khomeini as well as other Islamist leaders and whose relatively moderate temper and sophisticated attitude might well have served a positive purpose in the great feuds and hostilities which were to follow between the Islamists and their opponents.

The collapse of the former regime led to the assertion of old provincial grievances, at first in Gonbad and the Turkaman area east of the Caspian, in the Kurdish areas and later in Azerbaijan and among the Qashqa'i chiefs in Fars. The Turkaman clashes, which were supported by a group of Fada'i volunteers from Tehran, lasted only for a short while. On the other hand, the Kurdish demand for immediate autonomy had much deeper historical, ethnic and religious roots (most Iranian Kurds being Sunni Muslims), and led to an armed conflict which continued over several years, to end with the suppression of the Kurdish Democratic Party and (the less important) Komaleh group. The veteran KDP leader, Abdorrahman Qasemlu, was to be assassinated in Vienna in the late 1980s by unknown assailants, although the KDP and other opposition groups attributed the assassination to agents of the Islamic Republic. In 1992, four Kurdish leaders were assassinated in the Mykonos restaurant in Berlin, the German court later finding agents of the Islamic Republic responsible for the murder. There was no serious call for autonomy in Azerbaijan then or later; however, many if not most of its population were followers of Grand Ayatollah Shariatmadari, a senior *marja'* in Qom, and in later conflicts there was a revolt in Tabriz in his support which was abandoned on his advice. The Qashqa'i nomads in Fars did not lead a revolt, but in 1981, when their chieftain Khosrow Khan (who had been long in exile under the shah) tried to defy the government, he was seized and executed.[18]

The Turkaman and, much more importantly, Kurdish, conflicts had drawn the support of various Marxist-Leninist organizations and tendencies, and not least the Fada'is. An exception was the Tudeh Party, who were bending over backwards to prove their loyalty to Khomeini's leadership. With their leaders now returned from their long exile under the shah, the Tudeh Party was probably the least popular revolutionary grouping at the time, for various reasons. Their unpopularity was not due to their Marxist-Leninist ideology, which with some variations had adherents among other leftist organizations and their supporters. Some, both leftist and non-leftist, people saw them as being too dependent on the Soviet Union, if not downright Soviet agents. Others also had bad memories of their attitude and behaviour towards Mosaddeq's government, and still others of their erstwhile derision of Ayatollah Kashani, while most were critical of their conduct during and after the 1953 coup and their later cautious attitude towards the shah's regime following its rapprochement with the Soviet Union. On the other hand, they were very well organized and had an effective propaganda machine, used their Soviet connection to their advantage, gained a strong presence in intellectuals' and writers' organizations as well as women's and youth movements and, in time, penetrated the armed forces and organized a secret military network.

Upon the fall of the former regime both the Islamists and Marxist-Leninists began to arm themselves. They felt highly insecure both vis-à-vis each other and, no less, the imperial military, which was still largely intact, though demoralized. Within a short period, an official paramilitary organization was created to defend the new regime against all comers: the Revolutionary Guard Corps, generally known as Pasdaran. Beginning with 5,000 young men, this force was to grow rapidly in size and sophistication and become the most powerful and influential military force in the service of the Islamic Republic. A new radical Islamic political organization, the Organization of the Holy-Warriors of the Islamic Revolution (*Sazman-e Mojahedin-e Enqelab-e Eslami*) played an active role in organizing Pasdaran, their leading figure, Behzad Nabavi, being one of its early commanders. The Holy-Warriors Organization and Behzad Nabavi were later active in the reform movements of the 1990s and beyond. Another early commander of Pasdaran, Mohammad Mohsen Sazgara, likewise became a reformist but later completely fell out with the regime and joined its opposition in America.

The Fada'i guerrillas were by far the most popular Marxist-Leninist organization, attracting many leftist and activist youth of mainly the modern middle classes. Their freshness and the legends of their guerrilla activities before the revolution to some extent compensated for their limited theoretical knowledge and practical experience of politics. A small group of them who believed in permanent revolution broke away shortly after the February triumph, but the major split came over serious matters of ideology and strategy, the Majority Fada'is deciding to work within the new regime and soon falling under the influence of Tudeh leaders such as Nureddin Kiyanuri and Ehsan Tabari, and the Minority, later resorting to armed struggle against the regime and ending up in exile.

Another major militant and armed leftist force was Mojahedin-e Khalq, or Holy Warriors of the People. Having been seriously weakened by the ideological feud which had led to the departure of the Marxist-Leninist group *Peykar* (Struggle) from the organization, as well as by the successful operations of SAVAK against them (see Chapter 12), they began to rapidly recruit and build up their organization after February 1979. Their appeal was mainly to young revolutionaries from traditional middle-and lower middle-class families, who were attracted both by the organization's crypto-Marxist outlook and by its overt Islamic commitment. It was in many ways a unique phenomenon both in substance and style, and in hindsight it is not surprising that it ended up by becoming the main armed opposition to the Islamic Republic.

A large number of political (mainly left-wing) groupings had sprung up since the fall of the former regime, but almost all were short-lived. Bazargan's Freedom Movement as the main Mosaddeqite party with Islamic commitments was not widely based and did not have mass appeal either to the traditionals, because it was not Islamist, or to the moderns, because it was not sufficiently secular and/or leftist, although there was a strong leftist tendency among its younger members. Together with Sanjabi's National Front, which had an even smaller social base, they were contemptuously referred to as 'the liberals', an attribute that the Tudeh Party had turned into a pejorative political term and passed on to the other Marxist-Leninists as well as the Islamists. A new organization with some former National Front connections was the National Democratic Front, made up of relatively young Marxist and other socialist elements. It was popular for a while, but rapidly lost support and eventually had to go into exile.

The main Islamic protagonists at first were the Islamic Republic Party (IRP) and the Muslim People's Republican Party (MPRP). The IRP was the Islamist party par excellence and was led by clerics close to Ayatollah Khomeini, notably Ayatollah Seyyed Mohammad Beheshti and Hojjatoleslams Ali Akbar Rafsanjani, Mohammad Javad Bahonar and Seyyed Ali Khamenei. It attracted large numbers of Islamists of all ages who were especially devoted to Khomeini. In the few years that the party remained active it played a pivotal role in the politics of the Islamic Republic, and dissolved itself in 1987 when it had effectively become one with the government.[19] Another influential Islamist grouping was the Coalition of Islamic Societies (*Hey'at-ha-ye Mo'talefeh-ye Eslami*), the origins of which dated back to the early 1960s. It was a conservative organization with its main base in the upper stratum of the mercantile community.

The MPRP was IRP's main rival group among religious political organizations. It had the blessings of Ayatollah Shariatmadari, whose son Hasan Shariatmadari was among its leaders, and in terms of its broader political outlook it was not very different from the Freedom Movement, being a Muslim organization with democratic tendencies. It had its strongest following in Shariatmadari's ethnic Azerbaijan, and its fortunes were largely bound up with his position.

Qotbzadeh, Abolhasan Bani Sadr and Ebrahim Yazdi were men in their forties, with a Freedom Movement background; they had become Khomeiniites before the revolution and had served the Ayatollah himself in various capacities while he was in Paris. Yazdi was foreign minister in Bazargan's provisional government, and Bani Sadr became the republic's first president, as we shall see below. Qotbzadeh had been made the first head of the radio-television network – now described as the Voice and Face of the revolution – just after the revolution and, given his hard-headed attitude, had made many enemies in the media and among the intellectuals.

Indeed, one of the earliest causes of conflict among the triumphant revolutionaries was over the freedom of the press and media. The radio-television network was quickly turned into an Islamic institution. Most music and entertainment was replaced by Islamic talks and programmes, and women staff were made to wear the *hejab*. The main conflict, however, focused on freedom of the press, which was the domain of journalists, intellectuals and the Writers' Association. There were attacks and counter-attacks between Qotbzadeh and the press, but the matter extended far beyond that and was soon to involve various forces and individuals directly, including Khomeini himself. Having won press freedom towards the end of the shah's rule by strike action, some journalists entertained the utopian thought that 'there should be no limit on the freedom of expression and the pen', while the more realistic of them merely demanded pluralism so that all shades of opinion would have the opportunity to be heard. There were two broad criteria that defined acceptable press freedom. One was ideological, or better, revolutionary, requiring writers not to engage in 'counter-revolutionary' writing. In this, not just the Islamists but almost all the radical tendencies agreed, except that what was 'counter-revolution' to one party might well be regarded as revolutionary by some of the others. No less a person than Khomeini himself entered this debate when, late in March, barely a month and a half after the victory of the revolution, he said that while freedom of expression was permitted, there would be no room for 'conspiracy', saying that whereas some newspapers had pretended to be in the service of the revolution, in practice they had published material which was against it.[20]

The other criterion was the issue of legal constraints to press freedom, Khomeini himself pointing out that the press everywhere in the world was subject to law, and the law in Iran was the law of Islam. However, although a press law had been decreed, before a detailed body of rules regulating the press in clear ideological terms had come into existence, the invocation of Islamic law as the limit to press freedom was not very helpful, since outside a few obvious cases, it would not be clear in what sense a newspaper report or feature could be anti-Islamic. It was a running battle all through March to August – 'the spring of freedom' – involving many newspapers but notably *Kayhan* and *Ayandegan*, and it came to a head over the latter newspaper, which was banned. Some sixty other newspapers subsequently suffered the same fate. Khomeini himself set the seal of approval:

> After every revolution several thousand of these corrupt elements are executed in public and burnt, and the story is over. They are not allowed to publish newspapers. After so long, the [Bolshevik] October Revolution, still had no newspapers

[except those approved by the state] ... We all made mistakes. We thought we
were dealing with human beings. Evidently we are not. We are dealing with wild
animals. We will not tolerate them anymore.[21]

WOMEN

Women, both modern and traditional, had played an active role in the revolution, the modern women being inevitably more visible, although towards the
end of the former regime some of them began to wear light *hejab* as a gesture of
defiance against the regime. But they had not suspected that they would be
asked, and eventually forced, to adopt an Islamic dress code. Issues regarding
women went far beyond dress codes, however, eventually covering many aspects
of life such as marriage, divorce, the custody of the children, legal status and
ultimately such Islamic laws as those that regard the testimony of a woman, even
her life, worth half that of a man. The full extension and implications of
the status of women in the Islamic Republic took several years to come to light,
and both its politics and its sociology were to evolve through time. At first, the
1967 Family Protection Law – which among other things had limited polygamy
and made it possible for women to apply for divorce on certain grounds – was
abolished; but in response to the persistent campaigns of women its provisions
were fairly quickly reinstated, although the position still remained unequal.[22]
In these early struggles leading young women lawyers such as Shirin Ebadi
and Mehrangiz Kar as well as their supporters had to face traditional women
vigilantes who were led by one Zahra Khanom Cheraghi, the irony being that
the latter themselves had been liberated from their former status as mere
housewives.

The traditionalist conservatives, both clergy and lay, both man and woman,
believed that women should wear the *hejab*, be excluded from public employment at least at administrative and managerial levels and run the family at home.
This was partly at odds with the views of ideological Islamists, who would lead
unchaperoned Islamist women clad in black chadors while pressing submachine
guns to their chests in street demonstrations in support of the revolution and
Khomeini. Here as in many other areas, the Islamists were caught between the
requirements of traditional Shii Islam and its modern ideological interpretation,
which is clearly to be seen in the Islamic constitution. The dichotomy came
through the pronouncements of Ayatollah Khomeini himself, who, early in
March 1979 for example, angrily declared that the government offices were full
of 'naked women' and demanded that they should wear the Islamic *hejab* at
work;[23] and in addressing women he said:

You can be certain that you are in front line. You have proved you have a place
with men. Men have taken a lesson from you ... You are honoured by Islam ...
Islam wants to train you to be a perfect being so that you bring up other perfect
beings.[24]

The imposition of *hejab* came by stages, becoming obligatory at the completion of the Islamic revolution by the fall of Bani Sadr. The slogan of the club-wielding and chain-rattling Hezbollah at the time was '*Ya rusari ya tusari*' ('cover on the head, or a blow to the head'), ironically reminiscent of the forced unveiling under Reza Shah, when the police pulled scarves off the heads of women and tore them apart (see Chapter 9). However, the dress code was not completely uniform: women civil servants, students and others associated with state institutions had to wear the *maqna'eh*, which looked like a uniform, whereas others could wear trousers and a longer coat while covering their heads with a scarf. In both cases, only the woman's face and hands were not covered, although from the late 1990s it became possible to show some hair as well.

Both in theory and practice, the ideal Islamist woman turned out to be one who was a committed practising Muslim and an educated housewife who at the same time participated in social processes. Like so many other aspects of the theory and practice of Islamist ideology, the foundations of which were laid by Ayatollah Khomeini, it blended strong elements both of tradition and modernity. In a word, the pre-revolutionary traditional woman became modernized in certain basic respects, while the pre-revolutionary modern woman was forced to accept certain elements of traditionalism, at least in public. Through time, this made it possible for women in general to make significant social strides despite the laws which otherwise discriminated in favour of men. That was far from a situation which would have been remotely tolerable to Sheikh Fazlollah and other advocates of *mashru'eh* (Islamic government) in the Constitutional Revolution (see further Chapter 14).

THE CONSTITUTION

This dichotomy set in a formal form is most evident by the constitution of the Islamic Republic, which was finally approved in mid-November 1979 and put to popular vote shortly afterwards. It included features and principles that closely resembled the former constitution, which had been a product of the Constitutional Revolution, as well as precepts and provisions which were entirely Islamist, once again exposing the innovative and eclectic character of the modern Islamic ideology which Khomeini and his followers espoused and applied. It would not be entirely accurate to describe the system it produced as a theocracy, although it contained strong elements of clerical rule; it would be equally inaccurate to regard it as secular and/or democratic, which in some respects it resembled.[25]

The fact that it established an Islamic republic was not necessarily contradictory, since there is no Islamic law that requires the government to be monarchical. The contradictions were in the pronouncements and provisions which gave the sovereignty both to God and the people and which created three separate powers à la Montesquieu, including an elected president and a representative legislature, while at the same time establishing *velayat-e faqih*, or the

guardianship of the jurisconsult, which had been anticipated in Khomeini's treatise on Islamic government (see Chapter 12). The representative aspects of the
system were further constrained later when anyone deemed by the unrepresentative Council of Guardians of the constitution as not being of firm Islamic
commitment and character was disqualified from standing for presidency and
the parliament.

At first, this was applied to secular groups and individuals; later it was also
applied to any Muslim party or individual, such as Bazargan's Freedom
Movement, who did not expressly approve of the concept of *velayat-e faqih*,
despite the fact that this was disputed also by many leading *maraje'* and jurists.
Eventually, it was also applied to large numbers of reformist Islamists, such
as members of the Islamic Participation Front, which generally supported
President Khatami's government (see Chapter 14). Thus the system that came
into being was virtually unprecedented both in Iran and elsewhere, though in
some of its secular features it resembled the South African system under the
apartheid regime, which maintained representative government but only for
some of the population.

It was characteristic of the revolutionary conflicts of the time, and the fact that
the all-embracing nature of the revolution represented various ideologies,
programmes and agendas, that the constitution went through several drafts until
it reached the final form in which it was put to vote. The official preliminary draft,
published in June 1979, was close to the former constitution except that it envisaged the creation of a republic, as had been already established by popular vote.
But apart from a somewhat loftier, more moral and more idealistic tone, it applied
essentially the same principles and structures, which included the provision for a
guardian council of six civilian lawyers and five Islamic jurisprudents, elected by
the parliament and the *maraje'*, not automatically to judge whether laws passed by
the parliament are in conformity with the *shari'a* but only on request.[26]

Khomeini approved the draft constitution and, together with a few marginal
revisions of his own, suggested that it should be put to a referendum. But the non-
Islamist radicals and revolutionaries began to clamour for the election of a
constituent assembly, as had been promised by Bazargan when he had taken office.
This reflected both acute distrust and naive optimism on the part of many of the
mainly modern political forces. The Marxist-Leninists were concerned that a bourgeois liberal constitution was about to be imposed without thorough-going debate,
and both they and other secular forces were wary of its religious implications,
which, as noted, were in fact minimal. But in their optimism they overlooked the
fact that an election would return a landslide victory, not for them but for the
supporters of Khomeini. Indeed, Hashemi Rafsanjani pointed this out to Bani Sadr
and Ezzatollah Sahabi at the time, telling them that the resulting assembly would be
packed with backward and ignorant delegates from far corners of the country.[27]

The formal argument against calling a constituent assembly was that it would
take too long for it to be elected and that it would also take too long to deliberate
while the country was in urgent need of a constitutional framework to run

its affairs. However, feelings were running high and in the end an agreement – brokered by the liberal and popular Ayatollah Taleqani – was reached for establishing a select 'assembly of experts' to review and finalize the draft constitution.[28] Predictably, this assembly (of seventy-two members) was dominated by Khomeini's close supporters, who effectively set aside the draft document and rewrote it in the form described above, including the central and fundamental concept of *velayat-e faqih*, which merged religion and government into the formation of an ideological state.

Alarmed by the fact that they were exceeding both their mandate and the deadline by which they were due to report, Bazargan's government decided to dissolve the assembly, but Khomeini stopped them. The non-Islamists had had their chance with the draft constitution and spoiled it by insisting on calling a constituent assembly. It is extremely unlikely that such an assembly would have written a less – if not more – religious and ideological constitution than was produced by the assembly of experts. The fact is that Khomeini had the overwhelming support of the people and that had the others agreed to put the original official draft to the vote, it would have carried with Khomeini's endorsement. Once again in Iranian history, failure to compromise (the hated *sazesh*) led to a radical result.

From the outset, Bazargan's government had tried to return the country's economy and administration to a normal state, following what Bazargan described as a step-by-step (*gam beh gam*) policy. But it soon became clear that theirs was a government with much responsibility and little power and authority, and did not have Khomeini's confidence. Bazargan was neither anti-West nor did he believe in a root-and-branch Islamist (or leftist) revolution. The revolutionary courts were entirely independent and free to execute, jail and confiscate property at will. The Revolutionary Council was a power unto its own. 'The Imam's Committees', which had come into existence during the revolution to organize and coordinate actions such as providing food, had been turned into an executive body which could often overrule the government's decisions. Most of the leftists saw Bazargan as a 'friend of America' and 'representative of the well-to-do bourgeoisie' and were demanding unlimited freedom, class war and anti-imperialist struggles at one and the same time; and although many industries as well as banks and insurance companies had been nationalized under their and Islamists' pressure, they demanded greater state intervention in the economy. In the meantime, those moderns who had begun to lose faith in the revolution altogether were attacking Bazargan for not overthrowing the revolution itself. Seldom in history had a prime minister been given a task as hopeless and thankless as Bazargan's.[29]

HOSTAGE-TAKING

On 13 February 1979, two days after the fall of the former regime, an armed Fada'i group attacked the American embassy and occupied it for a short while but was driven out by forces loyal to the government.[30]

On 4 November 1979 a group of students describing themselves as 'Muslim student followers of the Line of Imam [i.e. Khomeini]' (*Daneshjuyan-e Mosalman-e Peyrov-e Khatt-e Emam*) attacked and occupied the American embassy and took its diplomats hostage. Shortly before, Bazargan had met America's national security advisor, Zbigniew Brzezinski, in Algiers, raising further typically Iranian suspicions in the minds of large numbers of people, especially the moderns and the Marxist-Leninists, not only that the 'liberals' wished to bury the hatchet with the United States but even that the revolution had been sold to America from the start, perhaps by Ayatollah Khomeini himself in Paris, where, among others, he had received a delegation by Ramsey Clark, a former US attorney general. On 22 October the shah had been admitted to the United States to follow treatment for his cancer, and Khomeini had denounced America as the Great Satan.

At the American embassy, the Line-of-Imam students released the women and African-American hostages at the outset, leaving fifty-three white men, one of whom was later released. They demanded that America return the shah to Iran 'to be tried and executed' and apologize for its part in the coup of August 1953 against Mosaddeq, despite the fact that they and like-minded people had been denouncing Mosaddeq supporters such as Bazargan as 'liberals' and 'friends of America'. When the hostage-taking dragged on and led to America's seizure of about $8 billion Iranian assets in retaliation, the students of the Line of Imam added the release of the assets to the list of their demands for releasing the hostages.

Various hostage-takers later claimed that they had intended to occupy the embassy for a few hours or a few days to make their point with the utmost international publicity. Within a few days, however, Khomeini endorsed their action, Bazargan's government had already resigned and the hostage-takers dug in for what turned out to be 444 days before the hostages were released. The efforts of many, in the meantime, including Yazdi and Qotbzadeh, to have the hostages released were frustrated, and the secret military action by America for their release met with bad luck and the loss of eight American soldiers in a desert storm in north-eastern Iran.

Khomeini's endorsement, which stopped any quick release of the hostages, led to renewed public frenzy comparable to the early days of the victory of the revolution. Everyone, modern and traditional, Marxist-Leninist and Islamist, rich and poor (except the few 'liberals') rallied to the anti-American battle cry. Many who had begun to be disillusioned by the decline of mass fervour and the spread of political conflict found a new channel in which to express their revolutionary zeal anew. The revolutionary slogan 'neither East nor West' – reminiscent of Khalil Maleki's old concept of the Third Force – which was meant to be an assertion of sovereignty and independence, had been turned into confrontation with America: once again the country was united over what it did not like, in this case America. That may not have been the original purpose of the hostage-taking, but it followed from Khomeini's endorsement of it.

The Line-of-Imam students did not just take hostages but began to piece together shredded documents which they had found in the American embassy, or the Nest of Espionage (*laneh-ye jasusi*) as they began to call it, exposing 'traitors', 'liberals' and 'friends of America', who, in one capacity or another, had had contact with the American embassy. Their greatest victim perhaps was Abbas Amir Entezam, Assistant Prime Minister and government spokesperson under Bazargan (and lately ambassador to the Scandinavian countries), one of the most serious charges against whom was the fact that, in a letter, an American diplomat had addressed him as '*Dear* Mr. Amir Entezam', apparently proving to his enemies that he was held as a person dear to American imperialism. He was put on trial, convicted as a spy and languished in various jails for many years.

It was in this atmosphere of fury and frenzy, on the one hand, and fear of persecution, on the other, that the constitution was put to the vote, making it impossible for the opponents of the institution of *velayat-e faqih* to present their arguments and criticisms as fully as they would have hoped. Not even the Marxist-Leninists raised any objection to this most fundamental constitutional principle, now that the struggle against American imperialism was in full sway. The Tudeh, the Fada'is and the Mojahedin all came out in full support of the hostage-taking while writers and intellectuals were busy collecting signatures in its defence. Many Iranian students, professionals and international civil servants in the West were doing the same, and demonstrations were held in various European cities, including London and Manchester, in support. As a recent author notes, however, 'many Iranians, including a number of the hostage takers, today view the episode as a monumental mistake that turned Iran into a pariah state in the eyes of the West and stunted its development for years to come'.[31] As various hopes for a reasonably quick release of the hostages were frustrated, America broke off its diplomatic relations with Iran.

A lonely voice was nevertheless raised against the hostage-taking as early as 12 November 1979, eight days after the event. In its press release in the English language, the London based Committee for the Defence and Promotion of Human Rights in Iran condemned the fact that American diplomats were 'being held against their own will . . . as pawns and hostages in a matter over which they themselves have no control whatsoever. This is both a case of an official violation of the most basic rights of man, and one which also involves a complete negation of elementary diplomatic immunities.' The statement concluded:

> We strongly protest against this mode of behaviour, not only in defence of those human beings who are thus subjected to sufferings and indignity, but also because such acts of complete lawlessness will easily create a precedent for further attacks on the basic rights of Iranian people themselves who cannot even claim diplomatic immunity in their own land.[32]

The hostages were eventually released on 20 January 1981, the day Ronald Reagan formally became president, after the Iranian-American Algiers Accords of 19 January. It took so long partly because of domestic expediencies and partly as a result of differences among rival factions concerning the terms and conditions of the release. The rumour seriously began to circulate among the opponents and critics of the regime, and also others who were becoming bored by the fact that no great millennium had dawned by the time the fervour of hostage-taking died out, that the hostage-taking had been carried out on President Carter's own orders. According to this conspiracy theory, Carter had planned the hostage-taking so that before the presidential election in November 1980 the hostages would be released and this would boost his vote in the election. It is quite possible that this rumour had a role in delaying the release of the hostages until Carter had lost the election.

Meanwhile, in the previous September Iraq had attacked Iran, thus starting a war which it took almost eight years and untold death and destruction to conclude.

THE FALL OF BANI SADR

In the charged atmosphere of the early days of the hostage-taking, the new Islamic constitution was put to the vote. This was followed by presidential and parliamentary elections. As the IRP was caught in confusion over its candidate, Abolhasan Bani Sadr, who had severed his roots with the Freedom Movement and was believed to be favoured by Khomeini, was elected president. Yet despite his closeness to Khomeini in Paris and Tehran, Bani Sadr, son of a provincial Ayatollah with a degree from the University of Tehran who had spent many years in Paris, was more of a Muslim democrat than an Islamist, closer in political sentiment and attitude to Bazargan than to Khomeini, and this was the root cause of his growing conflict with the Islamists as represented by the IRP and their strong man, Ayatollah Beheshti.[33] The IRP won the parliamentary majority, and gained the freedom to restrict presidential decisions according to the constitution. After a prolonged struggle, the Majlis imposed on Bani Sadr an Islamist prime minister, Mohammad Ali Raja'i. The conflict continued, almost like a slanging match, between the two sides, which included Bazargan and a few of his supporters who had found their way into the Majlis.

A favourite theme was an ongoing argument over ideological commitment (ta'ahhod) versus technical expertise (takhassos) in determining the qualifications of public employees, or whether preference should be given to Islamists (even if not technically qualified) or to modern educated people (even if they were not good Islamists, for example, if they shaved their beards and wore a tie). Bani Sadr began to attract some support from modern educated people, while others from this group held him partly responsible for a revolution they were beginning to regret. But unlike Khomeini and the IRP he did not have a popular base, nor was he supported in any significant way by those great ulama who did not agree with velayat-e faqih. After Iraq's attack and invasion of Iran, he began to spend much time at the front, partly to gain popularity and partly to avoid daily conflict in

Tehran. The Tudeh and other Marxist–Leninists saw him in quite the same light as they had Bazargan, the Tudeh being a staunch supporter of Khomeini and IRP in any case. Increasingly, Bani Sadr was drawn to the Mojahedin-e Khalq, who were well armed and well organized, with an extensive and devoted membership, but did not have a large popular following. Thus far they had defied Khomeini's insistence that they should voluntarily disarm themselves.

At first Khomeini seemed to be sitting on the fence and urging the two sides to compromise. At a later stage, the arbitration of his son-in-law, Ayatollah Eshraqi, did not manage to resolve the conflict. While Khomeini was naturally inclined towards Beheshti and the IRP, the overtures of Bani Sadr towards the Mojahedin made him both suspicious and angry and he eventually decided to abandon him. Bani Sadr was impeached by the parliament and, on 20 June 1981, the Mojahedin led a public revolt which resulted in armed conflict and many casualties. They were joined by members of some of the Marxist-Leninist groups such as Minority Fada'is and Peykar, though not Tudeh and Majority Fada'is. On 28 June a powerful bomb exploded in the IRP headquarters which killed more than seventy of its leading figures, including Beheshti. Two months later another bomb exploded in the presidential office, killing President Raja'i, who had replaced Bani Sadr, and Prime Minister Bahonar, who had replaced Raja'i. Both explosions were strongly suspected of being the work of the Mojahedin, though they did not confirm this themselves. The Islamists reacted by unleashing a reign of terror which was countered by Mojahedin assassinating Islamist politicians and religious figures. For a while the situation began to resemble an urban civil war, while the war with Iraq was still raging at the front. Meanwhile, Bani Sadr and Mas'ud Rajavi (the Mojahedin leader) escaped by plane to Paris, where they formed a coalition which later fell apart when the Mojahedin entered an agreement with Iraq.[34]

After Bani Sadr's fall the Islamization of social and political life began to be rapidly completed. Symbolically, the National Consultative Assembly (Majlis) was renamed the Islamic Consultative Assembly. From now on all women (and not just public employees) had to observe the Islamic dress code. A massive purge of government offices began, making redundant many non-Islamist employees and expelling the higher civil servants, in some cases confiscating their property as well. This was conducted largely by Islamist teenage boys sitting in government offices who, typically, would just enter on a printed expulsion form the name of the civil servant, describe his position in the department as 'agent of the hated Pahlavi regime' and his offence as 'looting the public treasury'. There was no charge, no hearing and no defence. This was followed by a thorough purge of the universities by the Council of Cultural Revolution, since most of the students and professors, whether leftist, liberal or non-political, did not conform to the political and educational requirements of Islamist ideology.[35]

At the same time, many political parties were outlawed, but not the Tudeh party and the Majority Fada'is. Their turn came in 1983 after the Tudeh Party's military network was exposed by Vladimir Kuzichkin, a KGB agent in the Soviet embassy in Tehran who defected to Britain in 1982.[36] Most of the party leaders and cadres were then arrested and tried for treason, some being executed while others received jail sentences. In a television interview, the leading party members confessed to having been Soviet agents for forty years, although they made these statements clearly under duress.[37] In the meantime many Tudeh and Majority members fled the country, mainly to the Soviet Union and Afghanistan, which was then under Soviet tutelage.

With the rise of the Islamic revolution and the radicalization of the domestic and international situation, first by the hostage-taking of November 1979 and later by the fall of Bani Sadr, the position of moderate organizations such as the MPRP decidedly weakened. In 1982, Sadeq Qotbzadeh confessed to planning a military coup, which would involve the bombing of Khomeini's residence, and implicated Shariatmadari in the plot.[38] Qotbzadeh was executed by firing squad and Shariatmadari was put under house arrest and lost all political power.

That is how the Islamic revolution, which had been proceeding since the hostage-taking of November 1979, was completed. And thus began the first major wave of emigration of many disillusioned, frightened and dispossessed (mainly but not entirely modern) Iranians from their country, largely to the West, from which the modern Iranian diaspora sprang.

Why did the Islamists triumph over the other revolutionary groups? Liberals of all kinds did not have a chance to gain power on their own because they had a small social base (most of the middle classes being committed to Khomeini until it was too late) and weak organizations. But, above all, it was because they were not armed and did not wish to eliminate others from politics. This left the Islamists and leftists, including the Mojahedin. The Islamists were well organized and used the networks of mosques and bazaars to their advantage. But so were most of the leftists, the fundamental difference being in the Islamists' mass appeal, which they could then employ in political action, including elections. None of the leftist groups and parties could draw on anything near the (active or passive) numbers of the Islamists, apart from the fact that the two biggest and best organized Marxist-Leninist parties – the Tudeh and Majority Fada'is – supported the Islamists until their own elimination because they held anti-Americanism to be their most sacred revolutionary objective. And when the Mojahedin's revolt came it did not last beyond a short period. The greatest secret of the triumph of the Islamists was the supreme popularity and legitimacy of Khomeini himself.

WAR

The war that had been started by Iraq in September 1980 was to rage for almost eight years, until Iran accepted the UN ceasefire resolution in July 1988. When it began, it further boosted the position of radical Islamists, who might otherwise not have won the contest with Bani Sadr as easily as they did. The Iranian revolution had made a deep impression on Muslim peoples almost everywhere, and notably among the Shia majority in Iraq, who had long been treated as second-class citizens. Encouraged by victory at home and the revolution's popularity abroad, Iranians – and not least Khomeini himself, who had long cherished the vision of a world Islamic order – at first openly spoke of exporting the revolution to other countries, although hard experience later removed such illusions, much as it had done after the French and Russian revolutions.[39]

Saddam Hussein, who had been deeply wounded by his 1975 surrender to the shah (see Chapter 11), now believed he had both the pretext and the power to renounce the Algiers accord, overrun the Shatt al-Arab waterway, annex parts of Khuzistan province and, he hoped, bring down the Islamist regime. In contemplating these objectives he was probably encouraged by the wishful thinking of some of his advisors among Iranian exiles, who underrated the strength of the revolutionary regime and the patriotic sentiments of Iranian people. He was also fearful of radical Shia movements in Iraq itself, which he savagely repressed, while expelling more than 100,000 Iraqis of Iranian extraction or known sympathies for Khomeini into Iranian territory.[40]

Saddam's undeclared invasion at first caught the Iranians by surprise, resulting in the ruin and loss of the border town of Khorramshahr, which was liberated by the Iranians late in May 1982, compelling Saddam to begin to sue for peace. Many volunteers joined the Revolutionary Guards, and a new and virtually self-sacrificing paramilitary force called *Basij* (lit. Mobilization) – also made up of volunteers, most of them below or above conscription age, including many teenage boys – was launched, and the regular army demonstrated its loyalty to the revolutionary regime by effective participation in the war. The heroism and quest for martyrdom of the Basiji boys became a daily event. Comparing them with the Republican fighters in the Spanish civil war described in George Orwell's report, a western journalist was to write two decades later:

> The confluence of religion and politics in their thin frames was a coming together of personal and universal interests. They too were fighting for earthly rewards, but that was not the sum of it. . . . Whenever a Basiji threw himself onto a rocket-propelled grenade that had landed in a crowded trench – and such acts of heroism were commonplace – he was doing his comrades the ultimate service. Yet he was doing himself a service too. He died smiling because he had convinced himself that going in a certain way, with certain words on his lips, would be in his own interest.[41]

The Islamic Republic turned down Saddam's peace moves in June 1982 and the Saudi Arabia-led plan of offering substantial reparations and indemnity to Iran. Anger, revolutionary fever and the hope of replacing Saddam's regime with an Islamic republic prompted Khomeini and his lieutenants to take the war into enemy territory. 'War War till Victory' (*Jang Jang ta Piruzi*) became a regular official slogan as long as the war lasted. Even as late as July 1988 when the war was drawing to a close, Khomeini was to declare:

We have repeatedly declared this truth about our Islamic foreign and international policy that we wish to extend Islam's influence in the world, and reduce
the dominion of the world-devourers (*jahan-kharan*, i.e the imperialist
powers). Now if the lackeys of America would like to describe this attitude as
expansionist and the idea of creating a world empire, we would not be deterred
by it, and would even welcome it.[42]

By 1984, Saddam's military objective changed from occupying Iranian territory
to preventing Tehran from making any major gain inside Iraq. He tried to increase
the cost of the war to Iran by buying more and better weapons, mainly from the
Soviet Union and France, and using chemical weapons against Iranian troop
concentrations. The chemical attacks were especially damaging, causing thousands
of deaths and injuries, but had little effect on Iranian morale. In March 1984
Iranians captured parts of the Majnun Islands, whose oil fields had economic as well
as strategic value. Iraqi chemical attacks continued to be supplemented by the war
of the cities, that is, Iraq initiating air attacks on Tehran and other Iranian cities and
Iran responding in like manner. Meanwhile, the tanker war and attacks on shipping,
begun by Iraq when it invaded the Iranian island of Kharg, raged in the Persian
Gulf; in this the United States later joined on the side of Iraq.

Iran's international isolation was a product and consequence of the radical
change in its foreign policy since the revolution, which had brought it immense
popularity among third world and particularly Muslim people but severely
weakened its relations with the world and regional powers. It broke off relations
with Israel, stopped the flow of Iranian oil to South Africa, joined the non-
aligned countries in the United Nations, advocated the liberation of the world
masses much as other revolutions had done before and asserted full autonomy
in its foreign relations. Yet, as noted, in the hostage-taking drama Iran had
overplayed its hand by holding on to the American hostages for too long
(though largely for domestic reasons), and ended up by making a financially
unfavourable settlement, having already paid a high diplomatic cost for its
policy. It was opposed to the Soviet policy in Afghanistan, yet it did try to some
extent to play off Russia against America. But this policy began to lose its force
from the mid-1980s when US–Soviet relations took a favourable turn.[43]

The war of attrition which began in 1984 was to go on for another four years,
Iraq depending mainly on weapons and credit from its Arab and western
backers, while Iran pushed nationalist sentiments, revolutionary zeal and the
Shiite cult of martyrdom to their utmost limits to compensate for their complete
isolation. Large population displacements took place both in the war zone and
elsewhere, growing numbers of people temporarily leaving the main cities to
escape the bombing, some of them coming back to see their houses ruined and
some of their dear ones dead, maimed or shell-shocked. Nothing as horrific as
this had been experienced by the country in recent centuries. It soon became a
'rose garden of martyrs' in name as well as fact, and the flower of its youth
destroyed by landmines and mustard gas.

WAR ISLAMISM

Yet despite its revolutionary enthusiasm, the Islamic Republic was confronted with hard realities regarding the conduct of the war, the running of the economy in the face of the decline and later collapse of petroleum prices from the early 1980s, the suppression of the militant domestic opposition and peaceful opponents of the continuation of the war and the hostility or indifference of virtually every regional and international power. The result was the emergence of a regime which may be best described as War Islamism, by analogy with the regime of War Communism which ruled over Russia during the civil and foreign intervention wars between 1918 and 1921.[44] The economy was largely geared to the war machine, shortages of consumer goods were inevitable and a system of rationing was introduced, which, although far from ideal from the public's point of view, was on the whole managed well. There was a sustained decline in the average standard of living; in 1988 alone, the last year of the war, the GDP shrank by almost 8 per cent.[45] There was a sharp rise in inflation and civilian unemployment and a continuing decline in the rate of exchange of the rial.[46] In general, the overall economic performance deteriorated, even though some sections of society might have become better off in consequence of the revolution.[47]

This was a politically repressive and economically *étatiste* regime. All opposition was effectively banned, and virtually all criticism described as 'aiding the enemy'. The second Majlis, elected in 1985, was packed with Islamists, not even a single Muslim non-Islamist such as Bazargan being any longer a member. Nevertheless, its members were officially or unofficially barred from raising sensitive questions, notably regarding Iran's secret contacts and deals with the United States, which, when exposed late in 1986, became known as the Iran-Contra affair or Irangate.[48] The main deal was the secret sale of limited US military equipment via Israel to Iran, in exchange for Iran's help in getting American hostages released in Lebanon, while the proceeds of the deal were used by the United States for financing the right-wing guerrilla operations against the government of Nicaragua. The exposure was particularly aimed at discrediting Majlis Speaker Hashemi Rafsanajni, who had been directly involved in the affair.[49] Some of the Iranian radical Islamists who exposed the deal via their contacts in Lebanon and were tried and executed[50] were close to Ayatollah Montazeri, whom the Assembly of Leadership Experts had earlier elected deputy and heir to Khomeini, but he was otherwise not implicated in the affair.[51]

Iran had become a corporate state. The government of Prime Minister Mir Hosein Mousavi (Musavi) consisted of young Islamist radicals with much passion for a state-run economy and egalitarian policies. The Majils was run by Ali Akbar Hashemi Rafsanjani, who was in effect in charge of the war effort, while President Seyyed Ali Khamenei, who was later to become supreme leader, acted as the overseer of the government's executive branch. The Foundation for the Downtrodden (*Bonyad-e Mostaz'afan*) became a large socio-economic conglomorate, and while its operations had a considerable impact on the economy, in practice it was not answerable to any official body.[52]

ABSOLUTE GUARDIANSHIP

If the political critics of the regime were weak and suppressed, it was different with those powerful bazaar merchants and other businessmen who increasingly disliked the government's *étatiste* attitude, which was translated into policies the most important of which had to be cleared through parliament. The government had the Majlis majority, but increasingly they had to face the resistance of the Council of Guardians, the constitutional body which vetted parliamentary legislation so as to ensure that it was consistent with Islamic and constitutional laws. There was thus a confrontation between the two most powerful faces of modern Islamism, the radical, *étatiste* and egalitarian and the conservative, capitalistic and market-orientated. This had already taken institutional form in the split of the radical Association of Militant Clerics (*Ruhaniyun-e Mobarez*) from the influential Society of Militant Clergy (*Ruhaniyat-e Mobarez*). After quite some time, when it looked as if part of the government's business was grinding to a halt, and following appeals for his intervention Khomeini sided with the radicals, although this did not result in their complete victory, as War Islamism was drawing to a close, let alone later when peace and Rafsanjani took over (see Chapter 14).

As the theorist of Islamic government, it was not surprising that Khomeini entered the controversy with his new conception of the Absolute Guardianship of the Jurisconsult (*Velayat-e Motlaqeh-ye Faqih*). The main point of the conflict had been the extent of the powers of the state over the rights of private property. In a long speech hitting at the traditionalist ulama and the business community, Khomeini was later to say that 'the authorities of the revolutionary Iranian regime should realize that some Godless people would describe anyone as communist and eclectic who works for the poor and needy, and treads the path of Islam and revolution',[53] and still later was to add that 'the genuine ulama of Islam have never accepted the yoke of capitalists, money-worshippers and khans ... The committed religious leadership are staunch enemies of blood-sucking capitalists.'[54]

In a fatva issued in December 1987 in response to a question put to him by the minister of labour and social affairs, Khomeini confirmed that the minister was well within his rights to go ahead with the ministry's proposed legislation (which favoured workers vis-à-vis employers). Prime Minister Mousavi quickly interpreted this as a general fatva confirming the extraordinary powers of the Islamic state.[55] This was incredible to a number of religious politicians and dignitaries. They took it to imply that the state was above the law and could take and implement arbitrary decisions. Thus, Ayatollah Lotfollah Safi, the Secretary of the Council of Guardians who was close to Grand Ayatollah Golpayegani, a senior *marja'* in Qom, wrote to Khomeini:

Certain people have concluded from your fatva that the government can use this power to substitute any social, economic, family, commercial, civil, agricultural or other system for the original and direct Islamic systems [and reverse the *shari'a* rules]. Clearly, as your blessed opinion has always acted as a general guideline, this time, too you will correct the mistake.[56]

Khomeini disappointed Safi by replying that there had been no mistake and that his fatva was 'applicable to all affairs which are under the dominion of the state'.[57] However, he ended his letter to Safi by saying that they should not 'pay any attention to rumours'. In an address at the Friday prayers in Tehran, President Khamenei tried to take advantage of Khomeini's vague reference to 'rumours' and interpreted his letter to Safi as meaning that speculations about the limitless powers of the state were nothing but rumours.[58] Khomeini's response to Khamenei was as clear as it was shocking:

It appears from your address at the Friday prayers that you do not regard government as legitimate in the sense of the Absolute Guardianship given to the most noble Prophet . . . Your interpretation of what I have said, in the sense that it simply means that the government has power only within the commandments of God, is entirely contrary to what I had intended.

I should point out that government [which is a branch of the Absolute Guardianship of the Prophet] is one of the primary rules of Islam, and has priority over all subsidiary rules, even including those governing prayers, fasting and hajj.[59]

And he went on to make plain the implications of his new theory for the day-to-day practice of government:

The [Islamic] government can ultimately break [even] those contracts which it had made with the people on the basis of *shari'a* rules, whenever the contract may be contrary to the expediency (*maslahat*) of the country and Islam. It can also stop any activity – be it spiritual or temporal – whose continuation would be contrary to the expediency of Islam.[60]

Finally, he emphasized that the fears expressed by Ayatollah Safi of the Council of Guardians that Islam's social and economic rules could be violated by the new order were irrelevant, for 'even if this was so, it is part of the powers of [Islamic] government'.[61]

The gates were thus opened for the longest-running and most intensive controversy within the regime since 1981, when it had finally purged itself of all of its members who were not fully committed to ideological Islam. In a seminar of jurisprudents and religious leaders which was shortly convened in Qom to discuss the concept of Absolute Guardianship, Ayatollah San'ei hit the nail on the head by asking 'Is the Guardianship itself law-giving or arbitrariness; is the

Guardianship . . . itself a law, or lawlessness?'[62] The question directly concerned the regime's political legitimacy, for, by definition, arbitrary rule cannot be legitimate. The notion of absolute rule had been already implicit in Khomeini's original concept of the Guardianship of the Jurisconsult because it meant that an unelected person or body of persons would lay down the law *within the framework of the shari'a* for an answerable government. It could therefore draw its legitimacy from the *shari'a*, despite the fact that it was absolute and unrepresentative.

But the new theory of Absolute Guardianship went categorically beyond this. It claimed for the jurisprudent the full authority of the Prophet in matters of both spiritual and temporal government, but was silent about the fact that the Prophet's authority had been legitimized only be divine revelation and inspiration and/or the concept of sinlessness and infallibility. If the Guardian was neither sinless nor infallible nor in direct communion with God, on what legal authority could he suspend, modify or replace fundamental *shari'a* laws whenever he judged them to be inexpedient or contrary to the interest of Islam? Was Islam itself subject to arbitrary definition by whoever happened to be in power? And, regarding the issue of political legitimacy, what was the difference between this and traditional arbitrary rule?[63]

However, a compromise was finally reached which led to the institution of the Council for Determining the Expediency of the Regime, according to which whenever there was persistent conflict between the Majlis and the Council of Guardians, the matter would be arbitrated and finally settled by the Expediency Council. This was not an unhelpful channel for settling such disputes, but it was a far cry from Khomeini's theory of Absolute Guardianship. What had triggered the whole controversy was, however, not a legal but a political matter. Therefore the establishment of such a council could do nothing to resolve the political conflict between radicals, moderates and conservatives.

CEASEFIRE

As noted, this controversy suddenly arose in the final months of the war, which had been going on at great human and material cost and with little or no achievement. A notable Iranian victory had been the capture of the Al-Faw peninsula in February 1986, which was retaken by the Iraqis in April 1988. The capture of Al-Faw was probably another good opportunity for Iran to present Iraq with peace terms favourable to itself. But the policy of 'War, War till Victory' was then still in full sway. In 1988 the biggest Iraqi chemical attack to date was launched in the battle for Halabja, a small Iraqi Kurdish city on the Iranian border whose people were suspected of disloyalty to Saddam. It infamously led to the death and serious injury of 5,000 Kurdish civilians alone. An international journalist was later to recall:

For years before this particular atrocity, only a handful of London-based reporters and regional specialists (including myself) condemned Saddam. Ours were lone and isolated voices. Most western media organisations lapped up the deliberately misleading agenda set by lobby briefings and the White House and State Department. In the words of Geoffrey Kemp, at the time the head of the Near & Middle East at the State Department, Saddam was 'our son of a bitch' . . .[64]

The Iranians flew an ITN camera crew, which happened to be in Tehran, straight into Halabja, together with agency photographers. It took three more weeks for the world to realize the full scale of the horror.[65] Even at this stage, Washington and London were not interested in taking the story any further: they continued to support Saddam. Whether Saddam deliberately targeted the Kurds, or whether they were caught in crossfire as Iraq targeted Iranian soldiers, the fact remains that whoever gave the orders – Saddam or one of his officers – was fully aware that the theatre of deployment for this horrendous weapon was a mass of civilian men, women and children.[66]

Iraq had been traditionally a client state of the Soviet Union and had had close ties with France, especially for rearmament. Now the Americans restored diplomatic relations with Iraq (broken off since the six-day Arab-Israeli war of 1967) and gave it increasing financial, material, diplomatic and logistical support. Apart from France, some other EU countries also helped Iraq's war machine, while the Arab countries of the Persian Gulf continued a massive flow of cash to the Iraqi government.

By mid-1988 the Iranians began to realize that in effect they had taken on the whole world single-handedly and that if there was to be any victory in that war it would not be theirs. Several hundreds of thousand people had been killed, maimed, disabled, displaced from their homes or afflicted with mental illness. Untold destruction had been caused and many economic resources had been wasted. The Iranians had fought with great courage and fortitude but at last they saw that this was not a war that they could possibly win. On 3 July 1988, the US navy cruiser USS *Vincennes*, whose captain later admitted that it had been in Iranian territorial waters at the time, shot down an Iranian passenger airliner with the loss of 290 passengers and crew. Nevertheless, the Iranians accepted UN Resolution 598 late in July 1988, and by 20 August the ceasefire came into effect. It was not a defeat, but it negated eight years of optimism and definite promise of victory to the Iranian people.[67]

After all this, only Khomeini could communicate the ceasefire decision to the Iranian people – and especially to those masses who held him virtually sacred – in such a way that he knew would minimize its disappointing and dispiriting effect. 'I have traded my honour and reputation with God' he said in a radio broadcast, and added:

Had it not been in the interests of Islam and Muslims, I would never have accepted this, and would have preferred death and martyrdom instead. But we have no choice and should give in to what God wants us to do . . . I reiterate that

the acceptance of this issue is more bitter than poison for me, but I drink this cup
of poison for the Almighty and for his satisfaction.[68]

But the guns did not entirely fall silent yet. The Mojahedin, who, backed by
Saddam Hussein, had been camping in Iraq for several years, launched an attack
after the Iranian government had accepted the ceasefire resolution. They
invaded western Iran and fought with the Pasdaran for the city of Kermanshah.
At first they benefited from Iraqi air cover, but once this was withdrawn under
international pressure, the operation quickly lost its momentum and ended in
the Mojahedin's defeat; they also lost several thousand of their fighters.

It looked as if the revolutionary fervour had died down and, to some extent at
least, been replaced with low morale in consequence of the acceptance of the UN
resolution. But this was not to last long. While a series of summary executions had
begun in Iranian jails, the British author Salman Rushdie's book *The Satanic Verses*
was published in September 1988, and gradually began to be seen by Muslims
across the world as a great insult to Islam, the Prophet, his wife and even Ayatollah
Khomeini. Public protests came first from British Muslims, then from Pakistan
and other countries with large Muslim populations. By February 1989 Ayatollah
Khomeini was alerted to the issue, and he issued a fatva 'that the author of the book
The Satanic Verses, which has been compiled, printed and published in opposition
to Islam, the Prophet and the Koran, and those publishers who were aware of its
contents, are sentenced to death.'[69] At a stroke, the lull was broken: there was great
excitement among Iranian and other Muslim peoples and fierce international
controversy returned, resulting in the deterioration of Anglo-Iranian relations just
at the time when they were about to be raised to ambassadorial level.

THE FALL OF MONTAZERI

Ayatollah Hosein Ali Montazeri, Khomeini's deputy and heir designate, was a
former student of Khomeini, a faithful disciple of his from the early 1960s and a
leading figure of the revolution who had spent many years in jail before being
released late in 1978. But he was more of a religious scholar than a politician, and
he believed that the Islamic Republic should have a wide social base, show a
higher degree of tolerance towards the non-committed and refrain from treating
its opponents too harshly.

His conflict of opinion with Khomeini began after the defeat of the Mojahedin
invasion late in July, when Khomeini had instructed the judicial and intelligence
authorities to execute many political prisoners held in jail.[70] The prisoners to be
executed included many who had already served or were about to finish serving
their jail sentences. In the event – and according to various estimates – 2,000 to
7,000 inmates were executed, some of them recently captured Mojaheds but
many also existing Mojahed and leftist prisoners.

In the first of three letters, addressed to Khomeini and dated 27 July 1988,
Montazeri explicitly protested against 'your recent order [to the authorities] to

execute the Hypocrites [i.e., the Mojahedin] who are held in prison', adding that while the execution of those involved in the recent attack may be 'acceptable to society', 'the execution of individuals who had been previously given lower sentences than capital punishment ... bypasses judicial principles and the decisions of the judges involved'. In a letter of 15 August to a number of judicial and security authorities Montazeri enjoined them to refrain from 'vengeance' and wondered whether 'all of our arguments in jurisprudence concerning caution in matters [which involve the spilling] of blood have been incorrect'. And in a subsequent letter on 3 September to Khomeini, he related the account of a *shari'a* judge who had watched impotently as a security official decided to execute a Mojahed who was both repentant and prepared to join the front against Iraq.[71]

Montazeri had seldom made a secret of his unhappiness with some of the regime's arbitrary and illiberal decisions. For example, in October 1988, he had gone as far as saying in public:

The respectable individuals who are in charge of the country and the revolution, and have themselves had the bitter taste of lack of freedom of expression in the unjust monarchical regime ... must not imagine that just because the [former] arbitrary regime has now been destroyed we no longer have any need for freedom of speech ... *None of us is sinless and infallible so as to be in no need of advice.*[72]

But now the leaking of his letters outside Iran, months after they had been written and just after the Salman Rushdie affair, led to Khomeini making a direct attack on Montazeri, and on 29 March 1989 the latter resigned his position. 'From the very beginning I myself was seriously opposed to my own appointment as Deputy Leader,' he wrote in a humble letter of resignation to the Leader, adding that 'if there have been any inevitable mistakes and weaknesses, they should hopefully be corrected under your guidance'.[73]

Overnight, his pictures disappeared from walls, and his official title of Exalted Jurisprudent (*Faqih-e Aliqadr*) and Grand Ayatollah was turned into Hojjataleslam, which in his case was highly contemptuous. Montazeri was to continue his criticism of the regime and virtually advocate democratic government in the next two decades, which often resulted in his words being censored and in him being put under house arrest.[74]

THE DEATH OF KHOMEINI

The Ayatollah passed away on 3 June 1989, a little more than two months after Montazeri's political disgrace. Khomeini had been suffering from chronic heart disease, and death occurred in consequence of a series of heart attacks. He was eighty-nine.

A jurisprudent, mystic, charismatic revolutionary leader and religious innovator, it would not be an exaggeration to say that he had the greatest impact on

Iranian history since the Constitutional Revolution. But he probably saw his mission as much beyond that: as a successor of the Prophet, his mission extended to the entire Islamic world. And although he did not establish a new Islamic world order, it cannot be denied that the Islamic world after Khomeini was considerably different from what it had been before him. His Islamic revolution impacted on the whole world of Islam in various ways.

Khomeini's funeral drew millions of mourners to the streets, and in the frenzy some of them died or were injured. Iran, a country of martyrs and mourners, had not seen such a huge or passionate and emotional funeral procession in living memory. It will be worth quoting from the direct observations of Tom Fenton, a senior American journalist who covered the event for CBS news on 5 June 1989:

> By mid-morning, the sun beating down on the mourners had pushed the temperature outside the glass case to nearly 38 degrees Celsius. The case was perched on a makeshift platform of truck containers draped with black cloth . . . Inside lay the body of Ayatollah Khomeini, coolly waiting to be buried . . . The Ayatollah's body was lying in state in a prayer ground in north-central Tehran, to allow his people to pay their last respects. In keeping with Moslem tradition for preparing a body for burial, Khomeini's feet were pointed towards Mecca. The black turban indicating his descent from the Prophet Mohammed lay on his chest . . . All around us in the dusty field were groups of women weeping in their black chadors and clusters of men beating their chests and heads. Men from the Revolutionary Guards Corps . . . were trying to cool down the crowd with fire hoses, but emotions were rising with the outside temperature . . . I knew it was going to be one of these events you never forget. Ayatollah Khomeini would be buried as he lived, in the eye of a religious storm.

Fenton went on to add that

> even though much of Iran's middle class had mixed feelings about his revolution, there was no question about his place in the hearts of millions of Iran's poor. He still held them in a spell, in death as he did in life . . .
>
> An endless stream of Iranians turned out on the morning of the funeral, which began on the open ground where his body was lying in state . . . The government planned to transport the body in a refrigerated truck from the prayer ground to the burial ground 15 miles south of the capital. That was not going to be easy. Roads out of the capital were clogged with mourners, all of them on foot. Much of the able bodied population of Tehran and hundreds of thousands of people from the surrounding countryside wanted to accompany their leader to the grave, and if possible to touch the corpse . . . When the prayers ended, reporters watched with astonishment as people ran forward and grabbed the Iranian flag draped on the open coffin, and a green cloth beneath the body. The coffin tilted as it was carried to the truck, threatening to spill the

body on the ground. The authorities were losing control. Frenzied mourners finally brought the funeral procession to a halt. Plans were changed, and a helicopter was called in to transport the body the rest of the way.

Fenton explained that 'Passions in the crowd below us had reached fever pitch': they saw two men being passed hand over hand by the crowd. Their eyes were wide open but they were lifeless. They had apparently beaten themselves to death.

Iranian television announced that the funeral had been postponed until tomorrow, and the crowd was asked to return home. Five hours later, when the burial ground had been cleared, a helicopter arrived carrying the Speaker of the Parliament, Ali-Akbar Hashemi-Rafsanjani, who had taken charge of arrangements. Minutes later, another helicopter landed carrying Khomeini's body, this time secure in a closed aluminium box that looked like an airline shipping container. Despite the ring of Revolutionary Guards surrounding the burial ground, there was another chaotic scene as clergymen and the Guards themselves pushed and shoved for the honour of carrying the box. The top was ripped off, and the body was removed and lowered into the grave. Khomeini was buried, as prescribed in the Muslim religion, wrapped only in a shroud. Stone slabs were placed over the corpse, and the grave was quickly filled as the burial ground overflowed with hysterical mourners. The box was ripped to pieces for relics. By the next morning, a black container stood over the grave. Flowers were placed on top of it. Mourners stroked the metal walls and wept. A huge mosque was eventually built on the site of the grave. And despite all the predictions (including my own) that chaos would follow, Iran remained remarkably calm after Khomeini's death.[75]

The predictions, mentioned by Fenton, that chaos would follow after Khomeini's death did not materialize because, despite certain superficial traits, this had not been a one-person rule, and the regime still had a wide social base, as witnessed by the funeral itself.

CHAPTER 14

Iran after Khomeini

Arbitrary Rule (estebdad) *and chaos* (harj-o-marj) *are two sides of the same coin.*

Seyyed Mohammad Khatami

IN 2008 IRAN WAS still in the news headlines, being described by the West and Israel as a threat to peace. Rumours were flying about an imminent American and/or Israeli attack on Iran's nuclear and military installations, while the country was admired in many Muslim and third world counties for standing up to America. It had undergone significant changes in all spheres of life since 1989, but at the same time all the major domestic and foreign problems had remained, and some even had intensified. The winds of change had been blowing since the death of Khomeini, but, as is familiar from Iranian history, in different and unpredictable directions. An important consequence of Khomeini's disappearance from the scene was the emergence or, better perhaps, coming to the surface of intra-regime conflicts, which were to widen as well as diversify in the next two decades, so that by mid-2008 there were serious divisions within the Islamists themselves, apart from the opposition of non-Islamist Iranians. The passing of Khomeini ended an Iranian short term and began another, but only within the regime itself, since otherwise the Islamic Republic continued to exist long after his death.

Khomeini was the overseer, arbiter and ultimate law-giver of the system but was not an arbitrary ruler in the style of the shah and traditional Iranian rulers. He drew his political legitimacy from the large number of people who looked upon him not just as a *marja'*, a traditional source of religious emulation, but primarily as a charismatic revolutionary religious leader. That is what made his position unique and irreplaceable, no matter who occupied the role of spiritual leader after him. A fundamental change in the mode and style of government, and the emergence of political conflicts and ideological disagreements, were therefore virtually inevitable.

CONSTITUTIONAL REVIEW

Shortly before his death, in April 1989, Khomeini set up a twenty-five-man council for the revision of the constitution, specifically instructing them to remove article 109 of the constitution, which laid down that the leader must be a *marja'*. The decision to revise the constitution was not a product of socio-political conflict either within or outside the regime but an acknowledgement that the constitution needed to be revised in the interest of greater clarity and efficiency. The main issues under discussion were the establishment of the machinery for the election of Khomeini's replacement and the encoding of the powers of the supreme leader in the constitution; the rationalization and central-ization of the executive and judiciary branches of the regime, given that there was a president, a prime minster and cabinet as well as a speaker of the parlia-ment (Rafsanjani) who had increasingly assumed executive responsibilities; the clarification of the position and the rights and duties of the Expediency Council; and the reform of the administration of the radio and television network.[1]

The new amendments granted the supreme leader extensive powers – for example, being commander-in-chief of the armed forces, appointing the head of the judiciary, appointing half of the membership of the Council of Guardians and so forth – that had already been enjoyed by Khomeini on his own personal authority, their significance now being in their formal extension to the office of the elected supreme leader, whoever he might turn out to be.

The amendments also provided for a new head of the judiciary, over and above the supreme court and chief justice. But by far the other most important constitu-tional amendment was the abolition of the office of prime minister and creation of an executive president, which brought into existence the necessary structures for a strategy of reform and reconstruction.[2] The fall of Ayatollah Montazeri a few months before had if anything proved that the regime was not ready for funda-mental change but only gradual development from the revolutionary, ideological period to a post-revolutionary, realist or pragmatist stage.

WINDS OF CHANGE

On 5 June 1989, two days after Khomeini's death, President Ali Khamenei was elected by the Assembly of Leadership Experts as the supreme leader, his religious rank being simultaneously raised from *hojattoleslam* – a lower rank – to ayatollah, although not yet to a *marja'* or grand ayatollah. He was to be declared a *marja'* in 1994 amidst conflict and controversy among the leading clerics.[3] As noted, no one could possibly have inherited Khomeini's authority, even if a grand ayatollah had been elected to replace him. But Khamenei's election in effect led to a separation of the leadership from the traditional *marja'iyat*, which had been largely united under Ayatollah Khomeini. This helped to reinforce the priority of the political over the purely religious qualifications of the supreme leadership. Put another way, the election of Khamenei demonstrated more clearly than before the fundamental

change in the position of the Shiite leadership itself that had occurred in consequence of Khomeini's Islamist as well as Islamic revolution. The new leader had
emerged not upon popular acclaim but as a result of being elected by an assembly
which also had the power to dismiss the leader.[4] Looking back, it marked a
growing tendency towards the separation of the traditional *marja'iyat* from the
Islamic government.

Khamenei was then a leading revolutionary Islamist with moderate views.
He came from a modest clerical background in Mashhad, had studied at the
Mashhad, Qom and Najaf seminaries but had stopped short of becoming a
mojtahed. As a devoted student of Ayatollah Khomeini, he had been active in
Islamist politics under the shah and had spent several years in jail and internal
banishment. With the triumph of the revolution he had emerged as one of the
younger members of the leading Islamist elite, and after a couple of stints in
government had been elected to the non-executive office of the presidency in
1981, having in the meantime lost the use of his right hand due to an assassination attempt by the Mojahedin-e Khalq. Yet despite the non-executive nature
of his office, he remained important and influential, not least as Tehran's Friday
Prayer Leader. It was in recognition of his loyalty, political experience and
closeness to the deceased leader that he was supported by a number of leading
Islamist figures, but especially Rafsanjani, for the position of supreme leadership.
He said in his inauguration address:

> I am an individual with many faults and shortcomings and truly a minor semi-
> narian. However, a heavy responsibility has been placed on my shoulders and I
> will use all my capabilities and all my faith in the Almighty to be able to bear
> this heavy responsibility.[5]

Since the presidential position had been vacated by the election of Khamenei
as leader, by the end of July Rafsanjani won an overwhelming victory in the fifth
presidential election. The election was held simultaneously with a referendum
for the recently drafted constitutional amendments, which had abolished the
office of prime minister and turned the presidential office into an executive presidency. Thus Khamenei became the supreme leader and Rafsanjani the head of
the executive and chairman of the cabinet.

Rafsanjani had been born into a well-to-do traditional provincial family and
been taught at the seminary in Qom by, among others, Ayatollah Khomeini, to
whom he had become a devoted disciple as a young man. He had become an
Islamist activist in the early 1960s and like Khamenei had spent several years in
prison. He had been one of the closest Islamist leaders to Khomeini during and
after the revolution, effectively in charge of the running of the war with Iraq and
Majlis speaker, with considerable influence in the conduct of foreign policy.
While being wholly committed to the Islamic regime, he was nevertheless a
pragmatist or realist regarding both domestic and international politics. As such,
he had gone along with the radicalization of events in consequence of the war

and revolutionary struggles during the 1980s, but now, after the ceasefire and the passing of Khomeini, his pragmatic outlook was set on social and economic reconstruction and improvements in regional and foreign relations. He said, for example, after the acceptance of the UN ceasefire resolution, which he among others had been supporting:

> The main thing is that we can stop making enemies without reason because of this new move. This has put a new path in front of us. There are many people who are currently giving help to Saddam [Hussein] who would not have done so if our foreign policy had been right.'[6]

This was reflected in the assistance he provided for the release of western hostages held in Lebanon.

Better relations with regional and international powers were one important objective which at the time large numbers of people and the majority of the country's leadership wished for. Iran had been terribly isolated in the region as well as the world at large, and the war had virtually exhausted the spiritual reserve of the people, whether Islamist or non-Islamist. The great loss of life, the extensive material damage, the highly illiberal and intolerant domestic politics, the dramatic fall in the standard of living and rationing had led to demands for normalization of the economy and society, especially as the human and material hardship and sacrifice of the long war had not resulted in any tangible victory.

THE EMERGENCE OF INDEPENDENT PROPERTIED CLASSES

Alongside steps taken towards a relatively more moderate approach to foreign relations, there was also a change of direction in economic policy against *étatisme* and corporatism and in favour of privatization and a more liberal outlook towards the domestic economy and foreign trade. There was planning for reconstruction, but there was also considerable space for the development of the private sector, dominated by the bazaar, or traditional business community, as a socio-economic community.[7] This marked the beginning of the emergence of merchant and capitalist groups as relatively *independent* social classes which, for the same reason, provided a social base for the state. The bazaar had indeed played an important role in the revolution and had continued to be the strongest property-owning base of the Islamic Republic after its triumph. But the decade of revolution and war and the concomitant radical turn of events had delayed the emergence of business classes as *independent* socio-political entities.

This is what began to take place in the 1990s for the first time since the rise of the shah's arbitrary rule in the mid-1960s. It may be recalled that from the early 1940s and the abdication of Reza Shah until the mid-1960s property-owning classes (at that time both landlords and merchants) began to reassert themselves as independent social classes, especially in the 1950s, after the 1953 coup had put an end to the chaotic trends of the 1940s and established a dictatorship. Apart from the small number of big merchants with a foot in modern industry and the expanding trade with the West, the bazaar was generally in opposition, while the landlords and the small and expanding modern business sector were generally behind the regime (see Chapter 10). The bazaar greatly benefited from the oil bonanza of the 1960s and 1970s, but this did not turn it into a social base for the shah's regime, mainly due to the absolute and arbitrary nature of that regime, which did not afford independence and participation to any social class, but partly also because of the bazaar's religious outlook and its alienation from official westernism. In other words, the bazaar's grievance against the shah's regime was largely political and cultural rather than economic, as some authors in the West have believed.

The oil bonanza also led to the growth of the modern business class, which, despite being the closest client of the state, was no more independent from it than the other social classes and therefore could not function as its social base (see Chapter 11). Hence it did not raise a finger to defend the state against the revolution, nor was it represented by any political movement or organization (see Chapter 12). That is also what crucially distinguished it from the 'bourgeois comprador' class, which has often been described as the class base of modern third world dictatorships.[8] The main pillars of the modern business sector, though perhaps no more than thirty businesses in number, were the losers in the Islamic revolution, some of them with debts to the banking system worth more than 50 per cent of the value of their assets. Most such properties were confiscated after the fall of Bani Sadr in 1981, and their owners left the country (see Chapter 13). But, contrary to the bourgeois comprador theory, this was not primarily in consequence of foreign trade connections – in which leading bazaar merchants had also been involved – but due to being dubbed as 'taghuti' by virtue of being modernists without religious roots while at the same time being closely dependent on the state.

The oil boom of the 1960s and especially 1970s had, as noted in Chapter 12, led to the rise of new social classes, which were generally alienated from and hostile to the Pahlavi state. They included newcomers to the traditional as well as modern middle class activities, including trade and the professions. With the fall of the former regime, it was they as well as the more established traditional communities who benefited from opportunities opened up by the Islamic state. It was not necessary for them to be active Islamists, and so long as they could not be accused of being 'taghuti' or 'liberal' they could enjoy promising professional placements or be active in the private accumulation of capital. And, crucially from the point of view of state–society relations, it was these social classes and communities which, especially from the 1990s, identified with the Islamic state and provided its most important social base. They were generally involved in domestic trade, foreign trade, modern industry and – to a lesser extent – modern agriculture.

It was not surprising then that the fundamentalist Islamist crowds – generally known as Hezbollah, later describing themselves as *Ansar-e Hezbollah*

(Supporters of Hezbollah) – taking to the streets to demonstrate against Rafsanjani's government, especially in its last two years (1995–7), often shouted the slogan 'Death to the capitalist' (*marg bar sarmayeh-dar*). There was little doubt as to the identity of 'the' capitalist, particularly as Rafsanjani himself was a rich businessman. But the matter went beyond that and, however symbolically, marked the appearance of classic class conflict within the Islamist fold. As noted, the Iranian Hezbollah, which literally means the Party of God, was a relatively shapeless crowd run by behind-the-scenes hardliners who would come out from time to time to demonstrate and shout harsh slogans or attack and break up the meetings of 'liberals' and reformers. Their similarity with the Lebanese Hezbollah was mainly in name rather than activity and organization.

THE FOUR MAIN FACTIONS

However, the forces behind Hezbollah were not the same as the radicals of the late 1980s and early 1990s who had lost a power struggle to the conservative-pragmatist alliance upon the ceasefire declaration, constitutional change, Khamenei's succession and Rafsanjani's election to presidency. In the earlier years of Rafsanjani's tenure, the old radicals were openly critical both of the new economic policy and the less hard-headed foreign policy. They believed in the continuation of illiberal economic policy and inflexibility in foreign relations. But in later years their differences with Rafsanjani's government were defined far less along economic or foreign policy lines and far more in the direction of a more open (though still Islamic) society. By the mid-1990s there were no longer three but four clearly identifiable Islamist factions which, in the absence of party political groupings, were largely represented by different newspapers and journals.

The factional struggle reached a climax twice in the early 1990s. In October 1990 the Council of Guardians (a conservative stronghold) required a number of well-established radicals, including Majlis Speaker Hojjatoleslam Mehdi Karroubi (Karrubi) and the former minister of the interior Hojjatoleslam Ali Akbar Mohtashemi-pur (both of them leading members of the Association of Militant Clerics), to sit for an examination to prove their proficiency in Islamic jurisprudence in order to qualify for nomination to the Assembly of Leadership Experts. This they regarded with disdain and refused to accept; and the acrimony surrounding the episode served to further bring into focus the conflict between the radicals and the then conservative- pragmatist alliance.[9]

The next and politically more severe clash of the radicals with the prevailing conservative-pragmatist alliance occurred over the approval of candidates for the 4th Majlis elections in 1992. The Council of Guardians, interpreting its constitutional right to 'oversee' or 'supervise' elections to include disqualification of 'undesirable' parliamentary and presidential candidates, disqualified a number of the old radicals from standing, including some deputies of the previous Majlis and former ministers and government officials. This led to loud protests by the candidates, who argued that supervision of elections did not confer the right to the Council to vet candidates. Besides, they demanded that the Council publish the reasons for which they had disqualified any candidate. Yet ever since, the Council has insisted on disqualifying 'undesirable' candidates for elected offices without stating its reasons. In the 2004 Majlis elections it resorted to wholesale disqualification of reformist deputies in the outgoing 6th Majlis. In 2008 many if not most reformist candidates were excluded from taking part in the 8th Majlis elections. The Council thus became the most effective single instrument for upholding the interest of the conservative groups in the Islamic Republic.

It was largely the radicals of the 1980s – such as Mehdi Karroubi, Mohammad Mousavi (Musavi) Kho'ini-ha, Abdollah Nouri (Nuri) and Behzad Nabavi – who, having been supplanted by Rafsanjani's conservative-pragmatist alliance first in the executive, then in the legislature, later in the 1990s made up the principal circle of the reformist movement that, in 1997, championed Mohammad Khatami's election to the presidency. In time, they were joined by such younger Islamist journalists and intellectuals as Abbas Abdi, Mashallah Shamolva'ezin, Hamidreza Jalaeipour and many others, some of whom had been among the Line of Imam students who had taken American diplomats hostage in 1979. The old radicals thus fundamentally changed from being associated with illiberal, étatiste and orthodox revolutionary attitudes and policies to a political community that, although still Islamist, increasingly resembled an Islamic humanist vision and a social-democratic attitude in their broader political outlook. Together with the Islamist intellectuals (Roshanfekran-e Dini) such as Abdolkarim Soroush, Mohsen Kadivar and Mohammad Mojtahed Shabestari, they began to argue that Islam was compatible with democracy, some of them even openly regretting their erstwhile opposition to the ageing Mehdi Bazargan, who had advocated the same view both before and after the revolution. Increasingly, this tended to become the 'liberal' face of the Islamist regime, especially in regard to domestic politics but also, to a lesser extent, vis-à-vis foreign relations, to the consternation of both the conservative and, particularly, the radical fundamentalist (Hezbollah) groups.

Their first popular daily newspaper was Salam, which began to publish in 1991 and 'soon turned into one of the most widely read newspapers, not least for its Alo, Salam (Hello, Salam) column, with questions and comments from the readers, some of which were in effect news reports provided to the paper by the public'.[10] Other influential journals which represented the new radical outlook were the Islamic intellectual bi-monthly Kiyan, published by Jalaeipour and edited by Shamsolvaezin (Shamsolva'ezin), which promoted the ideas of the religious reformist Soroush (Sorush), and the largely theoretical bi-weekly Asr-e Ma, run by Behzad Nabavi, a leading figure of the Organization of the Mojahedin of the Islamic Revolution. Both Nabavi and this organization (not to be confused with Mojahedin-e Khalq) had made a radical shift from their acute étatiste and anti-western position of the 1980s to one that advocated more political and economic freedom and better relations with outside powers. Together with the leading women's monthly *Zanan*, these were the main journals advocating the views of the reformed radicals who led the reform movement which, in 1997, brought Khatami to power. Their most important political organization was still the Association of Militant Clerics, which included Karroubi, Kho'ini-ha and Mohtashemi-pur.

The old radicals were then replaced by a new radical fundamentalist faction (or Hezbollah), which nostalgically looked back to the early revolutionary and war periods, advocating policies which included political illiberalism, populist egalitarianism, a command economy and a hard-line foreign policy. They were the main organizers of the street crowds, noted above, shouting 'death to the capitalist'. The daily newspaper *Kayhan* (later joined for a period by the daily *Sobh*) was the most energetic advocate of this faction's views. And though they did not have a clearly identifiable social base, they nevertheless managed to steal the show from the reformists, the pragmatists and the conservatives in the 2005 presidential election when Mahmoud Ahmadinejad, the candidate closest to them, was elected president. In time, Ayatollah Mesbah Yazdi emerged as their purest and most vocal spokesman among the ulama, arguing that Islam is incompatible with democracy, being critical of popular elections and maintaining that Islamic government is the domain of God, which must be run by jurisprudents as the guardians of the people.

Rafsanjani's pragmatist faction was at first mainly represented by the veteran daily *Ettela'at*, the only newspaper then to refer to him as ayatollah. It had a fairly wide base in the bazaar and among the new business classes as well as the expanding technocratic and bureaucratic group. Well-known figures in this faction were Kamal Kharrazi, then Iran's ambassador to the United Nations, and Vice-President Ataollah (Ata'ollah) Mohajerani, who, respectively, became foreign minister and minister of culture and Islamic guidance under Khatami. It was later represented by the newly formed Hezb-e Kargozaran-e Sazandegi (Agents of Reconstruction Party), which published the daily *Kargozaran*.

Finally, the conservative faction was made up of older and more powerful bazaar magnates, the more traditional Islamist ulama such as Ayatollah Meshkini in Qom and elsewhere and younger politicians who favoured a more liberal economic policy (hence their early alliance with the pragmatists) but were opposed to liberal political reforms and emphasized traditional religious values. The two most important organizations representing them were the relatively old Hei'at-ha-ye Mo'talefeh-ye Eslami (The Coalition of Islamic Societies), which mainly represented the bazaar conservatives and was later to be renamed Hezb-e Mo'talefe-ye Islami (Islamic Coalition Party), and the Society of the Militant Clergy (i.e., the Society of Combatant Clergy), which represented the Islamist conservative clerics. Among its younger and non-clerical adherents were Ahmad Tavakkoli and the brothers Ali and Mohammad Javad Larijani. The daily *Resalat* mostly represented conservative views, followed with some distance by *Jomhuri-ye Eslami*, which was closest to Khamenei.[11]

RAFSANJANI'S REFORMS

Rafsanjani took over the executive branch of a country that was ravaged by war and revolutionary struggles, had lost much of its inflated optimism of the late 1970s and early 1980s and was isolated in the region and the whole world. The revolution had not resulted in the millennium and the war had ended without conquest or compensation. Instead, the economy was in very poor shape and public morale was at its lowest since the late 1970s. Between the late 1970s and 1990, the standard of living had declined by half,[12] as a result of the steady fall in oil prices since the early 1980s from over \$31 in 1982 to less than \$19 in 1989[13] and the considerable rise in the annual rate of population growth from 2.7 per cent in the late 1970s to 3.6 per cent in the late 1980s, the total population having risen by 15 million from about 34 million to about 49.[14] Meanwhile, the cost of the war both in local currency and foreign exchange had left hardly any room for productive investment, while both war and revolutionary struggles had resulted in the flight of large amounts of capital and human resources. Inflation and unemployment rates were high and rising, money was scarce and international borrowing was extremely difficult due to the country's political isolation.

These were the circumstances in which Rafsanjani and his team launched their first Five Year Plan, trying to reduce the scale of government participation and intervention in the economy and relax some of the restrictions on the market. In typically Iranian fashion, they began with too much optimism and saw this as a panacea for all the country's economic ills, applying the new policy too fast and with too much zeal. The sudden opening up of the economy to the outside world led, among other things, to the accumulation of short-term debts to the tune of between \$20 and \$30 billion.[15] With its vast oil and gas resources there should have been no problem for Iran to raise its credit requirements in the world market, not least from the World Bank and the IMF, which would normally extend long-term credit on favourable terms to members of good financial standing. It was the Islamic Republic's unhappy foreign relations that provided a barrier against this, especially in the shape of the US economic sanctions, in which domestic US factors and Congressional legislation played the greater role. Notwithstanding his 'duel containment policy' vis-à-vis Iran and Iraq, President Clinton might have adopted a less punitive approach had such been allowed by American domestic lobbies and Congress.[16]

Meanwhile, as oil prices were showing no sign of picking up, hovering around \$15 to \$20,[17] the government and its licensees began to sell crude oil over and above the OPEC quota, sometimes for as little as \$8 per barrel. Thus, from the mid-1990s high foreign debts, a shortage of foreign credit, erratic changes in the foreign exchange regime and the rate of exchange, lessons from making too rapid and drastic changes for the circumstances and pressure from other Islamist factions for higher social welfare, lower inflation and lower unemployment left the government with little choice but to discontinue some of its trade liberalization policies.

The activities of such parastatal foundations as the *bonyads* (publicly owned giant charitable organizations) were also unhelpful to the process of economic policy change and management, since, given their size and importance in the economy, their virtually autonomous operations interfered with and reduced the efficacy of government decisions, for example for the control of the money supply. According to an extensive study of the *bonyads*, these foundations tended to prop up the revolutionary power centres and, using their influence in the 4th Majlis (1992-6), they managed to redirect the trend of privatization of state enterprises from the private sector to the para-governmental organizations.[18]

By 1995, two years into Rafsanjani's second term as president, a considerable amount of economic reconstruction, including repair of infrastructural damages caused by the long war, had been achieved, and Rafsanjani's supporters had given him the unofficial title of 'Commander of Reconstruction' (*Sardar-e Sazandegi*). Yet in the last two years of his tenure he increasingly looked like running a lame duck government, having largely abandoned his original strategic initiatives and lacking any clear line by which to move forward.

While there had been relatively less political turmoil since Rafsanjani's election to the presidency, there had also been little political development. It might have been difficult to initiate significant political change as early as 1989 even if the pragmatist-conservative alliance of the time had been favourable towards such a policy. This, however, remained the rule throughout Rafsanjani's eight-year presidency. The strategy of economic development without political liberalization began to be referred to as 'the Chinese model', and was resented by those Islamist and non-Islamist critics who had looked forward to a more open society. It is possible that Rafsanjani himself was somewhat in favour of such developments but his highly pragmatic style would not allow him to risk it too far beyond mentioning 'the practice of democracy' (*tamrin-e demokrasi*) from time to time. Regarding the position of women and young people, he made two celebrated gaffes, perhaps deliberately just to test the ground. One was when he said that if 'ladies' (*khanom-ha*) did not like the Islamic dress code they could wear two-piece suits instead. Facing the immediate outcry of the fundamentalists he explained that he had meant they should wear a chador as well. On the other occasion, he said that young men and women could enter a loving relationship through the Shia institution of temporary marriage, which he said they could enter upon verbal agreement. This time even some modern middle class women objected, saying that they would not be able to control the behaviour of their daughters when the country's president was encouraging this kind of 'licence'. The pragmatist president then backtracked, explaining that he meant they should go through a legal marriage ceremony.

As noted, Rafsanjani's government had been running out of steam in its last two years: his economic policy was in retreat; his foreign policy had reached a stalemate despite improved relations with the main regional players and the beginnings of a dialogue with EU countries (especially Germany and France), largely because of the continuing US–Iranian conflict; and the opposition of the other three factions (reformist, fundamentalist and now also conservative) to his government. In particular, the conservatives, who had supported Rafsanjani for some years, were now looking towards his replacement by one whom they could call truly their own. Being anxious about the prospects, Ataollah Mohajerani, a vice-president and the most liberal member of the government, even suggested, to the loud opposition of all the other factions, that the constitution should be amended to allow Rafsanjani to run for a third presidential term. All the signs indicated that the conservatives would win the 1997 presidential election, hardly anyone suspecting a highly unpredictable though historically familiar Iranian overturn of fortunes and refutation of predictions.

THE TIDE OF REFORMISM

23 May 1997 in the Iranian calendar was the 2nd of Khordad 1376. It was the day of the Islamic Republic's seventh presidential election in which Hojjatoleslam Seyyed Mohammad Khatami won a landslide victory. Khatami's election became known as the Epic of 23 May (*Hemaseh-ye Dovvom-e Khordad*), because of the high turnout and his 69 per cent of the votes but perhaps most of all because of the great enthusiasm with which most of the public, especially young people and women, both participated in and celebrated the victory. Six months earlier, there had been little doubt that Hojjatoleslam Ali Akbar Nateq Nuri, the Majlis speaker and conservative candidate, would be the next president. The reformist faction had been looking for a credible candidate just to put in a show but with little hope of winning the election. Their favourite candidate was Mir Hosein Mousavi, the 1980s prime minister under whom many of them had served in various capacities, but he was not ready to oblige, as indeed he did not eight years later in the 2005 elections.

It was relatively late in the day that the reformists turned to Khatami, who was known only among the political and intellectual elite. Born in 1943 in a town in the central southern Yazd province, he had read western philosophy at the University of Isfahan and education at the University of Tehran before attending the seminary in Qom and qualifying as a cleric. He had been a deputy in the 1st Islamic Majlis (1980–2) and had held other public posts, the most important of which was the portfolio of culture and Islamic guidance.

During his ministry press censorship was relaxed, a greater variety of journals appeared and there was an increase in the production of music, which Ayatollah Khomeini legalized along with playing chess and of which the traditional clerics did not approve. The Iranian film industry, led by such internationally renowned directors as Abbas Kia-Rostami, Mohsen Makhalbaf, Bahram Beizaei and including a growing number of younger talents, began to take off as a major local and international art form. But perhaps Khatami's greatest claim to fame among the elite, and the biggest single source of concern about his policies on the part of conservatives and hardliners, was his virtual ending of book censorship in the early 1990s.

'Western cultural onslaught' (*tahajom-e farhangi-ye gharb*) was a turn of phrase adopted by those circles who feared the loss of Islamist cultural austerity and the beginnings of a more open cultural sphere. Some of Khatami's admirers even began to talk about the emergence of a cultural renaissance, though that was a somewhat optimistic view. Combined conservative and fundamentalist pressure was put on both Rafsanjani and Khatami to apply greater restrictions. Khatami refused: rather than submitting to these demands, he resigned from office and was appointed to the politically insignificant directorship of the National Library. In a long resignation letter to Rafsanjani, which even some of the non-Islamist intellectuals described as 'a manifesto on freedom of expression', he defended cultural freedom while at the same time reiterating his commitment to the Islamic regime. He wrote:

> Unfortunately for a while now we are witnessing that in the field of cultural affairs all legal, religious, ethical, and secular norms are being violated ... Nowadays, every means is justified in the name of certain ends and as such the order of things is about to lose its logical and legal relevance ... The most immediate effect of this ambience is the discouragement and insecurity of fine and distinguished thinkers and artists, even those who are firm believers in the revolution and Islam.[19]

Khatami already had two books and several articles to his credit when his name was put forward as a presidential candidate. His pleasant looks, charming smile, sartorial neatness and, above all, fluent speech were important vote winners. His talk of the rule of law, tolerance, the development of the civil society and the rights and welfare of women and young people struck a strong chord with educated people, both modern and traditional, especially the young and women: a woman fully clad in ski gear, in a ski resort north of Tehran, said in English to a British TV reporter 'All women love Khatami!'

Having already taken important political, social, educational and cultural strides, women were now ready to push their efforts to higher levels for more rights and greater equality, especially before the law. Many if not most of the young were first-time voters; being the products of the baby boom of the late 1970s and early 1980s, they had not experienced the revolution, and were looking for jobs and new social and cultural opportunities. At the level of the political and intellectual elite, as noted, both the old radicals, who now made up the bulk of the reformists, and 'the religious intellectuals' (*roshanfekran-e dini*) had been advocating reform through their press, books and meetings, which mainly influenced the young people. All these agents and factors played a crucial role in Khatami's victory, not least the young volunteers for his campaign who, among other things, packed the streets, stopping cars to hand out election leaflets and loudly saying 'only Khatami' (*faqat Khatami*).

Yet all this did not quite make the sum. It was a general turn away from more of the same and a wish for a fresh start that turned the electoral table: many of those who voted for Khatami were religious, and some of them, from the lower strata, were to vote for Ahmadinejad eight years later. It was the combination of almost all the moderns and most of the traditionals that made Khatami's landslide victory possible, both then and in 2001. The public jubilation at the time of Khatami's victory was reminiscent, though on a much reduced scale, of February 1979. So shocked were some of the leading conservative clerics that they tried to pressurize the supreme leader, Ayatollah Khamenei, to cancel the election, but this he refused to do. Nevertheless, the highly significant difference in the light of Iranian history and society described in this volume was that one-third of the votes went another way.

Highly significant also was the great emphasis that Khatami and reform-minded journalists and intellectuals put on the rule of law. In so doing they were explicitly mindful of the legacy of the Constitutional Revolution, the revolution for law, almost a century before (see Chapter 8). Although absolute and arbitrary rule no longer functioned as in the past – since power was not concentrated, there were some checks and balances, and the regime had a social base – piecemeal arbitrary behaviour was still prevalent, not least in the treatment of peaceful political dissidents. They were often dragged from their homes, physically and mentally abused and brought in front of the television to admit the charges against them, and they sometimes died in custody, as in the case of Mozaffar Baqa'i and Ali Akbar Sa'idi Sirjani.[20] Such practices did not entirely cease under Khatami or afterwards, but the scale was considerably reduced. Most of the arrests were made following legal procedure, and Khatami always condemned official lawless behaviour whenever it was suspected. Still, given Khatami and the reform movement's acute and explicit awareness of the country's long tradition of arbitrary rule – Khatami often saying that 'arbitrary rule and chaos are two sides of the same coin' – the question of the rule of law went far beyond that, and the pitch went so high, that no less a person than the supreme leader himself emphasized it in his public speeches, and said more than once that no one, including himself, was above the law.

The extension and promotion of civil society was contingent on the rule of law, and it further required the extension of the public sphere and therefore greater freedom of expression and the press. As Hossein Shahidi wrote:

> During President Khatami's first year in office the number of publications rose to 850, with the total circulation exceeding two million a day; the Association of Iranian Journalists . . . was established; and there were changes in the make-up of the press jury . . . that resulted in more decisions in favour of journalists . . . The minister of culture and Islamic guidance . . . made a point of personally attending the meetings of the press supervisory board. Early into its operation, the new board awarded licences to two dailies, *Jame'eh* (Society) and *Zan* (Woman), both of which were innovators in post-revolutionary Iranian journalism and early participants in what was going to be a long and escalating confrontation between the Iranian judiciary and the press.[21]

As radio and television were controlled by the conservatives, journals (both daily and periodicals) became the lifeline of the reform movement, and so they and their writers came under continuing attack by the conservative-fundamentalist factions, which gradually managed to eliminate many of the journals and reduce the scale of criticism in those that remained in circulation. Run by Faezeh (Fa'ezeh) Rafsanjani, a daughter of the former president, *Zan* was an unusual Islamic newspaper, and it did not take very long for it to be banned. *Jame'eh* was published and edited by the aforementioned Hamidreza Jalaeipour and Mashallah Shamsolvaezin: in later years, when Shamsolvaezin was editing another newspaper much in line with *Jame'eh*, which by then had been banned, he was put on trial and served a jail sentence.

All this was part of a long process of emergence and elimination which might well be described as the 'battle of the press'. To a large extent the conservative-fundamentalist factions won this battle in the end, but not even under the anti-reformist presidency of Mahmoud Ahmadinejad was there a complete return to the status quo ante, that is, to the situation before Khatami, when, for example, vigilantes would beat unconscious a bookseller and set fire to his shop because he was selling an authorized book which they did not like or when the publication of the word *buseh* (kiss) in books was banned by the censors.[22]

Khatami's liberalization policies met with increasing resistance by his opponents, and by the time he had reached the fourth year of his first term he and the reformist movement had already lost significant ground. However, growing intra-reformist conflict and disillusionment began to emerge through his second term (2001–5).

TRADITIONALIST OPPOSITION

The reformists and their supporters were at first highly optimistic about the prospects for reform, but events proved them to have been too hopeful. They had won a landslide victory in which Rafsanjani played an effective role by preventing vote-rigging. They enjoyed the support of women and the young in particular. The Islamic Students Union and the Bureau of Reinforcing Unity, which included many activists, was behind them. Apart from their own organizations, a considerable number of prominent modern Islamic political theorists and 'religious intellectuals' such as Sa'id Hajjarian, Abbas Abdi, Akbar Ganji, Hasan Yousefi Eshkevari, Abdolkarim Soroush, Mohsen Kadivar, among many others, were campaigning for political and religious reform. Rafsanjani and his Agents of Reconstruction gave them support – Ataollah Mohajerani, one of their ranks, being Khatami's liberal minister of culture and Islamic guidance – although, as the reform movement became more radicalized, Rafsanjani was later to be alienated from them.

Another movement which gave the reformists critical support was the fellowship of various groups and individuals who were now dubbed the Melli-Mazhabis. Best described as religious democrats or religious Mosaddeqites, their

strongest organization was Bazargan's old Freedom Movement, which now, after
his death, was being led by Ebrahim Yazdi, who had been an old hand in the
party and Bazargan's foreign minister after the revolution (see Chapter 13).
Another leading figure among the Melli-Mazhabis was Ezattaollah Sahabi, also a
minister in Bazargan's cabinet, who had seen jail both before and after the
revolution. He was the publisher and editor of the influential bi-weekly journal
Iran-e Farda, which on the front cover of its first issue after Khatami's election
carried the headline 'The Big No!' Because of its relatively long history, its
religious commitment along with a commitment to parliamentary democracy
and its association with Mosaddeq's legacy, the Melli-Mazhabi movement was
qualitatively important. At the same time, it began to attract the attention of a
larger number of people, especially among the young, who were warming to
Mosaddeq's memory. This newly found popularity of the Melli-Mazhabis upset
not just the radical fundamentalists, who long before had described their politics
as 'liberal' and their religious attitude as 'American Islam', but also the conservative establishment. Thus the Melli-Mazhabis were subjected to judicial harassment, many of them were imprisoned for various terms and their publications
were eventually banned. Persecution of them intensified, especially between the
Majlis elections in the year 2000 and the presidential election (Khatami's second
term) in 2001, such that in the end they virtually ceased to have any significant
effect in the sphere of current politics.

Such was the strong show of support for the reform movement early after
Khatami's election in May 1997, after the 2nd of Khordad. Yet they tended to
underrate their opponents and the social, political and military forces they could
muster. Despite their serious electoral setback, the conservative establishment
was far from beaten. They had the Majlis majority (until the year 2000), the
Council of Guardians, the Expediency Council, the Assembly of the Leadership
Experts and the judiciary; the private economic sector was largely in their
hands; they controlled the *bonyad*s, the Revolutionary Guards and the regular
army; and radio and television were under the supreme command of the leader,
who was then following a centrist line but was essentially more inclined towards
the conservative establishment.

The reformists also faced the hostility of radical fundamentalists. Although
the latter did not have a large social base, they nevertheless controlled some
important newspapers, such as *Kayhan*, and could easily organize street gangs
described as Supporters of Hezbollah by themselves and by students and
reformists as 'plain-clothes men' (*lebas-shakhsi-ha*) or 'pressure groups' (*goruh-
ha-ye feshar*). Among other things, they used to attack authorized demonstrations by students and Khatami's supporters. Once in a public demonstration they
even beat up Mohajerani, the culture minister, and Abdollah Nouri (Nuri), the
interior minister, whom they pejoratively dubbed as 'liberals'. This prompted
critics to call Iranian society sarcastically a 'beating society' (*jamehe-ye zadani*)
rather than a 'civil society' (*jameh'eh-ye madani*). Not long afterwards, Nouri
spent three years in prison on the charge of insulting Islam.[23] Khatami was later

criticized by various groups for not having completely fulfilled his election promises (even though experience had made these promises more limited in his 2001 re-election), but it is unlikely that against the active opposition of his opponents, he could have achieved much more than he did, short of a violent clash with them, which he would not risk, nor could he have won even if he had attempted such a policy.

THE CAMPAIGN FOR DEMOCRACY

Along with 'civil society', 'public sphere' and other terms, a central concept that began to be hotly debated was the 'D word'. Was Islam compatible with democracy, and if so, should the Islamic Republic be reformed to become one? As noted, the religious intellectuals had made a beginning with this debate under Rafsanjani, but it was during the Khatami years that this became a central issue. The less radical writers argued that democracy was possible even within the terms of the existing constitution; others believed that it would not be possible without significant changes in the constitution. Both the secular fundamentalists and the Islamic fundamentalists argued that Islam and democracy were incompatible. The first group argued that democracy presumed the existence also of liberalism and secularism, and so it could not be applied in an Islamic framework; the second group held that the government of Islam was the domain of God and his representatives, and so the people would not have any say in it. Inevitably, this brought forward the sensitive question of *Velayat-e Faqih*, Guardianship of the Jurisconsult, which both involved a fundamental constitutional issue and concerned the position of the incumbent, Ayatollah Khamenei. Some authorities, such as Grand Ayatollah Montazeri, argued that the concept of guardianship had been misapplied and, if rightly interpreted, would be consistent with democratic government.[24]

Among other statements and activities, it was Montazeri's personal attack on the supreme leader that led to his house arrest in Qom for many years. Others rejected the Guardianship altogether. The late Ayatollah Ha'eri Yazdi, an Islamic philosopher and son of the highly respected founder of the Qom seminary, argued, in a book that was banned in Iran, that government in Islam was based on representation (*vekalat*), not guardianship (*velayat*).[25] Mohsen Kadivar, a leading clerical scholar who later went to jail, argued that eight of the ten traditions quoted from the Prophet Mohammad and Shii Imams as justification for the Guardianship were unreliable, and the remaining two did not prove the point.[26]

However, democracy and whether or not it was compatible with Islam and Shiism – 'the paradox of Islam and democracy' (*pardoks-e eslam va demokrasi*) as it came to be known – remained the central issue. Abdolkarim Soroush along with other reformist religious philosophers made use of modern hermeneutics to argue that the traditional readings of the Koran and Traditions were not necessarily the only possible or acceptable versions of the texts. Having rejected any and all conceptions of an Islamic ideology,[27] he went on to argue that proper readings of the principal sources show that there can be democracy in an Islamic society.[28] Further than this, Soroush declared that 'religious law [*sharia*] is not synonymous with the entirety of religion; nor is the debate on democratic religious argument a purely jurisprudential argument'[29]:

> Once the status of . . . reason has been established; once the theoretical, practical, and historical advances of humanity are applied to the understanding and acceptance of religion; once extra-religious factors find an echo within the religious domain; and finally, once religion is rationalized, then the way to epistemological pluralism – the centrepiece of democratic action – will be paved.[30]

Hasan Yousefi Eshkevari, the liberal cleric who was to be defrocked and imprisoned for several years after the Berlin Conference, was another tireless contributor to the debate on 'the paradox of Islam and democracy'. There were three theories, he said, each of which had its supporters in the Muslim world. One group believed in a 'religious government of the caliphate type' and 'consider democracy as permissiveness'; another believed in 'liberal democracy' in its western form:

> But the defenders of the third theory believe that there is no contradiction between religion and democracy that would compel us to forsake one for the sake of the other: [they hold] that Islamic government cannot be undemocratic . . . I defend the theory of 'Islamic democratic government', but I believe that basically in today's world, without following a democratic system, Islamic government is neither possible nor desirable.[31]

It was this third theory that Khatami was publicly advocating, calling it '*mardom-salari-ye dini*' in Persian. He did not claim that the exiting regime quite answered to that description, but, often repeating the view that 'democracy is not a programme but a process', he maintained that it was possible as well as desirable. It was this attitude which worried his traditionalist opponents most, and especially the extremists among them.

SERIAL KILLINGS

On 21 November 1998 the people of Iran were stunned by the official announcement that Daryush Foruhar, the veteran People of Iran party leader and labour minister in Bazargan's cabinet later turned an active dissident, had been viciously murdered together with his wife, Parvaneh Eskandari, also an active dissident, at their home in Tehran. For a few days various rumours about the possible perpetrators circulated in official circles, mainly hypothesizing that foreigners were involved; not only Israel but even Turkey was mentioned. Within the next twenty days the bodies of two dissident writers, Mohammad Mokhtari and Mohammad Ja'far Puyandeh, were found and identified, having been beaten and strangled. These murders shortly became known as serial killings or chain murders (*qatl-ha-ye zanjireh'i*). Tehran was gripped in horror, and fear spread everywhere that many intellectuals and reformist activists were on the killers' hit list. Describing the atmosphere resulting from the consecutive murders, the monthly reformist journal *Peyam-e Emruz*, wrote:

> The catastrophe of the murders through which Dariyush and Parvaneh Foruhar, from political groups, and Mokhtari and Puyandeh, from intellectual groups, were butchered and strangled, apart from worrying Iranian society and especially writers and intellectuals, was also followed by certain rumours. For example, there was a rumour about the existence of a list or lists which contained the names of those who were designated to be killed. The existence of such a black list swept like a wind what was left of the peace of the intellectual community. Many took precautionary measures . . . No one had confidence in the telephone anymore because it was believed that the murders were based on the knowledge of meetings arranged by telephone . . . The [official] investigation of the murders which gave society hope the culprits would be punished helped to reduce the scale of fear. But the murders . . . were so unprecedented, shocking and hateful to Iranian society that their effects can still be observed in society.[32]

It was widely believed that the murders were not just intended to terrorize reformist journalists, activists and the intellectual community into silence and inaction but that they were part of a plot to force Khatami to resign. The circulation of an unofficial hit list reminded some people of the kidnapping and murder of General Afshartus, Mosaddeq's police and security chief, when according to the authorities a hit list had existed in order to force Mosaddeq's resignation (see Chapter 11). Rumours were flying in every direction, and for several weeks society held its breath.

Before Khatami became president, there had been a number of highly suspicious deaths, mainly of writers and intellectuals for a number of years, perhaps the most important of them being Ahmad Tafazzoli, a world-famous professor of linguistics at the University of Tehran. There had also been an unsuccessful attempt to turn a bus carrying twenty-one intellectuals off the road and down a cliff. In all these cases it was suspected that the perpetrators were members of the intelligence organizations.

Early in January 1999, less than a month after the last two killings, the ministry of intelligence announced that they had uncovered the gang of murderers and that they were members of the staff of their own ministry. Although the revelation was shocking, it also brought quick relief to the community, since it showed that they were not going to be repeated and that the powers that be, and certainly the supreme leader, had approved of the revelation. Sa'id Emami, also known as Eslami, a senior official of the ministry of intelligence and one-time deputy minister for security,[33] and a number of ministry officials were arrested and charged with the killings. It was believed that Sa'id Hajjarian, a leading reformist theorist and journalist and one-time senior official of the intelligence ministry, had been instrumental in identifying the culprits. In the year 2000 he himself fell victim to an assassination attempt which left him paralyzed: this was apparently intended as revenge both for his role in exposing the serial killing suspects and his contribution to the reformists' landslide victory in the parliamentary elections for the 5th Majlis before the attempt on his life. It was later announced that the chief suspect, Sa'id Emami, had committed suicide in jail. The others were sentenced to up to ten years' imprisonment in their final appeal hearing. The victims' families boycotted the judicial process, arguing that the suspects were mere instruments and that there must be a search for those who had been behind the killings. More specifically, they believed that the perpetrators must secretly have sought and received a fatva or fatvas by one or more senior ayatollahs as religious sanction for the murders.

Another public figure who was suspected of being a subject of revenge by radical conservatives was the mayor of Tehran. Gholamhosein Karbaschi, an able and efficient administrator, had served in Isfahan before Rafsanjani made him the mayor of Tehran, where he was to found Iran's popular and all-colour newspaper *Hamshahri*, which was generally in line with the reform movement. He was controversial because of his unorthodox policies for the expansion and reconstruction of Tehran. These policies helped to rapidly expand and extend housing, urban highways and green space, but at the expense of increased congestion and pollution and the spread of high-rise buildings. However, these were not the main reasons for which he was tried in a court and sentenced to jail and a heavy fine. The main charge against him was the misappropriation of public funds, but the public, with whom he became more popular after his arrest, firmly believed that his real offence was the effective contribution he had made to Khatami's landslide victory.

A pattern emerged whereby the judiciary increasingly assumed the functions that used to be performed by the ministry of intelligence and the ministry of culture and Islamic guidance: control of publications, especially the press, and punishment of political offences. They would ban newspapers and journals for a short period or for ever, put publishers and other members of the press on trial and often jail and/or fine them, and in doing so often clash with the guidance ministry, which would accuse the judiciary of invading their administrative territory or otherwise defend the accused. It was the judiciary versus the executive, and later the legislature as well. In effect the judiciary had become the main vehicle for conservative efforts to contain the reform movement. In time, and after the landslide victory of the reformists in the sixth parliamentary elections in the year 2000, it even began to summon parliamentary deputies on political charges, certain of whom were interned for short periods.

STUDENT RIOTS AND THE BLOCKAGE

It was the judiciary's closure of the serious and influential newspaper *Salam*, the oldest and most influential reformist daily, published by Hojjatoleslam Kho'ini-ha and edited by Abbas Abdi, and the summoning of the former to the Special Court for Clerics which sparked off the second-most serious domestic crisis of the first term of Khatami's presidency. This subsequently became known as the 9 July (18 *Tir*) disaster. On 8 July 1999 the students at Tehran University, who at the time generally supported Khatami's government, held a demonstration without obtaining prior permission from the ministry of the interior to protest against the closure of *Salam*. That night, their halls of residence were attacked by a unit of riot police, backed up by a band of vigilantes who, while shouting religious slogans, assaulted any and all students resting in their rooms. The police action shook the government and the university authorities, who condemned it; the police denied having issued orders to the unit; and even the supreme leader publicly expressed regret at the incident. But the matter did not stop at that. The students reacted by holding angry demonstrations next day: these quickly spread into riots in which unemployed young people also took part; buildings were damaged and cars overturned. It took four days before calm returned to Tehran and other cities to which the unrest had spread.[34]

The eyes of the reformists were set on the parliamentary election for the 6th Majlis in February 2000. Some of their leading theorists, such as Hajjarian, were almost publicly saying that once they won the Majlis majority they would implement their entire reform programme, the central aim being the establishment of a form of democratic government. Events showed that once again, they were too hopeful. They did win a landslide victory but they had reckoned without the Guardian Council's power of veto and, ultimately, the supreme leader himself. Indeed, the first test came up very early in the day. The outgoing Majlis had banned a large number of reformist newspapers and journals. Therefore, the very first step that the new Majlis intended to take was to reverse that decision. But they had hardly begun the debate when the reformist Majlis speaker Hojjatoleslam Mehdi Karroubi presented the House with an edict by Ayatollah Khamenei which forbade the Majlis from going ahead with that legislation. The edict was described as a *hokm-e hokumati* (state ruling, or governmental ordinance) rather than a fatva because, according to the ideologues of the regime, a *hokm* was binding for the whole of society whereas a fatva had to be followed merely by the adherents of a given *marja'*.[35]

From then on, the conservative Guardian Council and the conservative-dominated Expediency Council vetoed virtually every government- or Majlis-initiated bill that was unacceptable to the conservative establishment. The judiciary, on the other hand, went on using its power to contain the reformist activists by various means, including arrest and imprisonment, which did not even quite exclude outspoken Majlis deputies. Meanwhile, the campaign of radical reformists against the election of Rafsanjani as a deputy for Tehran had largely resulted in his being alienated from the reform movement, thus narrowing its political base, although many of his Agents of Reconstruction did not withdraw their support from Khatami's government.

In time the obstructive decisions of the Guardian Council, the Expediency Council and the judiciary began to be referred to as *ensedad* (literally meaning 'blockage' or 'blocking'). In effect this revealed the inability of the executive and legislative branches – the two elected bodies – of government to implement policies to which the conservative establishment was strongly opposed. However, Khatami still retained much of his popularity despite such setbacks and despite his own observation that he had to face a crisis every nine days.[36]

One of the biggest of these was the fall-out from a meeting in Berlin, subsequently known as 'the Berlin Conference', early in April 2000. It was organized by the Heinrich Böll Institute as a 'post-election conference' and as a further contribution to the existing dialogue between the two countries. Those invited were invariably radical reformists and /or human rights activists. The conference was severely disrupted by a group of revolutionary immigrant Iranian dissidents, who condemned the reformist guest speakers as collaborators. The disruption took many forms, including a half-naked woman dancing and a man publicly taking off his clothes in the conference hall. There was a huge outcry by the anti-reformist factions and forces in Iran even before the conference participants had returned home. In particular, an edited videotape of the events had shown the speakers in a worse light from the conservatives' viewpoint. They were thus accused of treason both by the conservatives and their revolutionary opponents. Two of the seventeen participants did not return, but all of those who went back were put on trial in the revolutionary court. Eventually they were acquitted, but some of them were held in jail for a short period, including two of the four women defendants, the human rights lawyer Mehrangiz Kar and the feminist publisher Shahla Lahiji. Three of them, Akbar Ganji, Hasan Yousefi Eshkevari and Eazzatollah Sahabi, received jail sentences on other charges. Continuing his defiance from jail, Ganji was to serve his six-year sentence in full.[37]

KHATAMI'S TWIN BILLS

Notwithstanding these events, Khatami's popularity survived, not least because illiberal measures were clearly the work of those opposed to him. A few of his promises had been fulfilled but some others had been frustrated by his powerful opponents. His main domestic achievements had included a relatively more open society, a freer press than before, the emergence of a large number of NGOs, cultural advancement and more social (though not legal) rights and opportunities for women. One of his most crucial achievements in the promotion of local democracy was his legislation which, for the first time in their history, enabled Iranians to elect their own municipal councils and mayors. In the meantime many of the reformists had organized themselves into the

Participation Front (*Jebhe-ye Mosharekat*), a coalition of reformist organizations and activists led by one of the president's brothers, Mohammadreza Khatami.

Thus Khatami was elected for a second term in the presidential election of 2001. Once again, it was a landslide victory, with an even greater majority than in the 1997 election. Though he still had a large parliamentary majority, this did not impair the ability and the determination of the conservative establishment to block any executive decision or parliamentary legislation to which they had strong objections or the judiciary in effect largely assuming the role that, before Khatami's election, the ministry of intelligence had played in trying to deter the activities of dissidents and reformists. One episode that presented Khatami's government with another crisis and led to a considerable amount of public unrest, especially among the students, was the 2002 trial of the university teacher and reformist intellectual Seyyed Hashem Aghajeri for apostasy. Initially Aghajeri was sentenced to death; this was commuted to a jail sentence on appeal, although not before the supreme leader had publicly declared that Aghajeri had not committed a capital offence.[38]

Another trial which almost became a *cause célèbre* was the arrest and trial late in 2002 of three reformist activists and social researchers: Abbas Abdi, the former editor of the banned newspaper *Salam*, the reformist sociologist Hosein Ghaziyan and Behruz Geranpayeh, a professional pollster. They were accused of a variety of serious crimes, including fabricating polls and selling classified information to America. In fact, following an intense public debate on whether or not Iran should talk to America, they had been testing public opinion on certain domestic and international issues which, inter alia, had shown that 75 per cent of the respondents favoured negotiations with the United States. After the usual charges of crimes against the country's security, including espionage, and trial by the radical fundamentalist newspapers, eventually the supreme court dropped the charges of espionage and sentenced Abdi and Ghaziyan to imprisonment.[39]

All this was part of the judiciary's campaign for the containment of dissidents and reformists, the last major episode under Khatami being the death in custody of the Iranian-Canadian photojournalist Zahra Kazemi in July 2003. She had been arrested for taking photographs of the Evin prison during the students' unrest and was in the care of the judiciary when she died as a result of head injuries. Khatami asked no less than four of his ministers to investigate the case. The ministry of intelligence emphatically denied having been involved in the case, clearly implying that the judiciary was to blame; and one of their agents was later acquitted of the charge of Kazemi's murder. In November 2005, while the appeal court upheld the acquittal, it reopened the case for further investigation. In the meantime, Khatami's presidency had come to an end and Mahmoud (Mahmud) Ahmadinejad had been elected president. That ended any further investigation, the official explanation being that Kazemi's death had been due to accident, the judiciary's initial explanation shortly after the incident.[40]

Meanwhile, the *ensedad* or blocking of the executive and the parliament by the Council of Guardians had been going on much as before Khatami's second term of office. In order to face the unending challenge of the blockage and the judiciary, Khatami finally decided to take the bull by the horns. In September 2002 he submitted his 'twin bills' to the Majlis in the hope of enhancing the power of the Majlis and the presidency vis-à-vis the Council of Guardians and the judiciary. The bills gave the president the power to identify violations of the constitution and take those responsible to higher courts; they also ended the vetoing of legislation by the Council of Guardians and removed the Council's power to disqualify parliamentary and presidential candidates.

The bills brought much excitement among the reformist groups, the Majlis and the public in general, although there were still some who believed that the measures were not radical enough. The move may not have looked unduly radical, but if successful it would have radically altered the structure of power in favour of the reform movement. The bills were eventually passed by the pro-reform Majlis majority despite the filibustering tactics of the minority, which moved a large number of amendments. However, although passed by the Majlis, the bills had then to be ratified by the Council of Guardians itself, and predictably the Council – after applying some delaying tactics – refused to approve of the curtailment of its own power.[41] Indeed, Gholamhosein Elham, then head of the Council's research centre and later to become President Ahmadinejad's alter ego, said at the time when the bills were still being debated: 'This bill is supported by anti-revolutionary elements, and if approved, all the infidels, former Marxists, and non-Iranians with acquired Iranian nationality can enter parliament.'[42] Fearing the bills' rejection, the reformist deputies had been threatening that they would then hold a referendum. It was not quite clear what the subject of such a referendum would be and who would actually conduct it across the country. Perhaps it was for such reasons that the thought was abandoned.

Thus about one and a half years before the end of his presidential term, Khatami had virtually reached the end of his tether, knowing that he could not do much more to reform the political framework. His public credibility, already damaged among his frustrated constituency, began to decline further. The more idealistic reformists had already coined the phrase 'passing Khatami by' (obur az Khatami).[43] He took all the blame; but he still maintained a brave face. The dreaded consequence of the rejection of the twin bills came in January 2004. Vetting the candidates for the 7th Majlis elections due to be held in the next month, the Council of Guardians disqualified about 2,500 candidates (half the total number). However, the biggest blow to Khatami and the reformists was the disqualification of eighty sitting reformist deputies, most of them members and leaders of the Participation Front. At first they threatened to resign en masse; then they staged a bast or sit-in in the Majlis building, hoping perhaps for a strong show of public support, which however did not materialize. Not even the students made a move.[44] The mood of their constituency was at best described by the noted motto 'passing Khatami by' and at worst by total disappointment and disengagement from politics. The bast came to nothing, and the joint efforts of Khatami and the Majlis speaker Karroubi to rally the support of the supreme leader did not pay off.

The public's lack of enthusiasm had already been demonstrated the previous year by their quiet but highly effective boycott of the Tehran Council elections, resulting in a landslide conservative victory and the appointment of the little-known Mahmoud Ahmadinejad as mayor of Tehran. Not surprisingly, in the February 2004 parliamentary elections the turnout was relatively low (about 51 per cent, but less than 30 per cent in Tehran), and the conservatives won a handsome victory, partly for this reason and partly because approved reformist candidates were a small minority.

OTHER DOMESTIC ISSUES

Apart from students and young people, women had played an important role in the reformist camp, both as activists and as rank-and-file supporters. Two of their intellectual politicians, Elahe Koolaee (Kula'i) and Fatemeh Haghighatju (Haqiqatju), were outspoken deputies in the 6th Majlis and were disqualified from standing for the 7th. But there were others outside of the formal political framework who played a major rule in both the feminist and reformist movements. Some of the best known among them were Shahla Sherkat, publisher and editor of the monthly journal *Zanan* (Women, which was eventually banned in 2007); Shirin Ebadi, human rights lawyer, especially as it concerned women and children's rights; Mehrangiz Kar, human rights lawyer and activist; and Shahla Lahiji, feminist publisher and publicist. There were many others, including the feminist journalist Parvin Ardalan and the author/translator Nushin Ahmadi Khorasani, who were later to become more widely known. Ebadi[45] and Kar[46] were early advocates of reforms that would put women legally on a par with men. The issues included laws governing marriage and divorce, the age of marriage, the custody of children, children's rights, inheritance and, not least, punishment for murder where, in effect, the law valued the life of a woman at half that of a man. They wrote articles and booklets, held meetings, delivered public speeches defending their cause and were occasionally interned, though – under Khatami – not for any length of time.

The legal battle did not get very far. There was some improvement in marital laws; the *mehr*, or the money men were legally obliged to pay their wives on demand, was indexed to the rate of inflation; women's rights in case of divorce were somewhat improved, though they remained far from equal with men's; the age of majority for girls was considerably increased; and there were some other minor gains. But much remained to be achieved, and not least the equality of women's lives with men's in murder trials.

In the social sphere, women had been making rapid progress since the early 1990s. They went to schools and universities in much larger numbers than ever before, so that eventually female university students outnumbered male students. Both concurrently and as a result, there was a rapid growth of women engaged in the medical and legal professions, the academic and teaching professions, the civil, including diplomatic, service, arts and literature, social and municipal works and private business. There was also a significant increase in male–female contacts and friendships among young people. Although disproportionately, these advances included traditional as well as modern women, most traditional women benefitting by being able to leave home and take part in social events and processes, unaccompanied by men. The unprecedented fall in the population growth rate from 3.2 per cent eventually to 1.1 per cent, which mainly resulted from sustained and successful government campaigns, was significantly helpful to that process.[47]

Shirin Ebadi famously won the Noble Peace Prize in 2003.[48] It is worth quoting her brief assessment of Khatami's record on the demands of women up to 1999:

> The major problem of Iranian women must be found in Iranian laws. As president, Mr. Khatami does not have the right to change or reform the laws. This matter is in the hands of the Islamic Consultative Assembly (i.e., the Majlis) which has a conservative majority. Therefore Mr. Khatami did not in practice manage to do anything of importance in women's interest. What is more important, however, is that during Khatami's presidency an open space has been opened for the press, and so protest against anti-woman laws is conducted, and discussion of the injustice to which the law has subjected women proceeds with greater freedom than before. Besides, more opportunities are given to women in official appointments, and they are in a better position. For example, during his presidency women were appointed to university presidency, deputy presidency, directorship of the institute for the protection of environment and as presidential advisor. And many women became heads of departments and university professors.[49]

The situation remained more or less the same until the end of Khatami's term.[50]

Khatami's number one objective was political development in all its aspects. That was part of the reason why he did not score any noticeable goals regarding the economy. On the other hand, the economy had suffered from many structural and policy problems for a long time, and to begin to tackle such problems would have required expert advice and a minimum of political unity, which did not exist and was not realized: Khatami's powerful opponents were out to make life difficult for him in every respect; and the magnates of the private sector and the *bonyad*s had little sympathy for Khatami either. The criticism levelled at him mainly by radical fundamentalists that he did not pay sufficient attention to economic issues referred almost entirely to further social welfare measures, although the state was already subsidizing many food items and health services. In addition, such utilities as petrol, gas and water were so heavily subsidized that for all practical purposes they could be regarded as almost free.

As noted in Chapter 13, crude oil prices had been steadily declining since 1982. The average price picked up somewhat in 1989 – the year of Rafsanjani's election to presidency – at $18.33, and in the 1990s it remained generally low, seldom rising above $20. In 1998, the second year of Khatami's presidency, the average oil price fell to $11.91, its lowest level for two decades. Between 2000 and 2003 it hovered between $20 and $27. Between 2004 and 2005, the last years of Khatami's presidency, it jumped respectively to $37.41 and $50.04; but it was Ahmadinejad who was to reap the benefits of soaring oil prices.[51] Thus the economy under Khatami suffered from shortages of foreign exchange in relation to the consumption and investment requirements. His attempts at securing substantial foreign credit and investment, notably the construction of an oil refinery by Japan, were frustrated largely if not entirely as a result of the United States' opposition. This did not help projects for reducing the rates of inflation and unemployment, the latter being a particularly sensitive issue in view of the high rate of young people's entry into the job market.

Khatami's general economic policy was an extension and continuation of Rafsanjani's before him, but with greater emphasis on privatization and deregulation, in the hope that these would provide more encouragement and security for the private sector and thereby help economic growth and development. The annual growth rate was moderate and below the economy's potential. However, the basic structural and strategic factors against realizing that potential remained more or less intact. These included a combination of a large public sector, bureaucratic allocation of credit, limited domestic competition as well as a high level of protection from external markets.[52] According to Jalali-Naini, 'To generate higher incomes for the average household and to create a sufficient number of jobs to keep the rate of unemployment steady, the economy must grow at about 8 per cent per year, a feat that has not been achieved for a sustained period (three or more years) in the last 27 years.'[53] Karshenas and Hakimian concluded their study of oil resources and the economy, which was not just confined to the Khatami period, by noting that 'the oil dependence of the economy has increased. The technological gap between Iran and its peers . . . has widened, and economic diversification has stalled ... [T]hese trends do not paint a bright future for the long-term economic growth and prosperity of the country.'[54]

In a similar study of human resources and employment, Djavad Salehi-Esfahani concluded that 'on both sides of the political spectrum, policymakers increasingly realize that more flexibility for private employers is good for attracting domestic and foreign investment. If they were also to realize its importance for investment in human capital, they would be so much more likely to do something about it . . . Politics in Iran may have to mature further before it can produce agreements where common ground exists.'[55]

Finally, and taking a longer view, another economist noted that 'development requires not only *acquisition and innovation*, but also, and especially, *accumulation and preservation*, whether of wealth, of rights and privileges, or of knowledge and science ... The long-term [European] society makes possible long-term accumulation, precisely because the law and traditions that govern it, and its institutions, afford a certain amount of security by making the future reasonably predictable.'[56]

It was unlikely that such fundamental economic issues would be resolved without commensurate political development prior or, at least, parallel to them.

FOREIGN RELATIONS

Khatami had inherited a colossal amount of regional and international relations problems, even though the arch-realist Rafsanjani had done a good deal to resolve or reduce the scale of many of them. In fact, the realm of foreign relations showed more than any other the degree of conflict within the regime over important issues, the absence of a long-term mechanism for conducting foreign policy and the divided nature of political power, which made the successful resolution of policy differences extremely difficult. On the other hand, it became evident that neither did the United States, by far the most important of Iran's international adversaries, always act with realism or consistency when it came to dealing with Iran. Therefore while Khatami might have provided a golden opportunity for improvement of relations with the West, neither America nor his own domestic critics would help to provide an atmosphere conducive to significantly improved relations.

Khatami said at the beginning that he believed not in the clash but in the 'dialogue of civilizations', and the institute bearing this name which he founded in Tehran indicated his general foreign policy attitude. Within a relatively short period of time he managed to normalize relations with most other regional players and to resolve the Salman Rushdie conflict with Britain: the establishment of full diplomatic relations took place when Khatami's government declared that it would not implement or encourage the implementation of the sentence.

The EU powers revised their attitude towards Iran from 'critical dialogue' to 'constructive dialogue'. Khatami's interview with CNN in January 1998 in which he expressed regret about the hostage-taking incident and praised the values of American civilization received a positive response, a senior American official saying, 'When he says he regrets the hostage-taking and talks about America as a great civilization and these things get criticized in Iran, it is an indication to us that he's interested in breaking down this distrust and finding a way to engage with us.'[57] Likewise, Secretary of State Madeleine Albright's statement in March 2000 regretting past US interference in Iranian politics, especially regarding the 1953 coup, led to cautious optimism in Tehran: the Iranian foreign ministry spokesman was quoted as saying that her statement 'admits the mistakes of the past but also contains new and positive points'.[58] The Americans had already pleased Iran by putting the Mojahedin-e Khalq on their list of international terrorists.

Yet in practice not much came from any of this. There were not even the hoped-for 'cultural exchanges' let alone any 'government-to-government' dialogue.[59] Many factors may have worked to thwart a significant improvement in US–Iran relations, but the most important, and perhaps the most obvious, were the domestic forces in both countries which worked against rapprochement: in

Iran, radical fundamentalists and hard-line conservatives; in America, the Christian Right and pro-Israeli lobbies. Nevertheless, the closing years of the Clinton administration were clearly better times. But under President Bush, despite Tehran's optimism that his election would improve matters between them and Washington, the conflict was to escalate to mutual demonization and the threat of war.[60]

The presidency of George W. Bush made a slow beginning in foreign affairs, and no significant change occurred in US Middle East policy. The drama began with the great shock of the 9/11 terrorist attacks, which inaugurated a whole new era in America's domestic and foreign policy, and marked a clear watershed in America's foreign policy attitude and strategy, especially as regarded the Middle East and Islamic countries. It inaugurated the era of 'the war on terror', giving the impression that 'terror' was the exclusive domain of Muslim peoples. The rhetoric of 'the clash of civilizations' – that is, the inevitable clash of the West with Muslim peoples, or of Christianity with Islam – began to dominate ideological and strategic thinking, leading to regime change in Iraq and heightened confrontation and cold war with Iran.

President Bush said plainly in a speech that others could be either with or against America. Nevertheless, in the beginning it looked as if the American tragedy could act as a catalyst for improved relations between Iran and America. The virtually spontaneous sympathy displayed by Iranians – there were even candle-lit processions on the streets of Tehran – surprised American observers and commentators. Khatami sent a letter of condolence to Bush, and the mayor and fire chief of Tehran sent their condolences to their counterparts in New York. Apart from plain human emotion, the Iranian good wishes were due to the intense dislike of all Iranians, not just the Islamic regime, of the Taleban and their terrorist allies.

When the war in Afghanistan began in early October 2001, relations improved further, and for a couple of months it looked as if there would be opportunities for a rapprochement between the two countries. There was obvious mutual interest, but Iran's cooperation with US forces was not entirely due to that alone, since the US would have been able to accomplish their mission without Iran's help but perhaps over a longer period and at a higher cost. It looked as if not only Khatami but also the conservative establishment saw this as an honourable way of approaching the Bush administration for better relations. Whatever their motives, however, they – and especially Khatami – received a blow in President Bush's 'axis-of-evil' speech so soon after the fall of Afghanistan. Bush said in his State of the Union address on 29 January 2002 that 'Iran aggressively pursues these weapons [of mass destruction] and exports terror, while an unelected few repress the Iranian people's hope for freedom. States like these, and their terrorist allies, constitute an axis of evil, arming to threaten the peace of the world.'[61] This left Khatami badly exposed vis-à-vis his conservative and fundamentalist opposition.[62]

The main reason advanced for this sudden and vehement US change of attitude is that earlier in the month Israel had captured a ship carrying Iranian weapons bound for the Palestinian Authority. The Iranians denied any knowledge of this, and the matter has never been satisfactorily investigated, though some have attributed it to Iranian rogue elements.[63] However, it is unlikely that that incident was a determining factor in the president's vehement and uncompromising attack on the Islamic Republic, putting it on a par with Saddam Hussein's Iraq. In retrospect it looks more likely that, with their easy initial victory in Afghanistan, the neo-conservatives' minds had been set on regime change, not just in Iraq but also in Iran. This attitude was to continue through the rest of Khatami's term, even though Iranians did not make a fuss about the American and British invasion of Iraq – short of issuing critical verbal statements, of which France, Germany and Russia had been the most powerful forerunners. Yet relations took a turn for the worse in May 2003 when the United States linked the terrorist attack on the western compound in Saudi Arabia to al-Qaida Afghan refugees in Iran and demanded their extradition. Iran admitted that some such terrorists were in its jails, and said that it was ready to exchange them with the leaders of Mojahedin-e Khalq, who were under American protection in their Ashraf camp in Iraq. America rejected this condition and the Iranians did not oblige.[64]

It was also in May 2003 that, through the Swiss ambassador in Iran, the Iranians seriously offered to negotiate with America, suggesting an agenda which included all America's concerns, including Iran's nuclear programme.[65] The United States dismissed the offer. According to a report by the *Christian Science Monitor* in 2007:

> A package of concessions offered to the United States by Iran in 2003 was very close to what the United States is now asking from Tehran. The BBC reports that Iran offered, among other things, to end support for Lebanese and Palestinian militant groups and to help stabilize Iraq following the US-led invasion. But a former US senior official told BBC's *Newsnight* program that the package was rejected by Vice President Dick Cheney's office. One of the then Secretary of State Colin Powell's top aides told the BBC the state department was keen on the plan – but was overruled.[66]

Clearly, regime change was still at the top of the US agenda. The easily won American-led invasion and occupation of Iraq in the previous month is likely to have encouraged the dismissal of Iran's offer of negotiations, but events were to prove the victory in Iraq extremely costly and dangerous. Iran benefitted from the fall of Saddam Hussein, who was the Islamic Republic's most powerful adversary in the Muslim Middle East, just as it had benefitted by the fall of the Taleban, the enemy on its eastern frontiers. Thus, America had removed the country's troublesome neighbours in the east as well as west.

Regime change in Iraq had more far-reaching consequences for Iran, both because the majority of Iraq's population were Shia and because Iran had harboured within its borders the bulk of the Iraqi Shia revolutionary movements and armed groups during the long years of their struggle against Saddam Hussein. While the stabilization of the new (effectively Shia-led) Iraqi regime was both in the interest of Tehran and Washington, the situation was complicated by the militant Sunni–Shia confrontation in the country and Saudi Arabia's deep concern about a Shia-dominated Iraq. In later years, during Ahmadinejad's presidency, both Iran (or at least some elements within the Iranian military) and Saudi Arabia were involved in the arming of various Iraqi factions. Iran's involvement incurred the wrath of the United States, which claimed that therefore Iran was at least indirectly responsible for the killing of American soldiers in Iraq. Whatever the truth, this was part of America's intensifying cold war confrontation with Iran, the most important reason for which was Iran's success and persistence in its uranium enrichment programme under President Ahmadinejad (2005–8).

IRAN'S NUCLEAR PROGRAMME

Iran's nuclear programme became an increasingly controversial international issue under Khatami. The beginnings of the programme went back at least to the 1970s, when the shah took some preliminary steps towards building a nuclear power plant. In 1995, Iran signed a contract with Russia to resume work on the partially complete Bushehr plant.[67] In August 2002, a uranium enrichment facility in Natanz and a heavy water facility in Arak were discovered which had not been reported to the International Atomic Energy Agency (IAEA).

France, Germany and the United Kingdom (the 'EU-3') undertook a diplomatic initiative with Iran to resolve questions about its nuclear programme. The breakthrough came on 21 October 2003. The Iranian government and EU-3 foreign ministers meeting in Tehran issued a statement in which Iran agreed to cooperate with the IAEA, to sign and implement an additional protocol as a voluntary, confidence-building measure and to suspend its enrichment and reprocessing activities during the course of the negotiations. The EU-3, in return, explicitly agreed to recognize Iran's nuclear rights and to discuss ways Iran could provide satisfactory assurances regarding its nuclear power programme, after which Iran would gain easier access to modern technology. Iran signed an additional protocol on 18 December 2003, and agreed to act as if the protocol was in force, making the required reports to the IAEA and allowing the required access by IAEA inspectors, pending Iran's ratification of the protocol.[68]

On the question of whether Iran had a hidden nuclear weapons programme, the IAEA reported in November 2003 that it found no evidence that the previously undeclared activities were related to a nuclear weapons programme, but also that it was unable to conclude that Iran's nuclear programme was exclusively peaceful. However, Mohammad El-Baradei, the IAEA's Director General, later reported that most highly enriched uranium traces found in Iran by agency inspectors came from imported centrifuge components, apparently confirming Iran's claim that the traces were due to contamination.

Yet the brunt of western concern about Iran's programme was a belief that its pursuit of uranium enrichment was a prelude to nuclear armament, whereas the Iranian government kept insisting that it was a peaceful programme. Under the terms of the November 2004 Paris Agreement, Iran's chief nuclear negotiator, Hasan Rowhani (Runani), announced a voluntary and temporary suspension of its uranium enrichment programme, despite the fact that enrichment of uranium as such was not a violation of the Nuclear Proliferation Treaty. It was said at the time that this was a voluntary, confidence-building measure, to go on for a period of time (say, six months) as negotiations with the EU-3 continued.[69] Thus 'the dove of peace sat on the assembly' until Khatami's term of office came to an end. It was not to remain there for long.

Khatami's presidency had begun with high hopes but ended with the apathy if not frustration of many of his erstwhile supporters. Addressing Tehran University students on the occasion of Student's Day in November 2004, he had to face a hostile crowd shouting, 'Khatami, you liar, shame on you'.[70] When he went there again in 2007, the crowd were shouting 'Here comes the people's saviour'.[71] This was just a small reminder that the Iranian habit of 'short-termism' was still well in place.

TURN OF THE TIDE

Iranians are always good at surprising, which is essentially due to the habitual short-termness of their views and decisions regarding almost everything. That is the reason why serious attempts at reading the future, even the near future, run a big risk of ending up in frustration.

In June 2005 seven candidates stood for the presidency, five of them being regarded as possible winners. Rafsanjani was the favourite of pragmatic centrists, and most observers in Iran and abroad expected him to win. Mehdi Karroubi (Karrubi), the moderate reformist and twice Majlis speaker, had attracted the support of many of the reformists. Mohammad Bagher (Baqer) Ghalibaf (Qalibaf), a one-time revolutionary guard commander and former police chief, was rumoured to be the supreme leader's as well as the conservative establishment's favourite. Mostafa Moeen (Mo'in), a long-time minister of science, research and technology (formerly science and higher education), was a radical reformist and candidate of the Participation Front, backed by such non-Islamist organizations as the Freedom Movement and the Melli-Mazhabi Council. Mahmoud Ahmadinejad (Mahmud Ahmadinezhad), Mayor of Tehran, who had been appointed mayor as a result of a 12 per cent turn-out in the City Council elections, was closest to radical fundamentalists, apparently with a small social base and, of the five, the least likely to win.[72]

Polls had predicted a run-off between Rafsanjani and Moeen. But the split in the reformist vote between Karroubi and Moeen led to Ahmadinejad becoming second to Rafsanjani in the first round, with Karroubi in third place. Rafsanjani won 21 per cent of the votes, Ahmadinejad 19.5 per cent and Karroubi 17.3 per cent, while Moeen, who did not make it to the second round, gained 13.9 per cent.[73] These figures make it clear that had there been one reformist candidate instead of two, he would have been very likely to win in the run-off against Rafsanjani. The figures also show that if the reformist/pragmatist alliance of the first years of Khatami's presidency had endured, it would have won in the very first round. It is important to note that between themselves, Rafsanjani, Karroubi and Moeen had won more than 50 per cent of the votes in the first round.

The run-off therefore was between Rafsanjani and Ahmadinejad. Karroubi, and Rafsanjani later, after his defeat in the second round, complained of election irregularities, Karroubi in particular protesting that his real votes in the first round had been higher than Ahmadinejad's. The general complaint was about the Revolutionary Guards and especially Basij paramilitary volunteers having actively campaigned for Ahmadinejad and arranged his vote above Karroubi's in the first round. However that may be, in the run-off Ahmadinejad won 61.7 of the votes against Rafsanjani's humiliating 35.9 per cent.[74]

Sensing the serious possibility of Ahmadinejad winning in the second round, the reformist and Melli-Mazhabi leaders, even some leftist intellectuals who had probably boycotted the first round, rallied behind Rafsanjani. It was too late. It was more in the run-off that vast numbers of common voters warmed to Ahmadinejad, viewing him as one of themselves, a modest man of humble origins who had never been suspected of financial misappropriation as mayor or provincial governor before it, who was not himself well-to-do and who went round the provinces winning over rural and small-town votes by telling them that he would 'bring the oil money to the people's dinner spread (*sofreh*)'. And when it came to a clear choice between Ahmadinejad and Rafsanjani, not only the radical fundamentalists but also at least hard-line conservatives backed Ahmadinejad.[75]

When a child his family had moved to Tehran from a poor village, his father becoming a blacksmith in an underprivileged district of the city. Thanks to his native intelligence and the rising educational opportunities due to oil revenues he made it to school and a technical university, from which, over a long period, he obtained a doctorate in engineering. Meanwhile, he had joined the revolution as an Islamist and later served at the front in the Iran–Iraq war, and by the time he became mayor of Tehran he had been governor in several provinces.[76]

Predictably, Ahmadinejad filled his cabinet and other important public posts with men of radical fundamentalist backgrounds. But he did not stop at that. He replaced the existing Iranian ambassadors with his own men, and went as far as removing or retiring not just senior but even middle-ranking civil servants and public employees as well. This was the starkest example in recent times of the short-termness of society and of insecurity of government posts, to the extent that the rumour began to circulate that he had replaced everyone down to the doormen at government departments.

Having formally taken over the presidential office in August, one of his first acts as president was his attendance and speech at the UN General Assembly in

September, which impressed the audience more with his apocalyptic sentiments and wish for the urgent rise of the Mahdi-Messiah than his diplomatic skills.[77] On his return he told a leading cleric, Ayatollah Javadi Amoli, that a halo of light had surrounded him while delivering his UN speech.[78] This reflected the man's cultural and psychological simplicity despite the toughness of his character.

The same lack of political sophistication revealed itself in his making highly inflammatory remarks on Jerusalem Day (*Ruz-e Qods*) against Israel, and later convening an international Holocaust-denial conference. Also, his critical attitude towards the Israel–Palestine problem might have been expressed in ways that would have benefited his cause: in his years of presidency, Khatami had said more than once that he would not oppose any solution of the problem that is acceptable to the Palestinians.

Relations with Israel had been cut off since the 1979 Revolution, and Iranian rhetoric against Israel had remained uncompromising, although it had been significantly toned down under Khatami. In turn, Israel's rhetoric was also hostile to the Islamic Republic, despite the fact that the two sides recognized their priorities in the Iran–Iraq war when Israel sold military hardware to Iran. However, in the mid-1990s Iran became seriously concerned that the success of the Middle East peace process along the lines envisaged by Israel and America could result in its isolation in 'the new Middle East', which led to its rejection of the process, to an increase in its support for the Lebanese Hezbollah and, later, to encouragement of the Hamas government in Gaza.[79] Relations with the Persian Gulf monarchies (the GCC countries) had improved under Rafsanjani and, more, under Khatami. Under Ahmadinejad's presidency, the United States tried but did not succeed to rally Saudi Arabia and the other Arab countries of the Persian Gulf overtly against the Islamic Republic. Ahmadinejad's very friendly reception by the Saudi king in Riyadh and by the GCC summit in Qatar in 2007 clearly showed that they had their own independent agenda for their relations with Iran.[80]

Added to Ahmadinejad's simple and direct approach to politics was his highly messianic or Mahdist convictions about the imminent advent of the Hidden Imam to rid the world of injustice and corruption. Reference to this occurred in many of his speeches.[81] In mid-2008 he even made a habit of saying that Iran was being run by the Hidden Imam, despite the fact that He was still hidden from view.

Traditionally, many Shiites believed that the Hidden Imam would one day emerge from a hole or well in Samarra (in Iraq), but in very recent times the mosque in Jamkaran near Qom had also acquired that status.[82] Ahmadinejad had the mosque and its surroundings refurbished and redeveloped, and provided free transport at the weekends for civil servants to visit what was now a sacred place. Many of the pilgrims would throw large amounts of money and letters down the hole in Jamkaran in pursuit of miraculous help.

In early August 2005, almost as soon as Ahmadinejad formally took office, he ordered the seals on the uranium enrichment equipment in Isfahan to be removed. This was predictable in view of the fact that suspension of enrichment had been envisaged just for a few months to allow the IAEA's new monitoring devices to be installed. However, a few days later the EU-3, already engaged in negotiations with Iran, offered a package of incentives (which did not include a US pledge of non-aggression) in exchange for Iran's permanent cessation of enrichment. Iran rejected the offer, calling the plan insulting.[83] The new Iranian negotiator was Ali Larijani, former head of the radio and TV network, not a radical fundamentalist but a member of the conservative establishment.

Early in February 2006, the board of the IAEA voted to report Iran to the UN Security Council over its nuclear activities.[84] All the while, the United States had said that Iran was secretly engaged in making nuclear weapons, and the EU predicted that Iran's acquisition of nuclear technology could result in weaponiza-tion. Iran, on the other hand, kept insisting that its programme was purely for peaceful purposes, was transparent and was open to monitoring by IAEA inspec-tors. In late February 2006, the IAEA's director Mohammad El-Baradei suggested a compromise whereby Iran would stop industrial-scale enrichment and instead limit its programme to a small-scale pilot facility and import its nuclear fuel from Russia. Iran expressed interest in this compromise solution but the United States rejected it, thus making it clear that their real objection was not just to the possi-bility of Iran having a secret weaponization programme but Iran's acquisition of nuclear technology under any circumstances.[85] Two months later Ahmadinejad caught many, if not most, by surprise when he made a spectacular TV announce-ment that Iran had successfully enriched uranium.[86]

From that moment on, the acquisition of nuclear technology became a matter of national pride, so that even many of the opponents of Ahmadijead or the whole Islamic regime rallied behind the government in its pursuit of nuclear technology, the popular slogan being 'Nuclear technology is our inalienable right'. Strictly speaking Iran had not broken the law, since the Non-Proliferation Treaty (to which it was a signatory) did not forbid enrichment, only weaponiza-tion, which the Iranians insisted they were not pursuing. However, as noted, the United States in particular was opposed to Iran's enrichment even for peaceful purposes, being afraid that it might use the resource as such sometime in the future.

The success of Iran's uranium enrichment and its refusal to halt raised the stakes. There were numerous meetings and negotiations between the '5+1' (America, Britain, France, Russia and China plus Germany), the EU and the Iranians; at one stage Iran was offered a package of incentives, which it rejected. Finally, a series of UN sanctions was applied, the first one in December 2006, the second in March 2007 and the third (to date) in March 2008.[87] The sanctions would have been a good deal tougher had it not been for the moderating influ-ence of Russia and China, with whom Iran had good diplomatic and business relations.

In the meantime Larijani gave up his post as Iran's chief negotiator as a result of a disagreement or the difficulty of working with Ahmadinejad. However, the most unexpected and spectacular event regarding the conflict over Iran's nuclear programme was the publication in November 2007 of the consensus of the many US intelligence agencies, described as National Intelligence Estimate (NIE), that Iran had stopped efforts to make nuclear weapons since 2003. For a moment this seemed to take the teeth out of the constant threat of war and an American pre-emptive strike against Iran. One American journalist even described it as 'pre-emptive surgical strike by the intelligence community against the war party'.[88] But the stakes were higher than that, as *TIME* magazine indicated on 5 December 2007:

> The Rashomon-like battle to interpret the new National Intelligence Estimate (NIE) on Iran is well under way. All sides of the Iran nuclear dispute are working hard to make their own reading of the report the accepted one, and to emphasize the findings that best suit their agendas. Those agendas will remain unchanged by the NIE: Israel and Washington hawks want military action against a grave and gathering threat; the Bush administration is pursuing coercive diplomacy; the Europeans want to avoid war. And it is those agendas that will shape each player's response to the NIE in what promises to be a furious battle over Iran policy in the months to come.

This was not surprising because, as we have seen, the real objection was not just to Iran producing nuclear weapons but also to its acquiring the technology even if it was currently aimed at peaceful objectives. And besides, the Bush administration's concern over Iran went far beyond uranium enrichment and encompassed a whole range of hot issues, including Iran's formal and informal influence in Iraq, its support for Lebanon's Hezbollah (which proved highly effective in the Israel–Hezbollah war of July–August 2006), its support for the Palestinian Hamas and more generally what became known as 'Iran's rising power in the Middle East', in short, almost the very existence of the Islamic Republic.

In June and July 2008, the sound of war drums reached a high pitch. Israel was now assuming a higher profile than before in threatening war against Iran with or without America's participation. Iran responded to the Israeli military manoeuvres by saying that the 'manoeuvres aimed at warning Iran jeopardize global peace'.[89] Shortly afterwards the Iranians tested nine ground-to-ground missiles, which both the United States and Israel condemned, the State Department describing it as 'provocative',[90] although the suggestion that Iran might initiate a war with Israel was extremely far-fetched. This was followed by a meeting in Geneva between Iran and the EU, which raised hopes as it was also attended by a US assistant secretary of state, to discuss the 5+1's package of incentives in return for Iran's suspension of its uranium enrichment.[91] The apparent deadlock was still over the conditions of a comprehensive deal between Iran and America: Iran was prepared to start negotiating unconditionally; America would negotiate only if Iran suspended its uranium enrichment first.

Ahmadinejad's domestic popularity rated high in the first few months of his assumption of office since he was still good at employing his populist rhetoric – including the ever-escalating reference to the Mahdi (i.e., Mehdi), his blessing and his imminent advent – and had not yet been tested regarding the fulfilment of his promises. He described the group of people close to him as the Sweet Scent of Service (*Rayeheh-ye Khosh-e Khedmat*) but did not have a faction of his own in the Majlis, receiving his main support from a new conservative parliamentary coalition called the Principalists (*Osulgerayan*). The 7th Majlis was, as noted, dominated by the conservatives, who generally preferred Ahmadinejad to Rafsanjani and Karroubi but were not themselves radical fundamentalists and were rather wary of his frequent Mahdist slogans. Much of the bazaar and modern business community still made up the main social base of the regime, but Ahmadinejad's appeal was still directly to 'the people' – there would come a time when he would hold the Majlis as well as his own cabinet colleagues, the Central Bank and so on as responsible for the failure of his own policies, claiming that they had not given him full support.

Nowhere did his domestic policies more quickly and clearly yield negative results than his top priority objective of raising the ordinary people's standard of living, providing affordable housing for the masses and creating new jobs to reduce unemployment. With continuously soaring oil prices (which at one stage in 2008 peaked at $149 per barrel) he was well placed for achieving these goals if he had chosen appropriate economic policies. Being both a populist and a president who believed in the righteousness of his own policies, he had little time for expert economic advice, even though it was offered to him – free of charge – by the country's leading economists in a number of public statements. His economic words and deeds encouraged a substantial flight of capital to Dubai and other financially secure countries.

His vision of increasing social welfare resembled traditional charitable alms-giving in an otherwise complex political economy. He told the banks to give long-term low-interest loans for modest housing. The result was that directly or indirectly the money lent found itself in the hands of property speculators, leading to about a 100 per cent increase in property prices. Much of the money similarly lent to young people for starting small businesses to increase employment in fact found its way back to the banks: the young person would enjoy the 18 per cent interest on one-year loans and the bank would give further credit to business sharks and speculators. The result was soaring inflation (13 per cent according to Ahmadinejad, 25 per cent according to the Central Bank and probably 30 per cent or more in reality), especially as regarded housing and food prices. The unemployment rate went on rising, while the president was denigrating the successful policy of reducing the birth rate and saying that steps must be taken to encourage a higher population growth.

Clearly, this was not a vision or approach to the political economy of which the conservative establishment would approve, and it began to be reflected not just in reformist opposition dailies like *Eetemad-e Melli* (the organ of Karroubi's

National Trust Party) but also in mainstream conservative dailies such as
Resalat and *Jomhuri-ye Eslami*. Thus as early as December 2006, in the first tests
of public opinion, Ahmadeinejad's candidates scored low in the Tehran City
Council elections against the conservatives' independent list, while reformist
candidates performed better than expected.[92] And in the parallel elections held
for the influential Assembly of Experts, Rafsanjani, Ahmadinejad's bogeyman,
won by far the highest vote; the vote of the latter's religious mentor, Mesbah
Yazdi, was half of Rafsanjani's. In general the conservatives won most of the
seats, Karroubi's reformists performed reasonably well but Ahmadinejad's
fundamentalists did poorly.[93] The clearest demonstration yet of the conservative
establishment's doubts about Ahmadinejad came in September 2007, when the
Assembly of Experts elected Rafsanjani – who was already chairman of the
Expediency Council – as its chairman, defeating the radical fundamentalist
Ayatollah Jannati.[94]

Ayatollah Jannati was chairman of the Council of Guardians that vetted the
candidates for the 8th Majlis elections, held in March and April 2008, which
disqualified large numbers of reformist and independent candidates, including
a maternal grandson of Ayatollah Khomeini. Still, the new Majlis was far from
packed with hard-line fundamentalists, the sum of pragmatic conservatives,
reformists and independents making up the majority of the deputies.[95] And
the election of Ali Larijani – the prominent figure of the conservative establishment who had resigned as Iran's chief negotiator on its nuclear policy – to the
speakership of parliament did not reflect much confidence in Ahmadinejad's
government.[96]

The exact role of the supreme leader in all this was not easy to discern. He
certainly had wide constitutional powers, which included the supreme command
of the armed forces and the power to appoint the heads of the judiciary and the
radio and television networks. There was also little doubt that he had the last
word on major foreign policies, including and especially the nuclear policy. On
the other hand, there was no evidence that he intervened in less sensitive matters,
even including the government's economic policy – although he did say at least
once that Ahmadinejad's presidency had been the best of the Islamic Republic so
far. The Revolutionary Guards were a powerful force with extensive economic
and industrial activities of their own. They certainly were the principal military
arm of the Islamic Republic for both internal and external security, but, though
there were strong rumours on the subject, it was difficult to know the extent to
which they might directly interfere in political matters. As was noted above, it was
claimed that the *Basij*, the young militia under their command, had interfered in
the 2005 presidential election in favour of Ahmadinejad.

Regarding the political divisions in the regime, the evidence showed that
the four principal tendencies – conservative, pragmatist, reformist and radical
fundamentalist – noted above were still in place, there being a greater chance
of a conservative-fundamentalist alliance and reformist-pragmatist cooperation
when the lines were drawn. But it was clear that since the death of Ayatollah

Khomeini the conservative establishment had been the strongest single political force in the country.

More newspapers were closed under Ahmadinejad: it was the worst time for the reformist press, and the censorship of books and other cultural productions was intensified. Likewise, reformist activities and representation were considerably restricted, although this did not lead to the demise of the movement. Human rights and human rights activities also suffered more than before. Emadeddin Baghi (Emad al-Din Baqi), a leading human rights activist – especially in defence of prisoners' rights and against capital punishment – was tried by the Tehran revolutionary court and jailed in 2007 for the third time since 2000.[97]

Women's rights activists continued their campaign despite systematic harassment and imprisonment. It was centred on the 'one million signatures campaign' for the abolition of discriminatory laws'[98], led by a group of feminist activists, notably Parvin Ardalan and Noushin (Nushin) Ahmadi Khorasani, some of whom were sent to prison for a term. In March 2008 Ardalan received the 2007 Olof Palme Prize but was not allowed to travel abroad to receive it.[99]

As the summer of 2008 approached, 'exposures' and 'counter-exposures' broke out between Ahmadinejad's camp and its opponents within the conservative establishment. This episode was seen as an attempt by Ahmadinejad's supporters to discredit some, mainly clerical, members of the establishment, although the man who led the campaign was later imprisoned without trial.[100]

From August 2008, the oil price (which, as noted above, had reached an all-time high) began to crash in response to the world financial crisis and economic recession, at one point falling almost as low as $30, though gradually recovering to up to $70.[101] This put pressure on Ahmadinejad's government to revise their expenditure estimates in response to the considerable fall in expected oil revenues and foreign exchange receipt. As a result, it looked likely that there would be a significant drop in the rial's rate of exchange against other currencies sometime after the presidential election of June 2009. This would be tantamount to a devaluation of the rial and would fuel the existing inflationary pressures.

President Obama's election in November 2009 removed the short-term prospect of US military action against Iran since he repeated his election promise that his administration would be ready to negotiate with Iran without any preconditions. He went even further and sent a friendly as well as firm *Nawruz* (Persian New Year) message to the people and government of the Islamic Republic of Iran, emphasizing his readiness to hold direct talks and incidentally recognizing the Islamic Republic by naming it as such for the first time since the Revolution of February 1979.[102] The response of Iranian leaders, including Ayatollah Khamenei, was far from enthusiastic, emphasizing that they wished to see change in policy as well as in words. Both sides seemed to be awaiting the result of the forthcoming presidential election before deciding how to proceed.[103]

As it turned out, the Iranian presidential election of 12 June 2009 and the massive protest movement which followed it was the most dramatic event of 2009, heralding a new era in Iranian politics.

For months the reformist faction of the Islamic Republic had been looking for a viable candidate to challenge Ahmadinejad. Mehdi Karroubi had already declared his candidacy, but the mainstream reformists were in favour of Khatami and, failing that, Mir Hosein Mousavi. Khatami hesitated at first, then declared that he would stand as long as Mousavi didn't. When at last Mousavi's candidacy was declared, he stepped down, and joined Mousavi's campaign. As was noted above, some conservatives were not very happy with Ahmadinejad's fundamentalist policies, Mahdist vision and abrasive manner. For example, the conservative Association of Militant Clergy did not back his campaign, while the equally conservative Islamic Coalition Party did, explaining that they supported Ahmadinejad despite serious reservations, and solely to stop the reformists from winning. It was for the same reason that the large majority of conservatives rallied to Ahmadinejad's camp. The only independent conservative candidate, Mohsen Rezai, the Secretary of the Expediency Council and a former Revolutionary Guards commander, did not manage to attract much support even from his fellow conservatives.

Thus Ahmadinejad became the fundamentalist-conservative candidate once again, facing a coalition of the pragmatist and reformist factions who backed the two reformist candidates. This was an important change from 2005, when the reformists had had their own candidates, while Rafsanjani, as leader of the pragmatist faction, was also a candidate in his own right. As was argued above, if in that election the reformists and pragmatists had put up a single candidate, they might have won the election. Karroubi was supported by his National Trust Party, while Rafsanjani's Servants of Construction (*Kargozaran*), the Khatamist Participation Front and the more radical reformist Mojahedin of the Islamic Revolution (not to be confused with the opposition Mojahedin) backed Mousavi. However, the two reformist candidates and their supporters maintained friendly relations and spoke almost with one voice.

Mousavi's (and Karroubi's) main attraction for both Islamist reformist and secular voters was that they presented a moderate and liberal face, promising to give more freedom to students and young people, curb the power of the religious police, considerably extend freedom of the press and media, pursue rational economic policies and establish better relations with the West. At the same time the young people and urbanities opposed Ahmadinejad because of the limitations on political and cultural freedoms, his socio-economic policies, his confrontational attitude towards the West and, not least, his overly self-confident and abrasive personality.

The election campaigns had a slow start, but a couple of weeks before the election date they began to take off, especially in view of the televised debates between the candidates, which quickly made it clear that the real contest was between Ahmadinejad on the one hand and Mousavi (and Karroubi) on the other. These debates were lively, and sometimes even personal. The streets began to be packed with mostly pro-reformist election enthusiasts, holding open-air debates and discussions, shouting slogans, and even singing songs taunting Ahmadinejad. Within a week, Mousavi emerged as by far the most popular of the two reformist candidates, attracting a lot of support particularly among the young people. It was predicted that most of the voters in the big and bigger cities would vote for the reformists while small towns and rural areas would mainly back Ahmadinejad, especially in view of his policy of directly distributing cash and goods among them. Many domestic and international observers declared the election 'too close to call'.

A very large turnout was anticipated, which was believed to increase Mousavi's chances. In the event as many as 85 per cent of the electorate voted. The voters held their breaths. Many predicted that no candidate would score 50 per cent or more of the votes, and that there would therefore be a run-off, very likely between Mousavi and Ahmadinejad. Suddenly the government announced that Ahmadinejad had won a landslide victory, receiving more than 24 million (i.e. over 62 per cent) of the votes; Mousavi had scored more than 13 million (over 33 per cent) while Rezai and Karroubi had received a few hundred thousand votes each.[104]

The opposition was shocked. The totally unexpected gap between Ahmadinejad and Mousavi's votes convinced those who had voted for Mousavi and Karroubi that there had been massive vote rigging, some evidence for which began to appear in the following days. There was a huge outcry, and on 13 June, the day after the election, the opposition voters, largely Mousavi supporters, spontaneously took to the streets in their hundreds of thousands, protesting against the election results.[105] The clash with the security forces led to a number of deaths and injures, especially when members of the Basij militia and the notorious plain-clothes vigilantes attacked the universities of Tehran and Shiraz.[106]

The supreme leader had congratulated Ahmadinejad immediately after the election results were declared. On 19 June in his address after the Friday prayer he defended the election results and rejected Mousavi's and Karroubi's call, backed by street demonstrators, for a re-run of the election. Finally, he said that further demonstrations would not be tolerated.[107]

However both Mousavi and his supporters persisted,[108] and the next day there were bigger demonstrations across the country, which led to reports of up to twenty deaths and an unknown number of injuries in Tehran alone.[109] In particular, the death of a young woman, Neda Agha Soltan, became the worldwide symbol of the Iranian protest movement.[110] Meanwhile, the protesters had begun to shout 'Allaho Akbar' (God is the greatest) from the roof-tops, as they had done in the last weeks of the February 1979 Revolution, a stark déjà vu.

During the demonstrations, Faezeh Hashemi, the Ayatollah's daughter and a politician, was arrested together with her daughter and some relatives, but they were released shortly afterwards.[111] Between 400 and 500 opposition party leaders and activists, many of them former ministers, deputy ministers, assistant presidents as well as leading journalists were arrested during the protests. Strict measures were also taken to restrict the use of the internet and SMS (text) messages, the activities of foreign reporters, and access to foreign Persian broadcasts, especially the BBC and Voice of America. It became official habit to attribute much of the unrest to the machination of foreign powers and their media, and insist that they could not bring about a velvet revolution in Iran. At the same time both the EU and US governments (including the American president and the British prime minister) strongly condemned the Islamic Republic's treatment of the protesters. Iran expelled two British diplomats and Britain retaliated by expelling two Iranian diplomats.[112]

Meanwhile the opposition leaders had lodged formal complaints with the Council of Guardians, among whose constitutional function was to oversee all the elections. The Council admitted that the total number of votes counted in fifty constituencies was three million more than the total number of voters. Yet it added that even so this would nowhere close the gap of 11 million votes separating Ahmadinejad and Mousavi, and that hence it would not annul the election. Still later, the Council asked and received permission from the leader to extend their investigations by five more days. It said that it would recount 10 per cent of the votes, but this was rejected by the opposition. On 29 June, the Council concluded its investigation and confirmed Ahmadinejad's election. The opposition rejected the Council's decision.

In the meantime, the pro-reformist Association of Militant Clerics had demanded the annulment of the election. On the other hand, the heads of both 'the security forces' (i.e. riot police) and, more ominously, Revolutionary Guards had issued dire warnings to protesters to keep off the street. The mass demonstrations stopped, but there were still pockets of protesters in the streets, and the chant of 'Allaho Akbar' continued at night.

This was a major turning point in the history of the Islamic Republic: it had not experienced any such conflict since the fall of Bani Sadr, twenty-eight years before. Not just young people but people of all ages and from all walks of life came out in huge numbers. The confrontation was led not by disenchanted secular students but by some of the leading figures of the Islamic Revolution, who were now openly claiming that the regime was staging a 'coup' in order to abolish the republican and representatives principles of the system and turn it into an absolutist Islamic state.[113]

It was not only a crisis of authority but also of legitimacy. The Islamic Republic was split down the middle, not just in a contest but in a confrontation. Millions of people led by important Islamist forces appeared to be alienated from the system itself. The ministry of the interior raised the possibility of outlawing the reformist parties. The difference with 1979 was that not the whole of the society but a large part of it was confronting the state. Nevertheless a serious cleavage had occurred which would leave its marks on future developments.

Appendix: Iranian Society

Why Iran was not a feudal but an arbitrary society

T HAT IRAN WAS NOT a feudal but an arbitrary state and society is a fundamental point that will recur thoughout this study.

Feudalism describes a system which, though with a good deal of variation through time and place, was established for a thousand years from the fall of the Western Roman Empire to the Renaissance and the rise of absolutist states in Europe, although some of its features survived beyond that and, in the case of Russia, it both came late and was abolished too late. Some, especially western and western-inspired historians of Iran, have applied the term 'feudalism' extremely loosely, while pointing out that the system to which they refer was very different from European feudalism. Even the term 'nomadic feudalism' has been used, which is a contradiction in terms. In using the term loosely in the case of Iran, those historians have intended it as a shorthand notation for describing two historical facts: the existence of landlords, who collected the surplus product of sedentary agriculture, and the existence of nomadic tribes, led by their chieftains, who both reared livestock and raided and pillaged the settled population.

Some educated people, Iranian and others, may still be surprised to learn that Iran was never a feudal society. The reason for this misconception is that they often think of feudalism simply as a traditional system in which there are landlords and peasants. These are certainly some of the basic features of feudal society, but not all. If feudalism were to be described by these features alone, it could be claimed that virtually every society from the dawn of civilization until recent times has been feudal. This was not true even of Europe, where as noted, the feudal system flourished for ten centuries, being preceded by the classical Graeco-Roman system and followed by the Renaissance and absolutist states and other systems following them.

State and society

Feudal landownership in Europe was free and independent of the state. Land was owned by an aristocratic class that maintained its position on a long-term basis, even beyond the feudal period into modern times. This class originally lived in castles and manor houses, being virtual rulers in their territories, and later in sumptuous country houses and luxury residences in towns. None of that did or could exist in Iran precisely because landlords were basically creations of the state and did not have any *independent rights* of ownership, only the more or less temporary *privilege* of enjoying its benefits. This privilege could be withdrawn if and when the state so wished. Landowners could not automatically pass their estates on to their descendants. They did not form a long-term and continuous class because their possession normally lasted for a short period only, passing to others at the will of the state and its officials.

In contrast to mediaeval times, ancient European society was not feudal. Then society was divided between freemen or citizens and slaves who worked the land, the freemen themselves dividing into various independent classes, of which patricians and plebeians are well known. In every type of European society, even in the absolutist states of Europe between 1500 and 1900, the power of the state was to a greater or lesser extent constrained by laws or deeply entrenched traditions. For example, it was not normally possible even under absolutist rule for a prince, a member of the aristocracy, a leader of the Church or a member of the bourgeoisie to be killed at the whim of the king without charges, a hearing and trial. In Iran, on the other hand, all power was concentrated in the hands of the state, and more specifically the shah, who in the ultimate analysis owned the life and property of his subjects, his *ro'aya* (the plural of *ra'iyat*), literally meaning 'flocks'. Thus the most central characteristic of Iranian government – and of all social power – was that it was arbitrary, unconstrained by any long-term written or unwritten laws outside of itself.

In Europe, government was decentralized in the long feudal age, but in later periods it tended to become centralized. Thus the Renaissance states, which at the end of the fifteenth century replaced the feudal state, tended to be more centralized, and the absolutist states of the seventeenth to nineteenth centuries were still more centralized. Modern Iranian intellectuals therefore thought that Iran must have been feudal not only during the chaos of the early twentieth century or during parts of the Qajar era but ever since the beginning of its history. This was in any case a highly simplistic view of society and history – in regard to both Iran and Europe – but the fact that it was based on the assumption that the history and modes of development of Iran and Europe were the same was an even bigger misunderstanding. As observed above, Iranian states were more or less centralized depending on social, economic and cultural factors, but power was nevertheless always concentrated in the hands of the central government. This meant that even in the decentralized Qajar system, the provincial governor was appointed by the shah, ran his province arbitrarily at the shah's pleasure and would be dismissed any time the shah desired.

The myth of Divine Grace

The greatest single source on Divine Grace and its use in Persian literature and culture is *Shahnameh*, the ancient book of Iran's myths and legendary history, which now exists as a long poem by Abolqasem Ferdòwsi, the great Persian epic poet who flourished almost 1,100 years ago (see Chapter 1). In this work, rulers are said to have the right to succession because they possess Grace; their rule is both legitimate and just for the same reason; and they lose Grace and therefore their legitimacy when they become unjust. Rebellion in such cases is then justified, and, if successful, the rebel leader is deemed to have Grace and becomes the legitimate successor and leader.

The theory or myth of Divine Grace, and the consequences of its possession and loss in practice, recur throughout *Shahnameh*, even in the purely mythological, the heroic or epic and the 'historical' parts of the poem. Significantly, Grace takes a physical form on one occasion, and perhaps even more significantly this occurs in the 'historical' part, the story of Ardeshir, son of Babak, descendant of Sasan, and founder of the Sasanian empire (see Chapter 2).

It is clear from *Shahnameh* that the just ruler must hold and maintain Grace. In other words, the holding of Grace is both necessary and sufficient for a ruler to be legitimate. But, according to Ferdowsi's model, the *perfect* just ruler must have qualities of which Grace is only the necessary, but not sufficient, condition. The second condition is to be of 'pure seed', perhaps meaning of royal descent, though it has not been so specified. The third is the ability to learn from others and correct his mistakes rather than taking offence when offered good advice. Having laid down these three conditions, Ferdowsi then suggests a fourth for complete perfection: the wisdom or intellect (*kherad*) to be able to distinguish right from wrong, an apparently simple requirement but an extremely difficult one if it is to include the whole of a person's thoughts and deeds.

This seems to be the nearest that man may come to being divine, but for the fact that he is not immortal. Seen in this light, the concept does not seem to be too far from that of the Shiite Imams, although it is hardly necessary to emphasize the fact that – as shown in Chapter 3 – the imamate has its own theological basis, meaning and implications in the Shiite faith.

A just and legitimate ruler, then, does not have to be perfect, although he must have that most important quality, the possession of Divine Grace, a quality which is demonstrably a paranormal gift. Therefore, at least in the ultimate analysis, the shah's subjects had no rights (of life, property or anything else) independent from the will of the shah and those who acted in his name and on his authority. Or in other words, the state was not bound by any law outside of itself, applying the rules it made and breaking them at will. Therefore there could not exist any *long-term* social classes which would provide a social base for the state and on which the state depended. On the contrary, social classes were *short-term* categories and depended on the state for their status and fortune.

The proof of a ruler holding the *farr* and thus being legitimate was that he should be just. Throughout Iranian history a ruler was held to be just if he maintained peace and stability, secured the borders and did not allow his officials to act unjustly, that is, go beyond the power and authority that he had bestowed upon them to run the state on his behalf. Anushiravan the Just and Shah Abbas the Great are the quintessential examples of the just ruler in pre-Islamic and post-Islamic times, not because they were not arbitrary rulers of the most strict variety but because they stamped out conflict and chaos, brought peace and stability to the land, protected and extended the realm against foreign powers, improved public welfare and prosperity and most of all ruled the land with an iron fist.

Endnotes

ACKNOWLEDGEMENTS

1. 'Az in nameh, az namdaran-e shahr/Ali Deilam o Budolaf rast bahr,' though Ferdowsi goes on to add: 'I received no benefit from them but praise/My blood came to boil in their praise.'

INTRODUCTION: SELECT BIBLIOGRAPHY

Ahmadi, Hamid (ed.), *Iran: hoviyat, melliyat, qowmiyat*, Mo'asseseh-ye Tahqiqat va Tawseh'eh-ye Olum-e Ensani, Tehran, 2004

Brosius, Maria, *The Persians: An Introduction*, Routledge, London, 2006

Farhi, Farideh, 'Crafting a National Identity amidst Contentious Politics in Contemporary Iran', *Iranian Studies*, 38/1 (March 2005), reprinted in *Iran in the 21st Century*, ed. Homa Katouzian and Hossein Shahidi, Routledge, London and New York, 2008

Ferdowsi, Abolqasem, *Shahnameh*, vols 1–8, ed. Djalal Khaleghi-Motlagh (vol. 6 with M. Omidsalar, vol. 7 with A. Khatibi); vols 1–5, Mazda Publishers, Costa Mesa, CA and New York, in association with Bibliotheca Persica, 1990–7; vols 6–8, Bibliotheca Persica, New York, 2005–8

Frye, Richard N., *Persia*, Allen and Unwin, London, 1968

Garthwaite, Gene R., *The Persians*, Blackwell, Oxford, 2005

Gnoli, Gherardo, *The Idea of Iran: An Essay on its Origin*, Istituto Italiano per il Medio ed Estremo Oriente, Rome, 1989

Katouzian, Homa, 'Arbitrary Rule, a Comparative Theory of State, Politics and Society in Iran', *British Journal of Middle Eastern Studies*, 24/1 (1997)

——, *Iranian History and Politics, the Dialectic of State and Society*, paperback edn, London and New York, Routledge, 2007

——, 'Legitimacy and Succession in Iranian History', *Comparative Studies of South Asia, Africa and the Middle East*, 23/4 (December 2003)

——, 'The Aridisolatic Society: A Model of Long-term Social and Economic Development in Iran', *International Journal of Middle East Studies*, June 1983

——, 'The Short-Term Society: A Study in the Problems of Long-Term Political and Economic Development in Iran', *Middle Eastern Studies*, 40/1 (January 2004)

Kachuyan, Hosein, *Tatavvorat-e Gofteman-e Hoviyati-ye Iran*, Nashr-e Ney, Tehran, 2005

Lambton, Ann K. S., *Landlord and Peasant in Persia*, Oxford University Press, London, New York and Toronto, 1953

Meskub, Shahrokh, *Iranian Nationality and the Persian Language*, foreword and interview with author Ali Banuazizi; tr. Michael C. Hillmann; ed. John R. Perry, Mage Publishers, Washington DC, 1992

Soudavar, Abolala, *The Aura of Kings, Legitimacy and Divine Sanction in Iranian Kingship*, Mazda, Costa Mesa, CA, 2003

Taqizadeh, Seyyed Hasan, *Nameh-ha-ye London*, ed. Iraj Afshar, Farzan, Tehran, 1996.

UNESCO's Iranian National Commission, *IRANSHAHR, A Survey of Iran's Land, People, Culture, Government and Economy* (in Persian), Tehran University Press, Tehran, 1963

Vaziri, Mostafa, *Iran as Imagined Nation, the Construction of National Identity*, Paragon House, New York, 1993

CHAPTER 1: SELECT BIBLIOGRAPHY

Bausani, Alessandro, *The Persians, from the Earliest Days to the Twentieth Century*, tr. J. B. Donne, Elek Books, London, 1971

Briant, Pierre, *De la Grèce à l'Orient : Alexandre le Grand*, Gallimard, Paris, 1987

—— , *Histoire de l'Empire Perse de Cyrus à Alexandre*, Fayard, Paris, 1996

Curtis, J. E. and N. Tallis (eds), *Forgotten Empire: The World of Ancient Persia*, University of California Press, Berkeley, CA, 2005

Davidson, Olga, *Poet and Hero in the Persian Book of Kings*, Cornell University Press, Ithaca, NY and London, 1994

Davis, Dick (tr.), *Fathers and Sons*, Mage Publishers, Washington DC, 2000

—— (tr.), *Sunset of Empire*, Mage Publishers, Washington DC, 2004

—— (tr.), *The Legend of Seyavash*, Penguin, London, 1992

Ferdowsi, Abolqasem, *Shahnameh*, vols 1–8, ed. Djalal Khaleghi-Motlagh (vol. 6 with M. Omidsalar, vol. 7 with A. Khatibi); vols 1–5, Mazda Publishers, Costa Mesa, CA and New York, in association with Bibliotheca Persica, 1990–7; vols 6–8, Bibliotheca Persica, New York, 2005–8

Frye, Richard N., *The History of Ancient Iran*, C. H. Beck'sche Verlagsbuchhandlung, Munich, 1984

Gershevitch, Ilya (ed.), *The Cambridge History of Iran*, vol. 2 *The Median and Achaemenian periods*, Cambridge University Press, Cambridge, 1985

Girshman, R., *Iran: From the Earliest Times to the Islamic Conquest*, Penguin Books, London, 1961

Herodotus, *The Histories*, tr. Walter Blanco, ed. Walter Blanco and Jennifer Tolbert Roberts, Norton, New York and London, 1992

Ibnu'l Balkhi, *Farsnama*, eds G. L'Strange and R.A. Nicholson, Cambridge University Press, Cambridge, 1921

Levy, Reuben (tr.), *The Epic of Kings, Shah-Nama: The National Epic of Persia by Ferdowsi*, Routledge & Kegan Paul, London, 1967

Mashkur, Mohammadjavad, *Tarikh-e Iran Zamin*, Eshraqi, Tehran, 1987

Servatiyan, Behruz (ed.), *Khamseh-ye Nezami*, Ganjavi, Tus, Tehran, 1984

Shahbazi, Shapur, *Kurosh-e Bozorg, Zendegi va Jahandari-ye Bonyadgozar-e Shanhanshahi-ye Iran*, Daneshgah-e Pahlavi, Shiraz, 1970

Southgate, Minoo S. (tr.), *Eskandarnameh, a Persian Mediaeval Alexander-romance*, Columbia University Press, New York, 1978

Wiesehöfer, Josef, *Ancient Persia: From 550 BC to 650 AD*, tr. Azizeh Azodi, I.B. Tauris, London, 1996

Winchester, The Marchioness of, *Heroines of Ancient Iran*, Hutchinson, London, 1954

Yarshater, Ehsan (ed.), *The Cambridge History of Iran*, vol. 3: *The Seleucid, Parthian and Sasanian Periods*, Cambridge University Press, Cambridge, 1983

—— , *Dastan-ha-ye Iran-e Bastan*, Bongah-e Tarjomeh va Nashr-e Ketab, Tehran, 1965.

Zarrinkub, Abdolhosein, *Tarikh-e Mardom-e Iran: Iran-e Qabl az Islam*, Amir Kabir, Tehran, 1985

CHAPTER 2: SELECT BIBLIOGRAPHY

Bausani, Alessandro, *The Persians, from the Earliest Days to the Twentieth Century*, tr. J. B. Donne, Elek Books, London, 1971

Boyce, Mary, *Zoroastrianism, Its Antiquity and Constant Vigour*, Mazda Publishers, Costa Mesa, CA, 1993

—— , *Zoroastrianism, Their Religious Beliefs and Practices*, Routledge & Kegan Paul, London, 1979

Ferdowsi, Abolqasem, *Shahnameh*, vols 1–8, ed. Djalal Khaleghi-Motlagh (vol. 6 with M. Omidsalar, vol. 7 with A. Khatibi); vols 1–5, Mazda Publishers, Costa Mesa, CA and New York, in association with Bibliotheca Persica, 1990–7; vols 6–8, Bibliotheca Persica, 2005–8

Frye, Richard N., *The History of Ancient Iran*, C. H. Beck'sche Verlagsbuchhandlung, Munich, 1984

Gershevitch, Ilya (ed.), *The Cambridge History of Iran*, vol. 2, *The Median and Achaemenian Periods*, Cambridge University Press, Cambridge, 1985

Girshman, R., *Iran: From the Earliest Times to the Islamic Conquest*, Penguin Books, London, 1961

—— , *Iran: Parthians and Sassanians*, trs. Stuart Gilbert and James Emmons, Thames and Hudson, London, 1962

Ibnu'l Balkhi, *Farsnama*, eds G. L'Strange and R. A. Nicholson, Cambridge University Press, Cambridge, 1921

Pourshariati, Parvaneh, *Decline and Fall of the Sasanian Empire: The Sasanian-Parthian Confederacy and the Arab Conquest of Iran*, I.B. Tauris, London and New York, 2008

Wiesehöfer, Josef, *Ancient Persia: From 550 BC to 650 AD*, tr. Azizeh Azodi, I.B. Tauris, London, 1996

Yarshater, Ehsan (ed.), *The Cambridge History of Iran*, vol. 3: *The Seleucid, Parthian and Sasanian periods*, Cambridge University Press, Cambridge, 1983

Zaehner, R.C., *The Dawn and Twilight of Zoroastrianism*, Phoenix, London, 2002
—— , *Zurvan: A Zoroastrian Dilemma*, Clarendon Press, Oxford, 1995
Zarrinkub, Abdolhosein, *Tarikh-e Mardom-e Iran: Iran-e Qabl az Islam*, Amir Kabir, Tehran, 1985

CHAPTER 3: SELECT BIBLIOGRAPHY

Beihaqi, Abolfazl, *Tarikh-e Beihaqi*, ed. Ali Akbar Fayyaz, Ershad, Tehran, 1995
Browne, Edward Granville, *A Literary History of Persia*, vol. 1: *From the Earliest Times until Firdawsi*, Cambridge University Press, Cambridge, 1925
—— (tr.), *Revised Translation of the Chahar Maqala ('Four Discourses') of Nizami-i-Arudí of Samarqand, followed by an abridged translation of Mirza Muhammad's notes to the Persian text*, Luzac & Co., London, 1921
Bosworth, Edmund, *The Ghaznavids: Their Empire in Afghanistan and Eastern Iran*, Librairie du Liban, Beirut, 1973
Cole, Juan R. I., *Sacred Space and Holy War: The Politics, Culture and History of Shi'ite Islam*, I.B. Tauris, London and New York, 2002
Daftary, Farhad, *A Short History of the Ismailis: Traditions of a Muslim Community*, Edinburgh University Press, Edinburgh, 1998
Darke, Hubert (tr.), *The Book of Government, or, Rules for Kings: The Siyar al-Muluk or Siyasat-nama of Nizam al-Mulk*, Routledge & Kegan Paul, London and Boston, MA, 1978
Frye, Richard. N., *The Golden Age of Persia*, The Phoenix Press, London, 2000
—— (ed.), *The Cambridge History of Iran*, vol. 4, *The Period From the Arab Invasion to the Seljuks*, Cambridge University Press, Cambridge, 1975
Halm, Heinz, *Shi'ism*, tr. by Janet Watson and Marian Hill, Edinburgh, Edinburgh University Press, second edition, 2004
Katouzian, Homa, 'The Execution of Amir Hasank the Vazir', *Pembroke Papers*, 1 (1990), repr. in Charles Melville (ed.), *Persian and Islamic Studies in Honour of P. W. Avery*, University of Cambridge Centre of Middle Eastern Studies, Cambridge, 1990, repr. in Homa Katouzian, *Iranian History and Politics, The Dialectic of State and Society*, paperback edn, Routledge, London and New York, 2007
Kazemi Moussavi, Ahmad, *Religious Authority in Shi'ite Islam: From the Office of Mufti to the Instituion of Marja'*, International Institute of Islamic Thought and Civilization, Kuala Lumpur, 1996
Khomeini, Imam, *Writings and Declarations of Imam Khomeini*, tr. and annot. Hamid Algar, Mizan Press, Berkeley, CA, 1981; *Velayat-e Faqih (Hokumat-e Islami)*, Persian edn, n.p., new edn, 1979
Momen, Moojan, *An Introduction to Shi'i Islam: The History and Doctrines of Twelver Shi'ism*, Ronald, Oxford, 1985
Nezami, Aruzi, *Chahar Maqaleh*, ed. Mohammad Qazvini, Iranshahr, Berlin, 1927
Nezm al-Molk Tusi, *Siyar al-Muluk* or *Siyasatnameh*, ed. Hubert Darke, Bongah-e Tarjomeh va Nashr-e Ketab, Tehran, 1961
Rodinson, Maxime, *Mohammed*, tr. (from French) Anne Carter, Penguin, Harmondsworth, 1991
Rypka, Jan, *History of Iranian Literature*, D. Rydal Publishing Company, Dordrecht, Holland, 1968
Shaban, M. A., *The Abbasid Revolution*, Cambridge University Press, Cambridge, 1970
Shahidi, Seyyed Ja'far, *Tarikh-e Tahlili-ye Islam (az aghaz to nimeh-ye nakhost-e sadeh-ye chaharom)*, Markaz-e Nashr-e Daneshgahi, Tehran, 2004

CHAPTER 4: SELECT BIBLIOGRAPHY

Boyle, J. A. (ed.), *The Cambridge History of Iran*, vol. 5, *The Saljuq and Mongol Periods*, Cambridge University Press, Cambridge, 1968
Browne, Edward G., *A Literary History of Persia*, vols ii and iii, Cambridge University Press, Cambridge, 1928
Daftary, Farhad, *The Ismailis, Their History and Doctrines*, Cambridge University Press, Cambridge, 1990
Darke, Hubert (tr.), *The Book of Government or Rules for Kings: The Siyar al-Muluk or Siyasat-nama of Nizam al-Mulk*, Routledge & Kegan Paul, London and Boston, MA, 1978
Eqbal Ashtiyani, Abbas, *Tarikh-e Moghol: Az Hamleh-ye Changiz ta Tashkil-e Dawlat-e Teymuri*, Amir Kabir, Tehran, 1986
—— , *Vezarat dar Ahd-e Salatin-e Bozorg-e Saljuqi, Az Tarikh-e Tashkil-e in Selseleh ta Marg-e Sultan Sanjar*, [AH] *432–552*, Daneshgah-e Tehran, Tehran, 1960
Fazlollah, Rashid al-Din, *Jami' al-Tavarikh*, ed. Bahman Karimi, Eqbal, Tehran, 1959
Khwandmir, Ghiyath al-Din, *Habib al-Siyar*, ed. Mohammad Dabir Siyaqi, Khayyam, Tehran, 1974
Lambton, Ann K. S., *Continuity and Change in Mediaeval Persia: Aspects of Administrative, Economic and Social History, 11th–14th Century*, Persian Heritage Foundation, Albany, NY, 1988

—— , *Landlord and Peasant in Persia*, Oxford University Press, London, New York and Toronto, 1953
—— , *Theory and Practice in Mediaeval Persian Government*, Variorum Reprints, London, 1980
Morgan, David, *Mediaeval Persia 1040–1797*, Longman, London and New York, 1988
Mostawfi, Hamdollah, *Tarikh-e Gozideh*, ed. Abdolhosein Nava'i, Amir Kabir, Tehran, 1960
Nezam al-Molk Tusi, *Siyar al-Muluk*, ed. Hubert Darke, Bongah-e Tarjomeh va Nashr-e Ketab, Tehran, 1961
Ravandi, Soleiman, *Rahat al-Sudur va Ayat al-Surur dar Tarikh-e Al-e Seljuk*, ed. Mohammad Iqbal, rev. Mojtaba Minovi, Amir Kabir, Tehran, 1985

CHAPTER 5: SELECT BIBLIOGRAPHY

Abisaab, Rula Jurdi, *Converting Persia: Religion and Power in the Safavid Empire*, I.B. Tauris, London and New York, 2004
Browne, Edward G., *A Literary History of Persia*, vol. iv, Cambridge University Press, Cambridge, 1928
Falsafi, Nasrollah, *Zendegi-ye Shah Abbas Avval*, 5 vols, Ketab-e Kayhan, Tehran, 1955–73
Ferrier, Ronald W. (tr. and ed.), *A Journey to Persia: Jean Chardin's Portrait of a Seventeenth-Century Empire*, I.B. Tauris, London, 1996
Floor, Willem, *A Fiscal History of Iran in the Safavid and Qajar Periods*, Persian Studies, 17, Bibliotheca Press, New York, 1998
—— , *Safavid Government Institutions*, Mazda Publishers, Costa Mesa, CA, 2001
—— , *The Economy of Safavid Persia*, Reichert, Wiesbaden, 2000
Gabashvili, Valerain, N., 'The Undiladze Feudal House in the Sixteenth to Seventeenth-Century Iran According to Georgian Sources', *Iranian Studies*, 40/1 (February 2007), pp. 37–58
Jackson, Peter and Laurence Lockhart (eds), *The Cambridge History of Iran*, vol. 6, *The Timurid and Safavid Periods*, Cambridge University Press, Cambridge, 1986
Khwandmir, Amir Mahmud, *Iran dar Ruzegar-e Shah Isma'il va Shah Tahmasb Safavi*, ed. Gholamreza Tabtaba'i, Bonyad-e Mowqufat-e Doktor Mahmud Afshar Yazdi, Tehran, 1991
Matthee, Rudolph, *The Politics of Trade in Safavid Isfahan: Silk for Silver, 1600–1730*, Cambridge University Press, Cambridge, 1999
Melville, Charles (ed.), *Safavid Persia: The History and Politics of an Islamic Society*, I.B. Tauris, London, 1996
Monshi, Eskandar Beg, *Tarikh-e Alam Aray-e Abbasi*, ed. Mohammad Isma'il Rezvani, Donya-ye Ketab, Tehran, 1998
Morgan, David, *Mediaeval Persia, 1040–1797*, Longman, London and New York, 1988
Newman, Andrew J., *Safavid Iran, Rebirth of a Persian Empire*, I.B. Tauris, London, 2006
Nava'i, Abdolhosein, *Shah Abbas*, Entesharat-e Bonyad-e Farhang-e Iran, Tehran, 1974
—— , *Shah Ismai'l Safavi*, Entesharat-e Bonyad-e Farhang-e Iran, Tehran, 1968
Parsadust, Manuchehr, *Shah Isma'il Avval, Padshahi ba Asar-ha-ye Dirpay dar Iran va Irani*, Enteshar, Tehran, 1996
Savory, Roger, *Iran under the Safavids*, Cambridge University Press, Cambridge, 1980.
—— (tr.), *The History of Shah Abbas the Great*, 2 vols, Persian Heritage Series, 28, Boulder, CO, 1978
Stewart, Devin J., 'An Episode in the 'Amili Migration to Safavid Iran: Husayn b. 'Abd al-Samad 'Amili's Travel Account', *Iranian Studies*, 39/4 (December 2006), pp. 481–509
Turner, Colin, *Islam without Allah?: The Rise of Religious Externalism in Safavid Iran*, Curzon, Richmond, Surrey, 2000
Zarrinkub, Abdolhosein, *Tarikh-e Mardom-e Iran: Keshmakesh ba Qodrat-ha*, Amir Kabir, Tehran, 1985

CHAPTER 6: SELECT BIBLIOGRAPHY

Algar, Hamid, *Religion and State in Iran, 1785–1906, the Role of the Ulama in the Qajar Period*, University of California Press, Berkeley, CA, 1969
Amanat, Abbas, *Renewal and Reconstruction: The Making of the Babi Movement in Iran, 1844–1850*, Kalimat Press, Los Angeles, CA, 2005
Avery, Peter, Gavin Hambly and Charles Melville (eds), *The Cambridge History of Iran*, vol. 7, *From Nadir Shah to the Islamic Republic*, Cambridge University Press, Cambridge, 1991
Axworthy, Michael, *Sword of Persia: Nader Shah, From Tribal Warrior to Conquering Tyrant*, I.B. Tauris, London and New York, 2006
Floor, Willem (comp. and tr.), *The Afghan Occupation of Safavid Persia, 1721–1729*, Association pour l'avancement des études Iraniennes, Paris, 1998
Kelly, Laurence, *Diplomacy and Murder in Tehran: Alexander Griboyedov and Imperial Russia's Mission to the Shah of Persia*, I.B. Tauris, London and New York, 2002

Lambton, Ann K. S., *Qajar Persia: Eleven Studies*, I.B. Tauris, London, 1987

Lockhart, Laurence, *Nadir Shah*, Luzac, London, 1938

—— , *The Fall of the Safavid Dynasty and the Afghan Occupation of Persia*, Cambridge University Press, Cambridge, 1958

Moshiri, Mohammad (ed.), *Rostam al-Tavarikh*, Amir Kabir, Tehran, 1973

Mostawfi, Abdollah, *Sharh-e Zendegani-ye Man, Tarikh-e Ejtema'i va Edari-ye Dawreh-ye Qajariyeh*, vol. 1, Zavvar, Tehran, 1998

Perry, John, *Karim Khan Zand: A History of Iran, 1747–1779*, University of Chicago Press, Chicago, 1979

Savory, Roger, *Iran under the Safavids*, Cambridge University Press, Cambridge, 1980

Shamim, Ali Asghar, *Iran dar Dawreh-ye Saltanat-e Qajar*, Ibn Sina, Tehran, 1964

CHAPTER 7: THE DILEMMA OF REFORM AND MODERNIZATION

1. See further Fereydun Adamiyat, *Amir Kabir va Iran*, Kharazmi, Tehran, 1969.
2. Entry on Hasan Khan Salar in Mehdi Bamdad, *Sharh-e Hal-e Rejal-e Iran dar Qorun-e 12 o 13 o 14 Hejri*, vol. 1, Zavvar, Tehran, 1992, pp. 327–9.
3. See further Abbas Amanat, *Renewal and Reconstruction: The Making of the Babi Movement in Iran, 1844–1850*, Kalimat Press, Los Angeles, CA, 2005.
4. Mehdiqoli Hedayat (Mokhber al-Saltaneh), *Khaterat va Khatarat*, Zavvar, Tehran, 1984, pp. 56–7.
5. Ahmad Kasravi, *Baha'igari, Shi'igari, Sufigari*, ed. Alireza Samari, Isin, Nashr-e Nima, Germany, 2003.
6. See further Adamiyat, *Amir Kabir va Iran*.
7. Abdolhosein Nava'i (ed.), *Sharh-e Hal-e Abbas Mirza Molk Ara*, 2nd edn, Babak, Tehran, 1982. The letters have been published from the Iranian archives in Abbas Eqbal-e Ashtiyani's introduction to the book; see pp. 29–31, emphasis added.
8. See further the entry on Abbas Mirza Molk Ara in Bamdad, *Sharh-e Hal-e Rejal-e Iran*, vol. 2, pp. 222–7.
9. *Ruznameh-ye Khaterat E'temad al-Saltaneh*, ed. Iraj Afshar, Amir Kabir, Tehran, 1980, p. 821; Bamdad, *Sharh-e Hal-e Rejal-e Iran*, vol. 3, p. 403.
10. Hafiz Farmanfarmaian (ed.), *Khaterat-e Siyasi-ye Mirza Ali Khan Amin al-Dawleh*, Amir Kabir, Tehran, 1991, p. 6.
11. See further Abbas Amanat, *Pivot of the Universe: Nasir al-Din Shah Qajar and the Iranian Monarchy, 1831–1896*, I.B. Tauris, London, 1997.
12. Ibid.
13. Malkam Khan, 'Ketabcheh-ye Gheibi ya Daftar-e Tanzimat', in Mohammad Mohit-e Tabataba'i (ed.), *Majmu'eh-ye Asar-e Mirza Malkam Khan*, Tehran, Danesh, 1948, pp. 2–52. See also his other essays in Mohit-e Tabatab'i, *Majmu'eh-ye Asar*.
14. Ibid.; Homa Katouzian, 'European Liberalisms and Modern Concepts of Liberty in Iran', in *Iranian History and Politics, the dialectic of State and Society*, paperback edn, Routledge, London and New York, 2007.
15. Quoted in Abdollah Mostawfi, *Sharh-e Zendegani-ye Man*, vol. 1, Zavvar, Tehran, 1981, p. 123. See also Homa Katouzian, *State and Society in Iran: The Eclipse of the Qajars and the Emergence of the Pahlavis*, I.B. Tauris, paperback edn, London and New York, 2006, p. 27.
16. See further George Nathaniel Curzon, *Persia and the Persian Question*, Frank Cass, London, 1996.
17. Quoted from E'temad al-Saltaneh's *Khabnameh* in Bamdad, *Sharh-e Hal-e Rejal-e Iran*, vol. 4, p. 145.
18. See further Mahmud Farhad Mo'tamed, *Tarikh-e Siyasi-ye Dawreh-ye Sedarat-e Mirza Hosein Khan Moshir al-Dawleh, Sepahsalar-e A'azam*, Elmi, Tehran, 1946.
19. Nava'i (ed.), *Sharh-e Hal-e Abbas Mirza Molk Ara*, p. 175.
20. Hafiz Farmanfarmaian (ed.), *Khaterat-e Siyasi-ye Mirza Ali Khan Amin al-Dawleh*, pp. 86–8.
21. See further Vanessa Martin, *The Qajar Pact: Bargaining, Protest and the State in Nineteenth-Century Persia*, I.B. Tauris, London, 2005.
22. See for his biography Shirin Mahdavi, *For God, Mammon and Country: A Nineteenth Century Persian Merchant, Hajj Mohammad Hasan Amin al-Zarb (1834–1898)*, Westview, Boulder, CO and Oxford, 1999.
23. See further the entry on Amin al-Soltan in Bamdad, *Sharh-e Hal-e Rejal*, vol. 2, pp. 387–425.
24. Nazem al-Islam Kermani, *Tarikh-e Bidari-ye Iraniyan*, ed. Ali Akbar Sa'idi Sirjani, vol. 1, Agah, Tehran, 1983, pp. 22–39.
25. For a history of the movement see Nikki Keddie, *Religion and Rebellion in Iran, the Tobacco Protest of 1891–1892*, Frank Cass, London, 1966.
26. As noted, Malkam has been and still remains a controversial figure among historians and intellectual observers of the period. See for example Hamid Algar, *Malkum Khan, A Study in the History of Iranian Modernism*, California University Press, Berkeley, CA, 1973; Fereshteh Nura'i, *Mirza Malkam*

Khan Nazem al-Dawleh, Jibi, Tehran, 1973; Khan Malek-e Sasani, *Siyasatgaran-e Dawreh-ye Qajar*, n. p., Tehran, n. d. (date of preface, 1959); Ehtesham al-Saltaneh, *Khaterat-e Ehtesham al-Saltaneh*, ed. S. M. Musavi, Zavvar, 1988, Tehran; Mahmud Katira'i, *Feramasoneri dar Iran*, Eqbal, Tehran, 1968.

27. Albert Hourani, *Arabic Thought in the Liberal Age*, Oxford University Press, London, 1970.
28. See entry on Seyyed Jamal al-Din in Bamdad, *Sharh-e Hal-e Rejal*, vol. 1, pp. 257–81; E'temad al-Saltaneh, *Ruznameh-ye Khaterat*, ed. Iraj Afshar.
29. See for a biography of Seyyed Jamal al-Din, Nikki R. Keddie, *Sayyid Jamal al-Din al-Afghani: A Political Biography*, University of California Press, Berkeley, CA, 1972.
30. For an extensive description and analysis of the economy in the 19th century, see Homa Katouzian, *The Political Economy of Modern Iran*, Macmillan and New York University Press, London and New York, 1981, ch. 3; for an economic history of Iran in the 19th century see Charles Issawi, *The Economic History of Iran, 1800–1914*, University of Chicago Press, Chicago, IL, 1971; for a comprehensive study of Qajar as well as Safavid public finance, see Willem Floor, *A Fiscal History of Iran in the Safavid and Qajar Periods, 1500–1925*, Persian Studies, 17, Bibliotheca Persia Press, New York, 1998.

CHAPTER 8: THE REVOLUTION FOR LAW

1. Mohammad Ebrahim Bastani Parizi, *Asiya-ye Haft Sang*, Donya-ye Ketab, 1988, Tehran, p. 644.
2. Hajj Mokhber al-Saltaneh (Mehdiqoli Hedayat), *Khaterat va Khatarat*, Zavvar, Tehran, 1984 and *Gozaresh-e Iran: Qajariyeh va Mashrutiyat*, Noqreh, Tehran, 1984.
3. See entry on Mirza Mahmud Khan Hakim al-Molk in Bamdad, *Sharh-e Hal-e Rejal-e Iran*, vol. 5, pp. 35–9.
4. Abdolhosein Nava'i (ed.), *Yaddshat-ha-ye Malek al-Movarrekhin va Mer'at al-Vaqaye' Mozaffari*, Zarrin, Tehran, 1989, p. 267. The evidence of increasing disorder and chaos may be found in many contemporary and later sources, but it is seldom as specific and immediate as in these two books.
5. Ibid., pp. 306–7.
6. Ibid., pp. 20–2.
7. Ibid., pp. 23–6.
8. Ibid., pp. 26–7. Virtually all other primary sources describe Hakim al-Molk as a shameless money-grubber and an enemy of Atabak.
9. Ibid., pp. 27–8.
10. Ibid., p. 29.
11. Ibid., pp. 30–2.
12. Ibid., pp. 101–2.
13. Ibid., p. 184.
14. Ibid., p. 231.
15. Ibid., p. 248.
16. See further Afsaneh Najmabadi, *The Story of the Daughters of Quchan: Gender and National Memory in Iranian History*, Syracuse University Press, Syracuse, NY, 1998.
17. Nava'i (ed.), *Yaddasht-ha*, pp. 251–2.
18. Ibid. p. 26.
19. Ibid. p. 269.
20. Ibid. p. 271.
21. Ibid. p. 273.
22. Ibid. pp. 274 et seq.
23. Ibid. p. 338.
24. See the recently published Persian and English versions of his book in one volume, A. A. Seyyed-Ghorab and S. McGlinn, *The Essence of Modernity, Mirza Usof Khan Mustashar ad-Dowla Tabrizi's Treatise on Codified Law (Yak Kalame)*, Rozenberg Publishers and Purdue University Press, Amsterdam and West Lafayette, IN, 2008.
25. Mostashar al-Dawleh was much more a reformist than a revolutionary. It is illuminating that after the severe persecution to which he had been subjected and as late as 1893, in a death-bed letter to Mozaffar al-Din Mirza, the heir-designate, he still laid the emphasis on orderly government. See for his long, reasoned as well as impassioned letter, Nazem al-Islam Kermani, in Ali Akbar Sa'idi Sirjani (ed.), *Tarikh-e Bidari-ye Iraniyan*, vol. 1, pp. 172–7. See also Abdollah Mostawfi, *Sharh-e Zendegani-ye Man*, vol. 1, Zavvar, Tehran, 1981.
26. *Qanun*, 1 (20 February 1890), p. 1, quoted in Hossein Shahidi, 'Iranian Journalism and the Law in the Twentieth Century', *Iranian Studies*, 41/5 (December 2008), p. 741, emphasis added.
27. See further Fereydun Adamiyat, *Andisheh-ha-ye Mirza Fath'ali Akhnudzadeh*, Entesharat-e Kharazmi, Tehran, 1970 and *Andisheh-ha-ye Mirza Aqa Khan Kermani*, Payam, Tehran, 1978; Yahya Aryanpur, *Az Saba ta Nima*, vol. 1, book 2, Zavvar, Tehran, 1993, chs 3–7.

28. See further Homa Katouzian 'Towards a General Theory of Iranian Revolutions', in *Iranian History and Politics: The Dialectic of State and Society*, paperback edn, Routledge, London and New York, 2007.

29. Quoted in Ebrahim Bastani Parizi, *Zir-e in Haft Asman*, Javidan, Tehran, 1983, p. 55.

30. See further Edward G. Browne, *The Persian Revolution*, Frank Cass, London, 1966; Mohammad Ali Jamalzadeh *Sar o Tah Yek Karbas*, Ma'refat, Tehran, 1955; Homa Katouzian, 'All of the Same Cloth; Jamalzadeh's reminiscences of his boyhood in Isfahan', *Iranshenasi* (winter 2000).

31. For a recently published contemporary account of such conflicts see Mohammad Ali Tehrani Katouzian, *Tarikh-e Enqelab-e Mashrutiyat-e Iran*, ed. Naser Katouzian, Enteshar, Tehran, 2000, a hitherto unknown primary source on the Constitutional Revolution.

32. The influence of events in Russia may be seen clearly in the public statements put out by Iranian social democrats (*ejtem'iyun-e amiyun*), which vehemently supported the constitutional movement and, incidentally, were highly respectful of Tabataba'i. For the full text of the statements, see Nazem al-Islam Kermani, *Tarikh-e Bidari-ye Iranian*. See also Janet Afary, *The Iranian Constitutional Revolution, 1905–1911*, Columbia University Press, New York, 1996.

33. Tabataba'i's sermon from the pulpit in Nazem al-Islam Kermani, *Tarikh-e Bidari-ye Iraniyan*, where he details the grievances against Sho'a' al-Saltaneh and argues their case.

34. For a first-hand account of the incident see Tabataba'i's recently published notes in Hasan Tabataba'i (ed.), *Yaddasht-ha-ye Montasher Nashodeh-ye Seyyed Mohammad Tabataba'i*, Nashr-e Abi, Tehran, 2003.

35. For an extended description and analysis of the inappropriateness of Marx's European model to this case see Homa Katouzian, *State and Society in Iran, The Eclipse of the Qajars and the Emergence of the Pahlavis*, I. B. Tauris, London and New York, 2006, ch. 2.

36. Seyyed Mohammad Ali Jamalzadeh, 'Seyyed Jamal al-Din Va'ez-e Isfahani va Ba'zi Mobarezat-e U', in Ali Dehbashi (ed.), *Yad-e Mohammad Ali Jamazadeh*, Nashr-e Sales, Tehran, 1988, pp. 51–2. The quotation is directly from the contemporary journal *Al-Jamal*, 35 (1905).

37. See further Katouzian, 'Towards a General Theory'.

38. For the most recent first-hand account see Tabataba'i, *Yaddasht-ha*.

39. Hajj Mokhber al-Saltaneh (Mehdiqoli Hedayat), *Gozaresh-e Iran*.

40. E. G. Browne, *The Persian Revolution*, dates this incident to two weeks earlier.

41. For detailed descriptions of events see Ahmad Kasravi, *Tarikh-e Mashruteh ye Iran*, Amir Kabir, Tehran, 1976; Tehrani Katouzian, *Tarikh-e Mashrutiyat*, Nazem al-Isalm Kermani, *Tarikh-e Bidari*; Yaha Dawlat-Abadi, *Hayat-e Yahya*, Ferdowsi and Attar, Tehran, 1983; Browne, *The Persian Revolution*.

42. For a good, though characteristically brief, account of these conflicts see Mokhber al-Saltaneh, *Khaterat va Khatarat*.

43. On the coarse or obscene language of some of the newspapers and *shab-namehs* see especially Tehrani Katouzian, *Tarikh-e Enqelab-e Mashrutiyat* and Kasravi, *Tarikh-e Mashruteh*.

44. See Mokhber al-Saltaneh's first-hand account in *Khaterat va Khatarat* and Kasravi, *Tarikh-e Mashruteh*.

45. For details, see Homa Katouzian, 'Liberty and Licence in the Constitutional Revolution of Iran', *Journal of the Royal Asiatic Society*, 3/8 (July 1998), repr. in *Iranian History and Politics*.

46. For a comprehensive study of Britain and the Constitutional Revolution see Mansour Bonakdarian, *Britain and the Iranian Constitutional Revolution of 1906–1911: Foreign Policy, Imperialism and Dissent*, Syracuse University Press, Syracuse, NY, 2006.

47. For example, Tehrani Katouzian, *Tarikh-e Enqelab*.

48. Homa Katouzian, 'Seyyed Hasan Taqizadeh: Seh Zendegi dar Yek Omr', in *Iran-Nameh*, Vol. XXI, nos. 1–2, 2003, special issue on Taqizadeh (guest ed. H. Katouzian). Taqizadeh had expressed his regret on the matter to Iraj Afshar.

49. For an extensive account of Ephrem's career see W. Morgan Shuster, *The Strangling of Persia*, The Century Co., New York, 1912.

50. Iraj Afshar (ed.), *Mohammad Ali Mirza and Mohammad Ali Shah-e Makhlu' (55 sanad-e tazeh-yab)*, Nashr-e Abi, Tehran, 2009. For a description of the battles by one of their participants, see General Amir-Ahmadi's memoirs in Gholamhosein Zargarinezhad (ed.), *Khaterat-e Nakhostin Sepahbod-e Iran*, Mo'asseseh-ye Pazhuhesh va Mota le'at-e Farhangi, Tehran, 1994.

51. For the text of the great ulama's fatva, see Katouzian, *State and Society*, ch. 2.

52. Kasravi, *Tairkh-e Mashruteh*, contains the text of a number of such statements. For replies to them by the constitutionalist ulama see Nazem al-Islam, *Tarikh-e Bidari*.

53. See further Vanessa Martin, 'Aqa Najafi, Hajj Aqa Nurullah and the Emergence of Islamism in Isfahan, 1889–1908', *Iranian Studies*, 41/2 (April 2008).

54. Ibid. and Katouzian, 'Liberty and Licence'.

55. This occurs in a letter from Smart in Tehran to his former teacher Edward Browne in Cambridge. See Browne, *The Persian Revolution*, p.164. See also Vanessa Martin, *Iran and Modernism: The Iranian Revolution of 1906*, Syracuse University, Syracuse, NY, 1989.

56. See further Homa Katouzian, 'Problems of Democracy and the Public Sphere in Modern Iran', *Comparative Studies of South Asia, Africa and the Middle East*, 18/2 (1998), repr. in *Iranian History and Politics*.

57. On the language and conduct of the radical newspapers and publications see the text and n. 41 above.

58. See further Katouzian, *State and Society*, ch. 3.

59. Ahmad Matin Daftari, 'Andarz-ha-ye Baradaraneh beh Omum-e Daneshjuyan, Khosusan Dadresan va Ostadan-e Ayandeh', *A'in-e Daneshjuyan*, 2 (March 1945).

60. See further Shuster, *The Strangling of Persia*, pp. 171–2.

61. Ibid.

62. See further Taqizadeh Seyyed Hasan, *Zendegi-ye Tufani: Khaterat-e Seyyed Hasan Taqizadeh*, ed. Iraj Afshar, Elmi, Tehran, 1983, App. 5, p. 459.

63. For an extended description and analysis of the Shuster crisis, see Katouzian, *State and Society in Iran*, ch. 3.

64. For example, Ilse Itscherenska, 'Taqizadeh dar Alman-e Qeisari', *Iran Nameh*, 21/1–2 (spring and summer 2003); Jamshid Behnam, *Berlani-ha: Andishmandan-e Irani dar Berlan, 1915–1930*, Farzan, Tehran, 2000.

65. See further Wm. J. Olson, *Anglo-Iranian Relations during World War I*, Frank Cass, London, 1984.

66. Yahya Dawlat-Abadi, *Hayat-e Yahya*, vol. 3, p. 283; Baqer Aqeli, *Ruzshomar-e Tarikh-e Iran*, 3rd edn, Nashr-e Goftar, Tehran, p. 103.

67. Dawlat-Abadi, *Hayat-e Yahya*, vol. 3, ch. 32.

68. Many contemporary Iranian sources cover one or another aspect of Wassmus's operations. See in particular Abolqaem Kahhalzadeh, *Dideh-ha va Shenideh-ha*, ed. Morteza Kamran, Kamran, Tehran, 1984. See also Christopher Sykes, *Wassmuss, 'The German Lawrence'*, Longman, Green and Co., London and New York, 1936.

69. Ibid.; Mostawfi, *Sharh-e Zendegani-ye Man*, vol. 3, Zavvar, Tehran, 1998; Kasravi, *Tarikh-e Hijdahsaleh*; Olson, *Anglo-Iranian Relations*; Aqeli, *Ruzshomar*.

70. See further Mansoureh Ettehadieh, 'The Iranian Provisional Government', in Touraj Atabaki (ed.), *Iran and the First World War*, I.B. Tauris, London and New York, 2006.

71. On Kuchik Khan's movement see, for example, Ebrahim Fakhra'i, *Sardar-e Jangal, Mirza Kuchik Khan*, Javidan, Tehran, 1978; Mohammad Ali Gilak, *Tarikh-e Enqelab-e Jangal*, Nashr-e Gilak, Rasht, 1990.

72. For a discussion of the nationalist ideas of Akhudzadeh and Mirza Aqa Khan and the nationalist trends following their ideas see Homa Katouzian, *Sadeq Hedayat, The Life and Legend of an Iranian Writer*, I.B. Tauris, London and New York, 1991, chs 1 and 5. For a recent study see Afshin Marashi, *Nationalizing Iran: Culture, Power and the State, 1870–1940*, University of Washington Press, Seattle, WA, 2008.

73. See further Mohamad Tavakoli-Targhi, 'Narrative Identity in the Works of Hedayat and His Contemporaries', in Homa Katouzian (ed.), *Sadeq Hedayat, His Work and His Wondrous World*, Routledge, London and New York, 2007.

74. Abdorrahman Seif-e Azad (ed.), *Divan-e Aref*, Tehran, Seif-e Azad, 1948, pp. 262–3.

75. Katouzian, *Sadeq Hedayat*, p. 280; *Divan-e Aref*, p. 384.

76. For a more extensive and elaborate account of the rise of modern Iranian nationalism see Katouzian, *State and Society*, chs 3 and 11, and *Sadeq Hedayat*. See further Afshin Marashi, *Nationalizing Iran: Culture, Power and the State*.

77. Mohammad Gholi Majd, *The Great Famine and Genocide in Persia, 1917–1918*, University Press of America, Lanham, MD and Oxford, 2003.

78. For example, Abdorrahman Seif-e Azad (ed.), *Divan-e Aref*, p. 300.

79. Memorandum by Marling, 20/12/18, FO 371/3262.

80. For detailed evidence and analysis see Katouzian, *State and Society*, chs 4 and 5. See also Harold Nicolson, *Curzon, the Last Phase, 1919–1925: A Study in Post-war Diplomacy*, Constable, London, 1934.

81. For example, Viceroy (Foreign Department) to Secretary of State for India, FO 371/3262.

82. Among various telegrams and notes concerning this matter, Curzon noted that such payment 'is not merely exorbitant, it is corrupt'. Minute by Curzon added to Cox to Curzon, 17/7/19, FO 371/3861.

83. Cox later wired to Curzon that, among the three men involved in the negotiations, Vosuq had not asked for or insisted on the payment. See Cox to Curzon, *British Documents of Foreign Policy*, vol. iv, 720.

84. For the full text of the agreement see James Balfour, *Recent Happenings in Persia*, William Blackwood & Sons, Edinburgh and London, 1922, pp. 123–5.

85. See further Martin Sicker, *The Bear and The Lion*, Praeger, London, 1988, p. 39; Curzon to Cox, 19/8/19, *BDFP*, vol. 4, 782.
86. See, for example, the reports of Maj C.J. Edmonds, British political officer in the region, The Edmonds Papers, The Middle East Centre, St Antony's College, Oxford, such as the reports for January 1920 and March 1920.
87. See further 'The Revolt of Sheikh Mohammad Khiyabani', in Katouzian, *Iranian History and Politics*.
88. War Office to Baghdad, copy to General Champain, GOC, Norperforce, 28/2/20, WO 158/697.
89. See further Cyrus Ghani, *Iran and the Rise of Reza Shah: From Qajar Collapse to Pahlavi Power*, I.B. Tauris, London and New York, 1998, ch. 4; Katouzian, *State and Society*, ch. 6.
90. See further Lord Ironside (ed.), *High Road to Command: The Diaries of Major-General Sir Edmund Ironside, 1920–1922*, Leo Cooper, London, 1972; Richard H. Ullman, *Anglo-Soviet Relations*, vol. 3, *The Anglo-Soviet Accord*, Princeton University Press, Princeton, NJ, 1974; Ironside to Haldane, 24/10/20, WO 158/687; Norman to Curzon, 25/9/20, *BDFP*, 566; Norman to Curzon, 25/9/20, FO 371/4914.
91. See further Stephanie Cronin, *The Army and the Creation of the Pahlavi State in Iran, 1910–1926*, I.B. Tauris, London and New York, 1997; Katouzian, *State and Society*, ch. 5; Ullman, *The Anglo-Soviet Accord*.
92. Ironside, *High Road to Command*. See also Ghani, *Iran and the Rise of Reza Shah*.
93. Mohammad Ali Jamalzadeh, 'Taqrirat-e, Seyyed Zia and his "Black Book" ', pts 1, 2 and 7, *Ayandeh* (March 1980 and June 1981).
94. Ibid. and Colonel Qahremani's memoirs in M. T. Bahar, *Tarikh-e Mokhtasar-e Ahazab-e Siyasi dar Iran*, vol. 1, Jibi, Tehran, 1978, especially p. 82.
95. Jamalzadeh quoting Seyyed Zia, 'Taqrirat-e, Seyyed Zia and his "Black Book" '.
96. Ullman, *The Anglo-Soviet Accord*, p. 387.
97. Ghani, *Iran and the Rise of Reza Shah*, chapter 7; Katouzian, *State and Society*, ch. 9.
98. See, for example, Minute by G. P. Churchill, 'Persia: Political Situation' (37), FO 371/6409; Norman to the Foreign Office, 2/3/21, FO 371/6427.
99. Curzon to Norman, 14/3/21 *BDFP*, 696; Norman to Curzon 25/5/21, FO 371/6404.

CHAPTER 9: MODERN ARBITRARY RULE

1. For example, Mohammad Taqi Bahar, *Tarikh-e Mokhtasar-e Ahzab-e Siyasi dar Iran*, vol. 1, Jibi, Tehran, 1928; Hosein Makki, *Tarikh-e Bistsaleh-ye Iran*, vol. 2, Elmi, Tehran, 1995; Reza Niyazmand, *Reza Shah, Az Tavallod ta Saltanat*, Bonyad-e Motale'at-e Iran, Washington and London, 1996; Donald Wilber, *Riza Shah Pahlavi: The Resurrection and Reconstruction of Iran*, Exposition Press, New York, 1975; L. P. Elwell-Sutton, 'Reza Shah the Great', in George Lenczowski (ed.), *Iran under the Pahlavis*, Hoover Institution Press, Stanford, CA, 1978.
2. For example, the photocopy of his handwritten letter in 1918 in Nasrollah Seifpour Fatemi, *Ayeneh-ye Ebrat*, Nashr-e Ketab, London, 1989.
3. For example, Abdollah Mostawfi, *Sharh-e Zendegani-ye Man*, vol. 3; Reader Bullard, *Letters from Tehran*, ed. E. C. Hodgkin, I.B. Tauris, London and New York, 1991.
4. For Reza Khan's life before the 1921 coup, see, for example, Najafqoli Pesyan and Khosraw Mo'tazed, *Az Savadkuh ta Zhohnsburg*, Sales, Tehran, 1998; Bahar, *Tarikh-e Mokhtasar*, vol.1; Makki, *Tarikh-e Bistsaleh*, vol. 2; Mostawfi, *Sharh-e Zendegani-ye Man*, vol. 3.
5. For differing accounts and interpretations, see Gholamhosein Mirza Saleh (ed.), *Reza Shah: Khaterat-e Soleiman Behbudi, Shams Pahlavi and Ali Izadi*, Sahba, Tehran, 1983, pp. 396–9. Nasrollah Entezam, *Khaterat-e Nasrollah Entezam, Shahrivar-e 1320 az Didgah-e Darbar*, eds Mohammad Reza Abbasi and Behruz Tayarani, Sazman-e Asnad-e Melli-ye Iran, Tehran, 1992, pp. 75–80; Makki, *Tarikh-e Bistsaleh*, vol. 7, pp. 509–30; Baqer Aqeli, *Zoka al-Molk Forughi va Shahrivar-e 1320*, Elmi and Sokhan, Tehran, 1988, ch. 3.
6. For a definition and discussion of pseudo-modernism in Iran, see Homa Katouzian, *State and Society in Iran*, I. B.Tauris, London and New York, paperback edition, 2006 and *The Political Economy of Modern Iran, Despotism and Pseudo-Modernism*, Macmillan and New York University Press, London and New York, 1981.
7. See further Ebrahim Fakhra'i, *Sardar-e Jangal, Mirza Kuchik Khan*; Mohammad Ali Gilak, *Tarikh-e Enqelab-e Jangal*; Cosroe Chaqueri, *The Soviet Socialist Republic of Iran, 1920–1921: Birth of the Trauma*, Pittsburgh University Press, Pittsburgh, PA, 1995.
8. See further Kaveh Bayat, *Enqelab-e Khorasan*, Mo'asseseh-ye Pazhuhesh-ha-ye Farhangi, Tehran, 1991; Stephanie Cronin, 'An Experiment in Revolutionary Nationalism: The Rebellion of Colonel Mohammad Taqi Khan Pesyan', *Middle Eastern Studies*, 33/4 (October 1997); Ali Azari, *Qiyam-e Kolonel Mohammad Taqi Khan Pesyan*, Safi'ali Shah, Tehran, 1973.

9. See further Cronin, *The Army and the Creation of the Pahlavi State in Iran, 1910–1926*.

10. See further Kaveh Bayat, *Kudeta-ye Lahuti, Tabriz, Bahman 1300*, Shirzadeh, Tehran, 1997; Stephanie Cronin, 'Iran's Forgotten Revolutionary: Abolqasem Lahuti and the Tabriz insurrection of 1922', in *Reformers and Revolutionaries in Modern Iran*, ed. Stephanie Cronin, London and New York, RoutledgeCurzon, 2004.

11. For both speeches, Hosein Makki, *Doktor Mosaddeq va Notq-ha-ye Tarikhi-ye U*, Javidan, Tehran, 1985, pp. 130 and 139.

12. For details, see General Amir-Ahmadi's memoirs in Gholamhosein Zargarinezhad (ed.), *Khaterat-e Nakhostin Sepahbod-e Iran*, Mo'asseseh-ye Pazhuhesh va Motale'at-e Farhangi, Tehran, 1994; Katouzian, *State and Society*, ch. 10. See further Ahmad Kasravi, *Tarikh-e Hijdah Saleh-ye Azarbaijan*, Amir Kabir, Tehran, 1992; Bayat, Kevah, 'Riza Shah and the Tribes, an Overview', in Stephanie Cronin (ed.), *The Making of Modern Iran, State and Society under Riza Shah, 1921–1941*, Routledge, London and New York, 2003; Stephanie Cronin, *Tribal Politics in Iran*, Routledge, London and New York, 2007.

13. See further Gordon Waterfield, *Professional Diplomat, Sir Percy Loraine*, John Murray, London, 1973, especially chs 6–12; Katouzian, *State and Society*, ch. 10; several articles in various Soviet journals, including one in *Novyi Vostok* which described Reza Khan as 'the leader of the Persian national-revolutionary movement', cited in E. H. Carr, *The Bolshevik Revolution*, Penguin, Hanmondsworth, 1966, pp. 463–8; Radio Moscow's broadcasts in favour of Reza Khan and against Ahmad Shah, for example 21 October 1925, the eve of the fall of the Qajars, quoted in Makki, *Tarikh-e Bistsaleh*, vol. 3, pp. 427–8.

14. The details of 'the confession' were reported by the British envoy to the Foreign Office: 'Terror activities against the war minister (Sardar Sepah)', apparently a free translation of Persian press reports, FO 248/1369.

15. Ali Akbar Siyasi, *Gozaresh-e Yek Zendegi*, Siyasi, London, 1988.

16. In some sources this has been recorded as *Hezb-eTajddod* and translated into 'the Revival party'. See, for example, Peter Avery, Gavin Hambly and Charles Melville (eds), *The Cambridge History of Iran*, Cambridge University Press, Cambridge, 1991, p. 223.

17. For Eshqi's negative response, see Ali Akbar-e Moshir-Salimi (ed.), *Kolliyat-e Mosavvar-e Eshqi*, Moshir-Salimi, Tehran, c.1944, pp. 204–5.

18. Mohammad Taqi Bahar, *Divan*, ed. Mohammad Malekzadeh, vol. 1, Amir Kabir, Tehran, 1956, p. 358.

19. See further Bahar, *Tarikh-e Mokhtasar*, vol. 2; Makki, *Tarikh-e Bistsaleh*, vol. 2.

20. See further Habib Ladjevardi (ed.), *Kahaterat-e Mehdi Ha'eri Yazdi*, IranBooks, Bethesda, MD, 2001.

21. For example, Hajj Mirza Hosein Na'ini's letter to him mentioning the accompanying gift from the treasury of Imam Ali in Najaf. Makki, *Tarikh-e Bistsaleh*, vol. 3, p. 46.

22. See further Michael Zirinsky, 'Blood, Power and Hypocrisy: The Murder of Robert Imbrie and the American Relations with Pahlavi Iran, 1924', *International Journal of Middle East Studies*, 18/3 (1986); Dawlat-Abadi, *Hayat-e Yahya*, vol. 4, ch. 28; Makki, *Tarikh-e Bistsaleh*, vol. 3, ch. 15.

23. See further Katouzian, *State and Society*, ch. 10; Gordon Waterfield, *Professional Diplomat*.

24. For example, 'PERSIA', 23 /1 25, FO 371/10840; Katouzian, *State and Society*, ch. 10.

25. Dawlat-Abadi was the only one who declined to sign. Dalwat-Abadi, *Hayat-e Yahya*, vol. 4.

26. For example, ibid., chs 37 and 38; Makki, *Tarikh-e Bistsaleh*, vol. 3, chs 35–7; Ghani, *Iran and the Rise of Reza Shah*, ch. 13.

27. For the full proceedings, Makki, *Tarikh-e Bistsaleh*, vol. 3, pp. 556–655. For an analysis of the proceedings, Katouzian, *State and Society*, chs 10 and 11.

28. Witnessed by Yahya Dawlat-Abadi and Mohammad Mosaddeq. Dalwat-Abadi, *Hayat-e Yahya*, vol. 4, p. 343; Mosaddeq, *Taqrirat-e Mosaddeq dar Zendan*, notes by Jalil Bozorgmehr, ed. Iraj Afshar, Farhang-e Iranzamin, Tehran, 1980.

29. Mokhber al-Saltaneh (Mehdiqoli Hedayat), *Khaterat va Kahtarat*, p. 397.

30. Ibid., p. 386. See further Homa Katouzian, 'The Pahlavi Regime in Iran', in H. E. Chehabi and Juan J. Linz (eds), *Sultanistic Regimes*, The Johns Hopkins University Press, Baltimore, MD and London, 1998.

31. See Stephanie Cronin, 'Reza Shah, the Fall of Sardar Asad, and "the Bakhtiyari Plot" ', *Iranian Studies*, 38/2 (2005) and *Tribal Politics in Iran*; the entry on Sardar As'ad under 'Ja'farqoli', in Bamdad, *Sharh-e Hal-e Rejal-e Iran*, vol. 1.

32. See further Baqer Aqeli, *Nosrat al-Dawleh Firuz*, Nashr-e Namak, Tehran, 1994; the entry on Firuz, in Bamdad, *Sharh-e Hal-e Rejal*, vol. 4

33. For example, see Touraj Atabaki and Erik J. Zürcher (eds), *Men of Order: Authoritarian Modernization under Ataturk and Reza Shah*, 'Introduction', I.B. Tauris, London and New York, 2004; Afshin Marashi, 'Performing the Nation: The Shah's Official State Visit to Kemalist Turkey, June to July 1934',

in Cronin (ed.), *The Making of Modern Iran*. See also, Donald Wilber, *Riza Shah Pahlavi* and Amin Banani, *The Modernization of Iran*, Stanford University Press, Stanford, CA, 1961.

34. David Williamson, Secretary of the Legation, Tehran (2 May 1929), D. 81, DOS 891.00/1472, quoted in Michael Zirinsky, 'Riza Shah's Abrogation of Capitulations, 1927–1928', in Cronin (ed.), *The Making of Modern Iran*, p. 96.

35. See further Bahar, *Tarikh-e Mokhtasar*, vol. 2.

36. See further Vanessa Martin, 'Mudarris, Republicanism and the Rise to Power of Riza Khan, Sardar-i Sepah', in Cronin (ed.), *The Making of Modern Iran*; Ebrahim Khajeh-Nuri, *Bazigaran-e Asr-e Tala'i, Seyyed Hasan Modarres*, Javidan, Tehran, 1978.

37. See further Matthew Elliot, 'New Iran and the Dissolution of Party Politics under Reza Shah', in Atabaki and Zurcher, *Men of Order*.

38. See further Homa Katouzian, 'The Pahlavi Regime in Iran', in Chehabi and Linz (eds), *Sultanistic Regimes*.

39. Julian Bharier, *Economic Development in Iran 1900–1970*, Oxford University Press, Oxford, 1971, pp. 65–6, tables 4.1 and 4.2.

40. Katouzian, *The Political Economy of Modern Iran*, p. 114, table 6.2 and p. 130, table 7.2.

41. Charles Issawi, 'The Iranian Economy 1925–1975, Fifty Years of Economic Development', in Lenczowski, *Iran under the Pahlavis*, p. 131.

42. Stephanie Cronin, 'Riza Shah and the Paradoxes of Military Modernization, 1921–1941', in Cronin (ed.), *The Making of Modern Iran*, p. 40. See further Cronin, *The Army and the Creation of the Pahlavi State*, ch. 4, pp. 117–18.

43. Cronin, *The Army and the Creation of the Pahlavi State*, pp. 125–9; Banani, *The Modernization of Iran*, p. 55.

44. Mokhber al-Saltaneh (Mehdiqoli Hedayat), *Khaterat va Kahtarat*, pp. 375–6.

45. Wilber, *Riza Shah Pahlavi*, p. 129.

46. Mokhber al-Saltaneh (Mehdiqoli Hedayat), *Khaterat va Kahtarat*, pp. 377–8.

47. Banani, *The Modernization of Iran*, p.56.

48. Cronin, 'Riza Shah and the Paradoxes', p. 43.

49. Taqizadeh, *Zendegi-ye Tufani*, p. 364.

50. Ibid., pp. 212–16; Cronin, 'Riza Shah and the Paradoxes', pp. 42–52. See further on the fate of General Sheibani, in Iraj Afshar (ed.), *Nameh-ha-ye Paris az Mohammad Qazvini beh Seyyed Hasan Taqizadeh*, App. 4, Nashr-e Qatreh, Tehran, 2005.

51. Amir-Ahmadi's memoirs in Gholamhosein Zargarinezhad (ed.), *Khaterat-e Nakhostin Sephabod-e Iran*.

52. Stephanie Cronin, 'Riza Shah and the Disintegration of Bakhtiari Power in Iran', in Cronin (ed.), *The Making of Modern Iran*, p. 248 ff.

53. Kaveh Bayat, 'Riza Shah and the Tribes', in Cronin (ed.), *The Making of Modern Iran*.

54. Richard Tapper, 'The Case of the Shahsevans', in Cronin (ed.), *The Making of Modern Iran*.

55. See Stephanie Cronin, 'Riza Shah and the Disintegration of Bakhtiari Power', in Cronin (ed.), *The Making of Modern Iran*, especially pp. 261–5, and also Cronin, 'Riza Shah, the Fall of Sardar Asad'.

56. Bayat, 'Riza Shah and the Tribes', p. 217.

57. Banani, *The Modernization of Iran*, p. 60.

58. Zririnsky, 'Riza Shah's Abrogation of Capitulations'; Wilber, *Riza Shah Pahlavi*.

59. For example, Dawlat-Abadi, *Hayat-e Yahya*, vol. 1, chs 25–44.

60. For example, Isa Sadiq, *Yadgar-e Omr*, vol. 1, Sherkat-e Sahami-ye Tab'-e Ketab, Tehran, 1961, ch 4.

61. Katouzian, *Political Economy*, tables 6.2 and 7.2, based on Bharier, *Economic Development*, tables 4.1 and 4.2.

62. Ibid., ch. 2, table 5; Banani, *Modernization*, p. 108.

63. Cf. Banani, Bharier and Savory, 'Social Development in Iran during the Pahlavi Era', in Lenczcowski, *Iran under the Pahlavis*.

64. David Menasheri, *Education and the Making of Modern Iran*, Cornell University Press, Ithaca, NY and London, 1992, p. 110.

65. Sadiq, *Yadgar-e Omr*.

66. See further ibid.

67. Rudi Matthee, 'Transforming Dangerous Nomads into Useful Artisans, Technicians, Agriculturalists: Education in the Reza Shah Period', in Cronin (ed.), *The Making of Modern Iran*.

68. Banani, *Modernization*, pp. 103–7 and Savory, 'Social Development', p. 91.

69. Banani, *Modernization*, p. 111.

70. Gavin R. G. Hambly, 'The Pahlavi Autocracy: Riza Shah, 1921–1941' in Avery, Hambly and Melville (eds), *The Cambridge History of Iran*, vol. 7, p. 231.

71. Bharier, *Economic Development*, p. 37.
72. Isa Sadiq, *Yadgar-e Omr*, vol. 2, Amir Kabir, Tehran, 1966, p. 201 ff. Talinn Grigor, 'Re-cultivating "Good Taste": The Early Pahlavi Modernists and Their Society for National Heritage', *Iranian Studies*, 37/1 (March 2004).
73. Talinn Grigor, 'Re-cultivating "Good Taste"' and Sadiq, *Yadgar-e Omr*, vol. 2.
74. Sadiq, *Yadgar-e Omr*, vol. 2, p. 227. The proceedings of the conference were however not published until after the shah's abdication because they included a long article by Taqizadeh, who had been sacked as Iran's minister in Paris and, having criticised the proceedings of the official academy, had incurred the shah's wrath (see below). Ibid., pp. 216–17 and Taqizadeh, *Zendegi-ye Tufani*, p. 407.
75. Taqizadeh, *Zendegi-ye Tufani*, App. 14. Katouzian, entry on Taqizadeh, *Encyclopaedia Iranica*, forthcoming.
76. Sadiq, *Yadgar-e Omr*, vol. 2, pp. 236–7.
77. Wilber, *Riza Shah Pahlavi*, p. 146.
78. Houchang Chehabi, 'Dress Codes for Men in Turkey and Iran', in Atabaki and Zürcher, *Men of Order*.
79. Ibid., p. 225.
80. Mokhber al-Saltaneh, *Khaterat va Khatarat*, p. 407.
81. Makki, *Tarikh-e Bistsaleh*, vol. 6, pp. 279–87.
82. Aqeli, *Zoka al-Molk Forughi*.
83. Chehabi, 'Dress Codes for Men in Turkey and Iran', p. 193.
84. Moshir Salimi (ed.), *Kolliyat-e Eshqi*, p. 203.
85. Homa Katouzian, 'Iraj, the Poet of Love and Humour', *Iranian Studies*, 40/4 (September 2007); Mohammad-Ja'far Mahjub (ed.), *Divan-e Kamel-e Iraj-Mirza*, Sherkat-e Ketab, USA, 1986.
86. *Alam-e Nesvan*, 2/2 (September 1921), pp. 1–3.
87. Jasamin Rostam Kolayi, 'Expanding Agencies for the "New" Iranian Woman: Family Law, Work and Unveiling', in Cronin (ed.), *The Making of Modern Iran*, p. 158.
88. Mokhber al-Saltaneh (Mehdiqoli Hedayat), *Khaterat va Khatarat*, p. 407.
89. Chehabi, 'The Banning of the Veil and its Consequences', in Cronin (ed.), *The Making of Modern Iran*, p. 193.
90. Ibid.
91. Jalal Al-e Ahmad's short story 'Jashn-e Farkhondeh' (The Auspicious Festival) is a powerful fictional representation of the predicament of such men and women at the time. For documentation of orders and events, see Sazman-e Madarek-e Farhangi-ye Enqelab-e Eslami, *Vaqeh'eh-ye Kashf-e Hejab*, Mo'assehseh-ye Pazhuhesh-ha va Motale'at-e Farhangi, Tehran, 1992.
92. Bharier, *Economic Development*, ch. 4.
93. Wilber, *Reza Shah Pahlavi*, chs ix and x.
94. Bharier, *Economic Development*, pp. 70–4.
95. Ibid., ch. 6, table 6.
96. Banani, *The Modernization of Iran*, pp. 129–32.
97. Wilber, *Reza Shah Pahlavi*, p. 60.
98. Abolfazl Lesani, *Tala-ye Siayah ya Bala-ye Iran*, Amir Kabir, Tehran, 1978.
99. Mokhber al-Saltaneh (Mehdiqoli Hedayat, then prime minister), *Khaterat va Khatarat*, pp. 394–5.
100. Taqizadeh, *Zendegi-ye Tufani*, pp. 217–50 and App. 21. Katouzian, entry on Taqizadeh in *Encyclopaedia Iranica*, forthcoming.
101. Homa Katouzian, *Musaddiq and the Struggle for Power in Iran*, 2nd edn, I.B. Tauris, London and New York, 1999, ch. 7.
102. L. P. Elwell-Sutton, *Modern Iran*, G. Routledge and Sons, London, 1941, pp. 101–2.
103. Bharier, *Economic Development*, p. 178.
104. Ibid., p. 196.
105. Ann K. S. Lambton, *Landlord and Peasant in Persia*, Oxford University Press, London, New York and Toronto, 1953, ch. xii; Banani, *The Modernization of Iran*, pp. 119–29.
106. Ibid., pp. 62–7.
107. Homa Katouzian, 'The Poet-Laureate Bahar in the Constitutional Era', *IRAN*, British Institute of Persian Studies, London, 2002.
108. Katouzian, *Sadeq Hedayat: The Life and Legend of an Iranian Writer*, ch. 4.
109. Donné Raffat, *The Prison Papers of Bozorg Alavi: A Literary Odyssey*, Syracuse University Press, Syracuse, NY, 1985.
110. See Homa Katouzian, *Darbareh-ye Jamalzadeh va Jamalzadeh Shenasi*, Shahab, Tehran, 2003.
111. Mokhber al-Saltaneh (Mehdiqoli Hedayat), *Khaterat va Khatarat*, p. 397.
112. Homa Katouzian, 'Riza Shah's Political Legitimacy and Social Base', in Cronin (ed.), *The Making of Modern Iran* and entry on Jamalzadeh in *Encyclopaedia Iranica*, forthcoming.
113. Donald Wilber, *Iran Past and Present*, Princeton University Press, Princeton, NJ, 1958, pp. 100–1.

114. For full documentation see Houshang Sabahi, *British Policy in Persia 1918–1925*, Frank Cass, London, 1990; Katouzian, *State and Society*, chs 10 and 11.
115. Dawlat-Abadi, *Hayat-e Yahya*, vol. 4, p. 343.
116. Wilber, *Riza Shah Pahlavi*, p. 175.
117. Taqizadeh, *Zendegi-ye Tufani*, p. 246.
118. Ibid., p. 363.
119. Amir-Ahmadi, *Khaterat-e Nakhostin Sepahbod*.
120. Bharier, *Economic Development*, pp. 108 and 113.
121. Wilber, *Riza Shah Pahlavi*, pp. 174–5.
122. Afshar, *Nameh-ha-ye Paris*, pp. 273–5.
123. Taqizadeh, *Zendegi-ye Tufani*, pp. 253–5.

CHAPTER 10: OCCUPATION, OIL NATIONALIZATION AND DICTATORSHIP

1. Ahmad Faramarzi to Taqizadeh, *Nameh-ha-ye Tehran*, ed. Iraj Afshar, Farzan, Tehran, 2006, p. 352.
2. For example, Houchang Chehabi, 'The banning of the veil and its consequences', in Stephanie Cronin, *The Making of Modern Iran: State and Society under Riza Shah, 1921–1941*, London and New York, Routledge, 2003, p. 204.
3. See Abbasqoli Golsha'iyan, '*Yahddasht-ha-ye Abbasqoli-ye Golsha'iyan*', in *Yaddasht-ha-ye Doktor Qasem Ghani*, ed. Cyrus Ghani, vol. 4, Zavvar, Tehran, 1978, p. 557.
4. Reader Bullard, *The Camels Must Go: An Autobiography*, Faber & Faber, London, 1961 and the author's conversations with Sir Reader, Oxford, 1973.
5. Golsha'iyan, '*Yahddasht-ha*', pp. 560–3.
6. Ibid., pp. 562–4.
7. For a more elaborate discussion of this point see Homa Katouzian, 'Reza Shah's Political Legitimacy and Social Base', in Cronin (ed.), *The Making of Modern Iran*, pp. 32–3.
8. Hosein Makki, *Tarikh-e Bistsaleh-ye Iran*, vol. 7, Elmi, Tehran, 1985, pp. 214–16; Golsha'iyan, '*Yaddasht-ha*', p. 560.
9. For example, by Ali Dashti, quoted in Ebrahim Khajeh Nuri, *Bazigaran-e Asr-re Tala'i*, Jibi, Tehran, 1978, pp. 188–91; Soltan Ali Soltani, quoted in Hosein Kuhi Kermani, *Az Shahrivar-e 1320 ta Faje'eh-ye Azerbaijan*, vol. 1, Kuhi, Tehran, n. d., pp. 222–9.
10. Jalal Abdoh (public prosecutor in the cases brought against Reza Shah), *Chehel Sal dar Sahneh*, ed. Majid Tafreshi, Rasa, Tehran, 1989.
11. Golsha'iyan, '*Yaddasht-ha*', p. 568.
12. Ibid., p. 567.
13. Taqizadeh, *Zendegi-ye Tufani-ye Seyyed Hasan Taqizadeh*, p. 289.
14. Bullard to Eden, 26/5/42, FO371/34-31443; Denis Wright, *The English Amongst The Persians*, Heinemann, London, 1977; Sir Reader Bullard, *Letters From Tehran*, ed. E. C. Hodgkin, I.B. Tauris, London and New York, 1991; Baqer Aqeli, *Zoka'al-Molk-e Forughi va Shahrivar-e 1320*, Elmi, Tehran, 1988.
15. Press attaché to Bullard, 4/10/41, FO 416/99.
16. For the full text of his broadcast see Makki, *Tarikh-e Bistsaleh-ye Iran*, vol. 8, pp. 179–85, emphasis added.
17. FO 371 35117, quoted in Rose Greaves, '1942–1976: The Reign of Muhammad Riza Shah', in *Twentieth Century Iran*, ed. Hossein Amirsadeghi, assisted by R. W. Ferrier, Heinemann, London, 1977, p. 55.
18. Julian Bharier, *Economic Development in Iran*, p. 82, table 7.
19. See Katouzian, *The Political Economy of Modern Iran*, ch. 8.
20. Bharier, *Economic Development in Iran*, pp. 46–9, tables 3 and 4.
21. Quoted in Fakhreddin Azimi, *Iran, the Crisis of Democracy, 1941–1953*, I.B. Tauris, London, 1989, p. 82.
22. Persian and English sources on early Tudeh party history are now numerous. See, for example, Babak Amir Khosrovi, *Nazar az Darun beh Naqsh-e Hezb-e Tudeh-ye Iran*, Ettela'at, Tehran, 1996; Anvar Khameh'i, *Forsat-e Bozorg-e Az Dast Rafteh*, Hafteh, Tehran, 1983; Homa Katouzian, ed. and intro., *Khaterat-e Siyasi-ye Khalil Maleki*, 2nd edn, Enteshar, Tehran, 1989; Ardeshir Ovanessian, *Khaterat-e Ardeshir Ovanessian az Hezb-e Tudeh-ye Iran (1941–1947)*, ed. Babak Amir Khosrovi, Entesharat-e Hezb-e Demokratik-e Mardom-e Iran, Europe, 1990; Ervand Abrahamian, *Iran Between Two Revolutions*, Princeton University Press, Princeton, NJ, 1982; Sepehr Zabih, *The Communist Movement in Iran*, University of California Press, Berkeley, CA, 1966; Fakhreddin Azimi, *Crisis of Democracy*; Katouzian, *Musaddiq and the Struggle for Power in Iran*, I.B. Tauris, London and New York, 1990.

23. See their publications in *Majmu'eh-ye Entesharat-e Tablighat-e Islami*, Tehran, 1943.
24. For a detailed account of the early Islamist organizations see Mohamad Tavakoli-Targhi, '*Baha'i-setizi va Eslam-gera'i*', *Iran Nameh*, 19/1–2 (2001) and 'Anti-Baha'ism and Islamism in Iran', in *The Baha'is of Iran: Socio-historical Studies*, eds Dominic Parviz Brookshaw and Seena B. Fazel, Routledge, London and New York, 2008.
25. See further Karim Sanjabi's interview with Habib Ladjevardi, the Harvard Oral History Project, <www.fas.harvard.edu/~iohp/sanjabi.html>; Karim Sanjabi, *Omid-ha va Na-omidi-ha: Khaterat-e Siyasi*, Jebhe, London, 1989; Katouzian, *Musaddiq and the Struggle for Power in Iran*, pp. 86–7.
26. Ja'far Mehdi-niya, *Zendegi-ye Siyasi-ye Seyyed Zia al-Din Tabatab'i*, Mehdi-niya, Tehran, 1990; Azimi, *Crisis of Democracy* and *Quest for Democracy in Iran: A Century of Struggle against Authoritarian Rule*, Harvard University Press, Cambridge, MA, 2008.
27. For Mosaddeq's speech, Seyyed Zia's reply and other speeches on the subject see Hosein Key-Ostovan, *Siyasat-e Movazeneh-ye Manfai*, Key-Ostovan, Tehran, 1948.
28. See further Hamid Shawkat, *Dar Tir-res-e Hadeseh: Zendegi-ye Siyasi-ye Qavam al-Saltaneh*, Tehran, Bakhtaran, 2007; Aqeli, *Mirza Ahmad Khan Qavam al-Saltaneh*; Azimi, *Crisis of Democracy*; Katouzian, *Musaddiq and the Struggle for Power.*
29. For conflicting assessments of Millspaugh's mission in the 1940s see Arthur Chester Millspaugh, *Americans in Persia*, Brookings Institution, Washington, 1946; Ablohasan Ebtehaj, *Khaterat-e Abolhasan Ebtehaj*, ed. Alireza Arouzi, Ebtehaj, London, 1991.
30. Taqizadeh, *Nameh-ha-ye London*, ed. Iraj Afshar, Tehran, Farzan, 1996, p. 254.
31. Quoted in Rose Greaves, '1942–1976: The Reign of Muhammad Riza Shah', p. 66.
32. Taqizadeh, *Nameh-ha-ye London*; Homa Katouzian, '*Seyyed Hasan Taqizadeh: Seh Zendegi dar Yek Omr*', *Iran Nameh*, 21/1 & 2 (spring and summer 2003), repr. in *Hasht Maqaleh dar Tarikh va Adab-e Mo'aser*, Nashr-e Markaz, Tehran, 2006; 'Seyyed Hasan Taqizadeh', entry in *Encyclopedia Iranica*, forthcoming.
33. *Nameh-ha-ye London*, pp. 77–8.
34. Parliamentary speech quoted in Key-Ostovan, *Siyasat-e Movazeneh-ye Manfai*, vol. 1, p. 26.
35. Bullard to Eden, 21/12/42, FO 371/34-31443; see further Bullard to Eden, Report on Political Events of 1942, 26/3/1943, FO371/ 34-331 443; Ali Amini, *Khaterat-e Ali Amini*, ed. Habib Ladjevardi, Iranian Oral history Project, Centre for Middle Eastern Studies, Harvard University, Bethesda, MD and Ketabforushi-ye Iran, 1997, pp. 50–3; Bullard, *Letters From Tehran*; Baqer Aqeli, *Mirza Ahmad Khan Qavam al-Saltaneh*; Makki, *Tarikh-e Bistsaleh*, vol. 8.
36. For a comprehensive study of the Azerbaijan revolt see Louise L'Estrange Fawcett, *Iran and the Cold War: the Azerbaijan Crisis of 1946*, Cambridge University Press, Cambridge, 1992; see also, Touraj Atabaki, *Azerbaijan: Ethnicity and the Struggle for Power in Iran*, I.B. Tauris, London, 2000.
37. On Pishevari's relationship with Tudeh leaders, see Katouzian (ed.), *Khaterat-e Siyasi-ye Khalil Maleki.*
38. For a detailed study of the revolt of southern tribes see Reza Jafari, 'Centre-Periphery Relations in Iran: the Case of the Southern Rebellion in 1946', DPhil thesis, University of Oxford, Oxford, 2000.
39. Azimi, *Crisis of Democracy*, pp. 175–6.
40. Baqer Aqeli (ed.), *Khaterat-e Mohammad Sa'ed-e Maragheh'i*, Nashr-e Namak, Tehran, 1994.
41. For example, Jalal Al-e Ahmad, *Dar Khedmat va Khiyanat-e Roshanfekran*, Ravaq, Tehran, 1978; Anvar Khameh'i, *Forsat-e Bozorg-e Az Dast Rafteh.*
42. For the full speech see Key-Ostovan, *Siyasat-e Movazeneh.*
43. For details see Mostafa Fateh, *Panjah Sal Naft-e Iran*, Entesharat-e Peyam, Tehran, 1979.
44. See further Habib Ladjevardi, *Labor Unions and Autocracy in Iran*, Syracuse University Press, Syracuse, NY, 1985.
45. Fereidun Keshavarz, *Man Mottaham Mikonam*, Ravaq, Tehran, 1979; Anvar Khameh'i, *Az Ensh'ab ta Kudeta*, Entesharat-e Hafteh, Tehran, 1984.
46. Khameh'i, *Az Ensh'ab*, pp. 128–9; Ali Akbar Siyasi, *Gozaresh-e Yek Zendegi*, Siyasi, London, 1988, pp. 214–15; Aqeli (ed.), *Khaterat-e Mohammad Sa'ed.*
47. Katouzian, *Musaddiq*, ch. 6. For the full text of Qavam's letter to the shah objecting to the constitutional amendments see Ali Vosuq, *Chahar Fasl*, Vosuq, Tehran, 1982, pp. 33–43.
48. Bharier, *Economic Development*, ch. 5, table 1.
49. Ann K. S. Lambton, *Landlord and Peasant in Persia*, Oxford University Press, London and New York, 1953, p. 209; *The Persian Land Reform, 1962–1966*, The Clarendon Press, Oxford, 1969, p. 37.
50. Katouzian, *Musaddiq*, ch. 6; Azimi, *Crisis of Democracy*, ch. 14 and *Quest for Democracy in Iran: A Century of Struggle against Authoritarian Rule.*
51. Abolfazl Lesani, *Tala-ye Siyah ya Bala-ye Iran*, Amir Kabir, Tehran, 1978, pp. 136–7; Taqizadeh, *Zendegi-ye Tufani*; Katouzian, 'Seyyed Hasan Taqizadeh'.

52. See Mozaffar Baqa'i's interview with Habib Ladjevardi, the Harvard Oral History Project, <www.fas.harvard.edu/~iohp/BAGHAI09.PDF>; Hosein Makki, *Khal'-e Yad*, Bongah-e Trajomeh va Nashr-e Ketab, Tehran, 1981; Khameh'i, *Az Ensh'ab*.

53. Katouzian, *Musaddiq*; Mohammad Mosaddeq, *Musaddiq's Memoirs*, ed. and intro. Homa Katouzian, tr. Seyyed Hasan Amin and Homa Katouzian, Jebhe, London, 1988.

54. For a report on the day-to-day developments leading to the formation of the Front see *Zendeginameh-ye Siyasi: Neveshteh-ha va Sokhanrani-ha-ye Seyyed Ali Shayegan*, ed. Ahmad Shayegan, vol. 1, Agah, Tehran, 2006.

55. See further ibid.; Katouzian, *Musaddiq*, ch. 6; Azimi, *Crisis of Democracy*, ch. 14; *Bakhtar-e Emruz* (10 November and 7 December 1949).

56. For the shah's proposal of premiership through Jamal Emami see Mosaddeq's *Notq-ha va Moktubat*, various volumes, n.p., Paris, 1960s and 1970s. See further Mohammad Mosaddeq, *Musaddiq's Memoirs*, Book II.

57. For a more detailed account of Razmara's relations with the shah and the great powers see Azimi, *Crisis of Democracy*, ch. 16.

58. For the strongest arguments for the shah's involvement in the assassination see Mosavvar Rahmani, *Khaterat-e Siyasi: Bist-o-Panj Sal dar Khedmat-e Niru-ye Hava'i-ye Iran*, Ravaq, Tehran, 1984; Naser Qashqa'i, *Sal-ha-ye Bohran: Yaddasht-ha-ye Ruzaneh-ye Naser Sawlat Qashqa'i*, ed. Nasrollah Haddadi, Rasa, Tehran, 1987; Khameh'i, *Az Ensh'at ta Kudeta*.

59. Shepherd to the Foreign Office, 22/6/51, FO 248/1514.

60. See the Tudeh Party, *Nashriyeh Ta'limati*, 12 (1951).

61. For detailed documentation of British efforts between May and September 1951 to bring down Mosaddeq's government see Homa Katouzian, 'Kushesh-ha-ye Sefarat-e Inglis bara-ye Ta'in-e Nakhost Vazir-e Iran az Melli Shodan-e Naft ta Khal'-e Yad', in *Estebdad, Demokrasi va Nehzat-e Melli*, 3rd edn, Nashr-e Markaz, Tehran, 2002. For the documents in question see L. A. C. Fry (30 January 1951), FO 371/91452; Francis Shepherd (British ambassador to Tehran), FO 317/91452; Shepherd to FO (7 March 1951), FO 248/1518; Shepherd to Bowker (12 March 1951), FO 371, 91452; Shepherd, memo (21 March 1951), FO 371, 91452; Oliver Frank to FO (27 March 1951), FO 371, 91452; Shepherd, memo (1 April 1951) FO 248/1518; and all the following documents in FO 248/1518: Shepherd to FO (22 June 1951); Shepherd, report (1 July 1951); Pyman, memo (7 July 1951); Shepherd, report (12 July 1951); Pyman, report (10 July 1951); L. F. L. Pyman (9 August 1951); George Middleton, report (18 September 1951); Pyman, report (22 September 1951); Shepherd, report (22 September 1951).

62. For example, George McGee, *Envoy to the Middle World, Adventures in Diplomacy*, Harper and Row, New York, 1983.

63. The literature on the oil dispute and proposals for its resolution is quite extensive. See, for example, Katouzian, *Musaddiq and the Struggle* and *Musaddiq's Memoirs*, Book II, 'Oil boycott and the political economy, Musaddiq and the strategy of non-oil economics', in James Bill and Wm. R. Louis (eds), *Musaddiq, Iranian Nationalism, and Oil*, I.B. Tauris, London, 1988; Ronald W. Ferrier, 'The Anglo-Iranian oil dispute, a triangular relationship', in Bill and Louis, *Musaddiq*; George C. McGee, 'Recollections of Dr Musaddiq', in Bill and Louis, *Musaddiq*; Motafa Elm, *Oil, Power and Principle: Iran's Oil Nationalization and its Aftermath*, Syracuse University Press, Syracuse, NY, 1992; Kamran Dadkhah, 'The Oil Nationalization Movement, the British Boycott and the Iranian Economy', in Elie Kedourie and Sylvia G. Haim, eds, *Essays on the Economic History of the Middle East*, Frank Cass, London, 1988; Azimi, *Crisis of Democracy*; Mary Ann Heiss, *Empire and Nationhood: The United States, Great Britain, and Iranian Oil, 1950–1954*, New York, 1997; 'The International Boycott of Iranian Oil and the Anti-Mosaddeq Coup of 1953', in Mark J. Gasiorowski and Malcolm Byrne (eds), *Mohammad Mosaddeq and the 1953 Coup in Iran*, Syracuse University Press, Syracuse, NY, 2004; Farhad Diba, *Mohammad Mossadegh, a Political Biography*, Croom Helm, London, 1986. George McGee, *Envoy to the Middle World, Adventures in Diplomacy*; Mostafa Fateh, *Panjah Sal Naft-e Iran*; Fo'ad Ruhani, *Tarikh-e Melli Shodan-e San'at-e Naft-e Iran*, 2nd edn, Jibi, Tehran, 1974. For a detailed discussion and appraisal of the World Bank proposal and the Iranian government's responses to it see Homa Katouzian, 'Mosaddeq va Pishnhad-e Bank-e Jahani', *Mehregan* (spring 1992), repr. in *Estebdad, Demokrasi*.

64. See further Katouzian, *Musaddiq*, chs 10 and 11.

65. See note 61 above and Wm. Roger Louis, 'Britain and the Overthrow of the Mosaddeq Government', in Gasiorowski and Byrne, *Mohammad Mosaddeq*.

66. That Mosaddeq had intended to resign primarily in anticipation of failure at the International Court has emerged from a recent study. See Homa Katouzian, '*Dalil-e Asli-ye Est'fa-ye Mosaddeq dar Vaqeh'eh-ye Si-ye Tir*', in *Estebdad, Demokrasi*. See further *Musaddiq's Memoirs*, Book II.

67. The literature on the 21 July uprising and Qavam's ill-fated government is now quite extensive. See, for example, Khamehe'i, *Az Enshab ta Kudeta*; Katouzian, *Musaddiq* and *Estebdad, Demokrasi* and

Musaddiq's Memoirs, Book II; Azimi, *Crisis of Democracy*; Elm, *Oil, Power and Principle*; Shawkat, *Dar Tir-res-e Hadeseh*; Aqeli, *Mirza Ahmad Khan Qavam al-Saltaneh*.

68. See further Elm, *Oil, Power and Principle*; Heiss, *Empire and Nationhood* and 'The International Boycott of Iranian Oil and the Anti-Mosaddeq Coup of 1953', in Gasiorowski and Byrne (eds), *Mohammad Mosaddeq*; Fateh, *Panjah Sal Naft*; Fo'ad Ruhani, *Tarikh-e Melli Shodan-e San'at-e Naft-e Iran*; Katouzian, *Musaddiq and the Struggle for Power*.

69. Fakhreddin Azimi, 'Unseating Mosaddeq: The Configuration and Role of Domestic Forces', in Gasiorowski and Byrne (eds), *Mohammad Mosaddeq*; Katouzian, *Musaddiq*, ch. 12.

70. Khalil Maleki, *Khaterat-e Siyasi*; Homa Katouzian, 'The Strange Politics of Khalil Maleki', in Stephanie Cronin (ed.), *Reformers and Revolutionaries in Modern Iran: New Perspectives on the Iranian Left*, RoutledgeCurzon, London and New York, 2004.

71. The above brief is based on Katouzian, *Musaddiq*, ch. 12. See also, Azimi, 'Unseating Mosaddeq; Shahrough Akhavi, *Religion and Politics in Contemporary Iran: Clergy-State Relations in the Pahlavi Period*, State University of New York Press, Albany, NY, 1980; Farhad Kazemi, 'The Fada'iyan-e Islam: Fanaticism, Politics and Terror', in *From Nationalism to Revolutionary Islam*, ed. Said Amir Arjomand, Macmillan, London, 1984; Shams Qanat-Abadi, *Seyri dar Nehzat-e Melli Shodan-e Naft: Khaterat-e Shams Qanat-Abadi*, Markaz-e Asnad-e Tarikhi-ye Vezarat-e Ettela'at, Tehran, 1988. For a detailed study of the formation and role of religious groups and ulama see Ali Rahnema, *Niru-ha-ye Mazhabi bar Bastar-e Harekat-e Nehzat-e Melli*, Gam-e Naw, Tehran, 2005.

72. For example, Mosaddeq, 'Statement of April 1953', in *Musaddiq's Memoirs*, Book II, chs 2 and 7; Mohammad Reza Shah, *Mission for My Country*, Heinemann, London, 1960; Azimi, *Crisis of Democracy*; Katouzian, *Musaddiq*.

73. Mohammad Torkaman, *Tawte'eh-ye Robudan va Qatl-e Afshartus*, Torkaman, Tehran, 1984; Azimi, *Crisis of Democracy*; Katouzian, *Musaddiq*.

74. For example, Henderson to the Secretary of State, 20/5/53, 788.00/5-2053/982. See further Amir Khosrovi, *Nazar az darun*.

75. British embassy in Washington to Sir R. Matkins, 21/5/1953. For a photocopy of the document see *Doktor Karim Sanjabi, Omid-ha va Naomidi-ha*, p. 449.

76. Ali Dashti, *Avamel-e Soqut-e Mohammad Reza Pahlavi* (yadddasht-ha-ye montasher nashodeh-ye Ail Dashti), ed. Mehdi Mahuzi, Zavvar, Tehran, 2004, pp. 44–5.

77. Mark Gasiorowski, 'The 1953 Coup d'Etat Against Mosaddeq', in Gasiorowski and Byrne (eds), *Mohammad Mosaddeq* and the references therein.

78. CIA Clandestine Service History, 'Overthrow of Premier Mossadeq of Iran, November 1952–August 1953', (March 1954) by Dr Donald Wilber, <www.gwu.edu/~nsarchiv/NSAEBB/NSAEBB28/>.

79. Ibid.

80. For a detailed description of the events see Gasiorowski, 'The 1953 Coup d'Etat Against Mosaddeq'. See also Stephen Kinzer, *All the Shah's Men: An American Coup and the Roots of Middle East Terror*, John Wiley & Sons, Hoboken, NJ, 2003.

81. Katouzian, *Musaddiq*; *Poltical Economy*.

82. Ali Amini, *Khaterat-e Ali Amini*, pp. 82–90.

83. Lambton, *Persian Land Reform*, pp. 56–7.

84. George B. Baldwin, *Planning and Development in Iran*, The Johns Hopkins Press, Baltimore, MD, 1967, pp. 110–24

85. See further Abolhasan Ebtehaj, *Khaterat-e Abolhasan Ebtehaj*; Francis Bostock and Geoffrey Jones, *Planning and Power in Iran: Ebtehaj and Economic Development under the Shah*, Frank Cass, London, 1989; Ebtehaj's interview with Habib Ladjevardi, Iran Oral History Project, Harvard University Centre for Middle Eastern Studies, <www.fas.harvard.edu/~iohp/ebtehaj>.

86. Aqeli, *Ruzshomar-e Tarikh-e Iran*, Nashr-e Goftar, Tehran, 1995, vol. 2, p. 51.

87. See further Mohamad Tavakoli-Targhi, 'Baha'i-setizi' and 'Anti-Baha'ism'; *Khaterat va Mobarezat-e Hojjatoleslam Mohammad Taqi Falsafi*, intro. Hamid Ruhani, eds Ali Davani et al., Markaz-e Asnad-e Enqelab-e Eslami, Tehran, 1997.

88. Ibid., pp. 59–63. Katouzian, *Musaddiq*, ch. 12.

89. Mark J. Gasiorowski, *US Foreign Policy and the Shah: Building a Client State in Iran*, Cornell University Press, Ithaca, NY, 1991, pp. 93–109.

90. Katouzian, *Political Economy*, p. 205, table 10.2 and the sources therein.

91. See further Rouhollah Ramazani, *Iran's Foreign Policy, 1941–1973, A Study of Foreign Policy in Modernizing Nations*, University Press of Virginia, Charlottesville, VA, 1975; Shahram Chubin and Sepehr Zabih, *The Foreign Relations of Iran: A Developing State in a Zone of Great-Power Conflict*, University of California Press, Berkeley, CA, 1974; Shahram Chubin, *Soviet Policy towards Iran and the Gulf*, International Institute for Strategic Studies, London, 1980.

92. Based on *Seven Year Development Plan of Iran* and *Review of the Second Seven Year Pan Programme of Iran*, Tehran Plan Organization, 1956 and 1960, summarized in Katouzian, *Political Economy*, table 10.1, p. 203. See also Bostock and Jones, *Planning and Power*; George Baldwin, *Planning and Development in Iran*.
93. Katouzian, *Political Economy*, table 10.4, p. 206 and the sources therein.
94. See further Mark J. Gasiorowski, 'The Qarani Affair and Iranian Politics', *International Journal of Middle East Studies*, 25 (1993).
95. See further Abrahamian, *Iran between Two Revolutions* and Katouzian, *Political Economy*.
96. See further Katouzian, *Musaddiq*, ch. 16.
97. Bharier, *Economic Development*, p. 138. See further Lambton, *Persian Land Reform*; Eric J. Hooglund, *Land and Revolution in Iran, 1960–1980*, University of Texas Press, Austin, TX, 1982; Homa Katouzian, 'Land Reform in Iran, A Case Study in the Political Economy of Social Engineering', *Journal of Peasant Studies* (1974).
98. Ali Amini, *Khaterat-e Ali Amini*, pp. 132–7.
99. Ibid., p. 201.
100. Mohammad Gholi Majd, *Resistance to the Shah: Landowners and the Ulama in Iran*, University Press of Florida, Gainsville, FL, 2000.
101. See further Dashti, *Avamel-e Soqut*, especially his long letter of advice to the Shah.
102. Afshar (ed.), *Zendegi-ye Tufani*, p. 411.
103. Ibid.
104. For example, H. E. Chehabi, *Iranian Politics and Religious Modernism: The Liberation Movement of Iran under the Shah and Khomeini*, Cornell University Press, Ithaca, New York, 1990, ch. 4; Katouzian, *Political Economy*, ch. 11.
105. See 'October 27, 1964, The Granting of Capitulatory Rights to the US', in *Writings and Declarations of Imam Khomeini*, tr. and annot. Hamid Algar, Mizan Press, Berkeley, CA, 1981, pp. 181–4.

CHAPTER 11: THE WHITE REVOLUTION

1. See further Homa Katouzian, 'The Political Economy of Oil-Exporting Countries', *Mediterranean Peoples* (September 1979) and 'Oil and Economic Development in the Middle East', in *The Modern Economic History of the Middle East in its World Context*, Essays Presented to Charles Issawi, ed. Georges Sabagh, Cambridge University Press, Cambridge, 1989. See also Hossein Mahdavy, 'The Patterns and Problems of Economic Development in Rentier States: The Case of Iran', in Michael A. Cook (ed.), *Studies in the Economic History of the Middle East from the Rise of Islam to the Present-Day*, Oxford University Press, Oxford, 1970.
2. Martin F. Herz, *A View from Tehran: A Diplomatist Looks at the Shah's Regime in June 1964*, Institute for the Study of Diplomacy, Georgetown University, Washington DC, 1979, pp. 6–7, emphasis added.
3. For a psychological analysis of the Shah's attitude towards the United States, see Marvin Zonis, *Majestic Failure: The Fall of the Shah*, University of Chicago Press, Chicago and London, 1991.
4. See Asadollah Alam, *The Shah and I: The Confidential Diary of Iran's Royal Court, 1969–1977*, intro. and ed. Alinaghi Alikhani, trs Alinaghi Alikhani and Nicholas Vincent, I.B. Tauris, London and New York, 1991, p. 46
5. Ibid., p. 233.
6. Ibid., p. 236.
7. Ibid., pp. 277–8.
8. The Shah put this and similar points consistently in interviews with the international media since 1970. See, for example, William D. Smith, 'Price Quadruples for Iranian Crude Oil at Auction', *New York Times* (12 December 1973).
9. Alam, *The Shah and I*, pp. 347–9.
10. Ibid., p. 350.
11. Ibid., p. 239.
12. Ibid., p. 240.
13. Ibid., p. 176.
14. Ibid., p. 169.
15. Ibid., p. 197.
16. Ibid., p. 198.
17. Ibid., p. 341.
18. Ibid., p. 543.
19. See further Parviz C. Radji, *In the Service of the Peacock Throne: The Diaries of the Shah's Last Ambassador to London*, Hamish Hamilton, London, 1983.

20. Alam, *The Shah and I*, p. 331.
21. Ibid., p. 228.
22. Ibid., pp. 245–6.
23. Ibid., p. 360.
24. Mohammad Reza Shah Pahlavi, *Besu-ye Tamaddon-e Bozorg*, Markaz-e Pazhuhesh va Nashr-e Farhang-e Dawran-e Pahlavi, Tehran, 1975, pp. 248–9.
25. Ibid., p. 249.
26. Ibid., p. 252.
27. Ibid., p. 250.
28. Alam, *The Shah and I*, p. 365.
29. For a full-scale biography of Hoveyda see Abbas Milani, *The Persian Sphinx: Amir Abbas Hoveyda and the Riddle of the Iranian Revolution, A Biography*, I.B. Tauris, London and New York, 2000.
30. Ibid., pp. 210–11.
31. On the organization and activities of the Iran-e Novin party see Manuchehr Kalali (its first general secretary), Iranian Oral History Collection, Harvard University (henceforth Harvard Oral History).
32. Alam, *The Shah and I*, p. 232.
33. Homa Katouzian, 'The Pahlavi Regime in Iran', in H. E. Chehabi and Juan J. Linz (eds), *Sultanistic Regimes*, pp. 192–3.
34. Mohammad Reza Shah Pahlavi, *Mission for My Country*, Hutchinson, London, 1960, p. 173.
35. Abolhasan Ebtehaj in an interview with Habib Ladjevardi, Harvard Oral History, <www.fas.harvard.edu/~iohp/ebtehaj.html>.
36. General Fereydun Jam in an interview with Habib Ladjevardi, Harvard Oral History.
37. Ibid.
38. General Hasan Toufanian in an interview with Zia Sedghi, Harvard Oral History, <www.fas.harvard.edu/~iohp/toufanian.html>.
39. Admiral Amir Abbas Ramzi Atai in an interview with Shahla Haeri, Harvard Oral History.
40. General Jam, Harvard Oral history.
41. General Toufanian, Harvard Oral History.
42. General Jam, Harvard Oral History.
43. General Hasan Alavi-Kia, in an interview with Habib Ladjevardi, Harvard Oral History.
44. Armin Meyer, *Quiet Diplomacy: From Cairo to Tokyo in the Twilight of Imperialism*, Universe, Lincoln, NE, 2003, p.136.
45. See occasional remarks in Alam, *The Shah and I*.
46. For a comprehensive study of Iran-American relations in the period, see Mark J. Gasiorowski, *U.S. Foreign Policy and the Shah: Building a Client State in Iran*, Cornell University Press, Ithaca, NY, 1991. See further James A. Bill, *The Eagle and the Lion: The Tragedy of American-Iranian Relations*, Yale University Press, New Haven and London, 1988.
47. See further Rouhollah Ramazani, *Iran's Foreign Policy, 1941–1973, A Study of Foreign Policy in Modernizing Nations*; Shahram Chubin, 'Iran', in Yezid Sayigh and Avi Shlaim (eds), *The Cold War and the Middle East*, Clarendon Press, Oxford, 1997. Shahram Chubin and Sepehr Zabih, *The Foreign Relations of Iran: A Developing State in a Zone of Great-Power Conflict*, University of California Press, Berkeley, CA, 1974.
48. See further sources in n. 47 above.
49. See further Rouhollah K. Ramazani, *The Persian Gulf: Iran's Role*, University Press of Virginia, Charlottesville, VA, 1972; Roham Alvandi, 'National Identity and Iranian Foreign Policy: Resolving the Bahrain Question', M.Phil. dissertation, University of Oxford, Oxford, 2007; Hossein Heirani Moghaddam, 'The Anglo-Iranian Conflict over the Disputed Islands in the Persian Gulf, 1820–1971', DPhil dissertation, University of Oxford, Oxford, 2004.
50. For example, Mohammad Reza Pahlavi, *Answer to History*, Stein and Day, New York, 1980.
51. See further Massoud Karshenas, *Oil, State and Industrialization in Iran*, Cambridge University Press, Cambridge, 1990; Robert E. Looney, *Economic Origins of the Iranian Revolution*, Pergamon Press, New York, 1982; Katouzian, *Political Economy*; Jahangir Amuzegar, *Iran: An Economic Profile*, Middle East Institute, Washington DC, 1977; Jahangir Amuzegar and M. Ali Fekrat, *Iran: Economic Development under Dualistic Conditions*, The University of Chicago Press, Chicago, IL, 1971; George B. Baldwin, *Planning and Development in Iran*, The Johns Hopkins University Press, Baltimore, MD, 1967.
52. Katouzian, *Political Economy*, table 13.7, based on Central Bank of Iran, *Annual Report* (various issues).
53. Ann. K.S. Lambton, *The Persian Land Reform, 1962–1966*, Oxford: The Clarendon Press, ch. ix.
54. Ibid., p. 196.
55. Ibid., ch. xi; Homa Katouzian, 'Land Reform in Iran: A Case Study in the Political Economy of Social Engineering', *Journal of Peasant Studies* (1974).

56. Fatemeh Etemad Moghadam, *From Land Reform to Revolution: The Political Economy of Agricultural Development in Iran*, I.B. Tauris, London and New York, 1996, ch. 3; Lambton, *The Persian Land Reform*, chs xiv–xvi.
57. See further Homa Katouzian, 'Oil *versus* Agriculture: A Case of Dual Resource Depletion in Iran', *Journal of Peasant Studies* (April 1978).
58. Moghadam, *From Land Reform to Revolution*.
59. See further Homa Katouzian, 'The Agrarian Question in Iran', in A. K. Ghose (ed.), *Agrarian Reform in Contemporary Developing Countries*, Croom Helm, London, 1983.
60. Katouzian, 'Oil *versus* Agriculture'.
61. Fatemeh Etemad Moghadam, 'The Effect of Farm Size and Management System on Agricultural Production in Iran', DPhil thesis, University of Oxford, Oxford, 1978.
62. Ibid.
63. Moghadam, *From Land Reform to Revolution*, table 7.4.
64. See further Richard Tapper (ed.), *The Conflict of Tribe and State in Iran and Afghanistan*, Croom Helm and St Martin's Press, London and New York, 1983.
65. David Menasheri, *Education and the Making of Modern Iran*, ch. 9, table 5.
66. Ibid., table 8.
67. UNESCO Statistical Yearbook, Paris, 1977.
68. Ibid., pp. 128–76.
69. Ibid.
70. Menasheri, *Education and the Making of Modern Iran*, pp. 190–1.
71. Ibid., ch. 10, table 14.
72. Ibid., ch. 9, table 12.
73. Ibid., p. 235.
74. Ibid., ch. 10, table 14.
75. Ibid., pp. 218–19.
76. See further for details Asghar Schirazi, *The Constitution of Iran: Politics and the State in the Islamic Republic*, tr. John O'Kane, I.B. Tauris, London and New York, 1997, pp. 215–16.
77. Jahangir Amuzegar, *Iran: An Economic Profile*, tables v.3 and xiv.1
78. Computed from Central Bank of Iran, *Annual Report*, various years and other official publications.
79. Katouzian, *Political Economy*, tables 13.1 and 13.3.
80. Ibid., table 13.7.
81. Massoud Karshenas, *Oil, State and Industrialization in Iran*, App. table P.2; Robert E. Looney, *Economic Origins of the Iranian Revolution*, table 4.1.
82. For a study of the Iranian economy in the twentieth century see Hadi Salehi Esfahani and M. Hashem Pesaran, 'Iranian Economy in the Twentieth Century: A Global Perspective', *Iranian Studies*, 42/2, 2009.

CHAPTER 12: THE REVOLUTION OF FEBRUARY 1979

1. For example, his interview with Mike Wallace, <www.youtube.com/watch?v=66-jkx36BPc>.
2. See further Chehabi, *Iranian Politics and Religious Modernism*; Katouzian, *Musaddiq and the Struggle for Power in Iran*.
3. Mehdi Bazargan, *Modafe'at dar Dadgah*, Freedom Movement, Tehran, 1964; Chehabi, *Iranian Politics and Religious Modernism*.
4. For the full text of the highly charged report see Homa Katouzian, 'Khalil Maleki, the Odd Intellectual Out', in Negin Nabavi (ed.), *Intellectual Trends in Twentieth-Century Iran: A Critical Survey*, The University of Florida Press, Gainesville, FL, 2003, p. 45.
5. Ervand Abrahamian, *The Iranian Mojahedin*, Yale University Press, New Haven and London, 1989, p. 86, emphasis added.
6. See further Mehrzad Boroujerdi, *Iranian Intellectuals and the West: The Tormented Triumph of Nativism*, Syracuse University Press, Syracuse, NY, 1996, especially ch. 3, 'The othering of the west'.
7. See further Negin Nabavi, 'In Search of Culture and Authenticity: The Iranian Intellectuals vis-à-vis the State, 1953–1977', D.Phil. thesis, University of Oxford, Oxford, 1997. See also Ali Gheissari, *Iranian Intellectuals in the 20th Century*, University of Texas Press, Austin, TX, 1998.
8. Ahmad Kasravi, *A'in*, reprint, Nashr o Pakhsh-e Ketab, Tehran, 1977, pt 1, p. 6.
9. Ibid., pt 2, p. 13
10. Ibid., pt 1, p. 13.
11. Ibid., p. 47.
12. Seyyed Fakhreddin Shadman, *Taskhir-e Tamaddon-e Farangi*, Tehran, n. p., 1947, repr. in Abbas Milani (ed.), *Taskhir-e Tamaddon-e Gharbi*, Gam-e Naw, Tehran, 2003; Shadman, *Trazhedi-ye Farang*,

Tahuri, Tehran, 1967; Mohamad Tavakoli-Targhi's review of Mehrzad Borujerdi's *Iranian Intellectuals and the West: The Tormented Triumph of Nativism,* in *International Journal of Middle East Studies,* 32/4 (2000).

13. Jalal Al-e Ahmad, *Gharbzadegi,* 2nd edn 1964, repr., Ravaq, Tehran, 1978; Jalal Al-e Ahmad, *Gharbzadegi [Weststruckness],* tr. John Green and Ahmad Alizadeh, Mazda Publishers, Costa Mesa, CA, 1997; *Plagued by the West,* tr. Paul Sprachman, Caravan Books, Delmar, NY, 1982; Jalal Al-e Ahmad, *Occidentosis: A Plague from the West,* tr. R. Campbell, annot. and intro. by Hamid Algar, Mizan Press, Berkeley, CA, 1984.

14. Mohamad Tavakloi-Targhi, *Refashioning Iran: Orientalism, Occidentalism and Historiography,* Palgrave, Basingstoke and New York, 2001, pp. 118–22; *Tajddod-e Bumi va Bazandishi-ye Tarikh,* Nashr-e Tarikh-e Iran, Tehran, 2002, pp. 117–20.

15. Quoted in Lloyd Ridgeon (ed.), *Religion and Politics in Modern Iran, A Reader,* I.B. Tauris, London and New York, 2005, p. 166.

16. Quoted in ibid., pp. 172–3.

17. Jalal Al-e Ahmad, *Dar Khedmat va Khiyanat-e Rowshanfekran,* Kharazmi, Tehran, 1978.

18. See further Hamid Dabashi, *Theology of Discontent,* New York University Press, New York, 1993.

19. For a comprehensive account of Shariati's life and career see Ali Rahnema, *An Islamic Utopian: A Political Biography of Ali Shari'ati,* I.B. Tauris, London, 1998. For the circumstances of Shariati's death in England see p. 386.

20. Ibid., p. 24.

21. Abrahamian, *The Iranian Mojahedin,* ch. 4.

22. Rahnnema, *An Islamic Utopian,* p. 287.

23. See his *Marxism and Other Western Fallacies: An Islamic Critique,* tr. R. Campbell, Mizan Press, Berkeley, CA, 1980; Rahmena, *An Islamic Utopian,* ch. 22.

24. Ervand Abrahamian, 'The Working Class and the Islamic State in Iran', in *Reformers and Revolutionaries in Modern Iran, New Perspectives on the Iranian Left,* ed. Stephanie Cronin, RoutledgeCurzon, London and New York, 2004, p. 269.

25. Abrahamian, *The Iranian Mojahedin,* p. 119, quoted from *Entezar* (1980), p. 21.

26. Ibid., p. 116, quoted from *Bazgasht beh Khishtan* (n.d.), pp. 11, 30.

27. *Entezar: Mazhab-e Entezar,* quoted in Mohsen M. Milani, *The Making of Iran's Islamic Revolution: From Monarchy to Islamic Republic,* Westview Press, Boulder, CO and London, 1988, p. 133. See further Shahrough Akhavi, 'Shariati's Social Thought', in Nikki. R. Keddie (ed.), *Religion and Politics in Iran,* Yale University Press, New Haven and London, 1983.

28. See further Baqer Moin, *Khomeini, Life of the Ayatollah,* I.B. Tauris, London and New York, 1999; *Khaterat-e Ayatollah Pasandideh* (Khomeni's elder brother), ed. Mohammadjavad Moradi-niya, Mo'asseseh-ye Chap o Enteshar-e Hadith, Tehran, 1995.

29. See his *Kashf al-Asrar,* n.p., 1942, which is a critique of Ali Akbar Hakamizadeh's *Asrar-e Hezar Saleh* (Secrets of a Thousand Years), Tehran, 1942. See also Vanessa Martin, 'Religion and State in Khumaini's *Kashf al-Asrar*', *Bulletin of the School of Oriental and African Studies,* 56, pt 1 (1993).

30. *Writings and Declarations of Imam Khomeini,* tr. and annot. Hamid Algar, pp. 189–94.

31. See further Imam Khomeini, *Velayat-e Faqih (Hokumat-e Eslami),* new edn, n.p., 1979; English translation, *Writings and Declarations of Imam Khomeini,* tr. and annot. Hamid Algar, p. 42. See also Michael M. J. Fischer, *Iran: From Religious Dispute to Revolution,* Harvard University Press, Cambridge, MA, 1980.

32. *Writings and Declarations of Imam Khomeini,* p. 55.

33. Ibid., p. 57.

34. Ibid., p. 56.

35. Ibid., p. 62.

36. Ibid., p. 61.

37. Ibid., pp. 75–6.

38. Ibid., p. 49. See also Hamid Enayat, *Modern Islamic Political Thought: The Response of the Shi'i and Sunni Muslims to the Twentieth Century,* Macmillan, London, 1982.

39. For his biography and SAVAK documents and reports on him see *Yaran-e Imam beh Ravayt-e SAVAK: Shahid Ayatollah Seyyed Mohammad Reza Sa'idi,* Markaz-e Barresi-ye Asnad-e Tarikhi (Vezarat-e Ettela'at), Terhan, 1997.

40. Salehi Najaf-Abadi, *Shahid-e Javid,* 2nd edn, n.p., 1972, pp. xiv–xv (1st edn, 1970).

41. Quoted in Negin Nabavi, 'The Discourse of "Authentic Culture" in Iran in the 1960s and 1970s', in Negin Nabavi (ed.), *Intellectual Trends in Twentieth-Century Iran,* p. 91.

42. See further Afshin Matin-Asgari, *Iranian Student Opposition to the Shah,* Mazda Publishers, Costa Mesa, CA, 2002; Hamid Shawkat, *Konfederasion-e Jahani-ye Daneshjuyan va Mohasselin-e Iran (Etthehadiyeh-ye Melli),* Ata'i, Tehran, 1999.

43. He went much further than that, even saying that women were 'evil'. See Oriana Fallaci, *Interview with History*, Liveright Publishing, New York, 1976, pp. 270–2.
44. See also his 1974 interview with Mike Wallace in <www.youtube.com/watch?v=66-jkx36BPc>.
45. Maziar Behrooz, *Rebels with a Cause: The Failure of the Left in Iran*, I.B. Tauris, London and New York, 1999, p. 61.
46. See further Abrahamian, *The Iranian Mojahedin*; Behrooz, *Rebels with a Cause*.
47. Ibid., ch. 2.
48. See further Peyman Vahabzadeh, 'Mostafa Sho'aiyan: The Maverick Theorist of Revolution and the Failure of Frontal Politics in Iran', *Iranian Studies*, 40/3 (2007).
49. See further Kanun-e Gerdavari va Nashr-e Asar-e Jazani (eds), *Jongi darbareh-ye Zendegi va Asar-e Bizhan-e Jazani*, Khavaran, Paris, 1999; Peyman Vahabzadeh, 'Bizhan Jazani and the Problems of Historiography of the Iranian Left', *Iranian Studies*, 38/1 (2005).
50. Mahin Jazani and Abdolkarim Lahiji, in Kanun-e . Gerdavari va Nashr-e Asar-e Jazani (eds), *Jongi darbareh-ye . . . Bizhan Jazani*; Ahabzadeh, 'Bizhan Jazani'; Maziar Behrooz, *Rebels with a Cause*.
51. Jamshid Taheripur, 'Bizhan Jazani, Amuzegar-e Enqelab', in Kanun-e Gerdavari va Nashr-e Asar-e Jazani (eds), *Jongi darbareh-ye . . . Bizhan Jazani*.
52. Vahabzadeh, 'Bizhan Jazani and the Problems of Historiography of the Iranian Left'.
53. See further Bizhan Jazani, *Capitalism and Revolution in Iran*, tr. Iran Committee, Zed Press and Victas Publishing House, London and New Delhi, 1980; Baba Ali, in Kanun-e Gerdavari va Nashr-e Asar-e Jazani (eds), *Jongi darbareh-ye . . . Bizhan Jazani*.
54. See further Farhad Kazemi, *Poverty and Revolution in Iran: The Migrant Poor, Urban Marginality and Politics*, New York University Press, New York, 1980.
55. See further Nimah Mazaheri, 'State Repression in the Iranian Bazaar, 1975–1977: The Anti-Profiteering Campaign and an Impending Revolution', *Iranian Studies*, 39/3 (September 2006); Robert E. Looney, *Economic Origins of the Iranian Revolution*.
56. See further Saedi's interview with Zia Sedghi, Harvard Oral History Project, quoted in *Saedi, Az U va darbareh-ye U*, ed. Baqer Mortazavi, Forough, Cologne, 2007.
57. *Briefing Paper on Iran*, Amnesty International, November 1976.
58. Hossein Shahidi, *Journalism in Iran: From Mission to Profession*, Routledge, London and New York, 2007, p. 7.
59. See further Naser Mo'azzen (ed.), *Dah Shab: Shab-ha-ye She'r-e Sha'eran va Nevisandegan dar Anjoman-e Farhangi-ye Iran o Alman*, Amir Kabir, Tehran, 1979.
60. Baqer Moin, *Khomeini, Life of the Ayatollah*, ch. 10.
61. Sorush Publications, *Taqvim-e Tarikh-e Enqelab-e Eslami-ye Iran*, pp. 54–57, Sorush, Tehran, 1991, quoted in Hossein Shahidi, *Journalism in Iran*, pp. 9–10. See further Shaul Bakhash, 'Sermons, Revolutionary Pamphleteering and Mobilisation: Iran, 1978', in Said Amir Arjomand (ed.), *From Nationalism to Revolutionary Islam*, Macmillan, London, in association with St Antony's College, Oxford, 1984.
62. Ervand Abrahamian, *Iran between Two Revolutions*, Princeton University Press, Princeton, NJ, 1982, p. 517.
63. See further Annabelle Sreberny-Mohammadi and Ali Mohammadi, *Small Media, Big Revolution: Communication, Culture and the Iranian Revolution*, University of Minnesota Press, Minneapolis, 1994.
64. Katouzian, *Political Economy of Modern Iran*, p. 347; Shahidi, *Journalism in Iran*, p. 15.
65. Karim Sanjabi, *Omid-ha va Naomidi-ha, Kahaterat-e Doktor Karim Sanjabi*, Jebhe, London, 1989, p. 296.
66. Azhari-ye bichareh/olagh-e char setareh/bazam begu navareh/navar ken pa nadareh.
67. See the full text penned by Reza Ghotbi, Empress Farah's cousin and head of Iran's radio-television network, <persian.fotopages.com/?entry=46578> and Mehdi Bazargan, *Enqelab-e Iran dar daw Harekat*, Bazargan, Tehran, 1984, pp. 207–9.
68. See further William Shawcross, *The Shah's Last Ride*, Pan Books, London, 1990; Bazargan, *Enqelab-e Iran*.
69. Sanjabi, *Omid-ha va Naomidi-ha*, pp. 306–9.
70. Mohammad Reza Pahlavi, *Answer to History*, Stein and Day, New York, 1980, ch. 6.
71. Ibid. and Anthony Parsons, *The Pride and the Fall, Iran: 1974–1979*, Cape, London, 1984.
72. See further William H. Sullivan, *Mission to Iran*, Norton, New York, 1981.
73. See further Zbigniew Brzezinski, *Power and Principle: Memoirs of the National Security Adviser, 1977–1981*, Weidenfeld & Nicolson, London, 1983.
74. See further Cyrus R. Vance, *Hard Choices: Critical Years in America's Foreign Policy*, Simon and Schuster, New York, 1983.
75. See further Jimmy Carter, *Keeping Faith: Memoirs of a President*, Bantam Books, New York, 1982.

76. 'Nasr-e menallha va fathan qarib/Nang bar in saltanat e por farib'. The first part of the slogan is an idiomatic Koranic verse.
77. 'Ta shah kafan nashavad/In vatan vatan nashavad'.
78. Shahidi, *Journalism in Iran*, p. 15.
79. Sanjabi, *Omid-ha va Naomidi-ha*, pp. 310–12.
80. For the text of his resignation in which he declared the Royal Council 'illegal' see Davud Ali-Baba'i, *Bist o Panj Sal dar Iran Cheh Gozasht (Az Bazargan ta Khatami)*, vol. 1, Omid-e Farda, Tehran, 2005, p. 117.
81. Mehdi Bazargan, *Enqelab-e Iran*.
82. 'Bakhtiar, nawkar-e bi ektiyar'.
83. For example, Sullivan, *Mission to Iran*; Bazargan, *Enqelab-e Iran*; Sanjabi, *Omid-ha va Naomidi-ha*.
84. 'Baradar-e Arteshi/Chera Baradar-koshi?'
85. See further Carter, *Keeping Faith*; Brzezinski, *Power and Principle*; Sullivan, *Mission to Iran*. See also, Said Amir Arjomand, *The Turban for the Crown: The Islamic Revolution in Iran*, Oxford University Press, New York and Oxford, 1988, pp. 119–28.

CHAPTER 13: THE ISLAMIC REPUBLIC

1. Khomeini-ye azizam/Begu ta khun berizam.
2. Charles Kurzman, *The Unthinkable Revolution*, Harvard University Press, Cambridge, MA, 2004, pp. vii–viii.
3. See the foregoing chapters, especially the Introduction and Chapters 8 and 12.
4. Karl Popper, *The Poverty of Historicism*, Routledge, London, 2002.
5. See *Saedi, Az U, va darbareh-ye U*, ed., Baqer Mortazavi, Forough, Cologne, 2007, p. 101.
6. See for a report of Yazdi's speech at Washington's Middle East Institute in April 2008, <niacblog.wordpress.com/2008/04/07/former-leader-of-revolution-ebrahim-yazdi-calls-for-us-iran-talks-rips-into-voa-persian/>.
7. See further Homa Katouzian, 'Towards a General Theory of Iranian Revolutions', *Iranian History and Politics, The Dialectic of State and Society*, London and New York, Routledge, 2007.
8. See further Chapter 8.
9. See further Katouzian, 'Towards a General Theory'.
10. Mehdi Bazargan, *Enqelab-e Iran dar Daw Harekat*, Bazargan, Tehran, 1984, p. 92, n.1. He explains that the political atmosphere was such that freedom and democracy had been turned into dirty words.
11. See Sadeq (Sadeqi Givi) Khalkhali, *Ayyam-e Enzeva, Jeld-e Dovvom-, Khaterat-e Ayatollah Khalkhali*, Nashr-e Sayeh, Tehran, 2001, p. 81.
12. For a fairly detailed account of Hoveyda's trial and execution see Abbas Milani, *The Persian Sphinx: Amir Abbas Hoveyda and the Riddle of the Iranian Revolution, A Biography*, I.B. Tauris, London and New York, 2000.
13. See Khalkhali, *Ayyam-e Enzeva*, p. 78.
14. 'Hezb faqat Hezbollah/Rahbar faqat Ruhollah'.
15. 'Baray-e dafn-e shohada/Mehdi biya, Mehdi biya', 'Mehdi' being the Persian pronunciation of 'Mahdi', an attribute of the Hidden Imam.
16. 'Khodaya, Khodaya/Ta Enqelab-e Mehdi/Hatta Kenar-e Mehdi/Khomeini ra Negahdar'.
17. See Yunes Javanrudi, *Taskhir-e Kayhan*, Hashieh, Tehran, 1980, p. 81. A minor cleric apparently confessed to being a leader of Forqan, although there never was an official report on the group, its membership and its aims. See Davud Alibaba'i, *Bist-o-panj Sal dar Iran Cheh Gozasht*, vol. 1, Omid-e Farda, Tehran, 2002, p. 220.
18. For an early account of this see Eric Hooglund, 'Iran 1980–85: Political and Economic Trends', in *The Iranian Revolution and the Islamic Republic*, ed. Nikkie R. Keddie and Eric Hoogland, Syracuse University Press, Syracuse, NY, 1986.
19. See <www.hamshahrionline.ir/News/?id=48009> (accessed 26 April 2008).
20. See Sorush Publications, *Taqvim-e Tarikh-e Enqelab-e Eslami-ye Iran*, vol. 4, pp. 566–8, cited in Hossein Shahidi, *Journalism in Iran: From Mission to Profession*, Routledge, London, 2007, p. 31.
21. *Sahifeh-ye Nur*, vol. 8. p. 245, quoted in Baqer Moin, *Khomeini, Life of the Ayatollah*, p. 219.
22. See further for details Schirazi, *The Constitution of Iran*, pp. 216–19.
23. *Kayhan*, 6 March 1979.
24. *Saifeh-ye Nur*, vol iii, p. 410, quoted in Vanessa Martin, *Creating an Islamic State: Khomeini and the Making of a New Iran*, I.B. Tauris, London and New York, 2003, p. 155.
25. See further Schirazi, *The Constitution of Iran*, ch. 1.
26. Ibid., p. 22.
27. Abolhasan Bani Sadr, *Khiyanat beh Omid*, Bani Sadr, Paris, 1982; the author's conversations with Ezzatollah Sahabi, Tehran, April 2006.

28. Schirazi, *The Constitution of Iran*, ch. 2.
29. See further Abdol'ali Bazargan (ed.), *Moshkelat va Masa'el-e Avvalin Sal-e Enqelab az Zaban-e Mohandes Bazargan*, Bazargan, Tehran, 1981; Sa'id Barzin, *Zendeginameh-ye Mohandes Mehdi Bazargan*, Nashr-e Markaz, Tehran, 1995; Mehdi Bazargan, *Enqelab-e Iran dar Daw Harekat*; Kheirollah Esma'ili, *Dawlat-e Movaqqat*, Entesharat-e Markaz-e Asnad-e Enqelab-e Eslami, Tehran, 2002; Alibaba'i, *Bist- o- panj Sal*, vol. 1.; Shaul Bakhash, *The Reign of the Ayatollahs: Iran and the Islamic Revolution*, Unwin Paperbacks, London, 1985, ch. 3.
30. See <century.guardian.co.uk/1970–1979/Story/0,,106889,00.html> and William H. Sullivan, *Mission to Iran*.
31. Kasra Naji, *Ahmadinejad: the Secret History of Iran's Radical Leader*, I.B. Tauris, London and New York, 2008, p. 25.
32. The statement was released under the signature and academic address of the Committee's Secretary, Homa Katouzian. It has been reprinted in the Berlin publication *Hoghugh-e Baschar/Human Rights*, 18/1 (spring 2002), pp. 95–6.
33. Banisadr's views were a good deal more Islamist during the revolution than when he was president. See his *Eqtesad-e Eslami*, Paris, Bani Sadr, 1977. See further Homa Katouzian, 'Shi'ism and Islamic Economics: Sadr and Bani Sadr', in Nikki R. Keddie (ed.), *Religion and Politics in Iran, Shi'ism from Quietism to Revolution*, Yale University Press, New Haven, CT and London, 1983.
34. See further Bani Sadr, *Khiyanat beh Omid*; Bakhash, *The Reign of the Ayatollahs*, chs 5 and 6; Ervand Abrahamian, *The Iranian Mojahedin*.
35. See further Ali Rahnema and Farhad Nomani, *The Secular Miracle, Religion, Politics & Economic Policy in Iran*, Zed Books, London and New Jersey, 1990, ch. 5.
36. See Vladimir Kuzichkin, *Inside the KGB: Myth and Reality*, tr. Thomas B. Beattie, intro. Frederick Forsyth, Andre Deutsch, London, 1990.
37. See *Siyast va Sazman-e Hezb-e Tudeh az Aghaz ta Forupashi*, vol. 1, Mo'asseseh-ye Motal'eat va Pazhuhesh-ha-ye Siyasi, Tehran, 1991; Ehsan Tabari, *Kazh-raheh: Khaterati az Hezb-e Tudeh*, Amir Kabir, Tehran, 1988; Nureddin (Nur al-Din) Kiyanuri, *Khaterat-e Nureddin Kiyanuri*, Didgah, Tehran, 1992; Ervanad Abrahamian, *Tortured Confessions: Prisons and Public Recantations in Modern Iran*, University of California Press, Berkeley, CA, 1999.
38. For the text of Qotbzadeh's televised confessions see Alibaba'i, *Bist-o- panj Sal*, vol. 5, 2006, pp. 493–501.
39. See further David Menasheri (ed.), 'Khomeni's Vision: Nationalism or World Order', in *The Iranian Revolution and the Muslim World*, Westview, Boulder, CO, San Fransisco, CA, Oxford, 1990.
40. See further Shahram Chubin and Charles Tripp, *Iran and Iraq at War*, I.B. Tauris, London, 1988, ch. 2; Amazia Baram, 'The Impact of Khomeini's Revolution on the Radical Shi'i Movement of Iraq', in Menasheri (ed.), *The Iranian Revolution and the Muslim World*.
41. Christopher de Bellaigue, *In the Rose Garden of the Martyrs*, HarperCollins, London, 2004, p. 139.
42. *Kayhan-e Hava'i* (27 July 1988).
43. For a review of Iranian international relations at the time see, for example, Anoushiravan Ehteshami and Manshour Varasteh (eds), *Iran and the International Community*, Routledge, London and New York, 1991.
44. See, for example, Edward Hallett Carr, *The Russian Revolution: From Lenin to Stalin, 1917–1929*, Papermac, London, 1980 and *The Bolshevik Revolution, 1917–1923*, 3 vols, Macmillan, London, 1978; Maurice Dobb, *Soviet Economic Development Since 1917*, Routledge & Kegan Paul, London, 1966.
45. See Hassan Hakimian and Massoud Karshenas, 'Dilemmas and Prospects for Economic Reform and Reconstruction in Iran', in Parvin Alizadeh (ed.), *The Economy of Iran: Dilemmas of an Islamic State*, I.B. Tauris, London and New York, 2000, p. 45.
46. Parvin Alizadeh, 'Introduction', in Alizadeh (ed.), *The Economy of Iran*.
47. For a detailed empirical study of the economy, see Jahangir Amuzagar, *Iran's Economy under the Islamic Republic*, I.B. Tauris, London and New York, 1993, especially chs 14 and 15.
48. For example, Nehzat-e Azadi-ye Iran, *Velayat-e Motlaqeh-ye Faqih*, Nehzat-e Azadi, Tehran, ?1988, pp. 4–11.
49. Wilfried Buchta, *Who Rules Iran?: The Structure of Power in the Islamic Republic*, a joint publication of the Washington Institute for Near East Policy, Washington DC and the Konrad Adenauer Stiftung, Berlin, 2000, p. 92.
50. It turned out that Seyyed Mehdi Hashemi, the leading figure in the affair, and his accomplices had also been seasoned murderers. See further Mohammad Reyshahri, *Khaterat-e Siyasi, 1986–1987*, Mo'asseseh-ye Motal'at va Pazhuhesh-ha-ye Siyasi, Tehran, 1990.
51. See Homa Katouzian, 'Islamic Government and Politics: The Practice and Theory of the Absolute Guardianship of the Jurisconsult', in *After the War: Iran, Iraq and the Arab Gulf*, ed. Charles Davies, Carden Publications, Chichester, 1990.

52. For example, Ali A. Saeidi, 'The Accountability of Para-governmental Organizations (bonyads): The Case of Iranian Foundations', *Iranian Studies*, 37/1 (September 2004).
53. *Kayhan-e Hava'i*, 27 July 1988.
54. *Ettela'at*, 25 February 1989.
55. Iran Radio (Home Service), 9 December 1987, BBC Monitoring Service.
56. Iran Radio (Home Service), 23 December 1987, BBC Monitoring Service.
57. Ibid.
58. Ibid.
59. *Jomhuri-ye Eslami*, 9 January 1988.
60. Ibid.
61. Ibid.
62. *Jomhuri-ye Eslami*, 20 January 1988.
63. See further Katouzian, 'Islamic Government and Politics'.
64. Adel Darwish, 'Halabja: whom does the truth hurt? in <www.opendemocracy.net/conflict- journal-ismwar/article_1049.jsp>, first published on 17 March 2003.
65. Ibid.
66. For a detailed and highly informative account of the Halabja incident, see Joost R. Hiltermann, *A Poisonous Affair: America, Iraq and the Gassing of Halabja*, Cambridge University Press, Cambridge, 2007.
67. For full accounts of the Iran–Iraq war see further, for example, Shahram Chubin and Charles Tripp, *Iran and Iraq at War*; Dilip Hiro, *The Longest War: the Iran–Iraq Military Conflict*, Grafton, London, 1989.
68. Tehran Radio, 20 July 1988, quoted in Moin, *Khomeini, Life of the Ayatollah*.
69. Moin, *Khomeini*, pp. 282–3.
70. Moin, *Khomeini*, pp. 278–9
71. See further Katouzian, 'Islamic Government and Politics', pp. 258–9, quoting from photocopies of the original letters.
72. *Kayhan-e Hava'i*, 19 October 1988, emphasis added.
73. For the full text of the letter, see *Kayhan-e Hava'i*, 15 April 1989.
74. For the website of Montazeri's office, see <www.amontazeri.com/farsi/default.asp>.
75. See for the full account Tom Fenton, 'The Day They Buried the Ayatollah', *Iranian Studies*, 41/2 (April 2008).

CHAPTER 14: IRAN AFTER KHOMEINI

1. See further Anoushiravan Ehteshami, *After Khomeini: The Second Iranian Republic*, Routledge, London and New York, 1995, ch. 2.
2. See further Mohsen Milani, 'The Evolution of the Iranian Presidency: From Bani Sadr to Rafsanjani', *British Journal of Middle Eastern Studies*, 20/1 (1993).
3. In 1994, the death of Grand Ayatollah Araki at 103, a traditional senior cleric committed to the Islamist line, created something of a succsssion crisis. The Society of Instructors of the Qom Seminary (*Hawzeh*) nominated seven Shiite leaders, including Khamenei, for the office of *marja'-e taqlid*. Upon serious objections from leading pontiffs, Khamenei declared that he was a *marja'* only for the Shiites outside Iran. Montazeri believed that the supreme leader should be popularly elected. Others such as Rafsanjani suggested that the office should be run by a committee or council of jurisprudents. See further Homa Katouzian, 'Problems of Political Development in Iran: Democracy, Dictatorship or Arbitrary Rule?', *British Journal of Middle Eastern Studies*, 22/4 (1995); Wilfred Buchta, *Who Rules Iran?*, p.93.
4. See further Katouzian, 'Problems of Political Development in Iran'.
5. Speech given on Iranian television, 16 June 1989, quoted in Karim Sajjadpour, *Reading Khamenei: The World View of Iran's Most Powerful Leader*, Carnegie Endowment for International Peace, Washington DC, 2008, p. 7.
6. Quoted directly from BBC's Summary of World Broadcasts, ME/0218 (1 August 1988), in Ehteshami, *After Khomeini*, p. 28. For a study of the change in Iran's foreign policy attitude at the beginning of Rafsanjani's presidency see Rouhollah K. Ramazani, 'Iran's Foreign Policy: Contending Orientations', *The Middle East Journal*, 43/2 (spring 1989).
7. Ali Ansari has characterized the Rafsanjani years as a 'mercantile bourgeois republic'. See Ali M. Ansari, *Iran, Islam and Democracy, the Politics of Managing Change*, 2nd edn, Chatham House, London, 2006, ch. 4.
8. For a brief and qualified application of the bourgeois comprador theory see Ehteshani, *After Khomeini*; Ansari, *Iran, Islam and Democracy*.

9. See further David Menasheri, *Post-Revolutionary Politics in Iran*, Frank Cass, London and Portland, OR, 2001, ch. 2.
10. See further Hossein Shahidi, *Journalism in Iran*, p. 47.
11. The classification of Islamist political tendencies into the above four major factions (while acknowledging the existence of some subdivisions) belongs to this author, but see further Mehdi Moslem, *Factional Politics in Post-Khomeini Iran*, Syracuse University Press, Syracuse, NY, 2002; Saeed Barzin, *Jenahbandi-ye Siyasi dar Iran az Dahe-ye 60 ta Dovvom-e Khordad, Hamrah-e Mosahebeh ba Homayoun Katouzian*, Nashr-e Markaz, Tehran, 1998.
12. For example, Hakimian and Karshenas, 'Dilemmas and Prospects for Economic Reform and Reconstruction in Iran', in Parvin Alizadeh (ed.), *The Economy of Iran, Dilemmas of an Islamic State*.
13. For oil price changes see <www.ioga.com/Special/crudeoil_Hist.htm>.
14. For data on population and other demographic changes see <en.wikipedia.org/wiki/Demography; countrystudies.us/iran/32.htm>. See also <en.wikipedia.org/wiki/Family_planning_ in_Iran#cite_ note-0>; <www.nationbynation.com/Iran/Population.htm>. See further Hassan Hakimian, 'Population Dynamics in Post-revolutionary Iran: A Re-examination of Evidence', in Alizadeh (ed.), *The Economy of Iran*.
15. For example, Hashem Pesaran, 'Economic Trends and Macro-economic Policies in Post-revolutionary Iran', in Alizadeh (ed.), *The Economy of Iran*. See also Jahangir Amuzegar, *Iran's Economy under the Islamic Republic*, I.B. Tauris, London and New York, 1993.
16. See further Steven Wright, *The United States and Persian Gulf Security: The Foundations of the War on Terror*, Ithaca Press, Reading, 2007, pt 2, ch. 4.
17. See <www.ioga.com/Special/crudeoil_Hist.htm>.
18. Ali A. Saeidi, 'The Accountability of Para-governmental Organizations'. See further Suzanne Maloney, 'Agents or Obstacles? Parastatal Foundations and Challenges for Iranian Development', in Alizadeh (ed.), *The Economy of Iran*.
19. See 'Saranjam Doktor Khatami Raft', in *Adineh*, 72 (August 1992), p. 5, quoted in Mehrzad Boroujerdi 'The Paradoxes of Politics in Post-revolutionary Iran', in *Iran at the Crossroads*, eds John L. Esposito and R. K. Ramazani, Palgrave, New York, 2001, pp. 19–20.
20. For a detailed and graphic description of physical torture inflicted on them, see Habibollah Davaran and Farhad Behbahani, *Dar Mehmani-ye Hajji Aqa: Dastan-e Yek E'teraf*, Omid-e Farda, Tehran, 1999.
21. Hossein Shahidi, *Journalism in Iran*, p. 56.
22. See for example Homa Katouzian, *Buf-e Kur-e Hedayat* (a critical monograph), 1st edn, Nashr-e Markaz, Tehran, 1994–5, throughout which the word *buseh* is replaced by three dots.
23. For the text of Nouri's defence in his trial see his *Shawkaran-e Eslah: Defa'iyat-e Abdollah Nuri*, Tarh-e Naw, Tehran, 2000. See also *Naqdi bara-ye Tamam-e Fosul: Goftugu-ye Akbar Gani ba Abdollah Nuri*, Tarh-e Naw, Tehran, 2000; Ali M. Ansari, *Iran, Islam and Democracy*.
24. For example, Shahrough Akhavi, 'The Thought and Role of Ayatollah Hossein'ali Montazeri in the Politics of Post-1979 Iran', *Iranian Studies*, 41/5 (December 2008).
25. Mehdi Haeri Yazdi, *Hekmat va Hokomat*, Shadi Publications, London, 1995. See also *Memoirs of Mehdi Hairi-Yazdi: Theologian and Professor of Islamic Philosophy*, ed. Habib Ladjevardi, Iranian Oral History Project, Cambridge, MA, 2001
26. See further Mohsen Kadivar, *Hokumat-e Vela'i*, Nashr-e Ney, Tehran, 1999. For a study of Kadivar's thoughts see Yasuyuki Matsunaga, 'Mohsen Kadivar, an Advocate of Postrevivalist Islam in Iran', *British Journal of Middle Eastern Studies*, 34/3 (December 2007). See also Ansari, *Iran, Islam and Democracy*, pp. 181–6.
27. Abdolkarim Soroush, *Farbeh-tar az Ideolozhi*, Serat, Tehran, 1994.
28. For example, Vala Vakili/Sa'id Mohebbei, 'Goftogu-ye Din o Siysat dar Iran: Andishe-ha-ye Siyasi-ye Doktor Soroush', in Abdolkarim Soroush, *Siyasat-Nameh*, Serat, Tehran, 1999.
29. See his 'Tolerance and Governance: A Discourse on Religion and Democracy', in *Reason, Freedom and Democracy in Islam: Essential Writings of 'Abdolkarim Soroush*, tr., ed. and with a critical introduction by Mahmoud Sadri and Ahmad Sadri, Oxford University Press, New York and Oxford, 2000, p. 134. See further Behruz Ghamari-Tabizi, *Islam and Dissent in Postrevolutionary Iran: Abdolkarim Sorush, Relgious Poltics and Democratic Reform*, I.B. Tauris, London and New York, 2008.
30. Ibid., p. 133.
31. Ziba Mir-Hosseini and Richard Tapper, *Islam and Democracy in Iran: Eshkevari and the Quest for Reform*, I.B. Tauris, London and New York, 2006, pp. 75–7. See further Eshkevari's newspaper articles in Hasan Yousefi Eshakevari, *Yad-e Ayyam: Ruykard-ha-ye Siyasi dar Jonbesh-e Eslahat*, Gam-e Naw, Tehran, 2000.
32. See the direct quotation in Hamid Kaviyani, *Dar Jostoju-ye Mahfel-e Jenayatkaran: Bazkhani-ye Parvandeh-ye Qatl-ha-ye Siyasi*, Nashr-e Negah-e Emruz, Tehran, 1999.

33. See 'Sa'id Eslami Keh Bud?', in ibid.
34. See further Mohammad Ali Zakariya'i, *Vaqe'eh-ye Talkh-e Ku-ye Daneshgah beh Ravayat-e Majlis-e Panjom*, Salam, Tehran, 1999; <en.wikipedia.org/wiki/Majlis_of_Iran>.
35. See Benedict Steiner, 'Ayatollah Khamene'i and the Position of Marja'-e Taqlid: Religious and Political Authority in the Islamic Republic of Iran', MPhil. thesis, Modern Middle Eastern Studies, University of Oxford, Oxford, 2008, ch. 3.
36. Christopher de Bellaigue, *The Struggle for Iran*, New York Review of Books, New York, 2007.
37. For the text of Ganji's defence at his trial, see *Kimiya-ye Azadi: Defa'iyat-e Akbar Ganji dar Dadgah-e Konferans-e Berlin*, Tarh-e Naw, Tehran, 2001.
38. See for the text of Aghajeri's defence at his trial Seyyed Hashem Aghajari, *Din, Qodrart va Servat: Mohakemeh va Defa'iyat*, Zekr, Tehran, 2003; see also his *Hokumat-e Dini va Hokumat-e Demokratik: Majmu'eh-ye Maqalat*, Zekr, Tehran, 2003.
39. For more details of this case see, for example, <www.jstor.org/stable/1559282?seq=6>. See also de Bellaigue, *The Struggle for Iran*, ch. 3.
40. For CBC's coverage of the events, see <www.cbc.ca/news/background/kazemi/>.
41. De Bellaigue, *The Struggle for Iran*, ch. 2; <www.jstor.org/stable/1559282?seq=6>.
42. See the BBC report directly quoting the Iranian news agency IRNA, <news.bbc.co.uk/2/hi/middle_east/2405777.stm>.
43. For example, Mohsen Armin, *Obur az Khatami, Majmu'eh-ye Maqalat*, Zekr, Tehran, 2001.
44. Ahmad Sidiqi, 'Khatami and the Search for Reform in Iran', *Stanford Journal of International Relations*, 6/1 (Winter 2005).
45. For example, Shirin Ebaday (Ebadi), *History and Documentation of Human Rights in Iran*, tr. Nazila Fathi, Bibliotheca Press, New York, 2000.
46. For example, *Pazhuheshi darbareh-ye Khoshunat aleih-e Zanan dar Iran*, Rawshangaran va Motale'at-e Zanan, Tehran, 2000.
47. See for a report on Iranian family planning <www.nationbynation.com/Iran/Population.htm>. See further Djavad Saleh-Isfahani, 'Human Resources in Iran, Potentials and Challenges', in Homa Katouzian and Hossein Shahidi (eds), *Iran in the 21st Century*, Routledge, London and New York, 2008.
48. See further Shirin Ebadi and Azadeh Moaveni, *Iran Awakening: From Prison to Peace Prize, One Woman Struggle at the Crossroads of History*, Vintage, Canada, 2007.
49. Shirin Ebadi, 'Negaresh-e Sonnat va Moderniteh beh Barabri-ye Zan o Mard', in Noushin Ahmadi Khorasani (ed.), *Jens-e Dovvom*, Ahmadi Khorasani, Tehran, 1999, p. 38.
50. The literature on the situation of Iranian women and their campaigns is already vast. See, for example, Nikki R. Keddie, 'Iranian Women's Status and Struggles Since 1979', in *Journal of International Affairs*, 60/2 (Spring/Summer 2007); Ziba Mir-Hosseini, *Islam and Gender: The Religious Debate in Contemporary Iran*, I.B. Tauris, London, 1999; Azadeh Kian-Thiébaut, 'From Motherhood to Equal Rights Advocates: The Weakening of the Patriarchal Order', in Katouzian and Shahidi (eds), *Iran in the 21st Century*; Nayereh Tohidi, 'The Global-Local Interaction of Feminism in Muslim Societies: The Cases of Iran and Azerbaijan', *Social Research*, 69 (2002); Charles Kurzman, 'A Feminist Generation in Iran?', *Iranian Studies*, 41/3 (June 2008).
51. See further <www.ioga.com/Special/crudeoil_Hist.htm>.
52. See further Ahmad R. Jalali-Naini, 'Economic Growth in Iran, 1950–2000', <www.gdnet.org/pdf2/gdn_library/global_research_projects/explaining_growth/Iran_growth_final.pdf>.
53. Ahmad R. Jalali-Naini, 'Capital Accumulation, Financial Market Reform and Growth in Iran', in *Iran in the 21st Century*, pp. 237–8.
54. See further Massoud Karshenas and Hassan Hakimian, 'Managing Oil Resources and Economic Diversification in Iran', in ibid., pp. 214–15.
55. Djavad Salehi-Isfahani, ibid., p. 269.
56. Homa Katouzian, 'The Significance of Economic History and the Fundamental Features of the Economic History of Iran', in ibid., p. 284 (emphasis in the original).
57. *New York Times* (Wednesday, 10 January 1998).
58. BBC World Service (18 March 2000).
59. *New York Times* (Wednesday, 10 January 1998).
60. On Iran's false hopes about a greater 'realism' of a George Bush administration see Ali M. Ansari, 'Iran and the United States in the Shadow of 9/11: Persia and the Persian Question Revisited', in *Iran in the 21st Century*, p. 113.
61. See the president's State of the Union address in <www.whitehouse.gov/news/releases/2002/01/20020129-11.html>.
62. See further Ali M. Ansari, *Confronting Iran: The Failure of American Policy and the Roots of Mistrust*, Hurst and Company, London, 2006.

63. For example, Steven Wright, *The United States and Persian Gulf Security*, ch. 7.
64. Ibid.
65. For example, Glenn Kessler, 'In 2003, US Spurned Iran's Offer of Dialogue: Some Officials Lament Lost Opportunity', *Washington Post* (18 June 2006).
66. See further Tom Regan, 'Report: Cheney Rejected Iran's Offer of Concessions in 2003: A former US senior official says the offer was very close to what the US currently wants', *The Christian Science Monitor* (18 January 2007). For the BBC report, see <news.bbc.co.uk/2/hi/middle_east/6274147.stm>.
67. See Gawdat Bahgat, 'Nuclear Proliferation: The Islamic Republic of Iran', *Iranian Studies*, 39/3 (September 2006); <www.nti.org/e_research/profiles/Iran/Nuclear/index.html>.
68. See further Christopher de Bellaigue, *The Struggle for Iran*, ch. 4.
69. See Mark Leonard, *Can EU Stop Iran's Nuclear Programme?*, Centre for European Reform, 2005. For factual details see de Bellaigue, *The Struggle for Iran*, chs 4 and 5; <en.wikipedia.org/wiki/Nuclear_program_of_Iran>.
70. Khatami, dorugh-gu, khejalat!
71. Naji-ye mellat amad.
72. Anoushiravan Ehteshami and Mahjoob Zweiri, *Iran and the Rise of its Neoconservatives: The Politics of Tehran's Silent Revolution*, I.B. Tauris, 2007, London and New York, ch. II.
73. For the breakdown of votes see 'Iranian Presidential Election 2005', <en.wikipedia.org/wiki/Iranian_presidential_election,_2005>.
74. De Bellaigue, *The Struggle for Iran*, ch. 8.
75. See further Kasra Naji, *Ahmadinejad: The Secret History of Iran's Radical Leader*, I.B. Tauris, London and New York, 2008, ch. 2.
76. Ibid., ch. 1; Ehteshami and Zweiri, *Iran and the Rise of its Neoconservatives*, ch. III.
77. Naji; *Ahmadinejad*, ch. 3.
78. Ibid.; the report by Radio Farda based on the video of Ahmadinejad's account to Amoli in Baztab.com, <www.rferl.org/featuresarticle/2005/11/184CB9FB-887C-4696-8F54-0799DF747A4A.html>.
79. See further Trita Parsi, 'Israel-Iranian Relations Assessed: Strategic Competition from the Power Cycle Perspective', in Katouzian and Shahidi (eds), *Iran in the 21st Century*; <www.opendemocracy.net/democracy-irandemocracy/israel_2974.jsp>.
80. See further <english.farsnews.com/newstext.php?nn=8512130242>; <yaleglobal.yale.edu/display.article?id=8888>; <www.wjla.com/news/stories/1207/477463.html>.
81. See Naji, *Ahmadinejad*, ch. 3.
82. For more information about 'the sacred mosque of Jamkaran' see <jamkaran.info/fa/>.
83. BBC report: <news.bbc.co.uk/1/hi/world/middle_east/4131706.stm>.
84. BBC report: <news.bbc.co.uk/1/hi/world/middle_east/4680294.stm>.
85. For a report see <news.xinhuanet.com/english/2006-02/18/content_4197711.htm>.
86. See <www.usatoday.com/news/world/2006-04-12-irannuclear_x.htm>.
87. For details see Naji, *Ahmadinejad*, ch. 4; <www.globalpolicy.org/security/sanction/indxiran.htm>.
88. Muriel Mirak-Weissbach, <globalresearch.ca/index.php?context=va&aid=7722>.
89. See <www.monstersandcritics.com/news/middleeast/news/article_1412556.php>.
90. See <news.bbc.co.uk/1/hi/world/middle_east/7498214.stm>.
91. For the letter by the 5+1 to the Iranian foreign minister see <www.fco.gov.uk/en/newsroom/latest-news/?view=News&id=3772654>; for the latter's response see <globe.blogs.nouvelobs.com/media/00/02/cb7c0be018109bea88567d7c7839309b.pdf>.
92. Report and analysis in <www.citymayors.com/politics/iran_elections_06.html>.
93. Report and analysis in <en.wikipedia.org/wiki/Iranian_Assembly_of_Experts_election,_2006>.
94. Report and analysis in <www.washingtonpost.com/wp-dyn/content/article/2007/09/04/AR2007090400311.html>; <www.rferl.org/featuresarticle/2007/09/30135898-ce43-40e0--062-4e2d0cec060a.html>.
95. For the details of the election results in the two rounds see <en.wikipedia.org/wiki/Iranian_legislative_election,_2008>.
96. For example, Scott Macleod, 'Are Ahmadinejad's Days Numbered', *TIME* magazine (29 May 2008).
97. Emadeddin Baghi, *Jonbesh-e Eslahat-e Demokratik-e Iran: Enqelab ya Eslah?*, Nashr-e Sarayi, Tehran, 2004; *Trazhedi-ye Demokrasi dar Iran: Bazkhani-ye Qatl-ha-ye Zanjirhe'i*, Nashr-e Ney, Tehran, 2000.
98. In Persian: *Yek million emza' bara-ye taghiir-e qavanin-e tabiiz amiz*.
99. <en.wikipedia.org/wiki/One_Million_Signatures>
100. <www.persianhub.org/off-topic-free-talk-published/157993-sokhanane-abbas-palizdar-dar-morede-iran.html; www.ihrv.org/inf/?p=335>

101. <www.nyse.tv/crude-oil-price-history.htm>
102. <www.youtube.com/watch?v=0ee0wrjVtkk>
103. <www.youtube.com/watch?v=ZNg0A3PLdxQ>
104. <news.bbc.co.uk/1/hi/world/middle_east/8098305.stm>
105. <news.bbc.co.uk/1/hi/world/middle_east/8098896.stm>;
     <www.youtube.com/watch?v=m6rO9MEPyF0&NR=1>
106. <news.bbc.co.uk/1/hi/world/middle_east/8099952.stm>
107. <www.youtube.com/watch?v=Co2r-iNMpBs>;
     <news.bbc.co.uk/1/hi/world/middle_east/8108661.stm>
108. <news.bbc.co.uk/1/hi/world/middle_east/8108983.stm>
109. <news.bbc.co.uk/1/hi/world/middle_east/8111352.stm>;
     <en.wikipedia.org/wiki/2009_Iranian_election_protests>
110. <neda-aghasultan-youtube.toronews.ws/>;
     <www.nbcwashington.com/news/us_world/Neda-Becomes-Iran-Uprising-.html>
111. <www.smh.com.au/world/rafsanjanis-daughters-arrest--a-warning-20090622-ct6n.html>
112. <news.bbc.co.uk/1/hi/uk/8115358.stm>
113. <news.gooya.com/politics/archives/2009/06/090063.php>

Select Bibliography

ENGLISH

Abrahamian, Ervand, *Iran between Two Revolutions*, Princeton University Press, Princeton, 1982
—— , *The Iranian Mojahedin*, Yale University Press, New Haven and London, 1989
Afary, Janet, *The Iranian Constitutional Revolution, 1905–1911*, Columbia University Press, New York, 1996
Alam, Asadollah, *The Shah and I: The Confidential Diary of Iran's Royal Court, 1969–1977*, intro. and ed. Alinaghi Alikhani, tr. Alinaghi Alikhani and Nicholas Vincent, I.B. Tauris, London and New York, 1991
Al-e Ahmad, Jalal, *Gharbzadegi [Westsrtuckness]*, tr. John Green and Ahmad Alizadeh, Mazda Publishers, Costa Mesa, CA, 1997
Akhavi, Sharough, *Religion and Politics in Contemporary Iran: Clergy-State Relations in the Pahlavi Period*, State University of New York Press, Albany, NY, 1980
Algar, Hamid, *Malkum Khan: A Study in the History of Iranian Modernism*, University of California Press, Berkeley, CA, 1973
—— , *Religion and State in Iran, 1785–1906, the Role of the Ulama in the Qajar Period*, University of California Press, Berkeley, CA, 1969
Alizadeh, Parvin (ed.), *The Economy of Iran: Dilemmas of an Islamic State*, I.B. Tauris, London and New York, 2000
Amanat, Abbas, *Pivot of the Universe: Nasir al-Din Shah Qajar and the Iranian Monarchy, 1831–1896*, I.B. Tauris, London, 1997
Amir Arjomand, Said, *The Turban for the Crown: The Islamic Revolution in Iran*, Oxford University Press, New York and Oxford, 1988
Amuzegar, Jahangir, *Iran: An Economic Profile*, Middle East Institute, Washington DC, 1977
—— , *Iran's Economy under the Islamic Republic*, I.B. Tauris, London and New York, 1993
Ansari, Ali M., *Confronting Iran: The Failure of American Policy and the Roots of Mistrust*, Hurst and Company, London, 2006
—— , *Iran, Islam and Democracy: the Politics of Managing Change*, 2nd edn, Chatham House, London, 2006
Arberry, A. J., *Classical Persian Literature*, Clarendon Press, Oxford, 1958
—— (ed.), *The Legacy of Persia*, Clarendon Press, Oxford, 1953
Atabaki, Touraj (ed.), *Iran and the First World War*, I.B. Tauris, London and New York, 2006
—— and Erik J. Zürcher (eds), *Men of Order: Authoritarian Modernization under Ataturk and Reza Shah*, I.B. Tauris, London and New York, 2004
Axworthy, Michael, *Sword of Persia: Nader Shah, From Tribal Warrior to Conquering Tyrant*, I.B. Tauris, London and New York, 2006
Azimi, Fakhreddin, *The Quest for Democracy in Iran: A Century of Struggle against Authoritarian Rule*, Harvard University Press, Cambridge, MA, and London, 2008
Balfour, James, *Recent Happenings in Persia*, William Blackwood & Sons, Edinburgh and London, 1922
Bakhash, Shaul, *The Reign of the Ayatollahs: Iran and the Islamic Revolution*, Unwin Paperbacks, London, 1985
Banani, Amin, *The Modernization of Iran*, Stanford University Press, Stanford, CA, 1961
Bausani, Alessandro, *The Persians, from the Earliest Days to the Twentieth Century*, tr. J. B. Donne, Elek Books, London, 1971
Bayat, Kaveh, 'Riza Shah and the Tribes, an Overview', in Stephanie Cronin (ed.), *The Making of Modern Iran: State and Society under Riza Shah, 1921–1941*, Routledge, London and New York, 2003

Behrooz, Maziar, *Rebels with a Cause: The Failure of the Left in Iran*, I.B. Tauris, London and New York, 1999

Bharier, Julian, *Economic Development in Iran, 1900–1970*, Oxford University Press, Oxford, 1971

Bill, James A., *The Eagle and the Lion: The Tragedy of American–Iranian Relations*, Yale University Press, New Haven, CT and London, 1988

—— , and Wm. R. Louis (eds), *Musaddiq, Iranian Nationalism, and Oil*, I.B. Tauris, London, 1988

Bonakdarian, Mansour, *Britain and the Iranian Constitutional Revolution of 1906–1911: Foreign Policy, Imperialism and Dissent*, Syracuse University Press, Syracuse, NY, 2006

Boroujerdi, Mehrzad, *Iranian Intellectuals and the West: The Tormented Triumph of Nativism*, Syracuse University Press, Syracuse, NY, 1996

Bosworth, Edmund, *The Ghaznavids: Their Empire in Afghanistan and Eastern Iran*, Librairie du Liban, Beirut, 1973

Bostock, Francis and Geoffrey Jones, *Planning and Power in Iran: Ebtehaj and Economic Development under the Shah*, Frank Cass, London, 1989

Boyce, Mary, *Zoroastrianism, Its Antiquity and Constant Vigour*, Mazda Publishers, Costa Mesa, CA, 1993

Browne, E. G., *A Literary History of Persia*, vols 1–4, Cambridge University Press, Cambridge, 1920–4

—— , *The Persian Revolution*, Frank Cass, London, 1966

Buchta, Wilfried, *Who Rules Iran? The Structure of Power in the Islamic Republic*, The Washington Institute for Near East Policy, Washington DC, 2000

Bullard, Reader, *Letters from Tehran*, ed. E. C. Hodgkin, I.B. Tauris, London and New York, 1991

Cambridge History of Iran, vols 1–7, various editors, Cambridge University Press, Cambridge, 1968–91

Carr, E. H., *The Bolshevik Revolution*, Penguin, Harmondsworth, 1966

Chaqueri, Cosroe, *The Soviet Socialist Republic of Iran, 1920–1921: Birth of the Trauma*, Pittsburgh University Press, Pittsburgh, PA, 1995

Chehabi, H. E., 'The Banning of the Veil and its Consequences', in Cronin (ed.), *The Making of Modern Iran: State and Society under Riza Shah, 1921–1941*, Routledge, London and New York, 2003

—— , *Iranian Politics and Religious Modernism, The Liberation Movement of Iran under the Shah and Khomeini*, Cornell University Press, Ithaca, NY, 1990

—— and Juan J. Linz, *Sultanistic Regimes*, The Johns Hopkins University Press, Baltimore and London, 1998

Chubin, Shahram and Sepehr Zabih, *The Foreign Relations of Iran: A Developing State in a Zone of Great-Power Conflict*, University of California Press, Berkeley, CA, 1974

Cronin, Stephanie, 'An Experiment in Revolutionary Nationalism: The Rebellion of Colonel Mohammad Taqi Khan Pesyan', *Middle Eastern Studies*, 33/4 (October 1997)

—— , *The Army and the Creation of the Pahlavi State in Iran, 1910–1926*, I.B. Tauris, London and New York, 1997

—— (ed.), *The Making of Modern Iran: State and Society under Riza Shah, 1921–1941*, Routledge, London and New York, 2003

—— (ed.), *Reformers and Revolutionaries in Modern Iran*, RoutledgeCurzon, London and New York, 2004

—— , 'Reza Shah, the Fall of Sardar Asad, and "the Bakhtiyari Plot"', *Iranian Studies*, 38/2 (2005)

Curzon, George Nathaniel, *Persia and the Persian Question*, Frank Cass, London, 1996

Dabashi, Hamid, *Theology of Discontent*, New York University Press, New York, 1993

Darke, Hubert (tr.), *The Book of Government or Rules for Kings: The Siyar al-Muluk or Siyasat-nama of Nizam al-Mulk*, Routledge & Kegan Paul, London and Boston, MA, 1978

Davis, Dick (tr.), *Fathers and Sons*, Mage Publishers, Washington DC, 2000

—— (tr.), *Sunset of Empire*, Mage Publishers, Washington DC, 2004

—— (tr.), *The Legend of Seyavash*, Penguin, London, 1992

De Bellaigue, Christopher, *In the Rose Garden of the Martyrs*, HarperCollins, London, 2004

—— , *The Struggle for Iran*, New York Review of Books, New York, 2007

De Bruijn, J. T. P., *Persian Sufi Poetry: An Introduction to the Mystical Use of Classical Persian Poems*, Curzon, Richmond, 1997

Ehteshami, Anoushiravan and Mahjoob Zweiri, *Iran and the Rise of its Neoconservatives: The Politics of Tehran's Silent Revolution*, I.B. Tauris, London and New York, 2007

—— , *After Khomeini: The Second Iranian Republic*, Routledge, London and New York, 1995

Elliot, Matthew, 'New Iran and the Dissolution of Party Politics under Reza Shah', in Touraj Atabaki and Erik J. Zürcher (eds), *Men of Order: Authoritarian Modernization under Ataturk and Reza Shah*, I.B. Tauris, London and New York, 2004

Elwell-Sutton, L. P., *Modern Iran*, G. Routledge and Sons, London, 1942

—— , 'Reza Shah the Great', in George Lenczowski (ed.), *Iran under the Pahlavis*, Hoover Institution Press, Stanford, CA, 1978

Enayat, Hamid, *Modern Islamic Political Thought: The Response of the Shi'i and Sunni Muslims to the Twentieth Century*, Macmillan, London, 1982

Esposito, John L. and R.K. Ramazani (eds), *Iran at the Crossroads*, Palgrave, New York, 2001

Ettehadieh, Mansoureh, 'The Iranian Provisional Government', in Touraj Atabaki (ed.), *Iran and the First World War*, I.B. Tauris, London and New York, 2006

Fawcett, Louise L'Estrange, *Iran and the Cold War: The Azerbaijan Crisis of 1946*, Cambridge University Press, Cambridge, 1992

Fischer, Michael M. J., *Iran: From Religious Dispute to Revolution*, Harvard University Press, Cambridge, MA, 1980

Floor, Willem, *A Fiscal History of Iran in the Safavid and Qajar Periods*, Persian Studies, 17, Bibliotheca Press, New York, 1998

—— , *Safavid Government Institutions*, Mazda Publishers, Costa Mesa, CA, 2001

—— , *The Economy of Safavid Persia*, Wiesbaden, Reichert, 2000

Frye, Richard N., *The History of Ancient Iran*, C. H. Beck'sche Verlagsbuchhandlung, Munich, 1984

—— , *Persia*, London, Allen and Unwin, 1968

—— , *The Golden Age of Persia*, Phoenix, London, 2000

Garthwaite, Gene R., *The Persians*, Blackwell, Oxford, 2005

Gasiorowski, Mark J., *US Foreign Policy and the Shah: Building a Client State in Iran*, Cornell University Press, Ithaca, NY, 1991

Gasiorowski, Mark J. and Malcolm Byrne (eds), *Mohammad Mosaddeq and the 1953 Coup in Iran*, Syracuse University Press, Syracuse, NY, 2004

Ghani, Cyrus, *Iran and the Rise of Reza Shah: From Qajar Collapse to Pahlavi Power*, I.B. Tauris, London and New York, 1998

Gheissari, Ali, *Iranian Intellectuals in the 20th Century*, University of Texas Press, Austin, TX, 1998

Girshman, R., *Iran, From the Earliest Times to the Islamic Conquest*, Penguin Books, London, 1961

—— , *Iran: Parthians and Sassanians*, tr. Stuart Gilbert and James Emmons, Thames and Hudson, London, 1962

Grigor, Talinn, 'Re-cultivating "Good Taste": The Early Pahlavi Modernists and Their Society for National Heritage', *Iranian Studies*, 37/1 (March 2004)

Hillman, Michael C. (ed.), *Major Voices in Contemporary Persian Literature*, University of Texas, Austin, TX, 1980

Ironside, Lord (ed.), *High Road to Command: The Diaries of Major-General Sir Edmund Ironside, 1920–1922*, Leo Cooper, London, 1972

Issawi, Charles, *The Economic History of Iran, 1800–1914*, University of Chicago Press, Chicago, IL, 1971

Jamalzadeh, Mohammad Ali, 'Taqrirat-e Seyyed Zia and his "Black Book" ', pts 1 and 2, *Ayandeh* (March 1980 and June 1981)

Karshenas, Massoud, *Oil, State and Industrialization in Iran*, Cambridge University Press, Cambridge, 1990

Katouzian, Homa, 'Iraj, the Poet of Love and Humour', *Iranian Studies*, 40, 4 (September 2007)

—— , *Iranian History and Politics, the Dialectic of State and Society*, paperback edn, Routledge, London and New York, 2007

—— , 'Liberty and Licence in the Constitutional Revolution of Iran', *Journal of the Royal Asiatic Society*, 3/8 (July 1998), reprinted in *Iranian History and Politics*

—— , *Musaddiq and the Struggle for Power in Iran*, 2nd (paperback) edn, I.B. Tauris, London and New York, 1999

—— , 'Problems of Democracy and the Public Sphere in Modern Iran', *Comparative Studies of South Asia, Africa and the Middle East*, 18/2 (1998), reprinted in *Iranian History and Politics*

—— , 'Riza Shah's Political Legitimacy and Social Base', in Cronin (ed.), *The Making of Modern Iran, State and Society under Riza Shah, 1921–1941*, Routledge, London and New York, 2003

—— , *Sadeq Hedayat, The Life and Legend of an Iranian Writer*, paperback edn, I.B. Tauris, London and New York, 2002

—— , *Sa'di, The Poet of Life, Love and Compassion*, Oneworld Publishers, Oxford, 2006

—— , *The Political Economy of Modern Iran: Despotism and Pseudo-Modernism*, Macmillan and New York University Press, London and New York, 1981

—— , *State and Society in Iran: The Eclipse of the Qajars and the Emergence of the Pahlavis*, paperback edn, I.B. Tauris, London and New York, 2006

—— , 'The Pahlavi Regime in Iran', in H. E. Chehabi and Juan J. Linz (eds), *Sultanistic Regimes*, The Johns Hopkins University Press, Baltimore, MD and London, 1998

—— , 'The Poet-Laureate Bahar in the Constitutional Era', *Iran*, British Institute of Persian Studies, London, 2002

—— , 'The Short-Term Society: A Study in the Problems of Long-Term Political and Economic Development in Iran', *Middle Eastern Studies*, 40/1 January 2004)

—— , 'Towards a General Theory of Iranian Revolutions', in *Iranian History and Politics: The Dialectic of State and Society*, paperback edn, Routledge, London and New York, 2007

Keddie, Nikki R., *Religion and Rebellion in Iran, the Tobacco Protest of 1891–1892*, Frank Cass, London, 1966

—— , *Roots and Results of Revolution*, Yale University Press, New Haven, CT and London, 2003

—— , *Sayyid Jamal al-Din al-Afghani: A Political Biography*, University of California Press, Berkeley, CA, 1972

—— (ed.), *Religion and Politics in Iran: Shi'ism from Quietism to Revolution*, Yale University Press, New Haven, CT and London, 1983

Khomeini, Imam, *Writings and Declarations of Imam Khomeini*, tr. and annot. Hamid Algar, Mizan Press, Berkeley, CA, 1981

Kinzer, Stephen, *All the Shah's Men: An American Coup and the Roots of Middle East Terror*, John Wiley & Sons, Hoboken, NJ, 2003

Lambton, Ann K. S., *Continuity and Change in Mediaeval Persia: Aspects of Administrative, Economic and Social History, 11th–14th Century*, Persian Heritage Foundation, Albany, NY, 1988

—— , *Landlord and Peasant in Persia*, Oxford University Press, London, New York and Toronto, 1953

—— , *Persian Land Reform, 1926–1969*, The Clarendon Press, Oxford, 1969

—— , *Qajar Persia: Eleven Studies*, I.B. Tauris, London, 1987

Lockhart, Laurence, *Nadir Shah*, Luzac, London, 1938

—— , *The Fall of the Safavid Dynasty and the Afghan Occupation of Persia*, Cambridge University Press, Cambridge, 1958

Mahdavi, Shirin, *For God, Mammon and Country: A Nineteenth Century Persian Merchant, Hajj Mohammad Hasan Amin al-Zarb (1834–1898)*, Westview, Boulder, CO and Oxford, 1999

Majd, Mohammad Gholi, *The Great Famine and Genocide in Persia, 1917–1918*, University Press of America, Lanham, MD and Oxford, 2003

Marashi, Afshin, *Nationalizing Iran: Culture, Power and the State, 1870–1940*, University of Washington Press, Seattle and London, 2008

—— , 'Performing the Nation: The Shah's Official State Visit to Kemalist Turkey, June to July 1934', in Stephanie Cronin (ed.), *The Making of Modern Iran: State and Society under Riza Shah, 1921–1941*, Routledge, London and New York, 2003

Martin, Vanessa, 'Aqa Najafi, Hajj Aqa Nurullah and the Emergence of Islamism in Isfahan, 1889–1908', *Iranian Studies*, 41/2 (April 2008)

—— , *Creating an Islamic State: Khomeini and the Making of a New Iran*, I.B. Tauris, London and New York, 2003

—— , *Iran and Modernism: The Iranian Revolution of 1906*, Syracuse University Press, Syracuse, NY, 1989

—— , 'Mudarris, Republicanism and the Rise to Power of Riza Khan, Sardar-i Sepah', in Cronin (ed.), *The Making of Modern Iran: State and Society under Riza Shah, 1921–1941*, Routledge, London and New York, 2003

—— , *The Qajar Pact: Bargaining, Protest and the State in Nineteenth-Century Persia*, I.B. Tauris, London, 2005

Matthee, Rudi, 'Transforming Dangerous Nomads into Useful Artisans, Technicians, Agriculturalists: Education in the Reza Shah Period', in Cronin (ed.), *The Making of Modern Iran: State and Society under Riza Shah, 1921–1941*, Routledge, London and New York, 2003

Melville, Charles (ed.), *Safavid Persia: The History and Politics of an Islamic Society*, I.B. Tauris, London, 1996

Menasheri, David, *Education and the Making of Modern Iran*, Cornell University Press, Ithaca, NY and London, 1992

—— , *Post-Revolutionary Politics in Iran*, Frank Cass, London and Portland, OR, 2001

Meskub, Shahrokh, *Iranian Nationality and the Persian Language*, foreword and interview with the author by Ali Banuazizi, tr. Michael C. Hillmann, ed. John R. Perry, Mage Publishers, Washington DC, 1992

Milani, Abbas, *The Persian Sphinx: Amir Abbas Hoveyda and the Riddle of the Iranian Revolution, A Biography*, I.B. Tauris, London and New York, 2000

Milani, Farzaneh, *Veils and Words: The Emerging Voices of Iranian Women Writers*, I.B. Tauris, London, 1992

Milani, Mohsen M., *The Making of Iran's Islamic Revolution: From Monarchy to Islamic Republic*, Westview Press, Boulder, CO and London, 1988

Mir-Hosseini, Ziba and Richard Tapper, *Islam and Democracy in Iran: Eshkevari and the Quest for Reform*, I.B. Tauris, London and New York, 2006

Moin, Baqer, *Khomeini: Life of the Ayatollah*, I.B. Tauris, London and New York, 1999

Mosaddeq, Mohammad, *Musaddiq's Memoirs*, ed. and intro. Homa Katouzian, tr. Seyyed Hasan Amin and Homa Katouzian, Jebhe, London, 1988

Mosaddeq, *Taqrirat-e Mosaddeq dar Zendan*, notes by Jalil Bozorgmehr, ed. Iraj Afshar, Farhang-e Iranzamin, Tehran, 1980

Moslem, Mehdi, *Factional Politics in Post-Khomeini Iran*, Syracuse University Press, Syracuse, NY, 2002

Mottahedeh, Roy, *The Mantle of the Prophet: Learning and Power in Iran*, Chatto & Windus, London, 1986

Mozaffari, Nahid and Ahmad Karimi Hakkak (eds), *Strange Times My Dear: The Pen Anthology of Contemporary Iranian Literature*, Arcade Publishing, New York, 2005

Nabavi, Negin (ed.), *Intellectual Trends in Twentieth-Century Iran: A Critical Survey*, University Press of Florida, Gainesville, FL, 2003

Naji, Kasra, *Ahmadinejad, the Secret History of Iran's Radical Leader*, I.B. Tauris, London and New York, 2008

Najmabadi, Afsaneh, *The Story of the Daughters of Quchan: Gender and National Memory in Iranian History*, Syracuse University Press, Syracuse, NY, 1998

Nicolson, Harold, *Curzon, the Last Phase, 1919–1925: A Study in Post-war Diplomacy*, Constable, London, 1934

Olson, Wm. J., *Anglo-Iranian Relations during World War I*, Frank Cass, London, 1984

Pahlavi, Mohammad Reza Shah, *Answer to History*, Stein and Day, New York, 1980

—— , *Mission for My Country*, Heinemann, London, 1960

Rahnema, Ali, *An Islamic Utopian: A Political Biography of Ali Shari'ati*, I.B. Tauris, London, 1998

—— and Farhad Nomani, *The Secular Miracle: Religion, Politics & Economic Policy in Iran*, Zed Books, London and New Jersey, 1990

Raffat, Donné, *The Prison Papers of Bozorg Alavi: A Literary Odyssey*, Syracuse University Press, Syracuse, NY, 1985

Ramazani, Rouhollah, *Iran's Foreign Policy, 1941–1973: A Study of Foreign Policy in Modernizing Nations*, University of Virginia Press, Charlottesville, VA, 1975

Rostam Kolayi, Jasmin, 'Expanding Agencies for the "New" Iranian Woman: Family Law, Work and Unveiling', in Cronin (ed.), *The Making of Modern Iran, State and Society under Riza Shah, 1921–1941*, Routledge, London and New York, 2003

Rypka, Jan, *History of Iranian Literature*, D., Rydal Publishing Company, Dordrecht, Holland, 1968

Sabahi, Houshang, *British Policy in Persia, 1918–1925*, Frank Cass, London, 1990

Savory, Roger, *Iran under the Safavids*, Cambridge University Press, Cambridge, 1980

Schirazi, Asghar, *The Constitution of Iran: Politics and the State in the Islamic Republic*, tr. John O'Kane, I.B. Tauris, London and New York, 1997

Seyyed-Ghorab, A. A. and S. McGlinn, *The Essence of Modernity: Mirza Usof Khan Mustashar ad-Dowla Tabrizi's Treatise on Codified Law (Yak Kalame)*, Rozenberg Publishers and Purdue University Press, Amsterdam and West Lafayette, IN, 2008.

Shahidi, Hossein, *Journalism in Iran: From Mission to Profession*, Routledge, London and New York, 2007

—— , 'Iranian Journalism and the Law in the Twentieth century', *Iranian Studies*, 41/5 (December 2008)

Shuster, W. Morgan, *The Strangling of Persia*, The Century Co., New York, 1912

Soudavar, Abolala, *The Aura of Kings: Legitimacy and Divine Sanction in Iranian Kingship*, Mazda Publishers, Costa Mesa, CA, 2003

Sykes, Christopher, *Wassmuss, 'The German Lawrence'*, Longman, Green and Co., London and New York, 1936

Sicker, Martin, *The Bear and The Lion*, Praeger, London, 1988

Tapper, Richard, 'The Case of the Shahsevans', in Cronin (ed.), *The Making of Modern Iran: State and Society under Riza Shah, 1921–1941*, Routledge, London and New York, 2003

Tavakoli-Targhi, Mohamad, 'Narrative Identity in the Works of Hedayat and His Contemporaries', in Homa Katouzian (ed.), *Sadeq Hedayat, His Work and His Wondrous World*, Routledge, London and New York, 2007

—— , *Refashioning Iran: Orientalism, Occidentalism and Historiography*, Palgrave, Basingstoke and New York, 2001

Ullman, Richard H., *Anglo-Soviet Relations*, vol. 3: *The Anglo-Soviet Accord*, Princeton University Press, Princeton, NJ, 1974

Waterfield, Gordon, *Professional Diplomat, Sir Percy Loraine*, John Murray, London, 1973

Wilber, Donald, *Iran Past and Present*, Princeton University Press, Princeton, NJ, 1958

—— , *Riza Shah Pahlavi: The Resurrection and Reconstruction of Iran*, Exposition Press, New York, 1975

Wright, Steven, *The United States and Persian Gulf Security: The Foundations of the War on Terror*, Ithaca Press, Reading, 2007

Yarshater, Ehsan (ed.), *Persian Literature*, Bibliotheca Persica, Albany, NY, 1988

Zaehner, R.C., *The Dawn and Twilight of Zoroastrianism*, Phoenix, London, 2002

Zirinsky, Michael, 'Blood, Power and Hypocrisy: The Murder of Robert Imbrie and the American Relations with Pahlavi Iran, 1924', *International Journal of Middle East Studies*, 18/3 (1986)

PERSIAN

Adamiyat, Fereydun, *Amir Kabir va Iran*, Kharazmi, Tehran, 1969

—— , *Andisheh-ha-ye Mirza Fath'ali Akhnudzadeh*, Entesharat-e Kharazmi, Terhan, 1970

—— , *Andisheh-ha-ye Mirza Aqa Khan Kermani*, Payam, Tehran, 1978

—— , *Fekr-e Demokrasi-ye Ejtema'i dar Nehzat-e Mashrutiyat-e Iran*, Entesharat-e Peyam, Tehran, 1984

Afshar, Iraj (ed.), *Azadi va Siyast, Abdorrahim Talebov*, Entesharat-e Sahar, Tehran, 1979
—— (ed.), *Ruznameh-ye Khaterat E'temad al-Saltaneh*, Amir Kabir, Tehran, 1980
—— (ed.), *Nameh-ha-ye Paris az Mohammad Qazvini beh Seyyed Hasan Taqizadeh*, Nashr-e Qatreh, Tehran, 2005
—— (ed.), *Mohammad Ali Mirza and Mohammad Ali Shah-e Makhlu' (55 sanad-e tazeh-yab)*, Nashr-e Abi, Tehran, 2009
Ahmadi, Hamid (ed.), *Iran: hoviyat, melliyat, qowmiyat*, Mo'asseseh-ye Tahqiqat va Tawseh'eh-ye Olum-e Ensani, Tehran, 2004
Al-e Ahmad, Jalal, *Dar Khedmat va Khiyanat-e Rowshanfekran*, Kharazmi, Tehran, 1978
——, *Gharbzadegi*, 2nd edn (1964), Ravaq, Tehran, reprinted 1978
Amir Khosrovi, Babak, *Nazar az Darun beh Naqsh-e Hezb-e Tudeh-ye Iran*, Ettela'at, Tehran, 1996
Aqeli, Baqer, *Nosrat al-Dawleh Firuz*, Nashr-e Namak, Tehran, 1994
——, *Ruzshomar Tarikh-e Iran*, 3rd edn, Nashr-e Goftar, Tehran, 1990–1.
Aryanpur, Yahya, *Az Saba ta Nima*, vols. 1 and 2, Zavvar, Tehran, 1993
Ashraf, Ahmad, *Mavane'-eh Tarikhi-ye Roshd-e Sarmayehdari dar Iran: Doreh-ye Qajariyeh*, Zamineh, Tehran, 1980
Azari, Ali, *Qiyam-e Kolonel Mohammad Taqi Khan Pesyan*, Safi'ali Shah, Tehran, 1973
Bahar, Mohammad Taqi, *Divan*, ed. Mohammad Malekzadeh, vol. 1, Amir Kabir, Tehran, 1956
——, *Tarikh-e Mokhtasar-e Ahazab-e Siyasi dar Iran*, vol. 1, Jibi, Tehran, 1978
Bamdad, Mehdi, *Sharh-e Hal-e Rejal-e Iran*, vols 1–6, Zavvar, Tehran, 1992
Barzin, Saeed, *Jenahbandi-ye Siyasi dar Iran az Dahe-ye 60 ta Dovvom-e Khordad, Hamrah-e Mosahebeh ba Homayoun Katouzian*, Nashr-e Markaz, Tehran, 1998
Bastani Parizi, Mohammad Ebrahim, *Zir-e in Haft Asman*, Javidan, Tehran, 1983
——, *Asiya-ye Haft Sang*, Donya-ye Ketab, 1988, Tehran.
Bayat, Kaveh, *Enqelab-e Khorasan*, Mo'asseseh-ye Pazhuhesh-ha-ye Farhangi, Tehran, 1991
——, *Kudeta-ye Lahuti, Tabriz, Bahman 1300*, Shirzadeh, Tehran, 1997
Bazargan, Mehdi, *Enqelab-e Iran dar daw Harekat*, Bazargan, Tehran, 1984
——, *Modafe'at dar Dadgah*, Freedom Movement, Tehran, 1964
Behnam, Jamshid, *Berlani-ha: Andishmandan-e Irani dar Berlan, 1915–1930*, Farzan, Tehran, 2000
Beihaqi, Abolfazl, *Tarikh-e Beihaqi*, ed. Ali Akbar Fayyaz, Ershad, Tehran, 1995
Daftari, Ahamd Matin, 'Andarz-ha-ye Baradaraneh beh Omum-e Daneshjuyan, Khosusan Dadresan va Ostadan-e Ayandeh', *A'in-e Daneshjuyan*, 2 (March 1945)
Dawlat-Abadi, Yaha, *Hayat-e Yahya*, 4 vols, Ferdowsi and Attar, Tehran, 1983
Ehtesham al-Saltaneh, Mahmud, *Khaterat-e Ehtesham al-Saltaneh*, ed. S. M. Musavi, Zavvar, 1988, Tehran
Entezam, Nasrollah, *Khaterat-e Nasrollah Entezam, Shahrivar-e 1320 az Didgah-e Darbar*, eds Mohammad Reza Abbasi and Behruz Tayarani, Sazman-e Asnad-e Melli-ye Iran, Tehran, 1992
Eqbal Ashtiyani, Abbas, *Tarikh-e Moghol: Az Hamleh-ye Changiz ta Taskhir-e Dawlat-e Teymuri*, Amir Kabir, Tehran, 1986
Eslami, Sazman-e Madarek-e Farhangi-ye Enqelab-e, *Vaqeh'eh-ye Kashf-e Hejab*, Mo'assehseh-ye Pazhuhesh-ha va Motale'at-e Farhangi, Tehran, 1992
Fakhra'i, Ebrahim, *Sardar-e Jangal, Mirza Kuchik Khan*, Javidan, Tehran, 1978
Falsafi, Nasrollah, *Zendegi-ye Shah Abbas Avval*, 5 vols, Ketab-e Kayhan, Tehran, 1955–73
Farhad Mo'tamed, Mahmud, *Tarikh-e Siyasi-ye Dawreh-ye Sedarat-e Mirza Hosein Khan Moshir al-Dawleh, Sepahsalar-e A'azam*, Elmi, Tehran, 1946
Farmanfarmaian, Hafiz (ed.), *Khaterat-e Siyasi-ye Mirza Ali Khan Amin al-Dawleh*, Amir Kabir, Tehran, 1991
Fateh, Mostafa, *Panjah Sal Naft-e Iran*, Entesharat-e Peyam, Tehran, 1979
Fatemi, Nasrollah Seifpour, *Ayeneh-ye Ebrat*, Nashr-e Ketab, London, 1989
Fazlollah, Rashid al-Din, *Jami' al-Tavarikh*, ed. Bahman Karimi, Eqbal, Tehran, 1959
Ferdowsi, Abolqasem, *Shahnameh*, vols 1–8, ed. Djalal Khaleghi-Motlagh (vol. 6 with M. Omidsalar, vol. 7 with A. Khatibi); vols 1–5, Mazda Publishers, Costa Mesa, CA and New York, in association with Bibliotheca Persica, 1990–7; vols 6–8, New York, Bibliotheca Persica, 2005–8
Foruzanfar, Badi'ozzamn, *Sokhan va Sokhanvarn*, Kharazmi, Tehran, 1971
Ghani, Qasem, *Yaddasht-ha-ye Doktor Qasem Ghani*, ed. Cyrus Ghani, vols 1–8, Zavvar, Tehran, 1978
Gilak, Mohammad Ali, *Tarikh-e Enqelab-e Jangal*, Nashr-e Gilak, Rasht, 1990
Hedayat, Mehdiqoli, *Gozaresh-e Iran: Qajariyeh va Mashrutiyat*, Noqreh, Tehran, 1984
——, *Khaterat va Khatarat*, Zavvar, Tehran, 1984
Ibnu'l Balkhi, *Farsnama*, eds G. L'Strange and R. A. Nicholson, Cambridge University Press, Cambridge, 1921
Itscherenska, Ilse, 'Taqizadeh dar Alman-e Qeisari', *Iran Nameh*, 21/1–2 (spring and summer 2003)
Jamalzadeh, Mohammad Ali, *Sar o Tah Yek Karbas*, Ma'refat, Tehran, 1955
——, 'Seyyed Jamal al-Din Va'ez-e Isfahani va Ba'zi Mobarezat-e U', in Ali Dehbashi (ed.), *Yad-e Mohammad Ali Jamazadeh*, Nashr-e Sales, Tehran, 1988

Kahhalzadeh, Abolqasem, *Dideh-ha va Shenideh-ha*, ed. Morteza Kamran, Kamran, Tehran, 1984
Kasravi, Ahmad, *A'in*, Nashr o Pakhsh-e Ketab, Tehran, repr. 1977
—— , *Tarikh-e Mashruteh-ye Iran*, Amir Kabir, Tehran, 1976
—— , *Tarikh-e Hijdahsaleh-ye Azerbaijan*, Amir Kabir, Tehran, 1992
—— , *Baha'igari, Shi'igari, Sufigari*, ed. Alireza Samari, Isin, Nashr-e Nima, Germany, 2003
Katira'i, Mahmud, *Feramasoneri dar Iran*, Eqbal, Tehran, 1968
Katouzian, Homa, *Darbareh-ye Jamalzadeh va Jamalzadeh Shenasi*, Shahab, Tehran, 2003
—— , *Hasht Maqaleh dar Tarikh va Adab-e Mo'aser*, Nashr-e Markaz, Tehran, 2006
—— , 'Seyyed Hasan Taqizadeh: Seh Zendegi dar Yek Omr', in *Iran-Nameh*, special issue on Taqizadeh (guest ed. H. Katouzian), 21/1–2 (Spring and Summer 2003)
Katouzian, Mohammad Ali Tehrani, *Tarikh-e Enqelab-e Mashrutiyat-e Iran*, ed. Naser Katouzian, Enteshar, Tehran, 2000
Kermani, Nazem al-Islam, *Tarikh-e Bidari-ye Iraniyan*, ed. Ali Akbar Sa'idi Sirjani, vol. 1, Agah, Tehran, 1983
Khajeh-Nuri, Ebrahim, *Bazigaran-e Asr-e Tala'i, Seyyed Hasan Modarres*, Javidan, Tehran, 1978
Khomeini, Imam, *Velayat-e Faqih (Hokumat-e Eslami)*, new edn, Amir Kabir, Tehran, 1978
Ladjevardi, Habib (ed.), *Khaterat-e Mehdi Ha'eri Yazdi*, Iran Books, Bethesda, MD, 2001
Lesani, Abolfazl, *Tala-ye Siayah ya Bala-ye Iran*, Amir Kabir, Tehran, 1978
Mahjub (ed.), Mohammad-Ja'far, *Divan-e Kamel-e Iraj-Mirza*, Sherkat-e Ketab, USA, 1986
Makki, Hosein, *Doktor Mosaddeq va Notq-ha-ye Tarikhi-ye U*, Javidan, Tehran, 1985
—— , *Tarikh-e Bistsaleh-ye Iran*, vol. 2, Elmi, Tehran, 1995
Maleki, Khalil, *Khaterat-e Siyasi*, ed. and intro. Homa Katouzian, 2nd edn, Enteshar, Tehran, 1989
Mashkur, Mohammadjavad, *Tarikh-e Iran Zamin*, Eshraqi, Tehran, 1987
Milani, Abbas (ed.), *Taskhir-e Tamaddon-e Gharbi*, Gam-e Naw, Tehran, 2003
Mirza Saleh, Gholamhosein (ed.), *Reza Shah: Khaterat-e Soleiman Behbudi, Shams Pahlavi and Ali Izadi*, Sahba, Tehran, 1983
Mohit-e Tabataba'i, Mohammad (ed.), *Majmu'eh-ye Asar-e Mirza Malkam Khan*, Tehran, 1948
Moshir-Salimi, Ali Akbar-e (ed.), *Kolliyat-e Mosavvar-e Eshqi*, Moshir-Salimi, Tehran, c.1944
Mostawfi, Abdollah, *Sharh-e Zendegani-ye Man, Tarikh-e Ejtema'i va Edari-ye Dawreh-ye Qajariyeh*, 3 vols, Zavvar, Tehran, 1998
Nava'i, Abdolhosein (ed.), *Yaddshat-ha-ye Malek al-Movarrekhin va Mer'at al-Vaqaye' Mozaffari*, Zarrin, Tehran, 1989
Nezami Aruzi, *Chahar Maqaleh*, ed. Mohammad Qazvini, Iranshahr, Berlin, 1927
Nezm al-Molk Tusi, Khajeh, *Siyar al-Muluk* or *Siyasatnameh*, ed. Hubert Darke, Tarjomeh o Nashr-e Ketab, Tehran, 1961
Niyazmand, Reza, *Reza Shah, Az Tavallod ta Saltanat, Bonyad-e Motale'at-e Iran*, Washington and London, 1996
Nura'i, Fereshteh, *Mirza Malkam Khan Nazem al-Dawleh*, Jibi, Tehran, 1973
Pahlavi, Mohammad Reza Shah, *Besu-ye Tamaddon-e Bozorg*, Markaz-e Pazhuhesh va Nashr-e Farhang-e Dawran-e Pahlavi, Tehran, 1975
Pesyan, Najafqoli and Khosraw Mo'tazed, *Az Savadkuh ta Zhohnsburg*, Sales, Tehran, 1998
Ravandi, Soleiman, *Rahat al-Sudur va Ayat al-Surur dar Tarikh-i Al-e Saljuq*, ed. Mohammad Iqbal, rev. Mojtaba Minovi, Amir Kabir, Tehran, 1985
Sadiq, Isa, *Yadgar-e Omr*, vol. 1, Sherkat-e Sahami-ye Tab'-e Ketab, Tehran, 1961
—— , *Yadgar-e Omr*, vol. 2, Amir Kabir, Tehran, 1966
Safa, Zabihollah, *Tarikh-e Adabiyat dar Iran*, vols 1–5, v.p., Tehran, v.d. since 1956
Sanjabi, Karim, *Omid-ha va Na-omidi-ha: Khaterat-e Siyasi*, Jebhe, London, 1989
Sasani, Khan Malek, *Siyasatgaran-e Dawreh-ye Qajar*, n.p., Tehran, n.d. (date of preface, 1959)
Seif-e Azad, Abdorrahman (ed.), *Divan-e Aref*, Tehran, Seif-e Azad, 1948
Shadman, Seyyed Fakhreddin, *Taskhir-e Tamaddon-e Farangi*, n.p., Tehran, reprinted 1947
Siyasi, Ali Akbar, *Gozaresh-e Yek Zendegi*, Siyasi, London, 1988
Tabtaba'i, Hasan (ed.), *Yaddasht-ha-ye Montasher Nashodeh-ye Seyyed Mohammad Tabataba'i*, Nashr-e Abi, Tehran, 2003
Taqizadeh, Seyyed Hasan, *Nameh-ha-ye London*, ed. Iraj Afshar, Farzan, Tehran, 1996
—— , *Zendegi-ye Tufani: Khaterat-e Seyyed Hasan Taqizadeh*, ed. Iraj Afshar, Elmi, Tehran, 1983
Tavakoli-Targhi, Mohamad, *Tajddod-e Bumi va Bazandishi-ye Tarikh*, Nashr-e Tarikh-e Iran, Tehran, 2002
Zargarinezhad, Gholamhosein (ed.), *Khaterat-e Nakhostin Sepahbod-e Iran*, Mo'asseseh-ye Pazhuhesh va Motale'at-e Farhangi, Tehran, 1994
Zarrinkub, Abdolhosein, *Tarikh-e Mardom-e Iran: Keshmakesh ba Qodrat-ha*, Amir Kabir, Tehran, 1985

Index

Tegudar (Ahmad) 104, 105
Tehran 154–6, 163–6, 172–4, 177–83, 204–6, 239–44,
   370–3, 380–5
   Turkic spoken around 11
   urban architecture 17
   shrines 70
   becomes capital 139
   Aqa Mohammad Khan crowned 140
   revolutionaries fight Shah's Cossacks 186
   Tehran University 216, 289, 364, 393
   expansion 223
   religious establishment 226, 250, 288
   Pasteur Institute 227
   Tehran Conference (1943) 233
   permission needed from Shah for military operations
      275
   football celebrations 293
   Hoseiniyeh-ye Ershad 298
   house price inflation 310
   Council elections 377, 390
Tehran Conference 233
Tekkalu (Turkoman Qezelbash tribe) 119, 120
Teymurtash, Abdolhosein 95, 153, 209, 210, 212,
   217, 227
Thiepes (Chishpish) 29
Third Force 247, 296, 338
Tiflis 140, 143
Tigris 40, 41
Timur (Teymur) 106–10, 135
Tiyul 94, 123, 128
Tobacco Revolt 148, 163, 165, 177
Toghrol Beg 91, 92
Tokharistan 83
Tonokabon (Shahsavar) 274
Tonokaboni, Sepahdar-e (later,
   Sepahsalar-e) 181, 186, 190
Torkan Khatun 95, 99
Toufanian (Tufaniyan), General Hasan 275
Towards the Great Civilization (Besu-ye Tamaddon-e
   Bozorg) 263, 270
Trajan, Emperor 44
Transoxiana 77, 80, 83, 84, 88, 90, 101, 107–10,
   114, 135
Travelogue of Ebarhim Beg, The 176
Trucial States 279
Truman–Churchill proposal 248, 249
Tsitsianov, Prince 143
Tudeh Party 234–6, 240–5, 253
   Pishevari and 239
   on oil nationalization 247
   activists jailed 254
   Soviet Union 257
   Amini 259
   eliminated 288
   1948 split 290, 296
   losing credibility 305
   critics of 308
   showing loyalty to Khomeini 330
   unpopularity 331
   contempt for 'liberals' 332
   support hostage taking 339
   support Islamists as anti-American 342
Tunb (Greater and Lesser) islands 279, 292
Tunisia 276
Turanian(s, Turanianism) 12, 21–6
Turkaman 11, 87, 89, 108–15, 118, 120, 121, 137, 159,
   160, 173, 174, 330
Turkamanchai treaty 144, 145, 149
Turkistan 42, 135
Turkmenistan 9, 41, 65, 99

Turks 84–8, 90–7
   Turkic speakers 10–12
   soldiers used by Abbasids 75, 81
   cultural effect of Seljuks 100
   1820 war 146
   First World War 192
   Iranians and 195, 208, 219, 284
Tus 94, 217
Twelfth Imam see Mahdi

Umayyads 67, 68, 72–4, 79, 117
Umma 63
United Nations (UN) 232, 239, 246, 279, 292, 300, 342,
   344, 349, 350, 357, 361, 385–7
   General Assembly 385
   sanctions against Iran 387
   Security Council 239, 246, 387
United States 256–9, 266–9, 312–14, 324, 380–2
   perception by Iranians 16, 226–7
   hostility to Anglo–Iranian 1919 Agreement 197
   vice-consul Robert Imbrie lynched 206
   and role of Dr Arthur Millspaugh 211, 237
   Iranian students sent to 216
   Iranian attitudes to 227
   1946 strong protest to the Soviet Union 240
   support for Razmara 244
   Shah's attitude towards 245, 263, 278, 280, 321
   and oil nationalization dispute 247, 249
   encouragement for Mosaddeq 251–2
   Khomeini's depiction of 262, 338
   support for Shah 277
   a base for Confederation of Iranian Students 291, 305
   and Vietnam 304
   held responsible for the absolute and arbitrary
      government in Iran 305, 310
   growing concern over 1978 events in Iran 318
   leftists' perception of Bazargan as a 'friend of
      America' 337
   breaks off diplomatic relations with Iran 339
   and Islamic Republic 339, 344, 354, 386
   and Iran nuclear issue 387, 388
   criticism of Americanism 261, 293, 329
   Khomeini's attack on immunity for American
      personnel in Iran 262
   PM Mansur assassinated for granting immunity to
      American personnel in Iran 272
   Soviet Union hostility over 1959 Iranian–American
      defence treaty 278
   Iranians' widespread belief that the Shah was under
      'American masters' 292, 302
   young Iranians influenced by rebellion of young
      Europeans and Americans 304
   critics of Russia and the Tudeh Party described as
      'American Marxists' 308
   official Iranian circles regard 1977 protests as an
      'American plot' 313
   Carter emphasizing Iranian–American friendship
      and cooperation 314
   American opinion divided on Iran 321
   Anti-Americanism 329, 342
   Armed Fada'i group's brief occupation of embassy 337
   Muslim students' occupation of Embassy and hostage
      taking 338–9, 344, 372
   'Iran-Contra' affair 345
   restores diplomatic relations with Iraq 349
   American journalist, Tom Fenton, on Khomeini's
      burial 352
   rumours of American and/or Israeli attack on Iran 354
   Melli-Mazhabis' religious attitude described as
      'American Islam' 368